THE
ENDURING DEBATE

CLASSIC AND CONTEMPORARY READINGS IN
AMERICAN POLITICS

THE
ENDURING DEBATE

CLASSIC AND CONTEMPORARY READINGS
IN AMERICAN POLITICS

David T. Canon

Anne Khademian

Kenneth R. Mayer

W. W. NORTON & COMPANY

NEW YORK   LONDON

The text of this book is composed in Adobe Palatino.
Composition by PennSet, Inc.
Manufacturing by Courier Companies
Book design by Jack Meserole

Library of Congress Cataloging-in-Publication Data
The enduring debate : classic and contemporary readings in American
politics / David T. Canon, Anne Khademian, Kenneth R. Mayer,
[editors].
     p.   cm.
  ISBN 0-393-97134-1 (pbk.)
  1. United States—Politics and government.   I. Canon, David T.
II. Khademian, Anne M., 1961–   .   III. Mayer, Kenneth R., 1960–   .
JK21.E53   1997
320.473—dc21   97-28414

W. W. Norton & Company, Inc., 500 Fifth Avenue, New York, N.Y. 10110
http://www.wwnorton.com

W. W. Norton & Company Ltd., 10 Coptic Street, London WC1A 1PU

2 3 4 5 6 7 8 9 0

Contents

PART I The Constitutional System

CHAPTER 1 Constructing the Government—The   3
Founding and the Constitution

1 FROM *The Origins of the American Constitution*—MICHAEL
KAMMEN   3

2 *The Federalist*, No. 15—ALEXANDER HAMILTON   12

3 "The Paranoid Style in American Politics"—RICHARD
HOFSTADTER   17

THE DEBATE: AN ECONOMIC INTERPRETATION OF THE
CONSTITUTION   23

4 FROM *An Economic Interpretation of the Constitution
of the United States*—CHARLES A. BEARD   23

5 FROM *Charles Beard and the Constitution: A Critical Analysis
of "An Economic Interpretation of the Constitution"*—ROBERT
E. BROWN   28

CHAPTER 2 Federalism and the Separation of Powers: 34
Then and Now

6 *The Federalist*, Nos. 51 and 46—JAMES MADISON   34

7 FROM *The Price of Federalism*—PAUL PETERSON   43

8 "Guns, the Commerce Clause, and the Courts"—ROBERT
KATZMANN   52

9 Rules Committee Report on the Unfunded Mandate Reform
Act of 1995   55

10 "Unfunded Mandates: Balancing State and National Needs"
—JAMES R. ST. GEORGE   59

THE DEBATE: DOES THE SEPARATION OF POWERS MAKE
GRIDLOCK INEVITABLE?   66

11 "It Ain't Broke"—CHARLES O. JONES   66

12 FROM "[Does the System Need Fixing?] A Rationale"
—DONALD L. ROBINSON   72

CHAPTER 3   The Constitutional Framework and the
Individual: Civil Liberties and Civil
Rights   77

13 "The Perpetuation of Our Political Institutions"—ABRAHAM
LINCOLN   78

14 "Letter from Birmingham Jail, 1963"—MARTIN LUTHER
KING, JR.   83

15 "In Defense of Prejudice"—JONATHAN RAUCH   92

| THE DEBATE: SHOULD DRUGS BE LEGALIZED?   100

16 "The War on Drugs is Lost"—WILLIAM F. BUCKLEY and
STEVEN B. DUKE   101

17 "Legalization Madness"—JAMES A. INCIARDI AND CHRISTINE
A. SAUM   107

PART II   Institutions

CHAPTER 4   Congress: The First Branch   119

18 FROM *Congress: The Electoral Connection*—DAVID R. MAYHEW   119

19 "*Too* Representative Government"—STEVEN STARK   123

20 "By the Numbers"—VIVECA NOVAK   138

| THE DEBATE: SHOULD THE SENATE REFORM THE
| FILIBUSTER?   147

21 "Slaying the Dinosaur: The Case for Reforming the Senate
Filibuster"—SARAH A. BINDER AND THOMAS E. MANN   147

22 "Defending the Dinosaur: The Case for Not Fixing the
Filibuster"—BILL FRENZEL   155

CHAPTER 5   The President: From Chief Clerk to
Chief Executive   160

23 "The Power to Persuade" FROM *Presidential Power*
—RICHARD NEUSTADT   160

24 "The Search for the Perfect President—*The Economist*   170

25 "Presidents and Economics: One-Star Generalizations"
—HERBERT STEIN   177

| THE DEBATE: THE REACH OF PRESIDENTIAL POWER   184

26 "Perspectives on the Presidency" FROM *The Presidency in a
Separated System*—CHARLES O. JONES   184

27 "The Out-of-Control Presidency"—MICHAEL LIND   190

CHAPTER 6   Bureaucracy in a Democratic System   203

28 "The Study of Administration"—WOODROW WILSON   203

29 FROM *Bureaucracy: What Government Agencies Do and Why
They Do It*—JAMES Q. WILSON   212

30 "National Performance Review: An Analysis"—DONALD
KETTL   221

THE DEBATE: THE FEDERAL BUREAUCRACY: HIERARCHY VS.
DECENTRALIZATION   228

31 FROM "Report Regarding the Internal Investigation of
Shootings at Ruby Ridge, Idaho, During the Arrest of Randy
Weaver"—DEPARTMENT OF JUSTICE   229

32 FROM "The National Performance Review"—AL GORE   233

CHAPTER 7   The Federal Judiciary   240

33 *The Federalist*, No. 78—ALEXANDER HAMILTON   240

34 "The Court in American Life" FROM *Storm Center: The
Supreme Court in American Politics*—DAVID O'BRIEN   247

35 "The Color-Blind Court"—JEFFREY ROSEN   254

| THE DEBATE: ORIGINAL INTENT VS. JUDICIAL ACTIVISM   266

36 FROM *The Tempting of America*—ROBERT H. BORK   266

37 "Who's Right About the Constitution? Meese v. Brennan"
—STUART TAYLOR, JR.   270

PART III Political Participation

CHAPTER 8 Public Opinion and the Mass Media 283

38 "Polling the Public" FROM *Public Opinion in a Democracy*
—GEORGE GALLUP 283

39 "Why Americans Hate Politics and Politicians"—MICHAEL
NELSON 291

40 "The Presidency and the Press"—CHARLES JONES 297

| THE DEBATE: THE MEDIA: HOW INFLUENTIAL ARE THEY? 303

41 "Why Americans Hate the Media"—JAMES FALLOWS 303

42 "Civic Journalism: Involving the Public" —MARGARET T.
GORDON 315

43 "When News Media Go to Grass Roots, Candidates Often
Don't Follow"—HOWARD KURTZ 317

CHAPTER 9 Elections and Voting 322

44 "The Voice of the People: An Echo" FROM *The Responsible
Electorate*—V. O. KEY 322

45 " 'Give 'em Hell' These Days Is a Figure of Speech"—EILEEN
SHIELDS WEST 328

46 "What I Learned About How We Pick a President"—LAMAR
ALEXANDER 337

47 The "Motor-Voter" Debate: The National Voter Registration Act of
1993 341

THE DEBATE: SHOULD CAMPAIGN SPENDING LIMITS BE
INSTITUTED? 348

48 Testimony of Herbert E. Alexander, Ann McBride, and
Candice J. Nelson before the Senate Rules Committee on
Campaign Finance Reform 349

49 "Take the Wealth Primary to Court"—JOHN BONIFAX 361

CHAPTER 10 Political Parties 364

50 "The Decline of Collective Responsibility in American Politics"
—MORRIS P. FIORINA 364

51 "The People vs. the Parties"—KEVIN PHILLIPS   375

52 Forum: "A Revolution, or Business as Usual?"—*Harper's Magazine*   383

53 Third Parties and the Presidential Race—WALTER BERNS AND GORDON S. BLACK   400

THE DEBATE: PARTY POLITICS IN AMERICA: SHOULD THE TWO-PARTY SYSTEM BE STRENGTHENED?   405

54 "A Report of the Committee on Political Parties: Toward a More Responsible Two-Party System"—AMERICAN POLITICAL SCIENCE ASSOCIATION   406

55 "Of Political Parties Great and Strong: A Dissent"—EVERETT CARLL LADD   410

CHAPTER 11   Groups and Interests   424

56 "Political Association in the United States" FROM *Democracy in America*—ALEXIS DE TOCQUEVILLE   424

57 "The Logic of Collective Action" FROM *The Rise and Decline of Nations*—MANCUR OLSON   427

58 "Connections Still Count"—W. JOHN MOORE   437

THE DEBATE: PACs AND POLITICS: WAS MADISON RIGHT?   447

59 *The Federalist*, No. 10—JAMES MADISON   448

60 "The Alleged Mischiefs of Faction" FROM *The Governmental Process*—DAVID B. TRUMAN   454

61 "The Hyperpluralism Trap"—JONATHAN RAUCH   461

PART IV   Public Policy

CHAPTER 12   Politics and Policy   473

62 "The Science of 'Muddling Through' "—CHARLES E. LINDBLOM   473

63 "American Business, Public Policy, Case Studies, and Political Theory"—THEODORE J. LOWI   482

64 "Why Our Democracy Doesn't Work"—WILLIAM A. NISKANEN   489

| THE DEBATE: DOES THE DEFICIT MATTER?   496

65 "Should the Senate Pass a Balanced Budget Constitutional Amendment?"—LARRY E. CRAIG AND JAMES M. BUCHANAN   497

66 "The Balanced Budget Crusade"—ROBERT EISNER   504

CHAPTER 13   Government and the Economy   511

67 "Call for Federal Responsibility"—FRANKLIN D. ROOSEVELT   511

68 "Against the Proposed New Deal"—HERBERT HOOVER   515

69 "It's *Not* the Economy, Stupid"—CHARLES R. MORRIS   520

70 "If the GDP Is Up, Why Is America Down?"—CLIFFORD COBB, TED HALSTEAD, AND JONATHAN ROWE   533

| THE DEBATE: THE ROLE OF GOVERNMENT IN THE ECONOMY   543

71 "Gray Markets and Greased Pigs"—JOHN HOOD   543

72 "The Era of 'Big' Government: Why You'd Miss It If It Went"—E. J. DIONNE, JR.   546

CHAPTER 14   Government and Society   554

73 "A Program for Social Security"—FRANKLIN D. ROOSEVELT   554

74 "The Next New Deal"—NEIL HOWE AND PHILIP LONGMAN   558

75 "Remaking U.S. Social Policies for the 21st Century," FROM *Social Policy in the United States*—THEDA SKOCPOL   577

| THE DEBATE: WELFARE REFORM   583

76 "Putting Recipients to Work Will Be the Toughest Job" —JEFFREY L. KATZ   584

77 Debate on the Senate Floor on Welfare Reform —SENATORS JOHN SHELBY (R.-ALA.) AND ORRIN HATCH (R.-UT)   591

78 "Should the House Pass H.R. 4, the Personal Responsibility Act?"—REPRESENTATIVES BILL ARCHER (R.-TEX.), MICHAEL COLLINS (R.-GA.), AND WILLIAM J. COYNE   594

CHAPTER 15   Foreign Policy and World Politics   600

79 "The Sources of Soviet Conduct"—"X"[GEORGE KENNAN]   600

80 "An Outward-Looking Economic Nationalism"—ROBERT B. REICH   607

> THE DEBATE: AMERICAN FOREIGN POLICY: ISOLATIONISM OR INVOLVEMENT?   619
>
> *81* "The Intervention Dilemma"—BARRY M. BLECHMAN   620
>
> *82* "Why America Must Not Go into Bosnia" —CHARLES KRAUTHAMMER   629

APPENDIX OF SUPREME COURT CASES

Marbury v. Madison (1803)   635

McCulloch v. Maryland (1819)   640

Barron v. Baltimore (1833)   645

Roe v. Wade (1973)   647

Brown v. Board of Education (1954)   652

United States v. Nixon (1974)   654

Planned Parenthood of Southeastern Pennsylvania v. Casey (1992)   659

United States v. Lopez (1995)   665

Acknowledgments   673

PART I

The Constitutional System

CHAPTER 1

Constructing the Government: The Founding and the Constitution

1
From *The Origins of the American Constitution*

Michael Kammen

The Constitution is a remarkably simple document that has provided a frame-work of governance for the United States for more than two hundred years. It establishes a shared sovereignty between the states and the federal government, a separation and checking of powers between three branches of government, qualifications for citizenship and holding office, and a delineation of the rights considered so fundamental, their restriction by the government requires exten-sive due process and a compelling national or state concern. Yet the Constitu-tion's simple text produces constant controversy over its interpretation, and constant efforts to bend, twist, and nudge its application to changing economic markets, technology, social trends, and family structures. The document's du-rability and flexibility amid conflict and social change is a tribute not only to the men who drafted the Constitution in 1787, but to the American people and their willingness to embrace the challenges of self-governance at the time of the Revolution and today.

In the following article Michael Kammen argues that in order to begin to understand the Constitution and the continuous debate surrounding its inter-pretation, we must look to the history of American constitutionalism. Informed by John Locke's Treatise *of the social contract, the British constitution, and a colonial experience deemed an affront to basic liberties and rights, Americans plunged into the writing of constitutions as a means to delegate power from the sovereign people to their elected and appointed agents. It is, as Kammen notes, quite remarkable that the American states chose to draft state constitutions in the midst of a revolutionary battle for independence, rather than establishing provisional governments. It is similarly remarkable that these state constitutions have grown significantly in length over the years and are so readily amended and even rewritten, in contrast to the relatively succinct and difficult-to-amend Constitution of the United States.*

Kammen suggests that the Constitution's simplicity and durability lie in both the historic need for compromise between conflicted interests, and the surprising common ground that nevertheless existed over basic principles: the need to pro-tect personal liberty, the commitment to a republican form of government, and the importance of civic virtue for preserving citizen sovereignty. This embrace of basic governing principles could explain the deeper devotion to the U.S. Con-stitution, in contrast to the state documents, as well might the fear that an amended or completely altered Constitution might prove less malleable and ac-commodating for the governance of a diverse nation.

The Nature of American Constitutionalism

"Like the Bible, it ought to be read again and again." Franklin Delano Roosevelt made that remark about the U.S. Constitution in March 1937, during one of those cozy "fireside chats" that reached millions of Americans by radio. "It is an easy document to understand," he added. And six months later, speaking to his fellow citizens from the grounds of the Washington Monument on Constitution Day—a widely noted speech because 1937 marked the sesquicentennial of the Constitution, and because the President had provoked the nation with his controver-sial plan to add as many as six new justices to the Supreme Court—Roosevelt observed that the Constitution was "a layman's document, not a lawyer's contract," a theme that he reiterated several times in the course of this address.

It seems fair to say that Roosevelt's assertions were approximately half true. No one could disagree that the Constitution ought to be read and reread. Few would deny that it was meant to be comprehended by lay-men, by ordinary American citizens and aspirants for citizenship. Nev-ertheless, we must ponder whether it is truly "an easy document to understand." Although the very language of the Constitution is neither technical nor difficult, and although it is notably succinct—one nineteenth-century expert called it "a great code in a small compass"—abundant evidence exists that vast numbers of Americans, ever since 1787, have not understood it as well as they might. Even the so-called experts (judges, lawyers, political leaders, and teachers of constitutional law) have been unable to agree in critical instances about the proper application of key provisions of the Constitution, or about the intentions of those who wrote and approved it. Moreover, we do acknowledge that the Constitution developed from a significant number of compromises, and that the document's ambiguities are, for the most part, not acci-dental.

Understanding the U.S. Constitution is essential for many reasons. One of the most urgent is that difficult issues are now being and will

continue to be settled in accordance with past interpretations and with
our jurists' sense of what the founders meant. In order to make such
difficult determinations, we begin with the document itself. Quite often,
however, we also seek guidance from closely related or contextual documents, such as the notes kept by participants in the Constitutional Convention held at Philadelphia in 1787, from the correspondence of
delegates and other prominent leaders during the later 1780s, from *The
Federalist* papers, and even from some of the Anti-Federalist tracts written in opposition to the Constitution. In doing so, we essentially scruti-
nize the origins of American constitutionalism.

If observers want to know what is meant by constitutionalism, they
must uncover several layers of historical thought and experience in public affairs. Most obviously we look to the ideas that developed in the
United States during the final quarter of the eighteenth century—unquestionably the most brilliant and creative era in the entire history of
American political thought. We have in mind particularly, however, a
new set of assumptions that developed after 1775 about the very nature
of a constitution. Why, for example, when the colonists found themselves
nearly in a political state of nature after 1775, did they promptly feel
compelled to write state constitutions, many of which contained a bill of
rights? The patriots were, after all, preoccupied with fighting a revolution. Why not simply set up provisional governments based upon those
they already had and wait until Independence was achieved? If and
when the revolution succeeded, there would be time enough to write
permanent constitutions.

The revolutionaries did not regard the situation in such casual and
pragmatic terms. They shared a strong interest in what they called the
science of politics. They knew a reasonable amount about the history of
political theory. They believed in the value of ideas applied to problematic developments, and they felt that their circumstances were possibly
unique in all of human history. They knew with assurance that their
circumstances were changing, and changing rapidly. They wanted self-
government, obviously, but they also wanted legitimacy for their new-
born governments. Hence a major reason for writing constitutions. They
believed in the doctrine of the social contract (about which Jean-Jacques
Rousseau had written in 1762) and they believed in government by the
consent of the governed: two more reasons for devising written constitutions approved by the people or by their representatives.

The men responsible for composing and revising state constitutions
in the decade following 1775 regarded constitutions as social compacts
that delineated the fundamental principles upon which the newly
formed polities were agreed and to which they pledged themselves. They
frequently used the word "experiment" because they believed that they
were making institutional innovations that were risky, for they seemed
virtually unprecedented. They intended to create republican govern-

ments and assumed that to do so successfully required a fair amount of social homogeneity, a high degree of consensus regarding moral values, and a pervasive capacity for virtue, by which they meant unselfish, public-spirited behavior.

Even though they often spoke of liberty, they meant civil liberty rather than natural liberty. The latter implied unrestrained freedom—absolute liberty for the individual to do as he or she pleased. The former, by contrast, meant freedom of action so long as it was not detrimental to others and was beneficial to the common weal. When they spoke of *political* liberty they meant the freedom to be a participant, to vote and hold public office, responsible commitments that ought to be widely shared if republican institutions were to function successfully.

The colonists' experiences throughout the seventeenth and eighteenth centuries had helped to prepare them for this participatory and contractual view of the nature of government. Over and over again, as the circles of settlement expanded, colonists learned to improvise the rules by which they would be governed. They had received charters and had entered into covenants or compacts that may be described as proto-constitutional, i.e., cruder and less complete versions of the constitutional documents that would be formulated in 1776 and subsequently. These colonial charters not only described the structure of government, but frequently explained what officials (often called magistrates) could or could not do.

As a result, by the 1770s American attitudes toward constitutionalism were simultaneously derivative as well as original. On the one hand, they extravagantly admired the British constitution ("unwritten" in the sense that it was not contained in a single document) and declared it to be the ultimate achievement in the entire history of governmental development. On the other hand, as Oscar and Mary Handlin have explained, Americans no longer conceived of constitutions in general as the British had for centuries.

> In the New World the term, constitution, no longer referred to the actual organization of power developed through custom, prescription, and precedent. Instead it had come to mean a written frame of government setting fixed limits on the use of power. The American view was, of course, closely related to the rejection of the old conception that authority descended from the Crown to its officials. In the newer view—that authority was derived from the consent of the governed—the written constitution became the instrument by which the people entrusted power to their agents.[1]

* * *

Issues, Aspirations, and Apprehensions in 1787–1788

The major problems that confronted the Constitution-makers, and the issues that separated them from their opponents, can be specified by the key words that recur so frequently in the documents that follow in this collection. The Federalists often refer to the need for much more energy, stability, and efficiency in the national government. They fear anarchy and seek a political system better suited to America's geographical expanse: "an extensive sphere" was Madison's phrase in a letter to Jefferson.

The Anti-Federalists were apprehensive about "unrestrained power" (George Mason's words), about the great risk of national "consolidation" rather than a true confederation, about the failure to include a bill of rights in the new Constitution, about the prospect of too much power in the federal judiciary, about the "tendency to aristocracy" (see the "Federal Farmer"*), about insufficient separation of powers, and a government unresponsive to the needs of diverse and widely scattered people.

Because the two sides disagreed so strongly about the nature of the proposed government—was it genuinely federal or really national?—it is all too easy to lose sight of the common ground that they shared, a common ground that made it possible for many Anti-Federalists to support the Constitution fully even before George Washington's first administration came to a close in 1793. Both sides felt an absolute commitment to republicanism and the protection of personal liberty, as we have already seen. Both sides acknowledged that a science of politics was possible and ought to be pursued, but that "our own experience" (Madison's view, though held by "Brutus"† also) ought to be heeded above all. A majority on both sides accepted the inevitable role that interests would play in public affairs and recognized that public opinion would be a powerful force. The phrase "public opinion" appears eleven times explicitly in *The Federalist* papers, and many other times implicitly or indirectly.

The desire for happiness was invoked constantly. Although admittedly a vague and elusive concept, it clearly meant much more than the safeguarding of property (though the protection of property belonged under the rubric of happiness in the minds of many). For some it simply meant personal contentment; but increasingly there were leaders, such as George Washington, who spoke of "social happiness," which referred to harmony among diverse groups. David Humphreys's "Poem on the Happiness of America" (1786) provides an indication that this notion had national as well as individual and societal connotations.

Although both sides believed that the preservation of liberty was one of the most essential ends of government, the continued existence of chattel slavery in a freedom-loving society created considerable awkwardness for the founders. In 1775–1776, when the revolutionaries had explained the reasons for their rebellion, they frequently referred to a British plot to "enslave" Americans. The constant invocation of that

* [The pen name of Richard Henry Lee of Virginia, a noted Antifederalist.]
† [The pen name of Robert Yates, an Antifederalist.]

notion has puzzled many students because whatever the wisdom or un-wisdom of imperial policy in general, there most certainly was no con-spiracy in London to enslave America.

There really should be no mystery about the colonists' usage, how-ever, because as good Lockeans they knew full well the argument in chapter four of John Locke's *Second Treatise of Government*, entitled "Of Slavery" (an argument reiterated in Rousseau's *Social Contract*). "The lib-erty of man in society," Locke wrote, "is to be under no other legislative power but that established by consent in the commonwealth, nor under the dominion of any will or restraint of any law but what that legislative shall enact according to the trust put in it." The denial of *full* freedom quite simply meant "slavery."

Slavery and the international slave trade were discussed extensively in 1787 at the Constitutional Convention. By then, however, "slavery" was not often used as a theoretical and general synonym for unfreedom. It meant the permanent possession of one person (black) by another (white), usually for life, the slaveowner being entitled to own the chil-dren of his or her chattel as well. We must remember that the Convention met in secret session, and that the delegates agreed not to divulge infor-mation about their proceedings for fifty years. Consequently not very much was said publicly about slavery in 1787–1788 in connection with the Constitution. Not until 1840, when the U.S. government published James Madison's detailed notes on the Convention debates, did Ameri-cans learn just how much had been compromised at Philadelphia in or-der to placate South Carolina and Georgia. The Constitution essentially protected slavery where it existed, and remained mute about the legality of slavery in territories that might one day become additional states. Accommodation had prevailed in 1787, which meant, as it turned out, postponing for seventy-four years the moral and political crisis of the Union.

Legacies of American Constitutionalism

Although it is difficult for us fully to imagine the complexities of interest group politics, regional rivalries, and ideological differences in 1787, the instrumental achievement of that extraordinary Convention has gener-ally been appreciated over the years. Even such a sardonic mind as H. L. Mencken's conceded as much. "The amazing thing about the Con-stitution," he wrote, "is that it is as good as it is—that so subtle and complete a document emerged from that long debate. Most of the Fram-ers, obviously, were second-rate men; before and after their session they accomplished nothing in the world. Yet during that session they made an almost perfect job of the work in hand."

Their accomplishment was, indeed, remarkable. The distribution and separation of powers among three branches at the national level, and the development of federalism as a means of apportioning sovereignty between the nation and the states, have received broad recognition and the compliment of imitation by many other nations.

Equally appreciated is the fact that the U.S. Constitution is the oldest written national constitution in the world. (The Massachusetts Constitution of 1780, although amended and revised many times, is even older.) Its endurance is genuinely remarkable. We should therefore note that the framers deserve much of the credit for that endurance, not simply because they transcended their own limitations, . . . but because they contrived to restrict the ease with which the Constitution might be revised or reconsidered. There was considerable talk in 1787–1788 about holding a second convention in order to refine the product of the first. Anti-Federalists and many who were undecided wanted such a course of action. George Washington, however, regarded that idea as impractical. Hamilton, despite his dissatisfaction with many aspects of the Constitution, doubted whether a second convention could possibly be as successful as the first; and Madison feared a serious erosion of what had been accomplished in 1787.

It is easy to forget that the Philadelphia Convention vastly exceeded its authority, and that the men who met there undertook what amounted to a usurpation of legitimate authority. As [President] Franklin Delano Roosevelt pointed out on Constitution Day in 1937, contemporaries who opposed the newly drafted document "insisted that the Constitution itself was unconstitutional under the Articles of Confederation. But the ratifying conventions overruled them." The right of revolution had been explicitly invoked in 1776 and implicitly practiced in 1787. Having done their work, however, most of the delegates did not believe that it ought to be repealed or casually revised.

The complexity of changing or adding to the original document had profound implications for the subsequent history of American constitutionalism. First, it meant that in order to gain acceptance of their handiwork, the Federalists had to commit themselves, unofficially, to the formulation of a bill of rights when the first Congress met in 1789, even though many Federalists felt that such a list of protections was superfluous. They protested that a finite list of specified safeguards would imply that numerous other liberties might not be protected against encroachment by the government. The point, ultimately, is that promulgation of the U.S. Constitution required two sets of compromises rather than one: those that took place among the delegates to the Convention, and the subsequent sense that support for ratification would be rewarded by the explicit enumeration of broad civil liberties.

Next, the existence of various ambiguities in the Constitution meant that explication would subsequently be required by various authorities, such as the Supreme Court. The justices' interpretations would become part of the total "package" that we call American constitutionalism; but the justices did not always agree with one another, and the rest of the nation did not always agree with the justices. Those realities gave rise to an ongoing pattern that might be called conflict-within-consensus.

Some of those disputes and ambiguities involved very basic questions: What are the implications and limits of consent? Once we have participated in the creation of a polity and agreed to abide by its rules, then what? How are we to resolve the conflict that arises when the wishes or needs of a majority diminish the liberties or interests of a minority? This last question was the tough issue faced by the New England states in 1814, when they contemplated secession, and by South Carolina in 1828–1833 when a high tariff designed to protect northern manufacturing threatened economic distress to southern agricultural interests. And that, of course, was the thorny issue that precipitated southern secession and the greatest constitutional crisis of all in 1860–1861.

There is yet another ambiguity, or contradiction, in American constitutional thought—though it is less commonly noticed than the one described in the previous paragraph. As we have observed, the founders were not eager for a second convention, or for easy revisions or additions to their handiwork. They did provide for change; but they made the process complicated and slow. They did not believe that the fundamental law of a nation should be casually altered; and most Americans have accepted that constraint.

Nevertheless, on the *state* level Americans have amended, expanded, revised, and totally rewritten their constitutions with some frequency. A great deal of so-called positive law (i.e., legislative enactments) finds its way into state constitutions, with the result that many modern ones exceed one hundred pages in length. There is no clear explanation for this striking pattern of divergence between constitutionalism on the national and state levels. The curious pattern does suggest, however, that Americans have regarded the U.S. Constitution of 1787 as more nearly permanent than their state constitutions. Perhaps the pattern only tells us that achieving a national consensus for change in a large and diverse society is much more difficult than achieving a statewide consensus for change.

Whatever the explanation for this dualism in American constitutionalism, the paradox does not diminish the historical reality that writers of the federal as well as the first state constitutions all tried to establish charters clearly suited to the cultural assumptions and political realities of the American scene. Even though the founders explored the history of political thought in general and the history of republics in particular, they reached the commonsense conclusion that a constitution must be adapted to the character and customs of a people. Hence the debate in 1787–1788 over the relative merits of "consolidation" versus "confederation." Hence the concern about what sort of governmental system would work most effectively over a large geographical expanse. James

Madison conveyed this sense of American exceptionalism several times in a letter to Thomas Jefferson (then U.S. minister to France) in 1788, when a bill of rights was under consideration.

On August 28, 1788, a month after New York became the eleventh state to ratify the Constitution, George Washington sent Alexander Hamilton a letter from his temporary retirement at Mount Vernon. The future president acknowledged that public affairs were proceeding more smoothly than he had expected. Consequently, he wrote, "I hope the political Machine may be put in motion, without much effort or hazard of miscarrying." As he soon discovered, to put the new constitutional machine in motion would require considerable effort. It did not miscarry because the "machine" had been so soundly designed. A concerted effort would be required, however, to keep the machine successfully in operation. That should not occasion surprise. The founders had assumed an involved citizenry; and the governmental system they created functions best when their assumption is validated. That is the very essence of democratic constitutionalism.

DISCUSSION QUESTIONS

1. In your view, what would Kammen think about recent efforts to amend the Constitution to ban abortion, mandate a balanced budget, protect the flag against desecration, and protect victims' rights?

2. Although the flexibility of the Constitution helps explain its longevity, that flexibility comes at a price: ambiguity and gaps in constitutional language. What are some examples of constitutional language that is ambiguous? (The text of the Constitution is in the appendix.)

NOTES

1. Mary Handlin, *The Dimensions of Liberty* (Cambridge, Mass., 1961), p. 55.

2

The Federalist, No. 15 _we need strong central_

ALEXANDER HAMILTON - trying to convince N.Y to ratify the Constit

Federalists: Supported the Constitution

Despite the deference given the Constitution today, it did not command instant respect in 1787. The fight for ratification was bitter between the Federalists (those who supported the Constitution) and the Antifederalists (who feared that the new national government would become too powerful).

The Federalist papers, originally written as a series of newspaper editorials intended to persuade New York to ratify the Constitution, remains the most valuable exposition of the political theory underlying the Constitution. In The Federalist, No. 15, reprinted below, Alexander Hamilton (writing under the pseudonym Publius) is at his best arguing for the necessity of a stronger central government than that established under the Articles of Confederation. He points out the practical impossibility of engaging in concerted action when each of the thirteen states retains virtual sovereignty, and the need for a strong central government to hold the new country together politically and economically.

Such well-known patriots as Patrick Henry—"Give me liberty or give me death!"—opposed the new Constitution. The proposed national government was stronger than its predecessor, but this was precisely the problem for the Anti-federalists. A stronger national government could act in a more concerted manner in matters of foreign affairs and interstate commerce, but it also held the power to oppress the very people who gave it sovereignty.

In the course of the preceding papers I have endeavored, my fellow-citizens, to place before you in a clear and convincing light the importance of Union to your political safety and happiness. . . . [T]he point next in order to be examined is the "insufficiency of the present Confederation to the preservation of the Union." . . . There are material imperfections in our national system and . . . something is necessary to be done to rescue us from impending anarchy. The facts that support this opinion are no longer objects of speculation. They have forced themselves upon the sensibility of the people at large, and have at length extorted . . . a reluctant confession of the reality of those defects in the scheme of our federal government which have been long pointed out and regretted by the intelligent friends of the Union.

We may indeed with propriety be said to have reached almost the last stage of national humiliation. There is scarcely anything that can wound the pride or degrade the character of an independent nation which we do not experience. Are there engagements to the performance of which we are held by every tie respectable among men? These are the subjects of constant and unblushing violation. Do we owe debts to foreigners and to our own citizens contracted in a time of imminent peril for the preservation of our political existence? These remain without any proper or satisfactory provision for their discharge. . . . Are we in a condition to resent or to repel the aggression? We have neither troops, nor treasury, nor government. . . . Is public credit an indispensable resource in time of public danger? We seem to have abandoned its cause as desperate and irretrievable. Is commerce of importance to national wealth? Ours is at the lowest point of declension. Is respectability in the eyes of foreign powers a safeguard against foreign encroachments? The imbecility of our government even forbids them to treat with us. . . . Is private credit the friend and patron of industry? That most useful kind which relates to borrowing and lending is reduced within the narrowest limits, and this still more from an opinion of insecurity than from a scarcity of money. * * *

This is the melancholy situation to which we have been brought by those very maxims and counsels which would now deter us from adopting the proposed Constitution; and which, not content with having conducted us to the brink of a precipice, seem resolved to plunge us into the abyss that awaits us below. Here, my countrymen, impelled by every motive that ought to influence an enlightened people, let us make a firm stand for our safety, our tranquility, our dignity, our reputation. Let us at last break the fatal charm which has too long seduced us from the paths of felicity and prosperity.

* * * While [opponents of the Constitution] admit that the government of the United States is destitute of energy, they contend against conferring upon it those powers which are requisite to supply that energy. . . . This renders a full display of the principal defects of the Confederation necessary in order to show that the evils we experience do not proceed from minute or partial imperfections, but from fundamental errors in the structure of the building, which cannot be amended otherwise than by an alteration in the first principles and main pillars of the fabric.

The great and radical vice in the construction of the existing Confederation is in the principle of LEGISLATION FOR STATES OR GOVERNMENTS, in their CORPORATE OR COLLECTIVE CAPACITIES, and as contradistinguished from the INDIVIDUALS of whom they consist. Though this principle does not run through all the powers delegated to the Union, yet it pervades and governs those on which the efficacy of the rest depends. Except as to the rule of apportionment, the United States have an indefinite discretion to make requisitions for men and money; but they have no authority to raise either by regulations extending to the individual citizens of America. The consequence of this is that though in theory

-the problem with the A of C is that the states are separate. The Feds can't tell each of us what to do, only the states under A of C their resolutions concerning those objects are laws constitutionally binding on the members of the Union, yet in practice they are mere recommendations which the States observe or disregard at their option. * * *

There is nothing absurd or impracticable in the idea of a league or alliance between independent nations for certain defined purposes precisely stated in a treaty regulating all the details of time, place, circumstance, and quantity, leaving nothing to future discretion, and depending for its execution on the good faith of the parties. * * *

If the particular States in this country are disposed to stand in a similar relation to each other, and to drop the project of a general DISCRETIONARY SUPERINTENDENCE, the scheme would indeed be pernicious and would entail upon us all the mischiefs which have been enumerated under the first head; but it would have the merit of being, at least, consistent and practicable. Abandoning all views towards a confederate government, this would bring us to a simple alliance offensive and defensive; and would place us in a situation to be alternate friends and enemies of each other, as our mutual jealousies and rivalships, nourished by the intrigues of foreign nations, should prescribe to us.

But if we are unwilling to be placed in this perilous situation; if we still will adhere to the design of a national government, or, which is the same thing, of a superintending power under the direction of a common council, we must resolve to incorporate into our plan those ingredients which may be considered as forming the characteristic difference between a league and a government; we must extend the authority of the Union to the persons of the citizens—the only proper objects of government.

Government implies the power of making laws. It is essential to the idea of a law that it be attended with a sanction; or, in other words, a penalty or punishment for disobedience. If there be no penalty annexed to disobedience, the resolutions or commands which pretend to be laws will, in fact, amount to nothing more than advice or recommendation. This penalty, whatever it may be, can only be inflicted in two ways: by the agency of the courts and ministers of justice, or by military force; by the COERCION of the magistracy, or by the COERCION of arms. The first kind can evidently apply only to men; the last kind must of necessity be employed against bodies politic, or communities, or States. . . . In an association where the general authority is confined to the collective bodies of the communities that compose it, every breach of the laws must involve a state of war; and military execution must become the only instrument of civil obedience. Such a state of things can certainly not deserve the name of government, nor would any prudent man choose to commit his happiness to it.

There was a time when we were told that breaches by the States of the regulations of the federal authority were not to be expected; that a sense of common interest would preside over the conduct of the respective members, and would beget a full compliance with all the constitutional requisitions of the Union. This language, at the present day, would appear as wild as a great part of what we now hear from the same quarter will be thought, when we shall have received further lessons from that best oracle of wisdom, experience. It at all times betrayed an ignorance of the true springs by which human conduct is actuated, and belied the original inducements to the establishment of civil power. Why has government been instituted at all? Because the passions of men will not conform to the dictates of reason and justice without constraint. * * * ③

In addition to all this . . . it happens that in every political association which is formed upon the principle of uniting in a common interest a number of lesser sovereignties, there will be found a kind of eccentric tendency in the subordinate or inferior orbs by the operation of which there will be a perpetual effort in each to fly off from the common center. This tendency is not difficult to be accounted for. It has its origin in the love of power. Power controlled or abridged is almost always the rival and enemy of that power by which it is controlled or abridged. This simple proposition will teach us how little reason there is to expect that the persons intrusted with the administration of the affairs of the partic-ular members of a confederacy will at all times be ready with perfect good humor and an unbiased regard to the public weal to execute the resolutions or decrees of the general authority. * * *

People have a tendancy to do their own thing b/c they authority therefor the states don't follow what the Federal gov. tells them to do

If, therefore, the measures of the Confederacy cannot be executed without the intervention of the particular administrations, there will be little prospect of their being executed at all. . . . [Each state will evaluate every federal measure in light of its own interests] and in a spirit of interested and suspicious scrutiny, without that knowledge of national circumstances and reasons of state, which is essential to a right judgment, and with that strong predilection in favor of local objects, which can hardly fail to mislead the decision. The same process must be repeated in every member of which the body is constituted; and the execution of the plans, framed by the councils of the whole, will always fluctuate on the discretion of the ill-informed and prejudiced opinion of every part. * * *

④
The Fed. gov. needs to have power over individuals b/c states are biased + won't always listen to the Feds

In our case the concurrence of thirteen distinct sovereign wills is requisite under the Confederation to the complete execution of every important measure that proceeds from the Union. It has happened as was to have been foreseen. The measures of the Union have not been executed; and the delinquencies of the States have step by step matured themselves to an extreme, which has, at length, arrested all the wheels of the national government and brought them to an awful stand. Congress at this time scarcely possess the means of keeping up the forms of administration, till the States can have time to agree upon a more substantial substitute for the present shadow of a federal government. . . . Each State yielding to the persuasive voice of immediate interest or

⑤
13 states must agree to follow direction of the Feds for anything to happen

convenience has successively withdrawn its support, till the frail and tottering edifice seems ready to fall upon our heads and to crush us beneath its ruins.

PUBLIUS

DISCUSSION QUESTIONS

1. Do you think the national government is sufficiently held in check as Hamilton argues, or is the exercise of its authority so vast as to give credence to Antifederalist fears? In other words, would the Framers be dismayed or pleased with the scope of government powers today?

3
"The Paranoid Style in American Politics"

RICHARD HOFSTADTER

Michael Kammen noted above that in an effort to explain their rebellion against the British, the colonists "frequently referred to a British plot to 'enslave' Americans." And in their opposition to the proposed Constitution, Antifederalist writers forecast the oppression of the people at the hands of a new and powerful national government—a "thirteen-horned monster" whose complexity placed it beyond the reach of sovereign citizens.

Such political expressiveness is perhaps representative of the "paranoid style" of American politics, as defined by Richard Hofstader. The style, according to Hofstader, reflects "militant and suspicious minds" who perceive the threat of an entire system of values, and are "aroused" by the clash of interests thought to be "irreconcilable" and thus beyond the influence of a political process that promotes "bargain and compromise." Our constitutional framework has facilitated bargaining, compromise, and eventual progress on numerous passionately debated issues—public school desegregation and civil rights, regulation of the environment, establishment of a central bank. There are nevertheless numerous issues where antagonists stand in stark opposition, invoking the "paranoid style" to protect values thought to be irreconcilable: abortion rights, gun control, and the legalization of homosexual marriages, to name a few. The most recent version of this style of politics is the proliferation of various "militia" groups that renounce all ties to the federal government, refuse to pay taxes, and arm themselves for the coming revolution.

Although American political life has rarely been touched by the most acute varieties of class conflict, it has served again and again as an arena for uncommonly angry minds. Today this fact is most evident on the extreme right wing, which has shown, particularly in the Goldwater movement, how much political leverage can be got out of the animosities and passions of a small minority. Behind such movements there is a style of mind, not always right-wing in its affiliations, that has a long and varied history. I call it the paranoid style simply because no other word adequately evokes the qualities of heated exaggeration, suspiciousness, and conspiratorial fantasy that I have in mind. In using the expression "paranoid style," I am not speaking in a clinical sense, but borrowing a clinical term for other purposes. I have neither the competence nor the desire to classify any figures of the past or present as certifiable lunatics.

In fact, the idea of the paranoid style would have little contemporary relevance or historical value if it were applied only to people with profoundly disturbed minds. It is the use of paranoid modes of expression by more or less normal people that makes the phenomenon significant.

When I speak of the paranoid style, I use the term much as a historian of art might speak of the baroque or the mannerist style. It is, above all, a way of seeing the world and of expressing oneself. Webster defines paranoia, the clinical entity, as a chronic mental disorder characterized by systematized delusions of persecution and of one's own greatness. In the paranoid style, as I conceive it, the feeling of persecution is central, and it is indeed systematized in grandiose theories of conspiracy. But there is a vital difference between the paranoid spokesman in politics and the clinical paranoiac: although they both tend to be overheated, oversuspicious, overaggressive, grandiose, and apocalyptic in expression, the clinical paranoid sees the hostile and conspiratorial world in which he feels himself to be living as directed specifically *against him*; whereas the spokesman of the paranoid style finds it directed against a nation, a culture, a way of life whose fate affects not himself alone but millions of others. Insofar as he does not usually see himself singled out as the individual victim of a personal conspiracy, he is somewhat more rational and much more disinterested. His sense that his political passions are unselfish and patriotic, in fact, goes far to intensify his feeling of righteousness and his moral indignation.

Of course, the term "paranoid style" is pejorative, and it is meant to be; the paranoid style has a greater affinity for bad causes than good. But nothing entirely prevents a sound program or a sound issue from being advocated in the paranoid style, and it is admittedly impossible to settle the merits of an argument because we think we hear in its presentation the characteristic paranoid accents. Style has to do with the way in which ideas are believed and advocated rather than with the truth or falsity of their content.

A few simple and relatively non-controversial examples may make this distinction wholly clear. Shortly after the assassination of President Kennedy, a great deal of publicity was given to a bill, sponsored chiefly by Senator Thomas E. Dodd of Connecticut, to tighten federal controls over the sale of firearms through the mail. When hearings were being held on the measure, three men drove 2,500 miles to Washington from Bagdad, Arizona, to testify against it. Now there are arguments against the Dodd bill which, however unpersuasive one may find them, have the color of conventional political reasoning. But one of the Arizonans opposed it with what might be considered representative paranoid arguments, insisting that it was "a further attempt by a subversive power to make us part of one world socialistic government" and that it threatened to "create chaos" that would help "our enemies" to seize power.

Again, it is common knowledge that the movement against the fluoridation of municipal water supplies has been catnip for cranks of all kinds, especially for those who have obsessive fear of poisoning. It is conceivable that at some time scientists may turn up conclusive evidence that this practice is, on balance, harmful; and such a discovery would prove the anti-fluoridationists quite right on the substance of their position. But it could hardly, at the same time, validate the contentions of those among them who, in characteristic paranoid fashion, have charged that fluoridation was an attempt to advance socialism under the guise of public health or to rot out the brains of the community by introducing chemicals in the water supply in order to make people more vulnerable to socialist or communist schemes.

A distorted style is, then, a possible signal that may alert us to a distorted judgment, just as in art an ugly style is a cue to fundamental defects of taste. What interests me here is the possibility of using political rhetoric to get at political pathology. One of the most impressive facts about the paranoid style, in this connection, is that it represents an old and recurrent mode of expression in our public life which has frequently been linked with movements of suspicious discontent and whose content remains much the same even when it is adopted by men of distinctly different purposes. Our experience suggests too that, while it comes in waves of different intensity, it appears to be all but ineradicable.

I choose American history to illustrate the paranoid style only because I happen to be an Americanist, and it is for me a choice of convenience. But the phenomenon is no more limited to American experience than it is to our contemporaries. Notions about an all-embracing conspiracy on the part of Jesuits or Freemasons, international capitalists, international Jews, or Communists are familiar phenomena in many countries throughout modern history. One need only think of the response to President Kennedy's assassination in Europe to be reminded that Americans have no monopoly of the gift for paranoid improvisation. More important, the single case in modern history in which one might say that the paranoid style has had a consummatory triumph occurred not in the United States but in Germany. It is a common ingredient of fascism, and of frustrated nationalisms, though it appeals to many who are hardly fascists and it can frequently be seen in the left-wing press. The famous Stalin purge trials incorporated, in a supposedly juridical form, a wildly imaginative and devastating exercise in the paranoid style. In America it has been the preferred style only of *minority* movements. It can be argued, of course, that certain features of our history have given the paranoid style more scope and force among us than it has had in many other countries of the Western world. My intention here, however, is not to make such comparative judgments but simply to establish the reality of the style and to illustrate its frequent historical recurrence.

We may begin with a few American examples. Here is Senator

McCarthy, speaking in June 1951 about the parlous situation of the United States:

> How can we account for our present situation unless we believe that men high in this government are concerting to deliver us to disaster? This must be the product of a great conspiracy, a conspiracy on a scale so immense as to dwarf any previous such venture in the history of man. A conspiracy of infamy so black that, when it is finally exposed, its principals shall be forever deserving of the maledictions of all honest men. . . . What can be made of this unbroken series of decisions and acts contributing to the strategy of defeat? They cannot be attributed to incompetence. . . . The laws of probability would dictate that part of . . . [the] decisions would serve this country's interest.[1]

Now let us turn back fifty years to a manifesto signed in 1895 by a number of leaders of the Populist party:

> As early as 1865–66 a conspiracy was entered into between the gold gamblers of Europe and America. . . . For nearly thirty years these conspirators have kept the people quarreling over less important matters, while they have pursued with unrelenting zeal their one central purpose. . . . Every device of treachery, every resource of statecraft, and every artifice known to the secret cabals of the international gold ring are being made use of to deal a blow to the prosperity of the people and the financial and commercial independence of the country.[2]

Next, a Texas newspaper article of 1855:

> . . . It is a notorious fact that the Monarchs of Europe and the Pope of Rome are at this very moment plotting our destruction and threatening the extinction of our political, civil, and religious institutions. We have the best reasons for believing that corruption has found its way into our Executive Chamber, and that our Executive head is tainted with the infectious venom of Catholicism. . . . The Pope has recently sent his ambassador of state to this country on a secret commission, the effect of which is an extraordinary boldness of the Catholic Church throughout the United States. . . . These minions of the Pope are boldly insulting our Senators; reprimanding our Statesmen; propagating the adulterous union of Church and state; abusing with foul calumny all governments but Catholic; and spewing out the bitterest execrations on all Protestantism. The Catholics in the United States receive from abroad more than $200,000 annually for the propagation of their creed. Add to this the vast revenue collected here. . . .[3]

Finally, this from a sermon preached in Massachusetts in 1798:

> Secret and systematic means have been adopted and pursued, with zeal and activity, by wicked and artful men, in foreign countries, to undermine the foundations of this Religion [Christianity], and to overthrow its Altars, and thus to deprive the world of its benign influence on society. . . . These impious conspirators and philosophists have completely effected their purposes in a large portion of Europe, and boast of their means of accomplishing their plans in all parts of Christendom, glory in the certainty of their success, and set opposition at defiance. . . .[4]

These quotations, taken from intervals of half a century, give the key-note of the style of thought. In the history of the United States one finds it, for example, in the anti-Masonic movement, the nativist and anti-Catholic movement, in certain spokesmen for abolitionism who regarded the United States as being in the grip of a slaveholders' conspiracy, in many writers alarmed by Mormonism, in some Greenback and Populist writers who constructed a great conspiracy of international bankers, in the exposure of a munitions makers' conspiracy of the First World War, in the popular left-wing press, in the contemporary American right wing, and on both sides of the race controversy today, among White Citizens Councils and Black Muslims.

* * *

The recurrence of the paranoid style over a long span of time and in different places suggests that a mentality disposed to see the world in the paranoid's way may always be present in some considerable minority of the population. But the fact that movements employing the paranoid style are not constant but come in successive episodic waves suggests that the paranoid disposition is mobilized into action chiefly by social conflicts that involve ultimate schemes of values and that bring fundamental fears and hatreds, rather than negotiable interests, into political action. Catastrophe or the fear of catastrophe is most likely to elicit the syndrome of paranoid rhetoric.

In American experience, ethnic and religious conflicts, with their threat of the submergence of whole systems of values, have plainly been the major focus for militant and suspicious minds of this sort, but elsewhere class conflicts have also mobilized such energies. The paranoid tendency is aroused by a confrontation of opposed interests which are (or are felt to be) totally irreconcilable, and thus by nature not susceptible to the normal political processes of bargain and compromise. The situation becomes worse when the representatives of a particular political interest—perhaps because of the very unrealistic and unrealizable nature of their demands—cannot make themselves felt in the political process. Feeling that they have no access to political bargaining or the making of decisions, they find their original conception of the world of power as omnipotent, sinister, and malicious fully confirmed. They see only the consequences of power—and this through distorting lenses—and have little chance to observe its actual machinery. L. B. Namier once said that "the crowning attainment of historical study" is to achieve "an intuitive sense of how things do not happen." It is precisely this kind of awareness that the paranoid fails to develop. He has a special resistance of his own, of course, to such awareness, but circumstances often deprive him of exposure to events that might enlighten him. We are all sufferers from history, but the paranoid is a double sufferer, since he is afflicted not only by the real world, with the rest of us, but by his fantasies as well.

DISCUSSION QUESTIONS

1. The Founders were most concerned about the tyranny of the majority and the power to trample minority rights. Their response was to create a system that provided access to a variety of minority interests that would check each other. Do you think it is a strength or a weakness of our Constitution that those citizens and politicians—typically minority interests and often on the fringes of society—who espouse "paranoid" views about government policy receive public attention and often play a role in defining the government's relationship to society?

NOTES

1. *Congressional Record*, 82nd Congress, 1st session (June 14, 1951), p. 6602.
2. Reprinted from Frank McVey, "The Populist Movement," *Economic Studies*, I (August 1896), pp. 201–2.
3. *Texas State Times*, September 15, 1855.
4. Jedidiah Moore, *A Sermon Preached at Charlestown, November 29, 1798* (Worcester, Mass., 1799), pp. 20–1.

The Debate: An Economic Interpretation of the Constitution

One of the longest-running debates over the Constitution focuses on the motivation of the founders in drafting the document. Was the motivation ideological, based on beliefs of self-governance, the nature of a social contract, and the role of representation? Or was the motivation purely economic, based on a perceived need to preserve economic interests that were threatened under the system of governance of the Articles of Confederation? And if the motivation was economic, what economic interests divided the Antifederalists from the Federalists in their opposition to or support for the Constitution?

One of the earliest and most controversial efforts to answer the question was written by Charles Beard in 1913. Beard argued that those who favored the Constitution and played the primary role in its drafting were motivated by the need to better protect their substantial "personality" interests—money, public securities, manufactures, and trade and shipping (or commerce)—in contrast to its opponents, who were primarily small farmers (with small real estate holdings) and debtor interests. Not only was its motivation less than democratic, Beard argued, but the Constitution was ratified by only one-sixth of the male population because voting was limited to property owners.

Robert Brown takes strong opposition to Beard's thesis. His criticism focuses mainly on Beard's use of historical data and its interpretation, leaving the door open for other interpretations of the motivations behind the Constitution as well as the base of public support for the document.

Beard - Constitution for $, commerce etc. (the Anti-Feds had debt interests) ratified by 1/6 of males b/c only property owners could vote

Brown - opposes

4

From *An Economic Interpretation of the Constitution of the United States*

— people making Constitution were out for their own interests b/c they were elites - $ - public securities - trade/shipping - manufactures agrees w/ D + Z

Charles A. Beard

The requirements for an economic interpretation of the formation and adoption of the Constitution may be stated in a hypothetical proposition which, although it cannot be verified absolutely from ascertainable data, will at once illustrate the problem and furnish a guide to research and generalization.

It will be admitted without controversy that the Constitution was the creation of a certain number of men, and it was opposed by a certain number of men. Now, if it were possible to have an economic biography of all those connected with its framing and adoption,—perhaps about 160,000 men altogether,—the materials for scientific analysis and classi-fication would be available. Such an economic biography would include a list of the real and personal property owned by all of these men and their families: lands and houses, with incumbrances, money at interest, slaves, capital invested in shipping and manufacturing, and in state and continental securities.

Suppose it could be shown from the classification of the men who supported and opposed the Constitution that there was no line of prop-erty division at all; that is, that men owning substantially the same amounts of the same kinds of property were equally divided on the matter of adoption or rejection—it would then become apparent that the Constitution had no ascertainable relation to economic groups or classes, but was the product of some abstract causes remote from the chief busi-ness of life—gaining a livelihood.

Suppose, on the other hand, that substantially all of the merchants, money lenders, security holders, manufacturers, shippers, capitalists, and financiers and their professional associates are to be found on one side in support of the Constitution and that substantially all or the major portion of the opposition came from the non-slaveholding farmers and the debtors—would it not be pretty conclusively demonstrated that our fundamental law was not the product of an abstraction known as "the whole people," but of a group of economic interests which must have expected beneficial results from its adoption? Obviously all the facts here desired cannot be discovered, but the data presented in the following chapters bear out the latter hypothesis, and thus a reasonable presump-tion in favor of the theory is created.

* * *

The purpose of such an inquiry is not, of course, to show that the Constitution was made for the personal benefit of the members of the Convention. Far from it. Neither is it of any moment to discover how many hundred thousand dollars accrued to them as a result of the foun-dation of the new government. The only point here considered is: Did they represent distinct groups whose economic interests they understood and felt in concrete, definite form through their own personal experience with identical property rights, or were they working merely under the guidance of abstract principles of political science?

* * *

The Disfranchised

In an examination of the structure of American society in 1787, we first encounter four groups whose economic status had a definite legal expression: the slaves, the indented servants, the mass of men who could *4 economic groups:* not qualify for voting under the property tests imposed by the state *① slaves,* constitutions and laws, and women, disfranchised and subjected to the *② indentured servants* discriminations of the common law. These groups were, therefore, not *③ men who didn't qualify* represented in the Convention which drafted the Constitution, except *under property tests* under the theory that representation has no relation to voting. *④ women*

How extensive the disfranchisement really was cannot be determined. In some states, for instance, Pennsylvania and Georgia, propertyless mechanics in the towns could vote; but in other states the freehold qualifications certainly excluded a great number of the adult males.

In no state, apparently, had the working-class developed a consciousness of a separate interest or an organization that commanded the attention of the politicians of the time. In turning over the hundreds of pages of writings left by eighteenth-century thinkers one cannot help being impressed with the fact that the existence and special problems of a working-class, then already sufficiently numerous to form a considerable portion of society, were outside the realm of politics, except in so far as the future power of the proletariat was foreseen and feared.

When the question of the suffrage was before the Convention, Madison warned his colleagues against the coming industrial masses: "Viewing the subject in its merits alone, the freeholders of the Country would be the safest depositories of Republican liberty. In future times a great majority of the people will not only be without landed [property], but any other sort of property. These will either combine under the influence of their common situation; in which case, the rights of property and the public liberty will not be secure in their hands, or, which is more probable, they will become the tools of opulence and ambition; in which case there will be equal danger on another side."

* * *

It is apparent that a majority of the states placed direct property qualifications on the voters, and the other states eliminated practically all who were not taxpayers. Special safeguards for property were secured in the qualifications imposed on members of the legislatures in New Hampshire, Massachusetts, New York, New Jersey, Maryland, North Carolina, South Carolina, and Georgia. Further safeguards were added by the qualifications imposed in the case of senators in New Hampshire, Massachusetts, New Jersey, New York, Maryland, North Carolina, and South Carolina.

While these qualifications operated to exclude a large portion of the adult males from participating in elections, the wide distribution of real property created an extensive electorate and in most rural regions gave the legislatures a broad popular basis. Far from rendering to personal property that defence which was necessary to the full realization of its rights, these qualifications for electors admitted to the suffrage its most dangerous antagonists: the small farmers and many of the debtors who were the most active in all attempts to depreciate personalty [private property] by legislation. Madison with his usual acumen saw the inadequacy of such defence and pointed out in the Convention that the really serious assaults on property (having in mind of course, personalty) had come from the "freeholders."

Nevertheless, in the election of delegates to the Convention, the representatives of personalty in the legislatures were able by the sheer weight of their combined intelligence and economic power to secure delegates from the urban centres or allied with their interests. Happily for them, all the legislatures which they had to convince had not been elected on the issue of choosing delegates to a national Convention, and did not come from a populace stirred up on that question. The call for the Convention went forth on February 21, 1787, from Congress, and within a few months all the legislatures, except that of Rhode Island, had responded. Thus the heated popular discussion usually incident to such a momentous political undertaking was largely avoided, and an orderly and temperate procedure in the selection of delegates was rendered possible.

* * *

A survey of the economic interests of the members of the Convention presents certain conclusions:

A majority of the members were lawyers by profession.

Most of the members came from towns, on or near the coast, that is, from the regions in which personalty was largely concentrated.

Not one member represented in his immediate personal economic interests the small farming or mechanic classes.

The overwhelming majority of members, at least five-sixths, were immediately, directly, and personally interested in the outcome of their labors at Philadelphia, and were to a greater or less extent economic beneficiaries from the adoption of the Constitution.

1. Public security interests were extensively represented in the Convention. Of the fifty-five members who attended no less than forty appear on the Records of the Treasury Department for sums varying from a few dollars up to more than one hundred thousand dollars. [A list of their names follows.]

It is interesting to note that, with the exception of New York, and possibly Delaware, each state had one or more prominent representatives in the Convention who held more than a negligible amount of securities, and who could therefore speak with feeling and authority on the question of providing in the new Constitution for the full discharge of the public debt: [list of names]

2. Personalty invested in lands for speculation was represented by at least fourteen members: [list of names]

3. Personalty in the form of money loaned at interest was represented by at least twenty-four members: [list of names]

4. Personalty in mercantile, manufacturing, and shipping lines was represented by at least eleven members: [list of names]

5. Personalty in slaves was represented by at least fifteen members: [list of names]

It cannot be said, therefore, that the members of the Convention were "disinterested." On the contrary, we are forced to accept the profoundly significant conclusion that they knew through their personal experiences in economic affairs the precise results which the new government that they were setting up was designed to attain. As a group of doctrinaires, like the Frankfort assembly of 1848, they would have failed miserably; but as practical men they were able to build the new government upon the only foundations which could be stable: fundamental economic interests.

* * *

Conclusions

At the close of this long and arid survey—partaking of the nature of catalogue—it seems worth while to bring together the important conclusions for political science which the data presented appear to warrant.

[1.] The movement for the Constitution of the United States was originated and carried through principally by four groups of personalty interests which had been adversely affected under the Articles of Confederation: money, public securities, manufactures, and trade and shipping.

[2.] The first firm steps toward the formation of the Constitution were taken by a small and active group of men immediately interested through their personal possessions in the outcome of their labors.

[3.] No popular vote was taken directly or indirectly on the proposition to call the Convention which drafted the Constitution.

[4.] A large propertyless mass was, under the prevailing suffrage qualifications, excluded at the outset from participation (through representatives) in the work of framing the Constitution.

[5.] The members of the Philadelphia Convention which drafted the Constitution were, with a few exceptions, immediately, directly, and personally interested in, and derived economic advantages from, the establishment of the new system.

[6.] The Constitution was essentially an economic document based upon the concept that the fundamental private rights of property are anterior to government and morally beyond the reach of popular majorities.

[7.] The major portion of the members of the Convention are on record as recognizing the claim of property to a special and defensive position in the Constitution.

[8.] In the ratification of the Constitution, about three-fourths of the adult males failed to vote on the question, having abstained from the elections at which delegates to the state conventions were chosen, either on account of their indifference or their disfranchisement by property qualifications.

ratified by 1/6 of males

[9.] The Constitution was ratified by a vote of probably not more than one-sixth of the adult males.

7 of 5 states actually ratifying

[10.] It is questionable whether a majority of the voters participating in the elections for the state conventions in New York, Massachusetts, New Hampshire, Virginia, and South Carolina, actually approved the ratification of the Constitution.

[11.] The leaders who supported the Constitution in the ratifying conventions represented the same economic groups as the members of the Philadelphia Convention; and in a large number of instances they were also directly and personally interested in the outcome of their efforts.

personal interests vs. small debtor farmers

[12.] In the ratification, it became manifest that the line of cleavage for and against the Constitution was between substantial personalty interests on the one hand and the small farming and debtor interests on the other.

[13.] The Constitution was not created by "the whole people" as the jurists have said; neither was it created by "the states" as Southern nullifiers long contended; but it was the work of a consolidated group whose interests knew no state boundaries and were truly national in their scope.

5

From *Charles Beard and the Constitution:*
A Critical Analysis of "An Economic
Interpretation of the Constitution"

ROBERT E. BROWN

people hating the Constitution wouldn't fight for their own beliefs.

—framers are elites but they work equalitaharimism (= share of the pie)

Conclusions

At the end of Chapter XI Beard summarized his findings in fourteen paragraphs under the heading of "Conclusions" (pp. 324–25). Actually, these fourteen conclusions merely add up to the two halves of the Beard thesis. One half, that the Constitution originated with and was carried through by personalty interests—money, public securities, man-ufactures, and commerce—is to be found in paragraphs two, three, six, seven, eight, twelve, thirteen, and fourteen. The other half—that the Constitution was put over undemocratically in an undemocratic society—is expressed in paragraphs four, five, nine, ten, eleven, and fourteen. The lumping of these conclusions under two general headings makes it easier for the reader to see the broad outlines of the Beard thesis.

* * *

If historical method means the gathering of data from primary sources, the critical evaluation of the evidence thus gathered, and the drawing of conclusions consistent with this evidence, then we must con-clude that Beard has done great violation to such method in this book. He admitted that the evidence had not been collected which, given the proper use of historical method, should have precluded the writing of the book. Yet he nevertheless proceeded on the assumption that a valid interpretation could be built on secondary writings whose authors had likewise failed to collect the evidence. If we accept Beard's own maxim, "no evidence, no history," and his own admission that the data had never been collected, the answer to whether he used historical method properly is self-evident.

[margin note: Beard didn't use historical evidence]

* * *

Finally, the conclusions which he drew were not justified even by the kind of evidence which he used. If we accepted his evidence strictly at face value, it would still not add up to the fact that the Constitution was put over undemocratically in an undemocratic society by personalty. The citing of property qualifications does not prove that a mass of men were disfranchised. And if we accept his figures on property holdings, either we do not know what most of the delegates had in realty and personalty, or we know that realty outnumbered personalty three to one (eighteen to six). Simply showing that a man held public securities is not sufficient to prove that he acted only in terms of his public securities. If we ignore Beard's own generalizations and accept only his evidence, we would have to conclude that most of the property in the country in 1787 was real estate, that real property was widely distributed in rural areas, which included most of the country, and that even the men who were directly concerned with the Constitution, and especially Washington, were large holders of realty.

Perhaps we can never be completely objective in history, but certainly we can be more objective than Beard was in this book. Naturally the historian must always be aware of the biases, the subjectivity, the pitfalls that confront him, but this does not mean that he should not make an effort to overcome these obstacles. Whether Beard had his thesis before he had his evidence, as some have said, is a question that each reader must answer for himself. Certain it is that the evidence does not justify the thesis.

So instead of the Beard interpretation that the Constitution was put over undemocratically in an undemocratic society by personal property, the following fourteen paragraphs are offered as a possible interpretation of the Constitution and as suggestions for future research on that document.

1. The movement for the Constitution was originated and carried through by men who had long been important in both economic and political affairs in their respective states. Some of them owned person-alty, more of them owned realty, and if their property was adversely affected by conditions under the Articles of Confederation, so also was the property of the bulk of the people in the country, middle-class farmers as well as town artisans.

2. The movement for the Constitution, like most important movements, was undoubtedly started by a small group of men. They were probably interested personally in the outcome of their labors, but the benefits which they expected were not confined to personal property or, for that matter, strictly to things economic. And if their own interests would be enhanced by a new government, similar interests of other men, whether agricultural or commercial, would also be enhanced.

3. Naturally there was no popular vote on the calling of the convention which drafted the Constitution. Election of delegates by state legislatures was the constitutional method under the Articles of Confederation, and had been the method long established in this country. Delegates to the Albany Congress, the Stamp Act Congress, the First Continental Congress, the Second Continental Congress, and subsequent congresses under the Articles were all elected by state legislatures, not by the people. Even the Articles of Confederation had been sanctioned by state legislatures, not by popular vote. This is not to say that the Constitutional Convention should not have been elected directly by the people, but only that such a procedure would have been unusual at the time. Some of the opponents of the Constitution later stressed, without avail, the fact that the Convention had not been directly elected. But at the time the Convention met, the people in general seemed to be about as much concerned over the fact that they had not elected the delegates as the people of this country are now concerned over the fact that they do not elect our delegates to the United Nations.

4. Present evidence seems to indicate that there were no "propertyless masses" who were excluded from the suffrage at the time. Most men were middle-class farmers who owned realty and were qualified voters, and, as the men in the Convention said, mechanics had always voted in the cities. Until credible evidence proves otherwise, we can assume that state legislatures were fairly representative at the time. We cannot condone the fact that a few men were probably disfranchised by prevailing

property qualifications, but it makes a great deal of difference to an interpretation of the Constitution whether the disfranchised comprised ninety-five per cent of the adult men or only five per cent. Figures which give percentages of voters in terms of the entire population are misleading, since less than twenty per cent of the people were adult men. And finally, the voting qualifications favored realty, not personality. ⟵————

5. If the members of the Convention were directly interested in the outcome of their work and expected to derive benefits from the establishment of the new system, so also did most of the people of the country. We have many statements to the effect that the people in general expected substantial benefits from the labors of the Convention.

6. The Constitution was not just an economic document, although economic factors were undoubtedly important. Since most of the people were middle-class and had private property, practically everybody was interested in the protection of property. A constitution which did not protect property would have been rejected without any question, for the American people had fought the Revolution for the preservation of life, liberty, and property. Many people believed that the Constitution did not go far enough to protect property, and they wrote these views into the amendments to the Constitution. But property was not the only concern of those who wrote and ratified the Constitution, and we would be doing a grave injustice to the political sagacity of the Founding Fathers if we assumed that property or personal gain was their only motive.

7. Naturally the delegates recognized that the protection of property was important under government, but they also recognized that personal rights were equally important. In fact, persons and property were usually bracketed together as the chief objects of government protection.

8. If three-fourths of the adult males failed to vote on the election of delegates to ratifying conventions, this fact signified indifference, not disfranchisement. We must not confuse those who could *not* vote with those who *could* vote but failed to exercise their right. Many men at the time bewailed the fact that only a small portion of the voters ever exercised their prerogative. But this in itself should stand as evidence that the conflict over the Constitution was not very bitter, for if these people had felt strongly one way or the other, more of them would have voted.

Even if we deny the evidence which I have presented and insist that American society was undemocratic in 1787, we must still accept the fact that the men who wrote the Constitution believed that they were writing it for a democratic society. They did not hide behind an iron curtain of secrecy and devise the kind of conservative government that they wanted without regard to the views and interests of "the people." More than anything else, they were aware that "the people" would have to ratify what they proposed, and that therefore any government which would be acceptable to the people must of necessity incorporate much of what was customary at the time. The men at Philadelphia were practical politicians, not political theorists. They recognized the multitude of different ideas and interests that had to be reconciled and compromised before a constitution would be acceptable. They were far too practical, and represented far too many clashing interests themselves, to fashion a government weighted in favor of personalty or to believe that the people would adopt such a government.

9. If the Constitution was ratified by a vote of only one-sixth of the adult men, that again demonstrates indifference and not disfranchisement. Of the one-fourth of the adult males who voted, nearly two-thirds favored the Constitution. Present evidence does not permit us to say what the popular vote was except as it was measured by the votes of the ratifying conventions.

2/3 favored

10. Until we know what the popular vote was, we cannot say that it is questionable whether a majority of the voters in several states favored the Constitution. Too many delegates were sent uninstructed. Neither can we count the towns which did not send delegates on the side of those opposed to the Constitution. Both items would signify indifference rather than sharp conflict over ratification.

delegates were uninstructed

11. The ratifying conventions were elected for the specific purpose of adopting or rejecting the Constitution. The people in general had anywhere from several weeks to several months to decide the question. If they did not like the new government, or if they did not know whether they liked it, they could have voted *no* and there would have been no Constitution. Naturally the leaders in the ratifying conventions represented the same interests as the members of the Constitutional Convention—mainly realty and some personalty. But they also represented their constituents in these same interests, especially realty.

people had plenty of time to reject

12. If the conflict over ratification had been between substantial personalty interests on the one hand and small farmers and debtors on the other, there would not have been a constitution. The small farmers comprised such an overwhelming percentage of the voters that they could have rejected the new government without any trouble. Farmers and debtors are not synonymous terms and should not be confused as such. A town-by-town or county-by-county record of the vote would show clearly how the farmers voted.

if small farmers really objected it wouldn't have passed

13. The Constitution was created about as much by the whole people as any government could be which embraced a large area and depended on representation rather than on direct participation. It was also created in part by the states, for as the *Records* show, there was strong state sentiment at the time which had to be appeased by compromise. And it was created by compromising a whole host of interests throughout the country, without which compromises it could never have been adopted. If the intellectual historians are correct, we cannot explain the Constitution without considering the psychological factors also. Men are motivated by what they believe as well as by what they have. Sometimes

psychological

their actions can be explained on the basis of what they hope to have or hope that their children will have. Madison understood this fact when he said that the universal hope of acquiring property tended to dispose people to look favorably upon property. It is even possible that some men support a given economic system when they themselves have nothing to gain by it. So we would want to know what the people in 1787 thought of their class status. Did workers and small farmers believe that they were lower-class, or did they, as many workers do now, consider themselves middle-class? Were the common people trying to eliminate the Washingtons, Adamses, Hamiltons, and Pinckneys, or were they trying to join them?

As did Beard's conclusions, these suggestions really add up to two major propositions: the Constitution was adopted in a society which was fundamentally democratic, not undemocratic; and it was adopted by a people who were primarily middle-class property owners, especially farmers who owned realty, not just by the owners of personalty. At present these points seem to be justified by the evidence, but if better evidence in the future disproves or modifies them, we must accept that evidence and change our interpretation accordingly.

After this critical analysis, we should at least not begin future research on this period of American history with the illusion that the Beard thesis of the Constitution is valid. If historians insist on accepting the Beard thesis in spite of this analysis, however, they must do so with the full knowledge that their acceptance is founded on "an act of faith," not an analysis of historical method, and that they are indulging in a "noble dream," not history.

DISCUSSION QUESTIONS

1. Judging from these readings, do you think the Framers were governed by self-interest or a commitment to principle, or some combination, when they drafted the Constitution? Explain your answer.

CHAPTER 2

Federalism and the Separation of Powers: Then and Now

[handwritten: — "division of power" = dual federalism b/t state + national among judicial/ legislative, executive]

[handwritten: 6 — checks + balance]

The Federalist, Nos. 51 and 46

JAMES MADISON

Some of the most divisive and bitter political battles in our nation's history have occurred over interpretations of the constitutional principle of federalism, or the division of powers and functions between the state governments and the national government. The struggle for desegregation and the civil rights of minorities, the legalization of abortion, the selective incorporation of the Bill of Rights into the Fourteenth Amendment, slavery, and the Civil War all ultimately turned on the question, Who has the authority to govern, the states, or the national government? Our federal system is a delicate balance of power and shared responsibility between nation and states, each with constitutional authority to pass laws, levy taxes, and protect the interests and rights of citizens. It is a dynamic balance of power, easily destabilized by economic crises, political initiatives, and Supreme Court rulings, but often resolved in more recent years by the question, Who will pay the price for implementing and enforcing government policy?

    Arguments over this delicate balance of power animated debates over constitutional ratification. In The Federalist, *No. 51, James Madison argued that to achieve a "double security" against majority tyranny, the power of government must be divided across (between state and national governments) and within levels of government (among the courts, the president, and Congress). Such a division insured that if any one institution tried to become too powerful, the others would step in to counteract it.*

    This "double security" did not satisfy those who feared that the national powers would encroach on state sovereignty. In The Federalist *No. 46, Madison went to great lengths to reassure the states that they would continue to wield a high degree of power, arguing that "the first and most natural attachment of the people will be to the governments of their respective states." While recognizing the potential for conflicts between state and federal governments, Madison concluded that the power retained by the states would be sufficient to resist appropriation by the newly established national government.*

No. 51

To the People of the State of New York:

To what expedient, then, shall we finally resort for maintaining in practice the necessary partition of power among the several departments as laid down in the Constitution? The only answer that can be given is, that as all these exterior provisions are found to be inadequate, the defect must be supplied by so contriving the interior structure of the government as that its several constituent parts may, by their mutual relations, be the means of keeping each other in their proper places. Without presuming to undertake a full development of this important idea, I will hazard a few general observations, which may perhaps place it in a clearer light, and enable us to form a more correct judgment of the principles and structure of the government planned by the convention.

In order to lay a due foundation for that separate and distinct exercise of the different powers of government, which to a certain extent is admitted on all hands to be essential to the preservation of liberty, it is evident that each department should have a will of its own; and consequently should be so constituted that the members of each should have as little agency as possible in the appointment of the members of the others. Were this principle rigorously adhered to, it would require that all the appointments for the supreme executive, legislative, and judiciary magistracies should be drawn from the same fountain of authority, the people, through channels having no communication whatever with one another. Perhaps such a plan of constructing the several departments would be less difficult in practice than it may in contemplation appear. Some difficulties, however, and some additional expense would attend the execution of it. Some deviations, therefore, from the principle must be admitted. In the constitution of the judiciary department in particular, it might be inexpedient to insist rigorously on the principle: first, because peculiar qualifications being essential in the members, the primary consideration ought to be to select that mode of choice which best secures these qualifications; secondly, because the permanent tenure by which the appointments are held in that department must soon destroy all sense of dependence on the authority conferring them.

It is equally evident, that the members of each department should be as little dependent as possible on those of the others for the emoluments annexed to their offices. Were the executive magistrate or the judges not independent of the legislature in this particular, their independence in every other would be merely nominal.

But the great security against a gradual concentration of the several powers in the same department, consists in giving to those who administer each department the necessary constitutional means and personal motives to resist encroachments of the others. The provision for defence must in this, as in all other cases, be made commensurate to the danger of attack. Ambition must be made to counteract ambition. The interest of the man must be connected with the constitutional rights of the place. It may be a reflection on human nature, that such devices should be necessary to control the abuses of government. But what is government itself, but the greatest of all reflections on human nature? If men were angels, no government would be necessary. If angels were to govern men, neither external nor internal controls on government would be necessary. In framing a government which is to be administered by men over men, the great difficulty lies in this: you must first enable the government to control the governed; and in the next place oblige it to control itself. A dependence on the people is, no doubt, the primary control on the government; but experience has taught mankind the necessity of auxiliary precautions.

This policy of supplying, by opposite and rival interests, the defect of better motives might be traced through the whole system of human affairs, private as well as public. We see it particularly displayed in all the subordinate distributions of power, where the constant aim is to divide and arrange the several offices in such a manner as that each may be a check on the other—that the private interest of every individual may be a sentinel over the public rights. These inventions of prudence cannot be less requisite in the distribution of the supreme powers of the State.

But it is not possible to give to each department an equal power of self-defence. In republican government the legislative authority necessarily predominates. The remedy for this inconveniency is to divide the legislature into different branches; and to render them, by different modes of election and different principles of action, as little connected with each other as the nature of their common functions and their common dependence on the society will admit. It may even be necessary to guard against dangerous encroachments by still further precautions. As the weight of the legislative authority requires that it should be thus divided, the weakness of the executive may require, on the other hand, that it should be fortified. An absolute negative on the legislature appears, at first view, to be the natural defence with which the executive magistrate should be armed. But perhaps it would be neither altogether safe nor alone sufficient. On ordinary occasions it might not be exerted with the requisite firmness, and on extraordinary occasions it might be perfidiously abused. May not this defect of an absolute negative be supplied by some qualified connection between this weaker department and the weaker branch of the stronger department, by which the latter may be led to support the constitutional rights of the former, without being too much detached from the rights of its own department?

If the principles on which these observations are founded be just . . . and they be applied as a criterion to the several State constitutions and to the federal Constitution, it will be found that if the latter does not perfectly correspond with them, the former are infinitely less able to bear such a test.

There are, moreover, two considerations particularly applicable to the federal system of America, which place that system in a very interesting point of view.

First. In a single republic, all the power surrendered by the people is submitted to the administration of a single government; and the usurpations are guarded against by a division of the government into distinct and separate departments. In the compound republic of America, the power surrendered by the people is first divided between two distinct governments, and then the portion allotted to each subdivided among distinct and separate departments. Hence a double security arises to the rights of the people. The different governments will control each other, at the same time that each will be controlled by itself.

Second. It is of great importance in a republic not only to guard the society against the oppression of its rulers, but to guard one part of the society against the injustice of the other part. Different interests necessarily exist in different classes of citizens. If a majority be united by a common interest, the rights of the minority will be insecure. There are but two methods of providing against this evil: the one by creating a will in the community independent of the majority—that is, of the society itself; the other by comprehending in the society so many separate descriptions of citizens as will render an unjust combination of a majority of the whole very improbable, if not impracticable. The first method prevails in all governments possessing an hereditary or self-appointed authority. This, at best, is but a precarious security; because a power independent of the society may as well espouse the unjust views of the major, as the rightful interests of the minor party, and may possibly be turned against both parties. The second method will be exemplified in the federal republic of the United States. Whilst all authority in it will be derived from and dependent on the society, the society itself will be broken into so many parts, interests and classes of citizens, that the rights of individuals or of the minority will be in little danger from interested combinations of the majority. In a free government the security for civil rights must be the same as that for religious rights. It consists in the one case in the multiplicity of interests and in the other in the multiplicity of sects. The degree of security in both cases will depend on the number of interests and sects; and this may be presumed to depend on the extent of country and number of people comprehended under the same government. This view of the subject must particularly recommend a proper federal system to all the sincere and considerate friends of republican government, since it shows that in exact proportion as the territory of the Union may be formed into more circumscribed Confederacies or States, oppressive combinations of a majority will be facilitated; the best security under the republican forms for the rights of every class of citizens will be diminished; and consequently the stability and independence of some member of the government, the only other security, must be proportionally increased. Justice is the end [that is, the goal] of government. It is the end of civil society. It ever has been and ever will be pursued until it be obtained, or until liberty be lost in the pursuit. In a society under the forms of which the stronger faction can readily unite and oppress the weaker, anarchy may as truly be said to reign as in a state of nature, where the weaker individual is not secured against the violence of the stronger; and, as in the latter state even the stronger individuals are prompted, by the uncertainty of their condition, to submit to a government which may protect the weak as well as themselves; so, in the former state will the more powerful factions or parties be gradually induced by a like motive to wish for a government which will protect all parties, the weaker as well as the more powerful. It can be little doubted that if the State of Rhode Island was separated from the Confederacy and left to itself, the insecurity of rights under the popular form of government within such narrow limits would be displayed by such reiterated oppressions of factious majorities that some power altogether independent of the people would soon be called for by the voice of the very factions whose misrule had proved the necessity of it. In the extended republic of the United States and among the great variety of interests, parties, and sects which it embraces, a coalition of a majority of the whole society could seldom take place on any other principles than those of justice and the general good; whilst there being thus less danger to a minor from the will of a major party, there must be less pretext, also, to provide for the security of the former, by introducing into the government a will not dependent on the latter, or, in other words, a will independent of the society itself. It is no less certain than it is important, notwithstanding the contrary opinions which have been entertained, that the larger the society, provided it lie within a practical sphere, the more duly capable it will be of self-government. And happily for the *republican cause*, the practicable sphere may be carried to a very great extent by a judicious modification and mixture of the *federal principle*.

PUBLIUS

[handwritten margin note: —if we can collect rasti nat'l gov. from states those people will remember what the states wants & better represent it]

[handwritten margin note: —nat'l gov. won't get too strong, each rep. will represent the state]

No. 46

I proceed to inquire whether the federal government or the State governments will have the advantage with regard to the predilection and support of the people. Notwithstanding the different modes in which they are appointed, we must consider both of them as substantially dependent on the great body of the citizens of the United States. . . . The federal and State governments are in fact but different agents and trustees of the people, constituted with different powers and designed for different purposes. The adversaries of the Constitution seem to have lost sight of the people altogether in their reasonings on this subject; and to have viewed these different establishments not only as mutual rivals and enemies, but as uncontrolled by any common superior in their efforts to usurp the authorities of each other. These gentlemen must here be reminded of their error. They must be told that the ultimate authority, wherever the derivative may be found, resides in the people alone, and that it will not depend merely on the comparative ambition or address of the different governments whether either, or which of them, will be able to enlarge its sphere of jurisdiction at the expense of the other. Truth, no less than decency, requires that the event in every case should be supposed to depend on the sentiments and sanction of their common constituents.

Many considerations . . . seem to place it beyond doubt that the first and most natural attachment of the people will be to the governments of their respective States. Into the administration of these a greater number of individuals will expect to rise. From the gift of these a greater number of offices and emoluments will flow. By the superintending care of these, all the more domestic and personal interests of the people will be regulated and provided for. With the affairs of these, the people will be more familiarly and minutely conversant. And with the members of these will a greater proportion of the people have the ties of personal acquaintance and friendship, and of family and party attachments; on the side of these, therefore, the popular bias may well be expected most strongly to incline.

The remaining points on which I propose to compare the federal and State governments are the disposition and the faculty they may respectively possess to resist and frustrate the measures of each other.

It has been already proved that the members of the federal will be more dependent on the members of the State governments than the latter will be on the former. It has appeared also that the prepossessions of the people, on whom both will depend, will be more on the side of the State governments than of the federal government. So far as the disposition of each towards the other may be influenced by these causes, the State governments must clearly have the advantage. But in a distinct and very important point of view, the advantage will lie on the same side. The prepossessions, which the members themselves will carry into the federal government, will generally be favorable to the States; whilst it will rarely happen that the members of the State governments will carry into the public councils a bias in favor of the general government. A local spirit will infallibly prevail much more in the members of Congress than a national spirit will prevail in the legislatures of the particular States.

. . . What is the spirit that has in general characterized the proceedings of Congress? A perusal of their journals, as well as the candid acknowledgments of such as have had a seat in that assembly, will inform us that the members have but too frequently displayed the character rather of partisans of their respective States than of impartial guardians of a common interest; that where on one occasion improper sacrifices have been made of local considerations to the aggrandizement of the federal government, the great interests of the nation have suffered on a hundred from an undue attention to the local prejudices, interests, and views of the particular States. I mean not by these reflections to insinuate that the new federal government will not embrace a more enlarged plan of policy than the existing government may have pursued; much less that its views will be as confined as those of the State legislatures; but only that it will partake sufficiently of the spirit of both to be disinclined to invade the rights of the individual States, or the prerogatives of their governments.

Were it admitted, however, that the federal government may feel an equal disposition with the State governments to extend its power beyond the due limits, the latter would still have the advantage in the means of defeating such encroachments. If an act of a particular State, though unfriendly to the national government, be generally popular in that State, and should not too grossly violate the oaths of the State officers, it is executed immediately and, of course, by means on the spot and depending on the State alone. The opposition of the federal government, or the interposition of federal officers, would but inflame the zeal of all parties on the side of the State, and the evil could not be prevented or repaired, if at all, without the employment of means which must always be resorted to with reluctance and difficulty. On the other hand, should an unwarrantable measure of the federal government be unpopular in particular States, which would seldom fail to be the case, or even a warrantable measure be so, which may sometimes be the case, the means of opposition to it are powerful and at hand. The disquietude of the people; their repugnance and, perhaps, refusal to co-operate with the officers of the Union; the frowns of the executive magistracy of the State; the embarrassments created by legislative devices, which would often be added on such occasions, would oppose, in any State, difficulties not to be despised; would form, in a large State, very serious impediments; and where the sentiments of several adjoining States happened to be in unison, would present obstructions which the federal government would hardly be willing to encounter.

But ambitious encroachments of the federal government on the authority of the State governments would not excite the opposition of a single State, or of a few States only. They would be signals of general alarm. Every government would espouse the common cause. A correspondence would be opened. Plans of resistance would be concerted. One spirit would animate and conduct the whole. The same combinations, in short, would result from an apprehension of the federal, as was produced by the dread of a foreign, yoke; and unless the projected innovations should be voluntarily renounced, the same appeal to a trial of force would be made in the one case as was made in the other.

The only refuge left for those who prophesy the downfall of the State governments is the visionary supposition that the federal government may previously accumulate a military force for the projects of ambition. The reasonings contained in these papers must have been employed to little purpose indeed, if it could be necessary now to disprove the reality of this danger. That the people and the States should, for a sufficient period of time, elect an uninterrupted succession of men ready to betray both; that the traitors should, throughout this period, uniformly and systematically pursue some fixed plan for the extension of the military establishment; that the governments and the people of the States should silently and patiently behold the gathering storm and continue to supply the materials until it should be prepared to burst on their own heads must appear to everyone more like the incoherent dreams of a delirious jealousy, or the misjudged exaggerations of a counterfeit zeal, than like the sober apprehensions of genuine patriotism. Extravagant as the supposition is, let it, however, be made. Let a regular army, fully equal to the resources of the country, be formed; and let it be entirely at the devotion of the federal government: still it would not be going too far to say that the State governments with the people on their side would be able to repel the danger.

Besides the advantage of being armed, which the Americans possess over the people of almost every other nation, the existence of subordinate governments, to which the people are attached and by which the militia officers are appointed, forms a barrier against the enterprises of ambition, more insurmountable than any which a simple government of any form can admit of.

Let us not insult the free and gallant citizens of America with the suspicion that they would be less able to defend the rights of which they would be in actual possession than the debased subjects of arbitrary power would be to rescue theirs from the hands of their oppressors. Let us rather no longer insult them with the supposition that they can ever reduce themselves to the necessity of making the experiment by a blind and tame submission to the long train of insidious measures which must precede and produce it.

The argument under the present head may be put into a very concise form, which appears altogether conclusive. Either the mode in which the federal government is to be constructed will render it sufficiently dependent on the people, or it will not. On the first supposition, it will be restrained by that dependence from forming schemes obnoxious to their constituents. On the other supposition, it will not possess the confidence of the people, and its schemes of usurpation will be easily defeated by the State governments, who will be supported by the people.

On summing up the considerations stated in this and the last paper, they seem to amount to the most convincing evidence that the powers proposed to be lodged in the federal government are as little formidable to those reserved to the individual States as they are indispensably necessary to accomplish the purposes of the Union; and that all those alarms which have been sounded of a meditated and consequential annihilation of the State governments must, on the most favorable interpretation, be ascribed to the chimerical fears of the authors of them.

PUBLIUS

DISCUSSION QUESTIONS

1. According to Madison, the principles of "separation of powers" and "checks and balances" operate to limit the authority of the national government. How? Discuss at least one current issue involving these two principles and the constitutional issues at stake.

2. Is Madison right in saying that people are more attached to their state governments than to the national government? Why or why not? If not, would it facilitate the democratic process if they were?

7
From *The Price of Federalism*

Paul Peterson

In this concise overview of American Federalism, Paul Peterson argues that both the early and the more modern systems of shared sovereignty between the national government and the states have had their disadvantages. From the early period of "dual federalism" to the contemporary system of a dominant national government, the battle over national and state government jurisdiction and power has led to bloodshed and war; the denial of political, social, and economic rights; and regional inequalities among the states.

Nevertheless, Peterson argues, federalism has also facilitated capital growth and development, the creation of infrastructures, and social programs that have greatly improved the quality of life for millions of Americans. Once the national government took responsibility for guaranteeing civil rights and civil liberties, the states "became the engines of economic development." Not all states are equally wealthy, but the national government has gradually diminished some of these differences by financing many social and economic programs. The latest battle over the proper form of federal relations involved welfare policy. Most Republicans in Congress wanted to give back to states the power to devise their own programs, whereas most Democrats wanted to retain a larger degree of federal government control. A welfare reform bill that gave states more autonomy and control was passed by Congress and signed into law by President Clinton in August 1996.

The Price of Early Federalism

As a principle of government, federalism has had a dubious history. It remains on the margins of political respectability even today. I was recently invited to give a presentation on metropolitan government before a United Nations conference. When I offered to discuss how the federal principle could be used to help metropolitan areas govern themselves more effectively, my sponsors politely advised me that this topic would be poorly received. The vast majority of UN members had a unified form of government, I was told, and they saw little of value in federalism. We reached a satisfactory compromise. I replaced "federal" with "two-tier form of government."

Thomas Hobbes, the founder of modern political thought, would have blessed the compromise, for he, too, had little room for federalism in his understanding of the best form of government. Hobbes said that people agreed to have a government over them only because they realized that in a state of nature, that is, when there is no government, life becomes a war of all against all. If no government exists to put malefactors in jail, everyone must become a criminal simply to avoid being a victim. Life becomes "nasty, brutish and short." To avoid the violent state of nature, people need and want rule by a single sovereign. Division of power among multiple sovereigns encourages bickering among them. Conflicts become inevitable, as each sovereign tries to expand its power (if for no other reason than to avoid becoming the prey of competing sovereigns). Government degenerates into anarchy and the world returns to the bitter state of nature from which government originally emerged.

The authors of the *Federalist* papers defended dual sovereignty by turning Hobbes's argument in favor of single sovereignty on its head. While Hobbes said that anything less than a single sovereign would lead to war of all against all, the *Federalist* argued that the best way of preserving liberty was to divide power. If power is concentrated in any one place, it can be used to crush individual liberty. Even in a democracy there can be the tyranny of the majority, the worst kind of tyranny because it is so stifling and complete. A division of power between the national and state governments reduces the possibility that any single majority will be able to control all centers of governmental power. The national government, by defending the country against foreign aggression, prevents external threats to liberty. The state governments, by denying power to any single dictator, reduce threats to liberty from within. As James Madison said in his defense of the Constitution, written on the eve of its ratification,

> The power surrendered by the people is first divided between two distinct governments, and then the portion allotted to each subdivided among distinct and separate departments. Hence a double security arises to the rights of the people. The different governments will control each other, at the same time that each will be controlled by itself. [*The Federalist*, No. 51]

Early federalism was built on the principle of dual sovereignty. The Constitution divided sovereignty between state and nation, each in control of its own sphere. Some even interpreted the Constitution to mean that state legislatures could nullify federal laws. Early federalism also gave both levels of government their own military capacity. Congress was given the power to raise an army and wage war, but states were allowed to maintain their own militia.

The major contribution of early federalism to American liberties took place within a dozen years after the signing of the Constitution. Liberty is never established in a new nation until those in authority have peacefully ceded power to a rival political faction. Those who wrote the Constitution and secured its ratification, known as the Federalists, initially captured control of the main institutions of the national government:

Congress, the presidency, and the Supreme Court. Those opposed to the new constitutional order, the antifederalists, had to content themselves with an opposition role in Congress and control over a number of state governments, most notably Virginia's.

The political issues dividing the two parties were serious. The Federalist party favored a strong central government, a powerful central bank that could facilitate economic and industrial development, and a strong, independent executive branch. Federalists had also become increasingly disturbed by the direction the French Revolution had taken. They were alarmed by the execution of thousands, the confiscation of private property, and the movement of French troops across Europe. They called for the creation of a national army and reestablished close ties with Britain.

The antifederalists, who became known as Democratic-Republicans, favored keeping most governmental power in the hands of state governments. They were opposed to a national bank, a strong presidency, and industrial government. They thought the United States would remain a free country only if it remained a land of independent farmers. They bitterly opposed the creation of a national army for fear it would be used to repress political opposition. Impressed by the French Revolution's commitment to the rights of man, they excused its excesses. The greater danger, they thought, was the reassertion of British power, and they denounced the Federalists for seeming to acquiesce in the seizure of U.S. seamen by the British navy.

The conflict between the two sides intensified after George Washington retired to his home in Mount Vernon. In 1800 Thomas Jefferson, founder of the Democratic-Republican party, waged an all-out campaign to defeat Washington's Federalist successor, John Adams. In retrospect, the central issue of the election was democracy itself. Could an opposition party drive a government out of power? Would political leaders accept their defeat?

So bitter was the feud between the two parties that Representative Matthew Lyon, a Democratic-Republican, spit in the face of a Federalist on the floor of Congress. Outside the Congress, pro-French propagandists relentlessly criticized Adams. To silence the opposition, Congress, controlled by the Federalists, passed the Alien and Sedition Acts. One of the Alien Acts gave President Adams the power to deport any foreigners "concerned in any treasonable or secret machinations against the government." The Sedition Act made it illegal to "write, print, utter, or publish . . . any false, scandalous and malicious writing . . . against . . . the Congress of the United States, or the President."

The targets of the Sedition Acts soon became clear. Newspaper editors supporting the Democratic-Republicans were quickly indicted, and ten were brought to trial and convicted by juries under the influence of Federalist judges. Matthew Lyon was sentenced to a four-month jail term for claiming, presumably falsely, that President Adams had an "unbounded thirst for ridiculous pomp, foolish adulation, and selfish avarice." Even George Washington lent his support to this political repression.

Federalism undoubtedly helped the fledgling American democracy survive this first constitutional test. When the Federalists passed the Alien and Sedition Acts, Democratic-Republicans in the Virginia and Kentucky state legislatures passed resolutions nullifying the laws. When it looked as if Jefferson's victory in the election of 1800 might be stripped away by a Federalist-controlled House of Representatives, both sides realized that the Virginia state militia was at least as strong as the remnants of the Continental Army. Lacking the national army they had tried to establish, the Federalists chose not to fight. They acquiesced in their political defeat in part because their opponents had military as well as political power, and because they themselves could retreat to their own regional base of power, the state and local governments of New England and the mid-Atlantic states.

Jefferson claimed his victory was a revolution every bit as comprehensive as the one fought in 1776. The Alien and Sedition Acts were discarded, nullified not by a state legislature but by the results of a national election. President Adams returned to private life without suffering imprisonment or exile. Many years later, he and Jefferson reconciled their differences and developed through correspondence a close friendship. They died on the same day, the fiftieth anniversary of the Declaration of Independence. To both, federalism and liberty seemed closely intertwined.

The price to be paid for early federalism became more evident with the passage of time. To achieve the blessings of liberty, early federalism divided sovereign power. When Virginia and Kentucky nullified the Alien and Sedition Acts, they preserved liberties only by threatening national unity. With the election of Jefferson, the issue was temporarily rendered moot, but the doctrine remained available for use when southerners once again felt threatened by encroaching national power.

The doctrine of nullification was revived in 1830 by John C. Calhoun, sometime senator from South Carolina, who objected to high tariffs that protected northern industry at the expense of southern cotton producers. When Congress raised the tariff, South Carolina's legislature threatened to declare the law null and void. Calhoun, then serving as Andrew Jackson's vice-president, argued that liberties could be trampled by national majorities unless states could nullify tyrannical acts. Andrew Jackson, though elected on a state's rights ticket, remained committed to national supremacy. At the annual Democratic banquet honoring the memory of Thomas Jefferson, Calhoun supporters sought to trap Jackson into endorsing the doctrine. But Jackson, aware of the scheme, raised his glass in a dramatic toast to "Our federal union: it must be preserved!" Not to be outdone, Calhoun replied in kind: "The union, next to our liberty, most dear!"

A compromise was found to the overt issue, the tariff, but it was not so easy to resolve the underlying issue of slavery. In the infamous Dred Scott decision, the Supreme Court interpreted federalism to mean that boundaries could not be placed on the movements of masters and slaves. Northern territories could not free slaves that came within their boundaries; to do so deprived masters of their Fifth Amendment right not to be deprived of their property without due process of law. The decision spurred northern states to elect Abraham Lincoln president, which convinced southern whites that their liberties, most dear, were more important than federal union.

To Lincoln, as to Jackson, the union was to be preserved at all costs. Secession meant war. War meant the loss of 1 million lives, the destruction of the southern economy, the emancipation of African Americans from slavery, the demise of the doctrine of nullification, and the end to early federalism. Early federalism, with its doctrine of dual sovereignty, may have initially helped to preserve liberty, but it did so at a terrible price. As Hobbes feared, the price of dual sovereignty was war.

Since the termination of the Civil War, Americans have concluded that they can no longer trust their liberties to federalism. Sovereignty must be concentrated in the hands of the national government. Quite apart from the dangers of civil war, the powers of state and local governments have been used too often by a tyrannical majority to trample the rights of religious, racial, and political minorities. The courts now seem a more reliable institutional shelter for the nation's liberties.

But if federalism is no longer necessary or even conducive to the preservation of liberty, then what is its purpose? Is it merely a relic of an outdated past? Are the majority of the members of the United Nations correct in objecting to the very use of the word?

The Rise of Modern Federalism

The answers to these questions have been gradually articulated in the 130 years following the end of the Civil War. Although the states lost their sovereignty, they remained integral to the workings of American government. Modern federalism no longer meant dual sovereignty and shared military capacity. Modern federalism instead meant only that each level of government had its own independently elected political leaders and its own separate taxing and spending capacity. Equipped with these tools of quasi-sovereignty, each level of government could take all but the most violent of steps to defend its turf.

Although sovereignty and military capacity now rested firmly in the hands of the national government, modern federalism became more complex rather than less so. Power was no longer simply divided between the nation and its states. Cities, counties, towns, school districts, special districts, and a host of additional governmental entities, each with its own elected leaders and taxing authority, assumed new burdens and responsibilities.

Just as the blessings bestowed by early federalism were evident from its inception, so the advantages of modern federalism were clear from the onset. If states and localities were no longer the guarantors of liberty, they became the engines of economic development. By giving state and local governments the autonomy to act independently, the federal system facilitated the rapid growth of an industrial economy that eventually surpassed its European competitors. Canals and railroads were constructed, highways and sewage systems built, schools opened, parks designed, and public safety protected by cities and villages eager to make their locality a boomtown.

The price to be paid for modern federalism did not become evident until government attempted to grapple with the adverse side effects of a burgeoning capitalist economy. Out of a respect for federalism's constitutional status and political durability, social reformers first worked with and through existing components of the federal system, concentrating much of their reform effort on state and local governments. Only gradually did it become clear that state and local governments, for all their ability to work with business leaders to enhance community prosperity, had difficulty meeting the needs of the poor and the needy.

It was ultimately up to the courts to find ways of keeping the price of modern federalism within bounds. Although dual sovereignty no longer meant nullification and secession, much remained to be determined about the respective areas of responsibility of the national and state governments. At first the courts retained remnants of the doctrine of dual sovereignty in order to protect processes of industrialization from governmental intrusion. But with the advent of the New Deal, the constitutional power of the national government expanded so dramatically that the doctrine of dual sovereignty virtually lost all meaning. Court interpretations of the constitutional clauses on commerce and spending have proved to be the most significant.

According to dual sovereignty theory, article 1 of the Constitution gives Congress the power to regulate commerce "among the states," but the regulation of intrastate commerce was to be left to the states. So, for example, in 1895 the Supreme Court said that Congress could not break up a sugar monopoly that had a nationwide impact on the price of sugar, because the monopoly refined its sugar within the state of Pennsylvania. The mere fact that the sugar was to be sold nationwide was only "incidental" to its production. As late as 1935, the Supreme Court, in a 6 to 3 decision, said that Congress could not regulate the sale of poultry because the regulation took effect after the chickens arrived within the state of Illinois, not while they were in transit.

Known as the "sick chicken" case, this decision was one of a series in which the Supreme Court declared unconstitutional legislation passed in the early days of President Franklin Roosevelt's efforts to establish his New Deal programs. Seven of the "nine old men" on the Court had been appointed by Roosevelt's conservative Republican predecessors. By declaring many New Deal programs in violation of the commerce clause, the Supreme Court seemed to be substituting its political views for those of elected officials. In a case denying the federal government the right to protect workers trying to organize a union in the coal industry, the Republican views of the Court seemed to lie just barely below the surface of a technical discussion of the commerce clause. Justice George Sutherland declared, "The relation of employer and employee is a local relation . . . over which the federal government has no legislative control."

The Roosevelt Democrats were furious at decisions that seemed to deny the country's elected officials the right to govern. Not since Dred Scott had judicial review been in such disrepute. Roosevelt decided to "pack the court" by adding six new judges over and above the nine already on the Court. Although Roosevelt's court-packing scheme did not survive the political uproar on Capitol Hill, its effect on the Supreme Court was noticeable. In the midst of the court-packing debate, Justices Charles Hughes and Owen Roberts, who had agreed with Sutherland's opinion in the coal case, changed their mind and voted to uphold the Wagner Act, a new law designed to facilitate the formation of unions. In his opinion, Hughes did not explicitly overturn the coal miner decision (for which he had voted), but he did say: "When industries organize themselves on a national scale, . . . how can it be maintained that their industrial labor relations constitute a forbidden field into which Congress may not enter?" Relations between employers and their workers, once said to be local, suddenly became part of interstate commerce.

The change of heart by Hughes and Roberts has been called "the switch in time that saved nine." The New Deal majority that emerged on the court was soon augmented by judges appointed by Roosevelt. Since the New Deal, the definition of interstate commerce has continued to expand. In 1942 a farmer raising twenty-three acres of wheat, all of which might be fed to his own livestock, was said to be in violation of the crop quotas imposed by the Agricultural Adjustment Act of 1938. Since he was feeding his cows himself, he was not buying grain on the open market, thereby depressing the worldwide price of grain. With such a definition of interstate commerce, nothing was local.

The expansion of the meaning of the commerce clause is a well-known part of American political history. The importance to federalism of court interpretations of the "spending clause" is less well known. The constitutional clause in question says that Congress has the power to collect taxes to "provide for the . . . general welfare." But how about Congress's power to collect taxes for the welfare of specific individuals or groups?

The question first arose in a 1923 case, when a childless woman said she could not be asked to pay taxes in order to finance federal grants to states for programs that helped pregnant women. Since she received no benefit from the program, she sued for return of the taxes she had paid to cover its costs. In a decision that has never been reversed, the Supreme Court said that she had suffered no measurable injury and therefore had no right to sue the government. Her taxes were being used for a wide variety of purposes. The amount being spent for this program was too small to be significant. The court's decision to leave spending issues to Congress was restated a decade later when the social security program was also challenged on the grounds that monies were being directed to the elderly, not for the general welfare. Said Justice Benjamin N. Cardozo for a court majority: "The conception of the spending power . . . [must find a point somewhere] between particular and general. . . . There is a middle ground . . . in which discretion is large. The discretion, however, is not confided to the Court. The discretion belongs to Congress, unless the choice is clearly wrong."

The courts have ever since refused to review Congress's power to spend money. They have also conceded to Congress the right to attach any regulations to any aid Congress provides. In 1987 Congress provided a grant to state governments for the maintenance of their highways, but conditioned 5 percent of the funds on state willingness to raise the drinking age from eighteen to twenty-one. The connection between the appropriation and the regulation was based on the assumption that youths under the age of twenty-one are more likely to drive after drinking than those over twenty-one. Presumably, building more roads would only encourage more inebriated young people to drive on them. Despite the fact that the connection between the appropriation and the regulation was problematic, the Supreme Court ruled that Congress could attach any reasonable conditions to its grants to the states. State sovereignty was not violated, because any state could choose not to accept the money.

In short, the courts have virtually given up the doctrine of judicial review when it comes to matters on which Congress can spend money. As a consequence, most national efforts to influence state governments come in the form of federal grants. Federal aid can also be used to influence local governments, such as counties, cities, towns, villages, and school districts. These local governments, from a constitutional point of view, are mere creatures of the state of which they are part. They have no independent sovereignty.

The Contemporary Price of Federalism

If constitutional doctrine has evolved to the point that dual sovereign theory has been put to rest, this does not mean that federalism has come to an end. Although ultimate sovereignty resides with the national government, state and local governments still have certain characteristics and capabilities that make them constituent components of a federal system. . . . Two characteristics of federalism are fundamental. First, citizens elect officials of their choice for each level of government. Unless the authority of each level of government rests in the people, it will become the agent of the other. Second, each level of government raises money through taxation from the citizens residing in the area for which it is responsible. It is hard to see how a system could be regarded as federal unless each level of government can levy taxes on its residents. Unless each level of government can raise its own fiscal resources, it cannot act independently.

Although the constitutional authority of the national government has steadily expanded, state and local governments remain of great practical significance. Almost half of all government spending for domestic (as distinct from foreign and military) purposes is paid for out of taxes raised by state and local governments.

The sharing of control over domestic policy among levels of government has many benefits, but federalism still exacts its price. It can lead to great regional inequalities. Also, the need for establishing cooperative relationships among governments can contribute to great inefficiency in the administration of government programs.

DISCUSSION QUESTIONS

1. What is the constitutional basis for federalism?

2. How has the relationship between state governments and the national government changed since the early years of the republic?

3. Does a federal system serve our needs today? Does the federal government have too much power relative to the states? What would be the advantages and disadvantages of a reduced Federal presence in state matters?

8

"Guns, the Commerce Clause, and the Court"

Robert Katzmann

What is the proper balance between state and federal authority? Much of the controversy surrounds the so-called commerce clause (Article I, Section 8), which gives Congress the power to "regulate commerce . . . among the several states." Commerce among the several states—interstate commerce—is subject to federal government regulation, whereas intrastate *activity—that taking place entirely within one state—is a matter for the individual states. The question is, what kind of economic activity is actually related to "commerce," and when is it "interstate," making it legitimate for the U.S. Congress to regulate? Just how the Court has answered these questions has changed dramatically over the years, depending on its deference to legislative decisions and the philosophies of the different justices. In the twentieth century, however, the Court has taken a broad view of the commerce clause, allowing federal intervention in crime control, civil rights, and other important policies. Yet in a recent case involving the commerce clause, the Court took a step toward a narrower reading. In* United States v. Lopez, *the Court struck down a federal law making it a crime to possess a gun within one thousand feet of a school, holding that this sort of regulation was not sufficiently related to interstate commerce to be a proper area of federal control. Some analysts think the decision could signify an era of a more activist court, scrutinizing congressional decisions quite rigorously.*

If timing is often everything, the Supreme Court majority in *United States v. Lopez* 1995 might wish that its decision had been announced some other day. A week after the Oklahoma City bombing, with public concern about violent crime mounting, the High Court, by a vote of 5–4, declared that Congress had exceeded its commerce clause authority by enacting the Gun-Free Zones Act of 1990 prohibiting the possession of guns within 1,000 feet of a school. Reaction to *Lopez* was swift and intense because it unleashed passions about two highly charged issues —crime and the far-reaching power of the federal government to regulate through the commerce clause.

President Clinton warned that the Court's ruling "could condemn more of our children to going to schools where there are guns." Others, citing the more than 40 states that have outlawed guns in schools, wondered whether Congress should have passed the law in the first place.

Ultimately, however, ways will surely be found to enact federal legislation that survives Supreme Court review.

Beyond the debate about the role of the federal government in crime prevention and the merits of federalizing crime, the Court's decision raises important questions about the scope of Congress's regulatory powers. The Court's ruling, striking down for the first time in 60 years a federal regulation of private activity, casts a shadow over what had been taken for granted—the power of Congress to regulate all manner of activity through the commerce clause.

Writing for the majority, Chief Justice William Rehnquist declared that "we start with first principles," that the Constitution created a federal government of limited and enumerated powers. In distinguishing major precedents sustaining congressional regulation of economic activity, the Court concluded that some activities are too removed from interstate commerce to be upheld under the commerce clause. The 1990 law, the majority determined, was not related to interstate commerce, and in any case, Congress did not attempt to show that the activity affected commerce. Chief Justice Rehnquist further asserted that were the Court "to accept the Government's argument [that Congress could regulate all activities that might lead to violent crime], we are hard-pressed to posit any activity by an individual that Congress is without power to regulate."

Justice Stephen Breyer's dissenting opinion, joined by Justices Ruth Bader Ginsburg, David Souter, and John Paul Stevens, maintained that the Court "must ask whether Congress could have had a rational basis for finding a significant (or substantial) connection between gun-related school violence and interstate commerce." With a tour de force review of the literature (including a wide range of social science research), Justice Breyer concluded that the gun problem significantly undermines the quality of education that is critical to economic prosperity, that guns threaten the commerce to which teaching and learning are inextricably linked.

Champions of judicial restraint and adherence to precedent cannot fail to take note of *Lopez*. Deferring to rationally based legislative judgments, as Justice Souter observed, is a paradigm of judicial restraint. A possible consequence of *Lopez* is that such deference will be supplanted by a more active judicial presence as the court distinguishes between commercial and noncommercial transactions that have "substantial effect" on commerce. For the Republican Congress, there must be a special irony in a judicial decision, written by Chief Justice Rehnquist, portending greater scrutiny of its legislation. Although the congressional leadership speaks of its respect for state prerogatives, federalization is the trend in such areas as criminal and tort law. The decision is also likely to create uncertainty in an area that seemed for the most part settled. We can, for example, expect challenges to environmental laws based on this new reading of the commerce clause.

It is premature to gauge the full impact of *Lopez*. There does not seem to be a majority to support a radical change in the interpretation of the commerce clause. Apart from the four dissenters, at least two in the majority do not appear ready to sign on to a wholesale change. In his concurring opinion, joined by Justice O'Connor, Justice Kennedy wrote that "stare decisis [let the decision stand] operates with great force in counseling us not to call in question the essential principles now in place." Unless and until a Republican president replaces a couple of moderate justices with ideological conservatives, we are not likely to see a direct assault on the commerce clause. In any event, a prudent Congress would be well advised to make express findings as to the effects of its legislation on interstate commerce.

Discussion Questions

1. Do you agree with a broad or narrow interpretation of the commerce clause of the Constitution? That is, should Congress have the power to regulate matters having a direct relationship to interstate commerce (actual movement of goods or money, for example), or should Congress be allowed to regulate where the relationship is more indirect (for example, banning guns in schools on the basis of education's relationship to the economy, which was the issue in *U.S. v. Lopez*)?

9
Rules Committee Report on the
Unfunded Mandate Reform Act of 1995

Congress often passes laws requiring the states to implement a particular program or meet a mandated standard for environmental quality or highway safety, much of the time without appropriating money for implementation. The problem is intensified for the states by the willingness of federal courts to uphold national mandates as "supreme" to state priorities. To resist or ignore a national mandate or judicial decree is often to risk losing essential federal funding. When Congress mandated a drinking age of twenty-one in 1984, for example, states risked a loss of federal highway funds if the national mandate was not made state law and enforced.

Responding to the complaints of many state governors and legislatures, Congress passed the Unfunded Mandate Reform Act of 1995 to curb the use of unfunded mandates and to promote the federal funding of future mandates implemented by the states. Printed below is an excerpt from a report of the bill providing background on the congressional motivation for passing the legislation. The report cites the popular interest in shrinking the size of the federal government and its activities, as well as the financial burden imposed upon the states by many federal mandates.

UNFUNDED MANDATE REFORM ACT OF 1995

JANUARY 13, 1995.—Ordered to be printed

MR. SOLOMON, from the Committee on Rules,
submitted the following

REPORT

together with

ADDITIONAL AND MINORITY VIEWS

[To accompany H.R. 5]

The bill also establishes a Commission on Unfunded Federal Mandates to review existing unfunded Federal mandates and to make recommendations to the Congress and the President with respect to reconciling, terminating, suspending, consolidating or simplifying unfunded Federal mandates.

* * *

Background

H.R. 5 was introduced in response to the increased tendency on the part of Congress and the agencies of the Federal Government to enact laws and regulations imposing requirements on State and local governments without commensurate funding to carrying out those requirements.

One recent example of an unfunded Federal mandate is the National Voter Registration Act of 1993. It requires states to allow residents to register at motor vehicle offices, welfare offices and other state offices where public services are delivered. California Governor Pete Wilson estimates that enforcement of the law will cost the state more than $35 million annually. As a result, Governor Wilson has filed suit in federal court to bar the Justice Department from enforcing the law until the Federal Government gives the State adequate funds to put the law into effect.

The impetus for mandate reform was the election of Ronald Reagan as President of the United States in 1980. He made federalism a top policy priority and aggressively pursued an intergovernmental reform agenda that included shrinking the size and function of the Federal Government, creating Federal-local partnerships, reducing Federal regulation of State and local governments, and establishing greater reliance on private sector institutions to achieve national priorities.

State and local organizations have recently sponsored a number of events to spotlight the unfunded mandates issue, increase public awareness, and build support in Congress for mandate relief legislation. They sponsored a National Unfunded Mandates Day in October 1993, and Unfunded Mandates Week in 1994, and "Stop the Mandate Madness" rallies on the Capitol steps.

There have been a number of studies that attempted to identify unfunded Federal mandates and to determine their costs. According to a 1984 report of the Advisory Commission on Intergovernmental Relations (ACIR) entitled "Regulatory Federalism," Federal laws containing mandates that affect State and local governments as of 1980 include: the Age Discrimination Act of 1975, the Clean Air Act Amendments of 1970, the Emergency Highway Energy Conservation Act, the Family Educational Rights and Privacy Act of 1974, the Occupational Safety and Health Act, and the Wholesome Poultry Products Act of 1968.

Since 1980, according to a 1992 follow-up report of the ACIR entitled "Federal Regulation of State and Local Governments: Regulatory Federalism—A Decade Later," another 27 statutes were enacted that included mandates, including the Americans with Disabilities Act, the Cash Management Improvement Act of 1990, the Fair Housing Act Amendments of 1988, the Social Security Amendments of 1983, and the Voting Rights Act of 1982.

The National Association of Counties also constructed the following list of twelve unfunded mandates considered "most burdensome and costly":

Underground Storage Tanks;
Clean Water Act/Wetlands;
Clean Air Act;
Subtitle D of the Resource Conservation and Recovery Act;
Safe Drinking Water Act;
Endangered Species Act;
Superfund;
Americans with Disabilities Act;
Fair Labor Standards Act;
Davis-Bacon Act;
Arbitrage (municipal bonds);
Immigration Act.

Prospective legislation that might be considered unfunded mandates includes minimum wage increases for State and local employees, an increase in Social Security payroll taxes, welfare reform, health care reform, and crime control.

An October 1993 Price Waterhouse study for the U.S. Conference of Mayors, entitled "Impact of Unfunded Federal Mandates on U.S. Cities," contained a survey on the costs incurred by cities to implement the following ten unfunded Federal mandates:

1. Underground Storage Tanks;
2. Clean Water Act;
3. Clean Air Act;
4. Resource Conservation and Recovery Act;
5. Safe Drinking Water Act;
6. Asbestos Abatement;
7. Lead Paint Abatement;
8. Endangered Species Act;
9. Americans with Disabilities Act;
10. Fair Labor Standards Act.

The study estimated that the total cost of these mandates for 1993 was $6.5 billion, and the estimated costs for the years 1994 through 1998 would total $54 billion. The specific cost estimates identified in that study are noted in the following chart:

ESTIMATED COSTS OF UNFUNDED FEDERAL MANDATES TO CITIES
[Hours and costs in thousands]

Mandates	Fiscal year 1993				Fiscal years 1994–1998
	Estimated annual staff hours (excluding overtime)	Estimated annual staff costs	Estimated annual direct/indirect budget costs	Total costs	Projected total costs
1. Underground Storage Tank Regulations (UST)...................	862	$23,393	$137,755	$161,148	$1,040,627
2. Clean Water Act (CWA)/ Wetlands	57,378	1,185,549	2,426,984	3,619,533	29,303,379
3. Clean Air Act (CAA)............	12,138	195,526	208,294	403,820	3,651,550
4. Solid Waste Disposal/RCRA......	9,680	173,384	708,191	881,575	5,475,968
5. Safe Drinking Water Act (SDWA)	4,444	94,549	467,783	562,332	8,644,145
6. Asbestos (AHERA)	898	19,554	109,754	129,308	746,828
7. Lead Based Paint...............	374	7,875	110,342	118,217	1,628,228
8. Endangered Species.............	252	6,934	30,024	36,958	189,488
9. Americans With Disabilities Act...	4,701	114,935	240,746	355,681	2,195,808
10. Fair Labor Standards Act (Exempt Employee & Other Costs).........	1,227	22,765	189,358	212,123	1,121,524
Total	91,954	1,844,464	4,629,231	6,473,695	53,997,545

In response to the consequences of this extraordinary burden, unfunded mandate reform legislation has been endorsed by the National Governors Association, the U.S. Conference of Mayors, the National League of Cities, the Council of State Governments, the National Association of Counties, the National Conference of State Legislatures, the National Federation of Independent Businesses, the U.S. Chamber of Commerce and the National School Boards Association.

DISCUSSION QUESTIONS

1. How does the national government coerce states to comply with its mandates? How was this power changed by the 1995 act?

10
"Unfunded Mandates: Balancing State and National Needs"

JAMES R. ST. GEORGE

James St. George puts the argument on federal mandates in a different context. Not only is the setting of national standards (whether funded or not) a legitimate activity of the federal government, the federal government more than compensates for unfunded mandates through its funding of numerous social programs long considered the domain of the states. Before the states can quarrel with the federal government over unfunded mandates, St. George suggests, they should get their own houses in order and spend more time preparing for, or worrying about, the implications of a balanced budget amendment for the states.

Among its first acts, the new 104th Congress passed legislation to limit unfunded mandates. The legislation curbs the federal government's power to require state and local governments to undertake major new programs without providing the funding for those programs. Under the new law Congress must either pay for any newly mandated programs—and identify a federal agency charged with reducing or eliminating the mandate requirements if Congress fails to provide full financing—or cast a separate vote indicating its intent to impose an unfunded mandate.

Origins of Consensus

The speed with which Congress acted on this issue suggests something approaching a national consensus that Washington has been imposing undue burdens on states and localities. Indeed, state and local officials —urban and rural, liberal and conservative, Republican and Democrat —appear to be largely of one mind in challenging the legitimacy of federal unfunded mandates. Even when these officials accept the intent of a particular federal mandate, they argue that Washington is wrong to substitute its priorities for local preferences. In a world of limited resources, they say, states and localities are increasingly unable to implement their own policies because of the burdens and requirements imposed by the federal government.

In requiring states and localities to spend their own resources to fulfill the mandate, federal officials are not subject to normal political constraints. They do not have to impose higher taxes or make difficult decisions about spending priorities to pay for the public services they mandate. The result may be an inefficient allocation of resources. The new mandate legislation, by requiring a separate vote on any new unfunded mandate, attempts to reassert those political constraints. The congressional action explicitly signals voters regarding the level of government responsible for the taxes or spending choices required to finance unfunded mandates.

Consensus around unfunded mandates grew out of fiscal difficulties facing state and local officials in recent years. State and local policymakers confronted with budget deficits, spending cuts, and tax increases naturally began looking for the source of their troubles. They identified a range of potential causes, including the recent recession, the escalating costs of Medicaid and other health care programs, the public demand for new prisons, and unfunded federal mandates. Focusing on unfunded mandates had two advantages. First, it was a problem over which some measure of control was possible. Compared with stopping recessions or running counter to the popular appetite for new prisons and longer sentences, limiting the ability of Congress to impose unfunded mandates would be easy. Second, a drive to stop unfunded mandates would dovetail with the nation's anti-Washington, anti-Congress political mood. Surely the public would be willing to blame Washington for the problems state and local officials faced.

While drawing the attention of Congress and the public to the fiscal impact of unfunded mandates has been a valuable contribution to sound public policy, the attack on unfunded mandates has obscured several important policy issues. First, imposing unfunded mandates is in many cases a legitimate assertion of national standards and may be the most efficient means of achieving them. Second, the federal government provides substantial financial assistance to states and localities for services, such as education and public safety, traditionally viewed as state and local responsibilities. Third, a major cause of fiscal stress for states and localities has been the failure of their revenue systems to keep pace with a changing economy. Finally, the constitutional amendment proposed by Republicans in Congress to require a balanced federal budget could dwarf the fiscal impact of unfunded mandates.

The Legitimacy of National Standards

In many cases it is entirely reasonable to establish national standards that everyone—including private employers, businesses, and states and localities—must observe. Like other employers, for instance, state and local governments must obey minimum wage, child labor, and civil rights laws. Not even the most ardent opponents of unfunded mandates have suggested that state and local governments should be exempt from these laws or that Washington should finance the cost of compliance.

The new unfunded mandate legislation recognizes the value of certain unfunded mandates by exempting federal laws that protect constitutional or civil rights. Even though the exemption applies to laws that were once extremely controversial—and were attacked for imposing federal rules over "states' rights"—few today would dispute the federal government's right to impose these obligations on state and local governments.

Similarly, it may be appropriate to establish national standards to meet a range of policy goals that could be described broadly as public goods, that is, goods like education or transportation that benefit the society or community at large rather than particular individuals. Because the benefits of public goods are available to individuals who do not pay for them, governments tax people to ensure that an optimal level of the good is produced. In a particular jurisdiction, however, voters and taxpayers may not tax themselves sufficiently to provide an adequate level of some public goods without federal intervention because they may not perceive themselves as reaping the full benefit of those goods. In these cases federal mandates may be the only method of allocating public goods efficiently.

It is well documented, for example, that providing preventive medical care and ensuring good nutrition for children are cost-effective investments. Children whose education suffers because they are chronically hungry or sick are unlikely to become fully productive adults. Much of the cost of inadequate childhood health care or nutrition, however, must be paid years after the damage is done. And in an increasingly mobile society, the costs—unemployment benefits, welfare dependency, incarceration, medical treatment—might well be incurred outside the town or state where the child was reared. Thus, while it is in the public interest to ensure adequate health care and a healthy diet for every child, it may not be in the narrow self-interest of each community to invest the full resources necessary to do so. This is not to say that state or local officials are somehow indifferent to the needs of children in their community. It only suggests that to the extent that costs accrued and benefits received are part of the matrix of policymaking, the mobility of human capital implies that states and localities may provide a less than optimal investment in these public goods absent national standards.

Environmental protection is another area in which states and localities may not on their own allocate sufficient resources to public goods. Reducing pollution can be thought of as a public good, because dirty air and fouled water do not stop at municipal or state borders. Underground storage tanks can leak chemicals that contaminate drinking water in distant locales. Midwestern factories create acid rain that falls in New England lakes. While an industrial state may want to reduce the impact of pollution, it is unlikely to account fully for the damage done by its pollution in other states. Moreover, to the extent that states compete with each other for economic development opportunities, they have an incentive to reduce spending on programs without short-term, in-state benefits. Again, it may be that only national standards can ensure the appropriate and efficient level of these public goods.

It is argued that when national standards are appropriate, Congress should provide national funding. But it is not always efficient for Washington to finance its mandates; it may be important for the implementing level of government to have a stake in holding down costs. Without such an incentive, the federal costs of mandate legislation could grow beyond amounts necessary to achieve established goals because state and local governments could "game" the system to maximize their federal payments.

In recent years, for example, many states were so creative in taxing health care providers to increase their federal Medicaid reimbursements that Congress and the executive branch had to step in to restrict the use of provider taxes. In this case, the federal government was merely matching state expenditures; even so, states found a way to leverage additional and in some cases unwarranted federal dollars. Such episodes should give pause to anyone who doubts that state or local officials would manipulate funding opportunities inappropriately.

The cost of funding federal mandates could also be driven up by perverse incentives states and localities would face under an unfunded mandate ban. The practical effect of prohibiting unfunded mandates would be to reimburse state and local governments for the cost of complying with any new mandate less any costs they were bearing before the mandate was imposed. The greatest subsidies would go to governments that had deferred action in the area in question. Timely state or local action to address an emerging problem, although perhaps more cost effective, would reduce the potential for subsequent federal reimbursement, presumably in perpetuity. Thus states and localities would be tempted to delay solving new problems if they saw a reasonable chance of federal action in the future.

Federal Aid for States and Localities

In discussions of unfunded mandates and the costs they impose on states and localities, the considerable support Washington provides for state and local activities usually goes unmentioned. Federal aid to state and local governments amounted to $217 billion in 1994, one-third more than in 1980 after adjusting for inflation. Federal grants now subsidize a broad range of state and local responsibilities, including economic development, public safety, job training, wastewater treatment, transportation, and education. In fact, in 1992, the last year for which aggregate state and local revenue data are available, federal aid was the largest single source of state and local revenue, exceeding revenue generated by the sales tax, income tax, or property tax.

Attacks on unfunded mandates also ignore the substantial subsidy for state and local income and property taxes implicit in allowing such taxes to be deducted in determining federal income subject to tax. In fiscal year 1994, the deduction of state and local taxes, together with the exclusion of interest income earned from various forms of state and local debt, cost the federal government $66 billion. While the savings from these tax expenditures accrue directly to taxpayers rather than state and local governments, the tax expenditures reduce the cost of state and local income and property taxes for taxpayers who itemize on their federal returns. Washington in effect pays 40 percent of state and local income and property taxes for the highest-income taxpayers and lower shares for other taxpayers. The protests from state and local officials that greet any proposal to eliminate these tax expenditures are ample evidence of their awareness of the subsidy the tax expenditures provide for state and local services.

Precise comparisons of the benefits of federal aid and the cost of unfunded mandates are impossible because of a lack of good data on the cost of mandates. But the value of federal aid probably far exceeds the costs of unfunded mandates. In 1993 the U.S. Conference of Mayors estimated the cost of 10 of the largest and most prominent unfunded mandates in more than 300 cities at $6.5 billion. Given that the population in these cities accounts for half the total population of all cities with at least 30,000 residents, as well as the possibility that the self-assessment of the burden was overstated, it is certainly possible that the total cost of unfunded mandates to municipalities is less than the benefit cities realized from tax expenditures alone.

Similarly, the Advisory Commission on Intergovernmental Relations has estimated that the cost of all unfunded mandates passed between 1983 and 1990 totaled between $2.2 billion and $3.6 billion in 1992. Even if these estimates are seriously understated, it seems unlikely that states and localities spend more on unfunded mandates than they receive in financial aid and tax subsidies from the federal government.

Outdated State Revenue Systems

The focus on unfunded mandates also obscures other causes of fiscal stress over which state and local officials themselves have some control. According to a report issued jointly by the National Governors' Association and the National Conference of State Legislatures, *Funding State Services in the 1990s*, one cause of states' fiscal problems is their failure to update their revenue systems to reflect the changing American economy. Outdated revenue systems lead to structural deficits that require state officials to increase tax rates or cut spending on a recurring basis.

For example, consumers buy a far larger share of services relative to goods than they did 30 years ago. Yet state sales taxes typically apply only to certain services. One result—along with a potential tax advantage for service providers over goods producers—is that most states' sales taxes generate less revenue for each dollar of total consumption than they once did.

State revenue systems have also failed to keep up with the increasing prevalence of businesses operating across state borders. Tax codes largely constructed during the 1930s are poorly situated to collect taxes from complex interstate and international businesses. In addition, the growth of state tax expenditures—essentially, spending programs that operate automatically through the tax code—has drained state coffers while other spending needs go unmet. A recent report by the Center on Budget and Policy Priorities found that in 11 of the 15 states with data available for analysis, tax expenditures grew faster than on-budget spending between 1990 and 1992. Concentrating too narrowly on the problems caused by unfunded mandates may weaken the resolve of some state officials to try to update their own tax systems to reflect the modern global, service-oriented economy.

Impact of a Balanced Budget Amendment

The biggest threat to state and local governments, however, comes not from unfunded mandates or outdated revenue systems, but from proposals in Congress to cut taxes and balance the federal budget by fiscal year 2002. Congressional leaders have indicated that they will exempt about half of the federal budget—Social Security, defense spending, and legally binding interest payments on the debt—from cuts, with the result that federal aid to states and localities would be extremely vulnerable to cuts. A report released in January by the Center on Budget and Policy Priorities, *Holding the Bag*, found that if across-the-board spending cuts are enacted in the unprotected half of the budget, federal aid to states and localities would be cut $390 billion over the next seven years below the amount projected by the Congressional Budget Office under current law.

Congress is likely to begin efforts to eliminate the deficit immediately, subjecting states and localities to a loss in federal aid next year. If Congress follows a "glide path" of steady cuts over seven years, state and local governments could lose $11 billion in federal aid in 1996. This modest down payment on eliminating the deficit—only the first of seven such cuts in subsequent years—is more than three times the high estimate of the cost in 1992 of all federal mandates imposed between 1983 and 1990. By 1998, less than halfway toward a balanced budget, state and local aid would be cut by $37 billion—the equivalent of 12 percent of revenue from the state personal income tax, corporate income tax, and sales tax combined. According to these projections, unfunded mandates may be the least of worries for state and local officials in coming years.

A Delicate Balance

Unfunded federal mandates are, by any reasonable standards, a problem for state and local governments. New legislation limiting Congress's ability to impose future mandates and calling for a full accounting of the impact of already existing mandates is a reasonable compromise between the occasional need for national standards and the legitimate concerns of state and local officials. Federal officials, however, should not interpret the apparent consensus as meaning that unfunded mandates are somehow illegitimate. When the benefits of various spending programs accrue outside the borders of state or local jurisdictions, it may be necessary to require state and local officials to meet appropriate national standards. So long as federal officials are willing to acknowledge in a separate vote that they are imposing an unfunded mandate intentionally, the public will be able to judge the legitimacy of their actions.

At the same time, state and local officials should not focus so single-mindedly on eliminating unfunded mandates that they ignore fiscal problems that are within their purview to solve. State officials in particular should look carefully at the impact on their own budgets of eliminating the federal deficit while protecting half the federal budget before they ratify a balanced budget amendment. If Congress implements a plan to eliminate the deficit by 2002, state and local officials may discover that the loss of federal aid has shifted to states and localities a burden far greater than that of unfunded mandates.

DISCUSSION QUESTIONS

1. When should the federal government have the power to impose mandates on the states, if ever (for example, environmental laws, the "motor voter" bill, school desegregation, or special education)?

THE DEBATE: DOES THE SEPARATION OF POWERS MAKE GRID-LOCK INEVITABLE?

The founders carefully split the powers of the national government among three branches, providing each with a means to check the power of the others. While the system is an effective check on the excessive concentration of power, it is a cumbersome way to govern a nation. Conflict between the branches is inevitable—especially when one political party controls the Congress and another the presidency (divided government)—and the result, as pundits, politicians, and voters alike complain, is often gridlock.

But is this such a bad thing? Charles Jones argues that even though our system "always appears broken," it is working as intended, and better than we might think. Some of the most productive legislative periods in history occurred under divided government. More important, when party unity does speed legislation through the House or Senate, the system of separated powers eventually slows the debate and forces more deliberate consideration of national public policy change.

Yet while Donald Robinson notes the value of a separated system for purposes of checking the accumulation of power, he focuses upon the "sense of paralysis and corruption" that accompanies divided government, and the "evidence that people may be getting a little impatient with this pattern of our politics." His proposal, as a member of the Committee on the Constitutional System, is to simply synchronize the elections of president, House and Senate every four years to allow elected officials to act in a concerted manner to implement their campaign promises.

11
"It Ain't Broke . . ."

CHARLES O. JONES

The source of my title, is, of course, the pithy aphorism: "If it ain't broke, don't fix it." I would add this advisory: "If it is broke, choose your fixer carefully—and always get a second opinion." It is a quality of a separated powers system like ours that it always appears broken, thus encouraging professional fixers to ply their trade. Some political systems work with "clean" theories—the most pristine of which have proven to be very wrong. We dirty things up a bit by promoting access, propagating legitimate participation, and dispersing accountability, yet compelling agreement. None of it works very well, as Barber Conable has observed, "just as the founding fathers intended." The separated system doesn't show well along the way.

The stimulus to make changes in our political system often derives from a desire to have presidential government and strong political parties in the parliamentary mode. Congress gets in the way of achieving this end and is therefore the subject of much criticism and many reform proposals. The president should be strong, policy ambitious, and responsible so that he can form a government—well, at least those we agree with should be so endowed. The system at present is viewed as producing gridlock, a term applied when either the president or the House or the Senate exercises their constitutional prerogatives to check the other branch.

It is surely true that serious participation in a separated system is big-time politics. Not everyone is good at it—some, in fact, should seek other employment. Surely we know by now that partisanship is not sufficient. Consider how Madison and the lads disconnected the elections and varied the term lengths. House members who came in with the president are on their own in two years time. The one-third of the Senate elected with the president will never again see him on the ballot.

Therefore, most of the time presidents have to work hard to form cross-party coalitions, to convince members of Congress that what they want is good for them and their constituents. Ours is not a partisan, party-based system. Those who try to manage on a partisan basis typically fail. Nor do party members fall neatly into policy slots. And so cross-party coalitions on one issue may look very different from those on other issues. Building support is continuous. It requires that legitimate interests be heard and that deals then be made.

Otto von Bismarck is believed to have said: "If you like laws and sausages, you should never watch either one being made." That is fine for sausage, and probably for laws the way Bismarck made them. But that is nonsense for us. Take a look—a good look. Others do. Ours is the most watched system in the world, and should be. What you don't like can be changed only with your attention and participation—not with turning away. And instituting a system based on "clean" theory would do more harm than help.

One feature of a separated system that troubles critics is the potential for divided government or, as I prefer to label it, split-party government. If it is difficult to form a government in the parliamentary sense when one party has won the White House, the House of Representatives, and the Senate, then imagine the problems when each party wins a branch of government. First it is worth observing that such an outcome is a perfectly constitutional result, not a perversion. Then it is notable that voters have, in this age of modern, electronic communication, returned split-party government a majority of the time. When asked, they even profess a preference for that outcome.

Has split-party government resulted in gridlock? Not if measured by the production of major legislation, according to David R. Mayhew in his book *Divided We Govern*. There is no difference between single- and split-party government by his count. In fact, one of the most productive periods was 1973–74, when we believed at the time that government had virtually ceased to work because of Watergate.

My own detailed study of major legislation during the post–World War II period shows a rich variety of presidential-congressional interaction at all stages of lawmaking, with initiative coming from both parties and from all three elected institutions. Why should we not expect that variation in a scheme that propagates legitimate involvement by duly and independently elected representatives?

What about the system in the next century? I believe it will be more like it is and has been than what many want it to be. Reforms will be put in place, to be sure—many were in [the 104th] Congress. But present students of American politics will have no trouble recognizing their government twenty years from now. It will continue to be a separated system of diffused responsibility, broad access, institutional and federal-state competition, and cross-party alliances on issues. The strong party, presidency-centered advocates will be just as frustrated then as they are now, perhaps more so.

None of that is to say that the partisan balances will be the same. The 1994 elections resulted in a stunning reshuffling of power; displaying another variation is separated system politics. I will say something about those results since it is my belief that much is to be learned about the future from what is happening in the present.

One can sympathize with President Clinton as he struggles to find his place in the revised politics of the day. The president lost an election without being on the ballot—the only first-term elected Democrat in this century to lose both houses of Congress (Truman was not an elected president in 1946). He is experiencing what no Republican president could arrange over the past forty years—a Republican majority in the House. His present status and strategic options are defined by the congressional Republicans—not an enviable position. And so President Clinton has had to reshape a presidency that was not that well formed from the start, a challenge to cope with a rare form of split-party government.

But there is more that is historic. American political parties are criticized in presidential elections for offering, then ignoring, relatively flaccid party platforms. We surely don't expect to have explicit contracts with the voters during the state and local contests that make up a congressional midterm election.

In fact, despite the preference among many analysts for the strong party model of government, many were puzzled by Newt Gingrich's media extravaganza on September 27 when he brought House Republican candidates to Capitol Hill to sign the Contract with America. David Broder was one of the few commentators to recognize the effort as suited to party government: "Newt Gingrich . . . said at a press briefing, 'Our government operates on the party system. We are a team. And we're offering you a contract on what our team will do.' . . . That is a sound proposition. People need to be reminded that Congress writes the laws in a partisan setting . . . in which the opposing parties divide, not just for spite, but on philosophy, program and principle" (*Washington Post*, September 28, 1994, p. A23).

Most analysts were skeptical, if not mocking, of the exercise. E. J. Dionne reported: "Many Democratic strategists are gleeful because this document ties 'outsider' Republican candidates back into their congressional leadership and defines the Republicans as advocates of tattered Reagan-style tax cuts." Stanley Greenberg, Clinton's pollster, was quoted by Dionne as stating that the Republicans had made a mistake with the Contract in offering policy substance that was not popular (*Washington Post*, October 4, 1994, p. A17).

Paul Begala was quoted in the *New York Times* as very pleased with the Contract: "There is not a night I don't thank God for the contract" (October 9, 1994, p. A26). Editorial comment was scathing: "Reaganism in a rear-view mirror," "reckless," "deceptive," "duplicitous propaganda," "a gimmick." (*New York Times*, September 28, 1994, p. A20; *Washington Post*, September 28, 1994, p. A22).

Studies by my colleagues in political science will no doubt show that the Contract played a minor role with voters in the 1994 elections. In other respects, however, it was an historic development. A huge majority of Republican candidates signed the document and took it seriously. And tying "outsider" candidates into their congressional leadership is exactly what Gingrich and Co. had in mind as support for their consolidation of power in potential competition with new committee chairs.

Because much of reality is perceptual, the fact that House Republicans did much better than expected was bound to encourage talk of a mandate, that goofy concept for a separated system that is used in postelection analysis to make sense of what typically is not there. In this case the mandate was awarded to a leader who was very anxious to act.

The third historic aspect of the 104th Congress is in what was accomplished early. The House Republicans accomplished all of what they promised in the Contract—that is, to bring to a vote all of the legislative actions listed therein. More than that, they passed the overwhelming majority of the proposals brought to the floor within the time limit they set and with extraordinary party unity. Still more, they created an energy and momentum that is unprecedented for so early in a session. A president accomplishing this much in the first three months would have been labeled a political genius.

Is this a case of the effective working of the separated system? It is not. One-hundred-day deadlines are not well suited to our policy politics. Scorekeeping becomes an end in itself. There is a probable inverse relationship between a high score and good legislation. To say that the House Republicans achieved, even exceeded, the goals set in the Contract is not necessarily to point with pride to the results. Legislation by exhaustion is not recommended, nor is urgent large-scale testing of grand behavioral and structural theories of governing.

The House Republicans set an impressive agenda in this first one hundred days—one directed to basic questions about what government can do, which government ought to do it, as well as the capacity of the private sphere to solve public problems. It is surely the envy of any policy-ambitious president. But speculation abounds as to whether these will be the effects of political reform and policy change:

- Term limits will improve lawmaking.
- Denial of cash benefits will reduce teenage pregnancies.
- Block grants to the states will reduce bureaucracy.
- States are better at governing than is the nation.
- The item veto will reduce unnecessary expenditures.
- Cost-benefit analysis of regulations will limit government control.
- Capping punitive damages lowers medical care costs.
- "Loser pays" will reduce the number of frivolous lawsuits.
- Tax cuts are consistent with balancing the budget.
- A constitutional amendment will produce a balanced budget.

The quantity and complexity of legislation passed by the House and sent to the Senate in the first three months were awesome. The legislative pipeline was full even before the budget debates began. The House voted on final passage on twenty-six pieces of legislation—twenty-five wins and one loss.

Of these twenty votes on final passage, Republicans lost an average of 6 votes per bill (a range of 0 to 40, on term limits). They picked up an average of 83 Democratic votes (a range of 6 to 201). Party unity for House Republicans averaged 97 percent for the 26 votes (with a range of from 83 to 100 percent). Just one vote—term limits—fell below 90 percent unity. Republicans had 99 to 100 percent unity on 12 of the votes.

What is frightening about this record? Should we not be overjoyed that party government is here at last? It was precisely this type of lawmaking that concerned the Founders. Big questions have been answered by untested theories and with little time devoted to considering the consequences.

It is, indeed, a time for considering major shifts to achieve effectiveness of government at all levels. But in our system, devolution is to be achieved by evolution, not revolution.

That brings me to the reassurance offered by a separated system.

Speaker Gingrich likes to compare this period with that in 1933. Indeed, the lamentable one-hundred-day timetable emanates from that time. Democratic presidents are fond of invoking the one-hundred-day promise; President Clinton being the most recent example with his economic and health care proposals. So far as I am aware, this is the first time a congressional leader has proposed such an ambitious program on this schedule. And he did it.

The argument for acting quickly is familiar. President Johnson summarized it well in his memoirs: "A president must always reckon that his mandate will prove short-lived." He might have added, "because it wasn't real anyway."

The separated system was sure to kick in. The House Republicans seized the initiative in setting the agenda and in formulating proposals that were fed to the other elected institutions. This is no small achievement—it is historic, as I have already pointed out.

Whereas the Senate will abide by this agenda for the most part, it will function precisely as designed. Counterproposals will be developed, action will be more deliberate, the minority party will be substantially more influential in forcing compromises, alternative theories will be propounded to those used as a basis for bills in the House, senators will take time to display their plumage.

And representatives of the two chambers will then meet in conference when passions have cooled.

I stress again the importance of the role played by Speaker Gingrich and the House Republicans. But a mandate for one of the three elected institutions is very different from one assigned to all three as led by the president (for example, 1932, 1964, and 1980). Just as the president is not the presidency and the presidency is not the government, just so the Speaker is not the House and the House is not the government (or even Congress).

What of the president's role in this version of the separated system? Of course, it depends on the person serving in the Oval Office. A president with limited domestic policy goals or one whose goals have been achieved (such as Eisenhower or Reagan in their final two years or Bush virtually from the start) can accommodate rather well to these political circumstances. They can concentrate on foreign and national security matters, employ the veto to curb congressional excesses, and participate in domestic initiatives where political gain might be realized.

* * *

I close with these thoughts from a great and honored public servant:

> Perhaps the dominant feeling about government today is distrust. The tone of most comment, whether casual or deliberate, implies that ineptitude and inadequacy are the chief characteristics of government. I do not refer merely to the current skepticism about democracy, but to the widely entertained feel-

ing of the incapacity of government, generally, to satisfy the needs of modern society. But . . . we ask more from government than any society has ever asked. At one and the same time, we expect little from government and progressively rely on it more. We feel that the essential forces of life are no longer in the channels of politics, and yet we constantly turn to those channels for the direction of forces outside them. Generalizations like these elude proof because they are usually based on very subtle factors. But the large abstention from voting in our elections must certainly bespeak an indifference not without meaning. . . . We have not adjusted our thinking about government to the overwhelming facts of modern life, and so carry over old mental habits, traditional schoolbook platitudes and campaign slogans as to the role, the purposes, and the methods of government.

These words are a part of my reassurance. As contemporary as they sound, they were in fact delivered by Felix Frankfurter in a lecture sixty-five years ago this month. We ain't fixed yet, Mr. Justice, and probably never will be. But we ain't hopelessly broke either; and whatever we do by way of repairs, we need to be careful not to interfere too much with the current national conversation about government and its role in our lives. With regard to the structure of the separated system, be assured that the Founders built in sufficient protections to preserve even its most maddening features.

12
From "[Does the System Need Fixing?] A Rationale"

DONALD L. ROBINSON

The point of departure for reform[ing the constitutional system of separation of powers]—not just now but throughout American history and I suspect in the foreseeable future—must be people's suspicion and frustration with politics. Popular attitudes, deep and abiding in this culture, support a system that checks power. Public opinion sees advantages in such a system. Unless action is supported by large and durable majorities, it ought not to be taken. Thus, the Madisonian checks curtailed the New Deal and reigned in the Great Society. The same system saved Civil Rights in the 1980s. Now it protects the poor and the vulnerable, as well as the environment, from the mean-spirited and reckless legions in the House of Representatives.

At the same time we need to recognize that the status quo favors the rich and the well born, who are at great advantage by a system that stacks the odds against strong governmental and political action. Thus, when the left, from the 1930s through the 1960s, wanted to enact programs to redistribute wealth and opportunity, the system bent those programs out of shape. Now, when the populist right attempts to act on a presumed mandate to dismantle federal bureaucracy and strengthen the private sector and local governments, inertia again favors the status quo.

The American people generally approve of this moderating tendency of our political system. We want leadership, but we are also suspicious of it, and we resist the plebiscitary presidency.

Lately there is evidence that people may be getting a little impatient with this pattern of our politics. We are no longer as rich a nation as we used to be, comparatively, and we are certainly not as cocky. Our economy looks a little more vulnerable now that the dollar has fallen by 50 percent within five years against the yen; we look and feel vulnerable. Maybe we no longer can count on the abundance of this continent to ensure our position as the number one nation in the world.

Social relations also seem to be posing a more threatening challenge to our system. We wish we could protect our borders against illegal immigration. We are beginning to think we may need a stronger state than we have. At the same time, people want to hold the system more accountable. Of course, such a mood can fuel the politics of paranoia—an antidemocratic or anticonstitutionalist impulse. Thus, it behooves sensible people to ponder these moods and be ready with alternatives if the public begins to sense that panaceas like term limits and the item veto and Balanced Budget Amendments are not going to solve our problems.

Since its founding, the Committee on the Constitutional System has responded to this sense of systemic strain. We were galvanized originally in the beginning of the 1980s by a concern about deficits, which were opposed by everyone, and yet no one seemed to be able to do anything about them; and what was worse, there was no way to hold the government accountable for these deficits. There was a great deal of finger-pointing. The president was blaming Congress, Congress was blaming the president, and they were all blaming the Federal Reserve. There was no way for a voter who was concerned about deficits to punish those responsible.

In addition, we faced recurrent gridlock—a sense of paralysis and corruption, divided government. Thoughtful people banded together in the Committee on the Constitutional System to consider what could be done about these problems. There were relatively few academics involved. It was mostly people with experience in government who came together to form the committee and began to consider changes that were quite radical in the context of American history.

Now I want to relate what we have been doing to the worldwide movement around issues of constitutional form and democracy. Most of the world's constitutional systems have been parliamentary in form during the twentieth century. Many governments in Europe and nations under European influence were in crisis in the post–Second World War period, because they emphasized representation at the expense of authority and coherence and energy in government. Particularly in France and Italy, there was this sense that governments were representative to a fault and often near paralysis because they were unable to mobilize majorities to act.

The need, it was felt, was to strengthen the executive and to make it less vulnerable to majorities in the assemblies. One method was to give the prime minister power of dissolution, a whip hand, particularly in a two-party system. But many parliamentary systems withdrew from that alternative on the ground that strengthening the executive to that extent would make the prime minister too strong and invite extreme oscillations in public policy.

The trick was to keep the assembly representative (usually with a system of proportional representation)—to keep the prime minister on a short leash, vulnerable to motions of no confidence, but at the same time to find a way to give the regime strengthened executive power. The breakthrough, conceptually, came during the 1950s in France, when the Gaullists developed the model of the Fifth French Republic, which added a separately elected president to the parliamentary system of the Fourth Republic. There were other changes, too; but the essential change in the Fifth Republic was to add to the French parliamentary form of government a president, with authority in foreign affairs and able to intervene in emergencies and resolve great difficulties. A president could give government in France coherence, and energy, and the necessary authority to deal with crises.

A variant of the French form is seen in the German Federal Republic. Such "hybrid constitutionalism" (sometimes called "semi-presidentialism") is now the preferred model in Eastern Europe. The Eastern European regimes look not to the United States as the model of constitutional democracy, but instead to France and Germany. When they call on experts to come and offer counsel to them, frequently they seek folks from those Northern and Western European countries, rather than the United States.

The United States is not about to adopt a parliamentary system. We are immunized against it! We want checks and balances for the reasons I indicated earlier. At the same time, we are beginning to recognize that our government needs stronger political controls over the bureaucracy, a greater ability to act, and the voters' ability to hold the government accountable for what it does.

I have come to believe that the process adopted by parliamentary government—to think about what was wrong and adopt an institutional reform that moved it in the direction of the presidential system—is one that we ought to consider here. Perhaps there will be a convergence of constitutional forms. There is a great deal to be said for the accountability that a parliamentary system affords. Yet it lacks coherence and energy. There is much to be said for our system of separated powers, with its checks and balances. What we lack is the ability to hold executive power accountable, so that we can trust it to take leadership.

The reason we are skeptical about presidential leadership is that we are afraid we could not hold it accountable if we unleashed it from the system of separated powers. We will never trust a stronger presidency unless we are assured that we can hold it accountable. This is why, for example, we insist on retaining staggered elections. Staggered elections help to make the power of our system accountable.

One way to strengthen the president (an idea the Committee on the Constitutional System has explored a good deal) would be to coordinate the electoral cycles so that president, House, and Senate would be chosen together every four years. That would help to ensure that the government was empowered over a period of four years to enact a program, based on its electoral campaign. This idea is a good one if what we want to do is unleash presidential power for coherent leadership. But it is greeted with skepticism by the American people, because we are afraid to give presidential leadership so much power. And so, we have not had much luck in the Committee on the Constitutional System selling the idea of coordinated electoral cycles.

We will not have luck with the idea of coordinate electoral cycles until we build into the proposal some way to hold such a government to account, if within that four-year cycle it goes stray or otherwise violates the political promise in America. What we need is a system that would have enabled us, for example, in a year like 1930 or 1931, to judge that the government we put in place in 1928 was on the wrong track and needed to be reorganized.

Constitutional democracy is a quest. The jury is always out. There is certainly little impulse in the country at this time for even mild structural reform. But systems unravel quickly in this world, as we know from what happened to the Soviet Union and from seeing what is happening in Canada, Australia, and South Africa. Who could have predicted what has happened in South Africa?

We may soon, suddenly, want a government that can act—whether for left- or right-wing purposes, whether for communitarian or market-oriented goals. Americans, I trust, will never want direct, untrammeled democracy. The popular impulse must be tempered, and Americans deeply understand that. Until we are assured that referenda, for example, will not carry away our liberties, we are going to resist the impulse to move in the direction of referenda.

At the same time, we must not frustrate democracy overmuch. We need a government that can act effectively, and I hope we will insist on one we can hold accountable.

DISCUSSION QUESTIONS

1. Does our constitutional system inhibit effective governance? That is, does the separation of powers go too far in trying to limit the potential for abuse of power at the expense of the ability to govern?

2. Should we amend the Constitution to allow for greater presidential authority to build public policies from electoral mandates?

3. What would the Founders think of the current state of the political system that they created?

CHAPTER 3

The Constitutional Framework and the Individual: Civil Liberties and Civil Rights

In the next two selections, Abraham Lincoln and Martin Luther King, Jr. take opposing points of view about how to achieve peaceful change in a civil society. What happens when the fight for justice and equality comes into conflict with the rule of law? Are people ever justified in breaking laws for what they perceive to be the greater good? Is civil disobedience justified in some contexts?

In a speech that he delivered twenty-three years before becoming president, Lincoln argues that the laws must be followed, as without adherence to laws we have no civil society. Change, Lincoln stresses, must come from working within the system. King disagrees, arguing that although people have a moral obligation to follow just laws, they have an equally compelling duty to break unjust laws through nonviolent means. In his "Letter from the Birmingham Jail," which he addressed to more conservative religious leaders in the civil rights movement who were concerned about his tactics, King outlined procedures for distinguishing between just and unjust laws and for resisting those laws that are unjust. It is ironic that despite Lincoln's admonitions about working within the system, under under his leadership the nation fought its bloodiest war precisely because the central issues of states' rights and slavery could not be solved within the system. King, on the other hand, who argued in favor of breaking unjust laws, was actually instrumental in putting pressure on Congress (the "system") to change those laws that he and others in the civil rights movement considered unjust.

The current battle over abortion policy shows that the debate between Lincoln and King is in fact timeless. Many pro-life activists invoke King's name to justify their blocking access to abortion clinics. Many pro-choice advocates believe that pro-life forces, having lost the battle in the legislature and the courts, should not be able to take to the streets to impose their views unilaterally.

[Handwritten annotations at top of page:]

- Duty to obey laws in order to have a civil society
- Ways to change laws w/in the system (w/o breaking laws)
- People need to obey even bad laws to prevent anarchy + alienation

13
"The Perpetuation of Our Political Institutions"

Abraham Lincoln

In the great journal of things happening under the sun, we, the American People, find our account running, under date of the nineteenth century of the Christian era. We find ourselves in the peaceful possession, of the fairest portion of the earth, as regards extent of territory, fertility of soil, and salubrity of climate. We find ourselves under the government of a system of political institutions, conducing more essentially to the ends of civil and religious liberty, than any of which the history of former times tells us. We, when mounting the stage of existence, found ourselves the legal inheritors of these fundamental blessings. We toiled not in the acquirement or establishment of them—they are a legacy bequeathed us, by a *once* hardy, brave, and patriotic, but *now* lamented and departed race of ancestors. Theirs was the task (and nobly they performed it) to possess themselves, and through themselves, us, of this goodly land; and to uprear upon its hills and its valleys, a political edifice of liberty and equal rights; 'tis ours only, to transmit these, the former, unprofaned by the foot of an invader; the latter, undecayed by the lapse of time and untorn by usurpation, to the latest generation that fate shall permit the world to know. This task gratitude to our fathers, justice to ourselves, duty to posterity, and love for our species in general, all imperatively required us faithfully to perform.

How then shall we perform it? At what point shall we expect the approach of danger? By what means shall we fortify against it? Shall we expect some transatlantic military giant, to step the ocean, and crush us at a blow? Never! All the armies of Europe, Asia and Africa combined, with all the treasure of the earth (our own excepted) in their military chest; with a Buonaparte for a commander, could not by force take a drink from the Ohio, or make a track on the Blue Ridge, in a trial of a thousand years.

At what point then is the approach of danger to be expected? I answer, if it ever reach us, it must spring up amongst us. It cannot come from abroad. If destruction be our lot, we must ourselves be its author and finisher. As a nation of freemen, we must live through all time, or die by suicide.

I hope I am over wary; but if I am not, there is, even now, something of ill-omen, amongst us. I mean the increasing disregard for law which pervades the country; the growing disposition to substitute the wild and furious passions, in lieu of the sober judgment of Courts; and the worse than savage mobs, for the executive ministers of justice. This disposition is awfully fearful in any community; and that it now exists in ours, though grating to our feelings to admit, it would be a violation of truth, and an insult to our intelligence, to deny. Accounts of outrages committed by mobs, form the everyday news of the times. They have pervaded the country, from New England to Louisiana; they are neither peculiar to the eternal snows of the former, nor the burning suns of the latter; they are not the creature of climate—neither are they confined to the slaveholding, or the non-slaveholding States. Alike, they spring up among the pleasure hunting masters of Southern slaves, and the order loving citizens of the land of steady habits. Whatever, then, their cause may be, it is common to the whole country.

It would be tedious, as well as useless, to recount the horrors of all of them. Those happening in the State of Mississippi, and at St. Louis, are, perhaps, the most dangerous in example and revolting to humanity. In the Mississippi case, they first commenced by hanging the regular gamblers; a set of men, certainly not following for a livelihood, a very useful, or very honest occupation; but one which, so far from being forbidden by the laws, was actually licensed by an act of the Legislature, passed but a single year before. Next, negroes, suspected of conspiring to raise an insurrection, were caught up and hanged in all parts of the State: then, white men, supposed to be leagued with the negroes; and finally, strangers, from neighboring States, going thither on business, were, in many instances, subjected to the same fate. Thus went on this process of hanging, from gamblers to negroes, from negroes to white citizens, and from these to strangers; till, dead men were seen literally dangling from the boughs of trees upon every road side; and in numbers almost sufficient, to rival the native Spanish moss of the country, as a drapery of the forest.

Turn, then, to that horror-striking scene at St. Louis. A single victim was only sacrificed there. His story is very short; and is, perhaps, the most highly tragic, of anything of its length, that has ever been witnessed in real life. A mulatto man, by the name of McIntosh, was seized in the street, dragged to the suburbs of the city, chained to a tree, and actually burned to death; and all within a single hour from the time he had been a freeman, attending to his own business, and at peace with the world.

Such are the effects of mob law; and such are the scenes, becoming more and more frequent in this land so lately famed for love of law and order; and the stories of which have even now grown too familiar, to attract any thing more than an idle remark.

But you are, perhaps, ready to ask, "What has this to do with the perpetuation of our political institutions?" I answer, it has much to do with it. Its direct consequences are, comparatively speaking, but a small evil; and much of its danger consists, in the proneness of our minds, to regard its direct as its only consequences. Abstractly considered, the hanging of the gamblers at Vicksburg was of but little consequence. They constitute a portion of population that is worse than useless in any community; and their death, if no pernicious example be set by it, is never matter of reasonable regret with anyone. If they were annually swept from the stage of existence by the plague or small pox, honest men would, perhaps, be much profited by the operation. Similar too, is the correct reasoning, in regard to the burning of the negro at St. Louis. He had forfeited his life, by the perpetration of an outrageous murder, upon one of the most worthy and respectable citizens of the city; and had he not died as he did, he must have died by the sentence of the law, in a very short time afterwards. As to him alone, it was as well the way it was, as it could otherwise have been. But the example in either case was fearful. When men take it in their heads today, to hang gamblers, or burn murderers, they should recollect, that, in the confusion usually attending such transactions, they will be as likely to hang or burn someone who is neither a gambler nor a murderer as one who is; and that, acting upon the example they set, the mob of tomorrow, may, and probably will, hang or burn some of them by the very same mistake. And not only so; the innocent, those who have ever set their faces against violations of law in every shape, alike with the guilty, fall victims to the ravages of mob law; and thus it goes on, step by step, till all the walls erected for the defence of the persons and property of individuals, are trodden down, and disregarded. But all this even, is not the full extent of the evil. By such examples, by instances of the perpetrators of such acts going unpunished, the lawless in spirit are encouraged to become lawless in practice; and having been used to no restraint, but dread of punishment, they thus become absolutely unrestrained. Having ever regarded Government as their deadliest bane, they make a jubilee of the suspension of its operations; and pray for nothing so much as its total annihilation. While, on the other hand, good men, men who love tranquility, who desire to abide by the laws, and enjoy their benefits, who would gladly spill their blood in the defence of their country; seeing their property destroyed; their families insulted, and their lives endangered; their persons injured; and seeing nothing in prospect that forebodes a change for the better; become tired of, and disgusted with, a Government that offers them no protection; and are not much averse to a change in which they imagine they have nothing to lose. Thus, then, by the operation of this mobocratic spirit, which all must admit is now abroad in the land, the strongest bulwark of any Government, and particularly of those constituted like ours, may effectually be broken down and destroyed—I mean the *attachment* of the People. Whenever this effect shall be produced among us, whenever the vicious portion of population shall be permitted to gather in bands of hundreds and thousands, and burn churches, ravage and rob provision-stores, throw printing presses into rivers, shoot editors, and hang and burn obnoxious persons at pleasure, and with impunity, depend on it, this Government cannot last. By such things, the feelings of the best citizens will become more or less alienated from it; and thus it will be left without friends, or with too few, and those few too weak, to make their friendship effectual. At such a time and under such circumstances, men of sufficient talent and ambition will not be wanting to seize the opportunity, strike the blow, and overturn that fair fabric which for the last half century has been the fondest hope of the lovers of freedom, throughout the world.

I know the American People are *much* attached to their Government; I know they would suffer *much* for its sake; I know they would endure evils long and patiently, before they would ever think of exchanging it for another. Yet, notwithstanding all this, if the laws be continually despised and disregarded, if their rights to be secure in their persons and property are held by no better tenure than the caprice of a mob, the alienation of their affections from the Government is the natural consequence; and to that, sooner or later, it must come.

Here then, is one point at which danger may be expected.

The question recurs, "how shall we fortify against it?" The answer is simple. Let every American, every lover of liberty, every well-wisher to his posterity, swear by the blood of the Revolution never to violate in the least particular the laws of the country; and never to tolerate their violation by others. As the patriots of seventy-six did to the support of the Declaration of Independence, so to the support of the Constitution and Laws, let every American pledge his life, his property, and his sacred honor; let every man remember that to violate the law is to trample on the blood of his father, and to tear the character of his own, and his children's liberty. Let reverence for the laws be breathed by every American mother to the lisping babe that prattles on her lap—let it be taught in schools, in seminaries, and in colleges; let it be written in Primers, spelling books, and in Almanacs; let it be preached from the pulpit, proclaimed in legislative halls, and enforced in courts of justice. And, in short, let it become the *political religion* of the nation; and let the old and the young, the rich and the poor, the grave and the gay, of all sexes and tongues, and colors and conditions, sacrifice unceasingly upon its altars.

While ever a state of feeling, such as this, shall universally, or even, very generally prevail throughout the nation, vain will be every effort, and fruitless every attempt, to subvert our national freedom.

When I so pressingly urge a strict observance of all the laws, let me not be understood as saying there are no bad laws, nor that grievances may not arise, for the redress of which, no legal provisions have been made. I mean to say no such thing. But I do mean to say that, although bad laws, if they exist, should be repealed as soon as possible, still while they continue in force, for the sake of example they should be religiously observed. So also in unprovided cases. If such arise, let proper legal provisions be made for them with the least possible delay; but, till then, let them, if not too intolerable, be borne with.

There is no grievance that is a fit object of redress by mob law. In any case that arises, as for instance, the promulgation of abolitionism, one of two positions is necessarily true; that is, the thing is right within itself, and therefore deserves the protection of all law and all good citizens; or, it is wrong, and therefore proper to be prohibited by legal enactments; and in neither case, is the interposition of mob law, either necessary, justifiable, or excusable.

* * *

But this state of feeling *must fade, is fading, has faded,* with the circumstances that produced it.

I do not mean to say, that the scenes of the revolution *are now* or *ever will* be entirely forgotten; but that like everything else, they must fade upon the memory of the world, and grow more and more dim by the lapse of time. In history, we hope, they will be read of, and recounted, so long as the bible shall be read; but even granting that they will, their influence *cannot be* what it heretofore has been. Even then, they *cannot be* so universally known, nor so vividly felt, as they were by the generation just gone to rest. At the close of that struggle, nearly every adult male had been a participator in some of its scenes. The consequence was, that of those scenes, in the form of a husband, a father, a son or a brother, *a living history* was to be found in every family—a history bearing the indubitable testimonies of its own authenticity, in the limbs mangled, in the scars of wounds received, in the midst of the very scenes related— a history, too, that could be read and understood alike by all, the wise and the ignorant, the learned and the unlearned. But *those* histories are gone. They *can* be read no more forever. They *were* a fortress of strength; but, what invading foeman could *never do,* the silent artillery of time *has done;* the leveling of its walls. They are gone. They *were* a forest of giant oaks; but the all-resistless hurricane has swept over them, and left only, here and there, a lonely trunk, despoiled of its verdure, shorn of its foliage; unshading and unshaded, to murmur in a few more gentle breezes, and to combat with its mutilated limbs, a few more ruder storms, then to sink, and be no more.

They *were* the pillars of the temple of liberty; and now that they have crumbled away, that temple must fall, unless we, their descendants, supply their places with other pillars, hewn from the solid quarry of sober reason. Passion has helped us; but can do so no more. It will in future be our enemy. Reason, cold, calculating, unimpassioned reason, must furnish all the materials for our future support and defence. Let those materials be molded into *general intelligence, sound morality,* and, in particular, *a reverence for the constitution and laws:* and, that we improved to the last; that we remained free to the last; that we revered his name to the last; that, during his long sleep, we permitted no hostile foot to pass over or desecrate his resting place; shall be that which to learn the last trump shall awaken our WASHINGTON.

Upon these let the proud fabric of freedom rest, as the rock of its basis; and as truly as has been said of the only greater institution, *"the gates of hell shall not prevail against it."*

[handwritten: OK. to break law if it's unjust]
[handwritten: purpose of demonstrating is to bring attention to to the surface => negotiate]

14
"Letter from Birmingham Jail, 1963"

MARTIN LUTHER KING, JR.

[handwritten: • O.K. to demonstrate when there's no alternative (break law)]
[handwritten: • If you do break the law do it openly & be willing to accept consequences]
[handwritten: • duty to break laws if they're unjust]

The "Negro Revolution" of the 1950s and early 1960s, which in the public mind had its beginning in the 1954 Supreme Court decision desegregating public schools, generally followed two paths: lawsuits pressed in state and federal courts, and the direct action programs of such organizations as the National Association for the Advancement of Colored People (NAACP), Congress of Racial Equality (CORE), and the Southern Christian Leadership Conference (SCLC). The Reverend Martin Luther King, Jr., who urged the tactic of passive resistance—Negroes, he said, should meet "physical force with an even stronger force, namely, soul force"—assumed the presidency of the SCLC and leadership of the new nonviolent protest movement. King and his followers chose Birmingham, Alabama, as the target of their antisegregation drive of 1963. King explained the choice: "If Birmingham could be cracked, the direction of the entire nonviolent movement in the South could take a significant turn." While King's group was pressing a boycott that crippled business and forced Birmingham businessmen to negotiate a desegregation agreement, Attorney General Robert F. Kennedy acted to secure the immediate registration of more than 2,000 Birmingham Negroes previously denied voting rights. Federal courts upheld the right of Negroes to nonviolent protest in Birmingham and elsewhere, but not before King had been arrested and jailed. The following letter (reprinted here in part), written from his cell on April 16, 1963, contained King's answer to charges by a group of eight Birmingham clergymen that he was in their city as an "outside agitator."

Source: *Christian Century,* June 12, 1963.

My Dear Fellow Clergymen:

While confined here in the Birmingham City Jail, I came across your recent statement calling my present activities "unwise and untimely." Seldom do I pause to answer criticism of my work and ideas. If I sought to answer all the criticism that cross my desk, my secretaries would have little time for anything other than such correspondence in the course of the day, and I would have no time for constructive work. But since I feel that you are men of genuine goodwill and that your criticisms are sincerely set forth, I want to try to answer your statement in what I hope will be patient and reasonable terms.

I think I should indicate why I am here in Birmingham, since you have been influenced by the view which argues against "outsiders coming in." I have the honor of serving as president of the Southern Christian Leadership Conference, an organization operating in every Southern state, with headquarters in Atlanta, Georgia. We have some eighty-five affiliate organizations across the South, and one of them is the Alabama Christian Movement for Human Rights. Frequently, we share staff, educational, and financial resources with our affiliates. Several months ago the affiliate here in Birmingham asked us to be on call to engage in a nonviolent direct-action program if such were deemed necessary. We readily consented, and when the hour came we lived up to our promise. So I, along with several members of my staff, am here because I was invited here. I am here because I have organizational ties here.

But more basically, I am in Birmingham because injustice exists here. Just as the prophets of the 8th century B.C. left their villages and carried their "thus saith the Lord" far afield, and just as the apostle Paul left his village of Tarsus and carried the gospel of Jesus Christ to the far corners of the Greco-Roman world, so am I compelled to carry the gospel of freedom beyond my own hometown. Like Paul, I must constantly respond to the Macedonian call for aid.*

Moreover, I am cognizant of the interrelatedness of all communities and states. I cannot sit idly by in Atlanta and not be concerned about what happens in Birmingham. Injustice anywhere is a threat to justice everywhere. We are caught in an inescapable network of mutuality, tied in a single garment of destiny. Whatever affects one directly affects all indirectly. Never again can we afford to live with the narrow, provincial "outside agitator" idea. Anyone who lives inside the United States can never be considered an outsider anywhere within its bounds.

You deplore the demonstrations taking place in Birmingham. But your statement, I am sorry to say, fails to express a similar concern for the conditions that brought about the demonstrations. I am sure that none of you would want to rest content with the superficial kind of social analysis that deals merely with effects and does not grapple with underlying causes. It is unfortunate that demonstrations are taking place in Birmingham, but it is even more unfortunate that the city's white power structure left the Negro community with no alternative.

*   *   *

You may well ask, "Why direct action? Why sit-ins, marches, etc.? Isn't negotiation a better path?" You are quite right in calling for negotiation. Indeed, this is the very purpose of direct action. Nonviolent direct action seeks to foster such a tension that a community which has constantly refused to negotiate is forced to confront the issue. It seeks so to dramatize the issue that it can no longer be ignored. My citing the creation of tension as part of the work of the nonviolent resister may sound rather shocking. But I readily acknowledge that I am not afraid of the word "tension." I have earnestly opposed violent tension, but there is a type of constructive, nonviolent tension which is necessary for growth. Just as Socrates felt that it was necessary to create a tension in the mind so that individuals could shake off the bondage of myths and half-truths and rise to the realm of creative analysis and objective appraisal, so must we see the need for nonviolent gadflies to create the kind of tension in society that will help men rise from the dark depths of prejudice and racism to the majestic heights of understanding and brotherhood.

The purpose of our direct-action program is to create a situation so crisis-packed that it will inevitably open the door to negotiation. I therefore concur with you in your call for negotiation. Too long has our beloved Southland been bogged down in a tragic effort to live in monologue rather than dialogue.

* * *

We have waited for more than 340 years for our constitutional and God-given rights. The nations of Asia and Africa are moving with jetlike speed toward gaining political independence, but we still creep at horse-and-buggy pace toward gaining a cup of coffee at a lunch counter. Perhaps it is easy for those who have never felt the stinging darts of segregation to say "Wait." But when you have seen vicious mobs lynch your mothers and fathers at will and drown your sisters and brothers at whim; when you have seen hate-filled policemen curse, kick, and even kill your black brothers and sisters with impunity; when you see the vast majority of your 20 million Negro brothers smothering in an air-tight cage of poverty in the midst of an affluent society; when you suddenly find your tongue twisted as you seek to explain to your six-year-old daughter why she can't go to the public amusement park that has just been advertised on television, and see tears welling up when she is told that Funtown is closed to colored children, and see ominous clouds of inferiority beginning to form in her little mental sky, and see her beginning to distort her personality by unconsciously developing a bitterness toward white people; when you have to concoct an answer for a five-year-old son asking, "Daddy, why do white people treat colored people so mean?"; when you take a cross-country drive and find it necessary to sleep night after night in the uncomfortable corners of your automobile because no motel will accept you; when you are humiliated day in and day out by nagging signs reading "white" and "colored"; when your first name becomes "nigger," your middle name becomes "boy" (however old you are), and your last name becomes "John," and your wife and mother are never given the respected title "Mrs."; when you are harried by day and haunted by night by the fact that you are a Negro, never quite knowing what to expect next, and are plagued with inner fears and outer resentments; when you are forever fighting a degenerating sense of "nobodiness"—then you will understand why we find it difficult to wait. There comes a time when the cup of endurance runs over, and men are no longer willing to be plunged into an abyss of injustice where they experience the bleakness of corroding despair. I hope, sirs, you can understand our legitimate and unavoidable impatience.

You express a great deal of anxiety over our willingness to break laws. This is certainly a legitimate concern. Since we so diligently urge people to obey the Supreme Court's decision of 1954 outlawing segregation in the public schools, at first glance it may seem rather paradoxical for us consciously to break laws. One may well ask, "How can you advocate breaking some laws and obeying others?" The answer lies in the fact that there are two types of laws: just and unjust. I agree with St. Augustine that "an unjust law is no law at all."

* * *

Let us consider some of the ways in which a law can be unjust. A law is unjust, for example, if the majority group compels a minority group to obey the statute but does not make it binding on itself. By the same token, a law in all probability is just if the majority is itself willing to obey it. Also, a law is unjust if it is inflicted on a minority that, as a result of being denied the right to vote, had no part in enacting or devising the law. Who can say that the legislature of Alabama which set up that state's segregation laws was democratically elected? Throughout Alabama all sorts of devious methods are used to prevent Negroes from becoming registered voters, and there are some counties in which, even though Negroes constitute a majority of the population, not a single Negro is registered. Can any law enacted under such circumstances be considered democratically structured?

Sometimes a law is just on its face and unjust in its application. For instance, I have been arrested on a charge of parading without a permit. Now there is nothing wrong in having an ordinance which requires a permit for a parade. But such an ordinance becomes unjust when it is used to maintain segregation and to deny citizens the First Amendment privilege of peaceful assembly and protest.

I hope you are able to see the distinction I am trying to point out. In no sense do I advocate evading the law, as would the rabid segregationist. That would lead to anarchy. One who breaks an unjust law must do so *openly, lovingly,* and with a willingness to accept the penalty. I submit that an individual who breaks a law that conscience tells him is unjust and who willingly accepts the penalty of imprisonment in order to arouse the conscience of the community over its injustice is in reality expressing the highest respect for law.

* * *

I must make two honest confessions to you, my Christian and Jewish brothers. First, I must confess that over the past few years I have been gravely disappointed with the white moderate. I have almost reached the regrettable conclusion that the Negro's great stumbling block in his stride toward freedom is not the White Citizen's Counciler or the Ku Klux Klanner but the white moderate who is more devoted to "order" than to justice; who prefers a negative peace which is the absence of tension to a positive peace which is the presence of justice; who constantly says "I agree with you in the goal you seek, but I cannot agree with your methods"; who paternalistically believes he can set the timetable for another man's freedom; who lives by a mythical concept of time and who constantly advises the Negro to wait for a "more convenient season." Shallow understanding from people of goodwill is more frustrating than absolute misunderstanding from people of ill will. Lukewarm acceptance is much more bewildering than outright rejection.

I had hoped that the white moderate would understand that law and order exist for the purpose of establishing justice and that when they fail in this purpose they block social progress. I had hoped that the white moderate would understand that the present tension in the South is a necessary phase of the transition from an obnoxious negative peace, in which the Negro passively accepted his unjust plight, to a substantive and positive peace, in which all men will respect the dignity and worth of human personality. Actually, we who engage in nonviolent direct action are not the creators of tension. We merely bring to the surface the hidden tension that is already alive. We bring it out in the open where it can be seen and dealt with. Like a boil that can never be cured so long as it is covered up but must be opened with all its pus-flowing ugliness to the natural medicines of air and light, injustice must be exposed, with all the tension its exposure creates, to the light of human conscience and the air of national opinion before it can be cured.

* * *

You speak of our activity in Birmingham as extreme. At first I was rather disappointed that fellow clergymen would see my nonviolent efforts as those of an extremist. I began thinking about the fact that I stand in the middle of two opposing forces in the Negro community. One is a force of complacency made up of Negroes who, as a result of long years of oppression, are so completely drained of self-respect and a sense of "somebodiness" that they have adjusted to segregation, and of a few middle-class Negroes who, because of a degree of academic and economic security and because in some ways they profit by segregation, have unconsciously become insensitive to the problems of the masses. The other force is one of bitterness and hatred, and it comes perilously close to advocating violence. It is expressed in the various black nationalist groups that are springing up across the nation, the largest and best-known being Elijah Muhammad's Muslim movement. Nourished by the Negro's frustration over the continued existence of racial discrimination, this movement is made up of people who have lost faith in America, who have absolutely repudiated Christianity, and who have concluded that the white man is an incorrigible "devil."

I have tried to stand between these two forces, saying that we need emulate neither the "do-nothingism" of the complacent nor the hatred of the black nationalist. For there is the more excellent way of love and nonviolent protest. I am grateful to God that, through the influence of the Negro church, the way of nonviolence became an integral part of our struggle.

If this philosophy had not emerged, by now many streets of the South would, I am convinced, be flowing with blood. And I am further convinced that if our white brothers dismiss as "rabble-rousers" and "outside agitators" those of us who employ nonviolent direct action and if they refuse to support our nonviolent efforts, millions of Negroes will, out of frustration and despair, seek solace and security in black nationalist ideologies—a development that would inevitably lead to a frightening racial nightmare.

* * *

Let me take note of my other major disappointment. Though there are some notable exceptions, I have also been disappointed with the white church and its leadership. I do not say this as one of those negative critics who can always find something wrong with the church. I say this as a minister of the gospel, who loves the church; who was nurtured in its bosom; who has been sustained by its spiritual blessings and who will remain true to it as long as the cord of life shall lengthen.

When I was suddenly catapulted into the leadership of the bus protest in Montgomery, Alabama, a few years ago, I felt we would be supported by the white church. I felt that the white ministers, priests, and rabbis of the South would be among our strongest allies. Instead, some have been outright opponents, refusing to understand the freedom movement and misrepresenting its leaders; all too many others have been more cautious than courageous and have remained silent and secure behind stained-glass windows.

In spite of my shattered dreams I came to Birmingham with the hope that the white religious leadership of this community would see the justice of our cause and with deep moral concern would serve as the channel through which our just grievances could reach the power structure. But again I have been disappointed.

I have heard numerous Southern religious leaders admonish their worshipers to comply with a desegregation decision because it is the *law*, but I have longed to hear white ministers declare, "Follow this decree because integration is morally *right* and because the Negro is your brother." In the midst of blatant injustices inflicted upon the Negro I have watched white churchmen stand on the sideline and mouth pious irrelevancies and sanctimonious trivialities. In the midst of a mighty struggle to rid our nation of racial and economic injustice I have heard many ministers say, "Those are social issues with which the gospel has no real concern," and I have watched many churches commit themselves to a completely otherworldly religion which makes a strange, unbiblical distinction between body and soul, between the sacred and the secular.

We are moving toward the close of the twentieth century with a religious community largely adjusted to the status quo—a taillight behind other community agencies rather than a headlight leading men to higher levels of justice.

* * *

But the judgment of God is upon the church as never before. If today's church does not recapture the sacrificial spirit of the early church, it will lose its authenticity, forfeit the loyalty of millions, and be dismissed as an irrelevant social club with no meaning for the twentieth century. Every day I meet young people whose disappointment with the church has turned into outright disgust.

Perhaps I have once again been too optimistic. Is organized religion too inextricably bound to the status quo to save our nation and the world? Perhaps I must turn my faith to the inner spiritual church, the church within the church, as the true *ecclesia* and the hope of the world. But again I am thankful to God that some noble souls from the ranks of organized religion have broken loose from the paralyzing chains of conformity and joined us as active partners in the struggle for freedom. They have left their secure congregations and walked the streets of Albany, Georgia, with us. They have gone down the highways of the South on torturous rides for freedom. Yes, they have gone to jail with us. Some have been kicked out of their churches, have lost the support of their bishops and fellow ministers. But they have acted in the faith that right defeated is stronger than evil triumphant. Their witness has been the spiritual salt that has preserved the true meaning of the gospel in these troubled times. They have carved a tunnel of hope through the dark mountain of disappointment.

I hope the church as a whole will meet the challenge of this decisive hour. But even if the church does not come to the aid of justice, I have no despair about the future. I have no fear about the outcome of our struggle in Birmingham, even if our motives are at present misunderstood. We will reach the goal of freedom in Birmingham and all over the nation, because the goal of America is freedom.

*   *   *

Before closing I feel impelled to mention one other point in your statement that has troubled me profoundly. You warmly commended the Birmingham police force for keeping "order" and "preventing violence." I doubt that you would have so warmly commended the police force if you had seen its angry dogs sinking their teeth into six unarmed, nonviolent Negroes. I doubt that you would so quickly commend the policemen if you were to observe their ugly and inhuman treatment of Negroes here in the City Jail; if you were to watch them push and curse old Negro women and young Negro girls; if you were to see them slap and kick old Negro men and young boys; if you were to observe them, as they did on two occasions, refuse to give us food because we wanted to sing our grace together. I cannot join you in your praise of the Birmingham Police Department.

It is true that the police have exercised discipline in handling the demonstrators. In this sense they have conducted themselves rather "nonviolently" in public. But for what purpose? To preserve the evil system of segregation. Over the past few years I have consistently preached that nonviolence demands that the means we use must be as pure as the ends we seek. I have tried to make clear that it is wrong to use immoral means to attain moral ends. But now I must affirm that it is just as wrong, or perhaps even more so, to use moral means to preserve immoral ends. Perhaps Mr. Connor and his policemen have been rather nonviolent in public, as was Chief Pritchett in Albany, Georgia, but they have used the moral means of nonviolence to maintain the immoral end of racial injustice. As T. S. Eliot has said, there is no greater treason than to do the right deed for the wrong reason.

I wish you had commended the Negro sit-inners and demonstrators of Birmingham for their sublime courage, their willingness to suffer and their amazing discipline in the midst of great provocation. One day the South will recognize its real heroes. . . . One day the South will know that when these disinherited children of God sat down at lunch counters they were in reality standing up for what is best in the American dream and for the most sacred values in our Judeo-Christian heritage, thereby bringing our nation back to those great wells of democracy which were dug deep by the founding fathers in their formulation of the Constitution and the Declaration of Independence.

DISCUSSION QUESTIONS

1. Identify the main points of disagreement between the readings by Lincoln and King.

2. Many of those involved in social protest movements (from abortion rights opponents to environmental protesters) draw parallels between themselves and King's legacy of civil disobedience, in an effort to establish their right to disobey laws that they consider unfair. Are these legitimate applications of King's argument? Why or why not?

15
"In Defense of Prejudice"

JONATHAN RAUCH

Many democratic theorists have argued that democratic reformers the world over should focus not only on free and fair elections, but also on the means to preserve the "absolute value of the individual and the universal applicability of basic rights." Democracies, in other words, must not only prevent the intrusion of government on basic liberties, but must play a positive role in bolstering and protecting the rights of all of their citizens. The challenge is admirable, but difficult. In practice, governments are often faced with trade-offs between the two values.

Consider free speech, a right enshrined in the First Amendment. The right to speak freely is fundamental to democratic governance. Yet it is not absolute. Is there a line where my right to speak freely impinges on your wish not to hear what I have to say, particularly when my words are perceived as offensive, harmful, and prejudicial? What role should the government play in drawing the line, if any? Should it limit some speech in order to protect against the insult words can bring?

In the following article Jonathan Rauch stands "in defense of prejudice" and in opposition to those who call for government regulation of speech that "insults or stigmatizes an individual . . . on the basis of their sex, race, color, handicap, religion, sexual orientation or national and ethnic origin." In the workplace, universities, public school curricula, the media, and criminal law, speech is increasingly regulated by speech codes aimed at eradicating prejudice. Rauch argues that regulating speech this way is foolish. In his view, the only way to challenge and correct prejudice is through the additional free flow of speech, some of which we might not want to hear. Government is at its "liberal" best when it works to preserve rather than prevent the free flow of speech, no matter how distasteful or hurtful that speech may be.

The war on prejudice is now, in all likelihood, the most uncontroversial social movement in America. Opposition to "hate speech," formerly identified with the liberal left, has become a bipartisan piety. In the past year, groups and factions that agree on nothing else have agreed that the public expression of any and all prejudices must be forbidden. On the left, protesters and editorialists have insisted that Francis L. Lawrence resign as president of Rutgers University for describing blacks as "a disadvantaged population that doesn't have that genetic, hereditary background to have a higher average." On the other side of the ideological divide, Ralph Reed, the executive director of the Christian Coalition, responded to criticism of the religious right by calling a press conference to denounce a supposed outbreak of "name-calling, scapegoating, and religious bigotry." Craig Rogers, an evangelical Christian student at California State University, recently filed a $2.5 million sexual-harassment suit against a lesbian professor of psychology, claiming that anti-male bias in one of her lectures violated campus rules and left him feeling "raped and trapped."

In universities and on Capitol Hill, in workplaces and newsrooms, authorities are declaring that there is no place for racism, sexism, homophobia, Christian-bashing, and other forms of prejudice in public debate or even in private thought. "Only when racism and other forms of prejudice are expunged," say the crusaders for sweetness and light, "can minorities be safe and society be fair." So sweet, this dream of a world without prejudice. But the very last thing society should do is seek to utterly eradicate racism and other forms of prejudice.

I suppose I should say, in the customary I-hope-I-don't-sound-too-defensive tone, that I am not a racist and that this is not an article favoring racism or any other particular prejudice. It is an article favoring intellectual pluralism, which permits the expression of various forms of bigotry and always will. Although we like to hope that a time will come when no one will believe that people come in types and that each type belongs with its own kind, I doubt such a day will ever arrive. By all indications, *Homo sapiens* is a tribal species for whom "us versus them" comes naturally and must be continually pushed back. Where there is genuine freedom of expression, there will be racist expression. There will also be people who believe that homosexuals are sick or threaten children or—especially among teenagers—are rightful targets of manly savagery. Homosexuality will always be incomprehensible to most people, and what is incomprehensible is feared. As for anti-Semitism, it appears to be a hardier virus than influenza. If you want pluralism, then you get racism and sexism and homophobia, and communism and fascism and xenophobia and tribalism, and that is just for a start. If you want to believe in intellectual freedom and the progress of knowledge and the advancement of science and all those other good things, then you must swallow hard and accept this: for as thickheaded and wayward an animal as us, the realistic question is how to make the best of prejudice, not how to eradicate it.

Indeed, "eradicating prejudice" is so vague a proposition as to be meaningless. Distinguishing prejudice reliably and nonpolitically from non-prejudice, or even defining it crisply, is quite hopeless. We all feel we know prejudice when we see it. But do we? At the University of Michigan, a student said in a classroom discussion that he considered homosexuality a disease treatable with therapy. He was summoned to a formal disciplinary hearing for violating the school's policy against speech that "victimizes" people based on "sexual orientation." Now, the evidence is abundant that this particular hypothesis is wrong, and any American homosexual can attest to the harm that the student's hypothesis has inflicted on many real people. But was it a statement of prejudice or of misguided belief? Hate speech or hypothesis? Many Americans who do not regard themselves as bigots or haters believe that homosexuality is a treatable disease. They may be wrong, but are they all bigots? I am unwilling to say so, and if you are willing, beware. The line between a prejudiced belief and a merely controversial one is elusive, and the harder you look the more elusive it becomes. "God hates homosexuals" is a statement of fact, not of bias, to those who believe it; "American criminals are disproportionately black" is a statement of bias, not of fact, to those who disbelieve it.

Who is right? You may decide, and so may others, and there is no need to agree. That is the great innovation of intellectual pluralism . . . We cannot know in advance or for sure which belief is prejudice and which is truth, but to advance knowledge we don't need to know. The genius of intellectual pluralism lies not in doing away with prejudices and dogmas but in channeling them—making them socially productive by pitting prejudice against prejudice and dogma against dogma, exposing all to withering public criticism. What survives at the end of the day is our base of knowledge.

* * *

Pluralism is the principle that protects and makes a place in human company for that loneliest and most vulnerable of all minorities, the minority who is hounded and despised among blacks and whites, gays and straights, who is suspect or criminal among every tribe and in every nation of the world, and yet on whom progress depends: the dissident. I am not saying that dissent is always or even usually enlightened. Most of the time it is foolish and self-serving. No dissident has the right to be taken seriously, and the fact that Aryan Nation racists or Nation of Islam anti-Semites are unorthodox does not entitle them to respect. But what goes around comes around. As a supporter of gay marriage, for example, I reject the majority's view of family, and as a Jew I reject its view of God. I try to be civil, but the fact is that most Americans regard my views on marriage as a reckless assault on the most fundamental of all institutions, and many people are more than a little discomfited by the statement "Jesus Christ was no more divine than anybody else" (which is why so few people ever say it). Trap the racists and anti-Semites, and you lay a trap for me too. Hunt for them with eradication in your mind, and you have brought dissent itself within your sights.

The new crusade against prejudice waves aside such warnings. Like earlier crusades against antisocial ideas, the mission is fueled by good (if cocksure) intentions and a genuine sense of urgency. Some kinds of error are held to be intolerable, like pollutants that even in small traces poison the water for a whole town. Some errors are so pernicious as to damage real people's lives, so wrongheaded that no person of right mind or goodwill could support them. Like their forebears of other stripe—the Church in its campaigns against heretics, the McCarthyites in their campaigns against Communists—the modern anti-racist and anti-sexist and anti-homophobic campaigners are totalists, demanding not that misguided ideas and ugly expressions be corrected or criticized but that they be eradicated. They make war not on errors but on error, and like other totalists they act in the name of public safety—the safety, especially, of minorities.

The sweeping implications of this challenge to pluralism are not, I think, well enough understood by the public at large. Indeed, the new brand of totalism has yet even to be properly named. "Multiculturalism," for instance, is much too broad. "Political correctness" comes closer but is too trendy and snide. For lack of anything else, I will call the new antipluralism "purism," since its major tenet is that society cannot be just until the last traces of invidious prejudice have been scrubbed away. Whatever you call it, the purists' way of seeing things has spread through American intellectual life with remarkable speed, so much so that many people will blink at you uncomprehendingly or even call you a racist (or sexist or homophobe, etc.) if you suggest that expressions of racism should be tolerated or that prejudice has its part to play.

The new purism sets out, to begin with, on a campaign against words, for words are the currency of prejudice, and if prejudice is hurtful then so must be prejudiced words. "We are not safe when these violent words are among us," wrote Mari Matsuda, then a UCLA law professor. Here one imagines gangs of racist words swinging chains and smashing heads in back alleys. To suppress bigoted language seems, at first blush, reasonable, but it quickly leads to a curious result. A peculiar kind of verbal shamanism takes root, as though certain expressions, like curses or magical incantations, carry in themselves the power to hurt or heal—as though words were bigoted rather than people. "Context is everything," people have always said. The use of the word "nigger" in *Huckleberry Finn* does not make the book an "act" of hate speech—or does it? In the new view, this is no longer so clear. The very utterance of the word "nigger" (at least by a non-black) is a racist act. When a *Sacramento Bee* cartoonist put the word "nigger" mockingly in the mouth of a white supremacist, there were howls of protest and 1,400 canceled subscriptions and an editorial apology, even though the word was plainly being invoked against racists, not against blacks.

Faced with escalating demands of verbal absolutism, newspapers issue lists of forbidden words. The expressions "gyp" (derived from "Gypsy") and "Dutch treat" were among the dozens of terms stricken as "offensive" in a much-ridiculed (and later withdrawn) *Los Angeles Times* speech code. The University of Missouri journalism school issued a *Dictionary of Cautionary Words and Phrases*, which included "*Buxom*: Offensive reference to a woman's chest. Do not use. See 'Woman.' *Codger*: Offensive reference to a senior citizen."

As was bound to happen, purists soon discovered that chasing around after words like "gyp" or "buxom" hardly goes to the roots of the problem. As long as they remain bigoted, bigots will simply find other words. If they can't call you a kike then they will say Jewboy, Judas, or Hebe, and when all those are banned they will press words like "oven" and "lampshade" into their service. The vocabulary of hate is potentially as rich as your dictionary, and all you do by banning language used by cretins is to let them decide what the rest of us may say. The problem, some purists have concluded, must therefore go much deeper than laws: it must go to the deeper level of ideas. Racism, sexism, homophobia, and the rest must be built into the very structure of American society and American patterns of thought, so pervasive yet so insidious that, like water to a fish, they are both omnipresent and unseen. The mere existence of prejudice constructs a society whose very nature is prejudiced.

This line of thinking was pioneered by feminists, who argued that pornography, more than just being expressive, is an act by which men construct an oppressive society. Racial activists quickly picked up the argument. Racist expressions are themselves acts of oppression, they said. "All racist speech constructs the social reality that constrains the liberty of nonwhites because of their race," wrote Charles R. Lawrence III, then a law professor at Stanford. From the purist point of view, a society with even one racist is a racist society, because the idea itself threatens and demeans its targets. They cannot feel wholly safe or wholly welcome as long as racism is present. Pluralism says: There will always be some racists. Marginalize them, ignore them, exploit them, ridicule them, take pains to make their policies illegal, but otherwise leave them alone. Purists say: That's not enough. Society cannot be just until these pervasive and oppressive ideas are searched out and eradicated.

And so what is now under way is a growing drive to eliminate prejudice from every corner of society. I doubt that many people have noticed how far-reaching this anti-pluralist movement is becoming.

In universities: Dozens of universities have adopted codes proscribing speech or other expression that (this is from Stanford's policy, which is more or less representative) "is intended to insult or stigmatize an individual or a small number of individuals on the basis of their sex, race, color, handicap, religion, sexual orientation or national and ethnic origin." Some codes punish only persistent harassment of a targeted individual, but many, following the purist doctrine that even one racist is too many, go much further. At Penn, an administrator declared: "We at the University of Pennsylvania have guaranteed students and the community that they can live in a community free of sexism, racism, and homophobia." Here is the purism that gives "political correctness" its distinctive combination of puffy high-mindedness and authoritarian zeal.

In school curricula: "More fundamental than eliminating racial segregation has to be the removal of racist thinking, assumptions, symbols, and materials in the curriculum," writes theorist Molefi Kete Asante. In practice, the effort to "remove racist thinking" goes well beyond striking egregious references from textbooks. In many cases it becomes a kind of mental engineering in which students are encouraged to see prejudice everywhere; it includes teaching identity politics as an antidote to internalized racism; it rejects mainstream science as "white male" thinking; and it tampers with history, installing such dubious notions as that the ancient Greeks stole their culture from Africa or that an ancient carving of a bird is an example of "African experimental aeronautics."

In criminal law: Consider two crimes. In each, I am beaten brutally; in each, my jaw is smashed and my skull is split in just the same way. However, in the first crime my assailant calls me an "asshole"; in the second he calls me a "queer." In most states, in many localities, and, as of September 1994, in federal cases, these two crimes are treated differently: the crime motivated by bias—or deemed to be so motivated by prosecutors and juries—gets a stiffer punishment. "Longer prison terms for bigots," shrilled Brooklyn Democratic Congressman Charles Schumer, who introduced the federal hate-crimes legislation, and those are what the law now provides. Evidence that the assailant holds prejudiced beliefs, even if he doesn't actually express them while committing an offense, can serve to elevate the crime. Defendants in hate-crimes cases may be grilled on how many black friends they have and whether they have told racist jokes. To increase a prison sentence only because of the defendant's "prejudice" (as gauged by prosecutor and jury) is, of course, to try minds and punish beliefs. Purists say, Well, they are dangerous minds and poisonous beliefs.

In the workplace: Though government cannot constitutionally suppress bigotry directly, it is now busy doing so indirectly by requiring employers to eliminate prejudice. Since the early 1980s, courts and the Equal Employment Opportunity Commission have moved to bar workplace speech deemed to create a hostile or abusive working environment for minorities. The law, held a federal court in 1988, "does require that an employer take prompt action to prevent . . . bigots from expressing their opinions in a way that abuses or offends their co-workers," so as to achieve "the goal of eliminating prejudices and biases from our society." So it was, as UCLA law professor Eugene Volokh notes, that the EEOC charged that a manufacturer's ads using admittedly accurate depictions of samurai, kabuki, and sumo were "racist" and "offensive to people of Japanese origin"; that a Pennsylvania court found that an employer's printing Bible verses on paychecks was religious harassment of Jewish employees; that an employer had to desist using gender-based job titles like "foreman" and "draftsman" after a female employee sued.

On and on the campaign goes, darting from one outbreak of prejudice to another like a cat chasing flies. In the American Bar Association, activists demand that lawyers who express "bias or prejudice" be penalized. In the Education Department, the civil-rights office presses for a ban on computer bulletin board comments that "show hostility toward a person or group based on sex, race or color, including slurs, negative stereotypes, jokes or pranks." In its security checks for government jobs, the FBI takes to asking whether applicants are "free of biases against any class of citizens," whether, for instance, they have told racist jokes or indicated other "prejudices." Joke police! George Orwell, grasping the close relationship of jokes to dissent, said that every joke is a tiny revolution. The purists will have no such rebellions.

The purist campaign reaches, in the end, into the mind itself. In a lecture at the University of New Hampshire, a professor compared writing to sex ("You and the subject become one"); he was suspended and required to apologize, but what was most insidious was the order to undergo university-approved counseling to have his mind straightened out. At the University of Pennsylvania, a law lecturer said, "We have ex-slaves here who should know about the Thirteenth Amendment"; he was banished from campus for a year and required to make a public apology, and he, too, was compelled to attend a "sensitivity and racial awareness" session. Mandatory re-education of alleged bigots is the natural consequence of intellectual purism. Prejudice must be eliminated!

. . . "Nobody escapes," said a Rutgers University report on campus prejudice. Bias and prejudice, it found, cross every conceivable line, from sex to race to politics: "No matter who you are, no matter what the color of your skin, no matter what your gender or sexual orientation, no matter what you believe, no matter how you behave, there is somebody out there who doesn't like people of your kind." Charles Lawrence writes: "Racism is ubiquitous. We are all racists." If he means that most of us think racist thoughts of some sort at one time or another, he is right. If we are going to "eliminate prejudices and biases from our society," then the work of the prejudice police is unending. They are doomed to hunt and hunt and hunt, scour and scour and scour.

What is especially dismaying is that the purists pursue prejudice in the name of protecting minorities. In order to protect people like me (homosexual), they must pursue people like me (dissident). In order to bolster minority self-esteem, they suppress minority opinion. There are, of course, all kinds of practical and legal problems with the purists' campaign: the incursions against the First Amendment; the inevitable abuses by prosecutors and activists who define as "hateful" or "violent" whatever speech they dislike or can score points off of; the lack of any evidence that repressing prejudice eliminates rather than inflames it. But minorities, of all people, ought to remember that by definition we cannot prevail by numbers, and we generally cannot prevail by force. Against the power of ignorant mass opinion and group prejudice and superstition, we have only our voices. If you doubt that minorities' voices are powerful weapons, think of the lengths to which Southern officials went to silence the Reverend Martin Luther King Jr. (recall that the city commissioner of Montgomery, Alabama, won a $500,000 libel suit, later overturned in *New York Times v. Sullivan* [1964], regarding an advertisement in the *Times* placed by civil-rights leaders who denounced the Montgomery police). Think of how much gay people have improved their lot over twenty-five years simply by refusing to remain silent. Recall the Michigan student who was prosecuted for saying that homosexuality is a treatable disease, and notice that he was black. Under that Michigan speech code, more than twenty blacks were charged with racist speech, while no instance of racist speech by whites was punished. In Florida, the hate-speech law was invoked against a black man who called a policeman a "white cracker"; not so surprisingly, in the first hate-crimes case to reach the Supreme Court, the victim was white and the defendant black.

In the escalating war against "prejudice," the right is already learning to play by the rules that were pioneered by the purist activists of the left. Last year leading Democrats, including the President, criticized the Republican Party for being increasingly in the thrall of the Christian right. Some of the rhetoric was harsh ("fire-breathing Christian radical right"), but it wasn't vicious or even clearly wrong. Never mind: when Democratic Representative Vic Fazio said Republicans were "being forced to the fringes by the aggressive political tactics of the religious right," the chairman of the Republican National Committee, Haley Barbour, said, "Christian-bashing" was "the left's preferred form of religious bigotry." Bigotry! Prejudice! "Christians active in politics are now on the receiving end of an extraordinary campaign of bias and prejudice," said the conservative leader William J. Bennett. One discerns, here, where the new purism leads. Eventually, any criticism of any group will be "prejudice."

DISCUSSION QUESTIONS

1. Do you think that certain types of speech or groups of people need to be protected in the "marketplace of ideas"?

2. Would a campus newspaper be justified in rejecting a paid advertisement from (a) a group or individual who denied that the Holocaust occurred; (b) a group or individual who argued that minorities should not be given any preferences in admission or financial aid; (b) a group or individual who accused the university president of being a war criminal and murderer for accepting research funds from the Department of Defense? Would you support a "speech code" that prohibited someone from making these arguments on campus? Defend your answer.

THE DEBATE: SHOULD DRUGS BE LEGALIZED?

For more than twenty years the United States has conducted a "war on drugs" domestically and internationally to prevent the production, sale, and consumption of drugs. It is a war many critics (such as William F. Buckley) claim the government has lost, conducted at a cost of more than $75 billion each year.

What makes the debate so emotional is that the issue of drug legalization is fundamentally a question of how we exercise our civil liberties, and what role the government ought to play in regulating our freedoms, if at all, in order to protect or promote a broad social interest. In a *National Review* forum entitled, "The War on Drugs is Lost," the journal's editor, William F. Buckley, Jr., and Yale law professor Steven Duke argue that the social costs of the drug war—the pursuit, prosecution and imprisonment of drug producers, sellers, and users—far outweigh any social benefits. In fact, as Duke argues, the war on drugs has had the horrid consequences of making "criminals out of one in three African-American males, creating one of the highest crime rates in the world," "destroy[ing] our inner cities by making them war zones," and bringing about the "de facto repeal of the Bill of Rights." Drug consumption is, according to these two authors, a matter of individual responsibility. They believe the only role for the national government ought to be the regulation of drug sales to minors and the devolution of other (and perhaps all) regulatory issues to the states and localities.

James Inciardi and Christine Saum oppose legalization. Their argument is not based on individual freedom, but on the public consequences of legalization. Legalization, they argue, would result in an escalation of violent crime, along with greater physical illness and psychiatric problems for drug users and their families. More important, legalization would not reduce the unemployment, poor housing, physical abuse, and bad economic times that often prompt drug use in the first place. In the context of civil rights, Inciardi and Saum see a legitimate role for government in restricting an individual's right to take drugs in order to promote a greater public good.

— consistent standard
— civil liberties

16
"The War on Drugs Is Lost"

William F. Buckley, Jr.

We are speaking of a plague that consumes an estimated $75 billion per year of public money, exacts an estimated $70 billion a year from consumers, is responsible for nearly 50 per cent of the million Americans who are today in jail, occupies an estimated 50 per cent of the trial time of our judiciary, and takes the time of 400,000 policemen —yet a plague for which no cure is at hand, nor in prospect.

* * *

It isn't the use of illegal drugs that we have any business complaining about, it is the abuse of such drugs. It is acknowledged that tens of millions of Americans (I have seen the figure 85 million) have at one time or another consumed, or exposed themselves to, an illegal drug. But the estimate authorized by the federal agency charged with such explorations is that there are not more than 1 million regular cocaine users, defined as those who have used the drug at least once in the preceding week. There are (again, an informed estimate) 5 million Americans who regularly use marijuana; and again, an estimated 70 million who once upon a time, or even twice upon a time, inhaled marijuana. From the above we reasonably deduce that Americans who abuse a drug, here defined as Americans who become addicted to it or even habituated to it, are a very small percentage of those who have experimented with a drug, or who continue to use a drug without any observable distraction in their lives or careers. About such users one might say that they are the equivalent of those Americans who drink liquor but do not become alcoholics, or those Americans who smoke cigarettes but do not suffer a shortened lifespan as a result.

Curiosity naturally flows to ask, next, How many users of illegal drugs in fact die from the use of them? The answer is complicated in part because marijuana finds itself lumped together with cocaine and heroin, and nobody has ever been found dead from marijuana. The question of deaths from cocaine is complicated by the factor of impurity. It would not be useful to draw any conclusions about alcohol consumption, for instance, by observing that, in 1931, one thousand Americans died from alcohol consumption if it happened that half of those deaths, or more than half, were the result of drinking alcohol with toxic ingredients extrinsic to the drug as conventionally used. When alcohol was illegal, the consumer could never know whether he had been given relatively harmless alcohol to drink—such alcoholic beverages as we find today in the liquor store—or whether the bootlegger had come up with paralyzing rotgut. By the same token, purchasers of illegal cocaine and heroin cannot know whether they are consuming a drug that would qualify for regulated consumption after clinical analysis.

But we do know this, and I approach the nexus of my inquiry, which is that more people die every year as a result of the war against drugs than die from what we call, generically, overdosing. These fatalities include, perhaps most prominently, drug merchants who compete for commercial territory, but include also people who are robbed and killed by those desperate for money to buy the drug to which they have become addicted.

This is perhaps the moment to note that the pharmaceutical cost of cocaine and heroin is approximately 2 per cent of the street price of those drugs. Since a cocaine addict can spend as much as $1,000 per week to sustain his habit, he would need to come up with that $1,000. The approximate fencing cost of stolen goods is 80 percent, so that to come up with $1,000 can require stealing $5,000 worth of jewels, cars, whatever. We can see that at free-market rates, $20 per week would provide the addict with the cocaine which, in this wartime drug situation, requires of him $1,000.

*   *   *

Serious crime is 480 per cent higher than in 1965. The correlation is not absolute, but it is suggestive: crime is reduced by the number of available enforcers of law and order, namely policemen. The heralded new crime legislation, passed last year and acclaimed by President Clinton, provides for 100,000 extra policemen, even if only for a limited amount of time. But 400,000 policemen would be freed to pursue criminals engaged in activity other than the sale and distribution of drugs if such sale and distribution, at a price at which there was no profit, were to be done by, say, a federal drugstore.

So then we attempt to put a value on the goods stolen by addicts. The figure arrived at by Professor Duke is $10 billion. But we need to add to this pain of stolen property, surely, the extra-material pain suffered by victims of robbers. If someone breaks into your house at night, perhaps holding you at gunpoint while taking your money and your jewelry and whatever, it is reasonable to assign a higher "cost" to the episode than the commercial value of the stolen money and jewelry. If we were modest, we might reasonably, however arbitrarily, put at $1,000 the "value" of the victim's pain. But then the hurt, the psychological trauma, might be evaluated by a jury at ten times, or one hundred times, that sum.

But we must consider other factors, not readily quantifiable, but no less tangible. Fifty years ago, to walk at night across Central Park was no more adventurous than to walk down Fifth Avenue. But walking across the park is no longer done. . . . Is it fair to put a value on a lost amenity? If the Metropolitan Museum were to close, mightn't we, without fear of distortion, judge that we had been deprived of something valuable? What value might we assign to confidence that, at night, one can sleep without fear of intrusion by criminals seeking money or goods exchangeable for drugs?

Pursuing utilitarian analysis, we ask: What are the relative costs, on the one hand, of medical and psychological treatment for addicts and, on the other, incarceration for drug offenses? It transpires that treatment is seven times more cost-effective. By this is meant that one dollar spent on the treatment of an addict reduces the probability of continued addiction seven times more than one dollar spent on incarceration. Looked at another way: Treatment is not now available for almost half of those who would benefit from it. Yet we are willing to build more and more jails in which to isolate drug users even though at one-seventh the cost of building and maintaining jail space and pursuing, detaining, and prosecuting the drug user, we could subsidize commensurately effective medical care and psychological treatment.

I have spared you, even as I spared myself, an arithmetical consummation of my inquiry, but the data here cited instruct us that the cost of the drug war is many times more painful, in all its manifestations, than would be the licensing of drugs combined with intensive education of non-users and intensive education designed to warn those who experiment with drugs. We have seen a substantial reduction in the use of tobacco over the last thirty years, and this is not because tobacco became illegal but because a sentient community began, in substantial numbers, to apprehend the high cost of tobacco to human health, even as, we can assume, a growing number of Americans desist from practicing unsafe sex and using polluted needles in this age of AIDS. If 80 million Americans can experiment with drugs and resist addiction using information publicly available, we can reasonably hope that approximately the same number would resist the temptation to purchase such drugs even if they were available at a federal drugstore at the mere cost of production.

And added to the above is the point of civil justice. Those who suffer from the abuse of drugs have themselves to blame for it. This does not mean that society is absolved from active concern for their plight. It does mean that their plight is subordinate to the plight of those citizens who do not experiment with drugs but whose life, liberty, and property are substantially affected by the illegalization of the drugs sought after by the minority.

* * *

- OD's ↓ b/c drugs
wouldn't be as
potent
- ↓ crime rates
- save $ on welfare

STEPHEN B. DUKE

"The drug war is not working," says Bill Buckley. That is certainly true if we assume, as he does, that the purpose of the drug war is to induce Americans to consume only approved drugs. But as the war wears on, we have to wonder what its purposes really are.

If its purpose is to make criminals out of one in three African-American males, it has succeeded. If its purpose is to create one of the highest crime rates in the world—and thus to provide permanent fodder for demagogues who decry crime and promise to do something about it—it is achieving that end. If its purpose is de facto repeal of the Bill of Rights, victory is well in sight. If its purpose is to transfer individual freedom to the central government, it is carrying that off as well as any of our real wars did. If its purpose is to destroy our inner cities by making them war zones, triumph is near.

Most of the results of the drug war . . . were widely observed during alcohol prohibition. Everyone should have known that the same fate would follow if the Prohibition approach were merely transferred to different drugs.

* * *

For forty years following the repeal of alcohol prohibition, we treated drug prohibition as we did other laws against vice: we didn't take it very seriously. As we were extricating ourselves from the Vietnam War, however, Richard Nixon declared "all-out global war on the drug menace," and the militarization of the problem began. After Ronald Reagan re-declared that war, and George Bush did the same, we had a drug-war budget that was 1,000 times what it was when Nixon first discovered the new enemy.

The objectives of the drug war are obscured in order to prevent evaluation. A common claim, for example, is that prohibition is part of the nation's effort to prevent serious crime. Bill Clinton's drug czar, Dr. Lee Brown, testified before Congress:

> Drugs—especially addictive, hard-core drug use—are behind much of the crime we see on our streets today, both those crimes committed by users to finance their lifestyles and those committed by traffickers and dealers fighting for territory and turf. . . . Moreover, there is a level of fear in our communities that is, I believe, unprecedented in our history . . .

If these remarks had been preceded by two words, "Prohibition of," the statement would have been correct, and the political reverberations would have been deafening. Instead, Dr. Brown implied that drug consumption is by itself responsible for "turf wars" and the other enumerated evils, an implication which he and every other drug warrior know is false. The only possibility more daunting than that our leaders are dissembling is that they might actually believe the nonsense they purvey.

I have little to add to the catalogue of drug-war casualties in the other essays assembled here. I do, however, see another angle of entry for Mr. Buckley's efforts at "quantification." I have argued elsewhere that the drug war is responsible for at least half of our serious crime. A panel of experts consulted by *U.S. News & World Report* put the annual dollar cost of America's crime at $674 billion. Half of that, $337 billion, was the *total* federal budget as recently as 1975. The crime costs of drug prohibition alone may equal 150 per cent of the entire federal welfare budget for 1995.

I also think Mr. Buckley understates the nonquantifiable loss of what he quaintly refers to as "amenities." Not only is it nearly suicidal to walk alone in Central Park at night, it is impossible in sections of some cities safely to leave one's home, or to remain there. Some Americans sleep in their bathtubs hoping they are bullet-proof. Prohibition-generated violence is destroying large sections of American cities. We can have our drug war or we can have healthy cities; we cannot have both.

* * *

Let's take a look at the "benefit" side of the equation. Were it not for the drug war, the prohibitionists say, we might be a nation of zombies. The DEA pulled the figure of 60 million from the sky: that's how many cocaine users they say we would have if it weren't for prohibition. Joseph Califano's colleague at the Center on Addiction and Substance Abuse, Dr. Herbert Kleber, a former assistant to William Bennett, puts the number of cocaine users after repeal at a more modest 20 to 25 million. In contrast, government surveys suggest that only about 3 million Americans currently use cocaine even occasionally and fewer than 500,000 use it weekly.

The prohibitionists' scenarios have no basis either in our history or in other cultures. In many countries, heroin and cocaine are cheap and at least de facto legal. Mexico is awash in cheap drugs, yet our own State Department says that Mexico does "not have a serious drug problem." Neither cocaine nor heroin is habitually consumed by more than a small fraction of the residents of any country in the world. There is no reason to suppose that Americans would be the single exception.

Lee Brown used to rely on alcohol prohibition as proof that legalization would addict the nation, asserting that alcohol consumption "shot straight up" when Prohibition was repealed. He no longer claims that, it having been pointed out to him that alcohol consumption increased only about 25 per cent in the years following repeal. Yet even assuming, contrary to that experience, that ingestion of currently illegal drugs would double or triple following repeal, preventing such increased consumption still cannot be counted a true benefit of drug prohibition. After repeal, the drugs would be regulated; their purity and potency would be disclosed on the package, as Mr. Buckley points out, together with appropriate warnings. Deaths from overdoses and toxic reactions would be reduced, not increased. Moreover, . . . the drugs consumed after repeal would be less potent than those ingested under prohibition. Before alcohol prohibition, we were a nation of beer drinkers. Prohibition pushed us toward hard liquor, a habit from which we are still recovering. Before the Harrison Act,* many Americans took their cocaine in highly diluted forms, such as Coca-Cola.

We would also end the cruel practices . . . wherein we deny pain medication to those who need it, preclude the medical use of marijuana, and compel drug users to share needles and thus to spread deadly diseases. The proportion of users who would consume the drugs without substantial health or other problems would be greatly increased. In comparison to any plausible post-repeal scenario, therefore, there simply are *no* health benefits achieved by prohibition.

* * *

I should perhaps confess that I am not now, nor have I ever been, a conservative. As an outsider, therefore, perhaps I can be pardoned for my inability to see consistency in the positions conservatives commonly take on drugs and related issues. I can understand how one who believes that government should force us to lead proper lives can, albeit mistakenly, support drug prohibition. But I cannot comprehend how *any* conservative can support the drug war. That is my major mystery. I am also perplexed by some subordinate, mini-mysteries, of which here are a few:

- Why do so many conservatives preach "individual responsibility" yet ardently punish people for the chemicals they consume and thus deny the right that gives meaning to the responsibility? Many of these same conservatives would think it outrageous for the government to decree the number of calories we ingest or the kind of exercise we get, even though such decrees would be aimed at preserving our lives, keeping us productive, and reducing the drain on scarce medical resources. The incongruity of these positions is mystifying, and so is the willingness of conservatives, in order to protect people from their own folly, to impose huge costs in death, disease, crime, corruption, and destruction of civil liberties upon others who are entirely innocent: people who do not partake of forbidden drugs.
- Newt Gingrich, Charles Murray, and other conservatives are rightly concerned about the absence of fathers in the homes of so many of America's youngsters. Where are those fathers? At least half a million are in prison, often for nothing worse than possessing drugs.
- Countless conservatives revere the right to one's property. Yet many

* [1914 act that classified cocaine as an illegal substance.]

conservatives support drug forfeiture as gladly as liberals. Congress has made a criminal prosecution unnecessary for persons with property who are associated (even if indirectly) with illicit drugs. An apartment house may be forfeited if a tenant grows a marijuana plant in his bathroom. A grandmother's home may be forfeited if a grandson hides drugs in the basement which he sells to his friends. The Supreme Court has said that there are constitutional limits on forfeitures, but it has yet to find any. With the notable exception of Congressman Henry Hyde (see his book, *Forfeiting Our Property Rights*), most legislators are unconcerned about drawing a line.

- Many conservatives strongly support schemes to "devolve" matters from the Federal Government to state and local governments. Yet there does not appear to be a single conservative politician in America who applies this principle to drug prohibition. The mystery deepens when we remember that this is precisely the way we handled alcohol prohibition. When we repealed the Eighteenth Amendment, we didn't declare that all forms of alcohol distribution were beyond the reach of prohibition; in the Twenty-First Amendment, we simply let each state decide how it wanted to handle alcohol. Some remained dry. Many devolved the issue to cities and counties, some of which have elected to maintain prohibition to this very day. Judge Sweet and others make a powerful case for applying this approach to other drugs in addition to alcohol. Why hasn't any conservative in elective office at least suggested that it be *considered*?

The only benefit to America in maintaining prohibition is the psychic comfort we derive from having a permanent scapegoat. But why did we have to pick an enemy the warring against which is so self-destructive? We would be better off blaming our ills on celestial invaders flying about in saucers.

17
"Legalization Madness"

• against legalization of drugs
• knocks down all of the pros

JAMES A. INCIARDI AND CHRISTINE A. SAUM

Frustrated by the government's apparent inability to reduce the supply of illegal drugs on the streets of America, and disquieted by media accounts of innocents victimized by drug-related violence, some policy makers are convinced that the "war on drugs" has failed. In an attempt to find a better solution to the "drug crisis" or, at the very least, to try an alternative strategy, they have proposed legalizing drugs. They argue that, if marijuana, cocaine, heroin, and other drugs were legalized, several positive things would probably occur: (1) drug prices would fall; (2) users would obtain their drugs at low, government-regulated prices, and they would no longer be forced to resort to crime in order to support their habits; (3) levels of drug-related crime, and particularly violent crime, would significantly decline, resulting in less crowded courts, jails, and prisons (this would allow law-enforcement personnel to focus their energies on the "real criminals" in society); and (4) drug production, distribution, and sale would no longer be controlled by organized crime, and thus such criminal syndicates as the Colombian cocaine "cartels," the Jamaican "posses," and the various "mafias" around the country and the world would be decapitalized, and the violence associated with drug distribution rivalries would be eliminated.

By contrast, the anti-legalization camp argues that violent crime would not necessarily decline in a legalized drug market. In fact, there are three reasons why it might actually increase. First, removing the criminal sanctions against the possession and distribution of illegal drugs would make them more available and attractive and, hence, would create large numbers of new users. Second, an increase in use would lead to a greater number of dysfunctional addicts who could not support themselves, their habits, or their lifestyles through legitimate means. Hence crime would be their only alternative. Third, more users would mean more of the violence associated with the ingestion of drugs.

These divergent points of view tend to persist because the relationships between drugs and crime are quite complex and because the possible outcomes of a legalized drug market are based primarily on speculation. However, it is possible, from a careful review of the existing empirical literature on drugs and violence, to make some educated inferences.

Considering "Legalization"

Yet much depends upon what we mean by "legalizing drugs." Would all currently illicit drugs be legalized or would the experiment be limited to just certain ones? True legalization would be akin to selling such drugs as heroin and cocaine on the open market, much like alcohol and tobacco, with a few age-related restrictions. In contrast, there are "medicalization" and "decriminalization" alternatives. Medicalization approaches are of many types, but, in essence, they would allow users to obtain prescriptions for some, or all, currently illegal substances. Decriminalization removes the criminal penalties associated with the possession of small amounts of illegal drugs for personal use, while leaving intact the sanctions for trafficking, distribution, and sale.

But what about crack-cocaine? A quick review of the literature reveals that the legalizers, the decriminalizers, and the medicalizers avoid talking about this particular form of cocaine. Perhaps they do not want to legalize crack out of fear of the drug itself, or of public outrage. Arnold S. Trebach, a professor of law at American University and president of the Drug Policy Foundation, is one of the very few who argues for the full legalization of all drugs, including crack. He explains, however, that most are reluctant to discuss the legalization of crack-cocaine because, "it is a very dangerous drug. . . . I know that for many people the very thought of making crack legal destroys any inclination they might have had for even thinking about drug-law reform."

There is a related concern associated with the legalization of cocaine. Because crack is easily manufactured from powder cocaine (just add water and baking soda and cook on a stove or in a microwave), many drug-policy reformers hold that no form of cocaine should be legalized. But this weakens the argument that legalization will reduce drug-related violence; for much of this violence would appear to be in the cocaine-and crack-distribution markets.

To better understand the complex relationship between drugs and violence, we will discuss the data in the context of three models developed by Paul J. Goldstein of the University of Illinois at Chicago. They are the "psychopharmacological," "economically compulsive," and "systemic" explanations of violence. The first model holds, correctly in our view, that some individuals may become excitable, irrational, and even violent due to the ingestion of specific drugs. In contrast, taking a more economic approach to the behavior of drug users, the second holds that some drug users engage in violent crime mainly for the sake of supporting their drug use. The third model maintains that drug-related violent crime is simply the result of the drug market under a regime of illegality.

(1) *Psychopharmacological Violence* — irrational & violent due to injesting drugs

The case for legalization rests in part upon the faulty assumption that drugs themselves do not cause violence; rather, so goes the argument, violence is the result of depriving drug addicts of drugs or of the "criminal" trafficking in drugs. But, as researcher Barry Spunt points out, "Users of drugs do get violent when they get high."

Research has documented that chronic users of amphetamines, methamphetamine, and cocaine in particular tend to exhibit hostile and aggressive behaviors. Psychopharmacological violence can also be a product of what is known as "cocaine psychosis." As dose and duration of cocaine use increase, the development of cocaine-related psychopathology is not uncommon. Cocaine psychosis is generally preceded by a transitional period characterized by increased suspiciousness, compul-

economically compulsive: violence to support $ for drugs

sive behavior, fault finding, and eventually paranoia. When the psychotic state is reached, individuals may experience visual, as well as auditory, hallucinations, with persecutory voices commonly heard. Many believe that they are being followed by police or that family, friends, and others are plotting against them.

Moreover, everyday events are sometimes misinterpreted by cocaine users in ways that support delusional beliefs. When coupled with the irritability and hyperactivity that cocaine tends to generate in almost all of its users, the cocaine-induced paranoia may lead to violent behavior as a means of "self-defense" against imagined persecutors. The violence associated with cocaine psychosis is a common feature in many crack houses across the United States. Violence may also result from the irritability associated with drug-withdrawal syndromes. In addition, some users ingest drugs before committing crimes to both loosen inhibitions and bolster their resolve to break the law.

Acts of violence may result from either periodic or chronic use of a drug. For example, in a study of drug use and psychopathy among Baltimore City jail inmates, researchers at the University of Baltimore reported that cocaine use was related to irritability, resentment, hostility, and assault. They concluded that these indicators of aggression may be a function of drug effects rather than of a predisposition to these behaviors. Similarly, Barry Spunt and his colleagues at National Development and Research Institutes (NDRI) in New York City found that of 269 convicted murderers incarcerated in New York State prisons, 45 percent were high at the time of the offense. Three in 10 believed that the homicide was related to their drug use, challenging conventional beliefs that violence only infrequently occurs as a result of drug consumption.

Even marijuana, which pro-legalizers consider harmless, may have a connection with violence and crime. Spunt and his colleagues attempted to determine the role of marijuana in the crimes of the homicide offenders they interviewed in the New York State prisons. One-third of those who had ever used marijuana had smoked the drug in the 24-hour period prior to the homicide. Moreover, 31 percent of those who considered themselves to be "high" at the time of committing murder felt that the homicide and marijuana were related. William Blount of the University of South Florida interviewed abused women in prisons and shelters for battered women located throughout Florida. He and his colleagues found that 24 percent of those who killed their abusers were marijuana users while only 8 percent of those who did not kill their abusers smoked marijuana.

And Alcohol Abuse – b/c it's legal it's linked to violence more than any illegal drug

A point that needs emphasizing is that alcohol, because it is legal, accessible, and inexpensive, is linked to violence to a far greater extent than any illegal drug. For example, in the study just cited, it was found that an impressive 64 percent of those women who eventually killed their abusers were alcohol users (44 percent of those who did not kill their abusers were alcohol users). Indeed, the extent to which alcohol is responsible for violent crimes in comparison with other drugs is apparent from the statistics. For example, Carolyn Block and her colleagues at the Criminal Justice Information Authority in Chicago found that, between 1982 and 1989, the use of alcohol by offenders or victims in local homicides ranged from 18 percent to 32 percent.

Alcohol has, in fact, been consistently linked to homicide. Spunt and his colleagues interviewed 268 homicide offenders incarcerated in New York State correctional facilities to determine the role of alcohol in their crimes: Thirty-one percent of the respondents reported being drunk at the time of the crime and 19 percent believed that the homicide was related to their drinking. More generally, Douglass Murdoch of Quebec's McGill University found that in some 9,000 criminal cases drawn from a multinational sample, 62 percent of violent offenders were drinking shortly before, or at the time of, the offense.

It appears that alcohol reduces the inhibitory control of threat, making it more likely that a person will exhibit violent behaviors normally suppressed by fear. In turn, this reduction of inhibition heightens the probability that intoxicated persons will perpetrate, or become victims of, aggressive behavior.

When analyzing the psychopharmacological model of drugs and violence, most of the discussions focus on the offender and the role of drugs in causing or facilitating crime. But what about the victims? Are the victims of drug- and alcohol-related homicides simply casualties of someone else's substance abuse? In addressing these questions, the data demonstrates that victims are likely to be drug users as well. For example, in an analysis of the 4,298 homicides that occurred in New York City during 1990 and 1991, Kenneth Tardiff of Cornell University Medical College found that the victims of these offenses were 10 to 50 times more likely to be cocaine users than were members of the general population. Of the white female victims, 60 percent in the 25- to 34-year age group had cocaine in their systems; for black females, the figure was 72 percent. Tardiff speculated that the classic symptoms of cocaine use—irritability, paranoia, aggressiveness—may have instigated the violence. In another study of cocaine users in New York City, female high-volume users were found to be victims of violence far more frequently than low-volume and nonusers of cocaine. Studies in numerous other cities and countries have yielded the same general findings—that a great many of the victims of homicide and other forms of violence are drinkers and drug users themselves.

Economically Compulsive Violence –violence to support $ for drugs

Supporters of the economically compulsive model of violence argue that in a legalized market, the prices of "expensive drugs" would decline to more affordable levels, and, hence, predatory crimes would become unnecessary. This argument is based on several specious assumptions. First, it assumes that there is empirical support for what has been referred to as the "enslavement theory of addiction." Second, it assumes that people addicted to drugs commit crimes only for the purpose of supporting their habits. Third, it assumes that, in a legalized market, users could obtain as much of the drugs as they wanted whenever they wanted. Finally, it assumes that, if drugs are inexpensive, they will be affordable, and thus crime would be unnecessary.

With respect to the first premise, there has been for the better part of this century a concerted belief among many in the drug-policy field that addicts commit crimes because they are "enslaved" to drugs, and further that, because of the high price of heroin, cocaine, and other illicit chemicals on the black market, users are forced to commit crimes in order to support their drug habits. However, there is no solid empirical evidence to support this contention. From the 1920s through the end of the 1960s, hundreds of studies of the relationship between crime and addiction were conducted. Invariably, when one analysis would support the posture of "enslavement theory," the next would affirm the view that addicts were criminals first and that their drug use was but one more manifestation of their deviant lifestyles. In retrospect, the difficulty lay in the ways that many of the studies had been conducted: Biases and deficiencies in research designs and sampling had rendered their findings of little value.

Studies since the mid 1970s of active drug users on the streets of New York, Miami, Baltimore, and elsewhere have demonstrated that the "enslavement theory" has little basis in reality. All of these studies of the criminal careers of drug users have convincingly documented that, while drug use tends to intensify and perpetuate criminal behavior, it usually does not initiate criminal careers. In fact, the evidence suggests that among the majority of street drug users who are involved in crime, their criminal careers are well established prior to the onset of either narcotics or cocaine use. As such, it would appear that the "inference of causality"—that the high price of drugs on the black market itself causes crime—is simply false.

Looking at the second premise, a variety of studies show that addicts commit crimes for reasons other than supporting their drug habit. They do so also for daily living expenses. For example, researchers at the Center for Drug and Alcohol Studies at the University of Delaware who studied crack users on the streets of Miami found that, of the active addicts interviewed, 85 percent of the male and 70 percent of the female interviewees paid for portions of their living expenses through street crime. In fact, one-half of the men and one-fourth of the women paid for 90 percent or more of their living expenses through crime. And, not surprisingly, 96 percent of the men and 99 percent of the women had not held a legal job in the 90-day period before being interviewed for the study.

With respect to the third premise, that in a legalized market users could obtain as much of the drugs as they wanted whenever they wanted, only speculation is possible. More than likely, however, there would be some sort of regulation, and hence black markets for drugs would persist for those whose addictions were beyond the medicalized or legalized allotments. In a decriminalized market, levels of drug-related violence would likely either remain unchanged or increase (if drug use increased).

As for the last premise, that cheap drugs preclude the need to commit crimes to obtain them, the evidence emphatically suggests that this is not the case. Consider crack-cocaine: Although crack "rocks" are available on the illegal market for as little as two dollars in some locales, users are still involved in crime-driven endeavors to support their addictions. For example, researchers Norman S. Miller and Mark S. Gold surveyed 200 consecutive callers to the 1-800-COCAINE hotline who considered themselves to have a problem with crack. They found that, despite the low cost of crack, 63 percent of daily users and 40 percent of non-daily users spent more than $200 per week on the drug. Similarly, interviews conducted by NDRI researchers in New York City with almost 400 drug users contacted in the streets, jails, and treatment programs revealed that almost one-half of them spent over $1,000 a month on crack. The study also documented that crack users—despite the low cost of their drug of choice—spent more money on drugs than did users of heroin, powder cocaine, marijuana, and alcohol.

(3) *Systemic Violence* ~result of drug market + illegality

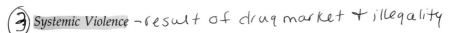

It is the supposed systemic violence associated with trafficking in cocaine and crack in America's inner cities that has recently received the attention of drug-policy critics interested in legalizing drugs. Certainly it might appear that, if heroin and cocaine were legal substances, systemic drug-related violence would decline. However, there are two very important questions in this regard: First, is drug-related violence more often psychopharmacological or systemic? Second, is the great bulk of systemic violence related to the distribution of crack? If most of the drug-related violence is psychopharmacological in nature, and if systemic violence is typically related to crack—the drug generally excluded from consideration when legalization is recommended—then legalizing drugs would probably *not* reduce violent crime.

Regarding the first question, several recent studies conducted in New York City tend to contradict, or at least not support, the notion that legalizing drugs would reduce violent, systemic-related crime. For example, Paul J. Goldstein's ethnographic studies of male and female drug users during the late 1980s found that cocaine-related violence was more often psychopharmacological than systemic. Similarly, Kenneth Tardiff's study of 4,298 New York City homicides found that 31 percent of the victims had used cocaine in the 24-hour period prior to their deaths. One of the conclusions of the study was that the homicides were not necessarily related to drug dealing. In all likelihood, as victims of homicide, the cocaine users may have provoked violence through their irritability, paranoid thinking, and verbal or physical aggression—all of which are among the psychopharmacological effects of cocaine.

Regarding the second question, the illegal drug most associated with systemic violence is crack-cocaine. Of all illicit drugs, crack is the one now responsible for the most homicides. In a study done in New York City in 1988 by Goldstein and his colleagues, crack was found to be connected with 32 percent of all homicides and 60 percent of all drug-related homicides. Furthermore, although there is evidence that crack sellers are more violent than other drug sellers, this violence is not confined to the drug-selling context—violence potentials appear to precede involvement in selling.

Thus, though crack has been blamed for increasing violence in the marketplace, this violence actually stems from the psychopharmacological consequences of crack use. Ansley Hamid, a professor of anthropology at the John Jay College of Criminal Justice in New York, reasons that increases in crack-related violence are due to the deterioration of informal and formal social controls throughout communities that have been destabilized by economic processes and political decisions. If this is the case, does anyone really believe that we can improve these complex social problems through the simple act of legalizing drugs?

Don't Just Say No

The issue of whether or not legalization would create a multitude of new users also needs to be addressed. It has been shown that many people do not use drugs simply because drugs are illegal. As Mark A. R. Kleiman, author of *Against Excess: Drug Policy for Results*, recently put it: "Illegality by itself tends to suppress consumption, independent of its effect on price, both because some consumers are reluctant to disobey the law and because illegal products are harder to find and less reliable as to quality and labeling than legal ones."

Although there is no way of accurately estimating how many new users there would be if drugs were legalized, there would probably be many. To begin with, there is the historical example of Prohibition. During Prohibition, there was a decrease of 20 percent to 50 percent in the ~prohibition~ number of alcoholics. These estimates were calculated based on a decline ~↓~ in cirrhosis and other alcohol-related deaths; after Prohibition ended, ~alcoholics~ both of these indicators increased.

Currently, relatively few people are steady users of drugs. The University of Michigan's *Monitoring the Future* study reported in 1995 that only two-tenths of 1 percent of high-school seniors are daily users of either hallucinogens, cocaine, heroin, sedatives, or inhalants. It is the addicts who overwhelmingly consume the bulk of the drug supply—80 percent of all alcohol and almost 100 percent of all heroin. In other words, there are significantly large numbers of non-users who have yet to even try drugs, let alone use them regularly. Of those who begin to use drugs "recreationally," researchers estimate that approximately 10 percent go on to serious, heavy, chronic, compulsive use. Herbert Kleber, the former deputy director of the Office of National Drug Control Policy, recently estimated that cocaine legalization might multiply the number of addicts from the current 2 million to between 18 and 50 million (which are the estimated numbers of problem drinkers and nicotine addicts).

This suggests that drug prohibition seems to be having some very positive effects and that legalizing drugs would not necessarily have a depressant effect on violent crime. With legalization, violent crime would likely escalate; or perhaps some types of systemic violence would decline at the expense of greatly increasing the overall rate of violent crime. Moreover, legalizing drugs would likely increase physical illnesses and compound any existing psychiatric problems among users and their family members. And finally, legalizing drugs would not eliminate the effects of unemployment, inadequate housing, deficient job skills, economic worries, and physical abuse that typically contribute to the use of drugs.

DISCUSSION QUESTIONS

1. Is drug use a matter of individual responsibility, or a social problem that should be regulated by the government?

2. Do you think legalization would reduce the violence and crime associated with drug use? Why or why not? Would it increase use? Why or why not?

PART II

Institutions

[Handwritten notes at top:]

- motivation by reelection (advertising, credit-claim)
- represent public/voters? elite/campaign donations?
- role is platforms for position-taking, credit-claiming, advertising

- structure enforces this desire for re-election
- power

CHAPTER 4

Congress: The First Branch

18
From *Congress: The Electoral Connection*

David R. Mayhew

Are members of Congress motivated by the desire to make good public policy that will best serve the public and national interest? The political scientist David Mayhew argues the motivation is not so idealistic or complex. Members of Congress simply want to be reelected, and most of their behavior—advertising, credit claiming, and position taking—is designed to make their reelection easier. Further, Mayhew argues that the structure of Congress is ideally suited to facilitate the reelection pursuit. Congressional offices and staff advertise member accomplishments, committees allow for the specialization necessary to claim credit, and the political parties in Congress do not demand loyalty when constituent demands run counter to the party line.

Mayhew's argument is not universally accepted. Many political scientists take his underlying premise as a given: Elected officials are self-interested, and this is manifest in their constant pursuit of reelection. But others disagree with the premise. Motivations, they argue, are far more complex than allowed for by such a simple statement or theory. People often act unselfishly, and members of Congress have been known to vote their consciences even if it means losing an election.

[1.] The organization of Congress meets remarkably well the electoral needs of its members. To put it another way, if a group of planners sat down and tried to design a pair of American national assemblies with the goal of serving members' electoral needs year in and year out, they would be hard pressed to improve on what exists. . . . [2.] Satisfaction of electoral needs requires remarkably little zero-sum conflict among members. That is, one member's gain is not another member's loss; to a remarkable degree members can successfully engage in electorally useful activities without denying other members the opportunity successfully to engage in them. In regard to credit claiming, this second point requires elaboration further on. Its application to advertising is perhaps obvious. The members all have different markets, so that what any one member does is not an inconvenience to any other. There are exceptions here—House members are sometimes thrown into districts together, senators have to watch the advertising of ambitious House members within their states, and senators from the same state have to keep up with each other—but the case generally holds. With position taking the point is also reasonably clear. As long as congressmen do not attack each other —and they rarely do—any member can champion the most extraordinary causes without inconveniencing any of his colleagues.

* * *

A scrutiny of the basic structural units of Congress will yield evidence to support both these . . . points. First, there are the 535 Capitol Hill *offices*, the small personal empires of the members. . . . The Hill office is a vitally important political unit, part campaign management firm and part political machine. The availability of its staff members for election work in and out of season gives it some of the properties of the former; its casework capabilities, some of the properties of the latter. And there is the franking privilege for use on office emanations. . . . A final comment on congressional offices is perhaps the most important one: office resources are given to all members regardless of party, seniority, or any other qualification. They come with the job.

Second among the structural units are the *committees*. . . . Committee membership can be electorally useful in a number of different ways. Some committees supply good platforms for position taking. The best example over the years is probably the House Un-American Activities Committee (now the Internal Security Committee), whose members have displayed hardly a trace of an interest in legislation. [Theodore] Lowi has a chart showing numbers of days devoted to HUAC public hearings in Congresses from the Eightieth through the Eighty-ninth. It can be read as a supply chart, showing biennial volume of position taking on subversion and related matters; by inference it can also be read as a measure of popular demand (the peak years were 1949–56). Senator Joseph McCarthy used the Senate Government Operations Committee as his investigative base in the Eighty-third Congress; later on in the 1960s Senators Abraham Ribicoff (D., Conn.) and William Proxmire (D., Wis.) used subcommittees of this same unit in catching public attention respectively on auto safety and defense waste. With membership on the Senate Foreign Relations Committee goes a license to make speeches on foreign policy. Some committees perhaps deserve to be designated "cause committees"; membership on them can confer an ostentatious identification with salient public causes. An example is the House Education and Labor Committee, whose members, in Fenno's analysis, have two "strategic premises": "to prosecute policy partisanship" and "to pursue one's individual policy preferences regardless of party." Committee members do a good deal of churning about on education, poverty, and similar matters. In recent years Education and Labor has attracted media-conscious members such as Shirley Chisholm (D., N.Y.), Herman Badillo (D., N.Y.), and Louise Day Hicks (D., Mass.).

Some committees traffic in particularized benefits.

* * *

Specifically, in giving out particularized benefits where the costs are diffuse (falling on taxpayer or consumer) and where in the long run to reward one congressman is not obviously to deprive others, the members follow a policy of universalism. That is, every member, regardless of party or seniority, has a right to his share of benefits. There is evidence of universalism in the distribution of projects on House Public Works, projects on House Interior, projects on Senate Interior, project money on House Appropriations, project money on Senate Appropriations, tax benefits on House Ways and Means, tax benefits on Senate Finance, and (by inference from the reported data) urban renewal projects on House Banking and Currency. The House Interior Committee, in Fenno's account, "takes as its major decision rule a determination to process and pass *all* requests and to do so in such a way as to maximize the chances of passage in the House. Succinctly, then, Interior's major strategic premise is: *to secure House passage of all constituency-supported, Member-sponsored bills.*"

* * *

Particularism also has its position-taking side. On occasion members capture public attention by denouncing the allocation process itself; thus in 1972 a number of liberals held up some Ways and Means "members' bills" on the House floor. But such efforts have little or no effect. Senator Douglas used to offer floor amendments to excise projects from public works appropriations bills, but he had a hard time even getting the Senate to vote on them.

Finally, and very importantly, the committee system aids congressmen simply by allowing a division of labor among members. The parceling out of legislation among small groups of congressmen by subject area has two effects. First, it creates small voting bodies in which membership may be valuable. An attentive interest group will prize more highly the favorable issue positions of members of committees pondering its fortunes than the favorable positions of the general run of congressmen. Second, it creates specialized small-group settings in which individual congressmen can make things happen and be perceived to make things happen. "I put that bill through committee." "That was my amendment." "I talked them around on that." This is the language of credit claiming. It comes easily in the committee setting and also when "expert" committee members handle bills on the floor. To attentive audiences it can be believable. Some political actors follow committee activities closely and mobilize electoral resources to support deserving members.

* * *

The other basic structural units in Congress are the *parties*. The case here will be that the parties, like the offices and committees, are tailored to suit members' electoral needs. They are more useful for what they are not than for what they are.

* * *

What is important to each congressman, and vitally so, is that he be free to take positions that serve his advantage. There is no member of either house who would not be politically injured—or at least who would not think he would be injured—by being made to toe a party line on all policies (unless of course he could determine the line). There is no congressional bloc whose members have identical position needs across all issues. Thus on the school bussing issue in the Ninety-second Congress, it was vital to Detroit white liberal Democratic House members that they be free to vote one way and to Detroit black liberal Democrats that they be free to vote the other. In regard to these member needs the best service a party can supply to its congressmen is a negative one; it can leave them alone. And this in general is what the congressional parties do. Party leaders are chosen not to be program salesmen or vote mobilizers, but to be brokers, favor-doers, agenda-setters, and protectors of established institutional routines. Party "pressure" to vote one way or another is minimal. Party "whipping" hardly deserves the name. Leaders in both houses have a habit of counseling members to "vote their constituencies."

DISCUSSION QUESTIONS

1. If members are motivated by the desire to be reelected, is this such a bad thing? Why or why not?

2. Does the constant quest for reelection have a positive or negative impact on representation? Explain. (The answer to this question obviously depends on your conception of representation.)

3. How could the institutions of Congress (members' offices, committees, and parties) be changed so that the collective needs of the institution would take precedence over the needs of individual members?

19

"*Too* Representative Government" — too many issues

STEVEN STARK

Over the past few decades, Congress has become more professional and capable. Members hire large, expert staffs to help them develop more informed legislation. Members respond to thousands of constituent requests for assistance and spend more time in their districts meeting with their constituents. Yet the public holds Congress in low esteem, and most voters look to elections as a means to reform, weed out, and fix all that ails the institution. Why?

Steven Stark argues Congress simply tries too hard to meet the schizophrenic demands of the American public. On the one hand, Americans complain that government is too big and costs too much. We want a balanced budget and lower taxes. But we still expect government to grapple with our biggest social problems—discrimination, social security benefits, disaster relief, health care, a clean environment. Stark argues that institutional reforms—changing legislative procedures, imposing term limits, or ratifying a balanced budget amendment—will not improve congressional performance. Members will still take on enormous challenges that they cannot meet in order to satisfy constituents who demand too much of their government at too little cost. Stark concludes that until both Congress and the nation accept a less ambitious agenda, and the fact that not every problem has a legislative solution, our distaste for the institution will continue to mount.

"Suppose you were an idiot," Mark Twain wrote during the Gilded Age. "And suppose you were a member of Congress. But I repeat myself." "Do you pray for the senators?" someone asked the chaplain of the Senate in 1903. "No, I look at the senators and pray for the country," he replied.

The more things change, the more they remain the same. The 104th Congress began work in January [1995], and talk of institutional revolution is once again in the air. It's not just that the Republicans—finally in control of both Houses for the first time in four decades—have begun reforming the least popular branch by taking such measures as applying all federal employment laws to Congress, cutting House committee staffs by a third, and requiring a 60 percent majority in the House to approve tax increases. Many critics, such as Kevin Phillips and Lamar Alexander, have discussed a number of rather radical proposals for recasting the institution—everything from term limits to increasing the size of Congress to cutting the length of the session in half to instituting national referenda.

One might argue that some of these changes would make Congress more effective, as would a few of the currently popular (but unlikely to pass) proposals for campaign-finance overhaul and restrictions on lobbying.

A number of scholars, former members of Congress, and other observers suggest, however, that even far-reaching reforms—not to mention the recent election results—are unlikely to quell the public's considerable discontent with Congress for long. In its attempts to lay the blame for that discontent at the feet of the Democrats, the new Republican majority is ignoring a fundamental reality that has come into being over the past generation: owing largely to the changing nature of representation, the expanding role of the federal government, and the influence of television, the public has arrived at new and often contradictory expectations of how Congress should act and what it should do. Until these contradictions are resolved, Congress is doomed to unpopularity and ineffectiveness, no matter who controls it.

There is, after all, an inevitable tension in any legislative system between deliberation and action, discretion and responsiveness. The job of a legislature is not only to get things done but also to air points of view and ensure the legitimacy of governmental action. These goals often conflict—as do the objectives of representing a constituency while exercising independent judgment, or looking out for both the national and the local interest. Throughout American history the pendulum has swung back and forth as legislators have tried to come to terms with these tensions. Today, however, voters apparently believe that the pendulum can be made to stop. In much the same way as the public seems to want a welfare state without picking up the tab, it wants the advantages of a legislative system without any of the costs.

Even if Congress adopts all the most ambitious reforms, this cannot be achieved. No matter how noble the goal, virtually any reform that seeks to change the makeup of Congress (such as term limits) or encourage debate or make members rely less on staff, so that they will draft their own bills and read those of others, will lead the institution to be even more dependent on special interests or to get less done. Almost any proposal that increases the institution's ability to act quickly, such as eliminating the filibuster or making it easier to "fast track" legislation, will tend to alienate those in the minority and cause some attempts at lawmaking to be less judicious and acceptable to the masses. Attempts to limit the length of the session will inevitably narrow the range of concerns that Congress can tackle. Although many of the current Republican proposals for institutional reform have surface appeal, chances are that they will eventually end up antagonizing at least as many voters as they please. And Congress will end up just as unpopular as it was when the Republicans took over, if not more so.

The Wired Congress — multiple connections 4 input

For the first four decades of the Republic, congressmen actually spent very little time in Washington. For the next century or so they had little contact with their districts once they were in Washington. (Senators, of course, were not even popularly elected until early in this century.) Theorists from Thomas Hobbes to Edmund Burke had debated the extent to which representatives should directly reflect the desires of their constituents, but that debate took place in a world in which a lot of groups couldn't vote, news was hard to come by, and no one really knew how to measure public opinion other than in an election. The difficulty of travel and the irregularity of mail delivery made communication between constituents and Congress problematic. Thus members inevitably had to exercise independent judgment on most issues, no matter where they stood philosophically on the representation question.

Today things have swung to the opposite extreme, and not just because the infamous lobbyists surround congressmen and senators. Daily polling, E-mail, 800 numbers, and call-in shows have exponentially increased the contact that representatives have with their constituents. "Many days I felt like nothing more than the end of a computer terminal," Elliott Levitas, a former representative from Georgia, told me in an interview. The danger today is not that representatives know too little about what the electorate feels but that they know too much. Like body temperature, public opinion can shift hourly without consequence. "The cooling-off process that used to exist isn't there any more," Dennis Eckart, a former representative from Ohio, says. "As a lover of democracy, I can appreciate that, but there was an advantage to having an electorate that couldn't figure out what was in a tax bill." What's more, polls are often misleading—in part because they can be manipulated, and in part because many issues are so complex that the public holds conflicting views of what it wants, and expects its representatives magically to resolve the conflict.

"Ultimately, there's very little clarity to all those poll numbers, even though a lot of analysts attach great significance to them," says Peter Smith, formerly a representative from Vermont and now the founding president of California State University at Monterey Bay. "Health care and welfare reform are abstractions, no matter what a poll says. People favor something in general. When you get down to specifics, however, they often don't." The debate last session over President Bill Clinton's health-care bill illustrated that principle once again.

The rise of constituency politics has also led the public to view legislators simply as instruments of its will. The political scientist David

— incapable challenge

Mayhew, of Yale University, is not alone in having observed that the job of a federal legislator changed dramatically with the rise of New Deal and Great Society programs. Now an increasing number of constituents look to their legislator not only to obtain valuable pork-barrel projects for their state or district but also to help them obtain personal benefits from the government and its bureaucracies.

This development has been exacerbated by the fact that representatives have to serve more constituents today than they did in the past. Sixty-five representatives served four million Americans in the first Congress—a ratio of approximately 1:60,000. Today, with 435 representatives serving a population of more than 260 million, the ratio is approximately 1:600,000. Offices in home states have proliferated, and legislative aides have increasingly been transformed into caseworkers, thereby accounting for a healthy proportion of the increase in the size of those vilified congressional staffs. (The Republican reforms haven't even touched House and Senate personal-staff members, almost 40 percent of whom now work in district or state offices.) It should be no surprise, then, that voters increasingly view their legislators almost as personal therapists—a perspective that hardly encourages representatives to show any independence from the will of their districts, or to act in the national interest when it conflicts with local concerns. If legislators now seem excessively parochial and preoccupied with day-to-day responsiveness, that is what they are hearing the public demand.

While these changes have been occurring, Congress has also been attracting members of a different kind, whether Republican or Democrat. Virtually everyone agrees that today's representatives tend to be far better educated and informed, more professional, and less graft-ridden than their predecessors. Yet many also believe that something is missing from this generation in Congress—even from the new Republicans. "What happened is that as the quality of the legislature went up, its performance went down," says Theodore Lowi, a professor of government at Cornell University. "These people are much more individual entrepreneurs; they have far less respect for party institutions and hierarchy." Or, as the former representative Al Swift, of Washington, puts it, "We'd be better off with four hundred and ten followers and twenty-five leaders than the other way around."

The new entrepreneurial style is blamed in part for the lack of collegiality in Congress and the proliferation of committee and subcommittee assignments on the Hill, which have increased for senators and nearly doubled for representatives since the 1950s. (The number of committees and subcommittees has actually shrunk, owing to reorganizations; the Republican Contract with America has consolidated even more committees.) It also helps account, Lowi says, for the fact that Congress has become so sensitive to short-term public opinion: "They don't have the party to hide behind anymore. Because they're more individually accountable, they feel much more vulnerable and they react accordingly."

Circular Cures — too many voices

Reversing the trend toward a professional class of legislators is the goal of the term-limits movement. Mark Petracca, a political scientist at the University of California at Irvine, has written that legislative professionalization runs counter to the basic values of representative government, because "a profession entails a set of role relationships between 'experts' and 'clients' " which are fundamentally at odds with the way Congress is supposed to work. Yet the desire for a "citizen legislature," embodied in the term-limits movement, may be as quixotic as the search for a doctor who still makes house calls. "Sure, Congress has changed, but so has the country," says Ronald Peters, the director of the Carl Albert Congressional Research and Studies Center, at the University of Oklahoma. "Things have become less hierarchical than they once were almost everywhere. Part of this is generational, but a lot of it is just the way we've changed as a people. Legislators are more autonomous, but so is everyone else in the culture. This institution may be more professional, but all disciplines are becoming more professionalized. This is all part of a larger pattern, which in one sense couldn't be more representative."

The current cultural preoccupation with inclusion has also had important effects. Opening up the process to everyone—by such means as expansion of voting rights, more primaries and referenda, and encouraging access to government services—could be characterized as the major theme of our politics over the past third of a century, and there's obviously a lot to be said for it. The congressional response to Watergate, for example, often focused on the process of government, not its substance: lawmakers passed "sunshine laws" to force government to be more open and ethical, and in a spasm of reform wiped out many seniority privileges to make Congress more egalitarian. Even today, when complaints about Congress focus on how process reforms have still failed to address the institution's underlying problems, many of the popular ideas about how to change Congress—such as term limits and more referenda—continue to focus on process. The problems caused by being more democratic and process-oriented, both Republicans and Democrats seem to be saying, can be solved by being even more democratic and process-oriented.

The more a system values giving everyone a voice, however, the less it can value speed and effectiveness. All those voices have to be heard, and frequently they have to be accommodated. The correlate of enabling more women and members of minorities to be part of the legislature— a laudable goal—is that their concerns must be addressed, even though some of these concerns have traditionally been ignored by most legislatures. Irwin Gertzog, in his book *Congressional Women*, finds that women in Congress are far likelier than their male colleagues to stress such issues as the treatment of rape victims, the problems of displaced homemakers, and funding for diagnostic tests for breast cancer. "Congress succeeds much better as a representative body than it used to," says Michael Mezey, a professor of political science at DePaul University, "which means it's probably somewhat less successful as a lawmaking body."

Democratizing the internal rules of Congress has also made it harder to accomplish anything substantive. The more a culture moves toward democracy, however, the more it empowers those forces that have the ability to manipulate public opinion or provide access. The rise in the importance of media consultants, the press, and special-interest money is directly proportional to the growth of democracy in the culture and in Congress over the past thirty years. Read the polls or listen to talk radio and you will find that the complaints today are as much about these new forces and what they have done to the process as about anything else. The urge to destroy elites has simply created another class of them; the solution has become the problem. And the Republicans are doing next to nothing to stop that.

The Buck Stops Nowhere

Congress once tended to pass relatively concrete, simple laws in relatively few areas, which meant that the results of any lawmaking were far easier to assess. For our first 140 years it dealt with economic issues primarily through tariffs and focused on the country's expansion, wars, and treaties. There was little money to spend, and the Constitution had been interpreted as allowing far less federal intrusion into the workings of the states than we know today. "Nineteenth-century Congresses actually worked better," Theodore Lowi says. "They just passed very limited, piecemeal laws." At the turn of the century the House had no staff members and the Senate only a few. (By 1991 the personal staffs of the two houses together numbered more than 11,000, and nearly another 3,500 people worked for the committees.)

The passage of a federal income tax early in this century was the first step toward the creation of the welfare state. Still, the concept of dealing with complicated economic and social-welfare problems on a systematic national basis really arose during the crisis presented by the Great Depression and then the Second World War. Congress's response in the 1930s and the three decades that followed was to cede to the executive branch (which had drafted most of the laws in the first place) the authority to solve most of these problems—and the creation of administrative agencies, along with the enlargement of administrators' responsibilities, was often part of the solution. The idea was that many problems were too complex or technical for a legislature and that a specialized agency such as the Federal Communications Commission, or an administrator such as the Secretary of Agriculture, could do a better job of solving them. These agencies were also created in an era when there was much intellectual support for the notion that decisions should be taken away from legislatures and given to experts, who knew better.

The typical congressional grant of authority to do this was quite brief, simple, and vague: "[to regulate] interstate and foreign commerce in communication by wire and radio"; to make agricultural marketing "orderly." In theory, Congress would strictly oversee the agency's performance. In reality, representatives were usually happy to pass the buck to someone else and leave the agency alone, except when they needed a favor. As it happened, legislators soon discovered that such a setup also allowed them to claim credit for a program and then, if things went awry, "run against the bureaucracy"—a bureaucracy they had created, to avoid having to deal with problems themselves. The buck stopped nowhere.

The Supreme Court put a stop to elements of Roosevelt's New Deal, on the grounds that the Constitution simply did not allow the federal government to act in many areas. Support for a further expansion of federal power, however, took hold in the public imagination in the 1950s and 1960s, with the civil-rights revolution, which ended up discrediting intellectual and legal arguments about "states' rights." Nelson Polsby, an expert on Congress and a professor of political science at the University of California at Berkeley, says, "It became an article of faith among liberals that you can't trust Mississippi, so you have to nationalize these things."

60,000 Pages ⎯ loss of local control, too many bills

For Lyndon Johnson's Great Society programs, in the mid-sixties, Congress was still using the New Deal agency as a model—with important differences. First, the traditional division between federal and state authority having been obliterated, Congress began moving into substantive areas, such as crime and housing, that had traditionally been beyond the purview of the federal government except in extreme emergencies. The early civil-rights laws were working, after all, and many of the nation's problems seemed rooted in its troubled racial past; a federal takeover seemed justified. Once involved in those areas, however, Congress kept expanding its grasp, eventually dictating to states on traditionally local questions—speed limits, for example. The result is that today Congress routinely passes laws dealing with local matters—crime, homelessness, education—and nobody even blinks at the loss of local control, which was once a cornerstone of our Jeffersonian public philosophy. As the former representative Al Swift puts it, "We've kind of blurred the distinction between a county sheriff and a congressman."

That's a recent and radical turn in our history, and one—"devolution" rhetoric to the contrary—that the Republicans show little sign of undoing. It is not simply that Speaker of the House Newt Gingrich may be misreading last year's election returns when he maintains that the public agrees it is time to dismantle much of the Great Society, or return programs to the states. The Contract With America, for example, promised a tougher anti-crime package, "strengthening rights of parents in their children's education," stronger child-pornography laws, and new rules to reform the welfare system, tort law, and product liability—efforts in many areas beyond what was seen as the purview of Congress when the Republicans last held both houses.

The 1960s blizzard of legislation came during an era when belief in the possibilities of governmental power may have been at a peak. In the 1965–1966 session alone nearly 20,000 bills were introduced. (The number in recent years has averaged fewer than 10,000 a session.) "If we can put a man on the moon, we can [fill in the blank]" seemed to characterize almost every politician's stump speech. Every problem, it seemed, had an effective legislative solution. Alan Ehrenhalt, the author of *The United States of Ambition*, finds that legislators of both parties still hold this belief. "Legislators are used to solving problems," he says. "Government tends to attract people who think government can solve problems. But once you get into things like crime, welfare, and education, you're trying to change human behavior, and that's much tougher to do. The New Deal was small potatoes compared to most of this stuff."

"Several things happen when the government gets into these areas," says James Q. Wilson, a professor of management and public policy at the University of California at Los Angeles. "First, no one really knows how to solve these problems. Second, the public itself is deeply conflicted about most of these issues; you rarely have a consensus from which to act. Third, these issues tend to be so complex that they overwhelm the process. And finally, when these measures fail to do much to solve something like crime—which is what inevitably happens—they greatly reinforce the general disillusionment with government. There's something to be said for sticking with what you know how to do."

During that legislative blizzard Congress was no longer just distributing money or dealing with problems in discrete areas (how to regulate the airwaves, or how to provide a supplemental income to senior citizens), and the grand problems it confronted, like poverty and crime, seemed to require a variety of coordinated strategies. "That was a key mistake," Theodore Lowi says. "Health and welfare are not holistic things; they're a collection of problems. The bills collapse of their own weight." Such bills also tend to be so elaborate that voters have difficulty understanding them—which means, at a minimum, that opponents have an easy time raising fears about them. Unsurprisingly, the public becomes more engaged when Congress is debating a seemingly straightforward issue like the Gulf War, in which voters can understand what is at stake.

Nonetheless, over time congressmen on both sides of the aisle began drafting longer, more comprehensive bills; the number of pages of law entered into the statute books during the relatively uneventful 1991–1992 session was two and a half times the number entered by the 1965–1966 Great Society Congress. With many legislators continually preoccupied by issues of openness and equal availability of services, access and due process became legislative focuses. That translated into greatly increased complexity and bureaucracy, not to mention a drain on the courts as litigants attempted to enforce their new rights. In 1936 there were 2,355 pages of regulations amplifying federal laws published in the Federal Register. By 1969 the number had risen to 20,464 pages; in the 1990s the register has been averaging about 60,000 pages a year.

No Amendments Wanted

Trying to solve a national megaproblem with one huge bill is still an American obsession, as the recent health-care debate showed. Still, by the late 1960s the old model of legislating had begun to fall out of favor, at least in one respect. The criticism, advanced by Ralph Nader and others, was that administrative agencies such as the Interstate Commerce Commission and the Federal Communications Commission inevitably became controlled by the forces they were supposed to regulate. Moreover, distrust of authority was expanding along with voting rights, and there was a corresponding lack of trust in the opinions of experts vis-à-vis "the people." As David Schoenbrod, a professor at New York Law School, has related in *Power Without Responsibility* (1993), what followed was a series of congressional statutes (beginning with the Clean Air Act, in 1970), passed with bipartisan support, that started to abandon the concept of open-ended delegation to independent agencies. Instead these laws essentially ordered the agency in question to take action and gave "elaborate instructions about the goals that it should achieve and the procedures for promulgating them." These instructions often placed administrative obligations on the states, while Congress took credit for the benefits of the legislation.

As a result of this legislative model statutes not only became lengthier and more complicated but also began running up hidden costs, while parochial and elite interests inevitably asserted their influence with help from both sides of the aisle: it was Alaska's Republican senator Ted Stevens, after all, who got grant money for Alaska to try to convert the aurora borealis into electricity. (As Congress-watchers point out, by the past session Congress was appropriating money for a University of Georgia study of city pests, ordering the Department of Health and Human Services to hire "six medium sedans" for transport, and adding what amounted to a gang-rehabilitation program to a flood-relief bill.) And over time Congress confronted many scientific or technical questions—such as how to clean the air—that were far beyond the expertise of most congressmen. So legislators of both parties hired more staff members to deal with these questions, and stopped reading much of their own legislation. Because members needed to rely on experts to draft these extensive and specific statutes, they also became increasingly reliant on "special interests"—if not to write the bills, then at least to tell them what the bills said before a vote. Cutting committee staff, as the Republicans have done, will hardly solve this problem, particularly for newer members, who tend to know less about technical problems than their more experienced colleagues.

The effect of an interstate-highway-building program or a Voting Rights Act—two legislative success stories from the 1950s and 1960s—can be assessed fairly easily. But, as Bruce Ackerman and Susan Rose-Ackerman, professors at Yale Law School, ask in *The Uncertain Search for Environmental Quality*, how does a deliberative body measure precisely the relationship between clean water and public health, let alone determine whether clean water could be had more cheaply by another method? What's more, even if a given approach makes sense now, things change over time. Once a bill gains a constituency—and all those that are enacted do, if only for economic reasons—it becomes very difficult to shift course.

The result has been a proliferation of vague or increasingly unworkable laws that judges cannot revise under current theories of statutory interpretation. (The same is not true of the common law.) These laws can also bankrupt the country, as the laws become ever more complex and costs mount. The Clean Air Act of 1970, complex as it was, filled forty-seven pages in the United States Code. The revision twenty years later filled more than 200 in the denser Congressional Record.

Having so many more constituents and areas of responsibility than it had in the past has also stymied Congress and shifted the way it operates. Besides muscling its way into areas once left to the states, Congress has spent an increasing amount of time over the past two decades on budgetary matters: the number of roll calls on budget questions in the House was almost six times as great in 1991 as it was in 1955—yet another trend that seems unlikely to change with Republican control. "The change in work load has affected the way Congress acts, which in turn has affected public perceptions," says Bruce I. Oppenheimer, a professor of political science at Vanderbilt University, who studies Congress. "In a time-constrained environment the opposition gains power. The filibuster wasn't used much before 1970, because it wasn't a very effective weapon. Who cared if you wasted time? Congress never ran out of time."

In a legislative world where time is scarce, democratic values also tend to collapse and mistakes to become more common. One of the purposes of deliberation, after all, is to achieve consensus and avoid error. Tellingly, bills for many of the major legislative achievements of the past sixty years, though contentious, ended up passing with large majorities. For example, the Social Security Act passed in 1935 with seventy-seven votes in the Senate; the Civil Rights Act in 1964 won seventy-three.

Yet one of the distinguishing characteristics of recent sessions, particularly in the House, is that what little deliberation did once occur has been virtually eliminated. That, in turn, has increased partisanship. In recent years a bill has had about half the chance of passage that it had fifty years ago. In part to speed things up—which is, after all, what the public says it wants—bills introduced on the floor increasingly restrict amendments. Although the Republicans have promised to address that, so far there has been no significant change. Debates now typically take place with no one listening in the chamber, as anyone who has ever watched C-SPAN knows. Even the much-praised Senate and House exchanges before passage of the Gulf War resolution, in January of 1991, consisted primarily of members' rising to deliver prepared speeches to a body in which virtually every mind was already made up. And this year? The Republicans have added many new wrinkles to Congress, but careful deliberation does not appear to be among them.

The Camera and Congress

too concerned w/ media rather than legislation

A different kind of congressional persona tends to flourish in the television age. Fifteen years ago Michael J. Robinson, a professor at Catholic University, wrote, "The increasingly greater reliance on the media for nomination, election, status in the Congress, and reelection is one sign of a new congressional character—one more dynamic, egocentric, immoderate, and, perhaps, intemperate." These telegenic figures, according to one source Robinson cited, were often more concerned with getting on television than with legislative mechanics—yet another reason for the lack of consensus, the emphasis on the illusion of results, and the expansion of staff to deal with the institution's real missions.

Because of its inherent biases, television has also subtly altered the way the public perceives Congress. C-SPAN, of course, has opened up the daily workings of Congress, but its effect is quite limited. C-SPAN's typical audience is minuscule compared with the audience that receives news about Congress from the major networks—which have greatly influenced the way print sources cover Congress.

The communications theorist Ernest Bormann once wrote that "television news coverage is, in many respects, an exercise in creative dramatics in which a cast of familiar characters assembles . . . and improvises a drama according to a stock scenario depending on the news event." By now the scenario involving Congress is very familiar. Because television is drawn to strong characters, it elevates the importance of the President and the speaker of the House vis-à-vis the institution of Congress. Because the medium is drawn to conflict, it denigrates the value of compromise, upon which legislatures depend, and plays up scandal or contentiousness. A recent study by S. Robert Lichter and Daniel R. Amundson, of the Center for Media and Public Affairs, has found that from 1972 to 1992 the proportion of network news stories concerning ethical lapses in Congress more than quadrupled, and the proportion of those portraying conflict between members nearly tripled from 1987 to 1992 (though, to be fair, conflict is up). Television is wedded to the dramatic gesture, and legislative bodies when legislating rarely act in a theatrical fashion. What's more, the legislative process is often messy and difficult; its lack of clear lines and packaging violates the whole spirit of scripted entertainment that has come to dominate the culture. The workings of Congress are complex and thus time-consuming to explain, and time is something that network television apparently cannot afford.

Changing the voters as much as the candidates, television creates a passive audience of viewer-voters who demand instant gratification and no loose ends. In a world where advertisers constantly proclaim, "You can have it all!" and "Just Do It!" voters have come to see government institutions as ones that should provide it all and just do it, Ross Perot–style. Commercial television also offers an implicit vision of the world in which it's not community or belief in an abiding principle that offers happiness but the acquisition of goods. No wonder, then, that as television became pervasive and the postwar consumer culture took root, voters came increasingly to view the purpose of Congress—if not of government—as guaranteeing their right to that happiness.

With Congress thus increasingly frustrated in its primary responsibility to develop and pass good laws, its members have turned to other tasks, many of them nurtured by television. Here, too, the Republicans have been no different from the Democrats. The memorable moments of the past three decades in Congress have naturally tended to come in front of the cameras—from the McCarthy hearings to Watergate to the Anita Hill–Clarence Thomas confrontation. Congress has been conducting investigations since the 1790s. Yet it is undeniable that congressional investigations have flourished in the television age, thereby appropriating more of Congress's time and attention. Unlike the typical lawmaking process, these hearings offer the broadcast media drama and compelling characters in a stately scene. And, as Daniel Boorstin pointed out nearly thirty-five years ago, in his book *The Image*, the real purpose of hearings is often difficult to discern. "In many cases," Boorstin wrote, "these committees have virtually no legislative impulse, and sometimes no intelligible legislative assignment."

And there is the confirmation process—another area that consumes increasing amounts of the Senate's energy, if only because the number of posts that require confirmation has risen from 149 to 310 since 1960. Confirmation fights are also part of our history, but dramatic confirmation *hearings* are mostly a media-age phenomenon. Here, too, the consensus is that the cameras have contorted the process into great TV drama but something of a well-documented travesty. In foreign policy, a stage that Presidents have long dominated, Congress has tried to share the television spotlight in recent decades, with the same mixed results and a commensurate loss of time to spend in other areas. In *War and Responsibility* (1993) the Stanford University law professor John Hart Ely argues that while Congress has appeared to try to take more responsibility for military action in recent decades, it has in fact happily abdicated to the President most of its powers in this area. This has allowed many members to claim credit when military ventures go well, but to hold accusatory hearings and press conferences before the cameras when they don't.

Congressional actions in the television age have thus come to join the category that Boorstin called "pseudo-events"—in which the illusion of results becomes far more significant in the culture than the results themselves. In legislative hearings that don't really look at legislation, in crime bills that almost everyone privately admits will do next to nothing to reduce crime, the appearance and the drama of the action overshadow the importance of the action itself. Pseudo-events, Boorstin said, are usually more interesting than real actions, and they therefore seem more compelling and often more real. He wrote,

> Once we have tasted the charm of pseudo-events, we are tempted to believe they are the only important events. . . . And the poison tastes so sweet that it spoils our appetite for plain fact. Our seeming ability to satisfy our exaggerated expectations makes us forget that they are exaggerated.

Tainted Prescriptions — these won't solve the problem

In the end it is always easy to romanticize the past, just as it is tempting to exaggerate how much a shift in control will change Congress. A fifty-two-seat shift in the House is unusual in modern times, but it may mean only that the country is returning to the electoral patterns of a century ago, when party control of Congress often shifted back and forth by large margins, while the body drew its share of criticism. "There was no golden age of legislation," says the Yale political scientist David Mayhew.

Agreement is almost universal that Congress could take a number of steps both to purge itself of the effects of special-interest money and to make the legislative process operate more efficiently. After last November there is a perception of hope that the new majority will at least try to do the latter. (The Republican Party has never been enthusiastic about campaign-finance or lobbying reform.) But the Republicans, while in some ways addressing the expanding role of the federal government, appear only slightly more aware than the Democrats before them of the real polarities of sentiment that will have to be addressed before Congress can truly be reformed.

Few of the proposed structural reforms, moreover, would have the effect their proponents suggest. The notion, for example, that a national referendum would be any less susceptible than the legislative process to special-interest influence is ludicrous; and studies on term limits suggest that imposing a twelve-year limit would increase the mean turnover rate in the House by all of one percent per election (though it might, for better or worse, change the type of person elected to Congress). Sending Congress home for six months a year, or cutting down on staff, means that legislators would do less, more slowly; eliminating the filibuster and instituting referenda would be designed to get more or different laws on the books more quickly.

These reforms would not solve "the problem" with Congress, because voters and their representatives are terribly confused about what that is. Voters say they want less government at lower cost, but they apparently want it to do much of what it now does—or more. Polls tell us that among the major complaints about Congress are that it doesn't represent the voters well enough and that it becomes gridlocked—failing to solve the nation's lingering problems, such as health care and welfare reform. Yet over the past two generations Congress has become far more representative and responsive than it used to be, and it now addresses issues that previous legislatures never dreamed of. Nevertheless, as public disillusionment increases, the impulse has been to become even more closely tied to public opinion and to find new legislative ways of attacking megaproblems more quickly and efficiently. The Republicans don't propose to turn all of crime control or tort-law reform over to the states; they propose to enact many of the sweeping reforms themselves, and do it better and faster than the Democrats. So the demands and the contradictions spiral on, out of control. The solutions are manifestations of the problem.

Ironically, what Congress may need is not more democracy but less, and the will to address not bigger problems faster but smaller ones in more-measured ways. Admittedly, much of the civil-rights legislation of the 1960s changed the country profoundly for the better, and subsequent efforts toward greater democracy and openness were implemented in good faith. Now it is time to declare these efforts a success—we have democratized the process!—and move on to developing a public philosophy to address some of the problems we have acquired from encouraging access to national government.

In the populist rush to extend the spirit of democracy that, as Alexis de Tocqueville reminded us 150 years ago, is part of the American character, today's voters and leaders often forget that this is, in the end, a republic. The founders feared the power of the mob and provided distance between the rulers and the ruled, so that our representatives could deliberate much like a jury and exercise collective judgment and even wisdom. Their job, in the words of *The Federalist Papers*, was to "refine and enlarge" the popular will. It is a hierarchical relationship; they are entrusted with power. No parents or teachers worth their salt poll their children or pupils constantly and then give in at the first sign of discontent—just as no legislators in their right minds would cut taxes while keeping government benefits the same. Yet that's what pure representation will do for us a lot of the time. Paradoxically, giving legislators the freedom to forget about public opinion once in a while would do much to restore the voters' faith in the integrity of their representatives. Similarly, few would quarrel with the success of much of the New Deal—and even some of the Great Society—and many of our problems do require national solutions. But they don't necessarily demand complicated, comprehensive solutions.

"If I could get legislators to do just one thing, it would be to take a political Hippocratic oath," the author Alan Ehrenhalt says. "First, do no harm. Just attack things you can do something about." Theodore Lowi concurs. "Congress should narrow its agenda to a few things it knows how to do," he says. "And it should quit writing these large bills which pretend to address a problem but really don't, and create unforeseen problems in their wake."

Those steps alone, it seems, would require a shift in sentiment, in both parties and in the nation at large, not simply because they might mean the passage of fewer complicated entitlement programs for the middle class, but also because they would spell the end of the notion that there can somehow be a risk-free society with a government solution to every problem. The public and the press would also be required to reevaluate whether a buzz of legislative activity really constitutes a "golden age," and whether gridlock—which often means doing nothing because nothing can be done or because we don't know what to do—is always such a terrible thing. Yet such a change would even benefit liberalism. Congress would do less, but might well do better what it did, thereby increasing confidence in the national government generally. And the body might then have the will, occasionally, to act in the national interest by expanding government, even if that meant temporarily rejecting public opinion.

DISCUSSION QUESTIONS

1. Is Congress too representative? How does Stark's argument square with the image of the "out of touch" Washington politician?

2. Do you agree that the American people expect the impossible from Congress? Does this account for Congress's image problem, or are there other contributing factors as well?

☞ Workload should be lessened

☞ Congress is a "machine"

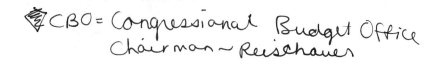
CBO= Congressional Budget Office
Chairman ~ Reischauer

20
"By the Numbers"

Viveca Novak

The Congressional Budget Office (CBO) has been a dependable player in the tumultuous world of Congressional politics. Created in 1974 as part of a budget reform law, its budgetary analyses and economic forecasts are respected by Republican and Democrat alike. When other Congressional institutions came under fire (especially the House Bank and Post Office) the CBO plugged along as one of Washington's real success stories. Because of its credibility, CBO plays a major role in policy debates. In the 1994 health care debate, for example, the CBO had to generate budgetary forecasts for all the rival plans.

Viveca Novak describes the institution, its transformation into the provider of respected nonpartisan analysis, and the grace and skill employed by CBO leaders in walking a fine line between partisans of both sides anxious over the CBO's analysis of legislation near and dear to their hearts.

It was quickly apparent that Robert D. Reischauer's mike was dead as facing the glare of hot lights and television cameras and the somewhat friendlier gazes of a half-dozen Senators, he began his synopsis of the Congressional Budget Office's (CBO) eagerly awaited annual economic and budget outlook.

Several failed fix-it attempts prompted Budget Committee chairman Jim Sasser, D-Tenn., to invite Reischauer to take a well-miked empty seat on the panel's dais to deliver his message. Maybe by chance, maybe not, Sasser indicated a chair on the Democratic side. The CBO director smiled and hesitated a half-beat. "Well, I could sit over there for half of my testimony, and over here for the other half," he said, pointing to the GOP side.

Reischauer's quip neatly summed up the delicate position he's often in: Trying to maintain the credibility of the analyses and projections the office is required to grind out while keeping most of his congressional masters happy and somehow dodging partisan sniper fire.

"We are an analytical institution that's asked to be objective and shoot straight and let the chips fall where they may," Reischauer said in an interview, "that is imbedded in an institution that is all politics. The danger always is that the host institution, when the stakes are very high, can't or doesn't want to accept politically damaging information and might choose to in a sense kill the messenger or banish the messenger."

For the most part, the CBO has walked the fine line steadily. But now, 20 years after the 1974 Congressional Budget Act brought it into being, the stakes have never been higher for the office. Nothing it has produced in the past has drawn as much pregame day pressure as its Feb. 8 analysis of Clinton's plan for overhauling the nation's health care system. And when all is said and done, it's likely that never will its decision-making process have been so intensively probed.

With its decision that the Clinton plan's numbers don't add up—instead of cutting the deficit by $58 billion over six years, the CBO said, it would swell it by $74 billion—the office gave ammunition aplenty to Republicans and proponents of other plans. And its treatment of the Clinton plan's mandated employer premium payments as part of the budget, rather than off-budget as the White House wanted, allows the GOP to roll out the T-word—a move that could pack big political punch.

Rep. Richard K. Armey, D-Texas, a frequent CBO critic, had said earlier that the office's integrity was "on the line" with this analysis. After he heard the news, he said that "Reischauer, agonized as he was, made a good-government decision that will maintain the veneer of a nonpartisan CBO."

Democrats hailed the CBO for saying that Clinton's plan would begin cutting the nation's health bill by 2000 and criticized it for wanting to include the premiums in the budget. Clinton's first reaction to that decision's impact on the deficit was, 'll fix that."

An uncomfortable Reischauer, meanwhile, urged Congress to balance the deficit projections with the advantages of universal health coverage.

Since last fall, the pressure on the CBO had built. For a while, the question of taxes or premiums, on-budget or off, were staples of small talk in Washington, where hipness is sometimes measured by one's glibness with acronyms of lesser-known government programs.

In late October, Republicans tried to tack on to temporary spending legislation a provision directing the CBO to count the health insurance premiums as taxes. That message was echoed in a Nov. 19 letter to Reischauer signed by three Republican House leaders and the ranking GOP members of all committees with health jurisdiction.

In early December, *The Washington Post*'s David S. Broder wrote that the CBO had already made its mind up to keep the bulk of the package off-budget. Reischauer denied it, but the report triggered a visit from five House Republicans, led by Minority Leader Robert H. Michel of Illinois. "He acted like a man who felt like he was on the rack," Thomas J. Bliley Jr. of Virginia, one of the five, said of Reischauer. "Let's face it, he was between Scylla and Charybdis. On the one hand was his credibility, on the other hand his job."

Days before the analysis was set for release, Reps. Wayne Allard, R-Colo., and Timothy J. Penny, D-Minn., introduced a resolution to require that all health care legislation be on-budget. "Do you believe the largest entitlement program in U.S. history should be off-budget?" Allard asked in a "Dear Colleague" note. A similar resolution was introduced by Sen. Judd Gregg, R-N.H.

During a Jan. 27 hearing on the CBO's economic outlook, four Republicans asked Reischauer about the health care analysis and told him where he should come out. "I wanted to publicly acknowledge that I'm fully aware of the pressure that you're going to face, and we in the minority will surely not want to lessen that pressure," said Sen. Pete V. Domenici of New Mexico, a onetime Budget Committee chairman.

House and Senate Democratic leaders, House Budget Committee chairman Martin Olav Sabo, D-Minn., and numerous other Members and key staff spoke with Reischauer and some of his team of 35 or so aides who were spending at least part of their time untangling and quantifying the bill. The White House funneled its pressures through congressional offices; of course, it couldn't have been clearer what it wanted. Alice M. Rivlin, the CBO's first director and now deputy director of the Office of Management and Budget (OMB), was in touch with Reischauer, her former aide from the CBO's early days.

At Last, A Little Respect

Oddly, it was less than two decades ago that the CBO's founders, of whom Reischauer was one, had to work to persuade Washington to pay attention to them. The CBO was hardly the focus of the 1974 budget law, and there was little definition to the office's portfolio when it opened its doors. But it quickly became a presence. The CBO was credited, or blamed, for sinking President Carter's welfare reform plan.

Eventually, the CBO's main activities became clear: Scoring bills for their budget impact (which did in Carter's welfare proposal), making economic and budget projections, analyzing program and policy issues affecting the budget and—since 1979—printing a widely distributed book of options for reducing the deficit.

The office's importance grew in 1981, as OMB became more politicized. After 1985, the CBO helped Congress assess its compliance with that year's Balanced Budget Act's deficit targets, further enhancing its status. Then, with the 1990 Budget Enforcement Act and its accompanying caps on discretionary spending and its pay-as-you-go rules in the entitlement and tax areas, the CBO and its numbers crunchers took on even broader authority.

"The caps and pay-as-you-go rules have all given CBO estimates new power," said Rudolph G. Penner, who was the office's second director and is now senior manager of KPMG Peat Marwick's policy economics group in Washington. "Legally, OMB estimates prevail, but as a practical matter, as Congress considers legislation, they rely on CBO.

"The budget process now endows CBO numbers with a power that means life or death for particular programs and is indeed affecting the design of programs," Penner said. Clinton's health care program is a case in point. "The Administration would not have put price controls in [its health reform plan] but for the hope that they would be scored" by the CBO as saving money.

Reischauer is constantly called on to tuck his rangy frame behind one witness table or another. In 1993, he appeared before congressional panels 23 times, and some years have been much more intensive, as '94 is likely to be. In a two-week period at the end of January and the beginning of February, Reischauer was on six witness lists.

The CBO's credibility has been enhanced by the fact that its economic and deficit projections, while generally too rosy, have been closer to the mark than OMB's over the years. In its forecasts of economic growth, for example, it beat OMB in 6 of the 10 years ending in 1992 and tied it in one.

Both OMB and the CBO grossly underestimated the impact and duration of the recession of the past few years, leading to overly optimistic revenue estimates and no sense of the massive demand on food stamps, medicaid and other government programs as a result.

Reischauer, a 53-year-old Harvard University graduate with a Columbia doctorate in economics, helped Rivlin set the place up. (The office staff remains at about 220, small enough for everyone to be on a first-name basis.) Rivlin guided it through two four-year terms, then Penner, a Republican, took charge from 1983–87. Reischauer, meanwhile, had left in 1981 to be a senior vice president of the Urban Institute, then a senior fellow at the Brookings Institution, where he once again was a colleague of Rivlin. The son of famed Japan scholar Edwin O. Reischauer, he has written extensively on social welfare issues, education, budget policy and state and local fiscal problems and was a domestic affairs adviser to Democratic presidential nominee Michael S. Dukakis in 1988.

It took two years of House-Senate scuffling after Penner's departure to choose a new director. Then-Speaker Thomas P. O'Neill Jr., D-Mass., had pushed Reischauer for the slot after Rivlin left, but he was considered too liberal by the Republicans who then controlled the Senate. He finally got the nod in 1989.

The CBO's leaders have all been widely respected. Still, there have always been accusations of bias—from both sides. Its three directors have faced threats of removal and warnings that the office itself would be dissolved. The numbers it issues are regularly picked apart.

A few Members, though, have questioned the CBO's claim to nonpartisanship for years now. When Clinton gave his first State of the Union speech in 1993, snickers came from the GOP side when he promised to use "the independent numbers of the Congressional Budget Office" in putting together his economic plan—as opposed to figures from OMB, which have always been thought more politically skewed. (This year's budget reverted to using OMB's numbers.)

The critics include Rep. Jim Kolbe, R-Ariz., a Budget Committee member, who has called the CBO a "budgetary brothel . . . little more than a campaign research tool for the majority." The *American Spectator* has tried to discredit it by pointing out that in 1992, a CBO aide was named to head the Democratic National Committee's opposition research team.

The CBO's most vocal detractor by far, though, has been Armey, an economist and chairman of the House Republican Conference. "These are generally very professional, well-trained people who would like to do their best work and maintain their standing in the profession," he said. "But they are under enormous pressures, and at times, they clearly have produced work product that has a partisan bias and has been used by the majority for political purposes."

Armey cites several examples of what he views as the CBO's kowtowing. Especially serious, to Armey, was a flap over calculations of income distribution in 1992—data that were then used by Massachusetts Institute of Technology economist Paul R. Krugman to show what many analysts had believed for some time—that the rich, unlike almost everybody else, got quite a bit richer during the 1980s. Democrats used the data to fuel the "fairness" theme in the 1992 campaign, and Clinton used it heavily against President Bush. But Armey and other conservative Republicans found fault with the CBO's definition of family income, its treatment of capital gains income and how it took account of income mobility.

Reischauer responded that even with adjustments, the general trend was the same: The rich did get disproportionately richer. Moreover, he said, private economists had found the same drifts. And the model the CBO used for its measurements was developed under former director Penner.

Contrary to Armey & Co.'s assertions, Penner said the flap has nothing to do with the degree of behavioral response built into the CBO's models versus others. "Congress should take these [distributional tables] as one bit of information, but not as defining. But when a table appears on the front page of *The New York Times* or *The Washington Post*, Congress is almost forced to take it as a truth from the gods," he said, lamenting press misinterpretation.

Armey also made much of errors in the CBO's estimates of capital gains income, which were off by more than 100 per cent in 1990 alone and helped kill efforts to reduce the capital gains tax rate. Reischauer admits to the CBO's "badly overestimating" capital gains for a three-year period but adds that in the previous four years it had underestimated them. "We are continually adjusting our models," he said, "and probably overcompensated just as capital gains went in the tank" with the collapse of the savings and loan industry and the real estate market and other changes in the economy.

Armey, frustrated with the CBO, the congressional Joint Committee on Taxation and the Joint Economic Committee, has turned elsewhere for numbers, setting up the Institute for Policy Innovation in Lewisville, Texas, which is underwritten in part by such conservative foundations as John M. Olin; its primary economists are known as supply-siders. But not even many other congressional Republicans have high regard for the group's work.

Armey introduced a bill in the previous Congress to give the ranking minority members of the Budget Committees a say in recommendations for new CBO directors. Currently, those panels send names to the House Speaker and Senate President Pro Tem, who make the decision; some Republicans have complained that the CBO can't help but be influenced by knowing who controls the directorship. The bill would also have created a bipartisan, 13-member oversight board to ride herd on the CBO's work. It died and was not reintroduced.

Some Democrats also complain about the CBO's alleged political fouls. In 1991, then-Finance Committee chairman Lloyd Bentsen, D-Texas, helped defeat a proposal by Sen. Daniel Patrick Moynihan, D-N.Y., to cut social security taxes with the assistance of a CBO report showing that such cuts would lower savings, drive inflation up and lead to slower growth of gross national product. Moynihan aide Eduard A. Lopez was furious when he found out the study had been finished for almost a month but that Bentsen had been able to save it for a strategic moment.

Mind the Teeth

Anyone who thinks the CBO's a lap-dog for the Democrats, however, need only review the past year. The office scored Clinton's budget $61.4 billion short of its goal over five years, giving conservative Democrats a chance to force more cuts in the bundle. In mid-November, the CBO exploded White House projections that the first leg of the Administration's reinventing-government initiative would save $5.9 billion over five years. Try $305 million, the CBO said. And its estimate of the five-year impact on the deficit of the huge budget package passed by Congress also fell short of what the Democrats were saying: $433 billion ($477 billion if it used the same baseline as the White House), as opposed to $496 billion.

Over all, far more Republicans than not respect the office, it seems. Many, like Domenici, are big boosters.

Even at the libertarian Cato Institute, which is economically conservative, there is a split. "It's more and more clear that if the Democrats have a program they want to justify, the CBO will give them the numbers to justify it," Cato president Edward H. Crane III said.

But Cato chairman William A. Niskanen Jr., who was a member of President Reagan's Council of Economic Advisers, calls the CBO "a quite responsible group.

"Its forecasts have typically been more accurate than those of the Administration," he said. "It seems like a government model of Brookings. They are basically responsive to the Democratic majority, but that doesn't mean they are entirely captive."

"There's no doubt about [the CBO's] integrity," said Mark A. Bloomfield, president of the American Council for Capital Formation—even though he disagrees with the office about the impact of tax policy on the economy.

"I'm a big fan of CBO; they do the best analytic work in this town, and they are willing to stick their necks out," said Ron Boster, a longtime minority budget expert and now administrative assistant to Rep. Rick A. Lazio, R-N.Y. "I'm absolutely convinced there's a healthy, dynamic, honest debate going on there."

Penner summed it up this way: "You get screamed at a lot by both sides. Some of it's public, but much more of it's private. If you're kicked from both sides, you stand up straight."

Reischauer said one of the main reasons the CBO has been able to continue drawing such good reviews is that it doesn't issue policy recommendations—unlike the General Accounting Office, another research arm of Congress that has garnered far worse notices for, in the words of a Republican House aide, "pandering to requesters" of its reports.

It's not that Reischauer never opines. Last fall, he testified against two-year budgeting, for example, saying it would force Members to rely too much on faulty longrange economic and budget forecasts. Members, he added, should be forced to confront the deficit every year and decide whether to act. Reischauer has said he feels like the Energizer bunny with his never-ending deficit remonstrations.

On welfare reform, Reischauer has said: "If you look at our current welfare system, we basically do what is the cheapest way of solving our guilt or our obligation. We put a little money out on the stump and don't provide many support services and say, 'Low-income people, you can take it.' "

Reischauer, in his January testimony on the economic outlook, included comments about the proposed balanced budget constitutional amendment, something he surely didn't have to do; he called it a "radical response," inappropriate for a time when "existing procedures and political pressures" were working. He also warned that the economy, while on the upswing, was still not going gang-busters—seeming to give Democrats implicit permission not to vote for another big round of budget cuts this year lest they slow the recovery. He backed off shy of an actual recommendation, though: "Exactly when you take the next bite out of the apple is really up to you."

On health care, many suspect Reischauer of personally favoring a single-payer system, with the government in charge, but if he does, he's been careful to watch his words. Still, it's clear that he thinks it's an issue that needs to be addressed. For years now, he's been telling Congress that the core of the deficit problem is health care costs. And he's said that reform is essential "not only from the standpoint of the impact . . . on the economy, but also from the standpoint of equity."

OK, Gang, Lighten Up!

It's perhaps ironic that two decades after the CBO and the budget process were created, there's growing suspicion among many analysts that everybody is making too much of it all.

"I think everybody who has anything to do with these numbers feels they have taken on an importance they probably don't deserve," Penner said. "This enormous, complex budget process is so complicated that we spend as many resources administering it and trying to satisfy it as we do trying to figure out what's good and bad policy." While the process has had a good disciplinary effect on Congress, he said, "The point is that we are getting too involved in the arbitrary matter of satisfying the budget process."

CBO deputy director James L. Blum cited a case in point: the current effort to develop buyout legislation to let federal agencies downsize by offering bonuses for early retirements and resignations. While over all, the projected savings far outweigh the costs of the program, the scheme doesn't satisfy current scoring rules. "This is a situation where a good case could be made for waiving the budget rules," Blum said.

Health care, of course, is a far more important example. "It really is madness to have this decision depend on what CBO can or cannot score," Penner said.

Reischauer has been issuing similar warnings since the fall, saying that over-emphasizing the short-term savings of something like health reform or an overhaul of the welfare system is shortsighted—especially because the CBO's, or for that matter anyone's, scoring of a complete revamping of a seventh of the U.S. economy is riddled with uncertainties. It matters little in the broad scheme of things whether something is labeled "taxes" or not—but it's enormously important politically.

Reischauer in September voiced doubts about the budget process itself, saying it "clearly restrains our ability to do some long-run, sensible changes."

"We're in this because we think we as a society spend too much on health care and think we could have basically the same outcomes or better devoting a smaller over-all portion of our resources to health care," Reischauer said.

Reischauer doesn't necessarily relish the limelight, especially these days. He'd be just as happy to have the CBO's importance wane, since that would probably mean that the deficit was under control.

In January, Reischauer was unusually welcome on Capitol Hill. The projections he presented for the next five years were far more optimistic about the deficit and the economy than those he'd given Members a year ago. Still, more often than not, he's been a bearer of bad news who's had to scramble not to get caught in the policy cross fire.

"This is an immensely politically charged environment we live in," he said. "We produce information, that information enlightens some, for others it is simply a spear or sword in a battle. There's very little we can do about that. On any single day, there are a large number of Members and interest groups around the country and people in the Administration who are concerned, upset, distressed by something we've done."

Reischauer was obviously uneasy about the health care reform report. "I have considerable foreboding," he told the House Ways and Means Committee, that "the CBO report might be used in destructive rather than constructive ways . . . to undercut a serious discussion of health reform alternatives."

He won't say so, but it seems likely that his decision about whether he'd like another term as the CBO's director—his is up early next year —will depend in part on the intensity of the fallout from the office's health care reform analysis. "I'd be ready for a tour of Bosnia after this job," he said with only a touch of irony.

DISCUSSION QUESTIONS

1. Why does the Congressional Budget Office stand out as a success story in Washington?

2. Are there any general lessons that Congress could learn from the success of the CBO? Explain.

THE DEBATE: SHOULD THE SENATE REFORM THE FILIBUSTER?

Is the Senate filibuster an essential tool for ensuring thoughtful consideration of an issue and serving as an essential check on majoritarian passions? Or is an outdated stall tactic that allows a committed minority of one to block legislation an overwhelming number of Americans want?

Sarah Binder and Thomas Mann argue that the filibuster should be eliminated, or at least reformed to prevent costly and undemocratic delays in the business of the Senate and, indeed, of the country. If the Senate still operated as a deliberative body governed by deference, the filibuster might serve its original purpose of extending debate and preempting hasty moves. But the filibuster is now too often used to stop legislation at any cost. Binder and Mann recommend: (1) prohibiting filibusters on motions to confirm presidential appointees; (2) limiting the number of opportunities to invoke a filibuster for any given bill; and (3) decreasing the number of Senate votes required to stop a filibuster.

Bill Frenzel, on the other hand, argues that the filibuster is used very much within the spirit of the Constitution and the intent of the founders. The Founders, he argues, had a "profound distrust of government." They intentionally built a system that could check majority passions and limit the government's ability to act. The filibuster, in his view, remains a key part of that system, and in any case is not the immovable force it is alleged to be. Filibusters fail when confronted with overwhelming support for a bill, and they often force compromises which actually smooth the way for legislation. If gridlock is the result of a filibuster, he concludes, so be it.

21

"Slaying the Dinosaur: The Case for Reforming the Senate Filibuster"

SARAH A. BINDER AND THOMAS E. MANN

During the 103rd Congress, when Democrats controlled both ends of Pennsylvania Avenue for the first time since Jimmy Carter was president, House Democrats bristled at the way the Senate filibuster was distorting the balance between the chambers and radically reshaping or killing legislation that enjoyed majority support. House Republicans might have been their immediate opponents, but the real enemy was the Senate—and its filibuster.

What a difference an election makes. Facing an awesome display of leadership and discipline by the new majority Republicans, former House critics of the Senate became its most ardent champions. The agonizingly slow pace of the Senate and its empowerment of individual senators and minority factions became a virtue, not a vice, as House Democrats and their supporters looked to the filibuster as the ultimate means of stemming the conservative policy tide.

The breathtaking reversal by House Democrats made all the more remarkable the move by two Democratic senators at the beginning of the 104th Congress to revamp the Senate's cherished filibuster. "There is no reform more important to this country and to this body than slaying the dinosaur called the filibuster," proclaimed Senator Tom Harkin (D-Iowa). "We need to change it so that we can really get back to what our Founding Fathers envisioned—a process whereby the minority can slow things down, debate them, but not kill things outright." As Harkin sees it, the Senate's venerable rules, which require either unanimous consent or 60 votes to limit debate and guarantee a vote, are no match for new political conditions in the Senate. Extreme individualism with unrestrained use of the filibuster has undermined the Senate's comparative advantage. The fierce protection of individual rights is costing the Senate its unique role as the world's greatest deliberative body.

Harkin is right. It is time to reform the filibuster.

Origins of the Filibuster

Observers and members of the Senate alike generally attribute the filibuster to the designs of the Framers. But delegates to the Constitutional Convention passed up the opportunity to dictate a set of Senate procedures that would ensure the protection of minority interests. Although the Senate was intended to be a restraining check against rash, popular majorities in the House, the Framers believed they had designed the Senate in such a way as to make unnecessary any procedural tools to ensure its role as the more deliberative and temperate assembly. Staggered six-year terms, equal representation of large and small states, indirect election—these and other features were deemed sufficient to distinguish the Senate from the more popular and populous lower chamber. In fact, in urging ratification of the new Constitution both James Madison and Alexander Hamilton argued that requiring supermajorities for action would exact an unbearable toll on the power of a legislative majority to act.

The right to filibuster through extended debate and amendment arose by accident. Like the House, the early Senate had a rule known as the previous question motion—a procedure it used, sparingly, to put off decisions on delicate matters. Because the rule was seldom used, however, the Senate eliminated it in 1806. Without a previous question motion—a rule the House soon revamped to force votes on favored legislation—the Senate had no way to limit debate and amendment short of getting the consent of every senator.

When partisan and sectional tensions rose later in the 19th century, Senate majorities often found themselves unable to pass favored policy measures. A single senator—often in concert with colleagues on either side of the aisle—could filibuster and obstruct legislation through endless amendments or extended debate. Senators also exploited the filibuster to block rules changes that would have empowered a majority to force votes on favored legislation. Only when bullied by President Woodrow Wilson and an outraged public on the eve of World War I in 1917 did the Senate adopt its current Rule 22, a procedure that allows a supermajority to invoke cloture and thereby limit debate and amendments on pending legislation. On a handful of occasions since then, the Senate has reduced the number of senators necessary to invoke cloture, requiring three-fifths of the chamber (or 60 votes) to do so today.

Historical Trends and Modern Problems

No one is sure precisely how many Senate filibusters have taken place over the years. Because it is nearly impossible to separate episodes of extended debate from actual filibusters, scholars have had to rely on historical accounts of the Senate to determine the number of filibusters in the 19th century. Even after the advent of Rule 22 in 1917, not every cloture vote can be taken as a signal that a filibuster was under way. At times, particularly in the last decade, Senate leaders have sought cloture to lend some predictability to the Senate schedule or to force the hand of senators threatening to filibuster.

Still, no one disputes that the incidence of filibusters has increased exponentially. By our count, the entire 19th century saw only 22 filibusters. In the 102nd Congress (1991–92) alone, there were 35. Although it is often thought that the early filibusters were exclusively sectional in nature (as senators aligned on a regional basis to fight legislation favored by northern and western senators), partisanship often pervaded early obstructionism as well. Democrats fighting Whig expansionism before the Civil War, as well as Democrats fighting Republican efforts to protect blacks in the postbellum period, availed themselves of the filibuster to block legislation their parties opposed.

The explosion in the number of filibusters began after the 1950s. Where the 1950s averaged one filibuster per Congress, the 1970s averaged 11 and the 1980s, 19. At the same time, the average number of cloture votes rose from fewer than 1 per Congress in the 1950s to 27 per Congress in the 1980s. Not only did the sheer number of filibusters and cloture votes climb, but the targets of filibustering senators expanded as well. In the 1950s, the filibuster was used almost exclusively by a coalition of conservative Republicans and southern Democrats to thwart civil rights legislation. That same coalition also took advantage of the filibuster to block further reform of Rule 22. So long as a supermajority of senators was required to alter chamber rules, opponents of civil rights legislation could prevent changes in the Senate cloture rule that would have otherwise made it easier for a majority to act. But by the end of the 1970s the filibuster was no longer the preserve of conservatives. Liberals discovered that the filibuster could block policy initiatives and court nominations of the Nixon administration. Last year [1994], matters ranging from reforming product liability and lobbying laws to protecting California deserts were targets of a filibuster.

Senators have turned increasingly to the filibuster to block Senate action because there are few incentives not to. As crystallized by political scientist Richard F. Fenno, Jr., the Senate's shift from a communitarian body in the 1950s to an individualistic one after 1970 has meant the demise of the old Senate—where incentives and norms encouraged quiet apprenticeship and deference to committee and chamber elders. In today's Senate, senators are encouraged to be more responsive to their own personal agendas than to the needs of their colleagues and party leaders. Explosions in interest group pressures, media attention, campaign costs, and constituency obligations have all combined to give senators an overwhelming incentive to exploit their procedural rights. And when party leaders in the 1970s began to adjust to this new style of Senate activism, their decision to "track" filibusters by setting contested bills aside and moving onto other pressing legislation only increased further the use of the filibuster.

As a result, holds by individual senators—in effect a threat to filibuster—have proliferated and filibusters and cloture votes have grown apace. Not only have senators been more willing to filibuster measures they oppose, they have also exploited their procedural prerogatives to filibuster bills at multiple stages—on the motion to proceed to their consideration, on amendments to the bill, and at all three steps of the otherwise pro forma motions to agree to go to conference with the House. Because Senate leaders depend on gaining unanimous consent to structure the floor agenda (unless they can easily muster 60 votes to invoke cloture—a rare feat for recent majority parties), a single senator's pet objections can throw off the entire Senate agenda. Given increases in legislative demands and senators' conflicting schedules, party leaders can ill afford to call the bluff of senators threatening to filibuster or to force senators to hold the floor continuously during a filibuster. Instead, the mere threat to filibuster is enough to block action on legislation potentially favored by a sizable majority. As one senator has put it colorfully, "You have to think of the Senate as if it were 100 different nations and each one had the atomic bomb and at any moment any one of you could blow up the place. So that no matter how long you've been here or how short you've been here, you always know you have the capacity to go to the leader and threaten to blow up the entire institution. And, naturally, he'll deal with you."

Filibusters and Popular Majorities

The most common defense of the filibuster is that legislation favored by a popular majority has never been killed by extended debate. Senators, so the argument goes, will be unable to sustain a filibuster if they lack broad support within and outside the chamber. But it is wildly unrealistic to imagine that a largely apolitical public can serve as a watchdog on the dozens of filibusters waged each year. Indeed, the routinization of the filibuster, and the information overload associated with it, effectively eliminates any meaningful role for public opinion in disciplining the behavior of minority factions in the Senate. Even on broadly salient issues Senate obstructionism has surely killed measures that would otherwise have passed. The 40-year journey for civil rights legislation starting with anti-lynching bills in the 1920s is strong evidence that the filibuster permits a minority of the Senate to bottle up measures enjoying majority support.

Moreover, in the 1980s the coalition favoring cloture on bills killed by a filibuster constituted on average 56 percent of the Senate—falling four votes short of the supermajority needed to invoke cloture under Rule 22. It seems safe to conclude that filibusters have routinely prevented a sizable majority from casting a vote on pending legislation. Although the filibuster may encourage a majority to moderate its position, it also regularly prevents a majority from expressing its will on the Senate floor.

A few examples from the last Congress [1993–1995] illustrate the effect of the filibuster on legislation with widespread support. Early on, both houses overwhelmingly passed bills to overhaul laws regulating the activities of lobbyists and to tighten limits on gifts to members of Congress. But Republican senators successfully filibustered the conference report when it came to the floor a few weeks before last November's [1994] elections. For partisan political purposes, Republican senators refused even to vote for cloture after Democrats offered to remove the offending grassroots lobbying section. As a result, despite a majority for cloture and earlier supermajorities for identical provisions, the filibuster successfully killed the prominent reform measures. A filibuster also prevented final passage of a compromise bill to raise grazing fees on western public lands. In a chamber in which rural interests are already overweighted, a coalition of 16 senators from sparsely populated western states attracted enough Republican support to sustain a filibuster on legislation with majority support in both chambers.

Statutory Debate Limits

Perhaps the strongest argument in favor of reform is that senators themselves have been quite willing to limit the right to filibuster when such limits serve their immediate policy interests. In more than three dozen instances in recent decades, Congress has placed into statute strict limits on debate and amending activity on House and Senate floors. These antifilibuster provisions, generally known as "expedited procedures," have been used to ensure that a vote can be taken on a resolution either approving or disapproving some action proposed by the president or other executive branch official. If the law requires that Congress formally approve some action by the executive branch before it can be implemented, filibustering the resolution of approval can kill the initiative. Conversely, if the law mandates that Congress must formally disapprove an executive branch initiative in order to kill it, a filibuster against the resolution of disapproval can protect the initiative. When senators have had a policy interest in voting on the proposed delegation of power to the executive branch, they have pointedly banned the filibuster on the relevant resolution.

"Fast-track" procedures often used to guarantee a final vote on trade packages negotiated by the president are probably the best known expedited procedures. A strict 30-hour debate limit with no chance for amendment in the past has been imposed during consideration of nontariff trade packages on the Senate floor, although legislation extending fast-track authority can be filibustered. Similarly, the 1974 Budget Act imposed a 20-hour debate limit for consideration of budget reconciliation bills. When such expedited procedures are in place, senators opposed to some provision in the package cannot filibuster a bill to kill the offending provision.

But expedited procedures are not reserved for simply the most politically salient legislation. Senate majorities have banned the filibuster across a host of issues that involve delegation of authority to the executive branch, including foreign assistance, arms control, and energy and environmental regulations. Already in the 104th Congress [1995–1997], a majority in the Senate has created new expedited procedures. Statutory debate limits have been included in legislation regulating unfunded mandates and in a bill to permit Congress to review newly issued agency regulations. Although senators tend to claim a principled commitment to preserving Senate tradition, they are quite willing to foreclose their rights to filibuster when such limits serve more immediate political and policy interests.

Proposals for Reform

To limit the harm done by the filibuster, the Senate should consider three approaches to reform. The first would limit the ability of senators to filibuster presidential nominations for executive and judicial branch positions. Consider the example of former Carter administration official Robert Pastor, who was nominated last year [1994] by President Clinton as ambassador to Panama. Although the Senate Foreign Relations Committee approved Pastor's nomination by a bipartisan vote of 16–3, the nomination was killed at the end of the 103rd Congress by a threatened filibuster by Senator Jesse Helms (R-NC). Pastor afterward argued forcefully that a single senator ought not to be able to prevent the Senate from casting a vote on presidential nominations. "The Constitution grants the Senate the power to advise and consent on ambassadorial nominees," argued Pastor in the *Washington Post*, "not to delay and obstruct." Just as senators have been willing to impose statutory limits on debate on trade, budget, and other issues, they should also consider expedited procedures for consideration of nominations. Such a move would protect the full Senate's power to advise and consent on nominations.

A second reform approach, advocated in the last Congress [1993–1995] by then Senate Majority Leader George Mitchell (D-Maine), would limit the number of stages at which a measure can be filibustered. Rule 22 provides six opportunities to filibuster a bill before the vote on final passage—including on the motion to proceed to consideration of a bill and on the three votes related to going to conference. In recent years, senators have increasingly been prone to target the motion to proceed. By launching a filibuster on the procedural motion, a senator can prevent the chamber from even taking up legislation he or she opposes. The mere threat of a filibuster in the form of registering a hold on the bill has been enough to convince Senate leaders to shelve the motion to proceed and with it the bill. Although senators often lift many such holds, a threat to filibuster the motion to proceed delays the Senate and confounds party leaders' ability to set the chamber's schedule.

Under the Mitchell proposals, debate on the motion to proceed would be limited to two hours, a move that would guarantee the majority a debate (if not a vote) on bills high on the Senate's agenda. Moreover, by limiting individual senators' right to obstruct the motion, the majority leader would no longer be forced to engage in extended negotiations over even the most routine bills on the Senate's agenda. Senators of both political parties, including Senator Robert Byrd (D-West Virginia), perhaps the Senate's greatest champion of the filibuster, have at times endorsed such a limit on the motion to proceed.

The Mitchell proposals would also consolidate into a single motion the three votes necessary to go to conference with the House. The filibuster would be permitted only during consideration of a measure, on the single motion to proceed to conference, and on the conference report itself. Although these reforms would not temper the incentive of senators to exploit their procedural prerogatives, they would make it easier for the majority leader to organize the Senate schedule, lend some predictability to the consideration of legislation on the Senate floor, and force opponents of bills to focus extended debate on the measure itself rather than the preceding procedural motion.

The third approach to reform, advocated by Senators Tom Harkin (D-Iowa) and Joseph Lieberman (D-Connecticut), would ratchet down over several days the number of senators required to invoke cloture. Early this year the Senate rejected Harkin and Lieberman's proposed reform of Rule 22 that would have set a four-vote procedure to attain cloture, with the requisite number of votes for cloture declining with each vote. The initial 60-vote requirement would be lowered to 57, 54, and 51 votes on the following three votes. Under this proposal, a large minority could delay consideration of a bill by extended debate over a minimum of eight days and more likely several weeks, but would eventually have to give way to a simple majority seeking to cast a vote on the measure. Ratcheting down the number of votes required to invoke cloture would both preserve the minority's right to be heard while boosting Senate leaders' ability to move forward on favored legislation.

The Filibuster and the Character of the Senate

Whenever proponents of Senate reform have sought limits on extended debate, defenders of the filibuster have accused them of trying to undermine the uniqueness of the Senate, particularly its original role as a moderating force on intemperate majorities in the House. But the filibuster can be reformed without imperiling the inherent distinctness of the Senate or the Madisonian system of separated institutions competing for shared power. Its members will still serve six-year terms, allowing them to take a more measured approach than House members under the perpetual gun of a reelection campaign. Only a third of the Senate will still be up for reelection in any given year, diluting the impact of strong electoral waves such as the one that gave Republicans control of Congress last November. And senators from large and small states alike will still be given an equal vote, retaining the overweighting of rural interests in the Senate. The trick, of course, in any set of reforms is to balance two goals: protecting the right of individuals and minorities to be heard and ensuring the right of the majority to act. The use of the filibuster in today's Senate serves the interests of the minority at the expense of the majority. Far from preserving the Senate's role as a deliberative assembly, the filibuster today encourages rampant individualism and obstructionism, endless delays and unfocused discussion, hardly conducive to the thoughtful consideration of measures to solve vexing problems of public policy.

22
"Defending the Dinosaur: The Case for Not Fixing the Filibuster"

BILL FRENZEL

Defending the filibuster may not be quite as nasty as taking candy from a baby, but neither is it a good route to popular acclaim. Few kind words are ever spoken in defense of filibusters. Conventional wisdom and political correctness have pronounced them to be pernicious. The very word is pejorative, evoking ugly images of antidemocratic activities.

During the last biennium [two-year session of Congress], filibusters became so unlovable that a group, including former senators, formed "Action, Not Gridlock!" to try to stamp them out. The public, which had tested both gridlock and action, seemed to prefer the former. The organization disappeared.

As that public reaction suggests, political correctness is a sometime thing and conventional wisdom oft goes astray. The American public may not be rushing to embrace the filibuster, but neither has it shown any inclination to root it out. The Senate's overwhelming vote earlier this year against changing the filibuster means that the practice won't go away soon, so it is worth examining. Despite its bad press, the story of the modern filibuster is not one-sided.

Filibusters, the Constitution, and the Framers

Filibuster haters claim they are contrary to the spirit of the Constitution because they require extraordinary majorities. The rationale is that the Framers, who created a majority system and rejected supermajorities, would be horrified by filibusters. Perhaps, but don't be too sure. Remember that no one has dug up a Framer lately to testify to the accuracy of this theory.

The Framers created our system based on their profound distrust of government. They loaded the system with checks and balances to make it work very slowly and with great difficulty. Their intention was to prevent swift enactment of laws and to avoid satisfying the popular whimsy of each willful majority. Maybe they would trade popular election for a filibuster rule.

Without any live Framers, we can only speculate about their feelings.

However, it is hard to believe that, having designed an extremely balky system, they would want to speed it up today. More likely, they would merely remind us that for more than 200 years major American policy-making has been based on "concurrent majorities" anyway.

Parliamentary Comparisons

Most of the parliaments of the world are copies, or variants, of Westminster [the British Parliament]. With only one strong house and no separated executive branch, they can usually deliver laws swiftly. But when their actions affront public opinion, there is a political price to be paid, often very quickly. The government that offends the people soon becomes the opposition.

In our regional system, our majorities, assisted by a wide range of taxpayer-paid perks, do not usually pay any price. Our members of Congress are unbeatable (even in the earthquake of 1994, more than 90 percent of them who sought reelection were reelected). Our majorities are not eternal, but they are long-lived, unlike the Westminster forms.

It might make sense to consider trading the filibuster for congressional mortality (perhaps through term limits), but it is probably unwise to accept the blockbuster majority power of the Westminster system without accepting its balance of political turnover in return.

Actually, filibusters are not unique to the United States. Other parliaments are finding new opportunities for dilatory practices. The Japanese upper house recently presented its "ox-step," and an appointed majority in the Canadian Senate frustrated the intentions of the prime minister and his government on the ratification of the U.S.–Canada Free Trade Agreement. The strokes are different for different folks, but we are not alone. Delay is a time-honored political exercise that transcends political boundaries.

The Filibuster and the Popular Will

The filibuster has been often indicted for denying the popular will, but over recent history, that point is hard to demonstrate. In the first place, it is not easy to get, and hold, 41 votes in the Senate under any circumstances. It is practically impossible to do so against a popular proposal. Filibusters simply do not succeed unless they have popular support or *unless* there is a lack of enthusiasm for the proposal being filibustered.

In 1993 Senator Bob Dole (R-KS) led a filibuster against the Clinton Emergency Spending Bill. It succeeded because the public liked the filibuster better than the spending. In the Bush years, Senator George Mitchell (D-ME) stopped a capital gains proposal by threat of filibuster. Senator Mitchell succeeded because the people saw no urgency in the proposal. In both cases, political reality prevailed.

If the public wants a vote, it tells its representatives. In 1994 Senate

Republicans tried to filibuster the Crime Bill. Based on hot flashes from home, more than 60 senators perceived that the bill was popular, so the filibuster was broken quickly. The same thing happened to the Motor Voter Bill, the National Service Bill, and five out of six presidential appointments. If any proposal has substantial public support, a couple of cloture votes will kill the filibuster. The political reality is: frivolous filibusters do not succeed. The modern filibuster can gridlock ideas that are not popular, but it has not gridlocked the people.

The Bicameral System

In our unique system, the two houses of Congress have developed similar, but not identical, personalities and processes. The House of Representatives, with 440 orators, is harder to manage and has therefore created a set of rules to limit debate. In recent years, its majority has handled bills under rules that permitted few, if any, amendments and only an hour or two of debate.

The Senate, with only 100 orators, has stayed with free debate and an open amendment system. That is not a bad division of process. One house has been too closed, the other too open. The House operates with the relentlessness of Westminster majority, and the Senate has more time to examine, to delay, to amend, and, if necessary, to kill. All are vital functions of any legislature.

The new majority in the House are pledged to operate under more open rules than their predecessors. They have done so. Even so, they have had to move their program, so debate and amendments have still been subjected to some limitations, less than the old House, but still much more than the Senate.

There is still a relatively open pipeline for bills flowing from the House. Nine out of ten "Contract" bills is a strong showing of majority power. Following the Framers' wisdom, it is prudent to have a sieve in the Senate to compete with that open pipe in the House. At least some of the worst legislative lumps may be smoothed out in the finer mesh. Only if unlimited debate and amendments were guaranteed for all House bills would it make sense to kill the Senate filibuster.

Key to Compromise

Many filibusters are not filibusters at all, but merely threats. Most are undertaken to notify the managers of the proposal that problems exist. They are a signal from a minority to a majority that negotiations are in order. Sometimes the majority tries a cloture vote or two before negotiating. Sometimes it negotiates. Sometimes it does not.

Most of these procedures end in a modified bill, not a dead bill. The Crime Bill noted above passed. The Dole filibuster of emergency spending did not prevent passage of many of its bits of pork in regular appropriations bills. The old Mitchell capital gains filibuster will no doubt be picked up by Senator Daschle (D-SD) this year. The predicted result will be some sort of negotiated agreement.

The filibuster surely gives a minority a little more clout, but it does not prevent a majority from passing reasonably popular proposals. It gives a minority the opportunity to negotiate what it believes is an intolerable proposal into one it can live with. That compromise may serve the needs of the majority tolerably well too.

No Need for a Heavy Hand

One political reality test for the filibuster is the congressional ingenuity in finding ways to avoid it when necessary. Trade and Reconciliation bills are considered under laws that obviate filibusters. When there is a good reason to finesse the filibuster, the Senate always seems to get the job done.

Many other Senate rules, only dimly understood by common folks, reduce the legislative pace. I do not mean to bless multiple efforts to filibuster the same proposal. Once on the bill and once on the conference report is enough. Unlimited amendment after cloture is also too much opportunity for mischief.

Former Senate Majority Leader Mitchell has left constructive proposals to speed the work of the Senate without damaging the filibuster. They ought to be considered. The minority needs rights for protection. The majority needs the ability to move its program. Both needs can be well served by the modern 60-vote cloture rule. It should not be changed.

Keep the Filibuster

The test of the filibuster ought to be whether it is fair, appropriate, and constructive. It may have been a killer in the old days, when it slew civil rights bills, but under the new 60-vote system, it is difficult to recall a filibustered proposition that stayed dead if it was popular.

Most antifilibuster noise comes from advocates of ideas that were going to fail anyway. It is not essential for every idea that comes bouncing up or down Pennsylvania Avenue to become law. The filibuster is a useful legislative tool, consistent with the goals of the Framers, that keeps whimsical, immature, and ultimately unpopular bills out of the statute books.

Both houses have new majorities this year [1995]. The House Republican majority has already enhanced minority rights. The Senate majority has protected its minority as well by defeating a proposal to eliminate the filibuster. That vote may come back to bite the Republican majority, particularly on capital gains legislation. But for our centrist American government and its centrist electorate, it was the right thing to do.

DISCUSSION QUESTIONS

1. Is the filibuster a necessary protection for minority rights, or does it give too much obstructionist power to tiny minorities? Explain.

2. What changes, if any, should be made for use of the filibuster in the U.S. Senate?

CHAPTER 5

The President: From Chief Clerk to Chief Executive

23
"The Power to Persuade" from
Presidential Power

RICHARD NEUSTADT

An enduring theme in analyses of the presidency is the gap between what the public expects of the office and the president's actual powers. Neustadt, who wrote the first edition of Presidential Power *in 1960, offered a new way of looking at the office. Neustadt's main point is that the formal powers of the presidency (the constitutional powers set out in Article II and the statutory powers that Congress grants) are not the most important resource. The president cannot, Neustadt concluded, expect to get his way by command—issuing orders to subordinates and other government officials, with the expectation of immediate and unquestioning compliance. In a system of "separate institutions sharing power," other political actors have their own independent sources of power and therefore can refuse to comply with presidential orders. Nobody, Neustadt argues, sees things from the president's perspective (or "vantage point"). Legislators, judges, cabinet secretaries, all have their own responsibilities, constituencies, demands of office, resources. Their interests and the president's will often be different. The key to presidential power is the power to persuade—to convince others that they should comply with the president's wishes because doing so is in their interest. Presidents persuade by bargaining: making deals, reaching compromise positions, in other words, the give and take that is part of politics. The question remains, as the following selection points out, whether our method of selecting presidents is appropriate to the job the winner must do.*

The limits on command suggest the structure of our government. The constitutional convention of 1787 is supposed to have created a government of "separated powers." It did nothing of the sort. Rather, it *institutions* created a government of separated institutions *sharing* powers. "I am part of the legislative process," Eisenhower often said in 1959 as a reminder of his veto. Congress, the dispenser of authority and funds, is no less part of the administrative process. Federalism adds another set of separated institutions. The Bill of Rights adds others. Many public purposes can only be achieved by voluntary acts of private institutions; the press, for one, in Douglass Cater's phrase, is a "fourth branch of government." And with the coming of alliances abroad, the separate institutions of a London, or a Bonn, share in the making of American public policy.

What the Constitution separates our political parties do not combine. The parties are themselves composed of separated organizations sharing public authority. The authority consists of nominating powers. Our national parties are confederations of state and local party institutions, with a headquarters that represents the White House, more or less, if the party has a President in office. These confederacies manage presidential nominations. All other public offices depend upon electorates confined within the states. All other nominations are controlled within the states. The President and congressmen who bear one party's label are divided by dependence upon different sets of voters. The differences are sharpest at the stage of nomination. The White House has too small a share in nominating congressmen, and Congress has too little weight in nominating Presidents for party to erase their constitutional separation. Party links are stronger than is frequently supposed, but nominating processes assure the separation.

The separateness of institutions and the sharing of authority prescribe the terms on which a President persuades. When one man shares authority with another, but does not gain or lose his job upon the other's whim, his willingness to act upon the urging of the other turns on whether he conceives the action right for him. The essence of a President's persuasive task is to convince such men that what the White House wants of them is what they ought to do for their sake and on their authority.

Persuasive power, thus defined, amounts to more than charm or reasoned argument. These have their uses for a President, but these are not *because* the whole of his resources. For the men he would induce to do what he *institutions* wants done on their own responsibility will need or fear some acts by *interests* him on his responsibility. If they share his authority, he has some share in theirs. Presidential "powers" may be inconclusive when a President commands, but always remain relevant as he persuades. The status and authority inherent in his office reinforce his logic and his charm.

* * *

A President's authority and status give him great advantages in dealing with the men he would persuade. Each "power" is a vantage point for him in the degree that other men have use for his authority. From the veto to appointments, from publicity to budgeting, and so down a long list, the White House now controls the most encompassing array of vantage points in the American political system. With hardly an exception, the men who share in governing this country are aware that at some time, in some degree, the doing of *their* jobs, the furthering of *their* ambitions, may depend upon the President of the United States. Their need for presidential action, or their fear of it, is bound to be recurrent if not actually continuous. Their need or fear is his advantage.

A President's advantages are greater than mere listing of his "powers" might suggest. The men with whom he deals must deal with him until the last day of his term. Because they have continuing relationships with him, his future, while it lasts, supports his present influence. Even though there is no need or fear of him today, what he could do tomorrow may supply today's advantage. Continuing relationships may convert any "power," any aspect of his status, into vantage points in almost any case. When he induces other men to do what he wants done, a President can trade on their dependence now *and* later.

The President's advantages are checked by the advantages of others. Continuing relationships will pull in both directions. These are relationships of mutual dependence. A President depends upon the men he would persuade; he has to reckon with his need or fear of them. They too will possess status, or authority, or both, else they would be of little use to him. Their vantage points confront his own; their power tempers his.

*   *   *

The power to persuade is the power to bargain. Status and authority yield bargaining advantages. But in a government of "separated institutions sharing powers," they yield them to all sides. With the array of vantage points at his disposal, a President may be far more persuasive than his logic or his charm could make him. But outcomes are not guaranteed by his advantages. There remain the counter pressures those whom he would influence can bring to bear on him from vantage points at their disposal. Command has limited utility; persuasion becomes give-and-take. It is well that the White House holds the vantage points it does. In such a business any President may need them all—and more.

*   *   *

This view of power as akin to bargaining is one we commonly accept in the sphere of congressional relations. Every textbook states and every legislative session demonstrates that save in times like the extraordinary Hundred Days of 1933—times virtually ruled out by definition at mid-century—a President will often be unable to obtain congressional action on his terms or even to halt action he opposes. The reverse is equally accepted: Congress often is frustrated by the President. Their formal powers are so intertwined that neither will accomplish very much, for very long, without the acquiescence of the other. By the same token, though, what one demands the other can resist. The stage is set for that great game, much like collective bargaining, in which each seeks to profit from the other's needs and fears. It is a game played catch-as-catch-can, case by case. And everybody knows the game, observers and participants alike.

*   *   *

Like our governmental structure as a whole, the executive establishment consists of separated institutions sharing powers. The President heads one of these; Cabinet officers, agency administrators, and military commanders head others. Below the departmental level, virtually independent bureau chiefs head many more. Under mid-century conditions, Federal operations spill across dividing lines on organization charts; almost every policy entangles many agencies; almost every program calls for interagency collaboration. Everything somehow involves the President. But operating agencies owe their existence least of all to one another—and only in some part to him. Each has a separate statutory base; each has its statutes to administer; each deals with a different set of subcommittees at the Capitol. Each has its own peculiar set of clients, friends, and enemies outside the formal government. Each has a different set of specialized careerists inside its own bailiwick. Our Constitution gives the President the "take-care" clause and the appointive power. Our statues give him central budgeting and a degree of personnel control. All agency administrators are responsible to him. But they *also* are responsible to Congress, to their clients, to their staffs, and to themselves. In short, they have five masters. Only after all of those do they owe any loyalty to each other.

"The members of the Cabinet," Charles G. Dawes used to remark, "are a President's natural enemies." Dawes had been Harding's Budget Director, Coolidge's Vice-President, and Hoover's Ambassador to London; he also had been General Pershing's chief assistant for supply in the First World War. The words are highly colored, but Dawes knew whereof he spoke. The men who have to serve so many masters cannot help but be somewhat the "enemy" of any one of them. By the same token, any master wanting service is in some degree the "enemy" of such a servant. A President is likely to want loyal support but not to relish trouble on his doorstep. Yet the more his Cabinet members cleave to him, the more they may need help from him in fending off the wrath of rival masters. Help, though, is synonymous with trouble. Many a Cabinet officer, with loyalty ill-rewarded by his lights and help withheld, has come to view the White House as innately hostile to department heads. Dawes's dictum can be turned around.

*   *   *

The more an officeholder's status and his "powers" stem from sources independent of the President, the stronger will be his potential pressure on the President. Department heads in general have more bargaining power than do most members of the White House staff; but bureau chiefs may have still more, and specialists at upper levels of established career services may have almost unlimited reserves of the enormous power which consists of sitting still. As Franklin Roosevelt once remarked:

> The Treasury is so large and far-flung and ingrained in its practices that I find it almost impossible to get the action and results I want—even with Henry [Morgenthau] there. But the Treasury is not to be compared with the State Department. You should go through the experience of trying to get any changes in the thinking, policy, and action of the career diplomats and then you'd know what a real problem was. But the Treasury and the State Department put together are nothing compared with the Na-a-vy. The admirals are really something to cope with—and I should know. To change anything in the Na-a-vy is like punching a feather bed. You punch it with your right and you punch it with your left until you are finally exhausted, and then you find the damn bed just as it was before you started punching.[1]

* * *

There is a widely held belief in the United States that were it not for folly or for knavery, a reasonable President would need no power other than the logic of his argument. No less a personage than Eisenhower has subscribed to that belief in many a campaign speech and press-conference remark. But faulty reasoning and bad intentions do not cause all quarrels with Presidents. The best of reasoning and of intent cannot compose them all. For in the first place, what the President wants will rarely seem a trifle to the men he wants it from. And in the second place, they will be bound to judge it by the standard of their own responsibilities, not his. However logical his argument according to his lights, their judgment may not bring them to his view.

The men who share in governing this country frequently appear to act as though they were in business for themselves. So, in a real though not entire sense, they are and have to be. When Truman and MacArthur fell to quarreling, for example, the stakes were no less than the substance of American foreign policy, the risks of greater war or military stalemate, the prerogatives of Presidents and field commanders, the pride of a pro-consul and his place in history. Intertwined, inevitably, were other stakes, as well: political stakes for men and factions of both parties; power stakes for interest groups with which they were or wished to be affiliated. And every stake was raised by the apparent discontent in the American public mood. There is no reason to suppose that in such circumstances men of large but differing responsibilities will see all things through the same glasses. On the contrary, it is to be expected that their views of what ought to be done and what they then should do will vary with the differing perspectives their particular responsibilities evoke.

Since their duties are not vested in a "team" or a "collegium" but in themselves, as individuals, one must expect that they will see things *for* themselves. Moreover, when they are responsible to many masters and when an event or policy turns loyalty against loyalty—a day by day occurrence in the nature of the case—one must assume that those who have the duties to perform will choose the terms of reconciliation. This is the essence of their personal responsibility. When their own duties pull in opposite directions, who else but they can choose what they will do?

* * *

Outside the Executive Branch the situation is the same, except that loyalty to the President may often matter *less*. . . . And when one comes to congressmen who can do nothing for themselves (or their constituents) save as they are elected, term by term, in districts and through party structures *differing* from those on which a President depends, the case is very clear. An able Eisenhower aide with long congressional experience remarked to me in 1958: "The people on the Hill don't do what they might *like* to do, they do what they think they *have* to do in their own interest as *they* see it. . . ." This states the case precisely.

The essence of a President's persuasive task with congressmen and everybody else, *is to induce them to believe that what he wants of them is what their own appraisal of their own responsibilities requires them to do in their interest, not his.* Because men may differ in their views on public policy, because differences in outlook stem from differences in duty— duty to one's office, one's constituents, oneself—that task is bound to be more like collective bargaining than like a reasoned argument among philosopher kings. Overtly or implicitly, hard bargaining has character- ized all illustrations offered up to now. This is the reason why: persua- sion deals in the coin of self-interest with men who have some freedom to reject what they find counterfeit.

Let me introduce a case . . . : the European Recovery Program of 1948, the so-called Marshall Plan. This is perhaps the greatest exercise in policy *agreement* since the cold war began. When the then Secretary of State, George Catlett Marshall, spoke at the Harvard commencement in June of 1947, he launched one of the most creative, most imaginative ventures in the history of American foreign relations. What makes this policy most notable for present purposes, however, is that it became effective upon action by the 80th Congress, at the behest of Harry Truman, in the elec- tion year of 1948.

Eight months before Marshall spoke at Harvard, the Democrats had lost control of both Houses of Congress for the first time in fourteen years. Truman, whom the Secretary represented, had just finished his second troubled year as President-by-succession. Truman was regarded with so little warmth in his own party that in 1946 he had been urged *not* to participate in the congressional campaign. At the opening of Congress in January 1947, Senator Robert A. Taft, "Mr. Republican," had somewhat the attitude of a President-elect. This was a vision widely shared in Washington, with Truman relegated, thereby, to the role of caretaker-on-term. Moreover, within just two weeks of Marshall's commencement address, Truman was to veto two prized accomplishments of Taft's congressional majority: the Taft-Hartley Act and tax reduction. Yet scarcely ten months later the Marshall Plan was under way on terms to satisfy its sponsors, its authorization completed, its first-year funds in sight, its administering agency in being: all managed by as thorough a display of executive-congressional cooperation as any we have seen since the Second World War. For any President at any time this would have been a great accomplishment. In years before mid-century it would have been enough to make the future reputation of his term. And for a Truman, at this time, enactment of the Marshall Plan appears almost miraculous.

How was the miracle accomplished? How did a President so situated bring it off? In answer, the first thing to note is that he did not do it by himself. Truman had help of a sort no less extraordinary than the outcome. Although each stands for something more complex, the names of Marshall, Vandenberg, . . . Bevin, Stalin, tell the story of that help.

In 1947, two years after V-J Day, General Marshall was something more than Secretary of State. He was a man venerated by the President as "the greatest living American," literally an embodiment of Truman's ideals. He was honored at the Pentagon as an architect of victory. He was thoroughly respected by the Secretary of the Navy, James V. Forrestal, who that year became the first Secretary of Defense. On Capitol Hill Marshall had an enormous fund of respect stemming from his war record as Army Chief of Staff, and in the country generally no officer had come out of the war with a higher reputation for judgment, intellect, and probity. Besides, as Secretary of State, he had behind him the first generation of matured foreign service officers produced by the reforms of the 1920's, and mingled with them, in the departmental service, were some of the ablest of the men drawn by the war from private life to Washington.

* * *

Taken together, these are exceptional resources for a Secretary of State. In the circumstances, they were quite as necessary as they obviously are relevant. The Marshall Plan was launched by a "lame duck" Administration "scheduled" to leave office in eighteen months. Marshall's program faced a congressional leadership traditionally isolationist and currently intent upon economy. European aid was viewed with envy by a Pentagon distressed and virtually disarmed through budget cuts, and by domestic agencies intent on enlarged welfare programs. It was not viewed with liking by a Treasury intent on budget surpluses. The plan had need of every asset that could be extracted from the personal position of its nominal author and from the skills of his assistants.

Without the equally remarkable position of the senior Senator from Michigan, Arthur H. Vandenberg, it is hard to see how Marshall's assets could have been enough. Vandenberg was chairman of the Senate Foreign Relations Committee. Actually, he was much more than that. Twenty years a senator, he was the senior member of his party in the Chamber. Assiduously cultivated by F.D.R. and Truman, he was a chief Republican proponent of "bipartisanship" in foreign policy, and consciously conceived himself its living symbol to his party, to the country, and abroad. Moreover, by informal but entirely operative agreement with his colleague Taft, Vandenberg held the acknowledged lead among Senate Republicans in the whole field of international affairs. This acknowledgement meant more in 1947 than it might have meant at any other time. With confidence in the advent of a Republican administration two years hence, most of the gentlemen were in a mood to be responsive and responsible. The war was over, Roosevelt dead, Truman a caretaker, theirs the trust. That the Senator from Michigan saw matters in this light, his diaries make clear. And this was not the outlook from the Senate side alone; the attitudes of House Republicans associated with the Herter Committee and its tours abroad suggest the same mood of responsibility. Vandenberg was not the only source of help on Capitol Hill. But relatively speaking, his position there was as exceptional as Marshall's was downtown.

* * *

At Harvard, Marshall had voiced an idea in general terms. That this was turned into a hard program susceptible of presentation and support is due, in major part, to Ernest Bevin, the British Foreign Secretary. He well deserves the credit he has sometimes been assigned as, in effect, co-author of the Marshall Plan. For Bevin seized on Marshall's Harvard speech and organized a European response with promptness and concreteness beyond the State Department's expectations. What had been virtually a trial balloon to test reactions on both sides of the Atlantic was hailed in London as an invitation to the Europeans to send Washington a bill of particulars. This they promptly organized to do, and the American Administration then organized in turn for its reception without further argument internally about the pros and cons of issuing the "invitation" in the first place. But for Bevin there might have been trouble from the Secretary of the Treasury and others besides.

If Bevin's help was useful at that early stage, Stalin's was vital from first to last. In a mood of self-deprecation Truman once remarked that without Moscow's "crazy" moves "we would never have had our foreign policy . . . we never could have got a thing from Congress." George

Kennan, among others, had deplored the anti-Soviet overtone of the case made for the Marshall Plan in Congress and the country, but there is no doubt that this clinched the argument for many segments of American opinion. There also is no doubt that Moscow made the crucial contributions to the case.

*   *   *

The crucial thing to note about this case is that despite compatibility of views on public policy, Truman got no help he did not pay for (except Stalin's). Bevin scarcely could have seized on Marshall's words had Marshall not been plainly backed by Truman. Marshall's interest would not have comported with the exploitation of his prestige by a President who undercut him openly, or subtly, or even inadvertently, at any point. Vandenberg, presumably, could not have backed proposals by a White House which begrudged him deference and access gratifying to his fellow-partisans (and satisfying to himself). Prominent Republicans in private life would not have found it easy to promote a cause identified with Truman's claims on 1948—and neither would the prominent New Dealers then engaged in searching for a substitute.

Truman paid the price required for their services. So far as the record shows, the White House did not falter once in firm support for Marshall and the Marshall Plan. Truman backed his Secretary's gamble on an invitation to all Europe. He made the plan his own in a well-timed address to the Canadians. He lost no opportunity to widen the involvements of his own official family in the cause. Averell Harriman the Secretary of Commerce, Julius Krug the Secretary of the Interior, Edwin Nourse the Economic Council Chairman, James Webb the Director of the Budget—all were made responsible for studies and reports contributing directly to the legislative presentation. Thus these men were committed in advance. Besides, the President continually emphasized to everyone in reach that he did not have doubts, did not desire complications and would foreclose all he could. Reportedly, his emphasis was felt at the Treasury, with good effect. And Truman was at special pains to smooth the way for Vandenberg. The Senator insisted on "no politics" from the Administration side; there was none. He thought a survey of American resources and capacity essential; he got it in the Krug and Harriman reports. Vandenberg expected advance consultation; he received it, step by step, in frequent meetings with the President and weekly conferences with Marshall. He asked for an effective liaison between Congress and agencies concerned; Lovett and others gave him what he wanted. When the Senator decided on the need to change financing and administrative features of the legislation, Truman disregarded Budget Bureau grumbling and acquiesced with grace. When, finally, Vandenberg desired a Republican to head the new administering agency, his candidate, Paul Hoffman, was appointed despite the President's own preference for another. In all of these ways Truman employed the sparse advantages his "powers" and his status then accorded him to gain the sort of help he had to have.

* * *

Had Truman lacked the personal advantages his "powers" and his status gave him, or if he had been maladroit in using them, there probably would not have been a massive European aid program in 1948. . . . The President's own share in this accomplishment was vital. He made his contribution by exploiting his advantages. Truman, in effect, lent Marshall and the rest the perquisites and status of his office. In return they lent him their prestige and their own influence. The transfer multiplied *his* influence despite his limited authority in form and lack of strength politically. Without the wherewithal to make this bargain, Truman could not have contributed to European aid.

* * *

DISCUSSION QUESTIONS

1. Using recent presidents (Clinton, Bush, Reagan), identify and discuss some examples of Neustadt's argument that presidents cannot get their way by "command," and that they must bargain to get what they want.
2. Is Neustadt right? Can presidents ever rely on "command?"

NOTES

1. Reprinted from Marriner S. Eccles, *Beckoning Frontiers* (New York: Knopf, 1951), p. 336.

• unattainable ideals
• idependent, can compromise
• unrealistic expectations

24
"The Search for the Perfect President"

THE ECONOMIST

Samuel Johnson, often good for a nineteenth-century sound bite, once defined second marriages as "the triumph of hope over experience." We might say the same thing about presidential campaigns, as every four years the country elects a president with a large portion of the public unhappy with the choices offered. This explains, in part, the periodic flirtation with third party candidates and nonpoliticians such as Ross Perot and Colin Powell. Yet this selection argues that the definition of an "ideal" candidate is both fluid and inconsistent, and concludes that our hope for the hero on horseback does not mesh with what the office requires: where the public wants moral certitude and steadiness, the office demands compromise and tradeoffs in daily measure. As a result, no candidate —not Bill Clinton, Bob Dole, Ross Perot, or Colin Powell—can live up to the unrealistic expectations the electorate imposes.

Most love affairs must end. Either age withers them, or one of the partners fails to reciprocate the passion. Colin Powell, try as he might, could not reciprocate the storm of longing that was being whipped up for him across the length and breadth of the United States. His retirement from the presidential scene leaves no shortage of candidates for the top job, not all of them implausible. But it also leaves an aching vacuum for someone better than the present field, and for something more. That "something more" is defined in all kinds of ways: stature, dignity, candour, morality, the ability to get things done. Rightly or wrongly, Mr Powell was seen as epitomising all these virtues. He was, in short, ideal.

Ideal for the times, that is. Throughout history notions of the ideal presidential candidates have varied wildly, from the populist frontiersman (Andrew Jackson) to the youthful fighter for justice (Bobby Kennedy) and from the imperialist swashbuckler (Teddy Roosevelt) to the Yankee curmudgeon (Calvin Coolidge) to the favourite uncle (Ronald Reagan). None of these men, and it is never a woman, would look ideal for the mid-1990s, when America appears to be demanding an impossible (but Powell-like?) blend of toughness and compassion, budget-slashing radicalism and comforting tradition. But each seemed to offer what many voters wanted, epitomising a mood that was afoot in the country, yet only glancingly reflected by the main political parties. Each looked like somebody who would be able to transform mere politics-as-usual.

These enthusiasms contain within themselves plentiful seeds of disappointment. Yet, despite that, they seem to be getting more frequent. It is a rare modern campaign that does not include a flirtation, however brief, with an "ideal" candidate. And the Founding Fathers would have roundly disapproved of it.

America's constitution, in fact, makes rather little of the role of the president. In keeping with the best Enlightenment thinking, he was envisioned as a man of decent character and adequate, but not extravagant, property: a country gentleman or small-town lawyer who, if the nation called him, would do his duty for a while and then return to his *moutons* [sheep]. The United States would always distrust the *caudillismo*, the love of a strong leader, that typified other countries of the hemisphere. Blessed with a well-balanced constitution, anti-monarchical convictions and a large dose of Anglo-Saxon phlegm, Americans would keep their leader firmly in his place.

Quite when the feeling changed is difficult to pin down. In some ways, it has not changed at all. Most presidents and seekers of the presidency have been, or are, lawyers and career politicians, reared for the job and enmeshed in the system. But that can get stultifying, and, to modern Americans, intolerable; so, over the decades, other elements of desirable character have gradually been added.

By the mid-19th century, when America was finally emerging as a nation as a result of wars with the British, the Indians and the Mexicans, a military career was thought a good grounding for office, and heroes of obscure battles could always be sure of generating waves at the party conventions. By the 20th century, when America was extending its hegemony more by commerce than warships, men who had been in trade or industry became presidential timber for the first time: Herbert Hoover was a mining engineer, Harry Truman a haberdasher. Their careers did not necessarily recommend them for the presidency—indeed, Truman while in office was often perceived as a small-town businessman unfitted to cope with the momentous decisions of the time; but they suggested (as farming had done a century earlier) the common touch, practicality, and common sense.

A Good Man in America

Occasionally, as in the past months, there have also been surges for men who seem to embody sheer uprightness and strength of character: morality, in short. These men seldom propose themselves as candidates; this, of course, reinforces their morality, and makes them all the more attractive. Martin Luther King, [Jr.,] with his dreams of racial harmony, was such a figure in the 1960s; William Bennett, former education secretary, drug czar and author of the bestselling "Book of [Virtues]," is one today.

According to the opinion polls, "values," vaguely but sentimentally defined, are now the first concern of the American electorate, above even crime and stagnant real wages. Curiously, then, the ideal candidate at the end of the 20th century is somebody whose stainless family life and dedication to his duty would also have been his highest recommendations for office in the earliest years of the republic.

There is, however, one essential difference. Modern presidents are expected to lead both their country and, to some degree, the world. Everything they do, from negotiating to saluting, is judged on a scale of Actions Appropriate to Leaders. And although the cult of personality is kept on a short leash in America, so that the fire-eating, populist campaigns of a Strom Thurmond or a Pat Buchanan soon encounter general ridicule, the ideal presidential candidate still displays elements of the miracle-worker and the strong man. Such a man not only makes the planes run on time, and faces down the country's enemies; he can also achieve the near-mystical, such as "making America feel good about itself." (It was morning again in America with Ronald Reagan.)

The perfect candidate, therefore, is often a leader first, but not in the forum of politics. Recently, business experience has been preferred. Chrysler's Lee Iacocca looked ideal for a while. Much of Ross Perot's appeal in 1992 was his no-nonsense corporate image as the head of Electronic Data Systems in Dallas. True, he was obsessive, megalomaniac and sometimes plain weird; he was known to have outlawed beards among his employees, and certain colours of shirts; but he had also been startlingly successful. Strutting on the stage, inveighing against deficits and foreign lobbyists, Mr Perot gave no doubt that he would do whatever he promised without fear of contradiction. But he remembered—just—where he was; he would do these things only as the humble servant of the American people.

This, of course, was sanctimonious rubbish, which left Congress out on an uncomfortable limb. Yet Mr Perot's image, of the man called in to fix the machine, is powerful in modern campaigns. The government is plainly broken, so here is a man to mend it. He knows how it works, but he is not of it; he can wield the wrench and spanner until Congress and its interest groups holler for mercy. His face and ideology hardly matter, or so he would have the voters believe. He is just a doer, selflessly spending his money for the good of the country.

Such a man might appear to fit the modern bill exactly. American presidents, ideally, are men who put the good of the country before the good of their ideological clique. They are independent thinkers, creatures of no party. They should be able to break through confining structures, such as written manifestos or the particular demands of fringe groups;

and they should be able to unite the country behind them in a haze of patriotic endeavour.

This last capacity, however, is not one that is easily found in businessmen. In the final analysis, money often talks too loudly in their lives; their methods can seem too autocratic for the White House, their horizons too limited to the bottom line. The job to be done is far more diverse, complex and spiritual than either politicians or corporate leaders can attempt. And for those apparently necessary presidential virtues—for patriotism, and courage, and the instilling of a national sense of duty and service—Americans have found themselves looking once again in a surprisingly non-American direction, to the ranks of the armed forces.

The Man on the White Horse

In all, seven generals have reached the White House. . . . A raft of presidents, besides, have used a stint of soldiering to burnish their résumés. Teddy Roosevelt's jungle-hopping imperialism was much enhanced by his earlier adventures with the Rough Riders and his charge up San Juan hill. George Bush derived what profit he could from being the youngest American pilot on second-world-war service in the Pacific. Bob Dole's withered arm, shot up in Italy, is his most reliable campaign credential.

The reason is clear. Soldiers do difficult things despite appalling danger; they, above all others, should be able to cut through the tape of bureaucracy and take faint-hearted nations by the scruff of the neck. When they are heroes, they are charismatic to the level of film stars. And even when, like General Powell, they are actually bureaucrats, their war experience still commends them. What would the victor over Iraq do with the budget deficit, welfare reform and Medicare? How many punks would dare walk the streets with a general in charge? The accuracy of those laser-guided bombs, dropped down Iraqi factory chimneys, would be as nothing to the general's needle-sharp penetration to the core of America's malaise.

And generals, of course, are also the quintessential non-politicians. From the very beginnings of the republic, America's armed forces have been kept under civilian control and carefully apart from political activity. This was for sound reasons, which Alexander Hamilton summed up as "an hereditary impression of danger to liberty" from military institutions. But whenever politics and cabals and corruption have become dirty words, as has happened repeatedly, it is extraordinary how the longing gaze of the voters turns towards the man in uniform, or only lately out of it.

Flirtations with generals tend to go in waves. In its first 40 years the American republic could stomach no general as president other than George Washington. After 1828, with a succession of wars against the Indians, Mexico and each other, Americans suddenly changed their tastes, and for 60 years military men were in fashion for both presidency and vice-presidency. Suspicion then set in again, and lasted until the "I Like Ike" campaigns of the 1950s. General Powell's ascendancy marked the end of a three-decade spell of biliousness, during which distrust of generals near power seemed epitomised by the reaction to General Alexander Haig's frenzied cry of "I'm in charge here!" after the shooting of President Reagan in 1981.

While it lasts, general-fever can be pretty indiscriminate. Almost any swashbuckler is preferable to grey politicians on either the Republican or the Democratic side of the aisle. Yet fevers do not always lead to consummation. William Tecumseh Sherman, lionised in the north after he had taught the South what total war was like (and burnt Atlanta to the ground), came under enormous pressure to run for "the thankless office" in 1884; he not only refused to do so but insisted that, if elected, he would not serve. Douglas MacArthur, the victor over Japan, was first idolised and then abandoned; he had become disconcertingly fond of ticker-tape parades, fascistic leather jackets and his own opinions.

At a deep level, politics did not matter to these men. It seldom does. If a candidate has been drafted, or presents himself, as the noble and disinterested servant of his country, what use can he have for factions and deal-making? Dwight Eisenhower refused (just like General Powell) to be drawn on any political issue; he was an independent for years before, at the last moment, he became a Republican. Ulysses Grant, propelled into politics on the strength of his stellar Civil War performance, had little choice but to be a Republican; but he had seldom voted and scarcely cared.

To voters tired of the status quo, this may be refreshing for a while. Yet it can wear off. Zachary Taylor, a non-voter all his life, did not bother to get his mind round the slavery question, which was to become important. In the 1868 campaign, Grant studiously avoided the burning topic of whether blacks should have the vote. In the 1950s, Eisenhower stayed away as long as he could from the issue of school desegregation, hoping the courts would sort it out for him.

As for the business of governing, the very simplicity and naivety that commends military men for office can become a disadvantage. Dealing with Congress is often especially hard. Heroic appeals to the people, or huddling with a select group of colleagues like officers round a battle-map, are one thing; throwing an issue open to legislative debate, which may end with the president's wishes being rejected, is quite another. As Truman remarked of Eisenhower (who made a great success of the presidency, but never achieved the stable-cleaning he had promised): "Poor old Ike. It won't be a bit like the army. He'll say do this, do that, and not a thing will happen."

The Ideal and Its Enemies

The perfect presidential candidate for the late 20th century thus appears to be neither the career politician, nor the corporate maverick, nor the military hero. The career politician—even if, like Bill Clinton, he has tried to be a reformer—is too tied in to vested interests, lobbyists and old party structures. Americans no longer want this; they seem willing, even keen, to trade expertise at playing the system for the chance that a man may rise above it and govern in the interests of the nation as a whole. To plump for a CEO or a general, however, may be to go too far. Such men, perhaps tripping on their own hubris, risk being out-smarted by the old hands; and besides, the longing for a national fixer and father-figure seems an outdated and faintly dangerous notion.

It is the man who essentially stands alone, carrying his own message clearly and directly to the people, who will be seen as the ideal candidate during an election campaign. But the man who becomes president must continuously wrestle and compromise in competition with the legislature and sometimes with the courts; and he must also tone down his idealism (as Mr Clinton did over Bosnia) once the hard realities of diplomacy begin to arrive on the doorstep.

It is instructive to return to what the founders wanted, for it has more appeal and relevance to the modern age than voters may sometimes realise. The powers of the president, as given in the Constitution, are briefly stated. He is commander-in-chief (but without the power to de-clare or pay for a war); he may grant pardons for offences against the United States; he may make treaties, provided that two-thirds of the Senate concurs; and "he shall from time to time give to the Congress information of the state of the Union, and recommend to their consid-eration such measures as he shall judge necessary and expedient."

The ideal president is therefore not a Newt Gingrich, but an occasional prodder towards reform; not a charismatic MacArthur, but a man who must humbly seek the approval of Congress and take the advice of his generals; a steadying and correcting influence on legislation, but not a constant irritant. At times of crisis, he must articulate what the nation feels and do what needs to be done: something all candidates blithely promise, without realising the seriousness of the obligation. And al-though he must be there whenever needed, able to take the lead, he must not be a showy parader on the national stage. Distance, as the founders intended, lends both dignity and democracy to the office.

Yet it is now well-nigh impossible for candidates to achieve this cal-culated distance. Modern campaigns and political careers insist on con-tinuous exposure, both on television and in marathon sessions of pressing the flesh with voters. In the process, Americans quickly tear down their ideal candidates, rendering them mere politicians who must either scramble to restore their own standing in the hearts of the citizenry, or else abandon the attempt. The democratic system itself makes its ideals unattainable; and the endless circle of frustration, hope, love and disappointment is doomed to begin again. Who's next?

Discussion Questions

1. What qualities do you think the "ideal" president should have?

2. Do we, as the electorate, expect too much from presidential candidates (and presidents)? Is the problem our expectation, or is the election system at fault?

— Prez. are unfamiliar w/economics
— don't fully understand
— intelligent
— can't rely on advisors

25

"Presidents and Economics:
One-Star Generalizations"

Herbert Stein

We know that the economy matters a great deal to presidents. But how do presidents make economic policy—or, perhaps more important, how well do presidents understand economics when they make decisions? Here, Herbert Stein, one of Richard Nixon's economic advisors, offers his impressions of how presidents decide economic policy questions: how much attention they pay to their advisors, how they assimilate information about complex economic problems. Stein argues that although presidents are typically unfamiliar with economics, they are intelligent people well versed in the details of economic policy. They may not comprehend Keynes, but they understand how government action affects the national economy. Ultimately, however, although the work of professional economists offers important information and guidance to presidents, Stein concludes that presidents cannot rely on it as a substitute it for their own judgment and political sense.

1   Prez aren't econ.

Presidents are not economists. They have little comprehension of economics as a scientific, academic discipline, and little interest in it. Economists who have served as advisers to presidents like to claim that "their" president was different, but that is mostly self-serving fantasy.

Herbert Hoover was probably the president most familiar with the scientific economics of his time. He had been secretary of commerce, which has a certain connection with economics; he was aware of the work on economic fluctuations going on at the National Bureau of Economic Research; and he sometimes consulted with Wesley Mitchell, the great expert on business cycles. His associates have left us the picture of Hoover alone at night in the Oval Office poring over charts and tables, trying to figure out when the Depression would end. Unfortunately, the economics of his time was inadequate and circumstances gave Hoover little latitude anyway.

Franklin Roosevelt was more cavalier about economics. At an early press conference he said that he was for "sound money," but when a reporter asked him what he meant by that he replied, "I don't intend to write a book about it." FDR was a co-conspirator in letting the Keynesian virus into the American body politic, but the only meeting between what many consider the greatest American president of the twentieth century and the greatest economist of that time was not a happy one. After their meeting in June 1934, Keynes told Frances Perkins, the secretary of labor, that he had "supposed the president was more literate, economically speaking." Roosevelt for his part said of Keynes: "He left a whole rigmarole of figures. He must be a mathematician rather than a political economist."

The most memorable statement by Harry Truman on the subject of economics was that he wished for a one-armed economist who would not say "on the one hand and on the other hand" all the time. This, of course, shows a deep misunderstanding of economics, too often shared by economists themselves.

No one ever accused Dwight D. Eisenhower of being an economist, although his economic policy showed considerable sophistication. He was accustomed to the military system of delegating responsibility and once told Arthur Burns* that he, Burns, would have been a good chief of staff in the army. Eisenhower had a certain facility for translating economic ideas into homespun language, like saying that there was no reason to balance the budget in the length of time it takes the earth to revolve around the sun. But there is no evidence that he had any interest in economics as a science.

John F. Kennedy is the president most credited by his advisers with having a personal interest in economics. I believe, however, that this is part of the mythology that developed around his figure. He once said that he could never remember the difference between fiscal and monetary policy, but he remembered that William McChesney Martin was chairman of the board of governors of the Federal Reserve System, and that Martin started with an "M," as did money, so he knew that the Federal Reserve was responsible for monetary policy. I have always wondered why he did not tell himself that Federal Reserve started with an "F" and therefore the Fed was in charge of fiscal policy. But the whole story does not sound to me like evidence of Kennedy's proficiency in economics.

I once asked Richard Nixon whether he had studied economics in college. He told me that he had taken an economics course at Whittier College, taught by the college preacher. According to Nixon, the preacher "didn't know the first thing about economics," and Nixon finished the course not knowing any more than that.

Nixon knew the names of the players in the field of economics—as he did in many other sports. He also liked the idea of being identified as sophisticated and modern about economics. That is why he was proud to say, after explaining the budget in 1971, "Now I am a Keynesian in

* [Chair of the President's Council of Economic Advisers]

economics." But that simply meant that he had found a rationalization for proposing an unbalanced budget. With all due respect, the most that can be said for Nixon and economic science is that he was tolerant of it and its practitioners.

Ronald Reagan majored in economics at Eureka College. He was also, more than any other president, associated with a unique brand of economics, "supply-side economics." But I believe the record will show that he came to the supply side out of political necessity before the 1980 campaign rather than out of, or at least prior to, intellectual conversion. Moreover, there is a question still about what Reagan meant by it. Did he mean that cutting taxes would actually raise revenues for the Treasury or that cutting taxes would reduce the revenue less than it would if there were no positive effect on taxable incomes? I once had the occasion to say that I hoped he would not oppose a tax increase on ideological grounds. He replied that his reason was not ideological. But he knew what a Moslem philosopher of the Middle Ages had said—that the king who came into office with high taxes left with low revenue. That suggested to me little knowledge of the basis of his own economic philosophy.

George Bush majored in economics at Yale. I attribute to his education there the most significant thing he ever said about economics, namely, his 1980 statement that the Reagan plan for tax reduction was "voodoo economics." He did not attain that height again.

To draw any conclusions at this time about Bill Clinton would be premature. We do not yet have the memoirs of his devoted advisers that will tell of pleasant conversations with the president about the theory of factor price equalization while jogging around the South Lawn. But one can say that up to this point Mr. Clinton's public discussion of economic policy, which is abundant, does not reveal consciousness of any economic theory.

2   *little experience*

A second generalization is that most presidents have had little experience in the private economy. Almost all have spent most of their adult lives in government. Ronald Reagan was the exception, partly because his adult life before coming into the presidency was unusually long. His experience was in a peculiar industry, motion pictures. The main lesson he derived from that experience was that if the tax rates were steeply progressive the movie stars would not make more than one picture a year.

The closest we have come to having a businessman in the White House recently was Ross Perot. Thinking about that possibility suggests why, although business experience may be useful, being only a businessman may be dangerous. A businessman has a single, clear, and objective goal—maximization of profits. His standard of performance is effectiveness in achieving that goal. That is exemplified by Mr. Perot's idea that what the president has to do is to lift up the hood, presumably of the economy, and fix it. The goal is known—to get the vehicle running. But the president has to exercise judgment about the priority to be given to each of a large number of competing goals. That calls for a person whose judgment we can trust, and business success is no indication of that.

3 Know enough

Many presidents know a great deal about the nuts and bolts of economic policy. To know economics is not to know all that needs to be known about economic policy. Most economists know little about the specific legislation that prescribes economic policy or about the administrative processes that carry it out. Many presidents know a great deal about that. This is especially true of presidents who have spent much time in Congress, as my own observation of Nixon and Ford confirms. Experience as governor has something, but less, to contribute. FDR, of course, dealt mainly with new programs that he had created himself, so his prior experience as governor of New York was of little value. Since Hoover we have had no president with much experience in the executive branch, unless Eisenhower's military experience is counted.

4 They're intelligent

A fourth broad generalization is that presidents are intelligent and capable people. They have won in a tough competition. Most show considerable ability in absorbing the part of an economic argument that is essential for their purposes, making decisions about it, and rearticulating the argument in a way that will be understandable and acceptable to the audience they care about—if not to the readers of *The American Economic Review*. I was always impressed by the ability of Richard Nixon to listen to a discussion among the Quadriad, which included three professional economists—George Shultz, Arthur Burns, and me—as well as Treasury Secretary John Connally, and at the end synthesize the discussion accurately and come to at least a tentative conclusion about it. I do not have such firsthand observation of other presidents, but I believe that many of them had that same ability.

5 not prepared

Presidents who come into office with specific promises are likely to be disappointed and disappointing. Preparation for office does not expose them to reality and campaigning encourages unrealistic and irresponsible promises.

We tend to forget that FDR campaigned in 1932 on a promise to balance the budget. Nixon, Reagan, and Bush failed to live up to the same promise. Kennedy came into office with a list of expenditure programs he was going to initiate or enlarge. When he could not get much of this agenda through Congress he turned to tax reduction, something that had not been part of his original plan. Nixon's turn to price and wage controls was, of course, diametrically opposite to his campaign talk about the free market. Clinton found that he had to raise taxes on the middle class, rather than cut them as he had promised. Probably the most famous reversal, because the promise had been made so emphatically, was Bush's abandonment of his "No new taxes!" pledge.

6 ~rely on members + advisors

Presidents have come increasingly to rely on members of their own administrations for economic advice. FDR, Truman, and Eisenhower looked to other political leaders, especially members of Congress, to businessmen, and to officials of labor unions. Kennedy sought the advice of Paul Samuelson, who was not in the government, and received, but did not seek, the advice of John Kenneth Galbraith, who was far enough away as ambassador to India to be called an outsider. But thereafter reliance on outside advice became less frequent.

The most formal effort to arrange outside advice was the establishment in 1981 under Reagan of the President's Economic Policy Advisory Board (PEPAB). This body consisted of about a dozen people, all of whom had been officials of previous Republican administrations and most of whom had been advisers in Reagan's 1980 campaign. PEPAB turned out to be mainly a claque telling the president how well he was doing.

The dominance of insiders in advising a president is perfectly natural. They see the president much more frequently than any outsiders could. The president has confidence that they share his interests; he chose them with that in mind and they have linked their futures to his. And on most subjects they have more information, or at least more up-to-date information, than outsiders do.

Still, outside advisers have something to contribute. The insiders have an inescapable tendency to believe that the policies they helped formulate are working, or will work, long after they have become doubtful. Outsiders are more likely to be objective in this regard.

7 ~~advised~~ advized from committee

The president usually gets his economic advice from a small special committee. On every major issue there are many officials who have something to say. Some presidents have tried to work with each of these officials separately and to synthesize their advice independently. This is said to have been Jimmy Carter's intention. But it is an unworkable procedure because it wastes the president's time and does not give him the benefit of a confrontation among the positions held by different officials.

At the opposite extreme is the effort to involve all the economic officials at once in all the big issues. Nixon tried that at the beginning of his [first] administration. He established a body called the Cabinet Committee on Economic Policy (CABCOMMECOPOL, as dubbed by William Safire) that included about a dozen people—about 10 cabinet secretaries, the director of the budget, and the chairman of the CEA [Council of Economic Advisers]. That also turned out to be unworkable. On any given subject it invited endless talk by people who were ignorant and had no responsibility.

Generally the advice-giving body has dwindled down to a small group that has as its core the three agencies whose advice the president wants on almost every economic matter—the Treasury, the Office of Management and Budget, and the Council of Economic Advisers. This group of three (the Troika) is supplemented as the occasion requires. For example, during the Nixon administration when we had both the price and wage controls and the energy crisis, officials responsible for those two areas usually joined the Troika. Umbrella organizations with more members often existed, but in those cases the work was done by subcommittees of the people most directly concerned with particular problems. The secretary of the treasury, as the senior economic official, usually served as chairman of the advisory group. There were, however, exceptions, as when Kenneth Rush, Nixon's own former law professor, served as leader in the final days of the Nixon administration, and William Seidman, [Gerald] Ford's old friend from Michigan, served in the Ford administration.

The Clinton administration has established a National Economic Council, and advertises it as evidence of the elevation of economic policy and coordination in the president's list of priorities. But this is evidence only of a characteristic that is common to most administrations—ignorance of historical precedents.

8   The prez makes economic policy, not economists

A final generalization is that economists do not make economic policy, presidents do. That is not to say that presidents reject the advice of their economists. It means two things.

First, the president has chosen his advisers. As Paul Samuelson once said, "The leaders of this world may seem to be led around through the nose by their economist advisers. But who is pulling and who is pushing? And note this: he who picks his own doctor from an array of competing doctors is in a real sense his own doctor. The prince often gets what he wants to hear."

Presidents tend to choose advisers who share their own values and views. When Nixon appointed Paul McCracken, Hendrik Houthakker, and me to his Council of Economic Advisers, McCracken said that the president had no choice, since we were the only three Republican economists in existence. That was a joke, for several reasons, one being that at the time I was a registered Democrat. But Nixon knew that we were against fine-tuning, and for budget balancing and free markets. So he chose the kind of advice he got, although we tried conscientiously to evaluate his options.

Second, even on the president's own team, among the advisers most sympathetic to him, there will be differences, and he will have to use his own judgment to choose among them. In fact, in most cases any single adviser, if he is behaving responsibly, will recognize that economics does not point unequivocally to one policy as being best. Then the president has to choose.

If well used, economics can serve a valuable function for a president. It can help him to see what his policy options are—both broadening and narrowing the list of options. That is, it may reveal some options that he might not have considered or rule out some options that are beyond the pale of eligibility. Economics can, up to a point, help the president to visualize the consequences of following different options. Beyond that, it is up to the president.

Discussion Questions

1. Compare and contrast Stein's argument about presidents and economic policy with Charles Morris's in Chapter 13 (see "It's Not the Economy, Stupid"). How much control over economic affairs does Stein think presidents have?

2. According to Stein, do presidents need to have a good understanding of economics to make good economic policy? What about other policy areas? How much policy-specific knowledge should presidents have?

THE DEBATE: THE REACH OF PRESIDENTIAL POWER

Just how powerful is the president? Have the fears of some of the Framers—that the president would degrade into an imperial despot—been realized, or does the separation of powers effectively check the President's ability to misuse the powers of office? We offer two perspectives here. In his chapter "Perspectives on the Presidency," Charles O. Jones argues that we should view the president as only one of the players in American government; the presidency exists only as one part of a set of institutions where responsibility is diffused, where the bulk of political activity takes place independent of the presidency, and where the different players and institutions learn to adjust to the others. Consider, for example, that the Republican 104th Congress and President Clinton managed to reach compromises on a number of important issues despite early predictions that they would never agree on anything.

Michael Lind, in contrast, believes that the presidents have far more power than they are given credit for, that the presidential office has grown to the point where it constitutes a "fourth branch" of government, and that the apparent weakness of recent presidents is an illusion. According to Lind, presidents remain supreme in foreign affairs (George Bush claimed the authority to carry out the Persian Gulf War with or without congressional authorization), they can interpret statutes according to their own whim, and they can rely on an enlarged staff that has grown into a "fourth branch" of government. Lind concludes that the apparent weakness of recent presidents is due more to transient political forces than any inherent institutional features; in fact, he believes that the imperial presidency "is merely waiting to be powered up and taken out of the hangar."

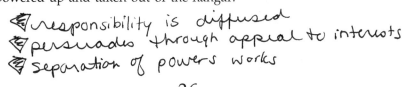

☑ responsibility is diffused
☑ persuades through appeal to interests
☑ separation of powers works

26
"Perspectives on the Presidency"
From *The Presidency in a Separated System*

CHARLES O. JONES

The president is not the presidency. The presidency is not the government. Ours is not a presidential system.

I begin with these starkly negative themes as partial correctives to the more popular interpretations of the United States government as presidency-centered. Presidents themselves learn these refrains on the job, if they do not know them before. President Lyndon B. Johnson, who had impressive political advantages during the early years of his administration, reflected later on what was required to realize the potentialities of the office:

> Every President has to establish with the various sectors of the country what I call "the right to govern." Just being elected to the office does not guarantee him that right. Every President has to inspire the confidence of the people. Every President has to become a leader, and to be a leader he must attract people who are willing to follow him. Every President has to develop a moral underpinning to his power, or he soon discovers that he has no power at all.[1]

To exercise influence, presidents must learn the setting within which it has bearing. President-elect Bill Clinton recognized the complexities of translating campaign promises into a legislative program during a news conference shortly after his election in 1992:

> It's all very well to say you want an investment tax credit, and quite another thing to make the 15 decisions that have to be made to shape the exact bill you want.
>
> It's all very well to say . . . that the working poor in this country . . . should be lifted out of poverty by increasing the refundable income tax credit for the working poor, and another thing to answer the five or six questions that define how you get that done.[2]

For presidents, new or experienced, to recognize the limitations of office is commendable. Convincing others to do so is a challenge. Presidents become convenient labels for marking historical time: the Johnson years, the Nixon years, the Reagan years. Media coverage naturally focuses more on the president: there is just one at a time, executive organization is oriented in pyramidal fashion toward the Oval Office, Congress is too diffuse an institution to report on as such, and the Supreme Court leads primarily by indirection. Public interest, too, is directed toward the White House as a symbol of the government. As a result, expectations of a president often far exceed the individual's personal, political, institutional, or constitutional capacities for achievement. Performance seldom matches promise. Presidents who understand how it all works resist the inflated image of power born of high-stakes elections and seek to lower expectations. Politically savvy presidents know instinctively that it is precisely at the moment of great achievement that they must prepare themselves for the setback that will surely follow.

Focusing exclusively on the presidency can lead to a seriously distorted picture of how the national government does its work. The plain fact is that the United States does not have a presidential system. It has a *separated* system. It is odd that it is so commonly thought of as otherwise since schoolchildren learn about the separation of powers and checks and balances. As the author of *Federalist* 51 wrote, "Ambition must be made to counteract ambition." No one, least of all presidents,

[margin note:] media & public

[margin note:] more focus on Prez

the Founders reasoned, can be entrusted with excessive authority. Human nature, being what it is, requires "auxiliary precautions" in the form of competing legitimacies.

The acceptance that this is a separated, not a presidential, system, prepares one to appraise how politics works, not to be simply reproachful and reformist. Thus, for example, divided (or split-party) government is accepted as a potential or even likely outcome of a separated system, rooted as it is in the separation of elections. Failure to acknowledge the authenticity of the split-party condition leaves one with little to study and much to reform in the post–World War II period, when the government has been divided more than 60 percent of the time.

Simply put, the role of the president in this separated system of governing varies substantially, depending on his resources, advantages, and strategic position. My strong interest is in how presidents place themselves in an ongoing government and are fitted in by other participants, notably those on Capitol Hill. The central purpose of this book is to explore these "fittings." In pursuing this interest, I have found little value in the presidency-centered, party government perspective, as I will explain below. As a substitute, I propose a separationist, diffused-responsibility perspective that I find more suited to the constitutional, institutional, political, and policy conditions associated with the American system of governing.

*   *   *

The Dominant Perspective

The presidency-centered perspective is consistent with a dominant and well-developed perspective that has been highly influential in evaluating the American political system. The perspective is that of party government, typically one led by a strong or aggressive president. Those advocating this perspective prefer a system in which political parties are stronger than they normally can be in a system of separated elections.

*   *   *

The party government perspective is best summarized in the recommendations made in 1946 by the Committee on Political Parties of the American Political Science Association.

> The party system that is needed must be democratic, responsible and effective. . . .
>
> An effective party system requires, first, that the parties are able to bring forth programs to which they commit themselves and, second, that the parties possess sufficient internal cohesion to carry out these programs. . . .
>
> The fundamental requirement of such accountability is a two-party system in which the opposition party acts as the critic of the party in power, devel-

oping, defining, and presenting the policy alternatives which are necessary for a true choice in reaching public decisions.[3]

Note the language in this summary: party in power, opposition party, policy alternatives for choice, accountability, internal cohesion, programs to which parties commit themselves. As a whole, it forms a test that a separated system is bound to fail.

I know of very few contemporary advocates of the two-party responsibility model. But I know many analysts who rely on its criteria when judging the political system. One sees this reliance at work when reviewing how elections are interpreted and presidents are evaluated. By this standard, the good campaign and election have the following characteristics:

- Publicly visible issues that are debated by the candidates during the campaign.
- Clear differences between the candidates on the issues, preferably deriving from ideology.
- A substantial victory for the winning candidate, thus demonstrating public support for one set of issue positions.
- A party win accompanying the victory for the president, notably an increase in the presidential party's share of congressional seats and statehouses so that the president's win can be said to have had an impact on other races (the coattail effect).
- A greater than expected win for the victorious party, preferably at both ends of Pennsylvania Avenue.
- A postelection declaration of support and unity from the congressional leaders of the president's party.

The good president, by this perspective, is one who makes government work, one who has a program and uses his resources to get it enacted. The good president is an activist: he sets the agenda, is attentive to the progress being made, and willingly accepts responsibility for what happens. He can behave in this way because he has demonstrable support.

It is not in the least surprising that the real outcomes of separated elections frustrate those who prefer responsible party government. Even a cursory reading of the Constitution suggests that these demanding tests will be met only by coincidence. Even an election that gives one party control of the White House and both houses of Congress in no way guarantees a unified or responsible party outcome. And even when a president and his congressional party leaders appear to agree on policy priorities, the situation may change dramatically following midterm elections. Understandably, advocates of party government are led to propose constitutional reform.

* * *

An Alternative Perspective

The alternative perspective for understanding American national politics is bound to be anathema to party responsibility advocates. By the rendition promoted here, responsibility is not focused, it is diffused. Representation is not pure and unidirectional; it is mixed, diluted, and multidirectional. Further, the tracking of policy from inception to implementation discourages the most devoted advocate of responsibility theories. In a system of diffused responsibility, credit will be taken and blame will be avoided by both institutions and both parties. For the mature government (one that has achieved substantial involvement in social and economic life), much of the agenda will be self-generating, that is, resulting from programs already on the books. Thus the desire to propose new programs is often frustrated by demands to sustain existing programs, and substantial debt will constrain both.

Additionally there is the matter of who *should* be held accountable for what and when. This is not a novel issue by any means. It is a part of the common rhetoric of split-party government. Are the Democrats responsible for how medicare has worked because it was a part of Lyndon Johnson's Great Society? Or are the Republicans responsible because their presidents accepted, administered, and revised the program? Is President Carter responsible for creating a Department of Energy or President Reagan responsible for failing to abolish it, or both? The partisan rhetoric on deficits continues to blame the Democrats for supporting spending programs and the Republicans for cutting taxes. It is noteworthy that this level of debate fails to treat more fundamental issues, such as the constitutional roadblocks to defining responsibility. In preventing the tyranny of the majority, the founders also made it difficult to specify accountability.

Diffusion of responsibility, then, is not only a likely result of a separated system but may also be a fair outcome. From what was said above, one has to doubt how reasonable it is to hold one institution or one party accountable for a program that has grown incrementally through decades of single- and split-party control. Yet reforming a government program is bound to be an occasion for holding one or the other of the branches accountable for wrongs being righted. If, however, politics allows crossing the partisan threshold to place both parties on the same side, then agreements may be reached that will permit blame avoidance, credit taking, and, potentially, significant policy change. This is not to say that both sides agree from the start about what to do, in a cabal devoted to irresponsibility (though that process is not unknown). Rather it is to suggest that diffusion of responsibility may permit policy reform that would have been much less likely if one party had to absorb all of the criticism for past performance or blame should the reforms fail when implemented.

Institutional competition is an expected outcome of the constitutional arrangements that facilitate mixed representation and variable electoral horizons. In recent decades this competition has been reinforced by Republicans settling into the White House, the Democrats comfortably occupying the House of Representatives, and, in very recent times, both parties hotly contending for majority status in the Senate. Bargains struck under these conditions have the effect of perpetuating split control by denying opposition candidates (Democratic presidential challengers, Republican congressional challengers) both the issues upon which to campaign and the means for defining accountability.

The participants in this system of mixed representation and diffused responsibility naturally accommodate their political surroundings. Put otherwise, congressional Democrats and presidential Republicans learn how to do their work. Not only does each side adjust to its political circumstances, but both may also be expected to provide themselves with the resources to participate meaningfully in policy politics.

Much of the above suggests that the political and policy strategies of presidents in dealing with Congress will depend on the advantages they have available at any one time. One cannot employ a constant model of the activist president leading a party government. Conditions may encourage the president to work at the margins of president-congressional interaction (for example, where he judges that he has an advantage, as with foreign and defense issues). He may allow members of Congress to take policy initiatives, hanging back to see how the issue develops. He may certify an issue as important, propose a program to satisfy certain group demands, but fail to expend the political capital necessary to get the program enacted. The lame-duck president requires clearer explication. The last months and years of a two-term administration may be one of congressional initiative with presidential response. The point is that having been relieved of testing the system for party responsibility, one can proceed to analyze how presidents perform under variable political and policy conditions.

* * *

In a separated system of diffused responsibility, these are the expectations:

- Presidents will enter the White House with variable personal, political, and policy advantages or resources. Presidents are not equally good at comprehending their advantages or identifying how these advantages may work best for purposes of influencing the rest of the government.
- White House and cabinet organization will be quite personal in nature, reflecting the president's assessment of strengths and weaknesses, the challenges the president faces in fitting into the ongoing government, and the political and policy changes that occur during the term of of-

fice. There is no formula for organizing the presidency, though certain models can be identified.

• Public support will be an elusive variable in analyzing presidential power. At the very least, its importance for any one president must be considered alongside other advantages. "Going public" does not necessarily carry a special bonus, though presidents with limited advantages otherwise may be forced to rely on this tactic.

• The agenda will be continuous, with many issues derived from programs already being administered. The president surely plays an important role in certifying issues and setting priorities, but Congress and the bureaucracy will also be natural participants. At the very least, therefore, the president will be required to persuade other policy actors that his choices are the right ones. They will do the same with him.

• Lawmaking will vary substantially in terms of initiative, sequence, partisan and institutional interaction, and productivity. The challenge is to comprehend the variable role of the president in a government that is designed for continuity and change.

• Reform will be an especially intricate undertaking since, by constitutional design, the governmental structure is antithetical to efficient goal achievement. Yet many, if not most, reforms seek to achieve efficiency within the basic separated structure. There are not many reforms designed to facilitate the more effective working of split-party government.

NOTES

1. Lyndon Baines Johnson, *The Vantage Point: Perspectives on the Presidency, 1963–1969* (New York: Holt, Rinehart and Winston, 1971), p. 18.
2. Ruth Marcus, "In Transition Twilight Zone, Clinton's Every Word Scrutinized," *Washington Post*, November 22, 1992, p. A1.
3. American Political Science Association, *Toward a More Responsible Two-Party System* (New York: Rinehart, 1950), pp. 1–2.

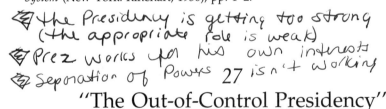

the Presidency is getting too strong
(the appropriate role is weak)
Prez works for his own interests
Separation of Powers 27 isn't working

"The Out-of-Control Presidency"

MICHAEL LIND

I

The president is shrinking. The institution of the presidency, magnified by half a century of world war and cold war, is rapidly diminishing in terms of both power and respect. The eclipse of Bill Clinton's

White House by Newt Gingrich's Republican Congress foreshadows what promises to be the new pattern. Meanwhile, Congress has become bloated and arrogant, swelling the ranks of its own staff while encroaching on the constitutional prerogatives of the White House. Congressional supremacy would be a disaster, particularly in foreign affairs. We cannot have 535 commanders in chief.

This tale of the decline of the presidency and the rise of Congress is the emerging conventional wisdom in Washington. It is familiar, widely believed—and wrong. In fact, the relative power of Bill Clinton and Newt Gingrich says more about the political abilities of those individual men during a passing moment in national life than about the relative legitimacy and effectiveness of the modern presidency and Congress. Congress actually continues to lose the long-term battle for legitimacy with the presidency, while the imperial presidency, thought to have perished during Watergate, is alive and well, having been quietly rehabilitated by Carter, Reagan and Bush.

And Clinton? The weakness of the Clinton administration is real. But that weakness is the result not of long-term trends but of a peculiar conjunction of politics and personality. Politically, a Democratic Party reduced to minority status and split into warring factions is facing a new Republican congressional majority intent, fleetingly, on electing a united Republican government in 1996. Personally, a president with no strong convictions confronts a speaker of the House who is a zealot.

When these patterns of politics and personality inevitably change, it will become clear that the presidency is still on top. Newt Gingrich, especially, does not represent traditional congressional power. The authority of the major speakers of the past was based on their control of their parties and their mastery of the House as an institution. Republican Joseph "Czar" Cannon, speaker during the 1900s, and Democrat Sam Rayburn, speaker during the 1940s and '50s, could take for granted enduring, parallel party and committee power structures in the House. Gingrich, by contrast, has spent his congressional career in the fluid environment of the post-Watergate House. He is a speaker like none before. In the 1970s, congressional reformers weakened the principle of seniority that had made possible the reign of powerful, often Southern, committee chairmen for most of the century. During the same period, the parties experienced a general decay: boss-dominated state and local party machines gave way to today's ideological factions, interest groups and media machines.

In this kaleidoscopic swirl, a strong speaker cannot rely on an established order; he has to improvise his own. Gingrich has done so, borrowing the techniques not of historic speakers of the House but of contemporary presidents. Gingrich resembles a president, for example, in that his formal party organization is but one instrument of his power. The others are his former personal patronage machine (GOPAC) that funds other members of Congress, his own corporate-funded think tank (the Progress and Freedom Foundation), extragovernmental conservative pressure groups and, not least, the media industries he manipulates so well. To the extent that Gingrich has predecessors in Congress, they are entrepreneurial types who have set up their own personally based organizations, such as the Hollywood liberal network of Henry Waxman and Howard Berman and Jesse Helms's ideological-conservative organization in North Carolina.

Gingrich has also adopted the sound-bite techniques of modern presidents and co-opted the presidential style in the 1994 congressional campaign, using the Contract with America in the manner of a presidential platform and, after victory, claiming a "mandate" from the people. (The mandate theory is implausible enough when presidents invoke it—only nineteen presidents have been elected with more than 50 percent of the vote. It is utterly absurd when applied to Congress, since a congressional majority can result from a shift of a few seats, in a few regions, and may say little or nothing about the national mood.)

That the speaker has been able to jury-rig a personal power base by borrowing the techniques of the plebiscitary presidency and maverick congressional ideologues testifies to the institutional weaknesses, not the strengths, of Congress. Indeed, the rise of Gingrich is a sign of the fall of Congress. Even in the unlikely event that Gingrich is followed by other Bonapartist speakers, the prominence of the speaker will likely prove to be temporary. A tribune-speaker like Gingrich would be no match for a tribune-president like Reagan.

* * *

The election of a Republican president, more than anything else, would show how illusory the apparent resurgence of Congress is. Republican or Democrat, the next president will be handed the Nixonian imperial presidency, with most of its powers intact and with a few new prerogatives added.

In foreign policy, the next president would discover that, like every president since Truman, he can wage war at will, without consulting Congress. Though he might consent to a congressional vote as a matter of public relations (as Bush did before the Gulf war), he is more likely to invoke his supposed "inherent" authority as commander-in-chief. If necessary, his aides will concoct legalistic rationalizations, citing dangers to U.S. citizens (Grenada, Panama), authorization by the United Nations (Somalia, Haiti), NATO treaty obligations (Bosnia) or anti-terrorism (Libya). Whether a liberal or a conservative, the next president will dismiss the War Powers Resolution as unconstitutional.

Nor is de facto presidential supremacy in foreign affairs limited to war-making, the next president will discover. Bush and Clinton will have bequeathed an important technique for ramming economic treaties through Congress with little debate: fast-track legislation, which limits the time allowed for debate and forbids amendments. The Senate, which the Founders wanted to have weigh treaty commitments deliberately, was granted a mere twenty hours to consider the treaty that committed the United States to the jurisdiction of the World Trade Organization (WTO). Perhaps the next president can insist that it be limited even further—to, say, half an hour or fifteen minutes.

In the domestic arena, the next president will find even greater enhancements of his prerogatives. Thanks to Jimmy Carter, who reformed the Senior Executive Service to give the White House more control over career bureaucrats, and Ronald Reagan, who politicized the upper levels of the executive branch to an unprecedented degree, the next president will find it easy to stack government with his spoilsmen or reward partisan bureaucrats. And he can thank George Bush for a technique that enhances presidential prerogative even further—signing laws while announcing he will not obey them.

Bush engaged in the greatest institutional power grab of any president since Nixon. In 1991 Bush, delivering a commencement address at Princeton, said: "[O]n many occasions during my presidency, I have stated that statutory provisions that violate the Constitution have no binding legal force." As Charles Tiefer points out in the *Semi-Sovereign Presidency*, Bush used "signing statements"—statements accompanying his signing of a bill, during which he announced he would not enforce this or that provision—to exercise an unconstitutional line-item veto.
. . . In one such instance, when Congress amended the Clean Air Act in 1990 to permit lawsuits by citizen groups against companies that had violated the act, Bush used a signing statement to declare, on supposed "constitutional grounds," that the executive branch would continue to act as though such citizen lawsuits were prohibited—nullifying the intent of Congress. Ironically, the "take care" clause of the Constitution was intended to compel the president to enforce laws he disapproved of (often, Colonial governors had refused to enforce parts of legislation passed by Colonial legislatures).

* * *

Yet another new instrument of arbitrary presidential power is the "czar." The institution of presidential commissars with vague, sweeping charges that overlap with or supersede the powers of department heads is utterly alien to the American constitutional tradition. Most famous is the celebrated position of "drug czar," . . . which arrogates duties that were previously handled perfectly adequately by agencies of Justice and other departments. Similarly, Vice President Dan Quayle acted as a "czar" as the head of Bush's Council on Competitiveness, designed to circumvent Cabinet heads and Congress in regulatory matters.

The White House staff that has ballooned since World War II seems close to becoming an extraconstitutional "fourth branch" of government. For obvious reasons, presidents have preferred to govern through their staffers, most of whom need not be confirmed by the Senate and many of whom are young and pliant, rather than deal with the heads of Cabinet departments and independent agencies, experienced people who are less likely to be mere tools of the president's will. Nor is it any accident that the major presidential scandals of the past generation—Watergate and Iran-contra—have involved attempts by shadowy and scheming courtiers of law-breaking presidents to circumvent or suborn the older, established executive departments. Every time the high-handed actions of White House courtiers drag a president into scandal, Congress, the press and the public denounce the courtiers—Nixon's plumbers, Ollie North—or the president and then, under a new president, sigh with relief: the system worked. That future presidents will almost certainly be tempted to use their White House staffers as Nixon and Reagan did is ignored.

The imperial presidency, then, is intact, merely waiting to be powered up and taken out of the hangar. If today's Congress has its way, the presidency will become even more imperial. Having captured Congress after half a century, the Republicans are hastening to give away the powers of the branch they control.

Some of these powers are formal, such as the line-item veto. States whose governors have the line-item veto don't balance their budgets any better than states without it. A line-item veto simply shifts the power to protect pork from a legislature to an executive. Giving the president the line-item veto would not balance the budget; it would merely permit the president to zero out the bounties of his enemies while keeping bounties for his allies. It would also wreck the constitutional design, which intended the branch closest to the people to have the last word on spending the people's money.

Other reforms backed by Republicans in Congress would weaken their institution indirectly. Term limits would reduce the expertise of representatives and senators—and boost their reliance on executive-branch experts, as well as on K Street lobbyists and think-tank flacks. Abolishing such independent congressional fact-finding agencies as the Office of Technology Assessment would hardly make a dent in the deficit but would make it easier for Congress to be hoodwinked by the executive branch it is supposed to oversee. A balanced budget amendment would shift the final arena of budgetary policy from the Capitol to federal courts, civil servants or White House staffers.

Why did the Republicans campaign so hard to win control of an institution whose powers they want to delegate to the White House? Most Republican members of Congress see themselves as members of their party first and members of Congress incidentally (as do most of their Democratic colleagues). The separation of powers was based on the assumption that, though there might be small factions in the different branches, there would not be permanent, large-scale parties intent on capturing all three branches of government simultaneously. Such simultaneous capture, of course, is the goal of the modern parties, each of which is organized primarily around electing presidents. The congressional Republicans are counting on a resumption of Republican presidential hegemony after what they hope will prove to be the interregnum of the Clinton years. Once a Republican is sworn in as president, his followers on Capitol Hill will rubber-stamp initiatives emanating from the White House. (That, at least, is the plan; as the troubles of FDR and LBJ show, the control of both branches by the same party does not mean even a strong president gets his way.)

* * *

II

James Madison, in a seldom-noted passage in Federalist No. 63, notes that American democracy differs from ancient republicanism not in replacing direct democracy with representative democracy but in the absence, from the American constitutional scheme, of politicians who could claim to represent the American people as a whole, in the manner of the Spartan Ephori and the Roman tribunes. There are no officers, Madison writes, "elected by the whole body of the people, and considered as the representatives of the people, almost in their plenipotentiary capacity. . . . The true distinction between these and the American governments lies in the total exclusion of the people in their collective capacity, from any share in the latter, and not in the total exclusion of the representatives of the people from the administration of the former." More pithily: the president does not "represent" the people as a whole. No officer and no branch "represents" the people as a whole. If one did, all other branches would seem parochial and illegitimate by comparison.

Madison and other Founders did not conceive of the president as a "representative" with a popular constituency at all. The president was to be a nonpartisan chief magistrate. The Founders designed the Electoral College with the expectation that presidents would frequently be chosen by the House, voting by states, from lists of candidates nominated by special state electors. The idea of the chief executive as chief representative is French, not American. As Louis Napoleon observed, his uncle Napoleon I "earnestly claimed the title of first Representative of the People, a title which seemed about to be given exclusively to members of the Legislative Body."

Andrew Jackson was the first president to claim, like the two Napoleons, to be a tribune of the masses: "The president is the direct representative of the American people." His attempt to act as a democratic monarch produced a backlash against such claims until the twentieth century. Lincoln justified his sweeping war powers using legal arguments, not the claim that he was the sole legitimate representative of the nation; indeed, this former Whig opponent of "King Andrew" Jackson was hesitant about suggesting legislation to Congress, for fear of arousing suspicions of executive supremacy. "My political education," he declared, "strongly inclines me against a very free use of any of these means [recommending legislation and using the veto], by the Executive, to control the legislation of the country. As a rule, I think it better that Congress should originate, as well as perfect its measures, without external bias."

The modern conception of the president as an all-powerful tribune of the people comes from Woodrow Wilson. Wilson preferred the British parliamentary system to the American system of separated powers: "It is, therefore, manifestly a radical defect in our federal system that it parcels out power and confuses responsibility as it does. The main purpose of the Convention of 1787 seems to have been to accomplish this grievous mistake." Wilson argued for a different, Rousseauian conception of democracy, in which the president is the nation personified: "The nation as a whole has chosen him, and is conscious that it has no other political spokesman." Wilson was the first president since Washington to address Congress in person. He argued that the American constitutional tradition should never obstruct an activist president: "If he rightly interpret the national thought and boldly insist upon it, he is irresistible; and the country never feels the zest of action so much as when its president is of such insight and caliber. Its instinct is for unified action, and it craves a single leader."

The Great Leader is to lead not only the United States but the world: "Our president must always, henceforth, be one of the great powers of the world, whether he act wisely or not." Not the United States, but the presidency itself, is to be a great power! Wilson called for the president to ignore the prerogatives of the House and the Senate in foreign policy and to present the legislature with treaties as faits accomplis [accomplished facts]. "He need disclose no step of negotiation until it is complete." This strategy backfired when Wilson tried to impose the League of Nations treaty on the Senate, but later presidents have used it effectively. Bush's military buildup in the Gulf more or less forced Congress to ratify his planned war against Iraq, while the Clinton administration followed its Republican predecessors in ramming through GATT and NAFTA by means of fast-track legislation.

The plebiscitary theory of the presidency, the theory that the president, like Napoleon I, is First Representative of the Nation, is shared by all presidents today, Republican or Democratic. Though most presidents are elected with a plurality, not a majority—meaning most voters wanted someone else—every president today claims a "mandate" from the "majority" of "the people," considered as an undifferentiated mass with one General Will. The nomination of today's presidential candidates by primaries, rather than by congressional caucuses (the first system) or brokered party conventions (the system from the 1830s to the 1960s), has reinforced the illusion that the president represents the popular will, unmediated by either government structures or party organizations. The plebiscitary president is free to run against Washington, and even against political parties, in the manner of Ross Perot.

Running against Washington means running against Congress and "the bureaucracy," which are treated as villains in a morality play. The virtuous heroes are the president, and (for conservatives) state governments and an idealized free market. Presidentialists build up the legitimacy of the presidency by grossly exaggerating the faults of Congress and the parts of the executive branch that the White House does not directly control, such as the civil service and the independent agencies.

Consider the myth that the budgets and staffs of Congress and federal agencies have been escalating out of control. The money spent on the entire legislative branch is minuscule compared to that which goes to the executive. As James Glassman has pointed out, "You can eliminate all of Congress . . . just get rid of the whole darn thing, you'd save exactly as much as you would save if you cut the defense budget by less than 1 percent." What's more, during the 1980s, appropriations for Congress actually fell, in real terms. U.S. representatives are paid much less than their counterparts in many other democracies, such as Japan, and their salaries compare unfavorably with those of professionals and corporate executives, many of whom have less onerous responsibilities. Congressional staff, though it has grown along with government in general, actually declined in the 1980s, while the number of employees in the executive and judicial branches expanded. As for turnover in Congress, the median length of terms for members of the House has been the same—four—from 1957 to the present. A twelve-year term limit for House members would hardly increase the present rate of turnover at all.

Why, then, do so many Americans believe Congress is a bloated, unresponsive, out-of-control institution? The American people have been misled by the propaganda of Republican members of Congress, who riddled the institution of Congress with bullet-holes in their bitter attack on the Democratic congressional majority. Voters have been misled, as well, by Democratic candidates, who profit in running against Congress and have no incentive to denounce the excesses of the office they hope to occupy.

Nor has the other half of the hated "Washington establishment," the federal bureaucracy, been growing out of control. Most Americans would be surprised to learn that in terms of manpower—around 2 million—the federal government has hardly grown at all since World

War II. State bureaucracies have grown faster, local bureaucracies even faster still. Federal funds, to be sure, have paid for much of the expansion of state and local bureaucracies, but conservatives have been concentrating their attacks not on federal funds, but on federal employees.

But, unlike Congress and the federal civil service, one federal institution does resemble the caricature of an ever-expanding, arrogant, corrupt bureaucracy. Since World War II, the White House staff and the Executive Office of the President have metastasized. Dwight Eisenhower made do with twenty-nine key assistants as his White House staff in 1960; Bush needed eighty-one in 1992. The Executive Office of the President, created in 1939, has grown to include thousands of bureaucrats functioning in a presidential court, a miniature executive branch superimposed on the traditional departmental executive envisioned by the Constitution.

Meanwhile, the number of presidential appointees and senior executives has ballooned an astonishing 430 percent between 1960 and 1992, from 451 to 2,393. Most of this growth has not been in jobs for the hated career civil servants, but in positions for upper-middle-class political activists who donated money to, or worked in, presidential campaigns, or roomed with somebody in college, or whatever.

Presidents have consistently sought to expand the number of these political appointees. Mostly from elite law, lobbying, business, banking or academic backgrounds, these courtiers have ever more elaborate titles: principal deputy assistant secretary, assistant associate office director. As the titles grow, the average tenure shrinks (down to eighteen months from three years during the Johnson years). The in-and-outers, once in, can't wait to get out and cash in their fancy titles for higher lobbyist fees or an endowed professorship of government. If conservatives are serious about cutting back government, why not abolish most of the post-'60s presidential branch? Where is the outcry against the expansion of the presidential bureaucracy? Why is a congressional barbershop a greater enormity than four White House staffers devoted to dealing with flowers?

Part of the answer may be that most politically active people in Washington long to get one of these mostly useless but impressive-sounding jobs. A stint as an assistant deputy secretary or associate division director can raise the fees of a lawyer or lobbyist in the private market or increase the prestige of a professor who returns to campus. By contrast, lawyers, lobbyists and professors do not salivate at the thought of jobs as congressional staffers. Some of Washington's elite journalists, too, rotate in —or have family members or friends connected to—jobs in the executive branch. While the presidency grows out of control, politicians and pundits bemoan the illusory expansion of Congress but never take aim at the White House.

Ideologues of all persuasions have an interest in promoting presidential prerogative. Why battle over years to build a congressional majority, when you can persuade a president to enact your favored reform—gays in the military or gays out of the military—with a stroke of a pen? This accounts for the spitting fury with which op-ed pundits, think tankers and spin doctors pounce on any president who does not use "the power of his office" to enact their pet projects by ukase,* preferably in the next few days or weeks.

Our press also helps the presidentialists of right and left by its obsessive focus on the person of the president at the expense of other executive branch officials, to say nothing of members of Congress and the judiciary. It makes for an easier story, of course, but laziness is no excuse for distorted coverage. Would the country crumble into anarchy if the major networks ignored the president for a week and followed the speaker, or the Senate majority leader, or the chief justice of the Supreme Court? Newspaper editors are just as bad. Several times, when I have written op-eds concerning government policy, I have been told by an editor, "You need to conclude by saying what the president should do."

Robert Nisbet has it right: "It is nearly instinctual in the political clerisy . . . to portray the president as the elected representative of the entire people . . . with congressmen portrayed as like mayors and city councilmen, mere representatives of wards, sections and districts." When appeals to plebiscitary legitimacy are insufficient, presidentialists can turn to the "court party" of legal and constitutional scholars, who are always ready with a defense of this or that supposed presidential prerogative. Judge Robert Bork, for example, has argued "that the office of the president of the United States has been significantly weakened in recent years and that Congress is largely, but not entirely, responsible." If one were comparing Reagan, Bush or Clinton to FDR at the height of his power, this might seem plausible. In a 200-year perspective it is absurd.

It is equally wrong to imagine cycles of presidential and congressional supremacy. As Theodore Lowi has pointed out, there have been only two eras: from 1789–1932, the U.S. was a congressional republic; after FDR, a presidential regime has been superimposed upon the former structure. In the remote era of the congressional republic, a president like William Henry Harrison could promise, as he did in his 1841 inaugural address, that he would: (a) refuse to run for a second term and support a constitutional amendment limiting presidents to a single term, (b) refuse to use the veto, except, in the manner of Washington and Madison, to send back laws he thought unconstitutional, and (c) seek to persuade Congress to remove the Treasury secretary from control by presidents, beginning with himself. All of this, in reaction to the "virtual monarchy" that Harrison and other Whigs perceived in the administration of An-

---

* [Edict, originally the imperial law of the Russian czar.]

drew Jackson, who never dreamed of wielding the power used routinely by even a modest contemporary president such as Bush.

III

That the views of a Harrison or a Madison seem so bizarre to us shows how hard it is to make the case for Congress today. Still, the case must be made. Presidential democracy is not democracy. In theory a single politician could be answerable to a constituency of hundreds of millions—but only in theory. In practice, the more presidential the U.S. government becomes, the less responsive it is to most Americans. Stunts like Jimmy Carter's "Phone the President" notwithstanding, any president will necessarily be remote from most citizens and accessible chiefly to concentric tiers of CEOs, big-money contributors, big-labor leaders, network anchors and movie stars. Any reader who doubts this should try to get appointments with both his or her representative and the president.

Under the Constitution of 1787, representative democracy in the United States means congressional democracy. Restoring congressional democracy must begin with discrediting in the public mind the plebiscitary theory of democracy. Americans must conclude that democracy does not mean voting for this or that elective monarch every four years and then leaving government to the monarch's courtiers. Democracy means continuous negotiation among powerful and relatively autonomous legislators who represent diverse interests in society.

This battle on the level of theory should be accompanied by a campaign at the level of symbolism. Congress, as an institution, is slighted by our public iconography. "We celebrate Presidents' Day," Thomas Langston notes in his new book about the presidency, *With Reverence and Contempt*. "Why not celebrate Speakers' Day? How about a Speakers' Memorial in Washington, D.C., . . . [or] proposing that famous speakers of the House, or senators, also ennoble our currency[?]" The royalism symbolized by pharanoic presidential libraries should be combated by a law requiring that all presidential papers hereafter be deposited permanently in a single, modest presidential library in Washington.

Changes in government organization would need to accompany changes in perceptions of congressional legitimacy. An electoral reform such as proportional representation for the House might actually strengthen the separation of powers; it would encourage a multiparty system, but the same multiparty coalition would not likely hold the House, Senate and White House at once. In a multiparty system, the president might also be forced to appoint coalition Cabinets, as in parliamentary regimes. He would have less influence over a Cabinet secretary of another party than over some servile functionary from his own.

As for the executive branch, the slow seeping of authority from Cabinet secretaries to courtiers needs to be halted and reversed. Congress could drastically cut the White House staff—if representatives aren't intimidated by the divinity that hedges our elected king. The depths of the reverence surrounding the presidential court became clear on Thursday, June 25, [1995] when a House Appropriations subcommittee released a plan to abolish the Council of Economic Advisers. "Democrats," *The New York Times* reported, "said they were startled at the lack of respect for a separate and equal branch of government displayed by the gesture, and even the subcommittee chairman, [Republican] Representative Jim Ross Lightfoot of Iowa, said he recognized that they could be accused of 'micromanagement' and lack of proper respect for the office of the president." It is as though the British parliament had threatened to cancel the changing of the guard at Buckingham Palace. The irony is particularly delicious since the Council of Economic Advisers was imposed on the presidency as part of the Employment Act of 1946 by conservatives in Congress hoping to check a free-spending White House.

The evolution of the council is typical of the process by which every augmentation of the executive branch in the interest of "efficiency" soon serves to enhance the power and prestige of the presidency. An even better example is the Office of Management and Budget, which was created after World War I as an independent agency (the Bureau of the Budget), drifted under presidential control during the administration of FDR and under Reagan became one of the White House's chief instruments of partisan control of executive agencies. Like a black hole, the presidency grows by absorbing ever more power and light.

Unlike a black hole, however, the presidency can be shrunk. Congress can not only scale back the White House to bring it in line with the staffs of prime ministers, but it can also make the heads of executive departments more independent of the president. The Founders expected department heads to carry out their duties more or less on their own (the Constitution gives the president the modest power to request reports in writing from department heads). The idea that department heads should be mere creatures of particular presidents is a modern misconception. Their duty is to use their own judgment to implement the laws passed by Congress, not to promote an imaginary "mandate" given the president by 40 or 45 percent of the voters. The Constitution permits Congress to vest the appointment of "inferior officers" in the heads of departments. Why not give it a try? It would strengthen their ties to their department head—and make it more likely that they would hang up when a White House staffer phoned to intervene, for the short-run political benefit of his boss, in the department's operations.

Reducing the president from a Latin American-style caudillo [military dictator] to something like a nineteenth- or eighteenth-century U.S. chief magistrate can be done, then, without revising the Constitution, merely by passing a few laws. It is hard to see how else the U.S. can avoid the completion of its slow evolution from a congressional republic into a full-fledged presidential state. The real trend in the world at the end of the twentieth century, it can be argued, is not so much from "dictatorship" to "democracy" as from unelected dictatorship to elective dictatorship—from Gorbachev to Yeltsin. The executive rulers have to face election, but rule by decree still tends to supplant rule by laws passed by representative legislatures. It could happen here—as the Founding Fathers feared it would. Ben Franklin, among others, predicted, "The Executive will always be increasing here, as elsewhere, till it ends in a monarchy." The new Republican majority in Congress should ponder that warning, as it sets about the further dismantling of the popular branch of government.

DISCUSSION QUESTIONS

1. Did the Framers succeed in establishing an executive with sufficient energy combined with sufficient checks to prevent abuse of power? What are some examples of how the system works? How it has broken down?

2. Examine Article II of the Constitution (in the appendix) and list the powers specifically granted to the president. Do these bear much relation to the powers identified by Jones and Lind? Judging from these readings, do you think the powers in the Constitution are sufficient or insufficient?

CHAPTER 6

Bureaucracy in a Democratic System

28
"The Study of Administration"

WOODROW WILSON

Until the late nineteenth century almost no one paid attention to how the government actually worked. Administrative positions were generally filled by political appointees who were supporters of elected officials, and there was little that resembled "management" in the contemporary sense. There was, however, a great deal of money distributed at the national level, and as scandals mounted over the manner in which the money was distributed, the demand for government accountability grew.

Reformers argued that government employees should be hired on the basis of their merit, rather than because of their political allegiance to one candidate or another. Others called for reforms in the administration of public programs. Nearly thirty years before he was president, Wilson, then a professor at Bryn Mawr College, wrote an article for the Political Science Quarterly *arguing that political scientists had neglected the study of public administration (or the problems involved in managing public programs). He contended that public administration should be carried out in accordance with scientific principles of management and efficiency, an argument that can be heard in contemporary debates over the need to "reinvent" government.*

It is the object of administrative study to discover, first, what government can properly and successfully do, and, secondly, how it can do these proper things with the utmost possible efficiency and at the least possible cost either of money or of energy. On both these points there is obviously much need of light among us; and only careful study can supply that light.

* * *

The science of administration is the latest fruit of that study of the science of politics which was begun some twenty-two hundred years ago. It is a birth of our own century, almost of our own generation.

Why was it so late in coming? Why did it wait till this too busy century of ours to demand attention for itself? Administration is the most obvious part of government; it is government in action; it is the executive, the operative, the most visible side of government, and is of course as old as government itself. It is government in action, and one might very naturally expect to find that government in action had arrested the attention and provoked the scrutiny of writers of politics very early in the history of systematic thought.

But such was not the case. No one wrote systematically of administration as a branch of the science of government until the present century had passed its first youth and had begun to put forth its characteristic flower of systematic knowledge. Up to our own day all the political writers whom we now read had thought, argued, dogmatized only about the *constitution* of government; about the nature of the state, the essence and seat of sovereignty, popular power and kingly prerogative; about the greatest meanings lying at the heart of government, and the high ends set before the purpose of government by man's nature and man's aims. . . . The question was always: Who shall make law, and what shall that law be? The other question, how law should be administered with enlightenment, with equity, with speed, and without fiction, was put aside as "practical detail" which clerks could arrange after doctors had agreed upon principles.

* * *

[However,] if difficulties of government action are to be seen gathering in other centuries, they are to be seen culminating in our own.

This is the reason why administrative tasks have nowadays to be so studiously and systematically adjusted to carefully tested standards of policy, the reason why we are having now what we never had before, a science of administration. The weightier debates of constitutional principle are even yet by no means concluded; but they are no longer of more immediate practical moment than questions of administration. It is getting to be harder to *run* a constitution than to frame one.

* * *

There is scarcely a single duty of government which was once simple which is not now complex; government once had but a few masters; it now has scores of masters. Majorities formerly only underwent government; they now conduct government. Where government once might follow the whims of a court, it must now follow the views of a nation.

And those views are steadily widening to new conceptions of state duty; so that at the same time that the functions of government are every day becoming more complex and difficult, they are also vastly multiplying in number. Administration is everywhere putting its hands to new undertakings. . . . Seeing every day new things which the state ought to do, the next thing is to see clearly how it ought to do them.

This is why there should be a science of administration which shall seek to straighten the paths of government, to make its business less businesslike, to strengthen and purify its organization, and to crown its dutifulness. This is one reason why there is such a science.

But where has this science grown up? Surely not on this side [of] the sea. Not much impartial scientific method is to be discerned in our administrative practices. The poisonous atmosphere of city government, the crooked secrets of state administration, the confusion, sinecurism, and corruption ever and again discovered in the bureaus at Washington forbid us to believe that any clear conceptions of what constitutes good administration are as yet very widely current in the United States.

* * *

American political history has been a history, not of administrative development, but of legislative oversight—not of progress in governmental organization, but of advance in law-making and political criticism. Consequently, we have reached a time when administrative study and creation are imperatively necessary to the well-being of our governments saddled with the habits of a long period of constitution-making. . . . We have reached . . . the period . . . when the people have to develop administration in accordance with the constitutions they won for themselves in a previous period of struggle with absolute power.

* * *

It is harder for democracy to organize administration than for monarchy. The very completeness of our most cherished political successes in the past embarrasses us. We have enthroned public opinion; and it is forbidden us to hope during its reign for any quick schooling of the sovereign in executive expertness or in the conditions of perfect functional balance in government. The very fact that we have realized popular rule in its fulness has made the task of *organizing* that rule just so much the more difficult. . . . An individual sovereign will adopt a simple plan and carry it out directly: he will have but one opinion, and he will embody that one opinion in one command. But this other sovereign, the people, will have a score of differing opinions. They can agree upon nothing simple: advance must be made through compromise, by a compounding of differences, by a trimming of plans and a suppression of too straightforward principles. There will be a succession of resolves running through a course of years, a dropping fire of commands running through a whole gamut of modifications.

* * *

Wherever regard for public opinion is a first principle of government, practical reform must be slow and all reform must be full of compromises. For wherever public opinion exists it must rule.

* * *

The field of administration is a field of business. It is removed from the hurry and strife of politics; it at most points stands apart even from the debatable ground of constitutional study. It is a part of political life only as the methods of the counting-house are a part of the life of society; only as machinery is part of the manufactured product. But it is, at the same time, raised very far above the dull level of mere technical detail by the fact that through its greater principles it is directly connected with the lasting maxims of political wisdom, the permanent truths of political progress.

The object of administrative study is to rescue executive methods from the confusion and costliness of empirical experiment and set them upon foundations laid deep in stable principle.

* * *

[A]dministration lies outside the proper sphere of *politics*. Administrative questions are not political questions. Although politics sets the tasks for administration, it should not be suffered to manipulate its offices.

* * *

There is another distinction which must be worked into all our conclusions, which, though but another side of that between administration and politics, is not quite so easy to keep sight of: I mean the distinction between *constitutional* and administrative questions, between those governmental adjustments which are essential to constitutional principle and those which are merely instrumental to the possibly changing purposes of a wisely adapting convenience.

* * *

A clear view of the difference between the province of constitutional law and the province of administrative function ought to leave no room for misconception; and it is possible to name some roughly definite criteria upon which such a view can be built. Public administration is detailed and systematic execution of public law. Every particular application of general law is an act of administration. The assessment and raising of taxes, for instance, the hanging of a criminal, the transportation and delivery of the mails, the equipment and recruiting of the army, and navy, etc., are all obviously acts of administration; but the general laws which direct these things to be done are as obviously outside of and above administration. The broad plans of governmental action are not administrative; the detailed execution of such plans is administrative. Constitutions, therefore, properly concern themselves only with those instrumentalities of government which are to control general law. Our federal constitution observes this principle in saying nothing of even the greatest of the purely executive offices, and speaking only of that President of the Union who was to share the legislative and policy-making functions of government, only of those judges of highest jurisdiction who were to interpret and guard its principles, and not of those who were merely to give utterance to them.

* * *

There is, [however,] one point at which administrative studies trench on constitutional ground—or at least upon what seems constitutional ground. The study of administration, philosophically viewed, is closely connected with the study of the proper distribution of constitutional authority. To be efficient it must discover the simplest arrangements by which responsibility can be unmistakably fixed upon officials; the best way of dividing authority without hampering it, and responsibility without obscuring it. And this question of the distribution of authority, when taken into the sphere of the higher, the originating functions of government, is obviously a central constitutional question.

* * *

To discover the best principle for the distribution of authority is of greater importance, possibly, under a democratic system, where officials serve many masters, than under others where they serve but a few. All sovereigns are suspicious of their servants, and the sovereign people is no exception to the rule; but how is its suspicion to be allayed by *knowledge*? If that suspicion could be clarified into wise vigilance, it would be altogether salutary; if that vigilance could be aided by the unmistakable placing of responsibility, it would be altogether beneficent. Suspicion in itself is never healthful either in the private or in the public mind. *Trust is strength* in all relations of life; and, as it is the office of the constitutional reformer to create conditions of trustfulness, so it is the office of the administrative organizer to fit administration with conditions of clear-cut responsibility which shall insure trustworthiness.

And let me say that large powers and unhampered discretion seem to me the indispensable conditions of responsibility. Public attention must be easily directed, in each case of good or bad administration, to just the man deserving of praise or blame. There is no danger in power, if only it be not irresponsible. If it be divided, dealt out in shares to many, it is obscured; and if it be obscured, it is made irresponsible. But if it be centered in heads of the service and in heads of branches of the service, it is easily watched and brought to book. If to keep his office a man must achieve open and honest success, and if at the same time he feels himself intrusted with large freedom of discretion, the greater his power the less likely is he to abuse it, the more is he nerved and sobered and elevated by it. The less his power, the more safely obscure and unnoticed does he feel his position to be, and the more readily does he relapse into remissness.

Just here we manifestly emerge upon the field of that still larger question—the proper relations between public opinion and administration.

To whom is official trustworthiness to be disclosed, and by whom is it to be rewarded? Is the official to look to the public for his meed of praise and his push of promotion, or only to his superior in office? Are the people to be called in to settle administrative discipline as they are called in to settle constitutional principles? These questions evidently find their root in what is undoubtedly the fundamental problem of this whole study. That problem is: What part shall public opinion take in the conduct of administration?

The right answer seems to be, that public opinion shall play the part of authoritative critic.

But the *method* by which its authority shall be made to tell? Our peculiar American difficulty in organizing administration is not the danger of losing liberty, but the danger of not being able or willing to separate its essentials from its accidents. Our success is made doubtful by that besetting error of ours, the error of trying to do too much by vote. Self-government does not consist in having a hand in everything, any more than housekeeping consists necessarily in cooking dinner with one's own hands. The cook must be trusted with a large discretion as to the management of the fires and the ovens.

* * *

The problem is to make public opinion efficient without suffering it to be meddlesome. Directly exercised, in the oversight of the daily details and in the choice of the daily means of government, public criticism is of course a clumsy nuisance, a rustic handling delicate machinery. But as superintending the greater forces of formative policy alike in politics and administration, public criticism is altogether safe and beneficent, altogether indispensable. Let administrative study find the best means for giving public criticism this control and for shutting it out from all other interference.

But is the whole duty of administrative study done when it has taught the people what sort of administration to desire and demand, and how to get what they demand? Ought it not to go on to drill candidates for the public service?

* * *

If we are to improve public opinion, which is the motive power of government, we must prepare better officials as the *apparatus* of government. . . . It will be necessary to organize democracy by sending up to the competitive examinations for the civil service men definitely prepared for standing liberal tests as to technical knowledge. A technically schooled civil service will presently have become indispensable.

I know that a corps of civil servants prepared by a special schooling and drilled, after appointment, into a perfected organization, with appropriate hierarchy and characteristic discipline, seems to a great many very thoughtful persons to contain elements which might combine to make an offensive official class—a distinct, semi-corporate body with sympathies divorced from those of a progressive, free-spirited people, and with hearts narrowed to the meanness of a bigoted officialism.

* * *

But to fear the creation of a domineering, illiberal officialism as a result of the studies I am here proposing is to miss altogether the principle upon which I wish most to insist. That principle is, that administration in the United States must be at all points sensitive to public opinion. A body of thoroughly trained officials serving during good behavior we must have in any case: that is a plain business necessity. But the apprehension that such a body will be anything un-American clears away the moment it is asked, What is to constitute good behavior? For that question obviously carries its own answer on its face. Steady, hearty allegiance to the policy of the government they serve will constitute good behavior. That *policy* will have no taint of officialism about it. It will not be the creation of permanent officials, but of statesmen whose responsibility to public opinion will be direct and inevitable. Bureaucracy can exist only where the whole service of the state is removed from the common political life of the people, its chiefs as well as its rank and file. Its motives, its objects, its policy, its standards, must be bureaucratic.

* * *

The ideal for us is a civil service cultured and self-sufficient enough to act with sense and vigor, and yet so intimately connected with the popular thought, by means of elections and constant public counsel, as to find arbitrariness or class spirit quite out of the question.

Having thus viewed in some sort the subject-matter and the objects of this study of administration, what are we to conclude as to the methods best suited to it—the points of view most advantageous for it?

Government is so near us, so much a thing of our daily familiar handling, that we can with difficulty see the need of any philosophical study of it, or the exact point of such study, should it be undertaken. We have been on our feet too long to study now the art of walking. We are a practical people, made so apt, so adept in self-government by centuries of experimental drill that we are scarcely any longer capable of perceiving the awkwardness of the particular system we may be using, just because it is so easy for us to use any system. We do not study the art of governing: we govern. But mere unschooled genius for affairs will not save us from sad blunders in administration. Though democrats by long inheritance and repeated choice, we are still rather crude democrats. Old as democracy is, its organization on a basis of modern ideas and conditions is still an unaccomplished work. The democratic state has yet to be equipped for carrying those enormous burdens of administration which the needs of this industrial and trading age are so fast accumulating.

* * *

We can borrow the science of administration [developed elsewhere] with safety and profit if only we read all fundamental differences of condition into its essential tenets. We have only to filter it through our constitutions, only to put it over a slow fire of criticism and distil away its foreign gases.

* * *

Our own politics must be the touchstone for all theories. The principles on which to base a science of administration for America must be principles which have democratic policy very much at heart. And, to suit American habit, all general theories must, as theories, keep modestly in the background, not in open argument only, but even in our own minds—lest opinions satisfactory only to the standards of the library should be dogmatically used, as if they must be quite as satisfactory to the standards of practical politics as well. Doctrinaire devices must be postponed to tested practices. Arrangements not only sanctioned by conclusive experience elsewhere but also congenial to American habit must be preferred without hesitation to theoretical perfection. In a word, steady, practical statesmanship must come first, closet doctrine second. The cosmopolitan what-to-do must always be commanded by the American how-to-do-it.

Our duty is to supply the best possible life to a *federal* organization, to systems within systems; to make town, city, county, state, and federal governments live with a like strength and an equally assured healthfulness, keeping each unquestionably its own master and yet making all interdependent and co-operative, combining independence with mutual helpfulness. The task is great and important enough to attract the best minds.

This interlacing of local self-government with federal self-government is quite a modern conception. . . . The question for us is, how shall our series of governments within governments be so administered that it shall always be to the interest of the public officer to serve, not his superior alone but the community also, with the best efforts of his talents and the soberest service of his conscience? How shall such service be made to his commonest interest by contributing abundantly to his sustenance, to his dearest interest by furthering his ambition, and to his highest interest by advancing his honor and establishing his character? And how shall this be done alike for the local part and for the national whole?

If we solve this problem we shall again pilot the world.

DISCUSSION QUESTIONS

1. Do you agree with Wilson's central proposition that politics and administration are separate things? Can you think of any examples where the two overlap? (Think about the differences and similarities between legislating and implementation.)

29

From *Bureaucracy: What Government Agencies Do and Why They Do It*

JAMES Q. WILSON

Woodrow Wilson was merely the first in a long line of reformers to suggest that government might be more efficient if it were run more like a business. The sentiment remains today. Perhaps a more "businesslike" government would issue our income tax refunds more promptly, protect the environment at lower cost, and impose fewer burdens on citizens. The catch is, we want all this at low cost and minimal intrusiveness in our lives, yet we want government bureaucracies to be held strictly accountable for the authority they exercise.

James Q. Wilson argues that government will never operate like a business, nor should it be expected to. His comparison of the Watertown, Massachusetts, Registry of Motor Vehicles (representing any government bureaucracy) with a nearby McDonald's (representing any private profit-seeking organization) shows that the former will most likely never service its clientele as does the latter. The problem is not bureaucratic laziness, but is instead due to the very different characteristics of public versus private enterprises. In order to understand "what government agencies do and why they do it," Wilson argues we must first understand that government bureaucracies operate in a political marketplace, rather than an economic one. The annual revenues and personnel resources of a government agency are determined by elected officials, not by the agency's ability to meet the demands of its customers in a cost-efficient manner. The government agency's internal structure and decision-making procedures are defined by legislation, regulation, and executive orders, while similar decisions in a private business are made by executive officers and management within the organization. And, perhaps most critical, a government agency's goals are often vague, difficult if not impossible to measure, and even contradictory. In business, by contrast, the task is simpler. The basic goal of a private business has always been to maximize the bottom line: profit. Although we should not approach the reform of government agencies the way we might a private bureaucracy, Wilson notes we should nevertheless try to make government bureaucracies operate more effectively and efficiently.

By the time the office opens at 8:45 A.M., the line of people waiting to do business at the Registry of Motor Vehicles in Watertown, Massachusetts, often will be twenty-five deep. By midday, especially if it is near the end of the month, the line may extend clear around the building.

Inside, motorists wait in slow-moving rows before poorly marked windows to get a driver's license or to register an automobile. When someone gets to the head of the line, he or she is often told by the clerk that it is the wrong line: "Get an application over there and then come back," or "This is only for people getting a new license; if you want to replace one you lost, you have to go to the next window." The customers grumble impatiently. The clerks act harried and sometimes speak brusquely, even rudely. What seems to be a simple transaction may take 45 minutes or even longer. By the time people are photographed for their driver's licenses, they are often scowling. The photographer valiantly tries to get people to smile, but only occasionally succeeds.

Not far away, people also wait in line at a McDonald's fast-food restaurant. There are several lines; each is short, each moves quickly. The menu is clearly displayed on attractive signs. The workers behind the counter are invariably polite. If someone's order cannot be filled immediately, he or she is asked to step aside for a moment while the food is prepared and then is brought back to the head of the line to receive the order. The atmosphere is friendly and good-natured. The room is immaculately clean.

Many people have noticed the difference between getting a driver's license and ordering a Big Mac. Most will explain it by saying that bureaucracies are different from businesses. "Bureaucracies" behave as they do because they are run by unqualified "bureaucrats" and are enmeshed in "rules" and "red tape."

But business firms are also bureaucracies, and McDonald's is a bureaucracy that regulates virtually every detail of its employees' behavior by a complex and all-encompassing set of rules. Its operations manual is six hundred pages long and weighs four pounds. In it one learns that french fries are to be nine-thirty-seconds of an inch thick and that grill workers are to place hamburger patties on the grill from left to right, six to a row for six rows. They are then to flip the third row first, followed by the fourth, fifth, and sixth rows, and finally the first and second. The amount of sauce placed on each bun is precisely specified. Every window must be washed every day. Workers must get down on their hands and knees and pick up litter as soon as it appears. These and countless other rules designed to reduce the workers to interchangeable automata were inculcated in franchise managers at Hamburger University located in a $40 million facility. There are plenty of rules governing the Registry, but they are only a small fraction of the rules that govern every detail of every operation at McDonald's. Indeed, if the DMV manager tried to impose on his employees as demanding a set of rules as those that govern the McDonald's staff, they would probably rebel and he would lose his job.

It is just as hard to explain the differences between the two organizations by reference to the quality or compensation of their employees.

The Registry workers are all adults, most with at least a high-school education; the McDonald's employees are mostly teenagers, many still in school. The Registry staff is well-paid compared to the McDonald's workers, most of whom receive only the minimum wage. When labor shortages developed in Massachusetts during the mid-1980s, many McDonald's stores began hiring older people (typically housewives) of the same sort who had long worked for the Registry. They behaved just like the teenagers they replaced.

Not only are the differences between the two organizations not to be explained by reference to "rules" or "red tape" or "incompetent workers," the differences call into question many of the most frequently mentioned complaints about how government agencies are supposed to behave. For example: "Government agencies are big spenders." The Watertown office of the Registry is in a modest building that can barely handle its clientele. The teletype machine used to check information submitted by people requesting a replacement license was antiquated and prone to errors. Three or four clerks often had to wait in line to use equipment described by the office manager as "personally signed by Thomas Edison." No computers or word processors were available to handle the preparation of licenses and registrations; any error made by a clerk while manually typing a form meant starting over again on another form.

Or: "Government agencies hire people regardless of whether they are really needed." Despite the fact that the citizens of Massachusetts probably have more contact with the Registry than with any other state agency, and despite the fact that these citizens complain more about Registry service than about that of any other bureau, the Watertown branch, like all Registry offices, was seriously understaffed. In 1981, the agency lost 400 workers—about 25 percent of its work force—despite the fact that its workload was rising.

Or: "Government agencies are imperialistic, always grasping for new functions." But there is no record of the Registry doing much grasping, even though one could imagine a case being made that the state government could usefully create at Registry offices "one-stop" multi-service centers where people could not only get drivers' licenses but also pay taxes and parking fines, obtain information, and transact other official business. The Registry seemed content to provide one service.

In short, many of the popular stereotypes about government agencies and their members are either questionable or incomplete. To explain why government agencies behave as they do, it is not enough to know that they are "bureaucracies"—that is, it is not enough to know that they are big, or complex, or have rules. What is crucial is that they are *government* bureaucracies. As the preceding chapters should make clear, not all government bureaucracies behave the same way or suffer from the same problems. There may even be registries of motor vehicles in other states that do a better job than the one in Massachusetts. But all government agencies have in common certain characteristics that tend to make their management far more difficult than managing a McDonald's. These common characteristics are the constraints of public agencies.

The key constraints are three in number. To a much greater extent than is true of private bureaucracies, government agencies (1) cannot lawfully retain and devote to the private benefit of their members the earnings of the organization, (2) cannot allocate the factors of production in accordance with the preferences of the organization's administrators, and (3) must serve goals not of the organization's own choosing. Control over revenues, productive factors, and agency goals is all vested to an important degree in entities external to the organization—legislatures, courts, politicians, and interest groups. Given this, agency managers must attend to the demands of these external entities. As a result, government management tends to be driven by the *constraints* on the organization, not the *tasks* of the organization. To say the same thing in other words, whereas business management focuses on the "bottom line" (that is, profits), government management focuses on the "top line" (that is, constraints). Because government managers are not as strongly motivated as private ones to define the tasks of their subordinates, these tasks are often shaped by [other] factors.

* * *

Revenues and Incentives

In the days leading up to September 30, the federal government is Cinderella, courted by legions of individuals and organizations eager to get grants and contracts from the unexpended funds still at the disposal of each agency. At midnight on September 30, the government's coach turns into a pumpkin. That is the moment—the end of the fiscal year—at which every agency, with a few exceptions, must return all unexpended funds to the Treasury Department.

Except for certain quasi-independent government corporations, such as the Tennessee Valley Authority, no agency may keep any surplus revenues (that is, the difference between the funds it received from a congressional appropriation and those it needed to operate during the year). By the same token, any agency that runs out of money before the end of the fiscal year may ask Congress for more (a "supplemental appropriation") instead of being forced to deduct the deficit from any accumulated cash reserves. Because of these fiscal rules agencies do not have a material incentive to economize: Why scrimp and save if you cannot keep the results of your frugality?

Nor can individual bureaucrats lawfully capture for their personal use any revenue surpluses. When a private firm has a good year, many of its officers and workers may receive bonuses. Even if no bonus is paid, these employees may buy stock in the firm so that they can profit from any growth in earnings (and, if they sell the stock in a timely manner, profit from a drop in earnings). Should a public bureaucrat be discovered trying to do what private bureaucrats routinely do, he or she would be charged with corruption.

We take it for granted that bureaucrats should not profit from their offices and nod approvingly when a bureaucrat who has so benefited is indicted and put on trial. But why should we take this view? Once a very different view prevailed. In the seventeenth century, a French colonel would buy his commission from the king, take the king's money to run his regiment, and pocket the profit. At one time a European tax collector was paid by keeping a percentage of the taxes he collected. In this country, some prisons were once managed by giving the warden a sum of money based on how many prisoners were under his control and letting him keep the difference between what he received and what it cost him to feed the prisoners. Such behavior today would be grounds for criminal prosecution. Why? What has changed?

Mostly we the citizenry have changed. We are creatures of the Enlightenment: We believe that the nation ought not to be the property of the sovereign; that laws are intended to rationalize society and (if possible) perfect mankind; and that public service ought to be neutral and disinterested. We worry that a prison warden paid in the old way would have a strong incentive to starve his prisoners in order to maximize his income; that a regiment supported by a greedy colonel would not be properly equipped; and that a tax collector paid on a commission basis would extort excessive taxes from us. These changes reflect our desire to eliminate moral hazards—namely, creating incentives for people to act wrongly. But why should this desire rule out more carefully designed compensation plans that would pay government managers for achieving officially approved goals and would allow efficient agencies to keep any unspent part of their budget for use next year?

Part of the answer is obvious. Often we do not know whether a manager or an agency has achieved the goals we want because either the goals are vague or inconsistent, or their attainment cannot be observed, or both. Bureau chiefs in the Department of State would have to go on welfare if their pay depended on their ability to demonstrate convincingly that they had attained their bureaus' objectives.

But many government agencies have reasonably clear goals toward which progress can be measured. The Social Security Administration, the Postal Service, and the General Services Administration all come to mind. Why not let earnings depend importantly on performance? Why not let agencies keep excess revenues?

*   *   *

But in part it is because we know that even government agencies with clear goals and readily observable behavior only can be evaluated by making political (and thus conflict-ridden) judgments. If the Welfare Department delivers every benefit check within 24 hours after the application is received, Senator Smith may be pleased but Senator Jones will be irritated because this speedy delivery almost surely would require that the standards of eligibility be relaxed so that many ineligible clients would get money. There is no objective standard by which the tradeoff between speed and accuracy in the Welfare Department can be evaluated. Thus we have been unwilling to allow welfare employees to earn large bonuses for achieving either speed or accuracy.

The inability of public managers to capture surplus revenues for their own use alters the pattern of incentives at work in government agencies. Beyond a certain point additional effort does not produce additional earnings. (In this country, Congress from time to time has authorized higher salaries for senior bureaucrats but then put a cap on actual payments to them so that the pay increases were never received. This was done to insure that no bureaucrat would earn more than members of Congress at a time when those members were unwilling to accept the political costs of raising their own salaries. As a result, the pay differential between the top bureaucratic rank and those just below it nearly vanished.) If political constraints reduce the marginal effect of money incentives, then the relative importance of other, nonmonetary incentives will increase. . . .

That bureaucratic performance in most government agencies cannot be linked to monetary benefits is not the whole explanation for the difference between public and private management. There are many examples of private organizations whose members cannot appropriate money surpluses for their own benefit. Private schools ordinarily are run on a nonprofit basis. Neither the headmaster nor the teachers share in the profit of these schools; indeed, most such schools earn no profit at all and instead struggle to keep afloat by soliciting contributions from friends and alumni. Nevertheless, the evidence is quite clear that on the average, private schools, both secular and denominational, do a better job than public ones in educating children. Moreover, as political scientists John Chubb and Terry Moe have pointed out, they do a better job while employing fewer managers. Some other factors are at work. One is the freedom an organization has to acquire and use labor and capital.

Acquiring and Using the Factors of Production

A business firm acquires capital by retaining earnings, borrowing money, or selling shares of ownership; a government agency (with some exceptions) acquires capital by persuading a legislature to appropriate it. A business firm hires, promotes, demotes, and fires personnel with considerable though not perfect freedom; a federal government agency is told by Congress how many persons it can hire and at what rate of pay, by the Office of Personnel Management (OPM) what rules it must follow in selecting and assigning personnel, by the Office of Management and Budget (OMB) how many persons of each rank it may employ, by the Merit Systems Protection Board (MSPB) what procedures it must follow in demoting or discharging personnel, and by the courts whether it has faithfully followed the rules of Congress, OPM, OMB, and MSPB. A business firm purchases goods and services by internally defined procedures (including those that allow it to buy from someone other than the lowest bidder if a more expensive vendor seems more reliable), or to skip the bidding procedure altogether in favor of direct negotiations; a government agency must purchase much of what it uses by formally advertising for bids, accepting the lowest, and keeping the vendor at arm's length. When a business firm develops a good working relationship with a contractor, it often uses that vendor repeatedly without looking for a new one; when a government agency has a satisfactory relationship with a contractor, ordinarily it cannot use the vendor again without putting a new project out for a fresh set of bids. When a business firm finds that certain offices or factories are no longer economical it will close or combine them; when a government agency wishes to shut down a local office or military base often it must get the permission of the legislature (even when formal permission is not necessary, informal consultation is). When a business firm draws up its annual budget each expenditure item can be reviewed as a discretionary amount (except for legally mandated payments of taxes to government and interest to banks and bondholders); when a government agency makes up its budget many of the detailed expenditure items are mandated by the legislature.

All these complexities of doing business in or with the government are well-known to citizens and firms. These complexities in hiring, purchasing, contracting, and budgeting often are said to be the result of the "bureaucracy's love of red tape." But few, if any, of the rules producing this complexity would have been generated by the bureaucracy if left to its own devices, and many are as cordially disliked by the bureaucrats as by their clients. These rules have been imposed on the agencies by external actors, chiefly the legislature. They are not bureaucratic rules but *political* ones. In principle the legislature could allow the Social Security Administration, the Defense Department, or the New York City public school system to follow the same rules as IBM, General Electric, or Harvard University. In practice they could not. The reason is politics, or more precisely, democratic politics.

* * *

Public versus Private Management

What distinguishes public from private organizations is neither their size nor their desire to "plan" (that is, control) their environments but rather the rules under which they acquire and use capital and labor. General Motors acquires capital by selling shares, issuing bonds, or retaining earnings; the Department of Defense acquires it from an annual appropriation by Congress. GM opens and closes plants, subject to certain government regulations, at its own discretion; DOD opens and closes military bases under the watchful guidance of Congress. GM pays its managers with salaries it sets and bonuses tied to its earnings; DOD pays its managers with salaries set by Congress and bonuses (if any) that have no connection with organizational performance. The number of workers in GM is determined by its level of production; the number in DOD by legislation and civil-service rules.

What all this means can be seen by returning to the Registry of Motor Vehicles and McDonald's. Suppose you were just appointed head of the Watertown office of the Registry and you wanted to improve service there so that it more nearly approximated the service at McDonald's. Better service might well require spending more money (on clerks, equipment, and buildings). Why should your political superiors give you that money? It is a cost to them if it requires either higher taxes or taking funds from another agency; offsetting these real and immediate costs are dubious and postponed benefits. If lines become shorter and clients become happier, no legislator will benefit. There may be fewer complaints, but complaints are episodic and have little effect on the career of any given legislator. By contrast, shorter lines and faster service at McDonald's means more customers can be served per hour and thus more money can be earned per hour. A McDonald's manager can estimate the marginal product of the last dollar he or she spends on improving service; the Registry manager can generate no tangible return on any expenditure he or she makes and thus cannot easily justify the expenditure.

Improving service at the Registry may require replacing slow or surly workers with quick and pleasant ones. But you, the manager, can neither hire nor fire them at will. You look enviously at the McDonald's manager who regularly and with little notice replaces poor workers with better ones. Alternatively, you may wish to mount an extensive training program (perhaps creating a Registration University to match McDonald's Hamburger University) that would imbue a culture of service in your employees. But unless the Registry were so large an agency that the legislature would neither notice nor care about funds spent for this purpose—and it is not that large—you would have a tough time convincing anybody that this was not a wasteful expenditure on a frill project.

If somehow your efforts succeed in making Registry clients happier, you can take vicarious pleasure in it; in the unlikely event a client seeks you out to thank you for those efforts, you can bask in a moment's worth of glory. Your colleague at McDonald's who manages to make customers happier may also derive some vicarious satisfaction from the improvement but in addition he or she will earn more money owing to an increase in sales.

In time it will dawn on you that if you improve service too much, clients will start coming to the Watertown office instead of going to the Boston office. As a result, the lines you succeeded in shortening will become longer again. If you wish to keep complaints down, you will have to spend even more on the Watertown office. But if it was hard to persuade the legislature to do that in the past, it is impossible now. Why should the taxpayer be asked to spend more on Watertown when the Boston office, fully staffed (naturally, no one was laid off when the clients disappeared), has no lines at all? From the legislature's point of view the correct level of expenditure is not that which makes one office better than another but that which produces an equal amount of discontent in all offices.

Finally, you remember that your clients have no choice: The Registry offers a monopoly service. It and only it supplies drivers' licenses. In the long run all that matters is that there are not "too many" complaints to the legislature about service. Unlike McDonald's, the Registry need not fear that its clients will take their business to Burger King or to Wendy's. Perhaps you should just relax.

If this were all there is to public management it would be an activity that quickly and inevitably produces cynicism among its practitioners. But this is not the whole story. For one thing, public agencies differ in the kinds of problems they face. For another, many public managers try hard to do a good job even though they face these difficult constraints.

DISCUSSION QUESTIONS

1. Wilson argues that McDonald's and the Department of Motor Vehicles operate differently because of the inherent differences between public and private organizations. Apply his reasoning to other cases, for instance the U.S. Postal Service and Federal Express, or any other public-private combination. Think about the goals of the organizations, who controls the organizations, how you distinguish success from failure, and the consequences of failure.

2. What would be the advantages and disadvantages of making government work more like a business?

30
"National Performance Review: An Analysis"

Donald Kettl

The most recent attempt to make government agencies more efficient and accountable is the "reinventing government" movement. Under the leadership of Vice President Al Gore, the National Performance Review (NPR) issued a report in 1993 suggesting ways to "reinvent" federal agencies. Citizens, the report argues, should be treated like valued customers; bureaucratic power should be decentralized, providing more authority to employees on the front line so that they can serve their "customers" more effectively; and excessive layers of management should be eliminated.

The political scientist Donald Kettl offers an analysis of the NPR report and its recommendations for the way in which government programs are managed. He reminds the reader of the critical importance of the political context within which any bureaucratic reform takes place. Prescriptions for bureaucratic reform based upon the operation of private sector organizations might make logical sense, but contrary to the argument made by Woodrow Wilson, politics cannot be removed from the administration of government. Hence, any effort to reform the administration of government, such as the NPR, will require the political support of elected officials, of bureaucrats affected by the changes, and of the American public.

Vice President Al Gore's National Performance Review (NPR), with a report issued in September 1993, promised nothing less than a revolutionary reinvention of the federal government. Critics dismissed it as hollow rhetoric, and some scholars criticized it as dangerous. In its first year, however, the NPR has produced impressive results and a genuine start on changing the culture of government simplification of some rules and procedures, especially by eliminating the onerous Federal Personnel Manual and the much-hated SF-171 job application form; a reform of the procurement process; improved top-level coordination of the government's management; and the stimulation of widespread innovation by federal managers through "reinvention labs."

The Short Term

The NPR produced more than almost anyone, including perhaps the reinventors themselves, believed possible. Even when the movement produced sketchy results, the problems it attacked usually were the right ones. To get the NPR moving, however, the reinventers made short-term tactical decisions to get quick wins. The quick wins, though, have come at the cost of building the foundation for lasting success. As a result, the NPR is not now self-sustaining. It has shown great potential, but the risk is that the NPR will become just a short-term political tactic instead of a lasting reform. Two problems, in particular, have plagued the NPR.

Preoccupation with Savings over Performance Improvement

Of course, a government that works better can cost less, as the NPR report's subtitle suggests. Streamlining procurement can save money, while a more customer-focused government can tailor programs more carefully to citizens' needs. In practice, however, seeking big savings in short order can undermine the broader effort for management improvement and increase costs in the long run. The largest single chunk of the NPR's promised $108 billion savings was to come from downsizing the federal work force ($40.4 billion). The downsizing was to be the product of the NPR's management improvements. The Clinton administration's eagerness for quick savings, however, led officials to shrink employment first and let the management improvements follow.

On one level, the focus on budget savings quickly alienated many government workers. The NPR had built a strong pro-bureaucrat case. It told public employees that the government's performance problems were the fault of the system, not of its workers. It also held out the promise of much greater flexibility for managers ("empowerment") and a reduction in red tape. The prospect of reducing federal employment by 272,900 workers, however, quickly preoccupied many managers, and, for many government workers, soon became the defining reality of the NPR.

On another level, the savings proved far easier to promise than to deliver. The administration has had recurring disputes with members of Congress and the Congressional Budget Office about the savings from individual proposals. These disputes diminished congressional support for the NPR and delayed pieces of the legislative program, especially the bill that provided buyout payments to employees who agreed to leave the federal service.

Moreover, the savings proved the hardest element of the NPR to judge. Some long-term savings required short-term investments, like the buyouts. Some short-term savings risked increasing long-term costs, especially if downsizing in the absence of a "reinvented" workplace led the wrong employees to leave or weakened government management. Beyond counting federal workers who left the government, putting hard numbers on the NPR's other savings required extraordinary feats of budgetary analysis. That complexity not only increased the difficulty of assessing the NPR's savings but also sometimes surrounded the NPR with debate of such technical detail as to undermine their political value. In the meantime, of course, the downsizing led many bureaucrats not to enlist in the NPR's revolution, but to hope that the NPR would soon go away. And since the public assumes that the NPR has long since produced the promised savings, the reinventers face the task of living up to the pledge as the task of achieving it—without undermining the rest of the movement—becomes ever greater.

Lack of an Explicit Strategy for Dealing with Congress

NPR officials initially believed that they could accomplish most of their reforms without seeking congressional approval. The lesson of the first year, however, is that virtually no reform that really matters can be achieved without at least implicit congressional support. The NPR has not yet developed a full strategy for winning it.

Congress embraced the broad downsizing initiative and, in fact, increased the reduction from 252,000 to 272,900 employees. For months, however, members stalled the buyout bill required to produce the savings, in part because of uncertainty about whether it would cost or save money in the short run. The House, meanwhile, voted to exempt the Veterans Health Administration, with 212,000 employees, from the downsizing, so as not to threaten veterans' health care. The Senate then voted to exempt federal criminal justice activities, so as not to jeopardize the war on crime. Many members of Congress supported the NPR in the whole, but then tugged at its individual threads in ways that threatened to unravel it.

In the beginning, the NPR had concentrated on launching its report. It had not developed a strategy for implementing its recommendations beyond trying to enlist legions of bureaucrats throughout the agencies in the cause and hoping that the power of the ideas would defuse opposition. Members of Congress had everything to gain from embracing the broad principles of reinvention and then protecting their constituents and favorite programs behind the scenes in committee rooms and little-noticed riders to complex bills.

In sum: The NPR, in its first year, accomplished far more than cynics suggested might be possible. It has launched a broad reform movement in the right direction, and it has been asking the right questions. Nevertheless, and this is the NPR's critical problem, the short-term accommodations it made to get the movement going weakened its chances for long-term success. It is not now a self-sustaining revolution, and considerable work needs to be done to move the invasion from a beachhead to a breakout, and then from a breakout to a conquest.

The Long Term

For the NPR to endure, it will need to build congressional support. That will require striking a different kind of bargain between the executive branch and Congress. The NPR's recommendations need congressional support while Congress needs a strategy for meaningful oversight. Both the president and Congress have a strong interest in attaining this uneasy balance. The stakes for the executive branch, both political and managerial, are clear. Moreover, especially in Congress's Governmental Affairs and Government Operations Committees,* there is fresh interest in defining a new congressional role in management. Without finding a new kind of bargain between the branches, it would be easy for the congressional micro-politics of the NPR to nibble away its key elements. Launching the reinvention revolution was the easy part. Sustaining the revolution will require much harder, and far less glamorous work. It will require considerable creativity, far more than either the reinventers or their critics have demonstrated, in recognizing and solving the four critical underlying problems that lie beyond the beachhead.

Tensions

There really is no such thing as *the* NPR. It has, in fact, been a three-front campaign: to shrink the size and cost of the government; to spread a new gospel of reinvention in areas like procurement reform and customer service; and to encourage an army of reinventers throughout the federal government. Its outside game, however, based on shrinking the government, undercut its efforts to transform the government's inside workers because it alienated many public employees. Long-term success requires the NPR to ensure that, on each of its fronts, its strategies complement—not disrupt—each other.

Capacity

The NPR report argued the need to bulldoze away overbearing forces of supervision, authority, and oversight. The report, however, was far weaker on what ought to spring up in their place. The overwhelming lesson of the last generation of policy experimentation in the United States is that government programs do not manage themselves. Rather, success depends on finding the institutions, processes, money, technology, and especially people—that is, the capacity—to do the job.

Will a reinvented government transform itself into a leaner govern-

---

* These are, respectively, the Senate and House committees with the formal responsibility of overseeing the management and administrative operations of the Executive branch. In 1995, the House changed the name of its committee from Government Operations to Government Reform and Oversight.

ment, faster on its feet and better able to adapt to the dizzying pace of change? Or will the legacy of reinvention be an even more hollow government with far less capacity to do its job, a government managed by employees with even less incentive to do their jobs well? The former would produce a truly revolutionary change. The latter would perpetuate the cycle of raised expectations, disappointing results, increased inefficiency, and public cynicism. Long-term success requires the NPR not only to explain what it wants to sweep away but, more important, to define what ought to spring up in the place of dysfunctional systems. Strengthening government capacity will require more than adherence to the broad themes of employee empowerment and customer service.

Ideas

The NPR built on ambitious ideas about cutting red tape, putting customers first, empowering employees, and cutting back to basics. Far less clear, however, was what those concepts actually meant. When do procedural due process and proper administrative safeguards become red tape? Who are the government's customers and how can they be served? Does customer service contradict other public goals? What would it take to empower employees, and what risks would empowerment create? Who decides what the basics are? In *Reinventing Government*, a driving spirit of the NPR, David Osborne and Ted Gaebler make the case that government should "steer, not row." But in what direction should government steer, and how good are the ideas that serve as its compass? The lessons from reinventions abroad and from private sector reform in the United States is that a clear sense of purpose and sharp guiding principles are critical to success. Long-term success requires the NPR to define, far more sharply, its purpose and guiding principles if it is to escape the quicksand of fuzzy rhetoric.

Glue

The NPR builds on a philosophy of "empowering" government workers to make better decisions. It argues for a more "entrepreneurial" philosophy, with a competition prescription replacing monopoly-based command-and-control management. In short, the NPR seeks to shift power from Congress to the bureaucracy and, within the bureaucracy, from top to bottom levels. If empowered bureaucrats behave entrepreneurially, what glue will prevent government from disintegrating into a vast network of quasi-independent operators? What processes will ensure democratic accountability to elected officials? What processes will ensure that the public interest dominates private behavior? Long-term success requires the NPR to build a force at the center of government, perhaps in the Office of Management and Budget, to focus government on results and to avoid having the reform spin off into scores of different, unconnected directions. It also requires that the NPR focus sharply on striking a new kind of bargain with Congress over government management.

Even more fundamentally, achieving the NPR's promise will require more clearly linking the question of what government ought to do with how government ought to do it. The NPR, in the report's own words, "focused primarily on how government should work, not on what it should do." The burden of a century of public management research, however, is that the distinction is artificial: the *how* powerfully shapes the *what* because means embody ends; from the beginning, the *how* has to be driven by the *what*.

To a greater degree than even political noncombatants stop to recognize, and certainly far more than government officials ever acknowledged, many public performance problems are often the product of what government sets out to do. Government in fact does many things very well, from delivering social security checks to providing weather satellite maps. Often, when things work badly, it is because it tries to do things that are very hard or impossible, like preventing drug abuse, training unemployed workers, cleaning up toxic waste, or providing welfare without creating dependence.

The Challenge

Improving performance on one level requires focusing government most clearly on what it does well and figuring out how to do those things better. The problem is that no one (and this includes the NPR) has thought clearly about what those things are. On another level, if we seek to do things well that are hard to do, we must be frank about the degree of difficulty and focus sharply on how to tackle the impossible. Many of the most basic questions to which the NPR has addressed itself revolve around such issues. If we choose to attack these problems at a superficial level, by focusing on the number of bureaucrats that can be eliminated or the dollars that can be saved, we will both miss the real issues and even further undercut government's ability to perform well.

The National Performance Review accomplished, in just its first year, far more than anyone thought possible. It energized employees, it attracted citizens, it drew media attention to government management, and it made the point that management matters. In the blush of success, however, the NPR failed to build the foundation for success in the long haul. It borrowed bits and pieces of management reform from both the public and private sectors and pasted them together in a patchwork that, while initially attractive, could not hold together. In the process, the NPR missed the most important lesson that other successful reforms teach: in the long run, management, matched to mission, matters most. The movement launched in September 1993, however promising, was not self-sustaining. Making it stick requires hard work on tough questions—work that, for the most part, has not begun.

DISCUSSION QUESTIONS

1. Is bureaucratic reform likely to succeed if the workers who staff the organizations are opposed to the reforms? Why or why not?

2. What advice would Woodrow Wilson have given to Al Gore? What advice would James Q. Wilson give?

The Debate: The Federal Bureaucracy: Hierarchy vs. Decentralization

In August of 1992 federal marshals attempted to arrest Randy Weaver, a white supremacist, on a weapons charge. Weaver resisted the arrest and a gunfight erupted in which Weaver's fourteen-year-old son and a U.S. marshal were killed. A week-long standoff ensued between Weaver's family and federal marshals and Federal Bureau of Investigation (FBI) agents; during the stalemate an FBI sniper killed Weaver's wife.

In the wake of Ruby Ridge, Attorney General Janet Reno created a task force to investigate the tragedy and the role of the FBI (a bureau within the Justice Department). The report, issued in 1994, was critical of the FBI's Hostage Rescue Team; it concluded that the FBI's "shoot on sight" policy was a violation of both the agency's own guidelines and Fourth Amendment restrictions on police powers. The report also offered recommendations for preventing a similar tragedy in the future. These recommendations are printed below.

What is most striking about the recommendations is their emphasis on stronger centralized oversight within the FBI, the need for greater specialization in the form of crisis response teams, and more stringent written rules for guiding the discretionary actions of FBI-agent behavior in the field. Each recommendation was designed to make FBI agents more accountable to their superiors and the agency heads more accountable to elected officials. Centralization is the goal. In contrast, the excerpt from "The National Performance Review," the report of the Reinventing Government task force, concludes that excessive centralization, extensive rules, and rigid procedures are precisely the problem with government agencies. The NPR recommendations thus run completely counter to those of the Ruby Ridge task force.

The difference between the two sets of recommendations is that one aims at maximizing accountability, whereas the other aims at maximizing performance and effectiveness. The problem is that we want both: We want agencies that are held closely in check for their actions, with a great deal of supervision to ensure their proper behavior, yet we are extremely critical of these same agencies when they are bogged down in their ability to perform by extensive written rules and procedures, specialized divisions that do not necessarily jell with the organization, and excessive layers of hierarchy that seem to diffuse accountability.

31
From *Report Regarding the Internal Investigation of Shootings at Ruby Ridge, Idaho, During the Arrest of Randy Weaver*

DEPARTMENT OF JUSTICE

V. Recommendations

Law enforcement officials confronted fundamental and recurring problems of crisis management at Ruby Ridge. Recently, the Department of Justice completed an exhaustive review of the government's response to the crisis at Waco, Texas.* The review included recommendations for managing barricade/hostage situations, coordinating law enforcement efforts, and dealing with persons whose motives and beliefs are unconventional.

Our recommendations expand on some of the ideas expressed in the Waco report, and, because each crisis presents its own particular difficulties, we offer recommendations emanating from the Ruby Ridge situation.

1. The Policy for the Use of Deadly Force and the Authorization Structure for Rules of Engagement Must be Standardized for All Federal Law Enforcement Agencies.

We believe that all federal law enforcement officers should be governed by a standard deadly force policy. Thus, we recommend that the Department of Justice establish a universal policy on the use of deadly force to govern the law enforcement components within the Department and to serve as a model for other agencies.

We have concluded that the special Rules of Engagement in force at Ruby Ridge violated the Constitution of the United States. We also found that the poorly drafted and ambiguous rules created confusion among those who were obliged to make instantaneous, life and death decisions while attempting to obey the requirements of the rules. In hostage/barricade situations, law enforcement officers need a clear definition of the conditions under which deadly force may be employed. It is critical that law enforcement personnel have a common and clear understanding

* [The government's armed standoff with the Branch Davidians, an extremist cult.]

of the rules governing their conduct. Moreover, when special rules of engagement are necessary, established review and authorization procedures must be in place.

Recently, the Department of Justice established the Office of Investigative Agency Policy, headed initially by the Director of the FBI. We suggest that Office may be best equipped to develop a standardized policy on the use of deadly force and to formulate procedures for formulating and authorizing special rules as needed.

2. Crisis Response Teams Need to be Created

As the authors of the Waco Report observed, it is imperative that specially trained crisis managers, familiar with relevant tactical, behavioral, and scientific disciplines, be available to respond to crises. FBI special agents in charge of particular geographical areas are not necessarily the best qualified individuals to supervise the government's response to crisis situations. We recommend that specially trained crisis managers should be deployed for that purpose. Expertise, not geography, should control. The recent consolidation of the FBI negotiations and tactical operations, as recommended in the Waco Report, will have an impact on the role both disciplines play in resolving crises.

We enthusiastically endorse the recent proposal by the Terrorism and Violent Crime Section of the Department of Justice that the FBI Crisis Response Team include specially trained prosecutors to provide legal support to tactical teams. Substantial difficulties confront prosecutors preparing a criminal case after a violent standoff between suspects and law enforcement. Law enforcement agents in such situations need to be mindful that a successful prosecution is one of the objectives of a favorable resolution of the crisis. The presence of prosecutors at crisis sites can contribute significantly to the ultimate success of the law enforcement effort within the criminal justice system.

Frequently, as at Ruby Ridge, the local FBI and local SWAT [strategic weapons and tactics] teams arrive at the scene before the HRT [hostage rescue team]. Therefore, we propose periodic joint training exercises by enhanced Crisis Response Teams, HRT, FBI SWAT teams and other federal and local law enforcement agencies. Such cross-training, as discussed in detail in the Waco Report, would have a number of benefits, including greater knowledge and appreciation of the contributions of each element of the response team.

3. A Multi-Agency Review with DOJ Representation Should be Established to Review Shooting Incident Reports

We found that the FBI review of the shooting incident at Ruby Ridge was not sufficiently thorough or accurate. We recommend that all internal reviews of shooting incidents by federal agencies be scrutinized by a board of representatives of law enforcement agencies prior to the close of the internal review process. The board should include at least one DOJ attorney with special expertise in this area.

The board could adopt the agency's findings and recommendations, return the report for additional inquiry, or refer the report to the appropriate component of the Department of Justice. The board would also be responsible for weighing recommendations made by the agency review team.

Such a process would encourage a higher quality of internal review throughout federal law enforcement agencies as well as increase public confidence in the review process.

4. Coordination Must Be Improved Between the FBI and Prosecutors in Regard to Discovery

Significant problems in the Ruby Ridge prosecution arose in the discovery process. The FBI delayed giving prosecutors the documents they needed for trial preparation and to provide to the defense in discovery. The delayed production of these documents to the defense occurred, in part, because of disputes between the FBI and the prosecutors about the material that was required to be produced. The delay in the production of the FBI Shooting Incident Report exemplifies this problem.

We recommend that the Department of Justice mandate that the FBI release to prosecutors Shooting Incident Reports and supporting documentation when a confrontation has resulted in death or serious injury. Moreover, the FBI should denominate a unit within the Bureau to coordinate and monitor discovery in a timely and thorough manner. Finally, the Department of Justice should establish guidelines governing the production of FBI material.

5. Coordination Among the FBI Crime Scene Investigation Team, the FBI Laboratory, and the Prosecutors Must Be Improved

Our report is critical of the crime scene investigation at Ruby Ridge. Because an experienced evidence response team was not used to recover and preserve evidence, the quality of the search and the resulting evidentiary analyses were compromised. To increase the chances of a successful prosecution, FBI Headquarters should mandate that its evidence response team be used in situations like Ruby Ridge to conduct systematic and thorough crime scene investigations.

The FBI Laboratory has for years been under conflicting pressures to perform analyses quickly for many different cases. Nonetheless, we believe that the problems that our inquiry has disclosed could have been avoided. The FBI Laboratory should not key its analyses to the trial date.

Prosecutors need laboratory analyses to develop a theory of their case, and analyses often suggest that additional examinations should be performed. We also recommend that the FBI assign an agent familiar with the theory of the case, the evidence, anticipated defenses, and FBI forensic capabilities to coordinate the prosecution's interaction with the Laboratory. In complex cases, this role may be exclusive of other responsibilities.

We also recommend that the FBI reevaluate its policy on memorializing witness interviews. We found inaccuracies in FD-302 interview reports of critical trail witnesses, which undermined their credibility at trial. The FBI needs to give consideration to other methods available that would more accurately memorialize witness interviews.

6. U.S. Attorneys' Offices Should Establish a Formal Indictment Review Process

The indictment drafted by Assistant U.S. Attorney Howen was reviewed and approved solely by U.S. Attorney Ellsworth. A number of defects in the indictment went undetected. We believe that significant indictments should be more carefully scrutinized.

We recommend that significant indictments be formally reviewed by a committee of Assistant U.S. Attorneys within a particular office, who have been thoroughly briefed on the theory of the case, the evidence, and anticipated defenses or problems. We do not suggest that such a process would resolve every factual or legal difficulty. However, it would encourage a more rigorous analysis of the relevant conduct and would probably ensure more appropriate charges.

7. Other Recommendations

We recommend that our analysis of the conduct of Assistant U.S. Attorney Ronald Howen be referred to the Executive Office for United States Attorneys for whatever action it deems appropriate.

Finally, we recommend that our findings concerning the events surrounding the shooting of Vicki Weaver by the FBI sniper/observer on August 22, 1992, and the Rules of Engagement under which he operated be referred to the appropriate component of the Department of Justice for an assessment of its prosecutive merit.

32

From "The National Performance Review"

AL GORE

Introduction

"Our goal is to make the entire federal government both less expensive and more efficient, and to change the culture of our national bureaucracy away from complacency and entitlement toward initiative and empowerment. We intend to redesign, to reinvent, to reinvigorate the entire national government." *President Bill Clinton, Remarks announcing the National Performance Review March 3, 1993*

Public confidence in the federal government has never been lower. The average American believes we waste 48 cents of every tax dollar. Five of every six want "fundamental change" in Washington. Only 20 percent of Americans trust the federal government to do the right thing most of the time—down from 76 percent 30 years ago. We all know why. Washington's failures are large and obvious. For a decade, the deficit has run out of control. The national debt now exceeds $4 trillion—$16,600 for every man, woman, and child in America.

But the deficit is only the tip of the iceberg. Below the surface, Americans believe, lies enormous unseen waste. The Defense Department owns more than $40 billion in unnecessary supplies. The Internal Revenue Service struggles to collect billions in unpaid bills. A century after industry replaced farming as America's principal business, the Agriculture Department still operates more than 12,000 field service offices, an average of nearly 4 for every county in the nation—rural, urban, or suburban. The federal government seems unable to abandon the obsolete. It knows how to add, but not to subtract.

And yet, waste is not the only problem. The federal government is not simply broke; it is broken. Ineffective regulation of the financial industry brought us the savings and loan debacle. Ineffective education and training programs jeopardize our competitive edge. Ineffective welfare and housing programs undermine our families and cities.

A Cure Worse Than The Disease

Government is not alone in its troubles. As the Industrial Era has given way to the Information Age, institutions—both public and private—have come face to face with obsolescence. The past decade has witnessed profound restructuring: In the 1980s, major American corporations reinvented themselves; in the 1990s, governments are struggling to do the same.

In recent years, our national leaders responded to the growing crisis with traditional medicine. They blamed the bureaucrats. They railed against "fraud, waste, and abuse." And they slapped ever more controls on the bureaucracy to prevent it. But the cure has become indistinguishable from the disease. The problem is not lazy or incompetent people; it is red tape and regulation so suffocating that they stifle every ounce of creativity. No one would offer a drowning man a drink of water. And yet, for more than a decade, we have added red tape to a system already strangling in it.

The federal government is filled with good people trapped in bad systems: budget systems, personnel systems, procurement systems, financial management systems, information systems. When we blame the people and impose more controls, we make the systems worse. Over the past 15 years, for example, Congress has created within each agency an independent office of the inspector general. The idea was to root out fraud, waste, and abuse. The inspectors general have certainly uncovered important problems. But as we learned in conversation after conversation, they have so intimidated federal employees that many are now afraid to deviate even slightly from standard operating procedure.

Yet innovation, by its nature, requires deviation. Unfortunately, faced with so many controls, many employees have simply given up. They do everything by the book—whether it makes sense or not. They fill out forms that should never have been created, follow rules that should never have been imposed, and prepare reports that serve no purpose—and are often never even read. In the name of controlling waste, we have created paralyzing inefficiency. It's time we found a way to get rid of waste and encourage efficiency.

The Root Problem: Industrial-Era Bureaucracies in an Information Age

Is government inherently incompetent? Absolutely not. Are federal agencies filled with incompetent people? No. The problem is much deeper: Washington is filled with organizations designed for an environment that no longer exists—bureaucracies so big and wasteful they can no longer serve the American people.

From the 1930s through the 1960s, we built large, top-down, centralized bureaucracies to do the public's business. They were patterned after the corporate structures of the age: hierarchical bureaucracies in which tasks were broken into simple parts, each the responsibility of a different layer of employees, each defined by specific rules and regulations. With their rigid preoccupation with standard operating procedure, their vertical chains of command, and their standardized services, these bureaucracies were steady—but slow and cumbersome. And in today's world of rapid change, lightning-quick information technologies, tough global competition, and demanding customers, large, top-down bureaucracies —public or private—don't work very well. Saturn isn't run the way General Motors was. Intel isn't run the way IBM was.

* * *

Many federal organizations are also monopolies, with few incentives to innovate or improve. Employees have virtual lifetime tenure, regardless of their performance. Success offers few rewards; failure, few penalties. And customers are captive; they can't walk away from the air traffic control system or the Internal Revenue Service and sign up with a competitor. Worse, most federal monopolies receive their money without any direct input from their customers. Consequently, they try a lot harder to please Congressional appropriations subcommittees than the people they are meant to serve. Taxpayers pay more than they should and get poorer service.

Politics intensifies the problem. In Washington's highly politicized world, the greatest risk is not that a program will perform poorly, but that a scandal will erupt. Scandals are front-page news, while routine failure is ignored. Hence control system after control system is piled up to minimize the risk of scandal. The budget system, the personnel rules, the procurement process, the inspectors general—all are designed to prevent the tiniest misstep. We assume that we can't trust employees to make decisions, so we spell out in precise detail how they must do virtually everything, then audit them to ensure that they have obeyed every rule. The slightest deviation prompts new regulations and even more audits.

Before long, simple procedures are too complex for employees to navigate, so we hire more budget analysts, more personnel experts, and more procurement officers to make things work. By then, the process involves so much red tape that the smallest action takes far longer and costs far more than it should. Simple travel arrangements require endless forms and numerous signatures. Straightforward purchases take months; larger ones take years. Routine printing jobs can take dozens of approvals.

This emphasis on process steals resources from the real job: serving the customer. Indeed, the federal government spends billions paying people who control, check up on, or investigate others—supervisors, headquarters staffs, budget officers, personnel officers, procurement officers, and staffs of the General Accounting Office (GAO) and the inspectors general. . . . Not all this money is wasted, of course. But the real waste is no doubt larger, because the endless regulations and layers of control consume every employee's time. Who pays? The taxpayer.

* * *

Consider but one example, shared with Vice President Gore at a meeting of federal employees in Atlanta. After federal marshals seize drug dealers' homes, they are allowed to sell them and use the money to help finance the war on drugs. To sell the houses, they must keep them presentable, which includes keeping the lawns mowed. In Atlanta, the employee explained, most organizations would hire neighborhood teenagers to mow a lawn for $10. But procurement regulations require the U.S. Marshals Service to bid out all work competitively, and neighborhood teenagers don't compete for contracts. So the federal government pays $40 a lawn to professional landscape firms. Regulations designed to save money waste it, because they take decisions out of the hands of those responsible for doing the work. And taxpayers lose $30 for every lawn mowed.

What would happen if the marshals used their common sense and hired neighborhood teenagers? Someone would notice—perhaps the Washington office, perhaps the inspector general's office, perhaps even the GAO. An investigation might well follow—hindering a career or damaging a reputation.

In this way, federal employees quickly learn that common sense is risky—and creativity is downright dangerous. They learn that the goal is not to produce results, please customers, or save taxpayers' money, but to avoid mistakes. Those who dare to innovate do so quietly.

This is perhaps the saddest lesson learned by those who worked on the National Performance Review: Yes, innovators exist within the federal government, but many work hard to keep their innovations quiet. By its nature, innovation requires a departure from standard operating procedure. In the federal government, such departures invite repercussions.

The result is a culture of fear and resignation. To survive, employees keep a low profile. They decide that the safest answer in any given situation is a firm "maybe." They follow the rules, pass the buck, and keep their heads down. They develop what one employee, speaking with Vice President Gore at a Department of Veterans Affairs meeting, called "a government attitude."

The Solution: Creating Entrepreneurial Organizations

* * *

Where we found success, we found many common characteristics. Early on, we articulated these in a one-page statement of our commitment. In organizing this report, we have boiled these characteristics down to four key principles.

1. Cutting Red Tape

Effective, entrepreneurial governments cast aside red tape, shifting from systems in which people are accountable for following rules to systems in which they are accountable for achieving results. They streamline their budget, personnel, and procurement systems—liberating organizations to pursue their missions. They reorient their control systems to prevent problems rather than simply punish those who make mistakes. They strip away unnecessary layers of regulation that stifle innovation. And they deregulate organizations that depend upon them for funding, such as lower levels of government.

2. Putting Customers First

Effective, entrepreneurial governments insist on customer satisfaction. They listen carefully to their customers—using surveys, focus groups, and the like. They restructure their basic operations to meet customers' needs. And they use market dynamics such as competition and customer choice to create incentives that drive their employees to put customers first.

By "customer," we do not mean "citizen." A citizen can participate in democratic decisionmaking; a customer receives benefits from a specific service. All Americans are citizens. Most are also customers: of the U.S. Postal Service, the Social Security Administration, the Department of Veterans Affairs, the National Park Service, and scores of other federal organizations.

In a democracy, citizens and customers both matter. But when they vote, citizens seldom have much chance to influence the behavior of public institutions that directly affect their lives: schools, hospitals, farm service agencies, social security offices. It is a sad irony: citizens own their government, but private businesses they do not own work much harder to cater to their needs.

3. Empowering Employees to Get Results

Effective, entrepreneurial governments transform their cultures by decentralizing authority. They empower those who work on the front lines to make more of their own decisions and solve more of their own problems. They embrace labor-management cooperation, provide training and other tools employees need to be effective, and humanize the workplace. While stripping away layers and empowering front-line employees, they hold organizations accountable for producing results.

4. Cutting Back to Basics: Producing Better Government for Less

Effective, entrepreneurial governments constantly find ways to make government work better and cost less—reengineering how they do their work and reexamining programs and processes. They abandon the obsolete, eliminate duplication, and end special interest privileges. They invest in greater productivity, through loan funds and long-term capital investments. And they embrace advanced technologies to cut costs.

These are the bedrock principles on which the reinvention of the federal bureaucracy must build—and the principles around which we have organized our actions. They fit together much like the pieces of a puzzle: if one is missing, the others lose their power. To create organizations that deliver value to American taxpayers, we must embrace all four.

Our approach goes far beyond fixing specific problems in specific agencies. Piecemeal efforts have been under way for years, but they have not delivered what Americans demand. The failure in Washington is embedded in the very systems by which we organize the federal bureaucracy. In recent years, Congress has taken the lead in reinventing these systems. In 1990, it passed the Chief Financial Officers Act, designed to overhaul financial management systems; in July 1993, it passed the Government Performance and Results Act, which will introduce performance measurement throughout the federal government. With Congress's leadership, we hope to reinvent government's other basic systems, such as budget, personnel, information, and procurement.

* * *

To deliver what the people want, we need not jettison the traditional values that underlie democratic governance—values such as equal opportunity, justice, diversity, and democracy. We hold these values dear. We seek to transform bureaucracies precisely because they have failed to nurture these values. We believe that those who resist change for fear of jeopardizing our democratic values doom us to a government that continues—through its failures—to subvert those very values.

Principles of the National Performance Review

We will invent a government that puts people first, by:

- Cutting unnecessary spending
- Serving its customers
- Empowering its employees
- Helping communities solve their own problems
- Fostering excellence

Here's how. We will:

- Create a clear sense of mission
- Steer more, row less
- Delegate authority and responsibility
- Replace regulations with incentives
- Develop budgets based on outcomes
- Expose federal operations to competition

- Search for market, not administrative, solutions
- Measure our success by customer satisfaction

Our Commitment: A Long-Term Investment in Change

This is not the first time Americans have felt compelled to reinvent their government. In 1776, our founding fathers rejected the old model of a central power issuing edicts for all to obey. In its place, they created a government that broadly distributed power. Their vision of democracy, which gave citizens a voice in managing the United States, was untried and untested in 1776. It required a tremendous leap of faith. But it worked.

DISCUSSION QUESTIONS

1. Are accountability and flexibility inversely related? That is, do you give up on one when you want more of the other? Can you maximize both at the same time?

2. Is it possible that we want different arrangements of accountability and flexibility for different kinds of bureaucracies? For example, would the organizational controls recommended for the FBI work for another agency, such as NASA, the Department of Agriculture, or the Marine Corps?

CHAPTER 7

The Federal Judiciary

33
The Federalist, No. 78

ALEXANDER HAMILTON

The judiciary, Hamilton wrote in defending the proposed constitution, "will always be the least dangerous to the political rights of the Constitution, because it will be least in a capacity to annoy or injure them." The lack of danger Hamilton spoke of stems from the Court's lack of enforcement or policy power: It must rely on the executive branch and state governments to enforce its rulings, and depends on the legislature for its appropriations and rules governing its structure. Critics of "judicial activism" (see Taylor and Bork, below) would likely disagree about the weakness of the Court relative to the other branches of government. Hamilton saw an independent judiciary as a key check on the other branches' ability to assume too much power.

To the People of the State of New York:

We proceed now to an examination of the judiciary department of the proposed government.

In unfolding the defects of the existing Confederation, the utility and necessity of a federal judicature have been clearly pointed out. It is the less necessary to recapitulate the considerations there urged, as the propriety of the institution in the abstract is not disputed; the only questions which have been raised being relative to the manner of constituting it, and to its extent. To these points, therefore, our observations shall be confined.

The manner of constituting it seems to embrace these several objects: 1st. The mode of appointing the judges. 2d. The tenure by which they are to hold their places. 3d. The partition of the judiciary authority between different courts, and their relations to each other.

First. As to the mode of appointing the judges; this is the same with that of appointing the officers of the Union in general, and has been so fully discussed in the two last numbers, that nothing can be said here which would not be useless repetition.

Second. As to the tenure by which the judges are to hold their places: this chiefly concerns their duration in office; the provisions for their support; the precautions for their responsibility.

According to the plan of the convention, all judges who may be appointed by the United States are to hold their offices *during good behavior;* which is conformable to the most approved of the State constitutions, and among the rest, to that of this State. Its propriety having been drawn into question by the adversaries of that plan, is no light symptom of the rage for objection, which disorders their imaginations and judgments. The standard of good behavior for the continuance in office of the judicial magistracy is certainly one of the most valuable of the modern improvements in the practice of government. In a monarchy it is an excellent barrier to the despotism of the prince; in a republic it is a no less excellent barrier to the encroachments and oppressions of the representative body. And it is the best expedient which can be devised in any government to secure a steady, upright, and impartial administration of the laws.

Whoever attentively considers the different departments of power must perceive, that, in a government in which they are separated from each other, the judiciary, from the nature of its functions, will always be the least dangerous to the political rights of the Constitution; because it will be least in a capacity to annoy or injure them. The Executive not only dispenses the honors, but holds the sword of the community. The legislature not only commands the purse, but prescribes the rules by which the duties and rights of every citizen are to be regulated. The judiciary, on the contrary, has no influence over either the sword or the purse; no direction either of the strength or of the wealth of the society; and can take no active resolution whatever. It may truly be said to have neither FORCE nor WILL, but merely judgment; and must ultimately depend upon the aid of the executive arm even for the efficacy of its judgments.

This simple view of the matter suggests several important consequences. It proves incontestably that the judiciary is beyond comparison the weakest of the three departments of power that it can never attack with success either of the other two; and that all possible care is requisite to enable it to defend itself against their attacks. It equally proves that though individual oppression may now and then proceed from the courts of justice, the general liberty of the people can never be endangered from that quarter; I mean so long as the judiciary remains truly distinct from both the legislature and the Executive. For I agree, that "there is no liberty, if the power of judging be not separated from the legislative and executive powers." And it proves, in the last place, that as liberty can have nothing to fear from the judiciary alone, but would have every thing to fear from its union with either of the other departments; that as all the effects of such a union must ensue from a dependence of the former on the latter, notwithstanding a nominal and apparent separation; that as, from the natural feebleness of the judiciary it is in continual jeopardy of being overpowered, awed, or influenced by its coördinate branches; and that as nothing can contribute so much to its firmness and independence as permanency in office, this quality may therefore be justly regarded as an indispensable ingredient in its constitution, and, in a great measure, as the citadel of the public justice and the public security.

The complete independence of the courts of justice is peculiarly essential in a limited Constitution. By a limited Constitution, I understand one which contains certain specified exceptions to the legislative authority; such, for instance, as that it shall pass no bills of attainder, no *ex-post-facto* laws, and the like. Limitations of this kind can be preserved in practice no other way than through the medium of courts of justice, whose duty it must be to declare all acts contrary to the manifest tenor of the Constitution void. Without this, all the reservations of particular rights or privileges would amount to nothing.

Some perplexity respecting the rights of the courts to pronounce legislative acts void, because contrary to the constitution, has arisen from an imagination that the doctrine would imply a superiority of the judiciary to the legislative power. It is urged that the authority which can declare the acts of another void must necessarily be superior to the one whose acts may be declared void. As this doctrine is of great importance in all the American constitutions, a brief discussion of the ground on which it rests cannot be unacceptable.

There is no position which depends on clearer principles than that every act of a delegated authority, contrary to the tenor of the commission under which it is exercised, is void. No legislative act, therefore, contrary to the Constitution, can be valid. To deny this would be to affirm that the deputy is greater than his principal; that the servant is above his master; that the representatives of the people are superior to the people themselves; that men acting by virtue of powers may do not only what their powers do not authorize, but what they forbid.

If it be said that the legislative body are themselves the constitutional judges of their own powers, and that the construction they put upon them is conclusive upon the other departments, it may be answered that this cannot be the natural presumption where it is not to be collected from any particular provisions in the Constitution. It is not otherwise to be supposed that the Constitution could intend to enable the representatives of the people to substitute their *will* to that of their constituents. It is far more rational to suppose that the courts were designed to be an intermediate body between the people and the legislature, in order, among other things, to keep the latter within the limits assigned to their authority. The interpretation of the laws is the proper and peculiar province of the courts. A constitution is, in fact, and must be regarded by the judges, as a fundamental law. It therefore belongs to them to ascertain its meaning, as well as the meaning of any particular act proceeding from the legislative body. If there should happen to be an irreconcilable variance between the two, that which has the superior obligation and validity ought, of course, to be preferred; or, in other words, the Constitution ought to be preferred to the statute, the intention of the people to the intention of their agents.

Nor does this conclusion by any means suppose a superiority of the judicial to the legislative power. It only supposes that the power of the people is superior to both; and that where the will of the legislature, declared in its statutes, stands in opposition to that of the people, declared in the Constitution, the judges ought to be governed by the latter rather than the former. They ought to regulate their decisions by the fundamental laws, rather than by those which are not fundamental.

This exercise of judicial discretion, in determining between two contradictory laws, is exemplified in a familiar instance. It not uncommonly happens that there are two statutes existing at one time, clashing in whole or in part with each other, and neither of them containing any repealing clause or expression. In such a case, it is the province of the courts to liquidate and fix their meaning and operation. So far as they can, by any fair construction, be reconciled to each other, reason and law conspire to dictate that this should be done; where this is impracticable, it becomes a matter of necessity to give effect to one in exclusion of the other. The rule which has obtained in the courts for determining their relative validity is, that the last in order of time shall be preferred to the first. But this is a mere rule of construction, not derived from any positive law but from the nature and reason of the thing. It is a rule not enjoined upon the courts by legislative provision but adopted by themselves, as consonant to truth and propriety for the direction of their conduct as interpreters of the law. They thought it reasonable, that between the interfering acts of an *equal* authority, that which was the last indication of its will should have the preference.

But in regard to the interfering acts of a superior and subordinate authority, of an original and derivative power, the nature and reason of the thing indicate the converse of that rule as proper to be followed. They teach us that the prior act of a superior ought to be preferred to the subsequent act of an inferior and subordinate authority; and that accordingly, whenever a particular statute contravenes the Constitution, it will be the duty of the judicial tribunals to adhere to the latter and disregard the former.

It can be of no weight to say that the courts, on the pretence of a repugnancy, may substitute their own pleasure to the constitutional intentions of the legislature. This might as well happen in the case of two contradictory statutes; or it might as well happen in every adjudication upon any single statute. The courts must declare the sense of the law; and if they should be disposed to exercise WILL instead of JUDGMENT, the consequence would equally be the substitution of their pleasure to that of the legislative body. The observation, if it prove any thing, would prove that there ought to be no judges distinct from that body.

If, then, the courts of justice are to be considered as the bulwarks of a limited Constitution against legislative encroachments, this consideration will afford a strong argument for the permanent tenure of judicial offices, since nothing will contribute so much as this to that independent spirit in the judges which must be essential to the faithful performance of so arduous a duty.

This independence of the judges is equally requisite to guard the Constitution and the rights of individuals from the effects of those ill humors, which the arts of designing men or the influence of particular conjunctures sometimes disseminate among the people themselves; and which, though they speedily give place to better information and more deliberate reflection, have a tendency, in the meantime, to occasion dangerous innovations in the government, and serious oppressions of the minor party in the community. Though I trust the friends of the proposed Constitution will never concur with its enemies in questioning that fundamental principle of republican government, which admits the right of the people to alter or abolish the established Constitution whenever they find it inconsistent with their happiness; yet it is not to be inferred from this principle that the representatives of the people, whenever a momentary inclination happens to lay hold of a majority of their constituents, incompatible with the provisions in the existing Constitution, would, on that account, be justifiable in a violation of those provisions; or that the courts would be under a greater obligation to connive at infractions in this shape, than when they had proceeded wholly from the cabals of the representative body. Until the people have by some solemn and authoritative act annulled or changed the established form, it is binding upon themselves collectively, as well as individually; and no presumption, or even knowledge, of their sentiments, can warrant their representatives in a departure from it, prior to such an act. But it is easy to see that it would require an uncommon portion of fortitude in the judges to do their duty as faithful guardians of the Constitution, where legislative invasions of it had been instigated by the major voice of the community.

But it is not with a view to infractions of the Constitution only that the independence of the judges may be an essential safeguard against the effects of occasional ill humors in the society. These sometimes extend no farther than to the injury of the private rights of particular classes of citizens by unjust and partial laws. Here also the firmness of the judicial magistracy is of vast importance in mitigating the severity and confining the operation of such laws. It not only serves to moderate the immediate mischiefs of those which may have been passed, but it operates as a check upon the legislative body in passing them; who, perceiving that obstacles to the success of iniquitous intention are to be expected from the scruples of the courts, are in a manner compelled by the very motives of the injustice they meditate to qualify their attempts. This is a circumstance calculated to have more influence upon the character of our governments, than but few may be aware of. The benefits of the integrity and moderation of the judiciary have already been felt in more States than one; and though they may have displeased those whose sinister expectations they may have disappointed, they must have commanded the esteem and applause of all the virtuous and disinterested. Considerate men of every description ought to prize whatever will tend to beget or fortify that temper in the courts; as no man can be sure that he may not be tomorrow the victim of a spirit of injustice by which he may be a gainer today. And every man must now feel that the inevitable tendency of such a spirit is to sap the foundations of public and private confidence, and to introduce in its stead universal distrust and distress.

That inflexible and uniform adherence to the rights of the Constitution and of individuals, which we perceive to be indispensable in the courts of justice, can certainly not be expected from judges who hold their offices by a temporary commission. Periodical appointments, however regulated or by whomsoever made, would, in some way or other, be fatal to their necessary independence. If the power of making them was committed either to the Executive or legislature, there would be danger of an improper complaisance to the branch which possessed it; if to both, there would be an unwillingness to hazard the displeasure of either; if to the people or to persons chosen by them for the special purpose, there would be too great a disposition to consult popularity, to justify a reliance that nothing would be consulted but the Constitution and the laws.

There is yet a further and a weightier reason for the permanency of the judicial offices, which is deducible from the nature of the qualifications they require. It has been frequently remarked, with great propriety, that a voluminous code of laws is one of the inconveniences necessarily connected with the advantages of a free government. To avoid an arbitrary discretion in the courts, it is indispensable that they should be bound down by strict rules and precedents, which serve to define and point out their duty in every particular case that comes before them; and it will readily be conceived from the variety of controversies which grow out of the folly and wickedness of mankind, that the records of those precedents must unavoidably swell to a very considerable bulk, and must demand long and laborious study to acquire a competent knowledge of them. Hence it is, that there can be but few men in the society who will have sufficient skill in the laws to qualify them for the stations of judges. And making the proper deductions for the ordinary depravity of human nature, the number must be still smaller of those who unite the requisite integrity with the requisite knowledge. These considerations apprise us that the government can have no great option between fit character; and that a temporary duration in office, which would naturally discourage such characters from quitting a lucrative line of practice to accept a seat on the bench, would have a tendency to throw the administration of justice into hands less able, and less well qualified, to conduct it with utility and dignity. In the present circumstances of this country and in those in which it is likely to be for a long time to come, the disadvantages on this score would be greater than they may at first sight appear; but it must be confessed that they are far inferior to those which present themselves under the other aspects of the subject.

Upon the whole, there can be no room to doubt that the convention acted wisely in copying from the models of those constitutions which have established *good behavior* as the tenure of their judicial offices, in point of duration; and that so far from being blamable on this account, their plan would have been inexcusably defective if it had wanted this important feature of good government. The experience of Great Britain affords an illustrious comment on the excellence of the institution.

PUBLIUS

DISCUSSION QUESTIONS

1. Was Hamilton correct in arguing that the judiciary is the least dangerous branch? Why or why not?

2. Critics of the Supreme Court often charge that it takes control of issues that should be properly decided in the legislature, while supporters claim that the Court is often the last check against the tyranny of the majority. Who has the stronger case? Can both sides be correct?

34

"The Court in American Life" from
Storm Center: The Supreme Court in American Politics

DAVID O'BRIEN

The "textbook" view of the federal judiciary is one in which judges sit in dispassionate review of complex legal questions, render decisions based on a careful reading of constitutional or statutory language, and expect their rulings to be adhered to strictly; the law is the law. This selection shows how unrealistic that picture is: O'Brien notes that the Supreme Court is very much a political institution, whose members pay more attention to the political cycle and public opinion than one might expect. O'Brien reviews the decision-making process in the famous Brown v. Board of Education of Topeka, Kansas, *in which the Court invalidated segregated public schools, as an example of how the Court fits itself into the political process. Throughout the case, justices delayed their decision, consolidated cases from around the country, and refused to set a firm timetable for implementation, relying instead on the ambiguous standard "with all deliberate speed." Far from being a purely objective arbiter of legal questions, the Court must pay close attention to its own legitimacy, and by extension the likelihood of compliance: it does no good to issue decisions that will be ignored.*

"Why does the Supreme Court pass the school desegregation case?" asked one of Chief Justice Vinson's law clerks in 1952. *Brown v. Board of Education of Topeka, Kansas* had arrived on the Court's docket in 1951, but it was carried over for oral argument the next term and then consolidated with four other cases and reargued in December 1953. The landmark ruling did not come down until May 17, 1954. "Well," Justice Frankfurter explained, "we're holding it for the election"—1952 was a presidential election year. "You're holding it for the election?" The clerk persisted in disbelief. "I thought the Supreme Court was supposed to decide cases without regard to elections." "When you have a major social political issue of this magnitude," timing and public reactions are important considerations, and, Frankfurter continued, "we do not think this is the time to decide it." Similarly, Tom Clark recalled that the Court awaited, over Douglas's dissent, additional cases from the District of Columbia and other regions, so as "to get a national coverage, rather than a sectional one." Such political considerations are by no means unique. "We often delay adjudication. It's not a question of evading at all," Clark concluded. "It's just the practicalities of life—common sense."

Denied the power of the sword or the purse, the Court must cultivate its institutional prestige. The power of the Court lies in the persuasiveness of its rulings and ultimately rests with other political institutions and public opinion. As an independent force, the Court has no chance to resolve great issues of public policy. *Dred Scott v. Sandford* (1857) and *Brown v. Board of Education* (1954) illustrate the limitations of Supreme Court policy-making. The "great folly," as Senator Henry Cabot Lodge characterized *Dred Scott*, was not the Court's interpretation of the Constitution or the unpersuasive moral position that blacks were not persons under the Constitution. Rather, "the attempt of the Court to settle the slavery question by judicial decision was simple madness." As Lodge explained:

> Slavery involved not only the great moral issue of the right of one man to hold another in bondage and to buy and sell him but it involved also the foundations of a social fabric covering half the country and caused men to feel so deeply that it finally brought them beyond the question of nullification to a point where the life of the Union was at stake and a decision could only be reached by war.

A hundred years later, political struggles within the country and, notably, presidential and congressional leadership in enforcing the Court's school desegregation ruling saved the moral appeal of *Brown* from becoming another "great folly."

Because the Court's decisions are not self-executing, public reactions inevitably weigh on the minds of the justices. Justice Stone, for one, was furious at Chief Justice Hughes's rush to hand down *Powell v. Alabama* (1932). Picketers protested the Scottsboro boys' conviction and death sentence. Stone attributed the Court's rush to judgment to Hughes's "wish to put a stop to the [public] demonstrations around the Court." Opposition to the school desegregation ruling in *Brown* led to bitter, sometimes violent confrontations. In Little Rock, Arkansas, Governor Orval Faubus encouraged disobedience by southern segregationists. The federal National Guard had to be called out to maintain order. The school board in Little Rock unsuccessfully pleaded, in *Cooper v. Aaron* (1958), for the Court's postponement of the implementation of *Brown's* mandate. In the midst of the controversy, Frankfurter worried that Chief Justice Warren's attitude had become "more like that of a fighting politician than that of a judicial statesman." In such confrontations between the Court and the country, "the transcending issue," Frankfurter reminded the brethren, remains that of preserving "the Supreme Court as the authoritative organ of what the Constitution requires." When the justices move too far or too fast in their interpretation of the Constitution, they threaten public acceptance of the Court's legitimacy.

* * *

When deciding major issues of public law and policy, justices must consider strategies for getting public acceptance of their rulings. When striking down the doctrine of "separate but equal" facilities in 1954 in *Brown v. Board of Education (Brown I)*, for instance, the Warren Court waited a year before issuing, in *Brown II*, its mandate for "all deliberate speed" in ending racial segregation in public education.

Resistance to the social policy announced in *Brown I* was expected. A rigid timetable for desegregation would only intensify opposition. During oral arguments on *Brown II*, devoted to the question of what kind of decree the Court should issue to enforce *Brown*, Warren confronted the hard fact of southern resistance. The attorney for South Carolina, S. Emory Rogers, pressed for an open-ended decree—one that would not specify when and how desegregation should take place. He boldly proclaimed:

> Mr. Chief Justice, to say we will conform depends on the decree handed down. I am frank to tell you, right now [in] our district I do not think that we will send—[that] the white people of the district will send their children to the Negro schools. It would be unfair to tell the Court that we are going to do that. I do not think it is. But I do think that something can be worked out. We hope so.

"It is not a question of attitude," Warren shot back, "it is a question of conforming to the decree." Their heated exchange continued as follows:

> CHIEF JUSTICE WARREN: But you are not willing to say here that there would be an honest attempt to conform to this decree, if we did leave it to the district court [to implement]?
> MR. ROGERS: No, I am not. Let us get the word "honest" out of there.
> CHIEF JUSTICE WARREN: No, leave it in.
> MR. ROGERS: No, because I would have to tell you that right now we would not conform—we would not send our white children to the Negro schools.[2]

The exchange reinforced Warren's view "that reasonable attempts to start the integration process is [sic] all the court can expect in view of the scope of the problem, and that an order to immediately admit all negroes in white schools would be an absurdity because impossible to obey in many areas. Thus, while total immediate integration might be a reasonable order for Kansas, it would be unreasonable for Virginia, and the district judge might decide that a grade a year or three grades a year is [sic] reasonable compliance in Virginia." Six law clerks were assigned to prepare a segregation research report. They summarized available studies, discussed how school districts in different regions could be desegregated, and projected the effects and reactions to various desegregation plans.

The Court's problem, as one of Reed's law clerks put it, was to frame a decree "so as to allow such divergent results without making it so broad that evasion is encouraged." The clerks agreed that there should be a simple decree but disagreed on whether there should be guidelines for its implementation. One clerk opposed any guidelines. The others thought that their absence "smacks of indecisiveness, and gives the extremists more time to operate." The problem was how precise a guideline should be established. What would constitute "good-faith" compliance? "Although we think a 12-year gradual desegregation plan permissible," they confessed, "we are not certain that the opinion should explicitly sanction it."

At conference, Warren repeated these concerns. Black and Minton thought that a simple decree, without an opinion, was enough. As Black explained, "the less we say the better off we are." The others disagreed. A short, simple opinion seemed advisable for reaffirming *Brown I* and providing guidance for dealing with the inevitable problems of compliance. Harlan wanted *Brown II* expressly to recognize that school desegregation was a local problem to be solved by local authorities. The others also insisted on making clear that school boards and lower courts had flexibility in ending segregation. In Burton's view, "neither this Court nor district courts should act as a school board or formulate the program" for desegregation.

Agreement emerged that the Court should issue a short opinion-decree. In a memorandum, Warren summarized the main points of agreement. The opinion should simply state that *Brown I* held racially segregated public schools to be unconstitutional. *Brown II* should acknowledge that the ruling created various administrative problems, but emphasize that "local school authorities have the primary responsibility for assessing and solving these problems; [and] the courts will have to consider these problems in determining whether the efforts of local school authorities" are in good-faith compliance. The cases, he concluded, should be remanded to the lower courts "for such proceedings and decree necessary and proper to carry out this Court's decision." The justices agreed, and along these lines Warren drafted the Court's short opinion-decree.

The phrase "all deliberate speed" was borrowed from Holmes's opinion in *Virginia v. West Virginia* (1911), a case dealing with how much of the state's public debt, and when, Virginia ought to receive at the time West Virginia broke off and became a state. It was inserted in the final opinion at the suggestion of Frankfurter. Forced integration might lead to a lowering of educational standards. Immediate, court-ordered desegregation, Frankfurter warned, "would make a mockery of the Constitutional adjudication designed to vindicate a claim to equal treatment to achieve 'integrated' but lower educational standards." The Court, he insisted, "does its duty if it gets effectively under way the righting of a wrong. When the wrong is deeply rooted state policy the court does its duty if it decrees measures that reverse the direction of the unconstitutional policy so as to uproot it 'with all deliberate speed.' " As much an apology for not setting precise guidelines as a recognition of the limitations of judicial power, the phrase symbolized the Court's bold moral appeal to the country.

Ten years later, after school closings, massive resistance, and continuing litigation, Black complained. "There has been entirely too much deliberation and not enough speed" in complying with *Brown*. "The time for mere 'deliberate speed' has run out." *Brown*'s moral appeal amounted to little more than an invitation for delay.

*   *   *

Twenty years after *Brown*, some schools remained segregated. David Mathews, secretary of the Department of Health, Education, and Welfare, reported to President Ford the results of a survey of half of the nation's primary and secondary public schools, enrolling 91 percent of all students: of these, 42 percent had an "appreciable percentage" of minority students, 16 percent had undertaken desegregation plans, while 26 percent had not, and 7 percent of the school districts remained racially segregated.

For over three decades, problems of implementing and achieving compliance with *Brown* persisted. Litigation by civil rights groups forced change, but it was piecemeal, costly, and modest. The judiciary alone could not achieve desegregation. Evasion and resistance were encouraged by the reluctance of Presidents and Congress to enforce the mandate. Refusing publicly to endorse *Brown*, Eisenhower would not take steps to enforce the decision until violence erupted in Little Rock, Arkansas. He then did so "*not* to enforce integration but to prevent opposition by violence to orders of a court." Later the Kennedy and Johnson administrations lacked congressional authorization and resources to take major initiatives in enforcing school desegregation. Not until 1964, when Congress passed the Civil Rights Act, did the executive branch have such authorization.

Enforcement and implementation required the cooperation and coordination of all three branches. Little progress could be made, as Assistant Attorney General Stephen Pollock has explained, "where historically there had been slavery and a long tradition of discrimination [until] all three branches of the federal government [could] be lined up in support of a movement forward or a requirement for change." The election of Nixon in 1968 then brought changes both in the policies of the executive branch and in the composition of the Court. The simplicity and flexibility of *Brown*, moreover, invited evasion. It produced a continuing struggle over measures, such as gerrymandering school district lines and busing in the 1970s and 1980s, because the mandate itself had evolved from one of ending segregation to one of securing integration in public schools.

Republican and Democratic administrations in turn differed on the means and ends of their enforcement policies in promoting integration.

Almost forty years after *Brown*, over 500 school desegregation cases remained in the lower federal courts. At issue in most was whether schools had achieved integration and become free of the vestiges of past segregation. Although lower courts split over how much proof school boards had to show to demonstrate that present *de facto* racial isolation was unrelated to past *de jure* segregation, the Court declined to review major desegregation cases from the mid-1970s to the end of the 1980s. During that time the dynamics of segregation in the country changed, as did the composition and direction of the Court.

* * *

"By itself," the political scientist Robert Dahl observed, "the Court is almost powerless to affect the course of national policy." Another political scientist, Gerald Rosenberg, goes much farther in claiming that "courts can *almost never* be effective producers of significant social reform." *Brown*'s failure to achieve immediate and widespread desegregation is instructive, Rosenberg contends, in developing a model of judicial policy-making on the basis of two opposing theories of judicial power. On the theory of a "Constrainted Court" three institutional factors limit judicial policy-making: "[t]he limited nature of constitutional rights;" "[t]he lack of judicial independence;" and "[t]he judiciary's lack of powers of implementation." On the other hand, a "Dynamic Court" theory emphasizes the judiciary's freedom "from electoral constraints and [other] institutional arrangements that stymie change," and thus enable the courts to take on issues that other political institutions might not or cannot. But neither theory is completely satisfactory, according to Rosenberg, because occasionally courts do bring about social change. The Court may do so when the three institutional restraints identified with the "Constrained Court" theory are absent and at least one of the following conditions exist to support judicial policy-making: when other political institutions and actors offer either (a) incentives or (b) costs to induce compliance; (c) "when judicial decisions can be implemented by the market;" or (d) when the Court's ruling serves as "a shield, cover, or excuse, for persons crucial to implementation who are *willing to act*." On the historical basis of resistance and forced compliance with *Brown*'s mandate, Rosenberg concludes that "*Brown* and its progeny stand for the proposition that courts are impotent to produce significant social reform."

Brown, nonetheless, dramatically and undeniably altered the course of American life in ways and for reasons that Rosenberg underestimates. Neither Congress nor President Eisenhower would have moved to end segregated schools in the 1950s, as their reluctance for a decade to enforce *Brown* underscores. The Court lent moral force and legitimacy to the civil rights movement and to the eventual move by Congress and President Johnson to enforce compliance with *Brown*. More importantly, to argue that the Court is impotent to bring about social change over-states the case. Neither Congress nor the President, any more than the Court, could have singlehandedly dismantled racially segregated public schools. As political scientist Richard Neustadt has argued, presidential power ultimately turns on a President's power of persuasion, the Court's power depends on the persuasiveness of its rulings and the magnitude of change in social behavior mandated. The Court raises the ante in its bid for compliance when it appeals for massive social change through a prescribed course of action, in contrast to when it simply says "no" when striking down a law. The unanimous but ambiguous ruling in *Brown* reflects the justices' awareness that their decisions are not self-enforcing, especially when they deal with highly controversial issues and their rulings depend heavily on other institutions for implementation. Moreover, the ambiguity of *Brown*'s remedial decree was the price of achieving unanimity. Unanimity appeared necessary if the Court was to preserve its institutional prestige while pursuing revolutionary change in social policy. The justices sacrificed their own policy preferences for more precise guidelines, while the Court tolerated lengthy delays in recognition of the costs of open defiance, building consensus, and gaining public acceptance. But in the ensuing decades *Brown*'s mandate was also transformed from that of a simple decree for putting an end to state-imposed segregation into the more vexing one of achieving integrated public schools. With that transformation of *Brown*'s mandate the political dynamics of the desegregation controversy evolved, along with a changing Court and country.

Discussion Questions

1. In what ways did the Court take "politics" into account in reaching the *Brown* decision? Was this appropriate? What was the alternative?

Notes

1. Letter to Charles Warren, July 19, 1923, Charles Warren Papers, Box 2, Library of Congress, Manuscripts Division, Washington, D.C.
2. Transcript of Oral Argument, Stanley Reed Papers, Box 43, University of Kentucky, Special Collections Library, Lexington, Kentucky.

35
"The Color-Blind Court"

Jeffrey Rosen

*This reading is an example of how O'Brien's view of Supreme Court "politics"
applies to contemporary jurisprudence. Rosen argues that the conservative
justices—Thomas, Scalia, Rehnquist, and Kennedy—have made explicitly political judgments in deciding that the Constitution is color blind. Their view is
that the law cannot properly take race into account in any form, and that affirmative action, congressional districts drawn in such a way to elect minority
representatives, and programs that set aside government contracts for minority
firms should be prohibited. Rosen's point is that these justices make selective
use of original intent when it supports their position, and ignore it when it does
not (compare, for example, Rosen's reading of the Reconstruction Amendments
to Taylor's later in this chapter). Ultimately, Rosen concludes that the Supreme
Court should simply refuse to get involved in these questions, leaving it to the
political branches to hammer out some resolution. The contemporary Court puts
itself in a position that the earlier Warren Court tried to avoid in the* Brown
*cases: attempting to resolve complex and controversial political issues on its
own, something that Scalia himself had argued the court is not equipped to do.*

The conservative justices are privately exuberant about the remarkable
Supreme Court term [of 1994–1995]. Surprised and slightly dazed by
the magnitude of their victory, they think they have finally exorcised the
ghost of the Warren Court, fulfilled the goals of the conservative judicial
revolution and vindicated the ideal of a color-blind Constitution for the
first time since Reconstruction. At least four justices—Clarence Thomas,
Antonin Scalia, William Rehnquist and Anthony Kennedy—have firmly
committed themselves to the proposition that government can almost
never classify citizens on the basis of race. They have signaled their
readiness to declare the Voting Rights Act unconstitutional by insisting
that the Fourteenth Amendment forbids states from using race as the
"predominant purpose" in drawing electoral districts. They have paved
the way for the judicial invalidation of most forms of affirmative action
by insisting that all racial preferences, whether passed by Congress or
the states, are presumptively unconstitutional unless narrowly designed
as a remedy for past discrimination. And they have made clear their
impatience with the court-ordered desegregation plans, the most tangible
legacy of *Brown v. Board of Education.* The lawyers will quibble, and the

president will implore everyone to search for common ground, but for the justices themselves, the victory is sweeter than they dared hope.

If the Court were Congress, it might be possible to admire what the justices have wrought. By following their consciences and the election returns, they have managed to represent the political mood of the country more faithfully than the people's elected representatives. The racialist remedies, such as minority set-asides and minority voting districts, that Democrats and Republicans briefly supported in the 1970s and 1980s have now lost favor among their former champions. And yet the new Republican Congress, afraid of the radical consequences of enacting the color-blind principle, is reluctant to repeal the programs it claims to oppose. The justices, by contrast, have plunged into the political thicket without worrying about the political consequences, and they have vindicated plebiscitary democracy more dramatically than the political branches themselves.

But the Court is not Congress; as conservatives never tire of reminding us, it is supposed to be a body of principle, not politics, committed to interpreting the law, not making it. So the great race cases of 1995 must be evaluated in light of the constitutional methodology that the conservatives themselves have chosen to embrace. For those of us, and I mean political liberals, who have been sympathetic to the conservative rhetoric of judicial restraint, strict constructionism and devotion to the original understanding of the Constitution, it's hard not to read the race decisions without feeling embarrassed and foolish and slightly duped, like an earnest child who discovers that fairy tales are not true. For the three race cases reveal the conservative judicial project to be unprincipled at its core.

In cases where they found it politically convenient, the conservatives were obsessively attentive to constitutional history. They exalted the understanding of the anti-federalists over the federalists, of Calhoun over Lincoln, and, with elaborate quotations from the late eighteenth century, revealed a Limbaughesque suspicion of federal power. In the *Lopez* case, they held, for the first time since the New Deal, that Congress lacked the power to enact a law; and, in the *Term Limits* case, they embraced a vision of state sovereignty that seemed to question the meaning of Reconstruction. In the desegregation case, Clarence Thomas went so far as to declare that "when an attack on the Constitution is followed by an open Federalist effort to narrow the provision, the appropriate conclusion is that the drafters and ratifiers of the Constitution approved the more limited construction offered in response." This is strict constructionism on steroids.

But in the three race cases there is a conspicuous silence. Discussions of the original meaning of the Reconstruction amendments—from which the conservatives claim to derive the principle that the Constitution is color-blind—are nowhere to be found. And no wonder. An examination of the historical evidence reveals that the original intentions of the radical Republicans in 1865 are flamboyantly inconsistent with the color-blind jurisprudence of the conservative justices in 1995. The selective historicism is so glaring that it calls to mind one of the most unfortunate eras in the Supreme Court's history—the civil rights cases of the 1870s and 1880s, when another band of conservative justices studiously ignored the original understanding of the Reconstruction amendments and struck down the laws passed by the Reconstruction Congress which guaranteed the civil equality of the freed slaves. The decisions to uphold segregation and to strike down affirmative action can hardly be compared, of course, despite Justice Thomas's suggestion that there is "a moral and constitutional equivalence . . . between laws designed to subjugate a race and those that distribute benefits on the basis of race." But, in their indifference to the original meaning of the Reconstruction amendments, the justices of the Waite Court and the Rehnquist Court are eerily similar.

How, precisely, did this remarkable term come to pass? In the most obvious sense, the conservatives triumphed in 1995 because four of them are committed to the principle that government can never make distinctions among citizens on the basis of race. And a fifth, Sandra Day O'Connor, has an impulse rather than an argument, whose precise contours she is unable to articulate, that racial classifications are in general a bad thing, except when they aren't. But the liberal justices, too, must bear some of the blame. After a false sense of confidence at the beginning of the term, when the newly appointed Clinton justices eked out narrow majorities in two death penalty cases, Justices Breyer, Souter, Ginsburg and Stevens failed, in the race cases, to make the historical arguments that might have helped their cause.

*   *   *

In one sense, 1995 was the year that Clarence Thomas found his voice, and he deserves credit for helping to forge the new conservative majority. By committing himself to the rhetoric of original intention with uncompromising vigor, by combining a few heartfelt beliefs—racial classifications are bad, state sovereignty is good—with the historical research of able clerks; and by displaying a willingness to overturn decades of precedent in the name of his methodology, he helped to shift the terms of debate for the entire court.

This makes it all the more unfortunate that, in the three race cases of 1995, Thomas and his colleagues presumed to transform the meaning of the Reconstruction amendments without pausing to examine their original meaning. So we must brace ourselves for the dark and lonely work of historical excavation. The antiquarian detour may seem tedious, but it is the only way to appreciate the unabashed opportunism that the conservative justices have displayed at their moment of triumph.

Writing for the conservative majority in *Miller v. Johnson*, Justice Kennedy held that apportionment decisions are constitutionally suspicious whenever race is "the predominant factor motivating the legislature's decision to place a significant number of voters" in a particular district. Repudiating O'Connor's muddled focus on appearances in *Shaw v. Reno*, Kennedy emphasized that a district need not look bizarre to violate the Constitution; instead, the question is whether "race for its own sake, and not other districting principles, was the legislature's dominant and controlling rationale." O'Connor provided a fifth vote but has still not sorted out her conflicted impulses. In an anxious concurrence—it was drafted, uncharacteristically, in her own hand—she tried to keep her options open by denying the obvious implications of the color-blind principle she had just endorsed. The Court's decision, she declared, "does not throw into doubt the vast majority of the Nation's 435 congressional districts, where presumably the States have drawn the boundaries in accordance with their customary districting principles." The adjective "presumably" is a plaintive touch; but it can't elide the fact that the decision plainly *does* throw into doubt the minority districts created to comply with the 1982 amendments to the Voting Rights Act. The "predominant purpose" test is cleverly designed to make race-based districting virtually impossible in practice, whether or not the Voting Rights Act survives in theory.

In 1982, of course, Congress's impulses were perversely conflicted. Although the amendments claim not to establish a right of proportional representation, they clearly require legislatures and courts to be exquisitely race-conscious and to use race as the "predominant purpose" in creating minority districts. In areas where blacks and whites vote in racially polarized blocs, black voters, by definition, "have less opportunity to elect representatives of their choice." To avoid violating the explicit commands of the Voting Rights Act, legislatures must create at least *some* districts where black voters constitute the majority rather than the minority (although the Bush and Clinton administrations were wrong to demand as many districts as possible). But, in the wake of *Miller*, any district created to comply with the Voting Rights Act is vulnerable to a constitutional challenge. Thus, every state is now trapped between what the Voting Rights Act requires and what Justice Kennedy says the Constitution forbids.

But never mind the prudential concerns about judges interjecting themselves into the thick of politics. The only question for a principled strict constructionist is whether the decision is supported by the original understanding of the framers of the Fourteenth Amendment. Although the Kennedy opinion contains not a word about history, the answer is perfectly clear.

Kennedy's notion that the Fourteenth Amendment prohibits states from using race as the "predominant purpose" in drawing electoral districts is hard to reconcile with the text of the Fourteenth Amendment itself. Section 2 of the amendment says that when the right to vote at any election is denied or abridged in any way, the basis of representation in the offending state shall be proportionately reduced. This was a brazenly partisan measure. The grant of citizenship to millions of freedmen in the South meant, the Reconstruction Republicans recognized, a dramatic increase in the number of congressional seats allocated to their opponents. If the Democratic legislatures continued to deny the vote to blacks—and everyone assumed that they would—then Democrats would soon have a congressional majority. By passing Section 2, the Republicans tacitly acknowledged that states were free to use race as the "predominant purpose" in denying or abridging the vote, as long as they were willing to pay the penalty.

During the heyday of the Warren era [1953–1969], the conservative judicial revolution was founded on the principle that the Fourteenth Amendment has nothing at all to say about apportionment. Dissenting in *Reynolds v. Sims*, the "one-man-one-vote case," Justice John M. Harlan, the high priest of modern judicial conservatives, reviewed the historical evidence exhaustively. He concluded: "The history of the adoption of the Fourteenth Amendment provides conclusive evidence that neither those who proposed nor those who ratified the Amendment believed that the Equal Protection Clause limited the power of the States to apportion their legislatures as they saw fit." A few months ago the Federalist Society, purveyor of law clerks and mischievous ideas to the conservative justices, sponsored a symposium in Chicago on Original Intent and the Constitution. One panel focused on the original understanding of the Reconstruction amendments. The panelists included some of the best conservative scholars of Reconstruction, and all of them agreed that the Scalia-Thomas insistence on color-blindness in matters of apportionment is impossible to reconcile with the history of the Reconstruction amendments. The Fourteenth Amendment plainly was *not* designed to forbid racial discrimination in all circumstances. In the odd nineteenth-century locution, it was designed to protect a limited set of civil rights, as opposed to political and social rights. There was some confusion about what these categories entailed, but everyone agreed that political rights included the right to vote, the right to hold office and the right to serve on juries. The committee report accompanying the Fourteenth Amendment explicitly stated that the amendment would have no effect on state authority over voting rights.

"At the heart of the Constitution's guarantee of equal protection lies the simple command that the Government must treat citizens as individuals, not as simply components of a racial, religious, sexual or national class," declares Justice Kennedy. Of course, the Reconstruction Republicans also talked about prohibiting caste legislation, which stigmatized and degraded blacks as a group. But even if one concedes Kennedy's point that the Fourteenth Amendment was individualist at its core, this is persuasive evidence that it has nothing to say about apportionment. Drawing electoral districts is a communal activity in which groups of representatives choose groups of constituents, not where individual constituents choose individual representatives.

It is also hard to identify what *injury* the individual white plaintiffs in the voting rights cases have suffered. Unlike the affirmative action cases, in which individual whites lose jobs to individual blacks, no voter has any *right* to be placed in a district where his or her preferred candidates are likely to win. Justice Kennedy claims that the placement of white voters in one district rather than another caused them "representational harms." But, as Justice Stevens pointed out in his dissent, the notion that white voters suffer "representational harms" when they are placed in a mostly black district rests on the very stereotypes Kennedy claims to abhor: that voters of a particular race "think alike, share the same political interests, and will prefer the same candidates at the polls." And why does Kennedy think that black districts have a race while white districts do not? For all these reasons, the Court's effort to regulate the collective activity of apportionment by invoking the individualist text of the Fourteenth Amendment is conceptually absurd.

The affirmative action case, *Adarand v. Pena*, is not quite as incoherent. But it, too, combines nervous hedging from Justice O'Connor with sweeping rhetoric that calls into question much of affirmative action as it is currently practiced. It reveals that at least two and perhaps four justices are willing to ban racial preferences in all circumstances. And it is impossible to reconcile with the original understanding of the Fourteenth Amendment.

Justice O'Connor, writing for the Court, held that all racial classifications, whether passed by Congress or the states, must be strictly scrutinized by judges and can only survive if they are "narrowly tailored" to accomplish a "compelling governmental interest." This is a daunting test: the last time five members of the Court upheld a racial classification under strict scrutiny was the Japanese internment case in 1944. But O'Connor, the former state legislator, makes clear that the scrutiny she has in mind is not quite so strict after all: "It is only by applying strict scrutiny that we can distinguish between unconstitutional discrimination and narrowly tailored remedial programs that legislatures may enact to further the compelling governmental interest in redressing the effects of past discrimination."

After a constitutional sea change, there is always a period of denial and confusion, as the politicians and the lawyers rub their eyes and try to absorb the meaning of the new order. Courts are notoriously weak engines of social change, and so perhaps the *Adarand* decision will, in the long run, be discreetly ignored. But, if the remedial model is followed to its logical conclusion, few affirmative action programs outside the university can survive. As Walter Dellinger, the assistant attorney general, emphasizes in a clear-eyed memorandum to federal agencies, all the most controversial racial preferences (such as the Federal Communications Commission's distress sale for minority broadcasters) are almost impossible to justify as a remedy for past discrimination. The largest federal affirmative action program—Executive Order 11,246, which requires federal contractors to adopt "goals and timetables" to correct "underutilization" of women and minorities—also appears to be unconstitutional under the new standard: there is little specific evidence of discrimination against minorities in most of the industries with which the federal government does business. And the federal set-asides for minority contractors are clearly doomed as well. Instead of succumbing to the O'Connorist impulse to deny the implications of the new order, President Clinton might do better to bow reluctantly to its radical force.

As a political matter, there is something appealing about the hard-headed skepticism of the *Adarand* opinion, which recognizes that Congress, no less than state legislatures, can be captured by cynical racial politics. Unlike the amorphous voting rights decisions, where judges have no objective standards for distinguishing permissible districts from impermissible ones, it's often possible, in the affirmative action cases, to identify real injuries to real victims.

As a constitutional matter, however, *Adarand* reveals the Achilles' heel of the jurisprudence of original understanding. The conservative justices have never begun to explain why the Fourteenth Amendment, which says that "*no state* shall abridge . . . the equal protection of the laws," should be construed to constrain the powers of Congress in any way. In his concurrence, Clarence Thomas declares that "under our Constitution, the government may not make distinctions on the basis of race." But Justice John Harlan's argument in the 1880s was much narrower. He did not claim that racial distinctions were forbidden in all circumstances but, rather, that the privileges and immunities of national citizenship can't be granted to one race and denied to another. And Harlan's argument would hardly justify striking down racial preferences for minority contractors. As John Harrison of the University of Virginia has illustrated, the privileges and immunities of national citizenship were originally understood as a narrow category of benefits and entitlements. They were uniform from state to state, and supported by general taxation. In the nineteenth-century idiom, they were fundamental rights, rather than discretionary privileges that could be granted or withdrawn at the government's pleasure. Being hired by the government to build highways, in short, was not among them. A true originalist, then, would allow government to discriminate against black contractors, as well as in favor of them, which is perhaps why the liberals didn't press the point.

Both Scalia and Thomas insist there is no constitutional or moral difference between racism and racialism, that racial classifications are unconstitutional in all circumstances. "In the eyes of government, we are just one race here. It is American," says Scalia. This is a Freudian slip disguised as a constitutional principle: the image of an "American race" conjures up visions of the late-nineteenth-century imperialists, of Brooks Adams and Ernest Renan, that should not trip easily off the tongue of an American conservative. "There can be no doubt that racial paternalism and its unintended consequences can be as poisonous and pernicious as any other form of discrimination," Thomas declares. "So-called 'benign' discrimination teaches many that because of chronic and apparently immutable handicaps, minorities cannot compete with them without their patronizing indulgence. . . . In my mind, government-sponsored racial discrimination based on benign prejudice is just as noxious as discrimination inspired by malicious prejudice."

At first, this proposition seems implausible. Surely Thomas doesn't mean to say that there are no moral or constitutional differences between the malicious discrimination that led to slavery and the benign discrimination that can lead, say, to a Supreme Court appointment. But, on reflection, Thomas's point seems provocative. It's plausible to argue that, regardless of its motivation, affirmative action can stigmatize and degrade minorities just as slavery did, because racial classifications of any kind promote racial castes. Perhaps not all affirmative action is stigmatizing; but anything short of an absolute ban would not adequately distinguish between racial classifications that produce stigma and those that don't. Because so much is stigmatizing, all must be banned.

But what about the original understanding of the Fourteenth Amendment? The only historical support Thomas offers for his argument is a sweeping citation to the Declaration of Independence. "There can be no doubt that the paternalism that appears to lie at the heart of this program is at war with the principle of inherent equality that underlies and infuses our Constitution. See Declaration of Independence." This is consistent with the natural law philosophy that Thomas embraced before his nomination, and more specifically, with the natural law rhetoric of some radical abolitionists. Charles Sumner believed, for example, that the Declaration of Independence was part of the Constitution and urged the Reconstruction Congress to adopt a resolution declaring that there shall be "no Oligarchy, Aristocracy, Caste or Monopoly invested with peculiar powers; but all persons shall be equal before the law, whether in the court room or at the ballot box." But Congress rejected Sumner's amendment and Thomas repudiated natural law at his confirmation hearings, declaring that it should play no role in constitutional adjudication. Thomas is trapped, in other words, between his personal impulses, which incline him toward Sumner, and his strict constructionist methodology, which tugs him back toward Calhoun. And without the shadowboxing rhetoric of original understanding, the *Adarand* decision might have been far more convincing.

The last case in the trilogy is *Missouri v. Jenkins*, which presages the end of court-ordered desegregation. The conservative five, speaking through Justice Rehnquist, held that the federal courts' power to remedy the effects of school desegregation does not extend very far beyond the elimination of segregation itself. A Kansas City district judge had ordered the state to pay more than $1.4 *billion* to create lavishly appointed magnet schools in the hope of attracting suburban whites into Kansas City public schools, which are almost 70 percent black. Rehnquist held that the district judge had exceeded his authority, because "[t]he proper response to an intradistrict violation is an intradistrict remedy." The sins of Kansas City could not be visited on the suburbs. Rehnquist also rejected the state's unlikely theory that the effects of segregation, rather than the effects of court-ordered integration, caused white flight to the suburbs. And he ridiculed the notion that the poor test scores of black students in the elaborately refurbished Kansas City schools—since the 1990s, they have included microcomputers, a planetarium, greenhouses, swimming pools and a 1,875-foot zoo—could be linked to the lingering effects of Jim Crow.

Of the three race decisions in 1995, *Jenkins* is, as a practical matter, the most important. Congress is unlikely to adopt new set-asides in the future; but hundreds of school districts remain under desegregation decrees. The decision also casts indirect light on the future of affirmative action, because it shows how narrowly the justices want to circumscribe the range of remedies for even the most egregious past discrimination. The proper goal, says Rehnquist, is to restore "the victims of discriminatory conduct to the position they would have occupied in the absence of that conduct."

Jenkins, moreover, is the most authentically conservative of the three race decisions, and, perhaps for this reason, it seems the most coherent and least arch. The five conservatives are brimming over with concern about the abuse of federal judicial power and the danger of empowering unelected judges to meddle in the politics of race—precisely the concerns that they overlooked in the reapportionment cases. "The necessary restrictions on our jurisdiction and authority . . . limit the judiciary's institutional capacity to prescribe palliatives for social ills," O'Connor announces. "At some point," adds Thomas, "we must recognize that the judiciary is not omniscient, and that all problems do not require a remedy of constitutional proportions."

Thomas contrasts his own color-blind vision with what he calls "a jurisprudence of black inferiority." He insists that voluntary segregation that results from private choices is not constitutionally troubling because it does not have the social meaning or stigmatic effects of state-imposed segregation. "It never ceases to amaze me that courts are so willing to assume that anything that is predominantly black must be inferior," he declares. "The mere fact that a school is black does not mean that it is the product of a constitutional violation," unless one is willing to accept the demeaning premise that racial separatism is itself unconstitutional. Thus, the black nationalism of Thomas's youth and the libertarianism of his early career intriguingly converge.

In his most personal contribution, Thomas goes on to confront the meaning and legacy of *Brown* v. *Board of Education*. *Brown*, of course, is the awkward subtext of the three race cases of 1995. As a law clerk forty years ago, William Rehnquist had written a memo to Justice Robert Jackson insisting that school segregation did not violate the Constitution and that *Plessy* v. *Ferguson* was correctly decided. Having converted to color-blindness, he is understandably wary about calling attention to his conversion. Thomas's views, however, are consistent, if hardly originalist. In a 1987 article in *The Howard Law Review*, "Toward a 'Plain Reading' of the Constitution—The Declaration of Independence in Constitutional Interpretation," he had criticized *Brown* for focusing on the psychological effects of segregated schools on black children, rather than on the social meaning of segregation: "Thus, the *Brown* focus on environment overlooks the real problem with segregation, its origin in slavery, which was at fundamental odds with the founding principles." In the *Jenkins* opinion, Thomas's argument is more formalistic: *Brown* "did not need to rely upon any psychological or social-science research in order to announce the simple yet fundamental truth that the government cannot discriminate among its citizens on the basis of race. . . . Psychological injury or benefit is irrelevant to the question whether state actors have engaged in intentional discrimination—the critical inquiry for ascertaining violations of the Equal Protection Clause."

To support his claim that *Brown* rests on firmer historical ground than the Warren Court acknowledged, Thomas cites an article by Michael McConnell of the University of Chicago, "Originalism and the Desegregation Decisions," recently published in *The Virginia Law Review*. But, in fact, McConnell's article is devoted to rejecting Thomas's broad color-blind premise. The Reconstruction Republicans did *not* accept Thomas's anachronistic notion that the equal protection clause was designed to root out intentional discrimination across the entire range of state action. Instead, they understood the *protection* of the laws as a relatively narrow guarantee, designed to ensure equal administration and enforcement of laws passed for the security of liberty and property. "To the supporters of the civil rights bills during the Reconstruction period," McConnell points out, "the focus was on an equality of rights—not on whether the processes of government were infected by discriminatory intent."

McConnell challenges the received wisdom, embraced by constitutional theorists from Ronald Dworkin to Robert Bork, that the *Brown* decision is inconsistent with the original meaning of the Fourteenth Amendment. Between 1870 and 1874, majorities in the House and Senate repeatedly voted in favor of school desegregation, on the theory that the amendment entitled all citizens to the same civil rights. For those who accepted the notion that education was a civil right (and this was a less controversial notion in the 1950s than in the 1870s), the Fourteenth Amendment required that it be extended to white and black citizens on exactly the same terms. But this evidence comes from the period *after* the Fourteenth Amendment was ratified, hardly the kind that Thomas is ordinarily willing to accept.

Thomas's defense of voluntary segregation is not entirely inconsistent with the vision of the Reconstruction Republicans, who saw no contradiction between public equality and private Negrophobia. Like them, Thomas seems to believe that social rights are beyond the regulatory power of the state and that social inequality—resulting from the private reluctance of whites to associate with blacks, or blacks with whites—should be left entirely to private choices. By contrast, both Thomas and the abolitionists believe that state-sponsored segregation should always be illegal and unconstitutional. Senator Sumner, crisply distinguishing between the private and public spheres, insisted that each person "is always free to choose who shall be his friend, his associate, his guest," but when he "walks the streets . . . he is subject to the prevailing law of equality."

But Thomas has boxed himself into a corner. In his *Jenkins* opinion he reiterates that, when an attack on a constitutional provision is followed by an attempt to narrow the provision, "the appropriate conclusion is that the drafters and ratifiers . . . approved the more limited construction offered in response." And there is no doubt that, during the debates over the Fourteenth Amendment itself, a prominent supporter stated unequivocally that it would not affect segregation. In the course of trying to reconstruct *Brown* v. *Board of Education*, in short, Thomas has committed himself to a methodology that compels him to reject it.

If the conservative justices had made an honest attempt to respect the intentions of the Reconstruction Republicans in the race cases of 1995, they would have voted for judicial restraint rather than judicial activism. Instead of declaring that the Constitution is color-blind in all circumstances, they would have concluded that the Fourteenth Amendment neither imposes any limits on race-conscious apportionment nor forbids set-asides for minority contractors. Nor does it necessarily forbid segregated schools—unless Justices Thomas and Scalia are willing to construe the historical evidence more expansively than they are willing to do in cases involving states' rights and federal powers.

But the race cases of 1995 are distressing in a way that transcends the methodological inconsistencies of conservative or liberal justices. For the second time in a century, the Supreme Court has presumed to forbid Congress from passing civil rights laws and creating voting districts for the benefit of blacks. As an example of judicial usurpation of Congress's prerogatives alone, this should make conservatives cringe. Already, liberals are eulogizing the decade that produced federal set-asides and the first black representatives from the South since the first Reconstruction as the second Reconstruction; and conservatives are celebrating the dawning of the color-blind age. Both claims seem hyperbolic. Perhaps the country is finally ready to embrace the color-blind ideal that was proposed and rejected by the 39th Congress [1865–1867]; but because the unelected justices have short-circuited the political debate, we may never know for sure.

"When a man has emerged from slavery," Justice Bradley declared in his notorious opinion striking down the public accommodations act of 1875, "and by the aid of beneficent legislation has shaken off the insep-arable concomitants of that state, there must be some stage in the pro-gress of his elevation when he takes the rank of a mere citizen, and ceases to be the special favorite of the laws." If the historic moment has arrived at last, the wrong heralds, once again, have trumpeted its arrival. Re-member Justice Scalia's cry of anguish in the last abortion case: "We should get out of this area, where we have no right to be, and where we do neither ourselves nor the country any good by remaining."

Discussion Questions

1. In what ways did the Court take "politics" into account in reaching the decisions discussed by Rosen? Was this appropriate? What was the alternative? Do these rulings indicate that the Court cannot only produce social reform, but undo it as well? Explain.

The Debate: Original Intent vs. Judicial Activism

Debates over the federal judiciary's role in the political process often focus on the question of how judges should interpret the Constitution. Should judges apply the document's literal meaning and the inferred intent of the Framers, or should they use a broader interpretive framework that incorporates their own attitudes and opinions? This debate intensified during Earl Warren's tenure as Chief Justice (1953–1969), because of Court decisions that expanded the scope of civil liberties and criminal rights far beyond what strict constructionists thought the Constitution's language authorized. The two readings in this section offer contrasting viewpoints. Robert Bork, who was nominated by Ronald Reagan to serve on the Supreme Court but rejected by the Senate, argues that judges must be bound by original intent, as it is the only neutral principle that allows the judiciary to function as a legal body instead of a political one. Stuart Taylor discusses the issue in the context of a public debate over the proper role of judges, between Edwin Meese, who was then Attorney General, and former Supreme Court Justice William Brennan. Taylor criticizes the original intent doctrine as fraught with inconsistencies, even as he faults Brennan for his willingness to rule on the basis of on his own moral convictions rather than the letter of the law. Taylor concludes that judges should adhere to a middle ground, recognizing that the meaning of the Constitution has to change over time while at the same time acknowledging that the specific language necessarily "imposes some bounds on judicial power."

36
From *The Tempting of America*

Robert H. Bork

The Original Understanding

W hat was once the dominant view of constitutional law—that a judge is to apply the Constitution according to the principles intended by those who ratified the document—is now very much out of favor among the theorists of the field. In the legal academies in particular, the philosophy of original understanding is usually viewed as thoroughly passé, probably reactionary, and certainly—the most dreaded indictment of all—"outside the mainstream." That fact says more about the lamentable state of the intellectual life of the law, however, than it does about the merits of the theory.

In truth, only the approach of original understanding meets the criteria that any theory of constitutional adjudication must meet in order to possess democratic legitimacy. Only that approach is consonant with the design of the American Republic.

The Constitution as Law: Neutral Principles

When we speak of "law," we ordinarily refer to a rule that we have no right to change except through prescribed procedures. That statement assumes that the rule has a meaning independent of our own desires. Otherwise there would be no need to agree on procedures for changing the rule. Statutes, we agree, may be changed by amendment or repeal. The Constitution may be changed by amendment pursuant to the procedures set out in article V. It is a necessary implication of the prescribed procedures that neither statute nor Constitution should be changed by judges. Though that has been done often enough, it is in no sense proper.

What is the meaning of a rule that judges should not change? It is the meaning understood at the time of the law's enactment. Though I have written of the understanding of the ratifiers of the Constitution, since they enacted it and made it law, that is actually a shorthand formulation, because what the ratifiers understood themselves to be enacting must be taken to be what the public of that time would have understood the words to mean. It is important to be clear about this. The search is not for a subjective intention. If someone found a letter from George Washington to Martha telling her that what he meant by the power to lay taxes was not what other people meant, that would not change our reading of the Constitution in the slightest. Nor would the subjective intentions of all the members of a ratifying convention alter anything. When lawmakers use words, the law that results is what those words ordinarily mean. If Congress enacted a statute outlawing the sale of automatic rifles and did so in the Senate by a vote of 51 to 49, no court would overturn a conviction because two senators in the majority testified that they really had intended only to prohibit the *use* of such rifles. They said "sale" and "sale" it is. Thus, the common objection to the philosophy of original understanding—that Madison kept his notes of the convention at Philadelphia secret for many years—is off the mark. He knew that what mattered was public understanding, not subjective intentions. Madison himself said that what mattered was the intention of the ratifying conventions. His notes of the discussions at Philadelphia are merely evidence of what informed public men of the time thought the words of the Constitution meant. Since many of them were also delegates to the various state ratifying conventions, their understanding informed the debates in those conventions. As Professor Henry Monaghan of Columbia has said, what counts is what the public understood. Law is a public act. Secret reservations or intentions count for nothing. All that counts is how the words used in the Constitution would have been understood at the time. The original understanding is thus manifested in the words used and in secondary materials, such as debates at the conventions, public discussion, newspaper articles, dictionaries in use at the time, and the like. Almost no one would deny this; in fact almost everyone would find it obvious to the point of thinking it fatuous to state the matter—except in the case of the Constitution. Why our legal theorists make an exception for the Constitution is worth exploring.

The search for the intent of the lawmaker is the everyday procedure of lawyers and judges when they must apply a statute, a contract, a will, or the opinion of a court. To be sure, there are differences in the way we deal with different legal materials, which was the point of John Marshall's observation in *McCulloch* v. *Maryland* that "we must never forget, that it is *a constitution* we are expounding." By that he meant that narrow, legalistic reasoning was not to be applied to the document's broad provisions, a document that could not, by its nature and uses, "partake of the prolixity of a legal code." But he also wrote there that it was intended that a provision receive a "fair and just interpretation," which means that the judge is to interpret what is in the text and not something else. And, it will be recalled, in *Marbury* v. *Madison* Marshall placed the judge's power to invalidate a legislative act upon the fact that the judge was applying the words of a written document. Thus, questions of breadth of approach or of room for play in the joints aside, lawyers and judges should seek in the Constitution what they seek in other legal texts: the original meaning of the words.

We would at once criticize a judge who undertook to rewrite a statute or the opinion of a superior court, and yet such judicial rewriting is often correctable by the legislature or the superior court, as the Supreme Court's rewriting of the Constitution is not. At first glance, it seems distinctly peculiar that there should be a great many academic theorists who explicitly defend departures from the understanding of those who ratified the Constitution while agreeing, at least in principle, that there should be no departure from the understanding of those who enacted a statute or joined a majority opinion. A moment's reflection suggests, however, that Supreme Court departures from the original meaning of the Constitution are advocated *precisely because* those departures are not correctable democratically. The point of the academic exercise is to be free of democracy in order to impose the values of an elite upon the rest of us.

If the Constitution is law, then presumably its meaning, like that of all other law, is the meaning the lawmakers were understood to have intended. If the Constitution is law, then presumably, like all other law, the meaning the lawmakers intended is as binding upon judges as it is upon legislatures and executives. There is no other sense in which the Constitution can be what article VI proclaims it to be: "Law." It is here that the concept of neutral principles, which Wechsler said were essential if the Supreme Court was not to be a naked power organ, comes into play. Wechsler, it will be recalled, in expressing his difficulties with the decision in *Brown* v. *Board of Education*, said that courts must choose principles which they are willing to apply neutrally, apply, that is, to all cases that may fairly be said to fall within them. This is a safeguard against political judging. No judge will say openly that any particular group or political position is always entitled to win. He will announce a principle that decides the case at hand, and Wechsler had no difficulty with that if the judge is willing to apply the same principle in the next case, even if it means that a group favored by the first decision is disfavored by the second. That was precisely what Arthur M. Schlesinger, Jr., said that the Black-Douglas wing of the Court was unwilling to do. Instead, it pretended to enunciate principles but in fact warped them to vote for interest groups.

The Court cannot, however, avoid being a naked power organ merely by practicing the neutral application of legal principle. The Court can act as a legal rather than a political institution only if it is neutral as well in the way it derives and defines the principles it applies. If the Court is free to choose any principle that it will subsequently apply neutrally, it is free to legislate just as a political body would. Its purported resolution of the Madisonian dilemma is spurious, because there is no way of saying that the correct spheres of freedom have been assigned to the majority and the minority. Similarly, if the Court is free to define the scope of the principle as it sees fit, it may, by manipulating the principle's breadth, make things come out the way it wishes on grounds that are not contained in the principle it purports to apply. Once again, the Madisonian dilemma is not resolved correctly but only according to the personal preferences of the Justices. The philosophy of original understanding is capable of supplying neutrality in all three respects—in deriving, defining, and applying principle.

The interpretation of the Constitution according to the original understanding, then, is the only method that can preserve the Constitution, the separation of powers, and the liberties of the people. Only that approach can lead to what Felix Frankfurter called the "fulfillment of one of the greatest duties of a judge, the duty not to enlarge his authority. That the Court is not the maker of policy but is concerned solely with questions of ultimate power, is a tenet to which all Justices have subscribed. But the extent to which they have translated faith into works probably marks the deepest cleavage among the men who have sat on the Supreme Bench. . . . The conception of significant achievement on the Supreme Court has been too much identified with largeness of utterance, and too little governed by inquiry into the extent to which judges have fulfilled their professed role in the American constitutional system."

Without adherence to the original understanding, even the actual Bill of Rights could be pared or eliminated. It is asserted nonetheless, and sometimes on high authority, that the judicial philosophy of original understanding is fatally defective in any number of respects. If that were so, if the Constitution cannot be law that binds judges, there would remain only one democratically legitimate solution: judicial supremacy, the power of courts to invalidate statutes and executive actions in the name of the Constitution, would have to be abandoned. For the choice would then be either rule by judges according to their own desires or rule by the people according to theirs. Under our form of government, under the entire history of the American people, the choice between an authoritarian judicial oligarchy and a representative democracy can have only one outcome. But this is a false statement of alternatives, for judicial interpretation of the Constitution according to its original understanding is entirely possible. When that course is followed, judges are not a dictatorial oligarchy but the guardians of our liberties.

Meese says the Const'n should be interpreted according to "Original Intent"

Liberals argue that times have changed so the Court should interpret the Const'n loosely.

Taylor says there's a middle ground. stick to main ideas (adhere to original intent) but some cases demand interp. according to modern times.

37 "Who's Right about the Constitution? Meese v. Brennan"

STUART TAYLOR, JR.

An activist jurisprudence, one which anchors the Constitution only in the consciences of jurists, is a chameleon jurisprudence, changing color and form in each era.

> The Constitution . . . is a mere thing of wax in the hands of the judiciary, which they may twist and shape into any form they please.

> If the policy of the Government upon vital questions affecting the whole people is to be irrevocably fixed by decisions of the Supreme Court, the instant they are made . . . the people will have ceased to be their own rulers.

> The Court . . . has improperly set itself up as . . . a super-legislature . . . reading into the Constitution words and implications which are not there, and which were never intended to be there. . . . We want a Supreme Court which will do justice under the Constitution—not over it.

Sounds like Ed Meese, doesn't it? Well, the first quotation is the attorney general's. But the second comes from Thomas Jefferson, the third from Abraham Lincoln, and the fourth from Franklin D. Roosevelt. When Meese assails government by judiciary, he is in good company.

Meese has denounced major Supreme Court rulings of the past 60 years and called for judges to look to "the original meaning of constitutional provisions" as "the only reliable guide for judgment." No attorney general in the past four decades has set out so deliberately to reduce the power of the judiciary or to screen the ideological credentials of new appointees.

Champions of liberal judicial activism have launched a ferocious counterattack. Justices William J. Brennan Jr. and John Paul Stevens retorted with pointed critiques of Meese's so-called "jurisprudence of original intention." Brennan said it was "arrogance cloaked as humility" for anyone "to pretend that from our vantage we can gauge accurately the intent of the Framers on application of principle to specific, contemporary questions." The real animus of advocates of this "facile historicism" he said, is a "political" agenda hostile to the rights of minorities.

Meese is certainly vulnerable to this sort of attack. He seems less a constitutional philosopher than a constitutional window-shopper, seeking to dress up his conservative political agenda as a principled quest for truth. His notion that judges can answer the hard questions raised by the Constitution without being "tainted by ideological predilection," simply by plugging in the intent of the Framers, is at best simpleminded and at worst disingenuous. When the Framers' intentions *are* clear, but contrary to a result Meese wants, he ignores them. While calling for restraint in the exercise of judicial power—especially enforcement of civil liberties—he pushes to aggrandize executive power.

Along the way, he has said some revealing things. "You don't have many suspects who are innocent of a crime," he told *U.S. News & World Report.* "That's contradictory. If a person is innocent of a crime, then he is not a suspect." This from a man who was himself suspected of several federal crimes until a special prosecutor cleared him last year—a man who then billed the government $720,824.49 for his defense lawyers. (He later confessed to a "bad choice of words.")

Meese also assailed as "intellectually shaky" and "constitutionally suspect" the Court's 60-year-old doctrine that most of the Bill of Rights, originally applicable only to the national government, was applied to the states by the 14th Amendment. Eminent Supreme Court justices criticized the doctrine too, but that was decades ago. When a Supreme Court ruling has "been affirmed and reaffirmed through a course of years," Lincoln said in 1857, "it then might be, perhaps would be, factious, nay even revolutionary, not to acquiesce in it as a precedent."

Nevertheless, the standard liberal retort to Meese is superficial. It caricatures his position as more extreme than it is. It ignores the long and honorable history of political attacks on judicial usurpation of power. Most important, its scorn for the "original intention" approach begs the question of where—if not from those who wrote and ratified the Constitution and its amendments—unelected judges get a mandate to override the will of the political majority by striking down democratically enacted laws.

For all his fumbling, Meese has spotlighted some of the real problems with the freewheeling judicial activism sometimes practiced by people like Brennan. Among these is a tendency to "find" in the Constitution rights (such as abortion rights) and social policies that can honestly be found neither in the language of the document, nor in the records left by those who wrote it, nor in any broad national consensus that has evolved since then. This is bad constitutional law even when you like the policies, as I sometimes do.

Meese deserves credit for bringing the deepest questions of constitutional law out of the law journals and into the newspapers. He surely has a political motive. But liberals who believe in democracy (anybody out there after two Reagan landslides?) should welcome the debate.

Too often liberals have taken the elitist view that ordinary voters are the natural enemies of civil liberties, and that only judges can be trusted to protect them. It is a shortsighted approach. As Justice Robert Jackson said four decades ago, "Any court which undertakes by its legal processes to enforce civil liberties needs the support of an enlightened and vigorous public opinion." Today most people confine their thinking about the Constitution to whether they like the policies the Court has decreed. The larger question of when courts should displace the ordinary policy-making role of elected officials gets little attention from anyone but law professors. Meese has begun to remind the public that in enforcing constitutional rights, federal judges are by definition restraining majority rule.

Within proper limits this is a noble function. Those who wrote the Constitution and its amendments saw them as bulwarks against oppression of minorities by a tyrannical majority. They specified certain fundamental rights shared by all Americans. They created special protections for minorities, especially blacks. They laid down these principles in majestic generalities meant to have continuing relevance in a changing society—freedom of speech, equal protection of the laws, due process of law. The federal courts—precisely because they are not answerable to the voters—are the logical bodies to enforce these rights against the majority.

Here, however, lies a difficult dilemma to which no wholly satisfactory solution exists. The Constitution being what the judges say it is, how can the judges be prevented from usurping the powers of elected officials and making political decisions? Meese's admonition to stick to original intent is only a starting point. The Constitution does tell judges to enforce certain broad principles such as "freedom of speech," but if these principles are to be enforced at all in a changing society, judges must supply much of their meaning.

The trouble is that judges of all political stripes have gone beyond applying the Constitution's principles to new circumstances. They have written their own moral and political values into it, pretending to have found them there. Sometimes they have "interpreted" the Constitution to forbid things explicitly allowed by its language.

Take Brennan, a hero to liberals—deservedly so—and Meese's principal foil in the current debate. In his speech belittling "original intention" theorists, Brennan denied writing his own views into the Constitution. "It is, in a very real sense, the community's interpretation that is sought," he said. "Justices are not platonic guardians appointed to wield authority according to their personal moral predilections."

But he gave these words a hollow ring when he explained why he always votes to strike down death penalty laws. He said they violate "the essential meaning" of the Eighth Amendment's prohibition against cruel and unusual punishment by denying "the intrinsic worth" of the murderers who are executed. Now, Brennan knows perfectly well that those who wrote that amendment had no intention of banning the death penalty, which was common at the time and was explicitly recognized in the Fifth and 14th Amendments.

So whence comes his mandate for invalidating the death penalty? "I hope to embody a community striving for human dignity for all, although perhaps not yet arrived," he explained. Translation: my moral convictions on this issue are so strong I would override the laws adopted by the people's elected representatives any way I could. Brennan admitted that most of his fellow countrymen and justices think the death penalty constitutional. As Judge Robert Bork has put it: "The truth is that the judge who looks outside the Constitution looks inside himself and nowhere else."

Well, what's so bad about that? If elected officials don't have the decency to end the death penalty (or antiabortion laws, or minimum-wage laws, or whatever else offends you), why shouldn't the judges do it?

The most important answer is that judicial legislation erodes democratic self-government. It converts judges into an unelected and illegitimate policy-making elite. Indeed, its more radical exponents evince a deep antipathy for the democratic process. But as Felix Frankfurter said, "Holding democracy in judicial tutelage is not the most promising way to foster disciplined responsibility in a people."

Defenders of judicial activism like to point out the vagueness of the Constitution's words and the futility of the quest for consensus on original intention. "And even if such a mythical beast could be captured and examined, how relevant would it be to us today?" asks Harvard law professor Laurence Tribe. He dismisses as a dangerous fallacy the notion that judges can be significantly restrained by the Constitution's text or history. The Supreme Court, he says, "just cannot avoid the painful duty of exercising judgment so as to give concrete meaning to the fluid Constitution."

Well, perhaps. But why can't the Court do something many law professors barely deign to discuss? When the Constitution's language and history provide little or no guidance on a subject, why can't it leave the law-making to legislatures? Those who work so hard to prove that the Constitution cannot supply the values for governance of modern society seem to think it follows that judges must do it, with a little help from their friends in academia. But their argument rebounds against the legitimacy of judicial review itself. Bork poses a question for which they have no good answer: "If the Constitution is not law—law that, with the usual areas of ambiguity around the edges, nevertheless tolerably tells judges what to do and what not to do— . . . what authorizes judges to set at naught the majority judgment of the American people?"

The activist approach of amending the Constitution in the guise of interpreting it goes hand in hand with a certain lack of candor about the enterprise. A judge who acknowledged that his goal was to strike down democratically adopted laws by rewriting the Constitution would risk impeachment. So we hear a lot about "finding" in the Constitution rights that had somehow gone unnoticed for more than a century.

There is no reason to suppose that unelected judges, using theories concocted by unelected law professors, will make better policies over time than elected officials. Nor that they will make more liberal policies. Judicial activism is not a game played only by liberals. Conservative judges rode roughshod over progressive and New Deal legislation for several decades ending about 1937. "Never . . . can the Supreme Court be said to have for a single hour been representative of anything except the relatively conservative forces of its day," Robert Jackson wrote in 1941.

Franklin Roosevelt changed that, ushering in an era of liberal judicial activism. Now the tables are turning again. Reagan and Meese are filling up the lower federal courts with conservatives and hoping to do the same with the Supreme Court. "I dream of a conservative Supreme Court striking down most federal legislation since the New Deal as unconstitutional," writes conservative columnist Joseph Sobran. Liberals may soon rediscover the virtues of judicial restraint, and find themselves urging a Reaganized judiciary to practice what Meese has been preaching.

Brennan and other liberal activist judges deserve the applause they have won for thrusting upon the nation some policies that were also triumphs of constitutional principle. Desegregation is one example. Protection of the rights of poor criminal defendants is another.

But liberal activism has gone to dubious extremes. Take the case of the man who approached a policeman in Denver and said he'd killed someone. The policeman told him about his rights to remain silent and have a lawyer. The man said he understood and proceeded with his confession, leading police to the scene where he said he had killed a 14-year-old girl. The sometime mental patient later told a psychiatrist that the voice of God had ordered him to confess. The Colorado Supreme Court threw out the confession on the ground that it was compelled by mental illness, and therefore involuntary. If he is ever tried, neither the confession nor, presumably, the other evidence ("fruits" of the confession) will be admissible. And he may go free.

Such judicial excesses are giving constitutional rights a bad name. Ed Meese is not alone in his outrage at judges who free criminals on the basis of technical rules that protect only the guilty, especially where they have little to do with deterring police abuse. The more this sort of thing happens, the greater the danger that the considerable public backlash may build to radical reaction.

There will always be cases in which judges must let criminals go free, and must defy public opinion, to vindicate the constitutional rights of innocent and guilty alike. Their ability to do so suffers when they squander the reservoir of goodwill they need for such occasions. "Liberty lies in the hearts of men and women," Learned Hand wrote. "When it dies there, no constitution, no law, no court can save it."

Judicial creation of new constitutional rights can also be mistaken even when much or most of the public approves. The best example is *Roe v. Wade*, the 1973 decision creating a constitutional right to abortion and striking down all state antiabortion laws. Abortion is one of the toughest moral issues around. If I were a legislator I might vote (with misgivings) to allow free access to abortion in the early stages of pregnancy, as the Supreme Court did. But the Court is not a legislature, and there is no plausible basis in the Constitution for it to take this issue away from the states, some of which had already legalized abortion before *Roe*.

Justice Harry Blackmun's opinion "found" a right to abortion within the vague, general "right to personal privacy." He said these rights were in the Constitution somewhere, though he was not sure where—probably the 14th Amendment's generalized protection of "liberty," maybe the Ninth Amendment. Blackmun (appointed by Richard Nixon) made no pretense that the Framers of these amendments intended to legalize abortion. History shows clearly that they did not. They were not thinking about abortion at all, although it was a familiar practice, illegal in some states, when the 14th Amendment was adopted. Nor do the words of the Constitution provide a shred of support for the detailed regulations the Court has drafted over time to curb state regulation of abortion.

Right-to-lifers are not the only people who deplore *Roe v. Wade*. Many liberal scholars—defenders of the pioneering Warren Court decisions so despised by Meese—have said the Burger Court went too far down the road of naked judicial legislation in that case. Among them are Archibald Cox, now retired from Harvard Law School, Dean John Hart Ely of Stanford Law School, and Dean Benno Schmidt of Columbia Law School, soon to be president of Yale. The abortion issue poses an excruciating clash between two moral imperatives: a woman's right to personal autonomy and protection of the unborn. Why every detail of local, state, and national policy on such a fundamental moral issue should depend on the personal philosophies of five or six judges escapes them, and me.

The disregard for the written Constitution that *Roe v. Wade* embodies is also a two-edged sword. President Reagan said in his debate with Walter Mondale that an unborn child is a living human being "protected by the Constitution, which guarantees life, liberty, and the pursuit of happiness to all of us." Well, there he goes again, quoting the Declaration of Independence and calling it the Constitution. But he was close enough: the 14th Amendment says no state may "deprive any person of life, liberty, or property, without due process of law." For those who believe a fetus is a "person" and abortion is murder, as Reagan does, it is possible to conclude that judges should strike down any state laws that allow it. Farfetched? Well, what if a state excluded homosexuals or handicapped children from the protection of its murder laws?

None of this means Meese's own approach to constitutional interpretation is adequate. It isn't. For starters, there is little evidence he has given the subject much thought. Beyond the high-sounding, platitudinous stuff about the Framers in the speeches his aides have written for him, he has had little specific to say about what he thinks their intentions were, or how broadly these intentions should be read. There is enormous room for disagreement here. The most important constitutional phrases, like "equal protection of the laws," are sweeping, vague, and only dimly illuminated by history.

Meese has tiptoed away from some of the few specific things he has said, including his attack on the doctrine that most of the Bill of Rights applies to the states through the 14th Amendment. It appeared in the written text of his July 9 speech to the American Bar Association. For some reason he omitted this point when he read the speech aloud. Moments afterward, reporters bearing tape recorders asked Meese whether he thought the Court had gone too far in applying the Bill of Rights to the states. "No," he responded. "I, well, I think this is something that's been done in 1925 and since, and so I don't think, ah, ah, I think, I do not have any particular quarrel at this stage of the game with what the Court has done in the intervening 60 years." Will the real Ed Meese please stand up?

Meese has stuck to his guns in denouncing as "infamous" major decisions upholding the rights of criminal defendants. One of his least favorites is *Mapp v. Ohio* (1961), which extended to the states the "exclusionary rule" barring use of evidence seized in violation of the

Fourth Amendment. Meese has said *Mapp* helps only "the guilty criminal," and has suggested abandoning the exclusionary rule in state and federal cases alike.

But Meese seems to have forgotten *Boyd v. U.S.*, which Justice Louis Brandeis said "will be remembered as long as civil liberty lives in the United States." The 1886 decision was the Supreme Court's first major Fourth and Fifth Amendment ruling. Unlike modern rulings, it was explicitly based on a detailed study of the Framers' intentions. *Boyd* held that the Framers intended the Fourth Amendment's ban on "unreasonable searches and seizures" to prohibit *all* governmental attempts to obtain a person's private papers or other property—even by warrant or subpoena—and to forbid their use as evidence to convict him. Innocence or guilt was irrelevant to this determination. The Court's confident assertion that this was the Framers' intention was based on a reading of their natural rights philosophy, on 18th-century case law, and on the fury at sweeping British searches that helped fuel the American Revolution.

If *Boyd* were the law today, it would place far greater restrictions on police than any imposed by the Warren Court, which Meese has denounced for its "expansive civil liberatarianism." The modern Court, unwilling to restrict official power so severely, has abandoned this broad vision. Its use of the exclusionary rule as a limited deterrent to police abuses is a pale remnant of the expansive rights the Court saw in the Fourth Amendment 99 years ago.

Meese's contention that the exclusionary rule helps only guilty criminals is demonstrably false. Of course, exclusion of improperly obtained but reliable evidence helps only the guilty in the immediate case at hand. But if officials knew they could search everyone indiscriminately and use any evidence they found, a lot of innocent people would be victims of illegal searches. The only way to take the profit out of police abuses is to bar use of the evidence found. This means letting some guilty criminals go free. It is one thing to say this is too high a price to pay in cases in which police inadvertently cross the line between marginally legal and marginally illegal searches. It is quite another to let officials use any and all illegally obtained evidence, as Meese would.

Meese's selectiveness in applying original intention is not limited to criminal law issues. If he really believed the Framers' specific intentions are "the only reliable guide for judgment," he would have to condemn *Brown v. Board of Education*, the landmark 1954 decision desegregating public schools. Anybody who did that today would be assailed as a segregationist crank. Meese recently applauded *Brown* as a case study in finding the original intention of the post–Civil War 14th Amendment. "The Supreme Court in that case was not giving new life to old words, or adapting a 'living,' 'flexible' Constitution to new reality," he declared. "It was restoring the original principle of the Constitution."

That's nice, but it's not true. The Congress that wrote the amendment had no intention of outlawing segregation, as Raoul Berger, Alexander Bickel, and others have demonstrated. The same Congress segregated its own Senate gallery and the District of Columbia schools, and rejected various desegregation bills. What the Court saw nearly 90 years later was that state-enforced segregation, relegating blacks to inferior schools and other facilities, had made a mockery of the 14th Amendment's central purpose: to put blacks and whites on an equal footing before the law. So the Court gave "new life to old words," to use Meese's mocking phrase, and threw out segregation.

The same Congress that drafted the 14th Amendment also passed some special welfare programs for recently freed slaves and other blacks in the South. These were, in modern parlance, affirmative action programs involving racial preferences, for blacks—sort of like the government hiring quotas that Meese has declared in violation of the 14th Amendment. Congress specifically excluded whites from some of these programs. Among them were federally funded, racially segregated schools for blacks only—a single program that contradicts the Meese view of the 14th Amendment's original intention on segregation and affirmative action alike. These programs were passed over the Meese-like objections that they discriminated against whites and included some blacks who were not personally victims of discrimination. But Meese's Justice Department, checking its slogans about judicial restraint at the door, has urged the Supreme Court to strike down every local, state, and federal government affirmative action program in the nation that prefers black employees over whites. Right or wrong, Meese's position on affirmative action is at war with his preachings about strict adherence to original intention.

The same is true of his position on a lot of issues. Many of the powers that his Justice Department exercises daily—reaching into every community with its wiretaps, its informers, its subpoenas—would have horrified the Framers. They feared centralized power more than anything but anarchy. They sought to limit severely the national government's law enforcement powers, leaving to state and local authorities jurisdiction over the all but genuinely interstate crimes.

What would Meese do about the strong historical evidence that the Framers intended to deny the government the power to issue paper money, which they saw as a threat to propertied interests? What about their intent to bar the president from launching military expeditions without congressional approval, except to repel attacks on United States territory?

And what about the First Amendment's religion clauses, as expounded by Joseph Story, a 19th-century justice whom Meese sometimes quotes on original intention? "The real object," Story said, "was not to countenance, much less to advance, Mahometanism, or Judaism, or infidelity, by prostrating Christianity; but to exclude all rivalry among Christian sects." Meese buys the "infidels" part when he says the Framers would have found "bizarre" the notion that government may not favor religion over nonreligion. He ignores the rest, of course. Any official who argued today that only Christians are protected by the religion clauses would be drummed out of office, and properly so.

The broader point is that sticking to the Framers' immediate goals as closely as Meese sometimes suggests is neither possible nor desirable. If *Brown v. Board of Education* was right, and it was, then a "jurisprudence of original intention" worthy of respect cannot mean enforcing constitutional rights only in the specific ways envisioned by the Framers. Such an approach would doom these rights to wither with the passage of time. The Framers' central purpose of preventing abuse of minorities would be strangled by narrow-minded attention to their more immediate concerns. As for the possibility of updating the Constitution by the formal amendment process, this takes a two-thirds majority in each house of Congress and approval by three-fourths of the states. Such majorities could rarely be mustered to deal with new threats to the rights of minorities.

New technologies such as wiretapping threaten liberties the Framers enshrined in ways that they could not have imagined. And the changing nature of society poses threats that the Framers did not foresee to the constitutional principles they established. Take libel law. Million-dollar libel suits by public officials were not prevalent in the 18th century, and it is fairly clear that the Framers did not intend the First Amendment (or the 14th) to limit private libel suits as the modern Court has done. But they did intend to protect uninhibited, robust, and wide-open debate about public affairs. And it seems to me proper for the Supreme Court to effectuate that broad purpose, in this litigious era, by imposing some curbs on libel suits.

Am I slipping into the kind of judicial revision of the Constitution I just rejected? I don't think so. There is a middle ground between narrow adherence to original intention and freewheeling judicial legislation. As Chief Justice John Marshall said in a famous 1819 decision, the Constitution is not a code of "immutable rules," but rather the "great outlines" of a system intended "to endure for ages to come, and, consequently, to be adapted to the various crises of human affairs." But it is for elected officials, as he said, to do most of the adapting. Judges should invalidate democratically enacted laws only, in John Ely's words, "in accord with an inference whose starting point, whose underlying premise, is fairly discoverable in the Constitution."

This approach will often set only loose outer boundaries around the Court's options in deciding specific issues. It requires judges in close cases to draw fine lines. And it does not pretend to purge their moral and political convictions entirely from the process. But its recognition that the Constitution imposes some bounds on judicial power—limits fleshed out more clearly by the accumulation of precedent—would channel the growth of the law in a more principled and therefore more legitimate direction.

At the outer limits of legitimacy are those cases in which the justices read into vague constitutional phrases like "due process" an emerging social consensus that seems contrary to the particular intentions of the Framers. This goes beyond applying old principles to new circumstances, and gets into tinkering with the principles or creating new ones. I think the Supreme Court should do it in a few rare cases, nudging society to progress in the common law tradition of gradually evolving principles against a background of continuity.

Brown v. Board of Education was such a case. It struck at the heart of a great evil. Though departing from the particular plans of the Framers, it honored their deeper, nobler intentions. And though overriding the democratic process, it crystallized an emerging national consensus that legally compelled racial segregation was unacceptable in modern America. That is the difference between judicial activism and judicial statesmanship, and why most of the fiercest critics of judicial activism don't dare criticize *Brown* today.

But the Court should attempt to lead only where the nation is prepared to follow. The creation of new constitutional values is a slippery slope, down which the courts should not travel too far too fast. At the bottom lies the kind of uninhibited and essentially lawless judicial legislation that Bork has justly assailed. The urge to do good is powerful, the urge to court greatness intoxicating. Judges should resist the sincere, but arrogant, assumption that they know best. Brandeis's words, aimed at Ed Meese's ideological predecessors, should also be heeded by his ideological adversaries: "The greatest danger to liberty is the insidious encroachment by men of zeal, well-meaning but without understanding."

DISCUSSION QUESTIONS

1. Critics of strict construction and original intent often point to ambiguities in the language of the Constitution (indeed, the readings in this section point out some examples). What are some examples of ambiguities in the Constitution (look at the Bill of Rights as a start)? What alternative interpretations can you develop?

2. Critics of judicial activism often argue that judges substitute their own reading of what they think the law *should* be for what the law *is*. What are the dangers of judges' assuming this role?

PART III

Political Participation

CHAPTER 8

Public Opinion and the Mass Media

38
"Polling the Public" from *Public Opinion in a Democracy*

George Gallup

Assessing public opinion in a democracy of 250 million people is no easy task. George Gallup, who is largely responsible for the development of modern opinion polling, argued that public opinion polls enhanced the democratic process by providing elected officials with a picture of what Americans think about current events. Despite Gallup's vigorous defense of his polling techniques and the contribution of polling to democracy, the public opinion poll remains controversial: critics charge that public officials pay too much attention to polls, making decisions based on fluctuations in public opinion rather than on informed, independent judgment.

We have a national election every two years only. In a world which moves as rapidly as the modern world does, it is often desirable to know the people's will on basic policies at more frequent intervals. We cannot put issues off and say "let them be decided at the next election." World events do not wait on elections. We need to know the will of the people at all times.

If we know the collective will of the people at all times the efficiency of democracy can be increased, because we can substitute specific knowledge of public opinion for blind groping and guesswork. Statesmen who know the true state of public opinion can then formulate plans with a sure knowledge of what the voting public is thinking. They can know what degree of opposition to any proposed plan exists, and what efforts are necessary to gain public acceptance for it. The responsibility for initiating action should, as always, rest with the political leaders of the country. But the collective will or attitude of the people needs to be learned without delay.

The Will of the People

How is the will of the people to be known at all times?

Before I offer an answer to this question, I would like to examine some of the principal channels by which, at the present time, public opinion is expressed.

The most important is of course a national election. An election is the only official and binding expression of the people's judgment. But, as viewed from a strictly objective point of view, elections are a confusing and imperfect way of registering national opinion. In the first place, they come only at infrequent intervals. In the second place, as [James] Bryce pointed out in *The American Commonwealth*, it is virtually impossible to separate issues from candidates. How can we tell whether the public is voting for the man or for his platform? How can we tell whether all the candidate's views are endorsed, or whether some are favored and others opposed by the voters? Because society grows more and more complex, the tendency is to have more and more issues in an election. Some may be discussed; others not. Suppose a candidate for office takes a position on a great many public issues during the campaign. If elected, he inevitably assumes that the public has endorsed all his planks, whereas this may actually not be the case.

* 　 * 　 *

The Role of the Elected Representative

A second method by which public opinion now expresses itself is through elected representatives. The legislator is, technically speaking, supposed to represent the interests of all voters in his constituency. But under the two-party system there is a strong temptation for him to represent, and be influenced by, only the voters of his own party. He is subject to the pressure of party discipline and of wishes of party leaders back home. His very continuance in office may depend on giving way to such pressure. Under these circumstances his behavior in Congress is likely to be governed not by what he thinks the voters of his State want, but by what he thinks the leaders of his own party in that State want.

* 　 * 　 *

Even in the event that an elected representative does try to perform his duty of representing the whole people, he is confronted with the problem: What is the will of the people? Shall he judge their views by the letters they write him or the telegrams they send him? Too often such expressions of opinion come only from an articulate minority. Shall the congressman judge their views by the visitors or delegations that come to him from his home district?

Pressure Groups and the Whole Nation

Legislators are constantly subject to the influence of organized lobbies and pressure groups. Senator Tydings . . . pointed out recently that the United States is the most fertile soil on earth for the activity of pressure groups. The American people represent a conglomeration of races, all with different cultural backgrounds. Sections and groups struggle with one another to fix national and international policy. And frequently in such struggles, as Senator Tydings pointed out, "self-interest and sectionalism, rather than the promotion of national welfare, dominate the contest." Senator Tydings mentions some twenty important group interests. These include labor, agriculture, veterans, pension plan advocates, chambers of commerce, racial organizations, isolationists and internationalists, high-tariff and low-tariff groups, preparedness and disarmament groups, budget balancers and spending advocates, soft-money associations and hard-money associations, transportation groups and states righters and centralizationists.

The legislator obviously owes a duty to his home district to legislate in its best interests. But he also owes a duty to legislate in the best interests of the whole nation. In order, however, to carry out this second duty he must *know* what the nation thinks. Since he doesn't always know what the voters in his own district think, it is just that much more difficult for him to learn the views of the nation. Yet if he could know those views at all times he could legislate more often in the interest of the whole country.

* * *

The Cross-Section Survey

This effort to discover public opinion has been largely responsible for the introduction of a new instrument for determining public opinion—the cross-section or sampling survey. By means of nationwide studies taken at frequent intervals, research workers are today attempting to measure and give voice to the sentiments of the whole people on vital issues of the day.

Where does this new technique fit into the scheme of things under our form of government? Is it a useful instrument of democracy? Will it prove to be vicious and harmful, or will it contribute to the efficiency of the democratic process?

The sampling referendum is simply a procedure for sounding the opinions of a relatively small number of persons, selected in such manner as to reflect with a high degree of accuracy the views of the whole voting population. In effect such surveys canvass the opinions of a miniature electorate.

Cross-section surveys do not place their chief reliance upon numbers. The technique is based on the fact that a few thousand voters correctly selected will faithfully reflect the views of an electorate of millions of voters. The key to success in this work is the cross section—the proper selection of voters included in the sample. Elaborate precautions must be taken to secure the views of members of all political parties—of rich and poor, old and young, of men and women, farmers and city dwellers, persons of all religious faiths—in short, voters of all types living in every State in the land. And all must be included in correct proportion.

* * *

Reliability of Opinion Surveys

Whether opinion surveys will prove to be a useful contribution to democracy depends largely on their reliability in measuring opinion. During the last four years [1935–1939] the sampling procedure, as used in measuring public opinion, has been subjected to many tests. In general these tests indicate that present techniques can attain a high degree of accuracy, and it seems reasonable to assume that with the development of this infant science, the accuracy of its measurements will be constantly improved.

The most practical way at present to measure the accuracy of the sampling referendum is to compare forecasts of elections with election results. Such a test is by no means perfect, because a preelection survey must not only measure opinion in respect to candidates but must also predict just what groups of people will actually take the trouble to cast their ballots. Add to this the problem of measuring the effect of weather on turnout, also the activities of corrupt political machines, and it can easily be seen that election results are by no means a perfect test of the accuracy of this new technique.

* * *

Many thoughtful students of government have asked: Why shouldn't the Government itself, rather than private organizations, conduct these sampling surveys? A few political scientists have even suggested the establishment of a permanent federal bureau for sounding public opinion, arguing that if this new technique is a contribution to democracy, the government has a duty to take it over.

The danger in this proposal, as I see it, lies in the temptation it would place in the way of the party in power to conduct surveys to prove itself right and to suppress those which proved it to be wrong. A private organization, on the other hand, must stand or fall not so much on what it reports or fails to report as on the accuracy of its results, and the impartiality of its interpretations. An important requirement in a democracy is complete and reliable news reports of the activities of all branches of the government and of the views of all leaders and parties. But few persons would argue that, for this reason, the government should take over the press, and all its news gathering associations.

* * *

Cloture on Debate?

It is sometimes argued that public opinion surveys impose a cloture on debate. When the advocates of one side of an issue are shown to be in the majority, so the argument runs, the other side will lose hope and abandon their cause believing that further efforts are futile.

Again let me say that there is little evidence to support this view. Every election necessarily produces a minority. In 1936 the Republicans polled less than 40 percent of the vote. Yet the fact that the Republicans were defeated badly wasn't enough to lead them to quit the battle. They continued to fight against the New Deal with as much vigor as before. An even better example is afforded by the Socialist Party. For years the Socialist candidate for President has received but a small fraction of the total popular vote, and could count on sure defeat. Yet the Socialist Party continues as a party, and continues to poll about the same number of votes.

Sampling surveys will never impose a cloture on debate so long as it is the nature of public opinion to change. The will of the people is dynamic; opinions are constantly changing. A year ago an overwhelming majority of voters were skeptical of the prospects of the Republican Party in 1940. Today, half the voters think the G.O.P. will win. If elections themselves do not impose cloture on debate, is it likely that opinion surveys will?

Possible Effect on Representative Government

The form of government we live under is a representative form of government. What will be the effect on representative government if the will of the people is known at all times? Will legislators become mere rubber stamps, mere puppets, and the function of representation be lost?

Under a system of frequent opinion measurement, the function of representation is not lost, for two reasons. First, it is well understood that the people have not the time or the inclination to pass on all the problems that confront their leaders. They cannot be expected to express judgment on technical questions of administration and government. They can pass judgment only on basic general policies. As society grows more complex there is a greater and greater need for experts. Once the voters have indicated their approval of a general policy or plan of action, experts are required to carry it out.

Second, it is not the province of the people to initiate legislation, but to decide which of the programs offered they like best. National policies do not spring full-blown from the common people. Leaders, knowing the general will of the people, must take the initiative in forming policies that will carry out the general will and must put them into effect.

Before the advent of the sampling referendum, legislators were not isolated from their constituencies. They read the local newspapers; they toured their districts and talked with voters; they received letters from their home State; they entertained delegations who claimed to speak for large and important blocs of voters. The change that is brought about by sampling referenda is merely one which provides these legislators with a truer measure of opinion in their districts and in the nation.

* * *

How Wise Are the Common People?

The sampling surveys of recent years have provided much evidence concerning the wisdom of the common people. Anyone is free to examine this evidence. And I think that the person who does examine it will come away believing as I do that, collectively, the American people have a remarkably high degree of common sense. These people may not be brilliant or intellectual or particularly well read, but they possess a quality of good sense which is manifested time and again in their expressions of opinion on present-day issues.

* * *

It is not difficult to understand why the conception of the stupidity of the masses has so many adherents. Talk to the first hundred persons whom you happen to meet in the street about many important issues of the day, and the chances are great that you will be struck by their lack of accurate or complete knowledge on these issues. Few of them will likely have sufficient information in this particular field to express a well founded judgment.

But fortunately a democracy does not require that every voter be well informed on every issue. In fact a democracy does not depend so much on the enlightenment of each individual, as upon the quality of the collective judgment or intelligence of thousands of individuals.

* * *

It would of course be foolish to argue that the collective views of the common people always represent the most intelligent and most accurate answer to any question. But results of sampling referenda on hundreds of issues do indicate, in my opinion, that we can place great faith in the collective judgment or intelligence of the people.

The New England Town Meeting Restored

One of the earliest and purest forms of democracy in this country was the New England town meeting. The people gathered in one room to discuss and to vote on the questions of the community. There was a free exchange of opinions in the presence of all the members. The town meeting was a simple and effective way of articulating public opinion, and the decisions made by the meeting kept close to the public will. When a democracy thus operates on a small scale it is able to express itself swiftly and with certainty.

But as communities grew, the town meeting became unwieldy. As a result the common people became less articulate, less able to debate the vital issues in the manner of their New England forefathers. Interest in politics lagged. Opinion had to express itself by the slow and cumbersome method of election, no longer facilitated by the town meeting with its frequent give and take of ideas. The indifference and apathy of voters made it possible for vicious and corrupt political machines to take over the administration of government in many states and cities.

The New England town meeting was valuable because it provided a forum for the exchange of views among all citizens of the community and for a vote on these views. Today, the New England town meeting idea has, in a sense, been restored. The wide distribution of daily newspapers reporting the views of statesmen on issues of the day, the almost universal ownership of radios which bring the whole nation within the hearing of any voice, and now the advent of the sampling referendum which provides a means of determining quickly the response of the public to debate on issues of the day, have in effect created a town meeting on a national scale.

How nearly the goal has been achieved is indicated in the following data recently gathered by the American Institute of Public Opinion. Of the 45,000,000 persons who voted in the last presidential election [1936], approximately 40,000,000 read a daily newspaper, 40,000,000 have radios, and only 2,250,000 of the entire group of voters in the nation neither have a radio nor take a daily newspaper.

This means that the nation is literally in one great room. The newspapers and the radio conduct the debate on national issues, presenting both information and argument on both sides, just as the townsfolk did in person in the old town meeting. And finally, through the process of the sampling referendum, the people, having heard the debate on both sides of every issue, can express their will. After one hundred and fifty years we return to the town meeting. This time the whole nation is within the doors.

DISCUSSION QUESTIONS

1. What are the advantages and disadvantages of modern public opinion polling?

2. How would our political system change if all public opinion polls were banned?

3. In 1980, the major networks declared Reagan the president-elect while the polls were still open in California. Television crews showed footage of people who were waiting in line to vote abandoning the polls. Does this event, or the more recent proliferation of "horse-race polling" up until the day of the election, undermine Gallup's argument that polls do not "impose cloture on debate"? All the networks, the campaigns, and most reporters know who has won a presidential election early on election day, because of sophisticated "exit polling" of people who have just voted. Should this information be kept secret, or should it be broadcast?

39
"Why Americans Hate Politics and Politicians"

Michael Nelson

Are the media to blame for America's cynical and antagonistic view of politics? Critics of the media argue that the airwaves are full of negative commentators bent on exposing every public official's moral warts; network news coverage of campaigns reduces complex issues to trivial, quick sound bites. For every critic who claims that the media has a liberal slant, another alleges a conservative bias. Nobody, it seems, is happy with media coverage of politics.

The problem, Michael Nelson argues, is not the media. It is also not the politicians, the political process, or the political parties. The problem is that Americans hold tightly to fundamental, but contradictory, values about the way in which the American political system should work. First, we believe that government ought to function according to a higher law or "ultimate standard of right." Second, Americans believe that government ought to function according to "popular sovereignty"—it ought to do what the people want. Nelson argues that the problem is these two values can and often do conflict: What the people want is not always the same as the principles set out in higher law. Consequently, when government inevitably fails to meet both standards, we do not blame our governing principles or ourselves, but rather the politicians, the institutions within which they exercise their authority, or the media.

Do psychiatrists still use word-association techniques with their patients? You know what I mean: Dr. Jungfreud says "food" and the patient says "mother," the doctor says "girls" and the patient says "mother," the doctor says "father" and the patient says "mother," and quickly they realize that the patient has a hangup with his mother. Modern psychiatric practices notwithstanding, I sometimes do a little word association on the first day of my introductory American government classes at Rhodes College. The first word I say is "politics" and back come the replies from the students (not "mother"): "corrupt," they say, "dirty," "games-playing," "ego trip," "a waste." (The nicest thing I heard the last time I did this was "boring.") Here is what they say in response to "politician": "selfish," "ambitious," "mediocre," "unprincipled."

*   *   *

Why do Americans hate politics and politicians? There is no scarcity of answers to this question. 1993 being the 30th anniversary of President John F. Kennedy's assassination and the 25th anniversary of the assassinations of his brother Robert and of Martin Luther King, Jr., much was made of the despair about politics that spread among the American people in the wake of those brutal deaths. Other explanations of our distrust and cynicism are grounded in the lies and half-truths the government told about the Vietnam war and about Watergate and all its many offspring: Koreagate, Irangate, Iraqgate, and, most recently, Whitewatergate, to name but a few. The media is another likely suspect—remodeled network evening news programs that treat politics and government with a sneer, now joined by new-style trash TV news shows and radio talk shows (Rush Limbaugh, can you hear me?) that are overtly hostile to politics and politicians. On top of all that, professional political consultants use the media to air their increasingly negative campaign ads, the cumulative effect of which, some argue, is to convince Americans that all the candidates in all our elections are bums.

Still other explanations of our cynicism and indifference may be found in two recent and very thoughtful books by journalists. E. J. Dionne of *The Washington Post*, in the book whose title I have adapted for this essay—*Why Americans Hate Politics*—blames the poverty of our prevailing political ideologies. "Liberalism and conservatism are framing political issues as a series of false choices. . . ." he writes. "On issue after issue, there is consensus [among the public] on where the country should move or at least on what we should be arguing about; [but] liberalism and conservatism make it impossible for that consensus to express itself." Most Americans agree, for example, that to help lift the underclass out of poverty will require some combination of government help *and* greater personal responsibility. But, Dionne argues, conservatives don't want to admit the need for government help and liberals don't want to tell poor people to take responsibility for their lives, so nothing is done. The progress of welfare reform in Washington will provide a good test of how far the political process has come on this issue.

Another journalist, Alan Ehrenhalt, turns his gaze to the politicians in a book called *The United States of Ambition*. Ehrenhalt argues that running for and serving in political office has become so time consuming and demanding that only people who are willing to become fulltime politicians can do it. Pernicious effects flow from this modern fact of political life. The talent pool from which leaders are drawn has narrowed—it now excludes the business or professional person (much less the blue collar or pink collar worker) who could spare some time for public service but not abandon a career or job to do so. The talent pool also includes many more liberals than conservatives, according to Ehrenhalt. Liberals, after all, like government and are more likely to be drawn to it on a fulltime basis. And with politics as their vocation, those who are elected in the modern era feel compelled to do everything they can to stay in office.

All of these explanations of why Americans hate politics and politicians have three things in common. First, they all point the blame away from the American people and fix it on somebody else—politicians, political consultants, the media, liberals, conservatives, assassins, and so on. (How convenient for us.) Second, they are all ahistorical, grounded almost entirely in recent events and developments. Third, they are all partial explanations—accurate, especially in explaining why antipolitical feelings are higher now than ever, but accurate only to a degree. In truth, there has never been a time when Americans were pro-politics and pro-politicians. Historically, the United States has lagged far behind other Western democracies in the development and extent of its welfare state. The American approach has been to regulate businesses rather than nationalize them. Political ideologies that exalt government—from fascism to communism—simply have not taken root in American soil; the United States is the only Western country in which Socialists were never able to form a leading political party. We seem to be antipolitical in our very bones.

II

Clearly another piece needs to be added to the great jigsaw puzzle that, once assembled, can reveal why Americans hate politics and politicians. This new piece would be a picture of us—of "we the people"—and not just of us in this generation but us through all the generations that, taken together, constitute the history of the United States. The label on the new piece would read: "American political culture."

American political culture consists of our longstanding, widely-shared, and deeply-felt values about how the political system ought to work (our process values) and the ends it ought to serve (our purpose values). It has become fashionable to speak of multiculturalism, and in many areas of American life it is accurate to do so as well. But when it comes to the purposes the political system ought to serve, almost everything that Americans in all their hyphenated variety have ever valued can be grouped under the headings "liberty" and "equality." One can argue—as Americans have for more than two centuries—about what these values mean and how they should be applied in specific situations. But liberty and equality are the banners under which such battles invariably are fought.

More pertinent to the question of why Americans hate politics and politicians are the process values of our political culture, our values concerning how the American political system ought to work, the rules of the game.

Deeply rooted in American political culture—that is, in us—is the belief that government ought to work in accordance with "higher law," some ultimate standard of right.

* * *

"Higher law" philosophy certainly prevailed in the America of 1776, when, as the historian Gordon Wood has shown, "the traditional covenant theology of Puritanism combined with the political science of the eighteenth century [Enlightenment] into an imperatively persuasive argument for revolution." (If that seems densely academic, does this sound more familiar? "We hold these *truths* to be *self-evident.*" That is higher law philosophy in a nutshell.) And it endures in the modern practice of inscribing our ideals into public policy.

* * *

But Americans' political process values include more than higher law. They also believe that the political system ought to operate in accordance with "popular sovereignty," a value that consists of the related beliefs that the only legitimate basis of political authority is the consent of the governed ("government of the people," to quote another greatest hit from American history) and that government is supposed to work in accordance with what the public wants ("government by the people"). The belief in popular sovereignty not only infuses virtually every political writing of the founding period, but it forms the philosophical foundation of the Constitution itself: "We the people . . . do ordain and establish this Constitution of the United States of America." . . . Since 1787, the belief in popular sovereignty has manifested itself in an endless and, by the standards of other Western nations, radical series of democratic reforms: universal suffrage; primaries, initiatives, referendums, recalls; and direct election of senators, presidential electors, and, in many states, judges, school boards, sheriffs, clerks, trustees, and commissioners—the American people are asked to speak authoritatively in so many ways. Popular sovereignty also underlies Americans' widely shared expectations of members of Congress and other legislators, whom we insist should vote in accordance with our wishes, not with their own considered judgments as to what is best.

Matters grow especially interesting when these two process values from the political culture are laid alongside each other, which is what most of us do, without thinking very much about it, in our own minds. Let's review the bidding. As Americans, we believe that government is supposed to work according to higher law—a fixed, external, eternal standard of right that is embodied in the Constitution. We also believe that it is supposed to work according to what the people want—popular sovereignty. An obvious problem arises. Which standard is supposed to prevail when what the higher law seems to require and what the people want are not the same? Never fear—Americans take pride in being great problem-solvers. And one of the most effective strategies for dealing with problems is to pretend that they do not exist. That is what we have done in this case. Listen, for example, to that great American problem-solver, Andrew Jackson:

> I believe that man can be elevated; man can become more and more endowed with divinity; and as he does he becomes more God-like in his character and capable of governing himself. Let us go on elevating our people, perfecting our institutions, until democracy shall reach such a point of perfection that we can acclaim with truth that the voice of the people is the voice of God.

Vox populi, vox dei—the voice of the people *is* the voice of God. How convenient the doctrine that allows us to believe that popular sovereignty will never conflict with the higher law.

And the doctrine endures, as reflected in comparative studies of civic competence and social trust in a number of Western democracies. To a far greater extent than Britons, Germans, Austrians, Netherlanders, Mexicans, Italians, and the French, Americans have been found to feel personally competent to participate intelligently in politics and to trust each other to do the same. In short, we see no contradiction between government of the people and by the people, and government for the people.

Americans also revere the Constitution. Ask a random sample of Europeans (as political scientists have done) what they are proudest of about their country and they are likely to mention its physical beauty or cultural achievements; ask Americans the same question and they will describe their form of government—democracy, freedom, "all men are created equal," etc. When Americans travel to Washington with their families (which most who can afford to do so eventually do), they are making pilgrimages of a sort. They visit the city's sacred shrines to Lincoln, Washington, Jefferson, Kennedy, and our fallen soldiers. They gaze upon its sacred texts—the Constitution and the Declaration of Independence—at the National Archives. They visit its temples of law and democracy—the Supreme Court, the Capitol, the White House. Their attitude is serious, even reverential; their gaze open-mouthed.

Why, then, do Americans hate politics and politicians? We hate them because we have left ourselves no alternative. When things go wrong, as most people think they have in the political system, we have no one else to blame. We can not blame the Constitution for what is wrong— far from it, it is our embodiment of higher law. And we certainly are not about to blame ourselves. And so we blame the only people who are left—the politicians. And they, wanting to please us, are only too happy to confirm us in our beliefs by pointing their own fingers of blame at each other.

* * *

DISCUSSION QUESTIONS

1. Do you agree with Nelson's assessment of why voters are so dissatisfied with politics? If we are to blame for our inconsistent expectations, how can those expectations be changed? Is it partly the responsibility of the media and politicians to "teach reality" (to place the blame somewhere else again)?

2. Do you think government should follow certain higher ends, or do what the people want? What happens when the two are in conflict?

40
"The Presidency and the Press"

Charles Jones

Both the president and the press have a role in pursuing the public interest. Yet, as Charles Jones writes in the following article, the two are in a competition to represent that interest, indeed, to represent the presidency and its officeholder. It is a relationship of necessity and tension. On the one hand the president needs the press to govern, to put issues and concerns before the voters, to present the president with stature and presence, while it is the role of a free press to report on the priorities and activities of the president. On the other, the independence of the press demands the rigorous reporting of the activities in the White House, including poor decisions, weak political agendas, and sometimes, scandals. Yet a press corps that is perceived as hostile to the president can have its access shut off.

The effort to balance this tension was the topic of a conference held in Washington, D.C., in 1995. Writing as an observer of the conference, Charles Jones reports on the "rules of engagement" adopted by presidents and the press corps as a means to balance the tension, the ways in which technological changes and changes in topics considered "permissible" to cover have altered the press and presidency relationship, and what the relationship has been between the Clinton White House and the press.

Few relationships better exemplify the inherent tensions of the politics of democracy than the vital association between presidents and the press. If democracy is about pursuing the public interest, and it is, then both presidents and the press can claim legitimate roles in that quest. Yet the two are bound to be in competition. As Gary Wills observed at a recent conference on this topic, "The fight over representing the presidency is a fight for representation of the entire nation." In a very real sense, both the president and the press properly view themselves as representatives—one elected, the other self-designated by reason of professional obligation.

All democrats would fight for preserving each. We want and need presidents and we want independent, even aggressive, reporting on what they do. Presidents and the press will be judged as performing well or poorly in this representational role, but of course, it is the criticism of the president that appears most often in print and over the airwaves. Thus, again quoting Gary Wills, "Sooner or later, all presidents blame their problems on the media, and they are right. The press and the president are linked in a natural enmity. They need each other and they resent that."

It was precisely because of this deliberate and requisite tension that a conference was held in Washington, D.C., on the presidency and the press. Presidential biographers, journalists, and historians discussed presidents and their interaction with the press. Three themes emerged from the conference:

1. This vital competition between the president and the press, and the resulting resentments, are characterized by enduring rules of engagement.
2. What changes in this relationship is the proficiency of presidents in dealing with the press, as well as the technology and permissible topics of coverage.
3. The Clinton presidency is a particularly rich illustration of the continuities and change, thus providing contemporary lessons about the representational rivalry of the two institutions.

In Competition to a Purpose: Rules of Engagement

Accepting that the relationship is competitive, the biographers identified several rules of engagement, discussed primarily from the perspective of the president. First and foremost is the civil and conversant acknowledgment by the president and his aides of the legitimate role played by the press. For example, Doris Kearns Goodwin stressed that Franklin Roosevelt fully understood how his position served as a focal point of political coverage. It is fair to say that he defined his job as incorporating press coverage of his performance despite animosity toward him among newspaper editors. He established rapport, he "kept to it," he fed them news. Likewise, Lou Cannon explained that Ronald Reagan's press officials, as well as the president himself, "understood what we did." Reagan experienced the importance of the press in the movie industry. His press aides were not as good as they thought, according to Cannon, but they worked at the job and had the advantage of the president's sense of humor. Richard Reeves explained that John F. Kennedy "read us and cared about us." The Kennedy White House systematically courted the press, even hiring some journalists along the way.

The second rule of engagement is the preservation of the dignity of the office and the protection of the reserve of personal bearing. For Roosevelt, who "always remained president," according to Kearns, this meant ensuring that the press not mistake good humor, cordiality, respect, and understanding for a kind of chumminess that might invite coverage of the president's physical handicap (an exclusion in reporting that would be unlikely today, however charming the president). A person as president somehow had to gain and maintain the stature of the presidency, a goal serving the purpose of professionals on both sides of the desk in the Oval Office (where FDR held his press conferences). For Dwight D. Eisenhower, according to [presidential biographer] Fred I. Greenstein, this protective veneer meant that the president should not be overexposed or too highly politicized. Reagan was, by profession, an actor and therefore prepared to play "the role of a lifetime" without revealing the actor as person.

The third rule of engagement was made less directly by the biographers; rather it is a reasonable inference from their discussion: Take honest advantage of the edge you have in occupying the place that will be a major source of news. Reeves and Cannon, both reporters as well as biographers, made this point in describing how the Kennedy and Reagan press operations sought to manage the news—guarding words carefully, being attentive always to the broader audience, providing the appropriate spin. All of the biographers provided illustrations.

Capitalizing on the advantage of the Oval Office naturally leads to a competence criterion as a fourth rule of engagement. Most of the biographers directly mentioned the need to have savvy press secretaries. Greenstein, who has studied one of the masters of the trade, James Hagerty for Eisenhower, was the most emphatic. Recommendations associated with this criterion include assurance that the press secretary is "in the loop" and that White House communications be centralized. John Mashek, a reporter with the *Boston Globe*, stressed that the keys to successful White House press operations are "openness, access, and reliability." Reeves characterized the Kennedy press operations just so, adding that reliability is enhanced if there is unity in the message coming from those in the White House. "Hire the right people" is sound advice in any endeavor. Clearly the competence criterion extends to an understanding on the part of others in the White House, including the president, of how important it is that the person standing before the White House press corps be reliable and knowledgeable.

These rules do not necessarily ensure favorable coverage. They are canons for constructive rivalry, not mutual admiration. As such, they form the basis of a taut professional relationship as well as a means for comparing presidents.

Some Do It Well; Some Do Not

"No president understands the true role of the press," Mashek says. Although that may be accurate enough from the perspective of the press corps, still it was apparent from the biographers that some presidents work harder and more sympathetically than others at the task and that certain presidents will fail however hard they try. As it happened, presidents who mostly followed the rules in their relationships with the press were oversampled in the session with the biographers. Four of the five

—Roosevelt, Eisenhower, Kennedy, and Reagan—had effective media operations for their time. The press was not uncritical; still, each was successful to a substantial degree in preserving the edge that is afforded the presidency as an institution.

It is true, of course, that communications technology changed dramatically during this time span, but the rules of engagement seem to be transferable from one era to the next, at least as chronicled by the biographers. What has changed is the level and diversity of competence to suit technological developments, thus making it more essential than ever that the White House press operations be supervised by skilled and experienced communication managers.

The exceptional case among the biographers, Richard M. Nixon, was discussed by Stephen Ambrose, who noted, "There was no love there." Nixon was "fixated on the press" to the point of exaggerating its power. The difficult relations were not for lack of attention but rather due to resistance to [Gary] Wills's formulation of competitive representation. Nixon and his staff were more likely to blame the press sooner than later, resenting their "need for each other" and therefore resisting the rules of engagement as acknowledged by others.

Although forever special in regard to press relations, Nixon is not the only president to experience serious problems. Had Harry Truman, Lyndon Johnson, Gerald Ford, and Jimmy Carter been represented at the conference by biographers, there may have been fuller representation of the range of presidential conceptions of the media role and the management styles of press secretaries. It is worth recording Greenstein's first key to successful press relations: Have a good product. Not all incumbents are good at the job of being president, and some have a style that obscures a good job being done. Bad press for the first group may be warranted for obvious reasons; bad press for the second may reasonably be attributed to poor reporting.

The Clinton Case

"We have not had a stranger relationship," said E.J. Dionne of the *Washington Post*. In Clinton, the press has a president of a new generation, of their generation for the most part. Like the Kennedy he professes to emulate, "he reads us." He is surely interesting, which, if not number one, is among the top three reasons for writing a story. Yet it was as if the discussion by the biographers was an invitation for a critique of Clinton press relations.

The wide-ranging discussion of President Clinton sought to explain his problematic relations with the press. Were these difficulties due to changes beyond the control of the White House or a result of inattention to the standard rules of engagement? Elizabeth Drew, who has written a critical account of the Clinton White House, subscribed to the view that the rules of engagement were ignored by Clinton and his aides or were ineffectually applied. For her, change outside was less explanatory than lack of competence of the White House in this sphere. Further, the president is overexposed, the message is unclear, and Bill Clinton has not achieved presidential stature.

Others also acknowledged that the Clinton White House press operations have been less than effective, but they identified a number of developments contributing to greater strain than in the past. Judy Woodruff of CNN stressed that the president is not so central a figure as before. Summits are not what they once were, the agenda has shifted to Capitol Hill, the president is but one of several candidates and must, therefore, fight for coverage. Dionne and Josette Shiner of the *Washington Times* were critical of the press and the public, observing changes judged to be unhealthy for both the presidency and the press: greater hostility and negativism, fewer limits on coverage of personal life, the sound-bite syndrome, unrealistic expectations. Dionne spoke of a "moral annihilation" that colors the treatment of major public figures, a view that resonated with others. George Stephanopoulos agreed that the Clinton White House got off to a bad start with the press. Not surprisingly, however, he also believes that significant changes make press relations substantially more arduous than in the past. Congress is more active in policy than in the past; television coverage focuses less on issues than on conflict; there has been a rise in attitude journalism, with the substance often lost in the analysis.

The discussion among the panelists was markedly less engaging than its title, "Clinton's Battles with the Press," might have foretold. Perhaps this reticence was because of the oversampling in the first session of presidents with tolerably good relations, combined with Richard Nixon representing a case of intolerably bad relations. Bill Clinton is no Richard Nixon, and thus there was not an obvious carryover comparative case. Whatever the reason, the strained relations we know to exist between the press and Clinton did not receive the kind of candid assessment that one might have expected, nor was closure achieved in regard to the competing explanations for what all acknowledge to be a competition more tense and difficult than would appear on the surface to be necessary or justified.

It is not obvious that the rules of engagement identified for other presidencies would fail to be effective for this president. Yet it is apparent that all of the rules were breached. The president imparted hostility, not understanding, to the press; he failed to establish presidential stature or bearing that could then be preserved; many in the press doubt the honesty of White House news management; and the White House press team failed the competence criterion during the administration's first two years. As the panelists noted, changes have occurred in communications technology, power distribution in Washington and the world, press attitudes and behavior, and general social deportment. Reason suggests that the rules found to be effective in the past are most in order under conditions of change and disorder. Yet they were, for the most part, ignored by the Clinton White House.

Gary Wills concluded by blaming us for "What's broke in our country." He may be correct in regard to many unfortunate trends in modern society, but that begs the issue raised in regard to Clinton's battles with the press. The puzzle of poor relations between two sets of same-generation, interdependent elites remains to be fully explained. Perhaps it is too soon to know with certainty; it cannot be too soon to inquire.

DISCUSSION QUESTIONS

1. Have the "rules of management" described by Jones solved the tension between the president and the press? Why or why not?

2. How is coverage of the presidency different from coverage of the other institutions of the national government?

The Debate: The Media—How Influential Are They?

The way in which politics is reported and what journalists choose to cover both play critical roles in facilitating the deliberative process of democracy. It should not be surprising, therefore, that critics of the media abound. James Fallows, Washington, D.C., editor of the *Atlantic Monthly*, argues that Americans hate the media because reporters are more interested in the "inside baseball" of Washington intrigue than in issues and public policies that are important to people. President Clinton's policy on health care, for example, is portrayed as merely a strategic move in a political game, rather than an attempt to put forth public policy that should be debated and discussed as a means to better serve America's health care needs. Although the interest in the "game" of politics and the effort to predict political outcomes might engage reporters inside the Beltway (the highway that surrounds Washington, D.C.), Fallows argues that they are woefully out of touch with the interests and concerns of most Americans. The result is a loss of credibility for the media, and more worrisome, a weak link in the deliberative process of democracy.

Margaret Gordon seconds Fallows' critique, arguing that the media don't provide voters with the information they need. She approves of an emerging trend called either "civic journalism" or "public journalism," in which newspapers in several cities are attempting to address the problems with political coverage and respond more directly to citizens' interests.

Howard Kurtz, the Washington Post media critic, is less convinced of the merits of this movement. In his view, public journalism puts reporters and editors in the uncomfortable position of openly taking sides in political debates, and candidates themselves tend to dislike unscripted encounters that are the hallmark of the process. At the same time, readers and other members of the public appear to support efforts to make the political process more participatory.

41
"Why Americans Hate the Media"

James Fallows

Not Issues But the Game of Politics

A generation ago political talk programs were sleepy Sunday-morning affairs. The Secretary of State or the Senate majority leader would show up to answer questions from Lawrence Spivak or Bob Clark, and after thirty minutes another stately episode of *Meet the Press* or *Issues and Answers* would be history.

Everything in public life is "brighter" and more "interesting" now. Constant competition from the weekday trash-talk shows has forced anything involving political life to liven up. Under pressure from the Saturday political-talk shows—*The McLaughlin Group* and its many disorderly descendants—even the Sunday-morning shows have put on rouge and push-up bras.

Meet the Press, moderated by Tim Russert, is probably the meatiest of these programs. High-powered guests discuss serious topics with Russert, who worked for years in politics, and with veteran reporters. Yet the pressure to keep things lively means that squabbling replaces dialogue.

The discussion shows that are supposed to enhance public understanding may actually reduce it, by hammering home the message that issues don't matter except as items for politicians to fight over. Some politicians in Washington may indeed view all issues as mere tools to use against their opponents. But far from offsetting this view of public life, the national press often encourages it. As Washington-based talk shows have become more popular in the past decade, they have had a trickle-down effect in cities across the country. In Seattle, in Los Angeles, in Boston, in Atlanta, journalists gain notice and influence by appearing regularly on talk shows—and during those appearances they mainly talk about the game of politics.

In the 1992 presidential campaign candidates spent more time answering questions from "ordinary people"—citizens in town-hall forums, callers on radio and TV talk shows—than they had in previous years. The citizens asked overwhelmingly about the *what* of politics: What are you going to do about the health-care system? What can you do to reduce the cost of welfare? The reporters asked almost exclusively about the *how*: How are you going to try to take away Perot's constituency? How do you answer charges that you have flip-flopped?

After the 1992 campaign the contrast between questions from citizens and those from reporters was widely discussed in journalism reviews and postmortems on campaign coverage. Reporters acknowledged that they should try harder to ask questions about things their readers and viewers seemed to care about—that is, questions about the differences that political choices would make in people's lives.

In January of 1995 there was a chance to see how well the lesson had sunk in. In the days just before and after Bill Clinton delivered his State of the Union address to the new Republican-controlled Congress, he answered questions in a wide variety of forums in order to explain his plans.

On January 31, a week after the speech, the President flew to Boston and took questions from a group of teenagers. Their questions concerned the effects of legislation or government programs on their communities or schools. These were the questions (paraphrased in some cases):

- "We need stronger laws to punish those people who are caught selling guns to our youth. Basically, what can you do about that?"
- "I notice that often it's the media that is responsible for the negative portrayal of young people in our society." What can political leaders do to persuade the media that there is good news about youth?
- Apprenticeship programs and other ways to provide job training have been valuable for students not going to college. Can the Administration promote more of these programs?
- Programs designed to keep teenagers away from drugs and gangs often emphasize sports and seem geared mainly to boys. How can such programs be made more attractive to teenage girls?
- What is it like at Oxford? (This was from a student who was completing a new alternative-school curriculum in the Boston public schools, and who had been accepted at Oxford.)
- "We need more police officers who are trained to deal with all the other different cultures in our cities." What can the government do about that?
- "In Boston, Northeastern University has created a model of scholarships and other supports to help inner-city kids get to and stay in college. . . . As President, can you urge colleges across the country to do what Northeastern has done?"

Earlier in the month the President's performance had been assessed by the three network-news anchors: Peter Jennings, of ABC; Dan Rather, of CBS; and Tom Brokaw, of NBC. There was no overlap whatsoever between the questions the students asked and those raised by the anchors. None of the questions from these news professionals concerned the impact of legislation or politics on people's lives. Nearly all concerned the struggle for individual advancement among candidates.

Peter Jennings, who met with Clinton as the Gingrich-Dole Congress was getting under way, asked whether Clinton had been eclipsed as a political leader by the Republicans. Dan Rather did interviews through January with prominent politicians—Senators Edward Kennedy, Phil Gramm, and Bob Dole—building up to a profile of Clinton two days after the State of the Union address. Every question he asked was about popularity or political tactics. He asked Phil Gramm to guess whether Newt Gingrich would enter the race (no) and whether Bill Clinton would be renominated by his party (yes). He asked Bob Dole what kind of mood the President seemed to be in, and whether Dole and Gingrich were, in effect, the new bosses of Washington. When Edward Kennedy began giving his views about the balanced-budget amendment, Rather steered him back on course: "Senator, you know I'd talk about these things the rest of the afternoon, but let's move quickly to politics. Do you expect Bill Clinton to be the Democratic nominee for re-election in 1996?"

The *CBS Evening News* profile of Clinton, which was narrated by Rather and was presented as part of the series *Eye on America*, contained no mention of Clinton's economic policy, his tax or budget plans, his failed attempt to pass a health-care proposal, his successful attempt to ratify NAFTA, his efforts to "reinvent government," or any substantive aspect of his proposals or plans in office. Its subject was exclusively Clinton's handling of his office—his "difficulty making decisions," his "waffling" at crucial moments. If Rather or his colleagues had any interest in the content of Clinton's speech as opposed to its political effect, neither the questions they asked nor the reports they aired revealed such a concern.

Tom Brokaw's questions were more substantive, but even he concentrated mainly on politics of the moment. How did the President feel about a poll showing that 61 percent of the public felt that he had no "strong convictions" and could be "easily swayed"? What did Bill Clinton think about Newt Gingrich? "Do you think he plays fair?" How did he like it that people kept shooting at the White House?

When ordinary citizens have a chance to pose questions to political leaders, they rarely ask about the game of politics. They want to know how the reality of politics will affect them—through taxes, programs, scholarship funds, wars. Journalists justify their intrusiveness and excesses by claiming that they are the public's representatives, asking the questions their fellow citizens would ask if they had the privilege of meeting with Presidents and senators. In fact they ask questions that only their fellow political professionals care about. And they often do so—as at the typical White House news conference—with a discourtesy and rancor that represent the public's views much less than they reflect the modern journalist's belief that being independent boils down to acting hostile.

The One-Track Mind

The limited curiosity that elite reporters display in their questions is also evident in the stories they write once they have received answers. They are interested mainly in pure politics and can be coerced into examining the substance of an issue only as a last resort. The subtle but sure result is a stream of daily messages that the real meaning of public life is the struggle of Bob Dole against Newt Gingrich against Bill Clinton, rather than our collective efforts to solve collective problems.

The natural instinct of newspapers and TV is to present every public issue as if its "real" meaning were political in the meanest and narrowest sense of that term—the attempt by parties and candidates to gain an advantage over their rivals. Reporters do, of course, write stories about political life in the broader sense and about the substance of issues—the pluses and minuses of diplomatic recognition for Vietnam, the difficulties of holding down the Medicare budget, whether immigrants help or hurt the nation's economic base. But when there is a chance to use these issues as props or raw material for a story about political tactics, most reporters leap at it. It is more fun—and easier—to write about Bill Clinton's "positioning" on the Vietnam issue, or how Newt Gingrich is "handling" the need to cut Medicare, than it is to look into the issues themselves.

Examples of this preference occur so often that they're difficult to notice. But every morning's newspaper, along with every evening's newscast, reveals this pattern of thought.

- Last February 1995, when the Democratic President and the Republican Congress were fighting over how much federal money would go to local law-enforcement agencies, one network-news broadcast showed a clip of Gingrich denouncing Clinton and another of Clinton standing in front of a sea of uniformed police officers while making a tough-on-crime speech. The correspondent's sign-off line was "The White House thinks 'cops on the beat' has a simple but appealing ring to it." That is, the President was pushing the plan because it would sound good in his campaign ads. Whether or not that was Clinton's real motive, nothing in the broadcast gave the slightest hint of where the extra policemen would go, how much they might cost, whether there was reason to think they'd do any good. Everything in the story suggested that the crime bill mattered only as a chapter in the real saga, which was the struggle between Bill and Newt.
- Last April, after the explosion at the federal building in Oklahoma City, discussion changed quickly from the event itself to politicians' "handling" of the event. On the Sunday after the blast President Clinton announced a series of new anti-terrorism measures. The next morning, on National Public Radio's *Morning Edition*, Cokie Roberts was asked about the prospects of the proposals' taking effect. "In some ways it's not even the point," she replied. What mattered was that Clinton "looked good" taking the tough side of the issue. No one expects Cokie Roberts or other political correspondents to be experts on controlling terrorism, negotiating with the Syrians, or the other specific measures on which Presidents make stands. But all issues are shoehorned into the area of expertise the most-prominent correspondents do have: the struggle for one-upmanship among a handful of political leaders.
- When health-care reform was the focus of big political battles between Republicans and Democrats, it was on the front page and the evening newscast every day. When the Clinton Administration declared defeat in 1994 and there were no more battles to be fought, health-care news

coverage virtually stopped too—even though the medical system still represented one seventh of the economy, even though HMOs and corporations and hospitals and pharmaceutical companies were rapidly changing policies in the face of ever-rising costs. Health care was no longer political news, and therefore it was no longer interesting news.

* * *

Pointless Prediction: The Political Experts

On Sunday, November 6, 1994, two days before the congressional elections that swept the Republicans to power, *The Washington Post* published the results of its "Crystal Ball" poll. Fourteen prominent journalists, pollsters, and all-around analysts made their predictions about how many seats each party would win in the House and Senate and how many governorships each would take.

One week later many of these same experts would be saying on their talk shows that the Republican landslide was "inevitable" and "a long time coming" and "a sign of deep discontent in the heartland." But before the returns were in, how many of the fourteen experts predicted that the Republicans would win both houses of Congress and that Newt Gingrich would be speaker? Exactly three.

What is interesting about this event is not just that so many experts could be so wrong. Immediately after the election even Newt Gingrich seemed dazed by the idea that the forty-year reign of the Democrats in the House had actually come to an end. Rather, the episode said something about the futility of political prediction itself—a task to which the big-time press devotes enormous effort and time. *Two days* before the election many of the country's most admired analysts had no idea what was about to happen. Yet within a matter of weeks these same people, unfazed, would be writing articles and giving speeches and being quoted about who was "ahead" and "behind" in the emerging race for the White House in 1996.

Spoon-Feeding: The White House Press Corps

In the early spring of last year [1995], when Newt Gingrich was dominating the news from Washington and the O. J. Simpson trial was dominating the news as a whole, *The Washington Post* ran an article about the pathos of the White House press room. Nobody wanted to hear what the President was doing, so the people who cover the President could not get on the air. Howard Kurtz, the *Post*'s media-writer, described the human cost of this political change:

> Brit Hume is in his closet-size White House cubicle, watching Kato Kaelin testify on CNN. Bill Plante, in the adjoining cubicle, has his feet up and is

buried in the *New York Times*. Brian Williams is in the corridor, idling away the time with Jim Miklaszewski.

An announcement is made for a bill-signing ceremony. Some of America's highest-paid television correspondents begin ambling toward the pressroom door.

"Are you coming with us?" Williams asks.

"I guess so," says Hume, looking forlorn.

The White House spokesman, Mike McCurry, told Kurtz that there was some benefit to the enforced silence: "Brit Hume has now got his crossword puzzle capacity down to record time. And some of the reporters have been out on the lecture circuit."

The deadpan restraint with which Kurtz told this story is admirable. But the question many readers would want to scream at the idle correspondents is *Why don't you go out and do some work?*

Why not go out and interview someone, even if you're not going to get any airtime that night? Why not escape the monotonous tyranny of the White House press room, which reporters are always complaining about? The knowledge that O.J. will keep you off the air yet again should liberate you to look into those stories you never "had time" to deal with before. Why not *read a book*—about welfare reform, about Russia or China, about race relations, about anything? Why not imagine, just for a moment, that your journalistic duty might involve something more varied and constructive than doing standups from the White House lawn and sounding skeptical about whatever announcement the President's spokesman put out that day?

What might these well-paid, well-trained correspondents have done while waiting for the O.J. trial to become boring enough that they could get back on the air? They might have tried to learn something that would be of use to their viewers when the story of the moment went away. Without leaving Washington, without going farther than ten minutes by taxi from the White House (so that they could be on hand if a sudden press conference was called), they could have prepared themselves to discuss the substance of issues that affect the public.

For example, two years earlier Vice President Al Gore had announced an ambitious plan to "reinvent" the federal government. Had it made any difference, either in improving the performance of government or in reducing its cost, or was it all for show? Republicans and Democrats were sure to spend the next few months fighting about cuts in the capital-gains tax. Capital-gains tax rates were higher in some countries and lower in others. What did the experience of these countries show about whether cutting the rates helped an economy to grow? The rate of immigration was rising again, and in California and Florida it was becoming an important political issue. What was the latest evidence on the economic and social effects of immigration? Should Americans feel confident or threatened that so many foreigners were trying to make their way in? Soon both political parties would be advancing plans to reform the welfare system. Within a two-mile radius of the White House lived plenty of families on welfare. Why not go and see how the system had affected them, and what they would do if it changed? The federal government had gone further than most private industries in trying to open opportunities to racial minorities and women. The Pentagon had gone furthest of all. What did people involved in this process—men and women, blacks and whites—think about its successes and failures? What light did their experience shed on the impending affirmative-action debate?

The list could go on for pages. With a few minutes' effort—about as long as it takes to do a crossword puzzle—the correspondents could have drawn up lists of other subjects they had never before "had time" to investigate. They had the time now. What they lacked was a sense that their responsibility involved something more than standing up to rehash the day's announcements when there was room for them on the news.

*   *   *

Out of Touch with America

In the week leading up to a State of the Union address White House aides always leak word to reporters that this year the speech will be "different." No more laundry list of all the government's activities, no more boring survey of every potential trouble spot in the world. This time, for a change, the speech is going to be short, punchy, and thematic. When the actual speech occurs, it is never short, punchy, or thematic. It is long and detailed, like all its predecessors, because as the deadline nears, every part of the government scrambles desperately to have a mention of its activities crammed into the speech somewhere.

In the days before Bill Clinton's address a year ago [1995] aides said that no matter what had happened to all those other Presidents, this time the speech really would be short, punchy, and thematic. The President understood the situation, he recognized his altered role, and he saw this as an opportunity to set a new theme for his third and fourth years in office.

That evening the promises once again proved false. Bill Clinton gave a speech that was enormously long even by the standards of previous State of the Union addresses. The speech had three or four apparent endings, it had ad-libbed inserts, and it covered both the details of policy and the President's theories about what had gone wrong with America. An hour and twenty-one minutes after he took the podium, the President stepped down.

Less than a minute later the mockery from commentators began. For instant analysis NBC went to Peggy Noonan, who had been a speech-writer for Presidents Ronald Reagan and George Bush. She grimaced and barely tried to conceal her disdain for such an ungainly, sprawling speech. Other commentators soon mentioned that congressmen had been slipping out of the Capitol building before the end of the speech, that Clinton had once more failed to stick to an agenda, that the speech probably would not give the President the new start he sought. The comments were virtually all about the tactics of the speech, and they were almost all thumbs down.

A day and a half later the first newspaper columns showed up. They were even more critical. On January 26 *The Washington Post*'s op-ed page consisted mainly of stories about the speech, all of which were withering. "ALL MUSH AND NO MESSAGE" was the headline on a column by Richard Cohen. "AN OPPORTUNITY MISSED" was the more statesmanlike judgment from David Broder. Cohen wrote: "Pardon me if I thought of an awful metaphor: Clinton at a buffet table, eating everything in sight."

What a big fat jerk that Clinton was! How little he understood the obligations of leadership! Yet the news section of the same day's *Post* had a long article based on discussions with a focus group of ordinary citizens in Chicago who had watched the President's speech. "For these voters, the State of the Union speech was an antidote to weeks of unrelenting criticism of Clinton's presidency," the article said.

> "Tonight reminded us of what has been accomplished," said Maureen Prince, who works as the office manager in her husband's business and has raised five children. "We are so busy hearing the negatives all the time, from the time you wake up on your clock radio in the morning. . . ."
> The group's immediate impressions mirrored the results of several polls conducted immediately after the president's speech.
> ABC News found that eight out of 10 approved of the president's speech. CBS News said that 74 percent of those surveyed said they had a "clear idea" of what Clinton stands for, compared with just 41 percent before the speech. A Gallup Poll for *USA Today* and Cable News Network found that eight in 10 said Clinton is leading the country in the right direction.

Nielsen ratings reported in the same day's paper showed that the longer the speech went on, the larger the number of people who tuned in to watch.

The point is not that the pundits are necessarily wrong and the public necessarily right. The point is the gulf between the two groups' reactions. The very aspects of the speech that had seemed so ridiculous to the professional commentators—its detail, its inclusiveness, the hyperearnestness of Clinton's conclusion about the "common good"—seemed attractive and worthwhile to most viewers.

"I'm wondering what so much of the public heard that our highly trained expert analysts completely missed," Carol Cantor, a software consultant from California, wrote in a discussion on the WELL, a popular online forum, three days after the speech. What they heard was, in fact, the speech, which allowed them to draw their own conclusions rather than being forced to accept an expert "analysis" of how the President "handled" the speech. In most cases the analysis goes unchallenged, because the public has no chance to see whatever event the pundits are describing. In this instance viewers had exactly the same evidence about Clinton's performance that the "experts" did, and from it they drew radically different conclusions.

In 1992 political professionals had laughed at Ross Perot's "boring" and "complex" charts about the federal budget deficit—until it became obvious that viewers loved them. And for a week or two after this State of the Union speech there were little jokes on the weekend talk shows about how out of step the pundit reaction had been with opinion "out there." But after a polite chuckle the talk shifted to how the President and the speaker and Senator Dole were handling their jobs.

Term Limits

As soon as the Democrats were routed in the 1994 elections, commentators and TV analysts said it was obvious that the American people were tired of seeing the same old faces in Washington. The argument went that those who lived inside the Beltway had forgotten what it was like in the rest of the country. They didn't get it. They were out of touch. The only way to jerk the congressional system back to reality was to bring in new blood.

A few days after the new Congress was sworn in, CNN began running an updated series of promotional ads for its program *Crossfire*. (Previous ads had featured shots of locomotives colliding head-on and rams locking horns, to symbolize the meeting of minds on the show.) Everything has been shaken up in the capital, one of the ads began. New faces. New names. New people in charge of all the committees.

"In fact," the announcer said, in a tone meant to indicate whimsy, "only one committee hasn't changed. The *welcoming* committee."

The camera pulled back to reveal the three hosts of *Crossfire*—Pat Buchanan, John Sununu, and Michael Kinsley—standing with arms crossed on the steps of the Capitol building, blocking the path of the new arrivals trying to make their way in. "Watch your step," one of the hosts said.

Talk about not getting it! The people who put together this ad must have imagined that the popular irritation with inside-the-Beltway culture was confined to members of Congress—and didn't extend to members of the punditocracy, many of whom had held their positions much longer than the typical congressman had. The difference between the "welcoming committee" and the congressional committees headed by fallen Democratic titans like Tom Foley and Jack Brooks was that the congressmen can be booted out.

"Polls show that both Republicans *and* Democrats felt better about the Congress just after the 1994 elections," a Clinton Administration official said last year. "They had 'made the monkey jump'—they were able to discipline an institution they didn't like. They could register the fact that they were unhappy. There doesn't seem to be any way to do that with the press, except to stop watching and reading, which more and more people have done."

Lost Credibility

There is an astonishing gulf between the way journalists—especially the most prominent ones—think about their impact and the way the public does. In movies of the 1930s reporters were gritty characters who instinctively sided with the common man. In the 1970s Robert Redford and Dustin Hoffman, starring as Bob Woodward and Carl Bernstein in *All the President's Men*, were better-paid but still gritty reporters unafraid to challenge big power. Even the local-TV-news crew featured on *The Mary Tyler Moore Show* had a certain down-to-earth pluck. Ted Knight, as the pea-brained news anchor Ted Baxter, was a ridiculously pompous figure but not an arrogant one.

Since the early 1980s the journalists who have shown up in movies have often been portrayed as more loathsome than the lawyers, politicians, and business moguls who are the traditional bad guys in films about the white-collar world. In *Absence of Malice*, made in 1981, an ambitious newspaper reporter (Sally Field) ruins the reputation of a businessman (Paul Newman) by rashly publishing articles accusing him of murder. In *Broadcast News*, released in 1987, the anchorman (William Hurt) is still an airhead, like Ted Baxter, but unlike Ted, he works in a business that is systematically hostile to anything except profit and bland good looks. The only sympathetic characters in the movie, an overeducated reporter (Albert Brooks) and a hyperactive and hyperidealistic producer (Holly Hunter), would have triumphed as heroes in a newspaper movie of the 1930s. In this one they are ground down by the philistines at their network.

In the *Die Hard* series, which started in 1988, a TV journalist (William Atherton) is an unctuous creep who will lie and push helpless people around in order to get on the air. In *The Bonfire of the Vanities* (1990) the tabloid writer Peter Fallow (Bruce Willis) is a disheveled British sot who will do anything for a free drink. In *Rising Sun* (1993) a newspaper reporter known as "Weasel" (Steve Buscemi) is an out-and-out criminal, accepting bribes to influence his coverage. As Antonia Zerbisias pointed out in the *Toronto Star* in 1993, movies and TV shows offer almost no illustrations of journalists who are not full of themselves, shallow, and indifferent to the harm they do. During Operation Desert Storm, *Saturday Night Live* ridiculed American reporters who asked military spokesmen questions like "Can you tell us exactly when and where you are going to launch your attack?" "The journalists were portrayed as ignorant, arrogant and pointlessly adversarial," Jay Rosen, of New York University, wrote about the episode. "By gently rebuffing their ludicrous questions, the Pentagon briefer [on *SNL*] came off as a model of sanity."

Even real-life members of the Washington pundit corps have made their way into movies—Eleanor Clift, Morton Kondracke, hosts from *Crossfire*—in 1990s releases such as *Dave* and *Rising Sun*. Significantly, their role in the narrative is as buffoons. The joke in these movies is how rapidly the pundits leap to conclusions, how predictable their reactions are, how automatically they polarize the debate without any clear idea of what has really occurred. That real-life journalists are willing to keep appearing in such movies, knowing how they will be cast, says something about the source of self-respect in today's media: celebrity, on whatever basis, matters more than being taken seriously.

Movies do not necessarily capture reality, but they suggest a public mood—in this case, a contrast between the apparent self-satisfaction of the media celebrities and the contempt in which they are held by the public. "The news media has a generally positive view of itself in the watchdog role," wrote the authors of an exhaustive survey of public attitudes and the attitudes of journalists themselves toward the press. (The survey was conducted by the Times Mirror Center for the People and the Press, and was released last May.) But "the outside world strongly faults the news media for its negativism. . . . The public goes so far as to say that the press gets in the way of society solving its problems. . . ." According to the survey, "two out of three members of the public had nothing or nothing good to say about the media."

The media establishment is beginning to get at least an inkling of this message. Through the past decade discussions among newspaper editors and publishers have been a litany of woes: fewer readers; lower "penetration" rates, as a decreasing share of the public pays attention to news; a more and more desperate search for ways to attract the public's interest. In the short run these challenges to credibility are a problem for journalists and journalism. In the longer run they are a problem for democracy.

42
"Civic Journalism: Involving the Public"

Margaret T. Gordon

It wasn't so long ago that most people believed what they read in the newspapers and saw on television. But now a substantial proportion of the public doesn't believe much of what it reads, hears, or watches— and many average citizens find the media as irrelevant to their lives as they find the politicians.

The key issue suggested by the public's declining ratings of both politicians' and journalists' honesty and ethical standards is that the public feels it has been "duped" by them all. People feel a need to "discount" what the politicians say—in person and in their political advertisements—and they also feel they must discount what the media say about politicians.

Why? Is it because they think journalists are biased toward one political party or the other? Perhaps, but there is another important factor. Most of the political news we get these days consists of information journalists have passed on to us—sometimes with little change—from marketers, spin doctors, handlers, press releases, politicians' press conferences, and staged pseudo events designed to get media attention.

The political stories that emerge after the editing and production processes are often "framed" in terms of a game or contest, a horse race, with the focus on who is winning and who is losing, not on the importance or effects of the issues the politicians support.

Sometimes, increasingly often it seems, political stories have an "edge" or a "zinger" added by the reporter to give it a little spice. They say their editors and producers want the spice, and they want it because marketing studies tell them the public wants it.

Is it true that the public wants horse-race political reporting and edge? Newspaper readership and television news viewership both have been declining for years. Maybe the marketers are wrong. Many people seem to have withdrawn from involvement, trusting only what they themselves see and experience. Perhaps they are seeking what is really truthful. A Times Mirror Center for the People and the Press study says that 34 percent of the electorate is not "detached" from the process, and 71 percent believe the media get in the way of our nation's solving its problems.

Is it the media's responsibility to help the nation solve its problems? No. But the news media, especially the print media, are protected by the

First Amendment of our Constitution because they have a sacred trust. They are supposed to protect the public from abuses of power by elected officials. They are supposed to give citizens the information we need to be informed, competent citizens. The media enjoy protection no other business has for that reason.

The media don't give us the information we need because marketers —seeking to reverse declining readership, listenership and viewership —say we don't really want it. Instead, we are overloaded with information and it seems increasingly difficult to find the information we really want.

The public understands that the media are businesses, driven by advertising, circulation and ratings figures, as well as the local and national economies. People know that many news decisions are made with the "bottom line" in mind rather than the "public good." And, despite the protection of the First Amendment, they see the media as like "any other business." Some members harbor special resentments though because they believe there is no way to make the media accountable, and that they mislead and misinterpret in order to sell more product.

For their part, the media owners argue they have rapidly increasing costs, especially investments in new technologies, and that they are assuming extraordinary risks. Perhaps, but it is also the media's responsibility to be accurate and to make the truth interesting.

During the past few years, several media outlets—including several in the Puget Sound area—have begun experimenting with what some say is a new form of journalism that may contain the seeds to a solution for this apparent dilemma. (Others say it's old-fashioned journalism in new clothes.)

It is called public journalism or civic journalism. It joins citizens and media together to interact on the political issues that concern the public. In some communities, civic journalism projects have drawn people together to identify problems, outline solutions, and work to implement them. In other communities, the focus has been on improving knowledge about the issues, candidates, and participation in elections. The practice of civic journalism, variously defined by different communities, does seem to promote greater citizen involvement.

It won't solve all the problems, or solve them quickly. The local experiments have been very tentative and not sweeping enough to be a real test of their usefulness. In fact, some people may have become so cynical about the press, so inattentive, that they might not have even known there was new journalistic activity in our midst.

What do we have to lose by encouraging the full development of civic journalism? Seattle doesn't have to imitate Charlotte, or Wichita—both cities where public journalism is practiced—or anywhere else. We can put a Northwest imprint on it.

The alternative seems to be a continuation of current trends that do not bode well for our local media, our communities, and for democracy.

43
"When News Media Go to Grass Roots, Candidates Often Don't Follow"

Howard Kurtz

A few days before the New Hampshire primary in February, Robert J. Dole said he was surprised to learn that jobs and economic insecurity were such big issues in the presidential campaign.

Had he read a series in the Boston *Globe* last November, he would have learned that "it's still the economy," according to town meetings, focus groups and polling in one New Hampshire town. The "People's Voice" series is one of dozens of grass-roots efforts in this campaign season by newspapers, and television and radio stations, rising from a growing movement called public journalism.

It is, in essence, an attempt by news organizations to fashion a citizens' agenda by orchestrating meetings and task forces—and, in some cases, drafting volunteers and pushing for solutions to local problems. While critics say this amounts to an abandonment of objectivity, supporters from Maine to California say the approach weans journalists from their dependence on political insiders and helps them forge new connections with their communities.

"It's not that different than going door to door" and interviewing voters, said *Globe* Editor Matthew Storin. "There's a little bit of a marketing spin to it. But I like doing this part of public journalism, even if it's being packaged as something new and it's not quite new. I can live with that. We're all trying to sell newspapers."

It might seem a rather obvious exercise for reporters to try to discover what voters are thinking. But in the wake of the 1992 campaign, when candidates used talk shows to bypass the mainstream press, newspapers in particular are searching for ways to remain relevant. And, with foundations handing out money for that very purpose, public journalism has become a handy way to grab the spotlight.

The movement's advocates argue that much of the public is disgusted with the usual horse-race coverage of politics. Consider the responses of focus-group participants in New Hampshire and Massachusetts in a study for the Pew Center for Civic Journalism:

"I think the media and politicians are connected. They are tied together by money and power and they just don't know about people like me."—Kathy, a homemaker.

"Most reporters give the editor or publisher what they want to hear."—Tony, a law enforcement officer.

"They care more about asking questions than listening to the answers."—Charlie, a salesman.

"They get away from the real issues of the campaign and don't tell us what a person really thinks."—Joyce, an accounting clerk.

Still, the notion that the news media should foster unscripted encounters between the public and the politicians has not been embraced by the candidates themselves. When the *Globe* and a Boston television and radio station sponsored a citizens' forum in Derry, N.H., only GOP candidates Richard G. Lugar, Robert K. Doman and Alan Keyes showed up. The major candidates also pulled out one day before a Des Moines forum, staged by Iowa Public Television and several other news organizations, when Senate Majority Leader Dole refused to participate.

Noncandidates, though, can use such forums to score political points. Hillary Rodham Clinton received upbeat coverage in March for joining a citizens' conference on the family, sponsored by the *Minneapolis Star Tribune* and a public television station. These are ambitious ventures: The *Star Tribune*, which last week convened a gathering of 400 people, says the purpose is "to help the state imagine a new kind of politics."

As public journalism has gained momentum in the last half-dozen years, it has taken on a variety of forms. Some news organizations have merely offered free pizzas to entice readers to attend meetings or fill out questionnaires. Others have joined forces with local universities that they also must cover. Still others have stretched the boundaries of what journalists ordinarily do.

The *Akron Beacon Journal* persuaded 22,000 citizens to mail in coupons pledging to work for improved race relations. The *Charlotte Observer* held inner-city town meetings in a "Taking Back Our Neighborhoods" campaign that prompted the city to tear down dilapidated buildings and open parks and recreational facilities. The Huntington, W.Va., *Herald-Dispatch* helped solicit volunteers for a half-dozen task forces on economic development and sponsored a visit to the state legislature to lobby on the issue.

"People are less concerned about the issue of reporting news versus making news," said Robert Gabordi, the *Herald-Dispatch* editor. "That's an old argument that doesn't stand up anymore. The more important question to ask is, are you being as aggressive a watchdog on a project you may have had a part in? We took a pretty hard look at the successes and failures of the whole project."

But Leonard Downie Jr., *The Washington Post*'s executive editor and a leading critic of public journalism, questioned the practice of "forcing politicians to appear at a forum of our choosing and to focus only on those questions we want to ask." He said it is "beyond the pale" for news organizations to get involved in advocating solutions, or even urging people to vote.

"That is a great danger to the credibility of the newspaper . . . even when the cause is the best possible cause," Downie said, adding: "It is very seductive, particularly for the top editors involved, who become celebrities through this process."

Some journalists expressed mixed feelings. *San Francisco Chronicle* reporter John King was at the center of a "Voice of the Voter" project during last year's mayoral race. He said he was surprised by "how thoughtful a lot of people are about the city" and contrasted it with his usual reporting: "You talk to your seven or eight appointed experts and they all say funny things that you slap in the paper. The more ridiculous the charge, the more space you give it."

At the same time, King said of the paper's practice of publishing reader comments verbatim: "It was really the Voice of the Yahoo. Instead of writing a crazy letter, people would call the voice mail and we'd run a 100-word rant from someone."

Some recent public journalism ventures have taken on a cookie-cutter flavor, in part because they work with such organizations as the Pew center and the Poynter Institute for Media Studies, which provide funding and technical assistance. Pew alone is financing such efforts in 17 cities this year. These often feature a catchy logo ("We the People," "Voices of Florida," "Front Porch Forum") and some polls and focus groups, with the findings splashed across the front page.

"There are superficial versions and there are more substantial versions," said Jay Rosen, director of New York University's Project on Public Life and the Press. "To me, proclaiming that you are 'the people's voice' is a problem unless you have made some extraordinary effort at public listening, to understand not only their votes but their lives in depth. Simply throwing ordinary people's voices into the paper is not worth a helluva lot."

Some efforts during the 1996 campaign have been worthwhile but low-risk. The *Des Moines Register* used the state's new fiber-optic network to allow high school students to question Republican candidates such as Malcolm S. "Steve" Forbes. "It wasn't front-page stuff," said David Yepsen, the paper's political editor. "Most of the questions were fairly predictable—positions on issues, that sort of thing. But it helped engage a segment of the electorate that's just getting interested in politics."

The Derry project—launched by the *Globe*, WABU-TV and WBUR-FM—is among the more ambitious. Some participants say it strikes at the heart of what is wrong with the news business.

"To me, civic journalism is simply a return to the roots of what journalism was originally," said Ted O'Brien, news director of WABU, a

UHF station owned by Boston University. "As you move into the larger markets, your life becomes very different from the mass of people who are watching. Since Watergate, you have a whole new group of reporters coming out of the upper middle class, and they're attracted by the glamour rather than the nitty-gritty."

The Derry effort zoomed in on the nitty-gritty, and that, for a business drawn to drama, was often a problem. "The challenge was trying to turn what we were hearing from people and learning about their lives into journalism," said Tara Murphy, project coordinator for WBUR, who conducted the Pew focus groups. "Some reporters feel kind of uncomfortable doing a story about something that has been organized. But these groups were not intended to be the story. They were listening posts for reporters."

Storin also found himself frustrated by the Derry participants. "They're not the clever, articulate people you're used to reading about in newspapers," he said. "We have to find a way to make them more interesting."

On separate occasions, Sens. Lugar (R-Ind.) and Phil Gramm (R-Tex.) and former Tennessee governor Lamar Alexander met with a half-dozen Derry residents at a local high school. Initially, the journalists said, the residents were a bit intimidated and did not ask follow-up questions. With some prodding from the reporters, that changed over time.

The basic, straightforward queries of ordinary citizens occasionally produced flashes of insight. When Priscilla Parten of Derry asked Alexander who would care for the elderly if the budget were cut, he spoke of "more personal responsibility in our own families." That drew a negative reaction, including a critical column by the *Globe*'s Ellen Goodman.

"It's easy to avoid a question from a reporter and not look bad, but you can't avoid a question from these people," O'Brien said. "You can't blow them off in the same way."

Months before Patrick J. Buchanan began surging in the polls with a populist economic message, the New Hampshire surveys found "that nearly 60 percent of potential voters felt they did not earn enough money, that 30 percent said they never will, and more than half worried that they might lose their homes and that their children will never have good jobs at good pay," the *Globe* reported.

In the focus groups, said Royal Ford, the *Globe*'s New Hampshire correspondent, "they didn't want to talk about moral issues. They wanted to talk about jobs, their future, their kids' future."

Ford found the exercise worthwhile, but added: "If the Boston *Globe* had said to me, 'Here's four months, roam around New Hampshire,' it probably would have produced the same thing." He also encountered skepticism within his own newspaper: "Some of the old Washington hands didn't think much of it. They asked how my obedient little voters were doing."

David Shribman, the Globe's Washington bureau chief, told Murphy that "most traditional reporters viewed it with dread and trepidation. . . . They were also repelled—not too strong a word—by the near-religious zeal of this new civic religion." But in the end, Shribman said, the project was viewed as "an absolute, bell-ringing, positive success."

Among Derry's 30,000 residents, the venture also drew rave reviews. "I thought it was wonderful," said Pat MacEachern, a volunteer teacher's aide, who expressed concern about education for her 5-year-old. "It focused more on what normal, everyday people are thinking about and what their concerns are. A lot of times, the global issues or what they're talking about in Washington isn't really relevant."

Vickie Buckley Chase, executive director of the Derry Chamber of Commerce, agreed. "It was an excellent opportunity to express our wants and desires without having the mass media coming down on us," she said. "It gave me an opportunity to see what might be in our future."

Some journalists say the movement's impact should not be oversold. "It's probably more effective as it gets more localized," King said. "The notion that it's going to affect the presidential race is pretty absurd."

But enthusiasts such as NYU's Rosen say it's no accident that public journalism has taken off in places such as Boston, Charlotte, Miami, Wichita, Madison and Norfolk.

"There's a growing breach between the national press corps and local and regional journalists who used to look upwards for their cues," he said. "I don't think people in the elite press quite understand this."

DISCUSSION QUESTIONS

1. Do you agree with Fallows and Gordon's critique of the media?

2. To what extent is the media's coverage of politics determined by the audience? People already have the option of watching the *The News Hour* on public TV or reading the *New York Times* or *Washington Post*, but few do. Would anyone watch the type of coverage favored by Fallows? Explain.

3. Should journalists take a more active role in the political process when they engage in "civic journalism"? Are critics correct in asserting that this crosses the line between reporting and advocacy? Or does civic journalism merely bring into the open the power of the media to set political and campaign agendas?

CHAPTER 9

Elections and Voting

44
"The Voice of the People: An Echo" from
The Responsible Electorate

V. O. KEY

The votes are cast, the tallies are in, the winning candidate claims victory and a mandate to govern—the people have spoken! But just what have the people said when they have cast a plurality of votes for one candidate? In the first chapter of his book The Responsible Electorate, *the political scientist V. O. Key, Jr., argued that the voice of the people is nothing more than an echo of the cacophony and hubbub of candidates and parties scrambling for popular support. "Even the most discriminating popular judgment," wrote Key, "can reflect only ambiguity, uncertainty, or even foolishness if those are the qualities of the input into the echo chamber."*

Hence, what was the logic of the voting decision? Why do people vote as they do? Key, writing thirty years ago, believed that voting decisions are more logical than is often believed, that voters look beyond the "images and cultivation of style," to "substance of politics." His reading of the evidence led to his famous conclusion that "voters are not fools," and that the electorate makes collective decisions based on a concern for public policy, the performance of government, and the personalities of the candidates.

In his reflective moments even the most experienced politician senses a nagging curiosity about why people vote as they do. His power and his position depend upon the outcome of the mysterious rites we perform as opposing candidates harangue the multitudes who finally march to the polls to prolong the rule of their champion, to thrust him, ungratefully, back into the void of private life, or to raise to eminence a new tribune of the people. What kinds of appeals enable a candidate to win the favor of the great god, The People? What circumstances move voters to shift their preferences in this direction or that? What clever propaganda tactic or slogan led to this result? What mannerism of oratory or style of rhetoric produced another outcome? What band of electors rallied to this candidate to save the day for him? What policy of state attracted the devotion of another bloc of voters? What action repelled a third sector of the electorate?

The victorious candidate may claim with assurance that he has the answers to all such questions. He may regard his success as vindication of his beliefs about why voters vote as they do. And he may regard the swing of the vote to him as indubitably a response to the campaign positions he took, as an indication of the acuteness of his intuitive estimates of the mood of the people, and as a ringing manifestation of the esteem in which he is held by a discriminating public. This narcissism assumes its most repulsive form among election winners who have championed intolerance, who have stirred the passions and hatreds of people, or who have advocated causes known by decent men to be outrageous or dangerous in their long-run consequences. No functionary is more repugnant or more arrogant than the unjust man who asserts, with a color of truth, that he speaks from a pedestal of popular approbation.

It thus can be a mischievous error to assume, because a candidate wins, that a majority of the electorate shares his views on public questions, approves his past actions, or has specific expectations about his future conduct. Nor does victory establish that the candidate's campaign strategy, his image, his television style, or his fearless stand against cancer and polio turned the trick. The election returns establish only that the winner attracted a majority of the votes—assuming the existence of a modicum of rectitude in election administration. They tell us precious little about why the plurality was his.

For a glaringly obvious reason, electoral victory cannot be regarded as necessarily a popular ratification of a candidate's outlook. The voice of the people is but an echo. The output of an echo chamber bears an inevitable and invariable relation to the input. As candidates and parties clamor for attention and vie for popular support, the people's verdict can be no more than a selective reflection from among the alternatives and outlooks presented to them. Even the most discriminating popular judgment can reflect only ambiguity, uncertainty, or even foolishness if those are the qualities of the input into the echo chamber. A candidate may win despite his tactics and appeals rather than because of them. If the people can choose only from among rascals, they are certain to choose a rascal.

Scholars, though they have less at stake than do politicians, also have an abiding curiosity about why voters act as they do. In the past quarter of a century [since the 1940s] they have vastly enlarged their capacity to check the hunches born of their curiosities. The invention of the sample survey—the most widely known example of which is the Gallup poll—

enabled them to make fairly trustworthy estimates of the characteristics and behaviors of large human populations. This method of mass observation revolutionized the study of politics—as well as the management of political campaigns. The new technique permitted large-scale tests to check the validity of old psychological and sociological theories of human behavior. These tests led to new hunches and new theories about voting behavior, which could, in turn, be checked and which thereby contributed to the extraordinary ferment in the social sciences during recent decades.

The studies of electoral behavior by survey methods cumulate into an imposing body of knowledge which conveys a vivid impression of the variety and subtlety of factors that enter into individual voting decisions. In their first stages in the 1930's the new electoral studies chiefly lent precision and verification to the working maxims of practicing politicians and to some of the crude theories of political speculators. Thus, sample surveys established that people did, indeed, appear to vote their pocketbooks. Yet the demonstration created its embarrassments because it also established that exceptions to the rule were numerous. Not all factory workers, for example, voted alike. How was the behavior of the deviants from "group interest" to be explained? Refinement after refinement of theory and analysis added complexity to the original simple explanation. By introducing a bit of psychological theory it could be demonstrated that factory workers with optimistic expectations tended less to be governed by pocketbook considerations than did those whose outlook was gloomy. When a little social psychology was stirred into the analysis, it could be established that identifications formed early in life, such as attachments to political parties, also reinforced or resisted the pull of the interest of the moment. A sociologist, bringing to play the conceptual tools of his trade, then could show that those factory workers who associate intimately with like-minded persons on the average vote with greater solidarity than do social isolates. Inquiries conducted with great ingenuity along many such lines have enormously broadened our knowledge of the factors associated with the responses of people to the stimuli presented to them by political campaigns.

Yet, by and large, the picture of the voter that emerges from a combination of the folklore of practical politics and the findings of the new electoral studies is not a pretty one. It is not a portrait of citizens moving to considered decision as they play their solemn role of making and unmaking governments. The older tradition from practical politics may regard the voter as an erratic and irrational fellow susceptible to manipulation by skilled humbugs. One need not live through many campaigns to observe politicians, even successful politicians, who act as though they regarded the people as manageable fools. Nor does a heroic conception of the voter emerge from the new analyses of electoral behavior. They can be added up to a conception of voting not as a civic decision but as

an almost purely deterministic act. Given knowledge of certain characteristics of a voter—his occupation, his residence, his religion, his national origin, and perhaps certain of his attitudes—one can predict with
a high probability the direction of his vote. The actions of persons are
made to appear to be only predictable and automatic responses to campaign stimuli.

*   *   *

Conceptions and theories of the way voters behave do not raise solely
arcane problems to be disputed among the democratic and antidemocratic theorists or questions to be settled by the elegant techniques of the
analysts of electoral behavior. Rather, they touch upon profound issues
at the heart of the problem of the nature and workability of systems of
popular government. Obviously the perceptions of the behavior of the
electorate held by political leaders, agitators, and activists condition, if
they do not fix, the types of appeals politicians employ as they seek
popular support. These perceptions—or theories—affect the nature of
the input to the echo chamber, if we may revert to our earlier figure, and
thereby control its output. They may govern, too, the kinds of actions
that governments take as they look forward to the next election. If politicians perceive the electorate as responsive to father images, they will
give it father images. If they see voters as most certainly responsive to
nonsense, they will give them nonsense. If they see voters as susceptible
to delusion, they will delude them. If they see an electorate receptive to
the cold, hard realities, they will give it the cold, hard realities.

In short, theories of how voters behave acquire importance not because of their effects on voters, who may proceed blithely unaware of
them. They gain significance because of their effects, both potentially and
in reality, on candidates and other political leaders. If leaders believe the
route to victory is by projection of images and cultivation of styles rather
than by advocacy of policies to cope with the problems of the country,
they will project images and cultivate styles to the neglect of the substance of politics. They will abdicate their prime function in a democratic
system, which amounts, in essence, to the assumption of the risk of trying to persuade us to lift ourselves by our bootstraps.

Among the literary experts on politics there are those who contend
that, because of the development of tricks for the manipulation of the
masses, practices of political leadership in the management of voters
have moved far toward the conversion of election campaigns into obscene parodies of the models set up by democratic idealists. They point
to the good old days when politicians were deep thinkers, eloquent orators, and farsighted statesmen. Such estimates of the course of change
in social institutions must be regarded with reserve. They may be only
manifestations of the inverted optimism of aged and melancholy men

who, estopped from hope for the future, see in the past a satisfaction of their yearning for greatness in our political life.

Whatever the trends may have been, the perceptions that leadership elements of democracies hold of the modes of response of the electorate must always be a matter of fundamental significance. Those perceptions determine the nature of the voice of the people, for they determine the character of the input into the echo chamber. While the output may be governed by the nature of the input, over the longer run the properties of the echo chamber may themselves be altered. Fed a steady diet of buncombe [bunkum], the people may come to expect and to respond with highest predictability to buncombe. And those leaders most skilled in the propagation of buncombe may gain lasting advantage in the recurring struggles for popular favor.

The perverse and unorthodox argument of this little book is that voters are not fools. To be sure, many individual voters act in odd ways indeed; yet in the large the electorate behaves about as rationally and responsibly as we should expect, given the clarity of the alternatives presented to it and the character of the information available to it. In American presidential campaigns of recent decades the portrait of the American electorate that develops from the data is not one of an electorate straitjacketed by social determinants or moved by subconscious urges triggered by devilishly skillful propagandists. It is rather one of an electorate moved by concern about central and relevant questions of public policy, of governmental performance, and of executive personality. Propositions so uncompromisingly stated inevitably represent overstatements. Yet to the extent that they can be shown to resemble the reality, they are propositions of basic importance for both the theory and the practice of democracy.

To check the validity of this broad interpretation of the behavior of voters, attention will center on the movements of voters across party lines as they reacted to the issues, events, and candidates of presidential campaigns between 1936 and 1960. Some Democratic voters of one election turned Republican at the next; others stood pat. Some Republicans of one presidential season voted Democratic four years later; others remained loyal Republicans. What motivated these shifts, sometimes large and sometimes small, in voter affection? How did the standpatters differ from the switchers? What led them to stand firmly by their party preference of four years earlier? Were these actions governed by images, moods, and other irrelevancies; or were they expressions of judgments about the sorts of questions that, hopefully, voters will weigh as they responsibly cast their ballots? On these matters evidence is available that is impressive in volume, if not always so complete or so precisely relevant as hindsight would wish. If one perseveres through the analysis of this extensive body of information, the proposition that the voter is not so irrational a fellow after all may become credible.

DISCUSSION QUESTIONS

1. When you go into the voting booth, how do you decide who to vote for? Is your decision ever affected by arguments raised during the political campaign? If so, how?

2. Did the 1996 presidential election support Key's view of the electoral process? That is, to what extent were the choices made in the election an "echo" of what the voters were presented with?

45

" 'Give 'em Hell' These Days Is a Figure of Speech"

Eileen Shields West

Voters are alienated by the negative campaigning and dirty politics that characterize so many electoral campaigns. To use Key's term, voters have become distraught with the "foolishness" on the other side of the echo chamber. Given the perception that mudslinging is at an all-time high, it is tempting to reminisce about the "good old days" when campaigns were focused on the issues of the days and certainly less vicious. Yet as Eileen Shields West makes clear, history reveals that campaigning today is positively tame by nineteenth-century standards. Just to put things in perspective, try to imagine Bob Dole claiming that "murder, robbery, rape, adultery and incest will be openly taught and practiced" if Bill Clinton was reelected in 1996. This was the warning issued by the opponents of Thomas Jefferson in 1800; they also labeled him a "mean-spirited, low-lived fellow, the son of a half-breed Indian squaw, sired by a Virginian mulatto father."

One of the big differences in campaigning in the two political eras is that today's media at least attempt to report news objectively, whereas nineteenth-century newspapers were propaganda machines for their favorite candidates. West is not trying to argue that campaigns today are substantive and issue based, in contrast to the past. It is simply useful to put things in a historical context.

This [1988] has been the year of the Seven Democratic Dwarfs and alleged wimpery, of demands for medical and military records, of titillated talk about monkey business afloat and lamentation at the cruelty of one campaign aide for blowing the whistle on oral plagiarism committed on TV. The race for the Presidency is getting too nasty, some people aver, and there is a tendency to blame it on what is seen as a tasteless and permissive age.

But whatever is wrong with American political campaigns, they have not become more salacious or more savage. Quite the reverse. "What respectable person today," political expert Paul Boller Jr. asks, "would think of calling one of the candidates for the highest office in the land a carbuncled-faced old drunkard? Or a howling atheist?" Or, for that matter, "a pickpocket, thief, traitor, lecher, syphilitic, gorilla, anarchist, murderer"? Nobody, of course. When the Senate minority leader, Robert

Dole, asked Vice President George Bush to stop lying about his (Dole's) political record, the country's pundits acted as if Dole had practically frothed at the mouth.

But in the good (or bad) old days, Dole's comment would have been the height of politesse. Starting with the Founding Fathers (Washington excepted), candidates for the Presidency or their cohorts verbally assaulted each other in ways today not only unspeakable but virtually unthinkable. Verbal violence during Presidential campaigns was as American as apple pie. President Martin Van Buren, for example, was charged with wearing corsets and taking more baths than a real man should. As late as 1888, trying to give folks back home an idea of what a Yankee political campaign was like, Britain's Lord Bryce described it as a "tempest of invective and calumny. . . . Imagine all the accusations brought against all the candidates for the 670 seats in the English Parliament," he wrote, "concentrated on one man, and read . . . daily for three months."

Starting in the election of 1800 (John Adams versus Thomas Jefferson) campaign songs appeared, too. By 1840, when plebeian beginnings in a log cabin appealed to the mob, the first full-scale campaign songbook helped the Whig candidate, William Henry Harrison, the hero of the Battle of Tippecanoe, defeat Van Buren by transforming Harrison from a Virginia aristocrat (who owned a Georgian mansion and sipped gentleman's whiskey) into a popular, log-cabin-dwelling, hard-cider-swigging hillbilly.

"He's a Little Squirt-wirt-wirt"

The tunefully reinforced image caught on and, try as they might, the Democrats could never discredit it, nor expunge another song-inspired inference that their own hapless candidate, President Van Buren, was a pantywaist. Democratic protests were drowned out by rousing choruses of "Old Tip he wears a homespun coat / He has no ruffled shirt-wirt-wirt / But Mat has the golden plate / And he's a little squirt-wirt-wirt." The wirt-wirts were embellished by spitting (usually tobacco juice) through the singer's teeth. It was that kind of campaign year. Out in Illinois a lawyer named Lincoln, running for the state legislature, could (and did) reach over to rip open his Democratic opponent's tightly buttoned cloth coat to reveal the ruffled silk shirt and velvet vest hidden beneath.

By then, political campaigning had become a staple of American entertainment. Politics is "the only pleasure an American knows," Alexis de Tocqueville wrote. "Even the women frequently attend public meetings and listen to political harangues as a recreation from their household labors." Men, and presumably women too, though they were 80 years from the vote, were mightily interested in the goings-on of the

1840 campaign, which notably contributed to what Lord Bryce would call the "booming" quality of American politics. The "boom," Bryce thought, struck the "imagination of those who in country hamlets read of the doings in the great city." American elections, Bryce held, were largely a matter of "booming."

More eligible voters (80 percent of about 2.4 million) cast their ballots in the 1840 campaign than had ever voted in a Presidential election, sweeping Harrison into office. It wasn't the public's fault that he was 68 years old, delivered an interminable Inaugural speech without a hat or coat, then died of pneumonia a month later. And though the rudeness of booming is now deplored, during the last half of the 19th century, when booming and outrageous incivility were at their peak, 75 to 85 percent of the electorate voted.

That figure compares sadly with all our recent elections when barely 50 percent of the eligible voters managed to get to the polls to choose the President. Every four years the experts sit around wondering why this is so. But most agree with political writer David Broder that Presidential campaigns, "whether or not they appeal to the mind at all, they don't stir people at the gut level the way they used to."

More than anything else, television gets blamed for what it has done to candidates and conventions, where the press seems to outnumber the politicians a thousand to one, and everybody grows accustomed to candidates trying to say as little as possible in answer to the same questions, asked again and again. Whatever the cause, a trip back to some of the most vicious campaigns—a time when libel suits were rare and incivility was in fine flower—provides a useful and diverting perspective.

By 1800, the aura that had somewhat protected the justly sacrosanct figure of George Washington had already given way to savage partisanship. His two terms were followed by one term for John Adams, a plump, brilliant but sometimes silly man who loved grand titles and was secretly mocked by enemies as "His Rotundity." The system of electoral votes, since modified, played strange tricks in the early Presidential races, especially since the candidate who came in second became Vice President. During his term (1797–1801), Adams was derided as the "President by three votes," because in 1796 he received only 71 electoral votes (to rival Jefferson's 68). When the Federalists chose to run Adams again, with Gen. Charles Cotesworth Pinckney of South Carolina as his running mate, the new Republican Party ran Jefferson with Aaron Burr.

"Head Itching for a Crowny"

The agrarian, egalitarian Republicans (who gradually became what history knows as Jeffersonian Democrats) swiftly spread a rumor that President Adams planned to marry one of his sons to the daughter of George III in order to start an American dynasty with economic ties to

England. Comic rumor even had it that George Washington himself got Adams to change his mind by donning his Revolutionary uniform and threatening to run him through with his patriot's sword. "See Johnny at the helm of State," Jeffersonians chorused, "Head itching for a crowny, / He longs to be, like Georgy, great, / And pulls Tom Jeffer downy!"

Adams had a sharp tongue. He once referred to Alexander Hamilton, his party's brilliant Secretary of the Treasury, as the "bastard brat of a Scotch pedlar." But under Republican onslaughts he often managed to stay cool. When it was put about that he had sent Pinckney to England in a U.S. frigate to procure four pretty girls as mistresses—for them both—Adams genially replied: "I do declare upon my honor, if this be true General Pinckney has cheated me out of my two."

Other Federalists fought back, questioning Jefferson's courage during the Revolution, mocking him as a dilettante inventor who dreamed up nothing but "Gim-Krackery." But that was the high road compared to this biographical précis of the sage of Monticello: "Tom Jefferson . . . a mean-spirited, low-lived fellow, the son of a half-breed Indian squaw, sired by a Virginia mulatto father . . . raised wholly on hoe-cake made of coarse-ground Southern corn, bacon and hominy, with an occasional . . . fricasseed bullfrog." Were he elected, an editorial in the Federalist *Connecticut Courant* warned readers, "Murder, robbery, rape, adultery and incest will be openly taught and practiced."

In a land still largely agrarian, the Republicans had won the support of country folk and (thanks largely to Jefferson's friend James Madison) were better organized. Even so, history records a neck-and-neck election result and bitter finagling because of the peculiar ground rules regarding the Presidency and the electoral votes. The two Republicans each got 73, Adams 65. This forced a runoff vote in the House of Representatives between Burr and Jefferson. On the 36th ballot, Jefferson was chosen. Federalists promptly cried "President by No Votes!" But the political power of the Northeast had been broken, at least for the moment. Years later a New York congressman mourned those good old days, "when a Federalist could knock a Republican down in the streets [of New York] and not be questioned about it."

In 1816 Gen. Andrew Jackson, surely one of the most combative men in American history, uncharacteristically wrote President-elect James Monroe, saying "Now is the time to exterminate the monster called party spirit." It was true that during the War of 1812, partisan loyalties, and to some extent sectional interests, had been submerged in a national desire to fight off the British. Americans felt good about themselves, as we would put it today, in part because of Jackson's astounding victory in the Battle of New Orleans. What has come to be known as the Era of Good Feelings was about to begin.

Largely thanks to Jackson, it did not last long. By 1824 he had run for President himself and got the most popular votes, only to be robbed, he thought, by the pesky Electoral College. In a runoff of the three leading candidates, the House of Representatives found itself having to choose between John Adams' diplomat son, John Quincy Adams; Secretary of the Treasury William Crawford; and Jackson. Henry Clay, Speaker of the House, had been eliminated and now used his influence to elect Adams.

What really stuck in Jackson's craw was, to him, the certain evidence that a deal had been struck between Adams and Clay, who was speedily appointed the new Secretary of State. Jacksonian anger at this "corrupt bargain," made, as he mildly put it, "by the Judas of the West" (Clay was from over the mountains in Kentucky), fueled the campaign of 1828. Adams' National Republicans, heirs to the old Federalists, stood for stronger central government, more federal expenditure and a higher tariff, but the issues took a backseat to a personality struggle between Adams, seen as an effete representative of Eastern power and privilege, and Old Hickory, a brawling, rough-tongued, frontier war hero, clearly a man of the people. The confrontation also helped create a new populist party, the Jackson Party, which swiftly became the new national Democratic Party. It also fueled a campaign almost too silly, too scurrilous to be believed.

Adams was a brilliant and dedicated public servant who rose at 5 each morning and worked pretty much without ceasing until 5 in the afternoon. But Democrats accused him of being a gambler because he once bought a secondhand billiard table for the White House. "When we find the fathers and mothers of our country . . . persuading young men from practices which lead to destruction," one Jacksonian editor soberly moralized, "we greatly fear that the too frequent answer will be, 'Why, the President plays billiards!' "

That was the polite part. They also asserted that the President and his wife had had premarital relations, and freely labeled him "The Pimp" on the strength of their unfounded charge that, during his term as ambassador to Russia (1809–14), Adams had procured an American girl for Czar Alexander I. Jackson was more vulnerable than Adams in this area, because he had been obliged to remarry his beloved wife Rachel when it turned out that her divorce (a scandal in itself) was not legal. He had to bear editorials and rhetorical speeches asking: "Ought a convicted adulteress and her paramour be placed in the highest offices of this free and Christian land?" Famous for a hot temper and for executing men during his military campaigns, he ground his teeth and listened as gleeful Adams supporters sang: "Oh, Andy! Oh Andy, / How many men have you hanged in your life? / How many weddings make a wife?"

Beside such things, routine charges that his mother was a "COMMON PROSTITUTE, brought to this country by the British soldiers!" perhaps set the celebrated duelist's adrenaline flowing. Nothing deterred the rolling wave of Jackson people from street demonstrations, barbecues and, above all, innumerable plantings of Jackson's symbol, the hickory pole, in parks and on street corners all over the country. On November 4, 1828, just before the election, Jackson's people tore up the sidewalk in front of Tammany Hall and the pro-Adams *New-York Spectator* sneered, "The pole was erected amid loud yells . . . the beer-barrels were rolled out; and it required no vivid imagination to distinguish in the uproar the yell of the hyæna, the cry of the panther and the whoop of the Winnebagoes."

The turnout was heavy, three times larger than in 1824. Old Hickory won by a comfortable margin. His Inauguration party, with common folk overrunning the White House, breaking furniture, spitting tobacco juice in corners and leaving muddy footprints on the carpets, is regarded as a classic symbol of democracy triumphant. But it was not only Jackson's victory, but his practices as President which insured that savage campaign partisanship would continue in Presidential politics. Jackson increased the power of the Presidency enormously. Unlike Adams, Jackson threw his cronies into office, ushering in a full-scale spoils system that used patronage mercilessly for political purposes, thus strengthening the hold of Democrats on power and preference. So much for exterminating the monster called party spirit.

The scene shifts past the Civil War, when the issues of slavery and the survival of the Union were agonizing and profound. By 1884 Reconstruction was over, America was exploding westward, business was booming and it was open season on campaign madness again. Republicans (a far different party from that of 1800) favored a protective tariff higher than the Democrats, but otherwise there was little difference between the party platforms. It was time for a campaign of pure theater or, as one critic has put it, a contest between the "copulative habits of one and the prevaricative habits of the other."

The one was Democrat Grover Cleveland, a Buffalo lawyer who, in three years, had leapfrogged from being his city's mayor to the governorship of New York to Presidential candidacy. The other was Republican James Blaine from Maine, an ex-Congressman and former Secretary of State.

Cleveland was a bit rough around the edges, a man reputed to wash down his dinner with beer and then relieve himself out of the window of his law office. (He had once been sued, in fact, by a passer-by who got in the way.) Cleveland was stoutly honest, though, and as a politician he had made many of the right enemies. His campaign slogan, "A Public Office is a Public Trust," stood in marked contrast to Blaine, a charming, sophisticated and sometimes funny man who campaigned as the "Plumed Knight," but who was also justly known as "Slippery Jim," a dishonest politician.

Blaine was a veteran legislator and skilled campaigner, of course, and his partisans soon were successfully poking fun at plodding Cleveland's inexperience and mushroomlike arrival on the political scene. Then on

July 21, the gods seemed to deliver the Presidency to Blaine on a silver platter. There, under a banner headline on the front page of the Buffalo *Telegraph* was the shocking revelation that Governor Cleveland had an illegitimate, 10-year-old son by Maria Halpin, a widow who had sewed collars for a living. Some of Cleveland's advisers rushed to Albany, expecting denial. But Cleveland had always told his associates, "Whatever you say, tell the truth," and that was exactly what he did now. Many years before, he admitted, he'd cavorted with Halpin, and had since supported the child, though he was never sure it was really his. When advisers wrung their hands at the political implications of the affair, he is said to have added, "I don't believe the American people want a gelding in the White House."

Republicans exulted and paraded around in knightly armor sporting brightly colored plumes, gleefully singing "Ma! Ma! Where's my Pa? Gone to the White House—Hah! Hah! Hah!" The president of Amherst College told his students that only voters with corrupt morals could support Cleveland, who was charitably characterized as a "coarse debauchee who would bring harlots to Washington."

How the campaign might have turned out if Cleveland's amorous proclivities had remained the major issue, no one knows. Just in time, letters turned up new evidence that Blaine had been engaged in some shady bond deals, one with the unheeded postscript: "Burn this letter." Blaine denied wrongdoing, while cartoonists like Thomas Nast pilloried him as a creature drenched in loot, wearing three very bedraggled plumes. It was the turn of Democrats to chant: "Blaine! Blaine! Jay Gould Blaine! The Continental Liar from the state of Maine!"

Cleveland won by a whisker—23,000 votes out of a total of 9.7 million cast for both candidates—and chortling Democrats sang: "Hurray for Maria! Hurray for the Kid! / I voted for Cleveland, and I'm damned glad I did!"

The election of 1896 was an amazing show, too. It was not scandalous, but rather a study in contrasting character and political style which illustrated the hold that Presidential campaigning had upon the American public. It also marked the permanent arrival in American politics of the prominent as well as powerful campaign manager in the person of Cleveland businessman Mark Hanna, who had helped his unprepossessing protégé, Republican William McKinley, become Governor of Ohio.

McKinley was a high-tariff man and wanted to campaign, as much as he wanted to campaign at all, on that issue. But his Democratic opponent, a 36-year-old Nebraska Congressman named William Jennings Bryan, wouldn't let him. As a Western agrarian and Populist with a golden voice, Bryan had a bimetallist bee in his bonnet. These were depression years and bimetallists, especially Bryan, believed with a crusading fervor that the poor would have more money and the economy would look up if the country went off the gold standard.

Speeches at the Rate of 30 a Day

McKinley believed that bimetallism, which called for unlimited coinage of silver, was nonsense and initially he refused to campaign about it. Quite a few conservative Democrats agreed and quit the party. To take his problem to the people, Bryan ran a whistle-stop campaign so successful that it forced succeeding Presidential candidates to follow suit. He traveled 18,000 miles, gave more than 600 speeches, sometimes at a rate of 30 a day, brought his message to five million people and laid a rhetorical mark on the American language with the ringing phrase: "You shall not press down upon the brow of labor this crown of thorns. You shall not crucify mankind upon a cross of gold."

McKinley was unimpressed, but Hanna grew nervous and urged his candidate to go on the road. McKinley refused to budge from his porch. "I might as well put up a trapeze on my front lawn and compete with some professional athlete," he said, "as go out speaking against Bryan." In the end, however, he agreed to have delegations come to him in Canton and said he would speak out for gold.

With a little help from Hanna, gold standard supporters began to appear. They wore gold neckties and gold hatbands and some rode gold-trimmed bicycles. They brought McKinley gifts: cheese, butter, watermelons and even live American eagles. Each delegation chairman would read a statement. McKinley would smile and listen, "like a child looking at Santa Claus." Then, his mother at his side, he stood on a chair in a long double-breasted coat with a carnation in his buttonhole and offered some pithy remark. One such message, succinct and economically sound: "Free silver will degrade your money."

By November 3 he and Hanna had outdone Bryan. Where the neat lawn had been, there was plain brown earth, looking "as if a herd of buffalo had passed that way." The white picket fence and grape arbor had long since been demolished by souvenir hunters. And the front porch threatened to collapse. But some 750,000 visitors had trooped past McKinley's home.

Democrats decried the special excursion rates the railroads had been induced to charge for a trip to Canton. Hanna was cartooned as pig-eyed and bloated, wearing a suit checkered with dollar signs. But the election turned out two million more voters than in 1892 and Bryan was decisively defeated.

"My relatives told me about the fun of packing up a wagon to hear William Jennings Bryan speak," the 60-ish national columnist and political commentator Hugh Sidey once told me. "It was like a neighborhood barn raising. Even when Franklin Roosevelt came through on the train in 1934, a lot of our neighbors went down in their Model A Fords, hoisted their kids up to see and brought a picnic lunch, instead of going to the movies."

Truman versus Republican "Bloodsuckers"

The excitement of such campaigns is now mainly a fading memory, and like Sidey's, most of the recollections are secondhand. Yet FDR was not the last President to go to the people in this way. That honor belongs to Harry Truman and the legendary "Give 'em hell, Harry" whistle-stop campaign of 1948, when Truman, refusing to believe newspapers, experts and straws in the wind, took off around the country, his rimless spectacles glittering, and let Tom Dewey and the "no-account, do-nothing, Republican, Eightieth Congress" have it.

Sometimes making 14 short speeches a day from the back platform of the train, he called the Republicans "bloodsuckers." Noting that they had "already stuck a pitchfork in the farmer's back," he told the folks in Missouri and Kansas and Iowa, "I wonder how many times you have to be hit on the head before you find out who's hitting you." All the rich Republicans would do, he said, was "let a little trickle down off the table like the crumbs that fell to Lazarus."

The press and the pundits wrote Truman off entirely. Though Alice Roosevelt Longworth said Dewey looked like the "bridegroom on a wedding cake," *Life* referred to him simply as "The next President," while the *Kiplinger Magazine* devoted an issue to what Dewey would do when, not if, he was elected. On the campaign train, one day, campaign adviser Clark Clifford tried to hide a copy of *Newsweek*, which had just polled 50 leading political commentators, reporting that not a single "expert" had picked Truman. But the President got hold of the copy anyway. He was not dismayed. "He looked at me," Clifford recalls, "and said, 'You know, not one of those 50 fellows has enough sense to pound sand in a rat hole!'"

And then came television.

Discussion Questions

1. Can you think of a few examples of negative campaigning or mudslinging in recent elections? How does it compare to the examples from the nineteenth century described by West?

2. What distinguishes mudslinging from legitimate attacks on a candidate's record? What makes an ad "negative"?

3. What steps can be taken to minimize the "mud" in our elections? Are the news media, the voters, parties, or the candidates primarily responsible?

46
"What I Learned About How We Pick a President"

Lamar Alexander

Running for president has always been an obstacle course. Candidates travel from small town to large city, deliver speech after speech, gather delegates for the nominating convention, press the flesh, develop public policy positions, plan for the possibility of governing—and do it all under the scrutiny of the media. As Eileen Shields West noted above, it is not now nor was it ever an easy task. In this first-hand sketch of the campaign process, Republican presidential candidate and former Tennessee governor Lamar Alexander maintains that running the obstacle course has become increasingly difficult, given the constant need to chase ever larger pots of campaign dollars while adhering to excessive campaign finance regulations, and the need to run dozens of state primary campaigns in twenty-five days, amid media coverage which has become terse, shallow, and mean spirited. Alexander offers several proposals for reforming the presidential nominating process.

While my wounds are fresh, let me offer several ways to fix how we nominate presidents. First, for those who only see it on *Inside Politics*, let me describe what running for president really feels like (especially when you have just lost). It is like scaling a cliff for three years in the dark to earn the privilege of shooting one NBA-range three-point shot, i.e., the New Hampshire primary. It is like walking above Niagara Falls on a swaying tightrope as the wind blows and the crowd shouts, "FALL!" This by itself is one reason to salute Bob Dole for making his way so well through such an obstacle course.

Now, to fix the process (although I should proclaim up front and loudly that it is the candidate who must accept responsibility for losing, not the process):

- *Report on those who are actually running for president.* It sometimes seemed that 90 percent of the political news during 1995 was about numerous Americans, estimable as they may have been, who had no intention of running or who couldn't win even if they did.
- *Ban the phrase "the motley crew."* Referring to those of us actually running, this phrase usually begins to appear after several months of stories about those who aren't running. Isn't it time after 200-plus years

of presidential elections to realize that any American looks better rocking on the porch than he (or she) does trudging through the mud bucknaked with spotlights turned on (another way to describe participation in the current presidential nominating process)?

- *Raise the limits on individual giving to campaigns from $1,000 to $5,000.* The well-intentioned $1,000 limit, placed into the federal law after Watergate, was meant to reduce the influence of money in politics. As with many federal laws, it has done just the opposite. For example, to raise $10 million in 1995 for my campaign, I attended 250 fund-raising events. This took about 70 percent of my time. I became unusually well acquainted with a great many good Americans capable of giving $1,000 (who probably represent a cross section of one percent of all the people in the country). Wouldn't I have been a better candidate—and the country better off had I been elected—if I had spent more time traveling around America and visiting our allies abroad? (I actually did this during 1994, when I was not meeting nice people who could give $1,000.)

- *Remove the state spending limits.* This is step two in the crusade to deal with the phenomenon of the zillionaire in politics. Think of it this way: Say the fifth-grade teacher organizes a contest for class president with water pistols as the weapon of choice; then some kid arrives with a machine gun. Either take away the new kid's machine gun (Bill Bradley suggests a constitutional amendment to limit what individuals can spend on their own campaigns) or give the rest of the fifth graders the freedom to raise and spend enough money to buy their own machine guns. In one week just before the New Hampshire primary, Steve Forbes bought 700 ads on one Boston television station in one week, most of them negative advertising against Dole (plus a few gentler ads against me). Forbes, let us remember, spent almost no time raising his money and had no limits on what he spent per state. The rest of us did. If New Hampshire is most of the ballgame in the presidential primaries, why shouldn't we be permitted to defend ourselves even if we use up all the money the government allows us to spend during the entire campaign?

- *Deregulate the election process.* The Federal Election Commission is full of competent people trying to do their jobs (several of whom are about to audit my campaign, which, if everything works out perfectly, will only take only about three years. I am not kidding). The campaigns are grossly overregulated. Of the $10 million our campaign raised during 1995, about $1 million went for accountants and lawyers for compliance with the federal rules. Is it really necessary, for example, for the federal government to decide that a candidate's campaign T-shirts need not bear the "Paid for by . . ." disclaimer? Fewer rules and full disclosure should be the bywords here.

- *Start the coverage earlier.* From the moment the networks began to cover the campaign (this year it was not until late January), you could feel the lift. As a candidate, you can also feel the collapse. I cannot help but think that there are ways—even many months out—to relate the day's news about, say, the failure of the Hartford school system's private-management contract to what the presidential candidates say about how schools should be run.

- *Spread it out.* At a breakfast in Washington in November, I said this to my friends in the news media: "If you guys were sportswriters, you would arrive during the last quarter of the Final Four championship game and claim you had covered the entire basketball season." You can imagine how many friends I made with this statement, but I was right. By my count, the news media covered the presidential race aggressively for just 21 days, from the Iowa caucus on February 10 until the South Carolina primary on March 2. Most of what went before consisted of asking people like me, "Why are you behind Bob Dole 72–3 in the polls?" at a time when everyone knew Dole and no one had ever heard of me. After South Carolina, the most frequently asked question was, "When are you going to get out?" So, most of us did. Let us hope the national political writers never decide to become umpires. The World Series wouldn't last more than one inning.

  Now, in defense of the media, it is hard to cover a 21-day wild rollercoaster ride, which is what the nominating process has become: 38 primaries in 25 days. Let's change this: Let Iowa and New Hampshire go it alone in February. Then, require all the other states to hold their primaries on the second Tuesday of March, April, or May. This would give winners a chance to capitalize on successes, voters a chance to digest new faces, and candidates a chance to actually meet voters. What do you think would have happened this year if after the surprising New Hampshire primary (Buchanan winning, Dole stumbling, me surging, Forbes falling) there had been three weeks to campaign before a March 12 primary in a bunch of states? Then another month until another set of primaries? Lots more interesting—and lots more conducive to sound judgment by the voters, too.

- *Create a new C-SPAN channel to cover the country outside Washington.* Chief executives from outside Washington sometimes make the best chief executives in the country. Why not a cable channel devoted entirely to Michigan governor John Engler's charter schools, San Antonio county executive Cyndi Krier's crime program, Milwaukee's school-choice program? Give these leaders as much C-SPAN face-time as members of Congress. This will give the public more exposure to state and local politicians who might then have a better chance of winning national office.

- *Let the candidates speak more often for themselves.* Praise the media here. C-SPAN's *Road to the White House* on Sunday nights set the pace. I was astonished how many told me they saw C-SPAN's 50-minute coverage in July of my walk across New Hampshire. The *New York Times* printed excerpts from candidates' speeches, even some very long excerpts. The networks all showed unedited stump speeches of the major candidates.

- *Find the good and praise it.* These were always the words of my friend the late Alex Haley. I can find the good easily about this process, even with its flaws. During the last year I walked across New Hampshire meeting several hundred people a day, spent 80 days in Iowa in maybe 200 meetings that ranged from 20 to 300 people, and had at least 50 meetings in Florida with the delegates to the Presidency III straw poll. During most of these meetings I was little known and unencumbered by news media. At least the news media presence was so small it did not disrupt the flow of the session.

I remember wishing time after time that anybody who had any sense of cynicism about our presidential selection process could be with me, as a fly on the wall—because they could not be cynical after hearing and seeing and feeling what I saw. The audience always listened carefully. Their questions went straight to the heart of what kind of country we could have, of our jobs, our schools, our neighborschools, and our families. In meeting after meeting, I came away certain that this is a nation hungry for a vision contest, not one willing to tolerate a trivial presidential election. There is a great market in the American electorate for a full-fledged discussion about what kind of country we can have in the year 2000 and beyond.

The reason to make certain we have a properly functioning presidential nominating process is that the presidency itself is our most important institution as we go into the new century, and the debate about who should be that president is our most useful national discussion.

DISCUSSION QUESTIONS

1. Do you think the reforms suggested by Alexander would bring about a different type of candidate, encourage more candidates to run, or allow presidents to govern differently during their first term? Why or why not?

2. What other reforms would you suggest to change the way we nominate our presidential candidates?

3. The current "front-loaded" primary season favors the front runner, as Robert Dole demonstrated in the 1996 primaries. What are the advantages and disadvantages of this feature of the nomination process?

47

The "Motor-Voter" Debate: The National Voter Registration Act of 1993

The United States was among the first nations to provide broad voting rights to all its citizens. Suffrage was initially limited to white males, but expanded gradually to include, in theory, everyone over eighteen save for a few minor exceptions (those convicted of federal felony crimes, for example). At each phase the expansion of the vote was controversial, but there was enough public support for repeated constitutional amendments to make the voting process more inclusive. Yet despite the effort to increase the number of voters, the percentage of eligible adults in the U.S. who vote is among the lowest in the developed world. Less than half of those eligible voted in the 1996 presidential race, and typically just over one-third bother to turn out in midterm congressional elections.

Political scientists have puzzled over the decline in voter turnout. Most point to imposed by registration that can dampen turnout by 7 to 10 percent. Proponents of the "motor-voter" bill reasoned that the best way to increase turnout is to make registration easier: by requiring that states give people an opportunity to register at motor vehicle and welfare offices, the bill could increase turnout by tens of millions of voters.

Broadening the base of potential voters, however laudable a goal, is a controversial issue. Registration requirements pose the biggest hurdle for the poor, minorities, inner city residents, and individuals without much education. People in these groups also tend to vote Democratic, so making it easier for them to register probably means more Democratic votes; as a result, a number of Republicans opposed "motor-voter." However, in the following excerpts from the debate over "motor-voter" on the House floor, this central political concern is never explicitly addressed by members of either political party. Democrats downplayed any anticipated political advantage from the bill, while Republicans argued that the bill would increase voter fraud, impose an unfair burden on states, and violate the principles of federalism. The Bill passed the House by a vote of 259–160 on February 4, 1993, and the Senate by 62–37 on March 17, 1993. After a conference committee ironed out differences in the two versions of the bill, President Clinton signed it into law on May 20, 1993.

MR. AL SWIFT (D-WA): Mr. Chairman, it sometimes seems strange that it takes so much work to do something so simple and so good for the American people as this measure will do. What we are trying to address here is the eradication of a rather unfortunate tradition in this country. We have used voter registration mechanisms in the United

States throughout many, many decades to prevent various groups who were from time to time and by certain groups considered undesirable, to make it very difficult for them to vote. At various times those have been eastern Europeans and southern Europeans, the Irish, African-Americans, and others.

There are very few people in this country today, who would condone establishing high registration thresholds for the purpose of discrimination against any American citizen, but we have grown out of that tradition to believe that it is government's right to establish high thresholds for registration; that, in short, government has the right to dictate high hurdles over which American citizens must jump in order to be qualified to vote on election day.

That is wrong. It is inconsistent with the fundamental beliefs and philosophy of this country, in which we believe that it is a God-given, not a government-given, right for a citizen of this country to vote.

The legislation which we have before us today suggests three specific ways to make it easier for citizens to register. All three are already in practice in this country. All three are working; all three are working well. There is nothing new; there is nothing untried here at all.

Ninety-two percent of Americans have a driver's license. The first thing this legislation does is to say that when one applies for a driver's license or renews the driver's license, they will also at that time have an opportunity to apply for registration to vote.

What of the other 8 percent? Why do they not have driver's licenses? Primarily either through physical disability that prevents them from driving, or economic disability, which prevents them from owning a car, so we do two other things in this legislation: we provide postcard registration, which is particularly useful to the disabled. That is a technique which is currently used by 28 States, a majority of the States. Most Americans today can register to vote through that technique.

For those who are in economic distress, we say in those agencies where they are most likely to seek help they will have an opportunity to apply for registration there as well.

Let me conclude this opening statement by making one other distinction that I think is terribly important. We use shorthand in our language and sometimes come to believe the accuracy of the shorthand. We say, "We register to vote." The truth is, all any of us do is apply to be registered to vote. The registrars register us.

Why is that distinction important? We have heard a lot of rhetoric around here about automatic registration. There is nothing in this bill that provides for that at all. Because whichever of the mechanisms in this bill are used by which to apply for registration, that application still goes, as any application does today, to a registration official who will screen that registration, that application, for eligibility. That is the way it is done now. That is the way it will be done under this legislation.

We do not have vote fraud because of any of these techniques now. There will be no vote fraud because these techniques will be used in every State, rather than in some. In short, this is simply an effort to make a citizen of this country more readily able to register, so come election day he or she will have no problem going into that voting booth and working his or her will.

*   *   *

MR. SONNY CALLAHAN (R-ALAB): Mr. Chairman, I rise in opposition to H.R. 2, the National Voter Registration Act, or motor-voter bill.

Voter registration officials in my State of Alabama are strongly opposed to the motor-voter bill because it is a gross infringement on States rights. It also imposes significant costs on the States without corresponding funding. I do not know about the other 49 States, but Alabama just cannot afford this expense, particularly when it will serve to promote voter fraud.

H.R. 2 will undoubtedly generate tremendous abuse in the election process. It will prevent any type of verification of postcard registration and encourage same-day registration. It also allows illegal aliens to register. Other questions persist: Can those under age 18 register? Can convicted felons register? I do not believe the supporters of this bill intend that fraud will prevail, but I do believe we should look very carefully at what will happen in reality. Widespread fraud is possible because the bill's safeguards are simply inadequate.

I agree that it is important to encourage participation in the democratic process. Voting is a fundamental right—indeed, it is a responsibility. The individual States are in a better position to determine how best to get people to register. I am not sure the Federal Government should have a major role in this process, but I do know this legislation is not the right method of involvement.

I urge my colleagues to join me in voting 'no' on the motor-voter bill.

*   *   *

Ms. ELEANOR HOLMES NORTON (D-WASH D.C.): Mr. Chairman, I do not envy the opponents of the National Voter Registration Act. It is bad enough to oppose increasing democratic participation. But Republicans, for whom Government efficiency and cost cutting have become a mantra, oppose those good things too when they oppose H.R. 2.

Like our economic productivity, our voter productivity needs an assist from modern methods and technology. A comparable law in the District of Columbia has yielded a 50-percent increase in new registrants since 1989.

Last year Americans went from cynical apathy to new levels of participation using new outlets. Let us put them in closer touch with the vote, the outlet that counts most in a democracy.

Support H.R. 2.

MR. HENRY HYDE (R-IL): Although it may come as a surprise to some we do not possess unlimited authority to impose our will and good intentions on the States or on the citizens of this Nation. This is not a body possessed with boundless authority, but a constitutionally created legislature with limited powers.

We have a solemn obligation to examine the Constitution to see what it says about the power of the Federal Government to regulate Federal and State elections and our authority to use the resources of State governments, without their consent, to implement a Federal regulatory scheme.

Article I, section 4 of the Constitution, gives Congress the authority to make regulations with respect to the "Times, Places and Manner of holding elections for Senators and Representatives." Section 2 of article I, provides that the electors for the House of Representatives in each State 'shall have the Qualifications requisite for Electors of the most numerous Branch of the State Legislature.'

Taken together, these two sections indicate that while Congress has authority to regulate Federal elections, States have the authority to conduct State elections and to set the qualifications for voters for State and Federal office, as long as they do not do so in a discriminatory fashion. In addition to these explicit references to voting, there is another section of the Constitution which is instructive. The 10th Amendment to the Constitution states that "the powers not delegated to the United States by the Constitution, nor prohibited by it to the States, are reserved to the States respectively, or the people."

* * *

This bill requires States to designate its offices that provide public assistance and unemployment compensation as voter registration agencies. Incredibly, States may not require Federal offices to share the load in implementing this Federal mandate. Federal offices have the option of deciding whether they can afford the commitment of time, resources, and personnel. They cannot be designated as voter registration agencies without their explicit agreement. Not only does this fly in the face of the 10th Amendment, it turns any traditional concept of federalism on its ear.

The goal of this bill—increase citizen participation in our Constitutional democracy—is one with which we all agree. We gain nothing, however, if in seeking to achieve that worthy goal, we trample on the very document which we are sworn to uphold.

MR. GENE GREEN (D-TX): Mr. Chairman, I appreciate the opportunity to be here.

* * *

Mr. Chairman, I want to ask the Members to support H.R. 2, because in an earlier life just 2 years ago, I served in the State senate in Texas, and for a number of years we talked about passing motor-voter. We finally did, and we have a bill in the State of Texas that is actually a little stronger than the one we are considering today. We heard the same concerns from a lot of Members from the other party about how it is going to hurt our voter registration and voter activity.

Well, I know that this last November election we had one of the highest turnouts in history in Texas, and I wish we could claim all of that from motor-voter. I think it helped, because we had an aggressive effort to register voters. We do it at driver's license locations.

One of the oppositions we heard in Texas was that it would slow down the driver's license lines. That is not true, because, frankly, we wait in lines already to renew our driver's licenses, and we just encouraged people to register to vote.

* * *

Every opportunity we can do, whether it be this bill or some other bill that would increase the participation of our citizens, we need to do that.

MR. CHARLES T. CANADY (R-FL): Mr. Chairman, I rise to speak in opposition to this bill—a bill which will perpetrate a massive fraud on the American people.

The bill under consideration will strike a devastating blow against constitutional order and the American system of democracy. Under the banner of reform, the bill would inaugurate a new era of abuse— an era in which millions of illegal aliens and other noncitizens will flood into the American electoral system.

Less than 1 month ago, the majority of this House trampled on the Constitution by granting voting rights on this floor to delegates from the territories and the District of Columbia. Now, the majority is prepared to assault the constitutional rights of American citizens once again.

In the name of democratic participation, access, and inclusion, this bill will open the floodgates to electoral fraud on an unprecedented scale. It would rob American citizens of their right to elect representatives in a free, open, and fair electoral process.

By encouraging the registration of persons not eligible to vote, the bill would dilute the voting power of American citizens. It would create an electoral system on a par with the rotten borough system of 18th century Britain.

This is not a reform—it is a sham. An ugly partisan attempt to skew the results of elections by corrupting the system for registering voters.

Americans who choose not to exercise their right to vote do so not because of legal barriers to registration—but because of frustration and apathy induced by a lack of confidence in the institutions of government in America—including a lack of confidence in the Congress.

The sorry spectacle of Congress effectively surrendering the franchise to illegal aliens and other noncitizens will only serve further to undermine the confidence of American citizens in their Government. It will produce a result exactly the opposite of the purported intent of this legislation.

* * *

MR. GERALD D. KLECZKA (D-WI): Mr. Chairman, H.R. 2 is the most important piece of legislation since the 1965 Voting Rights Act.

By simplifying the voter registration process and allowing eligible citizens to apply to register when they receive their driver's license, H.R. 2 ensures the voter registration process is responsive to the needs of voters, rather than Government bureaucrats.

* * *

During the committee consideration of this bill, I was one of the strongest and probably the most vocal proponent of this provision. I did so because my home State—Wisconsin—has same-day registration, and I am surprised that someone could suggest that this practice precludes meaningful verification and invites fraud, where no such proof exists.

In the 1992 Presidential election, the three States with same-day registration—Wisconsin, Maine and Minnesota—again ranked heads and shoulders above the national average. According to the election turnouts, Maine was first in the Nation with 72 percent turnout, followed by Minnesota with 71.6 percent. Wisconsin ranked fourth with 69 percent. Nationwide the average was 55.3 percent.

And I am proud to say that since Wisconsin adopted same-day registration in 1976, voter fraud has not been a problem, but long lines of voters at the polling places has [sic] been—that is exactly what we hope to achieve.

Mr. Chairman, with one-third of all eligible voters still unregistered, the need to make our political process more accessible to all Americans must be one of our priorities. H.R. 2 is a comprehensive compromise which will increase registration and maintain the integrity of the election process.

I urge all of my colleagues to join me in voting for this measure, and thank you, Mr. Swift, for allowing me to speak on behalf of this fine piece of legislation.

DISCUSSION QUESTIONS

1. The "motor-voter" law tackles one source of low voter turnout— institutional obstacles to registering. However, turnout has not increased in the past two federal elections. What do you think accounts for this continued lack of interest in electoral politics?

2. Voters between the ages of 18 and 25 have the lowest turnout rate of any group of voters. Why do you think this is the case? If you did not vote in the most recent election, why did you stay at home?

THE DEBATE: SHOULD CAMPAIGN SPENDING LIMITS BE INSTITUTED?

One of the most controversial and troubling aspects of the American electoral system is the amount of money candidates spend in the pursuit of office. In 1994, winning candidates spent an average of $4.5 million in the Senate and $450,000 in the House. Critics of the current system argue that wealthy candidates have an advantage, and that the need to raise such huge sums means candidates are beholden to the interest groups and individuals who contribute to their campaigns. Furthermore, challengers have a much harder time raising money than do incumbents, an imbalance that makes elections uncompetitive. One popular reform proposal would limit the amount that candidates can spend on campaigns. This poses some hard constitutional questions, since the Supreme Court has ruled that campaign spending is the equivalent of political speech and therefore cannot be limited. One way around this First Amendment hurdle is to make spending limits voluntary, by offering candidates something valuable (free television time or postage, for example) in return for an agreement to abide by a limit.

In the following selections, Herbert Alexander, Ann McBride and Candice Nelson offer varied critiques of a recent Senate effort to reform campaign finance based upon voluntary spending limits. McBride, the President of Common Cause, and Nelson, a professor of government, see a more level playing field for challengers and incumbents with spending limits. Alexander, a professor of political science, argues that political campaign spending can be viewed as the "tuition we pay for our education on the issues." Campaign spending limits might mean greater numbers of ill-informed voters and "negative" campaigning, which is thought to be more cost effective than "loftier" campaigns.

John Bonifax joins the debate as the director of the National Voting Rights Institute, arguing that the current system of electing a president through various state primaries is "the newest voting-rights barrier." He believes that because the only candidates who will survive the primary process are those able to raise sufficient funding, contributors able to give large sums of money play the key role in selecting candidates in the primary season. It is time, Bonifax argues, for the Supreme Court to review the current system of campaign finance.

48
Testimony of Herbert E. Alexander, Ann McBride, and Candice J. Nelson before the Senate Rules Committee on Campaign Finance Reform

Statement of Herbert E. Alexander

The goals of election law in a democracy should be to encourage political dialogue and citizen participation, while diminishing the advantages of wealthy individuals and special interests. Many of the far-reaching reforms that have been enacted, however, have sought to restrict and limit certain forms of electoral participation rather than to enlarge and expand it. Some of the reforms have become part of a politics of exclusion that should not be acceptable to a democratic society.

*   *   *

The purposes of legislation should be to regulate the problem areas widely perceived to be crucial; to seek to keep concentrations of power in check; to use government assistance where necessary, but with the least intrusion in the process; to ease fund raising and not make it harder, as the tendency is in this bill; to permit candidates and parties to spend ample money to campaign effectively and not seek to starve candidacies or parties financially; to diminish created dependencies on PACs and certain other financial sources by providing alternatives; to provide ample funding for the Federal Election Commission to administer and enforce the new law; to structure a system that is flexible and will not rigidify our politics; and to raise public confidence in the fairness of the system. The Senate bill falls short in some of these regards.

*   *   *

Political Costs

I think it useful to give some perspective on the premise of high political costs. The critics of high campaign costs are correct about the notable growth we have experienced in campaign spending—when calculated in aggregate dollars. According to figures compiled over the years by the Citizens' Research Foundation (CRF), total spending in the 1951–52 presidential election cycle amounted to $140 million. By 1991–92, such spending had reached $3.2 billion.

These figures include spending not only by presidential and congressional candidates in the predomination and general election campaigns but also spending by national and federally registered state and local political party committees; spending by nonparty political committees, such as PACs, and their sponsors; spending on campaigns for state and local elective offices; and spending on campaigns supporting or opposing state and local ballot issues.

The total amount spent in 1991–92, however, is less than the sums that the nation's two leading commercial advertisers—Procter and Gamble and Philip Morris—spent to proclaim the quality of their products. It represents a mere fraction of 1 percent of the $2.1 trillion spent in 1992 by federal, state, and local governments.

However, these aggregate amounts are not meant to suggest that for any given candidates at any given level of candidacy, amounts needed to be competitive may not be high. Political money remains a scarce resource. The remedy should be to make money easier to raise, not harder, and not to continually erode the private sector financial base by adding more restrictions.

There are five points to consider in determining whether we spend too much on elective politics and whether we should attempt to reduce or otherwise further regulate campaign spending.

1. There are no universally accepted criteria by which to determine when political campaign spending becomes excessive. No one knows precisely how much is too much, but it is clear that we spend a lot more on other endeavors, many of them arguably less important to the welfare of the republic than choosing our government leaders.

2. Inflation and more stringent reporting requirements account at least in part for some of the apparent increase in campaign spending. In presidential campaigns, while aggregate amounts spent have risen from $30 million in 1960 to $550 million in 1992, when the value of the dollar is held constant at 1960 value, the increase is fourfold, not the eighteen fold that the aggregate amounts would seem to indicate.

3. Gaining the favorable attention of potential voters has grown more expensive as the nature, technology, and requirements of election campaigning have changed.

4. The amounts of money candidates spend and the time they spend to raise it are due at least in part to laws enacted to broaden financial participation in campaigns and to limit the potential influence of large donors. The FECA limited individual contributions to $1,000 per federal candidate per election, prompting many candi-

dates and committees to rely on such fund-raising techniques as direct mail solicitations, which seek large numbers of relatively small contributors. Such appeals are expensive. Raising funds from many donors forces candidates to conduct a larger number of fund-raising events for a greater number of potential donors or to spend substantial amounts of campaign time dialing for dollars. A $1,000 contribution in 1975, when the limit was first enforced, is worth only $325 today.

5. Generally speaking, the larger the number of uncontested races, the lower the level of campaign spending. The higher the level of electoral competition, the more money is spent. In this sense, higher spending is desirable.

It is likely that campaign spending in congressional elections will continue to increase as the number of open seats increases. And the number of open seats surely will increase, at least in the short term, as incumbents participate in a sort of self-imposed term limitation by declining to run for re-election.

Expenditure Limitations

No issue has been as controversial as spending limits. While spending limitations can be shown to be illusory, ineffective, and damaging to competition, concern about high campaign costs has led many to seek their enactment. The problem with expenditure limits is that they reduce flexibility and rigidify the campaign process while inviting less accountable ways of spending, such as independent expenditures, issue campaigns related to the candidates' positions, and soft money.

The 1992 presidential general election provides a dramatic illustration of why spending limits are ineffectual. When the campaigns are analyzed, it becomes apparent that three distinct but parallel campaigns were conducted, either by each candidate or on each candidates' behalf. Only one of them operated under legally imposed spending limits.

In the first campaign, spending was limited by law to the $55.2 million provided in public funding, money supplemented by national party co-ordinated expenditures of $10.3 million. The total $65.5 million served as the spending limit.

In the second campaign, spending was provided for, but not limited under the law, to pay the legal, accounting and related costs the organization incurred in complying with the law; by soft money; by money spent on the nominees' behalf by labor unions, trade associations and membership groups on partisan communications with their constituencies; and in parallel campaigning or nominally nonpartisan activities directed to the general public.

In the third campaign, spending also was provided for by independent expenditures made without consultation or collaboration with the candidates and their campaigns.

At the very least, the development of these three parallel campaigns underlines the futility of attempting to impose a strict system of campaign spending limits. In our political system, which is animated by a variety of competing interests, each guaranteed freedom of expression, when the flow of money is restricted at any point in the campaign process, will inexorably carve new channels through which individuals and groups can seek to influence political campaigns and elections.

For another example: The current stories about Senator Dole bumping against the $37 million pre-nomination spending limit this year are well known, as well as the subterfuges to enable him to stay within the expenditure limit, by the RNC paying for staff, state parties picking up costs, and so on: another failure of expenditure limits!

The limits on the national nominating conventions are very low, and only supplemental spending by city and state host committees makes the conventions possible. Still another meaningless limit!

Hence there is accumulating evidence in all three phases of the presidential selection process that spending limits do not work. To enforce limits on hundreds of senatorial and congressional campaigns would require the Federal Election Commission to increase its staff at a time when FEC funding is being reduced, and would only add to the futility of trying to impose meaningful spending limits. Moreover, the spending limits the current bills would impose hinge on the advantages offered for those candidates who agree to comply. The bills [make] broadcasters and the Postal Service [pick up] the costs the Congress is unwilling to provide by appropriations or tax checkoff, the money for public financing; in any case, it is not certain that the courts would accept these as justification for the Buckley requirement* for providing spending limits.

The key is not to limit the amount of money candidates can spend but to assure that candidates are able to make their voices heard. It makes little sense to impose draconian limits on campaign contributions and expenditures. Far better to enable candidates to raise money from widely dispersed sources, thereby increasing interest and involvement in politics in the electoral system.

Yet another undesirable effect of spending ceilings is to encourage even more "negative campaigning" at a time when opinion polls reflect increasing public cynicism toward the political process. While voters often disdain such tactics in the abstract, negative campaigns persist because they have been shown to sway voter opinion in many instances. A candidate operating under spending ceilings likely will be more inclined to "go negative," since that type of tactic is a lot more cost-

---

* In *Buckley v. Valeo*, the Supreme Court allowed limitations on expenditures in national elections only if the limitations were part of a voluntary system of public financing.

effective than loftier forms of campaigning. A negative advertising barrage can quickly drive up an opponent's disapproval ratings, allowing the attacker to maximize the effect of his or her ability to use campaign cash under the limit.

To place limits on spending is to argue that campaigns cost too much. But how does one determine empirically how much is too much? And at what cost in terms of free speech?

Why not take a more expansive outlook, that elections are improved by well-financed candidates able to wage competitive campaigns? Political campaign spending should be considered the tuition we pay for our education on the issues. The most costly campaigns are those in which voters choose poorly because they are ill-informed.

Statement of Ann McBride

The present campaign finance system has played a central role in shaping an electoral landscape that is grossly unfair to challengers. Democracy depends on having real elections with real choices if people truly have the power to elect representatives who can be held accountable. Congressional incumbents now have such an extraordinary advantage over challengers that we are losing the ability to hold real elections for Congress.

Under the current system it is far easier for incumbents to raise money than challengers. In 1976, Senate winners spent an average of $610,000; in 1986, the average Senate winner spent $3 million. By 1994, that figure soared to $4.5 million.

For the past decade, the general rule has been that, on average, Senate incumbents outspent challengers in the general election by at least a 2-to-1 margin. For example, in 1992, while the average Senate incumbent spent almost $4.2 million for their campaign, the average challenger could only counter with less than $1.8 million. In that election year, Senate incumbents outspent their general election challengers in 27 out of 28 races, and only four incumbents lost.

In 1994, in an exception to the general rule, two challengers—Michael Huffington and Oliver North—had huge war chests. However, when those two races are excluded, the spending of an average Senate incumbent is again twice that of the average challenger.

The picture in the House is bleaker. By 1994, winning a seat in the House of Representatives cost an average of $450,000, and House incumbents outspent House challengers by a ratio of 2.6 to 1, or $549,801 on average spent by incumbents to $209,922 on average spent by challengers. In 1976, that ratio was 1.6 to 1. PAC contributions point up the fundraising advantage incumbents enjoy: in 1994, labor PACs gave 68 percent of their contributions to incumbents; business PACs on average gave 77 percent to incumbents.

It is also, in large part, for this reason that, even in the "revolutionary" 1994 election, the incumbent reelection rate in the House was still over 90 percent. Incumbents generally are able to vastly outraise challengers and typically swamp their challengers by outspending them. The need to raise this enormous amount of money makes elected officials dependent on those special interest groups and wealthy individuals with money to contribute and which want to use those political contributions to buy access and influence.

* * *

Voluntary Spending Limits

A poll taken this past summer found that 87 percent of Americans favor limiting the amount of money candidates can spend on a political campaign. Eighty-eight percent believe it will be effective to reduce the amount of money special interest groups can contribute to a candidate.

A system of voluntary spending limits combined with clean campaign resources will control congressional campaign spending—spending which gives advantages to incumbents over challengers.

S. 1219 establishes voluntary spending limits for Senate candidates based on a state's voting-age population. The spending limits range from $950,000 for candidates in smaller sates like Wyoming to $5.5 million in large sates like California.

By putting a cap on spending, the bill will hold down the costs of a campaign, will give challengers a fairer chance, and will reduce the pressure on candidates to raise every increasing amounts of money. As the Washington Post has noted, "At the moment, it is the absence of [spending] limits that hurts challengers. In 1994 incumbents outspent challengers in House races by better than 3 to 1. Properly set spending limits help challengers by preventing incumbents from burying them under money."

By inducing both incumbents and challengers to abide by a common spending cap, a spending limits system with real benefits will give challengers a real opportunity to compete with incumbents.

* * *

Opponents of Reform

Mr. Chairman, I'd like to take a few moments to respond to some arguments made by opponents of this important reform.

Speaker Gingrich has publicly opposed the companion bipartisan bill in the House. He also recently testified that there is too little money spent on political campaigns.

He argued that the total amount spent on House and Senate races in

1994, a record $724 million, was only twice as much as the advertising budgets for the three leading antacid manufacturers, and that this shows the money currently spent in politics is not excessive.

This view—not enough money is spent on politics—badly misses the point and is seriously wrong. The problem is not simply how much money is spent, but how much money must be raised and what candidates must do to raise it. The fundraising, the reliance on PACs and wealthy individuals, and the advantage of incumbents with access to money distort the political process.

For example, the pressure to raise the $4.5 million Senate average means that Senate candidates have to spend much of their time fundraising. Fundraising becomes an enormous distraction that interferes with Members doing the job they were elected to do. The $4.5 million the average Senate candidate must raise means a Senator must raise approximately $15,000 a week, every week for six years, starting the moment he or she is sworn into office.

As Senator Paul Simon noted, "A great many people visit the United States Senate, and they will see two or three of us on the floor debating some issue, and they get discouraged. . . . But they would be even more discouraged if they knew the reality. Probably at that point, there are more Senators on telephones trying to raise money. than there are on the floor of the United States Senate." The need to raise this enormous amount of money makes elected officials dependent on those special interest groups and wealthy individuals which have money to contribute —and who want to use those political contributions to buy access and influence.

Recent press reports indicate that part of Speaker Gingrich's proposed solution is to increase the influence of wealthy individuals by increasing the individual contribution limits five-fold. This increase would mean that one couple could give $20,000 to a congressional candidate—close to the average annual pay of working Americans.

There is not too little money in politics today, but too much—too much fundraising, too much spending, too much special interest money. And Mr. Gingrich's solution—raising the individual contribution limit five-fold—would only increase the influence of the wealthiest Americans at the expense of the average taxpayer.

To say that the current individual contribution limit is $1,000 actually understates the reality. The cycle limit on what an individual can contribute to a candidate is $2,000—$1,000 each for the primary and general election. And when, as is often the case, both spouses make the maximum contribution, a married couple thereby contributes $4,000 per candidate per election cycle. Thus, the existing contribution limit gives the very wealthy the ability to contribute a sum of money that is well beyond the capacity of average Americans. To increase the contribution limit— to $20,000 for a couple during an election cycle—is a change that would work to the benefit only of the very wealthy, and would further increase the disparity between the wealthy and average citizens in the relative ability to influence campaigns.

Speaker Gingrich also recently said that the number one problem in political campaigns is the wealthy candidate who spends his or her own money in a campaign.

There is no doubt that, under the existing campaign finance system, a wealthy candidate who is willing to spend an unlimited amount of his or her own personal fortune on a political campaign has an advantage today. It is difficult under existing rules for an opponent to raise the money necessary to compete with a wealthy candidate because spending by a wealthy candidate cannot be directly restricted due to constitutional limitations. Certainly this is an issue of concern but it is also an issue which can and should be addressed within the confines of the Supreme Court decision. S. 1219 provides valuable alternative resources to complying candidates that can be used to compete effectively with a wealthy opponent who chooses not to comply with the spending limits.

The broadcast provisions in S. 1219 give complying candidates running against wealthy candidates several advantages in response. Complying candidates are eligible to receive the free or reduced-rate broadcast time, and the wealthy candidate is not. The 50 percent discount on television means that $1 million of campaign funds spent on television is actually worth $2 million. Thus, complying candidates are able to buy an unlimited amount of broadcast time at half of the cost to the wealthy candidate purchasing the same amount of time. This is a significant advantage to complying candidates. Under S. 1219, wealthy candidates may continue to have an advantage, but opponents of wealthy candidates will be provided real resources with which to counter that wealth.

In truth, wealthy candidates who have spent their own money on their campaigns have not gotten much bang for their buck. While 14 Senate candidates each used $1 million or more of their own money in 1994 Senate races, only four of them were successful. Three of the four were incumbents—a group with a 90 percent reelection rate in any case. Overall, personal wealth accounted for only eight percent of 1994 Senate winners' campaign funds, while 20 percent of their funds came from PACs, according to the Congressional Research Service. In 1994 House races, 16 candidates each used $400,000 or more of their own personal wealth for their campaigns. Only two of the 16 won a seat in Congress. Overall, winners in 1994 House races relied on personal wealth for only one percent of their campaign funds, while raising 38 percent of their funds from their PACs. And in the one federal system with limits that does exist—the presidential system—only two of the major party candidates have elected not to participate in the spending limits system, and only one—current candidate Steve Forbes—has chosen to use his own money.

Another approach of opponents is to say that you do not need contribution limits but only disclosure. Of course, you could say the same thing about a bribe—don't make bribery a crime, just disclose it and let the voters decide. The fact is, however, that Americans want a political process that is based on standards of integrity and fairness, a process where big money cannot dominate. Disclosure is a critically important part of campaign finance regulation, but in itself will not make the campaign finance system fair, open and accountable. We have disclosure now, and that has not stopped wealthy individuals and special-interest groups from using campaign contributions to buy access and influence with elected officials. To remove contribution limits would say the sky is the limit. Mere disclosure of such corruption would not control it, but explode it. Disclosure of rampant corruption would serve only to increase public cynicism about politics and further the alienation of average voters from their government.

* * *

STATEMENT OF CANDICE J. NELSON

Mr. Chairman and Members of the Committee, thank you for the opportunity to testify with respect to S. 1219, the Senate Campaign Finance Reform Act of 1995.

First, I would like to commend Senators McCain and Feingold, as well as the other cosponsors of this legislation, for their bipartisan approach to this issue. For too long the debate over campaign finance reform has been clouded by partisanship. The cosponsors of this bill have set aside partisan differences to work towards a campaign finance reform bill that is bipartisan and can be debated on the substance of the issues involved, without partisan constraints.

This legislation, while not perfect, would go a long way towards "leveling the playing field" in Senate elections. This legislation would control the costs of campaigns, expand the resources available to Senate candidates, and increase accountability in Senate elections.

Controlling Campaign Costs

By establishing reasonable, voluntary spending limits the legislation would bring under control the money chase that candidates for the U.S. Senate currently endure. I was struck by the near uniform call for campaign finance reform among Senators who announced their retirement during the past year. Even Senators who have not been active proponents of campaign finance reform while in office denounced the current system of campaign finance and were nearly unanimous in citing the costs of running for office as one reason for their retirement.

While we can debate whether "too much" or "not enough" money is spent in Senate elections, what we do know is that the costs of Senate elections, and the time spent in raising the money to run for the U.S. Senate, takes time away from other activities and all too often discourages potential candidates from seeking congressional office. In the late 1980s the Center for Responsive Politics surveyed House and Senate members and staffers on a wide variety of legislative processes and procedures. When asked if the demands of campaign fundraising cut into the time spent on legislative work, over one-half, 52%, of Senators and their staffers replied that campaign fundraising significantly impacted their legislative work, and another 12% said that campaign fundraising had some effect on legislative time. Only 28% of Senators and staff, less than one-third, replied that campaign fundraising had no impact on legislative time.

Not only would spending limits control the costs of campaigns, and thus bring under control the amount of time spent raising that money, but spending limits would also reduce the discrepancy between incumbent and challenger spending in Senate elections. If the spending limits in this bill had been in effect for the 1994 elections, 23 of the 26 incumbents running would have exceeded the limits, compared to only 7 challengers, and two of those challengers were Oliver North and Michael Huffington, who spent $20 and $30 million respectively. Of those 19 challengers who spent less than the limits in the bill, 9 were Republicans and 10 were Democrats.

In 1994 there were 9 open seat races. In 5 of those races at least one candidate spent less than the spending limits, and in 2 of the races both candidates spent less than the spending limits. By placing a ceiling on the amount of money that could be raised and spent in Senate elections, this bill would curtail the endless money chase that candidates for the U.S. Senate currently have to endure.

Expanded Resources

Spending limits are not the only provisions in this bill which would help level the playing field in Senate elections. As you know, voter contact reaching potential voters to inform them about the candidates is the key element in a political campaign. A typical campaign will spend 70 to 75 percent of its budget on voter contact. The most expensive voter contact devices are mail and media, and this bill, by providing for discounted rates for both direct mail and paid media, would decrease the costs of voter contact and increase the abilities of candidates to communicate with the citizens of the state.

By providing a discounted postage rate for a number of pieces of direct mail equal to 2 times the voting age population of a state, candidates would be able to mail virtually all their direct mail at a discounted rate. As campaigns have become more specialized and targeting has become more sophisticated, direct mail has become an increasingly important voter contact device. For candidates to be able to do all of their mailings at a discounted rate would both increase the resources of the campaign and enable candidates with more limited resources to extend the purchasing power of those resources.

Similarly, the ability to purchase television time at 50 percent of the lowest unit rate would greatly increase candidates' opportunities to reach voters through paid media. Senate campaigns spend anywhere from two-fifths to three-quarters of their campaign budget on paid media, and, for most statewide campaigns, the majority of the paid media budget is for television. Typically, candidates do not pay the lowest unit rate for paid media, because they do not want to be preempted. By assuring candidates of reduced cost air time candidates who typically have little or no money for television advertising would have more opportunities to get their message to voters through paid media.

The thirty minutes of free media would likely be most useful to candidates near the end of the campaign. Whether candidates divided their time into six 5 minute spots or 60 thirty second spots, or some other mix of the time, the free time would at least allow all candidates some opportunity to reach voters, through television, with their campaign themes and messages.

This legislation will make it less expensive for candidates to communicate with potential voters through direct mail and paid television spots. For candidates who are able to raise and spend up to the spending limits of the bill, it may mean more voter contact than they currently engage in. For candidates who are not able to raise and spend up to the spending limits, it will mean that the money they do raise will allow them to do more voter contact than they are currently able to do. Their limited resources will be expanded. In either case, competition will increase, as both candidates will have the resources to communicate to voters that, under the current system, often only incumbents have.

Increased Accountability

This legislation, by requiring Senate candidates to raise 60 percent of their campaign contributions from constituents within their state, restores a balance between a candidate's electoral constituency and his or her financial constituency. Theories of representation argue that a Senator's most important constituency should be his or her electoral constituency—the men and women who voted him or her into office. However, the nationalization of campaign finance in congressional elections has meant that Senate candidates raise substantial sums of money outside their states. During one period in the 1980s 8 Senators raised more than 90 percent of their campaign contributions outside their state. By restricting the amount of money a Senate candidate can raise outside the state to 40 percent of the state spending limit, this legislation recognizes the importance of a Senate candidate raising the majority of his or her money from his electoral constituency. By not requiring more than 60 percent of campaign funds to be raised in-state, the legislation recognizes the existence of constituencies outside the state.

Finally, I would like to address the ban on soft money in federal elections. When I give talks on campaign finance, no matter who the audience, the most incomprehensible part of the current campaign finance system is the distinction between hard money and soft money. People in both this country and other countries do not understand why there are contribution limits for some activities but not others. That an individual can contribute $20,000 to a political party in hard dollars, yet can contribute unlimited amounts in soft money, seems to most Americans to undermine the existence of contribution limits. I commend the co-sponsors of this legislation for requiring all contributions to political parties for federal offices to fall under the contribution limits of the F.E.C.A.

Implementation

I would like to conclude my testimony by speaking briefly to the question of implementation of this legislation. This legislation, as I think it should, establishes a contingency provision for elections in which one candidate complies with the spending limits but the other candidate does not. Once the noncomplying candidate raises or spends in excess of 10 percent of the spending limit in a state the complying candidate's expenditure limit increases by 20 percent. Monitoring of compliance and noncompliance is to be done by the Federal Election Commission. I would urge you to make sure that the F.E.C. will have the resources to monitor compliance and to react to noncompliance in a timely fashion. If, late in the election cycle, one candidate in a race violates the spending limits, it will be imperative that the F.E.C. be able to know a violation has occurred and inform the complying candidate that his or her spending limit has been raised. If spending limits can be exceeded late in the campaign, and the contingency limits cannot be implemented in time to impact the election, the integrity of this legislation, in my opinion, will be seriously undermined.

Thank you for the opportunity to share my views on this bill with you.

49
"Take the Wealth Primary to Court"

JOHN BONIFAX

The courts in this country have a duty to protect the basic constitutional rights of all citizens in the political process. As a political strategy emerges around the country for building a democracy movement, so too must a legal strategy that will force the judiciary to address new constitutional questions about the campaign finance system. As with previous barriers to participation in our electoral process, the courts now have an obligation to intervene.

There are moments in our nation's history when a tradition we once thought constitutional becomes constitutional no more. The history of the right to vote in this country includes a series of such moments. Once held only by white male property owners, the right to vote has been continuously expanded as disenfranchised peoples have organized and struggled for an America that lives up to its legal and moral promise of democracy. Over time, the nation has seen the elimination of numerous barriers to voting rights—from property, race, sex, and age qualifications to exclusionary white primaries, poll taxes, high candidate filing fees, and vote dilution schemes.

Today, we must face up to the newest voting-rights barriers: the "wealth primary." The wealth primary is that exclusionary process, leading up to every party primary and every general election, in which those with money or access to money choose the candidates who almost invariably go on to govern. Those who do not raise enough money—that is, those who lose the wealth primary—almost always fail to win office.

The rest of us, the vast majority of American people, are shut out of this process. Because we have, ultimately, little to say in the outcome of elections, our right to vote is debased and undermined. Our system of financing electoral campaigns is constitutional no more.

For years, the campaign finance question has been posed in the courts as a question of the First Amendment rights of well-financed candidates and wealthy contributors. The Supreme Court helped frame it that way in its (highly controversial) 1976 decision in *Buckley* v. *Valeo*, striking down on First Amendment grounds mandatory congressional limits on overall congressional campaign expenditures, on candidates' expenditure of their personal wealth, and on "independent" expenditures.

But the constitutional question posed by the wealth primary is not about the First Amendment rights of the wealthy. It is about the Equal

Protection rights of all voters and candidates who are left behind in the fundraising process because of their lack of money and access to money. No federal court in the nation has ever ruled on this critical question.

Nearly 30 years ago, in the midst of the civil rights movement, the Supreme Court stated that wealth cannot serve as a barrier to the right to vote. In *Harper* v. *Virginia State Board of Elections*, two years after the Twenty-Fourth Amendment had banned poll taxes in federal elections, the Court struck down a poll tax of $1.50 in Virginia state elections. The Court found that "a State violates the Equal Protection Clause of the Fourteenth Amendment whenever it makes the affluence of the voter or payment of any fee an electoral standard. Voter qualifications have no relation to wealth."

Six years later, in *Bullock* v. *Carter*, the Court again stated that wealth cannot be a barrier in the electoral process. This time, the question concerned a system of high filing fees that the state of Texas required candidates to pay in order to appear on the primary ballot. The fees ranged from $150 to $8,900.

The Court invalidated the system on equal protection grounds. It found that, with the high filing fees, "potential office seekers lacking both personal wealth and affluent backers are in every practical sense precluded from seeking the nomination of their chosen party, no matter how qualified they might be and no matter how enthusiastic their popular support."

The "exclusionary character" of the system also violated the constitutional rights of non-affluent voters. "We would ignore reality," the Court stated, "were we not to find that this system falls with unequal weight on voters, as well as candidates, according to their economic status."

The Court has further held that not only processes mandated by statute, but also any process that is integral to the overall election of public officials—which becomes "part of the machinery" for getting elected (*Terry* v. *Adams*)—is a process that, under the constitutional guarantee of Equal Protection, must be open to all. Like the white primary of the past, today's exclusionary wealth primary is unconstitutional and should be struck down.

A legal strategy that challenges the constitutionality of the wealth primary can help redefine campaign financing as a bedrock democracy issue. It can play an important role in building the case for a system that protects the constitutional rights of all candidates and voters regardless of economic status—a system of democratically financed elections where we the people control and own the process. Just as the courts 30 years ago helped change the makeup of congressional and legislative districts through declaratory judgment so that they comported with the principle of one person, one vote, so the courts today can help break down the newest voting rights barrier.

DISCUSSION QUESTIONS

1. After reading the various perspectives on the role of money in political campaigns, do you see a need for campaign finance reform? If you think reform is needed, do you see the *amount* of money or the *source* of money as the main problem?

2. Some politicians, such as Newt Gingrich, have argued that we spend too *little* on political campaigns, not too much. He argues that challengers would be hurt more than incumbents by spending limits. Do you agree? Explain.

3. If you think reform is necessary, what kinds of changes would you suggest in how money is raised and spent? How would your reforms withstand the scrutiny of the Supreme Court, which has struck down mandatory spending limits?

CHAPTER 10

Political Parties

50
"The Decline of Collective Responsibility in American Politics"

Morris P. Fiorina

For more than three decades political scientists have studied the decline of the political parties. Morris P. Fiorina argues that the decline not only weakens political participation, but eliminates the motivation for elected members of the parties to define broad policy objectives. Instead, he argues, policies are aimed at serving the narrow interests of the various single-issue groups that now dominate politics. Without strong political parties to provide electoral account-ability, American politics has suffered a "decline in collective responsibility."

In the effort to reform the often corrupt political parties of the late 1800s— often referred to as "machines" that dominated the electoral process in many cities—it is important to ask whether we have eliminated the best way to hold elected officials accountable at the ballot box. The Republican Party's victory in 1994, in conjunction with its clear party platform contained in the Contract With America, prompted many to argue we were witnessing a party resurgence. History is yet to judge whether this was in fact the case.

Though the Founding Fathers believed in the necessity of establishing a genuinely national government, they took great pains to design one that could not lightly do things *to* its citizens; what government might do *for* its citizens was to be limited to the functions of what we know now as the "watchman state."

* * *

Given the historical record faced by the Founders, their emphasis on constraining government is understandable. But we face a later historical record, one that shows two hundred years of increasing demands for government to act positively. Moreover, developments unforeseen by the Founders increasingly raise the likelihood that the uncoordinated actions of individuals and groups will inflict serious damage on the nation as a whole. The by-products of the industrial and technological revolutions impose physical risks not only on us, but on future generations as well. Resource shortages and international cartels raise the spectre of economic ruin. And the simple proliferation of special interests with their intense, particularistic demands threatens to render us politically incapable of taking actions that might either advance the state of society or prevent foreseeable deteriorations in that state. None of this is to suggest that we should forget about what government can do *to* us—the contemporary concern with the proper scope and methods of government intervention in the social and economic orders is long overdue. But the modern age demands as well that we worry about our ability to make government work *for* us. The problem is that we are gradually losing that ability, and a principal reason for this loss is the steady erosion of *responsibility* in American politics.

*   *   *

Unfortunately, the importance of responsibility in a democracy is matched by the difficulty of attaining it. In an autocracy, individual responsibility suffices; the location of power in a single individual locates responsibility in that individual as well. But individual responsibility is insufficient whenever more than one person shares governmental authority. We can hold a particular congressman individually responsible for a personal transgression such as bribe-taking. We can even hold a president individually responsible for military moves where he presents Congress and the citizenry with a *fait accompli*. But on most national issues individual responsibility is difficult to assess. If one were to go to Washington, randomly accost a Democratic congressman, and berate him about a 20-percent rate of inflation, imagine the response. More than likely it would run, "Don't blame me. If 'they' had done what I've advocated for *x* years, things would be fine today."

*   *   *

American institutional structure makes this kind of game-playing all too easy. In order to overcome it we must lay the credit or blame for national conditions on all those who had any hand in bringing them about: some form of *collective responsibility* is essential.

The only way collective responsibility has ever existed, and can exist given our institutions, is through the agency of the political party; in American politics, responsibility requires cohesive parties. This is an old claim to be sure, but its age does not detract from its present relevance. In fact, the continuing decline in public esteem for the parties and continuing efforts to "reform" them out of the political process suggest that old arguments for party responsibility have not been made often enough or, at least, convincingly enough, so I will make these arguments once again in this essay.

A strong political party can generate collective responsibility by creating incentive for leaders, followers, and popular supporters to think and act in collective terms. First, by providing party leaders with the capability (e.g., control of institutional patronage, nominations, and so on) to discipline party members, genuine leadership becomes possible. Legislative output is less likely to be a least common denominator—a residue of myriad conflicting proposals—and more likely to consist of a program actually intended to solve a problem or move the nation in a particular direction. Second, the subordination of individual officeholders to the party lessens their ability to separate themselves from party actions. Like it or not, their performance becomes identified with the performance of the collectivity to which they belong. Third, with individual candidate variation greatly reduced, voters have less incentive to support individuals and more incentive to support or oppose the party as a whole. And fourth, the circle closes as party-line voting in the electorate provides party leaders with the incentive to propose policies that will earn the support of a national majority, and party back-benchers* with the personal incentive to cooperate with leaders in the attempt to compile a good record for the party as a whole.

In the American context, strong parties have traditionally clarified politics in two ways. First, they allow citizens to assess responsibility easily, at least when the government is unified, which it more often was in earlier eras when party meant more than it does today. Citizens need only evaluate the social, economic, and international conditions they observe and make a simple decision for or against change. They do not need to decide whether the energy, inflation, urban, and defense policies advocated by their congressman would be superior to those advocated by [the president]—were any of them to be enacted!

The second way in which strong parties clarify American politics follows from the first. When citizens assess responsibility on the party as a whole, party members have personal incentives to see the party evaluated favorably. They have little to gain from gutting their president's program one day and attacking him for lack of leadership the next, since they share in the president's fate when voters do not differentiate within the party. Put simply, party responsibility provides party members with a personal stake in their collective performance.

Admittedly, party responsibility is a blunt instrument. The objection immediately arises that party responsibility condemns junior Democratic representatives to suffer electorally for an inflation they could do little

---

* [Back-benchers are junior members of the Parliament, who sit in the rear benches of the House of Commons. Here, the term refers to junior members of political parties.]

to affect. An unhappy situation, true, but unless we accept it, Congress as a whole escapes electoral retribution for an inflation they *could* have done something to affect. Responsibility requires acceptance of both conditions. The choice is between a blunt instrument or none at all.

* * *

In earlier times, when citizens voted for the party, not the person, parties had incentives to nominate good candidates, because poor ones could have harmful fallout on the ticket as a whole. In particular, the existence of presidential coattails (positive and negative) provided an inducement to avoid the nomination of narrowly based candidates, no matter how committed their supporters. And, once in office, the existence of party voting in the electorate provided party members with the incentive to compile a good *party* record. In particular, the tendency of national midterm elections to serve as referenda on the performance of the president provided a clear inducement for congressmen to do what they could to see that their president was perceived as a solid performer. By stimulating electoral phenomena such as coattail effects and mid-term referenda, party transformed some degree of personal ambition into concern with collective performance.

* * *

The Continuing Decline of Party in the United States

Party Organizations

In the United States, party organization has traditionally meant state and local party organization. The national party generally has been a loose confederacy of subnational units that swings into action for a brief period every four years. This characterization remains true today, despite the somewhat greater influence and augmented functions of the national organizations. Though such things are difficult to measure precisely, there is general agreement that the formal party organizations have undergone a secular decline since their peak at the end of the nineteenth century. The prototype of the old-style organization was the urban machine, a form approximated today only in Chicago.

* * *

[*Fiorina discusses the reforms of the late nineteenth and early twentieth century.*]

In the 1970s two series of reforms further weakened the influence of organized parties in American national politics. The first was a series of legal changes deliberately intended to lessen organized party influence in the presidential nominating process. In the Democratic party, "New Politics" activists captured the national party apparatus and imposed a series of rules changes designed to "open up" the politics of presidential nominations. The Republican party—long more amateur and open than the Democratic party—adopted weaker versions of the Democratic rules changes. In addition, modifications of state electoral laws to conform to the Democratic rules changes (enforced by the federal courts) stimulated Republican rules changes as well.

* * *

A second series of 1970s reforms lessened the role of formal party organizations in the conduct of political campaigns. These are financing regulations growing out of the Federal Election Campaign Act of 1971 as amended in 1974 and 1976. In this case the reforms were aimed at cleaning up corruption in the financing of campaigns; their effects on the parties were a by-product, though many individuals accurately predicted its nature. Serious presidential candidates are now publicly financed. Though the law permits the national party to spend two cents per eligible voter on behalf of the nominee, it also obliges the candidate to set up a finance committee separate from the national party. Between this legally mandated separation and fear of violating spending limits or accounting regulations, for example, the law has the effect of encouraging the candidate to keep his party at arm's length.

* * *

The ultimate results of such reforms are easy to predict. A lesser party role in the nominating and financing of candidates encourages candidates to organize and conduct independent campaigns, which further weakens the role of parties. . . . [I]f parties do not grant nominations, fund their choices, and work for them, why should those choices feel any commitment to their party?

Party in the Electorate

In the citizenry at large, party takes the form of a psychological attachment. The typical American traditionally has been likely to identify with one or the other of the two major parties. Such identifications are transmitted across generations to some degree, and within the individual they tend to be fairly stable. But there is mounting evidence that the basis of identification lies in the individual's experiences (direct and vicarious, through family and social groups) with the parties in the past. Our current party system, of course, is based on the dislocations of the Depression period and the New Deal attempts to alleviate them. Though only a small proportion of those who experienced the Depression directly are active voters today, the general outlines of citizen party identifications much resemble those established at that time.

Again, there is reason to believe that the extent of citizen attachments to parties has undergone a long-term decline from a nineteenth-century high. And again, the New Deal appears to have been a period during which the decline was arrested, even temporarily reversed. But again, the decline of party has reasserted itself in the 1970s.

* * *

As the 1960s wore on, the heretofore stable distribution of citizen party identifications began to change in the general direction of weakened attachments to the parties. Between 1960 and 1976, independents, broadly defined, increased from less than a quarter to more than a third of the voting-age population. Strong identifiers declined from slightly more than a third to about a quarter of the population.

* * *

Indisputably, party in the electorate has declined in recent years. Why? To some extent the electoral decline results from the organizational decline. Few party organizations any longer have the tangible incentives to turn out the faithful and assure their loyalty. Candidates run independent campaigns and deemphasize their partisan ties whenever they see any short-term electoral gain in doing so. If party is increasingly less important in the nomination and election of candidates, it is not surprising that such diminished importance is reflected in the attitudes and behavior of the voter.

Certain long-term sociological and technological trends also appear to work against party in the electorate. The population is younger, and younger citizens traditionally are less attached to the parties than their elders. The population is more highly educated; fewer voters need some means of simplifying the choices they face in the political arena, and party, of course, has been the principal means of simplification. And the media revolution has vastly expanded the amount of information easily available to the citizenry. Candidates would have little incentive to operate campaigns independent of the parties if there were no means to apprise the citizenry of their independence. The media provide the means.

Finally, our present party system is an old one. For increasing numbers of citizens, party attachments based on the Great Depression seem lacking in relevance to the problems of the late twentieth century. Beginning with the racial issue in the 1960s, proceeding to the social issue of the 1970s, and to the energy, environment, and inflation issues of today, the parties have been rent by internal dissension. Sometimes they failed to take stands, at other times they took the wrong ones from the standpoint of the rank and file, and at most times they have failed to solve the new problems in any genuine sense. Since 1965 the parties have done little or nothing to earn the loyalties of modern Americans.

Party in Government

If the organizational capabilities of the parties have weakened, and their psychological ties to the voters have loosened, one would expect predictable consequences for the party in government. In particular, one would expect to see an increasing degree of split party control within and across the levels of American government. The evidence on this point is overwhelming.

* * *

The increased fragmentation of the party in government makes it more difficult for government officeholders to work together than in times past (not that it has ever been terribly easy). Voters meanwhile have a more difficult time attributing responsibility for government performance, and this only further fragments party control. The result is lessened collective responsibility in the system.

What has taken up the slack left by the weakening of the traditional [party] determinants of congressional voting? It appears that a variety of personal and local influences now play a major role in citizen evaluations of their representatives. Along with the expansion of the federal presence in American life, the traditional role of the congressman as an all-purpose ombudsman has greatly expanded. Tens of millions of citizens now are directly affected by federal decisions. Myriad programs provide opportunities to profit from government largesse, and myriad regulations impose costs and/or constraints on citizen activities. And, whether seeking to gain profit or avoid costs, citizens seek the aid of their congressmen. When a court imposes a desegregation plan on an urban school board, the congressional offices immediately are contacted for aid in safeguarding existing sources of funding and in determining eligibility for new ones. When a major employer announces plans to quit an area, the congressional offices immediately are contacted to explore possibilities for using federal programs to persuade the employer to reconsider. Contractors appreciate a good congressional word with DOD procurement officers. Local artistic groups cannot survive without NEA funding. And, of course, there are the major individual programs such as social security and veterans' benefits that create a steady demand for congressional information and aid services. Such activities are nonpartisan, nonideological, and, most important, noncontroversial. Moreover, the contribution of the congressman in the realm of district service appears considerably greater than the impact of his or her single vote on major national issues. Constituents respond rationally to this modern state of affairs by weighing nonprogrammatic constituency service heavily when casting their congressional votes. And this emphasis on the part of constituents provides the means for incumbents to solidify their hold on the office. Even if elected by a narrow margin, diligent service activities enable a congressman to neutralize or even convert a portion of those who would otherwise oppose him on policy or ideological grounds. Emphasis on local, nonpartisan factors in congressional voting enables the modern congressman to withstand national swings, whereas yesteryear's uninsulated congressmen were more dependent on preventing the occurrence of the swings.

*   *   *

[The result is the insulation of the modern congressional member from national forces altogether.]

The withering away of the party organizations and the weakening of party in the electorate have begun to show up as disarray in the party in government. As the electoral fates of congressmen and the president have diverged, their incentives to cooperate have diverged as well. Congressmen have little personal incentive to bear any risk in their president's behalf, since they no longer expect to gain much from his successes or suffer much from his failures. Only those who personally agree with the president's program and/or those who find that program well suited for their particular district support the president. And there are not enough of these to construct the coalitions necessary for action on the major issues now facing the country. By holding only the president responsible for national conditions, the electorate enables officialdom as a whole to escape responsibility. This situation lies at the root of many of the problems that now plague American public life.

Some Consequences of the Decline of Collective Responsibility

The weakening of party has contributed directly to the severity of several of the important problems the nation faces. For some of these, such as the government's inability to deal with inflation and energy, the connections are obvious. But for other problems, such as the growing importance of single-issue politics and the growing alienation of the American citizenry, the connections are more subtle.

Immobilism

As the electoral interdependence of the party in government declines, its ability to act also declines. If responsibility can be shifted to another level or to another officeholder, there is less incentive to stick one's neck out in an attempt to solve a given problem. Leadership becomes more difficult, the ever-present bias toward the short-term solution becomes more

pronounced, and the possibility of solving any given problem lessens.
. . . [P]olitical inability to take actions that entail short-run costs ordinarily will result in much higher costs in the long run—we cannot
continually depend on the technological fix. So the present American
immobilism cannot be dismissed lightly. The sad thing is that the American people appear to understand the depth of our present problems and,
at least in principle, appear prepared to sacrifice in furtherance of the
long-run good. But they will not have an opportunity to choose between
two or more such long-term plans. Although both parties promise tough,
equitable policies, in the present state of our politics, neither can deliver.

Single-Issue Politics

In recent years both political analysts and politicians have decried the
increased importance of single-issue groups in American politics. Some
in fact would claim that the present immobilism in our politics owes
more to the rise of single-issue groups than to the decline of party. A
little thought, however, should reveal that the two trends are connected.
Is single-issue politics a recent phenomenon? The contention is doubtful;
such groups have always been active participants in American politics.
The gun lobby already was a classic example at the time of President
Kennedy's assassination. And however impressive the antiabortionists
appear today, remember the temperance movement, which succeeded in
getting its constitutional amendment. American history contains numerous forerunners of today's groups, from anti-Masons to abolitionists to
the Klan—singularity of purpose is by no means a modern phenomenon.
Why, then, do we hear all the contemporary hoopla about single-issue
groups? Probably because politicians fear them now more than before
and thus allow them to play a larger role in our politics. Why should
this be so? Simply because the parties are too weak to protect their members and thus to contain single-issue politics.

In earlier times single-issue groups were under greater pressures to
reach accommodations with the parties. After all, the parties nominated
candidates, financed candidates, worked for candidates, and, perhaps
most important, party voting protected candidates. When a contemporary single-issue group threatens to "get" an officeholder, the threat
must be taken seriously.

* * *

Not only did the party organization have greater ability to resist
single-issue pressures at the electoral level, but the party in government
had greater ability to control the agenda, and thereby contain single-issue
pressures at the policy-making level. Today we seem condemned to go
through an annual agony over federal abortion funding. There is little
doubt that politicians on both sides would prefer to reach some reason-

able compromise at the committee level and settle the issue. But in today's decentralized Congress there is no way to put the lid on. In contrast, historians tell us that in the late nineteenth century a large portion of the Republican constituency was far less interested in the tariff and other questions of national economic development than in whether German immigrants should be permitted to teach their native language in their local schools, and whether Catholics and "liturgical Protestants" should be permitted to consume alcohol. Interestingly, however, the national agenda of the period is devoid of such issues. And when they do show up on the state level, the exceptions prove the rule; they produce party splits and striking defeats for the party that allowed them to surface.

In sum, a strong party that is held accountable for the government of a nation-state has both the ability and the incentive to contain particularistic pressures. It controls nominations, elections, and the agenda, and it collectively realizes that small minorities are small minorities no matter how intense they are. But as the parties decline they lose control over nominations and campaigns, they lose the loyalty of the voters, and they lose control of the agenda. Party officeholders cease to be held collectively accountable for party performance, but they become individually exposed to the political pressure of myriad interest groups. The decline of party permits interest groups to wield greater influence, their success encourages the formation of still more interest groups, politics becomes increasingly fragmented, and collective responsibility becomes still more elusive.

Popular Alienation from Government

For at least a decade political analysts have pondered the significance of survey data indicative of a steady increase in the alienation of the American public from the political process. . . . The American public is in a nasty mood, a cynical, distrusting, and resentful mood. The question is, Why?

If the same national problems not only persist but worsen while ever-greater amounts of revenue are directed at them, why shouldn't the typical citizen conclude that most of the money must be wasted by incompetent officials? If narrowly based interest groups increasingly affect our politics, why shouldn't citizens increasingly conclude that the interests run the government? For fifteen years the citizenry has listened to a steady stream of promises but has seen very little in the way of follow-through. An increasing proportion of the electorate does not believe that elections make a difference, a fact that largely explains the much-discussed post-1960 decline in voting turnout.

Continued public disillusionment with the political process poses several real dangers. For one thing, disillusionment begets further disillusionment. Leadership becomes more difficult if citizens do not trust their leaders and will not give them the benefit of a doubt. Policy failure becomes more likely if citizens expect the policy to fail. Waste increases and government competence decreases as citizens disrespect for politics encourages a lesser breed of person to make careers in government. And "government by a few big interests" becomes more than a cliché if citizens increasingly decide the cliché is true and cease participating for that reason.

Finally, there is the real danger that continued disappointment with particular government officials ultimately metamorphoses into disillusionment with government per se. Increasing numbers of citizens believe that government is not simply overextended but perhaps incapable of any further bettering of the world. Yes, government is overextended, inefficiency is pervasive, and ineffectiveness is all too common. But government is one of the few instruments of collective action we have, and even those committed to selective pruning of government programs cannot blithely allow the concept of an activist government to fall into disrepute.

Of late, however, some political commentators have begun to wonder whether contemporary thought places sufficient emphasis on government *for* the people. In stressing participation have we lost sight of *accountability*? Surely, we should be as concerned with what government produces as with how many participate. What good is participation if the citizenry is unable to determine who merits their support?

Participation and responsibility are not logically incompatible, but there is a degree of tension between the two, and the quest for either may be carried to extremes. Participation maximizers find themselves involved with quotas and virtual representation schemes, while responsibility maximizers can find themselves with a closed shop under boss rule. Moreover, both qualities can weaken the democracy they supposedly underpin. Unfettered participation produces Hyde Amendments and immobilism.

Discussion Questions

1. How could political parties provide "collective responsibility"? What are the obstacles standing in the way of strong parties that could provide such accountability?

2. Are strong parties in the interest of individual politicians? Can you think of instances where members of Congress either agreed to strong parties or distanced themselves from party leadership?

51
"The People vs. the Parties"

KEVIN PHILLIPS

Phillips is less sanguine than Fiorina about the impact political parties have on the electoral system, maintaining that the two-party system no longer speaks for the vast majority of voters. The result of this disconnection is cynicism and mistrust of government. The key to party politics is recapturing the center.

For the past two decades Democrats have been labeled "tax-and-spend" supporters of big government and as the captives of minorities, labor, gays, and feminists on the left fringe. The 1992 presidential election appeared to be a brief interruption of this trend as Bill Clinton and the Democrats regained the center by staking out a "New Democratic" agenda that was rooted in the popular concerns of welfare reform, health care, crime, and the deficit. The 1994 midterm elections, however, showed that voters were not convinced the Democrats had really changed. The failure of Clinton's health care reform effort seemed to embody the chasm between the campaign promises of the New Democrats and their ability to bring those promises to fruition.

Phillips points out that despite their success in 1994, Republicans have their share of coalitional problems. For the Republicans, the challenge is how to deal with the right wing of the party, made up largely of religious conservatives who favor school prayer, oppose abortion, and support limited government. The 1992 Republican presidential convention reflected this agenda, and pushed many moderate Republicans and "Reagan Democrats" to the Democratic party; the struggle over the abortion plank in the 1996 GOP platform showed that these questions are far from settled. This division, and efforts to define a future agenda that can bridge the gap, are evident in the Harper's Magazine *forum reprinted below (see p. 383). But unless the Republican party achieves a more broadly based agenda, it will continue to cater to elitist extremes while ignoring the bipartisan middle, just as the Democrats did in the 1970s and 1980s. This, Phillips argues, is the primary problem with the parties and the reason many voters are alienated from the political process.*

Massachusetts pundits and periodicals like to pour great debates from parochial pitchers. The big question of 1992 was whether Democratic ex-Senator Paul Tsongas could merchandise his hairshirt economics west of New England (no, as it turned out). Looking ahead to 1996, the wonderment is whether a cultural moderate liberal and fiscal conservative like GOP Governor William Weld can sell his own Eastern elite ideology to a nominating convention dominated by Indianapolis and Oklahoma City. Probably not.

These questions suggest a broader one: Can the current party system nominate anybody interesting or useful? Can either the Republicans or Democrats plausibly choose a nominee who will openly offer the elite viewpoint on a critical public policy smorgasbord: moderate liberalism on cultural issues, a budget-cutting approach to middle-class entitlements, sophisticated internationalism, and distrust of popular or plebiscitary politics and government? If not, isn't that limitation a deficiency of the system?

Now consider two other variations. Can a libertarian triumph in either Democratic or Republican clothing? Could either side nominate a committed theorist of a lesser role for government? Then, in another vein, can the case for rule by the people be offered and heard? Would either party put an establishment-baiting populist at the top of the ticket? Would the Republicans or Democrats willingly embrace a practitioner of cultural and institutional outsiderism (Religious Right activism, anti-Washington sentiment, or both), someone who also endorses middle-class economic interests or tax revolts, nationalism or neo-isolationism, and a wide range of populist mechanisms like term limits, recalls, initiatives and referenda, and ballot propositions to allow the public to vote on tax increases? I can't imagine any such candidate, even though national polls show the electorate tilting in many (even most) of these populist directions and in some libertarian ones. In fact, politicians who begin to embrace two or three of these populist views or any comparable libertarian ideas usually become pariahs in establishment circles.

So it is not surprising that artifice is emerging as the best White House qualification. The typical Democratic presidential nominee, based on 1988 and 1992, can be described as a technocrat or meritocrat with elite tendencies. The caveat is that such a person can't win in November's general election without muting his cultural liberalism and internationalism, reaffirming his party's traditional economic commitment to growth, labor, and middle-class entitlements, yet simultaneously deploring bureaucrats and special interests and donning at least a partial mask of populism and outsiderism. Dukakis couldn't handle the mix and lost. Clinton, who understood better, shaded in these various directions and won the White House. The Republican version of this quadrennial deception is to placate the Religious Right and their social-issue allies with cultural commitments unlikely to be fulfilled, while also beating tax-revolt and nationalist drums and likewise assuming some mask of populism and outsiderism. Tsongas couldn't perform the right Democratic dance steps in 1992; the odds are that Weld probably won't be able to do the GOP waltz in 1996, either.

The bipartisan irony is that once the populist rhetoric and pretension of the campaign has subsided, most presidents of both parties govern on the elite model or close to it. Not surprisingly, they lose credibility with voters for broken promises. Bush did, and the same thing is now happening to Clinton. Back in the 1960s, George Wallace overstated by contending that there wasn't a dime's worth of difference between the parties. There most certainly is. On a penny-to-dollar scale, the "difference" can be pegged at about 30 to 45 cents. This is hardly a strict tweedle-dum/tweedle-dee situation; rather, it results from shared lackluster thinking and intermittent collusion that provides no basis for serious innovation or for purge-Washington-every-decade-or-so government. The unproductive dynamics are all too simple. Popular frustration blocks elite remedies, and the elites block populist or libertarian prescriptions.

Party Poopers

Over the last several decades, the entrenchment of Washington's political classes arguably have made the two-party system part of America's late 20th century problem and probably not part of any 21st century solution, which is a focus of my new book (*Arrogant Capital*, published by Little, Brown, and Company). My purpose here is to pursue a different point: that the present U.S. party system cannot serve as a vehicle for the wisdom, such as it is, of the U.S. political, economic, and cultural elites, or for the populist anger or reformism of the masses. What the current system now produces under either party is shifty, back-stage bipartisanship and failed presidencies. Ronald Reagan was a partial exception, but both major opportunities of which he took advantage in the early 1980s—to proclaim "Morning Again in America" and to do so on a credit card—have been used up.

Scoffers will dispute the notion that the U.S. elites lack the political wherewithal to get their way. To be sure, they have enormous access to the media. And, yes, in this era of semi-corrupt politics, the hard and soft dollars of their campaign contributions buy massive influence in the executive and legislative branches alike. Their lobbyists throng Washington, winning quiet favors through obscure regulations or legislative amendments. However, with so much cynicism and frustration abroad in the land, both major parties, each standing for so little that excites public loyalty, are obliged to heed America's swing electorate of angry and suspicious independents. Furthermore, while both parties rely on powerful elites, they also rely on powerful anti-elites. These anti-elites are not comfortable with pin-striped Gucci centrism, and this is where much of the 30–45 cents worth of party difference originates.

Take the Democratic Party. Its economic policy is strongly influenced by anti-elite blue-collar workers, farmers, pensioners, critics of business and finance, and those ordinary folk who support rapid economic growth even at some risk of inflation. It's in cultural policy that the Democratic Party leans towards the views of what can fairly be called elites: the secular, nonchurch-going intelligentsia, the glitterati of Hollywood, fashion and the arts, gays, journalists and communicators, foundation and think-tank executives, and so forth. The Republicans more or less reverse the equation. They represent the elite upper-income and business viewpoint in economic policy, but to flesh out the party coalition, on cultural issues the national GOP has to bow to social-issue conservative and Religious Right constituencies. All of this is well known. Less attention is paid to another central truth: both parties are elite-dominated, which is why they find it so hard to represent ordinary Americans.

This overlapping of elites is where the not-a-dime's-worth-of-difference thesis deserves serious attention. Each party has well-known figures who take a moderate or centrist approach that combines relatively elite (in this case, somewhat conservative) economics with relatively elite (here somewhat liberal) cultural positions. These worthies are usually staunch internationalists, and rarely do they advocate populism. On the Republican side, the last 30 years have produced presidential ambitions in this vein from the likes of Pennsylvania Governor William Scranton (1964), New York Governor Nelson Rockefeller (1968), Representative John Anderson (1980), and now the minor wannabe crop of 1996—Weld and Senator Arlen Specter, for example. Politicians who represent a kindred mix have emerged on the Democratic side, too, and it is no ideological coincidence that some of the most prominent were once Republicans or came from Republican families: Massachusetts' Tsongas, Senator Bob Kerrey of Nebraska, White House chief of staff and former Congressman Leon Panetta, New Jersey Senator Bill Bradley, and even ex-Colorado Senator Gary Hart.

We should consider why this brand of Democrat hasn't been any more successful in reaching the Oval Office than were the old moderate Republicans of 1960 to 1980. In a nutshell, their media attention exceeds their intra-party popular support. Their principal socioeconomic appeal is to upper-bracket suburbanites, college students, venture capitalists, white-collar professionals, and the financial community—instead of core Democratic voters interested in bread-and-butter economic growth and distribution issues. Economically, they verge on crypto-Republicanism; this kind of New Democrat would rather meet with money managers or central bankers than with labor leaders (which, of course, isn't as "new" as it seems). At the same time, liberal leanings on culture and lifestyle issues make these politicos much less interested than the average Republican officeholder in upholding the fiscal and cultural interests of run-of-the-mall suburban constituencies. Indeed, fiscal new Democrats, epitomized by Tsongas and Kerrey, are particularly likely to deplore federal "pandering" to the middle class and to blame the middle class and its federal benefits programs for the nation's problems.

This fiscal revisionism hasn't exactly been a road to the White House.

Hart didn't pan out in 1984; neither did Dukakis four years later. Dukakis, who didn't want to use the term "country club" as a pejorative, insisted the election was about competence, not ideology. (He also came from a Republican family.) Then in 1992, Kerrey and Tsongas both miscarried with their early-stage, blame-the-middle-class themes. Tsongas did well in New England, with its tradition of puritanism and guilt, but as the campaign moved south and west, toward heavy industry, minorities, farmers, and pensioners, the Tsongas vote shrank with the ratio of Volvos and home delivery of the *New York Times*. By the Maryland, Florida, and Illinois primaries, Tsongas support shriveled towards a small affluent core. Clinton tapped the dominant Democratic anti-elite by lauding the middle class, defending pensioners and entitlements, and reiterating his attacks on the rich.

In 1996, Tsongas will not run against Clinton, but Kerrey might; if he does, it will be an interesting campaign. As a Medal of Honor winner in Vietnam, Kerrey could spotlight Clinton's foreign policy weakness. He might also run to Clinton's right on other issues, such as health care, on which he's already done an about-face. The centerpiece of Kerrey's 1992 presidential bid was a national health insurance plan that was to the left of Clinton's. Though his plan included a 5 percent payroll tax with no phase-in or exclusions, he now opposes Senator George Mitchell's delayed, contingent, 50 percent employer mandate, which excludes small firms.

Kerrey's weakness is his mix of neo-Republican economics and scapegoating of middle-class benefits. Recent reports also have had him getting his tax policy advice from billionaire investor Warren Buffett. Unless Clinton is a political basket case by 1996, the outline of a primary counterattack against a Kerrey candidacy is obvious. Although the president no longer has the credibility with the middle class that he enjoyed in 1992, he should be able to rally the majority of the Democratic electorate that responds to anti-elite economics.

If the prospect of an openly elite-oriented Democrat winning the White House in 1996 on a platform of ending Social Security as we know it is slim, the prospect of one of their GOP cousins gaining the Republican nomination is even thinner. Here the elite that rank-and-file voters reject is cultural. Weld is already changing some of his colors and re-attuning his 1994 Massachusetts reelection campaign to Catholic big-city swing Democrats, but it's hard to see his nomination playing west of Williamstown and Great Barrington. Weld's place on the national ticket probably depends on an acceptable GOP presidential nominee following in the footsteps of William McKinley and Richard Nixon by choosing a Cabot Lodge or Teddy Roosevelt–like running mate.

Weld's maneuvers also speak volumes about the unacceptability of politicos with libertarian leanings as nominees in either of the major parties. True, both sides have an overlap with part of the libertarian viewpoint. Reagan-type Republicans have broad streaks of what could be called Marlboro Man libertarianism: cap taxes and roll back government so that its regulations and taxes don't get in the way of ranchers, loggers, miners, and other entrepreneurs. But such Republicans, unlike full-menu libertarians, often favor government involvement in promoting defense industries, conservative morality, and religion in the schools. Liberal Democrats, in turn, have elements of what could be called Marijuana Man libertarianism: free up morality, grow what you want, and keep government out of the bedroom. But such liberals generally favor an activist government in other areas from affirmative action to stronger enforcement of environmental laws and regulations and higher taxes. The result is that each party can take a flavoring of libertarian thinking in a nominee, but no more. Across-the-board libertarianism is anathema to central constituencies.

Harvard man Weld, for example, captured favor in elite circles with a libertarian mix that blended tolerance on social issues with an Old Money investment banker's enthusiasm for reductions in estate and capital gains taxes. The power of the Religious Right in the GOP all but rules out any such 1996 candidate profile.

Moderate Variations

Former New Hampshire Senator Warren Rudman, who also blends social liberalism and fiscal conservatism, has tried to organize moderate Republicans to stymie the Religious Right. In 1992 he suggested that if the deficit were not brought under control there would soon be a new party. Probably not, because the issue is losing oomph.

But a broader new movement to limit government could come in three flavors. The first would repackage Perot centrism: tough on fiscal policy, fairly liberal on social issues, nationalist rather than internationalist, and populist on questions like town meetings and national referendums. The second would be the bipartisan elite version: liberal on social issues, budget-minded with a preference for sandblasting middle-class entitlements, internationalist and skeptical of populist mechanisms. If Tsongas and Rudman, who do bipartisan speeches together, formed a new party together, they would take this second option, although their mixture would probably not do as well as Perot's. Indeed, a Tsongas-Rudman ticket might well draw no more than the 7 percent that rallied around John Anderson's 1980 campaign, likewise maximizing in the Volvo and high-tech suburbs from Portland, Oregon to Portland, Maine, with detours to include university towns and upper-bracket playgrounds from Aspen to Nantucket. A third possibility for defunding big government would have a Pat Buchanan-type coloration and display the trappings of cultural war, America First nationalism, and various populist ideas.

So many varieties exist because so many of these viewpoints now find little real voice. This suggests a valid concern: the present party system fails not only to provide an effective public showcase for a bipartisan elite viewpoint, but also to offer any platform for serious libertarianism or populism because of the enormous private influence of the elites. Politicos like Perot and Buchanan, with their nationalism, culture wars, anti-Washington crusades, and support for bypassing the elites and going to the people are anathema to the establishments of both parties. So are the left-populist insurgencies of Jesse Jackson, Ralph Nader, and Jerry Brown. Even a more sophisticated version of populist or reformist insurgency may have to go outside the Republican-Democratic framework.

Which helps explain why the party system so shaky. America's bipartisan centrist elites are frustrated, and legitimately, at how neither party can showcase their ideas because of seething populism and the role of anti-elites within both parties. The bipartisan centrists find themselves obliged to use bipartisan commissions or summits to pursue policies that they presumably would prefer to press directly with the electorate. Unfortunately (and undemocratically), these mechanisms are designed to suspend the ordinary rules and retributions of politics to let the elites in both parties team up to recommend and often enact measures that have little public support. Prior examples range from the Greenspan Commission's 1983 insistence on major Social Security tax increases to the early 1990s deal between the parties to raise congressional salaries with as much camouflage as possible. The Bipartisan Commission on Entitlements, chaired by Kerrey, is the latest in this long line. Those who give it bipartisan cheer and a steady flow of memos see it as a way to make the middle class pay for deficit reduction with entitlement cuts, consumption taxes, and spending cuts, while promoting tax changes friendly to investors—in short, more self-serving policy-making by the upper bracket.

No wonder voters think that the interests of ordinary Americans are not represented in Washington. Their economic interests certainly aren't. Whenever bipartisan elites meet backstage in Washington, they are usually seeking to sidestep public opinion, not uphold it. Critics of Rush Limbaugh should broaden their concern. Precious few talk-show hosts can match the effect of senior members of our two-party system in breeding national cynicism.

A second related failure of this party system is the bipartisan need to pander. George Bush and Bill Clinton, while miles apart in their socioeconomic and ideological origins, reached the White House the same way: by promising the American people they would do things either that they never intended to do or that required populist battles for which they lacked the stomach. How could such governance not breed widespread popular contempt?

In 1988 and thereafter during the Bush administration, and in 1992 and then during the Clinton administration, the U.S. electorate has seen these shortcomings dominate each party in turn. Small wonder that voters are beginning to wonder about how well the two-party system serves the public interest. It is a debate that is likely to grow in 1995–96 as we watch what is rapidly becoming the saddest spectacle in American democracy: how so few, if any, of our Republican and Democratic wannabes are also oughtabes.

DISCUSSION QUESTIONS

1. Do you think a third party could fill the vacuum described by Phillips, or will the two parties respond with a more centrist agenda? In your opinion, which of these developments would be better for the average citizen?

52
Forum: "A Revolution, or Business as Usual?"

HARPER'S MAGAZINE

Running campaigns based on a party platform is one thing. Bringing the plat-form to fruition through governance is another. In the case of the Republican Party in 1994, the challenge has been not only to follow through on the promises made in the Contract With America, but also to define a vision and a strategy for the future that will appeal to voters for the long term and to provide a basis for holding together the various factions of the party. In March of 1995, two months after the Republicans took the reins of leadership in the House and Senate, Harper's Magazine *brought together six of the Republican Party's most prominent strategists to debate the future of the Republican Party. The discussion is one of ideals that ought to guide Republican efforts to steer the country and redefine the role of the federal government, mixed with pure polit-ical strategy aimed at bringing about those ideals and simply trying to hang on to a majority position in Congress. Some of the strategizing is blunt and brazen, offering the reader an inside look at the effort to make political ideals and cam-paign promises real.*

The mood these days in Washington's Republican salons is one of triumph and euphoria; plans are being made to occupy the capital for the next generation. But beneath the surface, signs of concern are starting to show. The staff director of the House Budget Committee re-cently admitted, "I don't know how many people thought we'd really have to implement these ideas."

As the Gingrich Congress debates the minutiae of term limits and capital-gains tax cuts, a new conversation is beginning among the back-room strategists whose memos and focus groups helped bring the party to power. How do Republicans placate an angry and fickle electorate that wants government to be slashed—as long as the cuts don't affect them? How do Republicans appease the ideologues who look at the No-vember victory not as an opportunity for incremental economic reform but as a mandate for cultural war?

To cast some light on the next act of Washington's political drama, *Harper's Magazine* invited six of the party's leading theoreticians to gather together over lamb filet and crab cakes and debate the future of Republicanism.

Paul Tough served as moderator.

Paul Tough is a senior editor of Harper's Magazine.

David Frum is the author of Dead Right. He has worked as an editor for the editorial page of the Wall Street Journal and as a columnist for Forbes. Currently, he is a weekly commentator for National Public Radio's Morning Edition and a monthly columnist for the American Spectator.

William Kristol is the chairman of Project for the Republican Future. He served as Vice President Dan Quayle's chief of staff during the Bush Administration.

Frank Luntz is the president of Luntz Research. He has worked as an adviser to Newt Gingrich and as a pollster for Ross Perot and Pat Buchanan. He conducted the voter research used to market the Contract With America.

Mike Murphy is a senior partner of the Murphy Pintak Gautier Agency, a media consulting firm. He has provided campaign strategy and political advertising for Oliver North, Michigan Governor John Engler, and New Jersey Governor Christine Todd Whitman. He [was] the chief strategist for Lamar Alexander for President.

James P. Pinkerton is a lecturer at the Graduate School of Political Management at George Washington University and a columnist for Newsday. He served as a domestic policy adviser in the Bush White House, where he invented the New Paradigm, a strategy for an activist conservative government.

Ralph Reed [was until 1997] the executive director of the Christian Coalition, an organization "dedicated to mobilizing and training Christians for effective political action." He has consulted on twenty-five congressional campaigns.

Bold Incrementalism and Public Decapitations

PAUL TOUGH: The newly elected Republican Congress has, in the Contract With America, a more specific agenda than any Congress in recent history. But I want to ask you to go beyond the contract, to sketch out some larger themes for this Congress and for the Republican Party in the long term. Is there a single unifying idea that the party should devote itself to?

MIKE MURPHY: We were elected to make fundamental radical changes in the size of the federal government. That's the idea we campaigned on, and that's what we've got to do.

JAMES P. PINKERTON: But we could also lay out a couple of principles. For example, we ought to have an affluence test on government spending and government benefits. To listen to Bill Archer, the Republican Ways and Means Committee chairman, say that we can cut everything except Social Security, which means Ross Perot and the

Rockefellers will get their checks while people are getting thrown out on the streets—

FRANK LUNTZ: Wait a second. If we touch Social Security in the next two years, we will give credence to everything that Bill Clinton said about the Republicans—that if we became a majority we were going to mess with Social Security. Philosophically, you're right, and I don't think there's anyone at this table who would disagree with you. In fact, most of us would probably say that Social Security is heading into a crisis. But politically, we can't do anything for at least two years, until we gain the public's confidence.

WILLIAM KRISTOL: Part of being the majority is getting to the point where we can go after entitlements in a big way. Take Roosevelt as an example. He didn't do everything at once. He phased in most of his big programs. Similarly, we are going to have to be both bold in the vision we hold out for America and somewhat prudent—if I can use a discredited Bush Administration word—and incremental. We need a kind of bold incrementalism that leads people along step by step, so that a year from now they'll be saying, "They really did cut some programs this year, and we like it."

RALPH REED: The most important thing for the Republicans to do right now, in order to rebuild the trust of the electorate, is simply to do what they said they would do. What they said they would do is honor the Contract With America. The Republicans have got to resist every temptation to get off that message. The great temptation right now, in the euphoria and giddiness after the election, is to begin to think of lots of other ideas, to begin to raise expectations even higher and try to do many other things that weren't in that contract. If the contract is successfully redeemed, then we will have built an enormous reservoir of political capital that we can carry into these other battles. So let's concentrate on the contract for now.

DAVID FRUM: But the contract isn't enough. Look, the 104th Congress has to pass two budgets. There's no way around it. They can either pass budgets that look essentially like the budgets that Congress has passed for the last decade, or they can pass budgets that cut a lot of the programs that deserve to be cut.

MURPHY: Absolutely. If we do not pass a budget that dramatically cuts spending, the kind that the *Washington Post* and the *New York Times* will term a catastrophe, and pay that short-term price, then in the long term we're going to be destroyed, because we will have lied to America. We've got political momentum. If we don't use it right away to make significant cuts, we will be failures.

PINKERTON: The question is, where to begin? I heard David Frum say on TV that we ought to start by taking some big obnoxious spending program for the rich and ceremoniously, publicly decapitating it.

KRISTOL: I agree. Farm subsidies.

PINKERTON: Farm subsidies are a perfect candidate. We can't really go to poor black people and throw them off welfare if we haven't first gone to rich white farmers and thrown *them* off welfare.

TOUGH: How far are you going to go with these cuts? Walk me down the streets of Washington, D.C., ten years from now. What's left here?

FRUM: What I hope we'll see is a government whose social-welfare functions are essentially confined to insuring people against the uninsurable catastrophic risks of ordinary life—catastrophic illness, short periods of unemployment, indigence. I also hope that we will have gotten government out of the business of monkeying around in the private economy, which means that virtually all of the Department of Commerce and the Department of Energy will be gone, as well as a lot of the Department of Transportation.

TOUGH: Where does the ax fall first?

FRUM: The big programs, like welfare, Medicaid, and Medicare, will take a little time to get rid of. But there are a lot of little ones that we can get rid of right away. Let's start with President Clinton's favorite, his advanced-technology project. If you have a plan for some technological breakthrough, the government will give you federal money to promote it—on one condition, which is that it can make a profit. In other words, if you can prove that you do not need a government subsidy, the government will give you one. That has to go. Washington is giving $70 million a year to General Motors, Ford, and Chrysler to build an electric car. That goes. When people hear that Republicans are taking money away from big auto-makers, that will help us politically.

LUNTZ: And we eliminate funding for the arts, the humanities, the Corporation for Public Broadcasting. Those cuts we do right away as well.

FRUM: Sure. And here's how I think we should do it. Instead of cutting incrementally—a little here, a little there—I would say that on a single day this summer we eliminate three hundred programs, each one costing a billion dollars or less. Maybe these cuts won't make a big deal of difference, but, boy, do they make a point. And you can do them right away, because, unlike Medicare, Medicaid, and welfare, they're not intellectually challenging.

TOUGH: So we're planning a day of public executions. What goes to the guillotine?

FRUM: The Rural Electrification Administration. The Department of Commerce's program to underwrite the advertising expenses of American corporations in foreign markets. The electric-car project. All programs to promote research on fuel efficiency. The Small Business Administration. Export promotion. Advanced-technology projects. The commercial space program. A lot of the Department of Transportation's demonstration projects. I mean, these things are just embarrassing.

TOUGH: Are farm subsidies in there?

Balancing the Budget—What Gets Cut

Most proponents of a balanced budget are understandably vague when it comes to the specific programs that would need to be cut. This is not the case for Representative Gerald Solomon (R., N.Y.), the new chair of the House Rules Committee, who last year issued a proposed budget that would balance income and expenditures by the end of the decade, without raising taxes or cutting Social Security. (The proposal would also allow for a substantial increase in defense spending.) It is, in Representative Solomon's words, "painful as hell." His Balanced Budget Task Force itemized more than five hundred specific cuts to be implemented over the next five years; a few are listed below, along with the amount that their implementation would save from the 1999 federal budget. In total, spending in that year's $1.6 trillion budget would be $221 billion below current Congressional Budget Office projections.

PROPOSED CHANGE	SAVINGS
Implement managed care for Medicaid beneficiaries	$13 billion
Cut Medicaid payments to hospitals	$8.9 billion
End all commodity subsidies (except dairy)*	$6.8 billion
Eliminate Community Development Block Grants	$4.8 billion
Restrict Medicaid coverage for noncitizens	$2.7 billion
Increase civil-service retirement age	$2.5 billion
Cancel plans to build the space station	$2.4 billion
Reduce subsidies for mass transit	$2.2 billion
Adjust food-stamp eligibility	$1.6 million
Reduce foreign aid to developing countries	$1.3 billion
Cancel all bilateral assistance to Russia	$1.2 billion
Freeze funding for the National Institutes of Health	$1.2 billion
Reduce medical care for veterans	$910 million
Cut funds for child-nutrition programs	$790 million
Abolish the Geological Survey	$710 million
Reduce Amtrak subsidies	$650 million
Cut funding for NEA, NEH, Smithsonian, National Gallery of Art, and CPB in half	$610 million

Cut funding for programs that pay for prenatal and preventive care, immunization, etc.	$590 million
Limit U.S. contributions to the U.N.	$400 million
Abolish the National Service Program	$390 million
Reduce FBI salaries and expenses	$350 million
Freeze funding for social services for the elderly	$110 million
Eliminate the Economic Development Administration	$36 million
Eliminate funding for the John F. Kennedy Center for the Arts	$24 million
Reduce spending on magnetic-levitation trains	$22 million
Eliminate the U.S. Travel and Tourism Administration	$18 million

Representative Solomon's district in upstate New York is known for its thriving dairy industry.

FRUM: Yes. Although that's a much bigger program, and one that's politically a lot harder to cut. A lot of the people who get hurt are our voters. But intellectually, farm subsidies are indefensible. They're pure political pork, and cutting them would send a very powerful message.

REED: I think we also need to cut something early on that is dramatic and symbolic and sort of dramaturgical, something that has the same kind of political impact that the air-traffic controllers' strike had for Reagan in 1981. Sure, it may have been a small union, it may have been a relatively insignificant labor dispute in the broad scale of labor history, but it was a significant moment because it demonstrated that Reagan was no longer going to allow the labor unions to tell the government what to do. If you pick a small agency that has a very formidable constituency, it would help pave the way for a lot of these other ventures. The Legal Services Corporation, which provides legal aid for the poor, would be a great one to cut.

Two Years in Hell

TOUGH: Frank, it's the summer of 1995. It's David Frum's day of the long knives. Three hundred programs are executed. Politically, how do you deal with the reaction when he eliminates the Small Business Administration and farm subsidies and the Corporation for Public Broadcasting and the National Endowment for the Arts and student loans—

LUNTZ: He's going to cut student loans?

FRUM: Yup.

LUNTZ: The whole program?

FRUM: Yes.

LUNTZ: Then people are going to cry. Well, David and I are going to go out to Kansas, and I'm going to watch him announce to a group of farmers that he's eliminating the farm-subsidies program. And I'm going to stand far, far away from him.

TOUGH: Won't the public's enthusiasm for these cuts dim once they realize that you're cutting not just welfare programs but programs that are directly benefiting them?

MURPHY: Look, we can't make everybody happy.

KRISTOL: People are so distrustful of government right now that we may have crossed some sort of magic threshold where people are willing to say, "Look, I'll even give up these programs that allegedly help me, because (a) they don't really help me much and (b) I do understand that we have a deficit and the whole thing is sprawling out of control. I'll give up my chunk of government benefits if everyone else is giving up his."

LUNTZ: That's the key. If everyone is giving up something at the same time, you're okay. But if we make the farmers go first, we're going to get killed in the farm community. We've all got to go together.

REED: According to our polling data, the first thing people want Congress to do is to reform welfare. So if you go out there early and pass a tough and strong and dramatic welfare-reform bill that encourages work and marriage and discourages out-of-wedlock birth, then rhetorically you can say, "Look, we've asked the least among us to sacrifice so that we can have a smaller government, so that we can have a more civil society, so that we don't have this spiraling debt. We can't ask the least among us to get out of the wagon and start pulling unless you get out, too." That's my argument on the NEA and the National Endowment for the Humanities. How can you go to a single mother in the inner city and say, "You're going to have to start carrying more weight" if you don't also go to the tuxedo and evening-gown crowd and say, "You're going to have to start paying for your own symphony." By starting with welfare, we can turn these cuts into a populist program that will actually work to our advantage.

MURPHY: What I'm advocating, with all due respect to my friend Frank, is that we ban pollsters for two years. Because the only thing the polls are going to tell us is what we can't do. In 1991, the Engler Administration in Michigan cut welfare. They just eliminated general assistance altogether. There was a huge war. Governor Engler cut arts funding. Our fat-cat donors didn't like that at all. Engler got his reelect number down to 19 percent. And last November he won reelection by a landslide. Let's face it: we are in for two years of political hell. There is simply no happy way for us to keep our promises. Yes, we can try to be clever and make sure everybody pays his fair share, but no matter how clever we are tactically, we're going to get a coalition of people really mad about what we're doing. People in focus groups are always very happy about cutting spending and cutting programs—except programs for themselves. So our success is going to be a function of how much courage we show, because we're going to get no credit for years.

LUNTZ: And with all due respect to Mike, what I'm afraid of is the media consultants. They're going to put together a thirty-second ad with no words, just film of some homeless person walking across the street with superimposed words saying, "Republicans did this to you. Now you do it to them." I am afraid of what the media is going to do to us. Look at the *New York Times*. A week ago, there were two pages of pictures of homeless people on Madison Avenue. A week earlier on the front page was a picture of two elderly people rummaging through garbage for food. They're getting ready to blame the Republicans. They run the big story on the GOP's plans right next to the photograph. They haven't linked the two yet, but it's only a matter of time.

TOUGH: But the sort of cuts you're talking about are going way beyond homeless people on Madison Avenue. There are going to be people who can't afford to go to college; small businesses are going to fail.

KRISTOL: Some of these cuts will have some effect, but most of these programs are so ineffectual that not many people are actually going to be hurt very much. The reason we don't like these programs, after all, is that we think they're ineffectual. If we thought they helped a lot of people, we wouldn't be conservative Republicans.

REED: And you're not just taking money away; you're also saying to the small-business community, "We're going to freeze federal regulations on small business for the next two years." You've now got 50 to 55 percent of the country receiving a check from the government in some way. And they've learned that with that money come all kinds of intrusive regulations on their freedom, on their liberty, and on their right to go out and earn a dollar and raise a family and have their children believe in the values they believe in. So if you don't just cut the money but you also pull back all of this intrusive government regulation, I think you can make it work.

TOUGH: So, Frank, does that reassure you enough for 1996? Do you think we can make those cuts?

LUNTZ: Absolutely. I just don't want to blunder into them. I think the timing is important, and I think we can finesse it.

FRUM: Are you sure you want to use the word "finesse"? Wasn't one of the ways we got into trouble in the late 1980s that we were constantly being, under the Bush Administration, so damn clever?

LUNTZ: I'll explain it in one sentence: I don't want to deliver bad news from a golf course in Kennebunkport. That's what I mean by finesse.

KRISTOL: That's why Frank gets the big bucks.

MURPHY: The tactics, which are what Frank and I do for a living, are just not that important. We have to do something big and unpopular, and it doesn't matter if we do it from a closed steel mill. It's still going to be unpopular. Sure, we ought to announce it from a closed steel mill as opposed to a golf course, but the political reality is that we're going to have to take a whack at the entitlement state, which includes a lot of programs that benefit the middle class. There's no easy, simple strategy to make that fact go away. We have never had our bluff called on spending. Now it's called. We better move fast.

Stewing in Brezhnevian Juices

TOUGH: Ralph, you said that the place to start cutting is welfare programs. Whether or not that helps the poor in the long run, in the short run there are going to be people who are really going to suffer; there are going to be families who will become homeless and children who are going to be put in orphanages. How much should that concern us?

PINKERTON: The Republicans need to come to grips with the real issue in underclass welfare dependency, which is the value of work. The Republicans ought to say that the transcendent value all Americans can agree on is work.

REED: And marriage and childbirth in marriage.

PINKERTON: Well, I want to go with the lowest common denominator. So I'll just stick with work. I'm not sure everybody wants to get married; I'm not sure everybody wants to have kids. But everyone wants to work.

LUNTZ: I don't know if that's true anymore. Particularly among black youth in the inner city, a lot of people would not say that work is a basic fundamental desire any longer.

PINKERTON: All right, then let's say the *Republicans* believe in work. Anybody who doesn't believe in work can be a Democrat. An emphasis on work puts some distance between us and the Michael Milkens and the junk-bond traders. In some areas of Republican ideology, there is a sense that the highest value is not work but just making money. We have to say that's wrong, that there is more merit to a person getting up every morning and going to work than someone just inheriting a fortune. Now, I can't imagine a welfare plan that doesn't involve us saying, "If you can work, you have to work. There's no more welfare." But in order to be successful, we're going to have to create some sort of program like Roosevelt's Civilian Conservation Corps to guarantee that although nobody gets a check for doing nothing, nobody is starving.

REED: So we're dismantling the New Deal by creating a new one.

LUNTZ: The government is going to pay for these jobs?

PINKERTON: That's right. We give a job to anyone who wants one. Franklin Roosevelt summoned 8 million people to work during the Depression; we can do the same.

TOUGH: Who runs this program?

PINKERTON: I'd ask someone like Colin Powell or Norman Schwarzkopf. The leadership cadre for a new CCC already exists: all the drill sergeants and NCOs who are being demobilized out of the military. We scoop them up and get them involved. The military used to be a lot of people doing simple tasks. Now the military is a few people doing complicated tasks. Let's go back to a lot of people doing simple tasks, but instead of having them fight wars, let's have them doing peaceful construction or planting trees or unpaving the Everglades. We're going to spend billions of dollars to take up all those levees down in the Everglades. Rather than turning the operation over to some contractor, let's make it labor-intensive and put disadvantaged inner-city youth to work.

KRISTOL: But no one believes that the federal government could run such a program.

PINKERTON: You believe the military can organize large bodies of people to do this sort of thing.

KRISTOL: To fight wars. That's a bit different. Don't you think, practically speaking, that the Republican position on welfare is going to crystallize around the idea of large-scale devolution to the states? Fine, let some governors experiment with a statewide public-works program. Other states would go with a tough cut-them-off approach.

REED: And after ten years you'll know which states have done a better job of encouraging work and discouraging illegitimacy.

PINKERTON: The problem is, we don't have ten years to sort this out.

KRISTOL: Don't you think most people would be thrilled if we got welfare down to the states?

PINKERTON: Well, yes. To use your phrase, many people *would* be thrilled. But there is a national consciousness on this above all other issues. The Republican message has to be totally clear: Nobody is going to starve. Everybody's going to make it. Everybody is going to work. I'm all for devolving education and housing and transportation and road building to the states. I just think that on this one issue of welfare, you need a federal guarantee.

TOUGH: Does that sound like such a radical idea, for the federal government to guarantee that people don't starve to death? Can't we all agree on that?

KRISTOL: It depends what it means in practice.

PINKERTON: It means we guarantee work. We guarantee honest labor.

KRISTOL: That doesn't guarantee that people won't starve, because people won't show up for work. You cannot in practice have a federal guarantee that people won't starve. Practically, the question is, Are you going to maintain federal entitlement programs or not? My preference is not to have federal entitlement programs but to send them all down to the states, let the states experiment much more, and have private charities take care of people. I don't believe, in fact, that people would starve. We could have federal leadership on these issues that is compassionate and says, "We think this is better for the poor."

REED: We live in a country with the most generous people in the entire world. The problem is that we've centralized charity and welfare, and things have actually gotten worse, not better. People want to return to nongovernmental solutions to poverty. We've got to challenge the churches, the synagogues, and the families to dig deeper and do more.

LUNTZ: Enormous government programs are what the other side offered. The public rejected that. They're ready to embrace us if we just do the things we promised.

PINKERTON: The issue is whether we go further. The issue is how to take apart the institutions that are wrecking this country. If we simply pass the Contract With America, which is essentially a pro-business agenda, and don't go further, then the top half of the economy will be liberated from government control and will prosper and the bottom half will continue to stew in its Brezhnevian juices. And two years from now we'll have an even more radical skew—both electoral and economic—than we did in the 1980s. The moral credibility of capitalism will be further undercut by another round of homeless stories, which will ultimately retard the Republican progress. People will say, "Yeah, we're all getting rich, but what about this poor child here on TV?" I'm not saying that if Republicans take bold steps to help the poor we can immediately expect to harvest a lot of votes from the inner city, but we'll reassure the rest of America that we do, in fact, have a plan for everyone. Right now, when you listen to Jesse Helms and Newt Gingrich, you don't really get the feeling that either man aspires to be a leader for the entire country.

TOUGH: Well, what about those inner-city voters? If you want to represent the whole country, doesn't that mean trying to attract black voters as well as whites?

PINKERTON: There's a significant part of our program that will appeal to African-American voters. We can go to blacks and say, "School vouchers, own your own home, American dream—"

LUNTZ: And that ain't gonna do it. It ain't gonna do it.

TOUGH: Why not?

LUNTZ: In our polling, we find very different priorities in the white and the nonwhite communities. The black community has become very dependent on the government to provide services, and it expects government to get involved and fix America's ills. At the same time, the white community has become particularly hostile about the government and the services it provides.

TOUGH: What does that mean for the Republican Party?

LUNTZ: That the black community is not ripe for picking. The black community's policies and beliefs are actually very closely aligned with the Democratic Party. Blacks are making a rational decision by voting Democratic. If the black community thinks it's better off and the country's better off with a Democratic administration, then its members should vote that way. The rest of America doesn't think so.

Backslappers in a Warrior-Like Frenzy

TOUGH: Aren't people going to be bothered by photos of poor homeless people showing up at City Hall, saying that they want to work and that they don't have food to feed their families?

FRUM: I agree with Jim that it's dangerous for the party to seem callous. But people's attitudes about the poor have changed significantly in the last decade. People are tired of the constant moaning they hear about the poor. A lot of middle-class taxpayers feel that they're paying more and more for the poor and that the poor are behaving worse and worse. And people are not sure that they're as sympathetic as they used to be. I don't think we should go out of our way to be callous. But there is no way that the Republican Party is going to be able to remain true to its principles without being accused of being callous. In the current environment, being accused of callousness might even be to our advantage. Jack Kemp spent a lot of time trying to come up with ideas that would both be conservative and avoid these accusations, and he failed.

KRISTOL: Republicans obviously should be strategic and clever about how to cut spending. We should be careful to target middle-class subsidies and big-business subsidies as much as we target programs that allegedly benefit the poor. But David's right: no matter what we do, the fairness card will be played against us, and if Republicans get spooked the first time someone tries to demagogue that issue, we will be in deep trouble. Republicans will need to have thick skins to survive the fairness attack that will be launched on us during the course of 1995.

MURPHY: And the reason we have to have thick skins is that the media hates us. We just won a huge victory, but Newt's numbers are 20 to 28 fave/unfave because he gets smeared every day in the press. Today, I saw my third newsweekly cover photo of Gingrich, like, strangling a kid. It's amazing. Qaddafi gets better press. The point is that we can do all this strategic stuff, we can hold great photo ops and all that, and the folks who write the CBS national news are still going to say, "Meet Mrs. X. She's dying tonight because of the Republican plan." If our folks lose it and freak and stampede, then we're going to blow the whole thing. Remember, we have a lot of backslapping nice guys in our caucus who've never been on the firing line. I worked with a lot of Republican politicians during the 1994 election, and everybody's real tough on the contract until some little old lady comes up to him at the plant gate and yells at him. Then he says, "Well, I don't really mean *all* of it." It's the natural way of politicians to be scared to do radical things. We have to whip our guys up into a warrior-like frenzy, or they're going to back off on day fourteen.

PINKERTON: Well, okay, that's one plan, to take a bunch of natural backslappers and whip them into a warrior-like frenzy. But another strategy that might work is to isolate a few core programs that the federal government will maintain that will guarantee that nobody falls through the cracks. I would rather buck up Mike's backslapping guys by giving them something to be *for*, which means a program like the CCC that guarantees that poor people are not going to starve.

FRUM: You're underestimating the opposition we're going to face. You're suggesting that the only thing that our legislators are afraid of is somebody saying, "There are hungry people, so we've got to have a program for hunger." That's not the accusation. There are going to be students who can't afford college. There are going to be electric cars not being built. There are going to be symphonies closing all over America.

PINKERTON: I'm saying there is a qualitative difference between those accusations. I think Republicans can withstand the symphony closures.

FRUM: The Republicans are much more afraid of angry symphony-goers than they are of people starving to death.

PINKERTON: Maybe so. Which exactly epitomizes the problem. If the Republicans are more afraid of symphony closures than of poor people starving, that says a lot about the Republican Party.

FRUM: It's just political reality. The sort of people who love the opera and support their local arts organizations are also the sort of people who make $100,000 donations to the Republican Party. We're not going to be fighting with uneducated destitute people; we're going to be fighting with the most powerful people in American society.

PINKERTON: But we've got to set some priorities. If this is a country with a sense of compassion, then there ought to be a clearly articulated national policy that says, "We don't want anybody to starve, but we believe in work." We lay it out just like Franklin Roosevelt did on this one narrow issue, and we campaign on that.

MURPHY: We tried this in 1974, after Watergate: "Republicans are people too." It's pure defense. The slogan appeals: "We're for work and we're against starvation." But the *New York Times* is still going to find people who are starving, even if we have WORK NOT STARVATION bumper stickers all over the place.

TOUGH: What if you start making all these cuts and President Clinton goes on television and gives a speech in which he says, "The Republican Party is attacking you. They won't let me give you the money that I want to give you to make your life better." And what if we're in a recession in 1995 and 1996, and people want some sort of economic stimulus? In 1992, George Bush was deemed out of touch for not responding to those calls. If we've got 500,000 people marching on Washington demanding that these cuts be reinstated, is it going to be as easy to ignore that as it is to ignore the *New York Times*?

MURPHY: Oh, it will be incredibly hard. But if we let the Democrats set the agenda, they're going to grind us up and they'll be back in power. We've got to say that we believe in personal responsibility; we don't believe people need a big government to organize them; people can do it for themselves. I mean, that's why we're Republicans. We've got to say that over and over and over again. It's the only choice we have.

KRISTOL: And Clinton cannot make the speech you're talking about. He totally lacks credibility with the American people. It's an interesting question whether another liberal could make that speech, Dick Gephardt or maybe a fresher face. Mario Cuomo out of retirement a year from now. With a new candidate, the Democrats could get 43 percent of the vote again. And if it's a three- or four-way race in 1996, that could lead to a Democratic victory. I don't think any of us discounts that possibility. In fact, I think Clinton has made a mistake by conceding so many of our premises. I mean, all he's doing now is cutting taxes and cutting spending. He's been harsher on public-housing programs than any conservative I can think of, which is a terrible concession for him to have made. He may have created room for some liberal to stand up and say, "Look, liberalism does have an honorable tradition. Roosevelt helped people. Johnson helped people. We're for civil rights. The Republicans are rich and mean-spirited. I'm going to defend these federal programs." Within the Democratic primary process, that would be a very attractive message from a fresh liberal face. I think it's a message that would defeat Bill Clinton in 1996.

Taking off the Jackboots

TOUGH: So far we've been talking about economic programs. But aren't a lot of voters attracted to the Republican Party because of your cultural agenda? Why aren't you talking about those issues?

REED: We have been. Welfare reform is a cultural and moral issue. It's not an economic issue. If we eliminate welfare altogether, it's not going to balance the budget or get us anywhere near there. It's about encouraging work and discouraging out-of-wedlock birth. It's about ending the chaos and the social dysfunction of our inner cities. There are critics who will try to get the Republican Party to accept the notion that there is a dichotomy between our social agenda and our economic agenda. It's absolutely, totally untrue.

PINKERTON: But our moderator is onto something, which is that we are doing something that the Republican Party didn't used to be good at doing. Instead of hectoring people about values, like we did at the Houston convention in 1992, we are talking about changing people's lives by changing their economic reality. I think the reason that the Republicans are on the edge of success is that we have found a common denominator of economically driven issues that enable people to create their own cultural superstructure.

FRUM: The great conservative hope is contained in a phrase that goes back thirty years: "In a conservative country, the libertarian method yields traditionalist results." Go through Ralph Reed's mailing list, and you'll find an awful lot of old Wallace voters, people who stood for trying to achieve conservative results through authoritarian methods. And a lot of them still favor authoritarian methods—maybe not authoritarian with jackboots, but authoritarian nonetheless. The great contribution Ralph Reed has made is that he has convinced a lot of those people that a libertarian approach is going to achieve the same results, and that it's an approach we can run and win on.

REED: I think those people, by the way, ended up in David Duke's file, not mine.

PINKERTON: Well, there were a lot of them. There were 10 million of them in 1968.

FRUM: And they aren't all horrible people. I think that one of the reasons the Republican Party now is such a disciplined organization, certainly as compared with its competition, is that everyone—even people with strong cultural agendas—has agreed to hope for the moment that we can use libertarian means to achieve traditionalist ends.

PINKERTON: The question is whether Ralph is going to be able to go to all those people who originally paid attention to Pat Robertson because he's a faith healer who averts hurricanes and predicts apocalypses and say to them, "Look, your real friends in this world are Wall Street tycoons, because trickle-down economics is the only kind of economics left." If he can sell that argument, that the haves and the have-nots share a common ethos, then the Republicans really will be the majority party forever.

MURPHY: What the pundits here in Washington don't understand is that these cultural issues are important to people. People see the whole concept of right and wrong eroding in this country. They see a kind of nihilistic society in which "values" is a dirty word and everything is okay. And that scares them. They want it to change. Politicians are afraid to talk about right and wrong because they are told by the intellectual culture that right and wrong isn't an issue. But voters are demanding that folks start addressing personal responsibility. Our party ought to address those things.

KRISTOL: As part of a broader conservative vision for the future, it's very important to emphasize that we have concrete ideas about how to revitalize civic society and how to strengthen families. But I tend to agree that the way in which this is reconciled politically is by making the political agenda mostly a neolibertarian, federalizing, get-government-off-our-backs agenda, and then letting communities and families, with some encouragement from the government but without authoritarian coercion, work on the reconstitution of civil society.

REED: That's right. You can't be part of a movement for limited government without accepting limits to what government can do. That's one of the things that I think separates conservatives from liberals. We genuinely believe that some of the greatest work, the most productive and fruitful work that will be done in society to improve people's lives, will be done by institutions other than the government.

LUNTZ: And that's why this is the beginning of a Republican majority, and a relatively long-term one. When you can have the lion and the lamb lie down together, when the Perot voter and the Christian conservative find more that unites them than divides them, you're looking at 55, 57 percent of America that is behind our program.

TOUGH: What about the possibility of a third party? Is that a threat to this coalition?

PINKERTON: I think that it is a threat, especially if the Republicans fall into the rut of complacency and smugness, looking after the top half and letting the bottom half sink into Gephardtian resentment. It's a more difficult challenge for the Republicans than simply doing a good job. Because in an era of post-party factionalization, there is not a lot stopping some ambitious egomaniac with a billion dollars from saying, "I don't care if I have any issues or not, I just want to be president." I think we're going to see a whole slew of them: Ross Perot/Silvio Berlusconi types, out there running just for the hell of it. This is how all our plans for coalitions and cleverness could come crashing down.

FRUM: I'm a lot less impressed by this threat. There aren't that many people in America with a billion dollars and an out-of-control ego.

PINKERTON: You haven't looked at the Forbes 400 list recently.

KRISTOL: But they won't get any votes unless Republicans fail. If Republicans succeed as the congressional majority, the chance of a third party is diminished radically. If Republicans fail on Capitol Hill, then you could have genuinely chaotic, postmodernist, deconstructionist politics in America. The interesting thing about the 1994 election is that by conventional analysis, it shouldn't have happened. It was an old-fashioned party election. It looked like elections from the 1890s, for God's sake. Maybe it's an aberration, maybe it can't last. Maybe a year from now we'll be back into chaos and into Perot squared. But maybe it really was a decisive moment and successful governance by the Republican majority will move us toward a generational realignment. At this point, I think those are basically the two alternatives: Republican success or political chaos.

DISCUSSION QUESTIONS

1. If you had been present at that meeting of Republican strategists, what advice would you have offered?

2. Have the coalitional and strategic problems for the Republican party changed since that March 1995 meeting? If so, how?

3. How do you think a similar meeting would play out for the Democratic party if it were held today? What are the Democrats' strategic and coalitional problems? How should those problems be solved?

4. Did you see much discussion among these strategists that would address Fiorina's or Phillips's concerns? Explain.

53
Third Parties and the Presidential Race

Walter Berns and Gordon S. Black

Why aren't third parties more prominent in the electoral process? Walter Berns argues that the primary reason is the electoral college, which "deflates the strength of minor parties and inflates the margin of the winning party." Rather than achieving an outright victory, however, a third party candidate could draw enough support away from a major party candidate to prevent any one candidate from winning a majority of the electoral college votes. Berns describes the constitutional provision for determining the next president in the event that a third-party candidate does prevent a clear winner in the race for president: members of the House of Representatives cast their votes collectively as members of state delegations; for victory, a candidate requires the votes of at least 26 state delegations.

Gordon Black offers another take on the question of third-party prominence. The problem, he indicates, lies with the candidates on a third-party ticket. Candidates the media identifies as "perfect" for the challenge, such as Colin Powell during the early months of the 1996 presidential campaign, can be quite removed from the concerns of voters that give rise to the need for a third party in the first place. On the other hand, a candidate who understands these concerns and will push for reform can be too much of an outsider and lack long-standing appeal to the voters and the media.

Third Party Candidates Face a High Hurdle in the Electoral College

Walter Berns

In the century and a half since the emergence of our current two-party system the United States has avoided any crisis in selecting a new president and vice-president—in part because the electoral college amplifies the margin of victory in the popular vote. This amplification gives us a clear winner even when the popular vote is close enough to be called a "photo-finish." John Kennedy, for example, won only one-third of a percent more popular votes than Richard Nixon in 1960, but collected

38 percent more electoral votes. Bill Clinton, who garnered just 43 percent of the popular vote in 1992's three-way race, captured nearly 70 percent of the electoral college.

It is always possible that a third-party candidate, by taking a state or two, may prevent either of the major party candidates from winning an electoral college majority, but this has not happened in the last 170 years. In such an event, the Constitution specifies that the election is thrown into the House of Representatives. It is quite likely, however, that in the weeks between the election and the gathering of the electoral college, the third-party candidate would entertain "bids" for his electors from one of the leaders—in return for policy or personnel concessions.

This was the express purpose in 1968 of George Wallace, who hoped to become kingmaker to either Richard Nixon or Hubert Humphrey. Deadlocking the vote in the electoral college will always be a ticklish undertaking, however. A third party not only must capture some states, but must be careful elsewhere not to draw votes from only one of the two major candidates, thus giving the other a landslide.

Wallace's campaign turned out to be the most successful third-party bid in over 50 years. Yet while Nixon and Humphrey each received only 43 percent of the vote (Nixon just over and Humphrey just under), Nixon nonetheless picked up a decisive 56 percent of the electoral vote.

This occurred because the voting procedure of the electoral college deflates the strength of minor parties and inflates the margin of the winning party. By state law, all electoral votes (except Maine's and Nebraska's) are awarded on a winner-take-all basis to the candidate who captures the most votes within that state. To have any electoral effect, then, a party must win outright within states. Regional third-party challenges generally fare better under this system. Southern favorite Wallace actually captured 46 electoral votes. Yet the electoral college still deflated his challenge. Although he had received nearly 14 percent of the popular vote, he got only eight percent of the electoral vote. Some 4.1 million Wallace votes cast outside the states he carried were "wasted."

A third party with an even national appeal but lacking plurality support within any state will be stymied by the electoral college. Millard Fillmore and the Know-Nothings won 21 percent of the popular vote in 1856, but received only 2 percent of the electoral vote. Republican William Howard Taft was the choice of 23 percent of the voters in 1912, but of less than 2 percent of the electoral college. That same year, Theodore Roosevelt mounted the biggest third-party challenge of the twentieth century, taking 28 percent of the popular vote, yet he ended up with just 17 percent of the electoral vote. Most recently, we had Ross Perot's 1992 campaign, when he won nearly 20 percent of the popular vote but didn't earn a single electoral vote.

The fear of vote-wasting is the main psychological burden imposed by the electoral college's deflation of third-party efforts. As election day approaches, third-party candidates often see their support fade, because voters don't want to squander their ballot on someone who won't win. This happened to both Wallace and Perot.

Despite the failures of Theodore Roosevelt, George Wallace, Ross Perot, and others, it is always possible that a third-party candidate may prevent either of the major party candidates from winning the electoral college majority required by the Constitution. Recent changes in the law make this easier. Court decisions have made ballot access for third-party candidates simpler, and the Federal Election Campaign Act ensures public funding, in advance of an election, for any minor party that received at least 5 percent of the vote in the previous presidential race.

If ever someone mounts a third-party campaign that prevents an electoral college victory by one of the major parties, a little-known set of constitutional, statutory, and parliamentary rules governing the choice of a president and vice president would kick in: the newly sworn-in members of the House of Representatives, with one vote per state delegation, would choose the president from among the top three vote-getters in the electoral college. Support of at least 26 state delegations is required for a president to be selected. Simultaneously, the newly sworn-in members of the Senate would vote individually for vice president, choosing among the top two vote-getters in the electoral college, with 51 votes required for victory.

These mechanisms would produce a president and a vice president with unchallengeable constitutional claims to those offices. In a world where government succession is often bent to the dictates of force, the importance of this cannot be exaggerated.

Third Party Candidates Won't Necessarily Bring Reform

Gordon S. Black

Periodically in American politics an election takes on unusual significance. The 1936 race between Franklin Roosevelt and Alf Landon was such an election. The issues fought out then—passive vs. activist government, free markert vs. government redistribution—defined for the future what it meant to be a Republican or a Democrat. Enduring party loyalties were forged on that battlefield.

These turning-point elections generally center around issues rather than personalities. They grow out of problems that have festered for a long time, frustrating large numbers of Americans. And they involve clashes between contestants who promise to take the country in distinctly different directions.

The 1996 campaign has the potential to become precisely this kind of election. The broadest question at issue is whether elected officials will be permitted to continue the three-decades-long process of pillaging public treasuries in order to extend their own period in office. Will Americans permit incumbents of both parties to mortgage our future to pay off the interests that finance their elections?

In addition to the candidates offered for president at this critical juncture by the two major parties, there are third party possibilities. . . .

The media presented Colin Powell as a "perfect" candidate, but he is someone with a weak understanding of the unhappiness of contemporary Americans. There is a real rebellion welling up in American politics, and Powell has so far operated as if he is totally oblivious to this fact. He looks and sounds like a leader, but he doesn't have anything to say about the issues over which Americans are in revolt.

In Ross Perot, on the other hand, we have an imperfect candidate with a shrewd understanding of the discontent in American politics. The national establishment dislikes Perot every bit as much as they love Powell, but Perot says what the discontented middle wants to hear. Now he faces the decision of whether to run at the top of the new political party whose state-by-state founding he has committed himself to funding.

One thing Perot's move to create a national party for independents has done is to virtually preclude a Powell run at the head of a third party. Unless Powell is prepared to do business with Perot, which seems unlikely, there is probably no room for him as an independent. (For that matter, I doubt he could have won the primary nomination of the Republican party this year.) The most likely option for Colin Powell is to run as vice-president.

I believe, however, that Perot is the third player who will shape much of the content of the 1996 race, as he did in 1992. If he wants the issues about which he cares presented to the American public, I think Perot has no choice but to run. When he does, he will attack the two parties for their persistent failures over the past generation. His themes—breaking the hold of lobbyists on Washington, restoring choice to elections, ending budget deficits, reducing mandates and unfunded liabilities—resonate with Americans. Perot will spend liberally to get these messages across.

The problem for Perot is that voters like much of the message but not necessarily the messenger. Perot doesn't seem much to care about this, but he should. Voters who dislike Perot will not tune in to his television presentations, regardless of the content. He doesn't have the curiosity factor going for him that he did in 1992. Moreover, Americans intuitively understand that governing is a collective enterprise, and they will rebel against the idea of Perot in the White House unless he broadens the visible leadership within his campaign.

The more successful Perot is, the more likely it is that the election will be defined by reform issues—whereas a run by Colin Powell would have focused the election away from issues onto personalities. Powell probably doesn't think of himself as the enemy of reform, but his general popularity coupled with his insulation from the discontent in America make him just that. Electing Colin Powell would have enormously set back reform in Washington. At least Clinton and Dole and today's other candidates have the public sensitivity to acknowledge that Americans are massively discontented.

Discussion Questions

1. Are the obstacles to the formation of third parties structural and institutional (as Berns argues), or more rooted in the type of candidates who run as third party candidates (as Black suggests)? Explain.

2. What impact would a strong third party have on the political process? What impact did minor parties have on the presidential campaign in 1996?

THE DEBATE: PARTY POLITICS IN AMERICA: SHOULD THE TWO-PARTY SYSTEM BE STRENGTHENED?

Should the Republican and Democratic parties be stronger organizations, playing a more definitive role in government and in the determination of voter choices? Could our democracy be improved and citizen participation increased by the creation of a third or even a fourth party that could offer alternative policy and candidate choices not currently embraced by the two major parties? Or does the system work fine just the way it is—and even as the founders intended it to?

In 1950, the Committee on Political Parties within the American Political Science Association (the professional organization for political scientists) put forth the definitive defense of the two-party system and argued for making the system stronger. A "responsible two-party system," it argued, was essential to insure a broad base of political support for the winning party—a necessary characteristic of democratic governance. In the committee's view, not only did third parties contradict political tradition in the United States, but if they could not offer a strong challenge to the party in power, they could not offer voters a meaningful choice. A strong opposition, instead, was more likely under a two-party system. More important, a strong party was necessary to govern in the contemporary political world. Winning parties must be able to define broad programs and policies that integrate the vast activities of modern government.

The connection between stronger political parties and bigger government, according to Everett Carll Ladd, is precisely the reason why we should *not* work to strengthen the two major political parties. Ladd argues that rather than drawing Americans into the political process, stronger political parties will only increase the discontent with a national government that tries to do too much, poorly. Parties able to define, pass, and implement broad public policies are not necessarily any more appealing to voters than parties caught in a system of separated powers and checks and balances. Comparisons between voter satisfaction with European parties and elected officials, and parties and officials in the United States, Ladd claims, bears out this point. More important, Ladd argues, voters seem to prefer government divided between the two parties in the Congress and the White House, rather than government by one party with a mandate to pursue broad policy changes. Although parties have been weakened in some respects, Ladd states that they have also been strengthened in others. "They remain," he concludes, "about as much of a presence as the public wants or will abide."

Two recent developments would please the APSA of 1950. First, in 1994, the Republicans played the role of a strong opposition party, offering voters the Contract With America, an alternative platform for governing the country. Congressional Democrats also followed this strategy in the 1996 elections with their "Families First" agenda. This renewed focus on serious policy platforms suggests the two-party system is alive and well, offering voters clear alternatives and some confidence that the positions will be acted upon. Second, a 1996 Supreme Court decision, *Colorado Republican Federal Campaign Committee et al. v. Federal Election Commission*, was a major victory for political parties. The Court held that "soft money" expenditures targeted at "party-building activities" could not be limited by the state. This ensures that political parties will continue to play an important role in political campaigns.

54
"A Report of the Committee on Political Parties: Toward a More Responsible Two-Party System"

AMERICAN POLITICAL SCIENCE ASSOCIATION

The Need for Greater Party Responsibility

The Role of the Political Parties

1. *The Parties and Public Policy* Throughout this report political parties are treated as indispensable instruments of government. That is to say, we proceed on the proposition that *popular government in a nation of more than 150 million people requires political parties which provide the electorate with a proper range of choice between alternatives of action.* The party system thus serves as the main device for bringing into continuing relationship those ideas about liberty, majority rule and leadership which Americans are largely taking for granted.

For the great majority of Americans, the most valuable opportunity to influence the course of public affairs is the choice they are able to make between the parties in the principal elections. While in an election the party alternative necessarily takes the form of a choice between candidates, putting a particular candidate into office is not an end in itself. The concern of the parties with candidates, elections and appointments is misunderstood if it is assumed that parties can afford to bring forth aspirants for office without regard to the views of those so selected. Actually, the party struggle is concerned with the direction of public affairs. Party nominations are no more than a means to this end. In short, party politics inevitably involves public policy in one way or another. *In order to keep the parties apart, one must consider the relations between each and public policy.*

This is not to ignore that in the past the American two-party system has shown little propensity for evolving original or creative ideas about public policy; that it has even been rather sluggish in responding to such ideas in the public interest; that it reflects in an enlarged way those differences throughout the country which are expressed in the operation of the federal structure of government; and that in all political organizations a considerable measure of irrationality manifests itself.

Giving due weight to each of these factors, we are nevertheless led to conclude that the choices provided by the two-party system are valuable to the American people in proportion to their definition in terms of public policy. *The reasons for the growing emphasis on public policy in party politics are to be found, above all, in the very operations of modern government.* With the extraordinary growth of the responsibilities of government, the discussion of public affairs for the most part makes sense only in terms of public policy.

2. *The New Importance of Program*   One of the most pressing requirements of contemporary politics is for the party in power to furnish a general kind of direction over the government as a whole. *The crux of public affairs lies in the necessity for more effective formulation of general policies and programs and for better integration of all of the far-flung activities of modern government.*

Only large-scale and representative political organizations possess the qualifications needed for these tasks. The ascendancy of national issues in an industrial society, the impact of the widening concern of government with problems of the general welfare, the entrance into the realm of politics of millions of new voters—all of these factors have tended to broaden the base of the parties as the largest political organizations in the country. *It is in terms of party programs that political leaders can attempt to consolidate public attitudes toward the work plans of government.*

Modern public policy, therefore, accentuates the importance of the parties, not as mere brokers between different groups and interests, but as agencies of the electorate. Because it affects unprecedented numbers of people and because it depends for its execution on extensive and widespread public support, modern public policy requires a broad political base. That base can be provided only by the parties, which reach people touched by no other political organization.

3. The Potentialities of the Party System *The potentialities of the two-party system are suggested, on the one hand, by the fact that for all practical purposes the major parties monopolize elections; and, on the other, by the fact that both parties have in the past managed to adapt themselves to the demands made upon them by external necessities.*

Moreover, in contrast with any other political organization today in existence, the major parties even now are forced to consider public policy at least broadly enough to make it likely for them to win elections. If public esteem of the parties is much less high than it might be, the depressed state of their reputation has resulted in the main from their past indifference to broadly conceived public policy. This indifference has fixed in the popular mind the idea of spoils, patronage and plunder. It is hence not astonishing when one hears a chosen representative assert for the public ear that in his state "people put principles above party." Much of the agitation for nonpartisanship—despite the impossibility of nonpartisan organization on a national level—is rooted in the same attitudes.

Bad reputations die hard, but things are no longer what they used to be. Certainly success in presidential campaigns today is based on broad national appeals to the widest possible constituencies. To a much greater extent than in the past, elections are won by influences and trends that are felt throughout the country. *It is therefore good practical politics to reconsider party organization in the light of the changing conditions of politics.*

It appeared desirable in this report to relate the potentialities of the party system to both the conditions that confront the nation and the expected role of the parties. *Happily such an effort entails an application of ideas about the party system that are no longer unfamiliar.*

Consideration of ways and means of producing a more responsible party system leads into the hazards of political invention. This is a challenge that has usually been accepted with misgivings by political scientists, who are trained to describe what is and feel less well qualified to fashion innovations. We hope that our own effort will stimulate both other political scientists and participants in practical politics to attempt similar undertakings on their own account. Only by a continuous process of invention and adjustment can the party system be adapted to meet the needs of our day.

What Kind of Party System Is Needed?

There is little point to talking about the American party system in terms of its deficiencies and potentialities except against a picture of what the parties ought to be. Our report would be lacking in exactness without an indication of the sort of model we have in mind.

Americans are reasonably well agreed about the purposes served by the two major parties as long as the matter is discussed in generalities.

When specific questions are raised, however, agreement is much more limited. We cannot assume, therefore, a commonly shared view about the essential characteristics of the party system. But we can and must state our own view.

In brief, our view is this: *The party system that is needed must be democratic, responsible and effective*—a system that is accountable to the public, respects and expresses differences of opinion, and is able to cope with the great problems of modern government. Some of the implications warrant special statement, which is the purpose of this section.

A Stronger Two-party System

1. *The Need for an Effective Party System* In an era beset with problems of unprecedented magnitude at home and abroad, it is dangerous to drift without a party system that helps the nation to set a general course of policy for the government as a whole. In a two-party system, when both parties are weakened or confused by internal divisions or ineffective organization it is the nation that suffers. When the parties are unable to reach and pursue responsible decisions, difficulties accumulate and cynicism about all democratic institutions grows.

An effective party system requires, first, that the parties are able to bring forth programs to which they commit themselves and, second, that the parties possess sufficient internal cohesion to carry out these programs. In such a system, the party program becomes the work program of the party, so recognized by the party leaders in and out of the government, by the party body as a whole, and by the public. This condition is unattainable unless party institutions have been created through which agreement can be reached about the general position of the party.

Clearly *such a degree of unity within the parties cannot be brought about without party procedures that give a large body of people an opportunity to share in the development of the party program.* One great function of the party system is to bring about the widest possible consent in relation to defined political goals, which provides the majority party with the essential means of building public support for the policies of the government. Democratic procedures in the internal affairs of the parties are best suited to the development of agreement within each party.

2. *The Need for an Effective Opposition Party* The argument for a stronger party system cannot be divorced from measures designed to make the parties more fully accountable to the public. *The fundamental requirement of such accountability is a two-party system in which the opposition party acts as the critic of the party in power, developing, defining and presenting the policy alternatives which are necessary for a true choice in reaching public decisions.*

Beyond that, the case for the American two-party system need not be restated here. The two-party system is so strongly rooted in the political traditions of this country and public preference for it is so well established that consideration of other possibilities seems entirely academic. When we speak of the parties without further qualification, we mean throughout our report the two major parties. The inference is not that we consider third or minor parties undesirable or ineffectual within their limited orbit. Rather, we feel that the minor parties in the longer run have failed to leave a lasting imprint upon both the two-party system and the basic processes of American government.

In spite of the fact that the two-party system is part of the American political tradition, it cannot be said that the role of the opposition party is well understood. This is unfortunate because democratic government is greatly influenced by the character of the opposition party. The measures proposed elsewhere in our report to help the party in power to clarify its policies are equally applicable to the opposition.

The opposition most conducive to responsible government is an organized party opposition, produced by the organic operation of the two-party system. When there are two parties identifiable by the kinds of action they propose, the voters have an actual choice. On the other hand, the sort of opposition presented by a coalition that cuts across party lines, as a regular thing, tends to deprive the public of a meaningful alternative. When such coalitions are formed after the elections are over, the public usually finds it difficult to understand the new situation and to reconcile it with the purpose of the ballot. Moreover, on that basis it is next to impossible to hold either party responsible for its political record. This is a serious source of public discontent.

* * *

55
"Of Political Parties Great and Strong: A Dissent"

EVERETT CARLL LADD

For most of this century, political science orthodoxy has held that American political parties need strengthening, to the end of improving the quality of the nation's democracy. For the last twenty years [since 1975], the Committee for Party Renewal has carried high the torch for stronger parties with this message embodied in its statement of principles: "Parties are indispensable to the realization of democracy. The stakes are no less than that."

The committee believes that party organization must be revitalized and refurbished, that political parties need to be more coherent and programmatic participators in government, and that the ties of individual voters to parties need to be made deeper and more evidently influential in voting decisions. In this view, a bigger party presence is the *sine qua non* [essential condition] of improving governmental performance and thus of restoring citizen confidence in the political system.

My own dissatisfaction with this view has been rising steadily. Over the years I have come to realize that the argument for stronger parties is at its base an argument for a larger government. It rests on a bundle of normative assumptions about what government should do, not on inherent democratic requirements. It goes hand in hand with arguments that the United States needs more government to solve problems, that the checks and balances system has been a terrible barrier to getting needed programs enacted, and finally that, in general, the good society requires a big polity. Political science has been making a statement about desired ends with regard to government's role instead of a hard analysis of the kind of party roles an effective democracy requires. This is not to say that parties are unneeded as representative institutions or that their continued weakening is desirable. Parties are needed. However, much of the contemporary unease with politics and government does not result from a diminished party role; indeed, a strengthening of parties might well exacerbate present discontent.

Tocqueville and "Great Parties"

Political scientists advocating stronger parties have often found comfort in the commentary of Alexis de Tocqueville. Tocqueville did not deal with the strength of voter ties to parties or the internal discipline of parties in government. But he did seem to come down on the side of an enlarged party presence in his discussion of "large" or "great" and "minor" or "small" parties. "The political parties that I style great," he wrote in the first volume of *Democracy in America*, "are those which cling to principles rather than to their consequences; to general and not to special cases; to ideas and not to men. These parties are usually distinguished by nobler features, more generous passions, more genuine convictions, and a more bold and open conduct than the others. In them private interest, which always plays the chief part in political passions, is more studiously veiled under the pretext of the public good. . . ." Large parties, then, are ones with a larger reach in ideas and principles, which contend with one another to determine the fundamental direction of a polity. The Washington-Adams-Hamilton Federalists were in Tocqueville's view a great party, as were Jefferson's Republicans.

In contrast, the America of Andrew Jackson's presidency, which Tocqueville visited, had, in the Frenchman's view, only "small" parties. "[I]t happens that when a calm state succeeds a violent revolution," he wrote, "great men seem suddenly to disappear and the powers of the human mind to lie concealed." He paints a rather despairing picture of small parties. Thus, they "are generally deficient in political good faith. As they are not sustained or dignified by lofty purposes, they ostensibly display the selfishness of their character in their actions. They glow with a factitious zeal; their language is vehement, but their conduct is timid and irresolute. The means which they employ are as wretched as the end at which they aim."

It's easy to see what Tocqueville had in mind by these references. The party activity he witnessed in the 1830s often seemed petty. It involved a highly developed interest in patronage, but often failed to aim for loftier goals. It was a time of consummate party "wheeler-dealers." "Party bosses" made their appearance on our political stage then. The reach of the conflict between the "Jackson men" and the "Adams men" seemed to Tocqueville petty in comparison to the struggle between the Federalists and the Antifederalists over the institutional future of the American Revolution—and so, of course, it was.

But great intuitive thinker that he was, Tocqueville recognized a flaw in his own reasoning and preferences, which led him to qualify his initial distinction. "Society is convulsed by great parties," he continued, [but] "it is only agitated by minor ones; it is torn by the former, by the latter it is [only] degraded. . . . America has had great parties, but has them no longer; and if her happiness is thereby considerably increased, her morality has suffered."

Narrow, often self-serving patronage parties are not an ideal many of us wish to defend, and Tocqueville certainly did not defend them. Still, he felt compelled to argue that the absence of great parties in the United States of the 1830s meant that the nation's "happiness is thereby considerably increased." And, seeing much to commend in the earlier American experience with great parties, he felt obliged to observe nonetheless that society in general "is convulsed" by them. Whatever was he talking about?

Just this. There is real splendor in seeing a party of large reach and high principle do battle in a time of great transition in a polity. The spectacle is all the more attractive, naturally, if that truly great party wins. Tocqueville's European experience made him keenly aware, of course, that it was by no means certain it would win.

Beyond this, nineteenth-century liberal that he was, Tocqueville recognized that having people consumed by politics is not a proper goal for the polity in the long run. There will be times when they must be so absorbed, and one devoutly hoped the parties of that day would serve them well in their search for better government. But much of the time a more prosaic existence has its attractions. This is what Tocqueville meant when he said that a kind of normalization of politics in Jacksonian America contributed to the happiness of the people. A less "politicized" environment has its virtues—in contentment if not grandeur.

From Great Parties to Strong Parties . . . and Strong Government

It is not by chance that the United States, where political parties are institutionally weaker than in any other industrial democracy, is also the country where the reach of the national government—though it has expanded greatly in recent decades—is still the most restricted. More collectivist, less individualist political outlooks encourage the formation of stronger, more elite-directed parties, and such parties are in turn powerful instruments for state action. Granted, a strong, disciplined party may on occasion be used, as it was in part in Margaret Thatcher's Britain, to dismantle programs enacted by earlier governments, Labour and Conservative alike. But on the whole, one wants strong parties in order to advance "positive" government—to enact and enlarge programs. E. E. Schattschneider made the point clearly in his classic *The Struggle for Party Government* in 1948:

"As a nation we have had little opportunity to prepare ourselves for the realization that it is now necessary for the government to act as it has never acted before. . . . The essence of the governmental crisis consists of a deficiency of the power to create, adopt, and execute a comprehensive plan of action in advance of a predictable catastrophe in time to prevent and minimize it. . . . The central difficulty of the whole system—the difficulty which causes all of the difficulties—is the fact the government characteristically suffers from a deficiency of the power to govern."

While the proposition has rarely received systematic empirical examination, some political scientists have at least questioned whether strong parties have in fact been associated with sounder policy. Leon D. Epstein has observed, for instance, that both Don K. Price and Pendleton Herring concluded at the end of the Depression decade that the disciplined party leadership found in the United Kingdom might well have produced far less desirable policy results than America's relatively weak and decentralized parties operating in a system of vastly separated and checked authority. Whether strong parties tend to advance sounder policy is, admittedly, a huge and complex empirical question. But until it is seen as an empirical question, treatment of it cannot advance much beyond the position—"Well, that's what I want anyway!" I find nothing in the canon of American political science that gives more empirical weight to the critics of the present workings of the separation of powers than to the proponents. Evidence seems at least as strong for the argument that America's system of separated power, relatively uncurbed by strong and disciplined parties, has improved public policy by helping to slow the rush of government expansion and lessen the likelihood of ill-considered, precipitant actions.

Questioning the Ideal of "Maximalist Politics"

The idea that "more politics" is more or less automatically desirable is deeply entrenched in contemporary political commentary—in the writings of political scientists, journalists, and other analysts. We see this in the literature on nonvoting. With some notable exceptions, much of the work on voter turnout sees low turnout as a huge problem, as a failure of democracy.

One may advocate efforts to promote vigorous citizenship—including encouraging voting—without subscribing to the argument that the relatively low turnout in the United States—about 56 percent of the adult resident population cast votes for president in 1992, for example—is on its face evidence of a grievous weakness in our democratic life. But many have argued that it does indicate just that. Thus Arthur T. Hadley wrote, "America's present problem . . . is an apathetic, cross-pressured society with strong feelings of political impotence, where more and more people find their lives out of control, believe in luck, and refrain from voting. These growing numbers of refrainers hang over our democratic process like a bomb, ready to explode and change the course of our history. . . . For us, now, an increase in voting is a sign of political health." Gary R. Orren argues that "if the health of a democracy can be measured by the level of popular participation in its electoral system, ours is ailing."

The argument is riddled with flaws. Consider, for example, Hadley's view that America is beset by an increasingly widespread decline of social obligation and participation—a surge in the number of "refrainers." This is simply not true. Voter turnout *has* declined from the 1960 level —the highest in this century. (Even here, it's worth noting that turnout in 1992 was almost exactly the same as it was in 1936—a presidential election in which Franklin Roosevelt and the New Deal had presumably galvanized the population to action.) But outside of voting, the data do not support an argument that participation is in decline. A study done in 1990 under the direction of Sidney Verba, Kay L. Schlozman, Henry R. Brady, and Norman H. Nie, showed once again a populace that is highly participatory in most areas of political activity (such as contributing money to political organizations, getting in contact with government officials, and the like) and even more so in nonpolitical public affairs (from a vast variety of organizational memberships to charitable giving and voluntary action).

Similarly, new findings in the United States and in Western Europe show that (1) charitable giving and voluntary action levels are increasing, not decreasing, in the United States, and (2) the levels dwarf those in Western Europe.

Returning to the matter of voter turnout as such, many different factors account for the American experience of relatively low participation. Not all of these are cause for concern. Ivor Crewe notes, for example, that while turnout in a given national election in the United States falls below that in Western Europe, Americans go to the polls far more often than the citizens of any other democracy. Not surprisingly, no one election is much of a novelty. The frequency of our elections probably reduces the turnout in any one of them.

Some factors that encourage high turnout are surely undesirable. Extreme fear can be a powerful incentive to vote—so as to prevent the feared outcome. Columnist George F. Will has reminded us that in the two presidential ballots conducted in Germany in 1932, 86 and 84 percent of the electorate cast ballots. In 1933, 89 percent voted in the assembly election in which the Nazis triumphed. Will asked: "Did the high 1933 turnout make the Nazi regime especially legitimate? Were the 1932 turnouts a sign of the health of the Weimar Republic?" His answer is the right one: "The turnouts reflected the unhealthy stakes of politics then: elections determined which mobs ruled the streets and who went to concentration camps." Americans are less inclined to fear massive upheaval or a dramatic discontinuity resulting from any particular election. In this environment, some people who are less interested in politics apparently feel a degree of security sufficient to permit them not to vote.

Raising these points is not a defense of nonvoting, but an argument instead that "more politics" is not automatically a good thing. A condition in which many people feel free to concentrate their energies on other aspects of life—raising families, working in churches, volunteering their time, and giving money to charitable institutions—has much to commend it. If better citizenship education and changes in electoral processes can help more people vote as well, so much the good. But let's not in the process claim that relatively low voter turnout is a sign of an apathetic populace generally abandoning its common and collective responsibilities.

The American ideological tradition has from the country's forming insisted on the need for a large public sector and a relatively small state. Properly construed, "public sector" refers to matters of common concern and action. The public sector hardly need be just governmental. The American idea has been that our common or public concerns as a people require vigorous activity outside the sphere of government. Tocqueville remarked on this at length a century and a half ago. He noted, for example, the extraordinary interest-group activity on behalf of all kinds of issues and objectives. "The political associations that exist in the United States," he wrote, "are only a single feature in the midst of the immense assemblage of associations in that country. . . . The Americans make associations to give entertainments, to found seminaries, to build inns, to construct churches, to diffuse books, to send missionaries to the antipodes; in this manner they found hospitals, prisons, and schools. . . . Wherever at the head of some new undertaking you see the government in France, or a man of rank in England, in the United States you will be sure to find an association."

In the first volume of *Democracy*, Tocqueville had given the classic statement of the fact that—far from holding back collective energy and participation—American individualism was its very source: "In the United States associations are established to promote the public safety, commerce, industry, morality, and religion. There is no end which the human will despairs of attaining through the combined power of individuals united into a society."

Today's Public Assess Government

Over the last several decades, Americans have been expressing increasingly ambivalent feelings about the scope of government and the quality of governmental performance.

On the one hand, we have remained—despite our complaints about government's record—an optimistic people who believe that problems are something to be solved, not endured. Thus, in an age of considerable national affluence, we have fairly high expectations with regard to action in areas as wide-ranging as the environment, crime, schools, health care, and poverty. We want action in these areas and usually see governmental action as one part of the necessary response.

On the other hand, all kinds of indicators reveal doubts about the wisdom of continuing to expand government's reach. Ever since the passage of Proposition 13 in California in 1978, tax protests have been a common part of the American political experience, and a highly democratic one at that. That is, the strongest insistence that tax hikes be curbed has often come from the lower half of the income spectrum, not from the upper half. In general, at the same time we are endorsing major interventions by government, we are calling government too big, too inefficient, too intrusive. Given the choice between government that does more and costs more, and that which does less and costs less, we are indicating a strong preference for the latter.

Many Americans are evidently angry about the performance of the country's political institutions. Consider, for example, judgments about Congress. Surveys from the 1940s through the 1960s consistently showed the national legislature getting pretty good marks. When Gallup asked in 1958 whether Congress was doing a good or poor job, it found only 12 percent saying poor. In a June 1970 survey, Gallup showed its respondents a card on which there were 10 boxes, numbered from +5 (for institutions "you like very much") down to –5 ("dislike very much").

Only 3 percent assigned Congress to the –4 and –5 boxes, and only 10 percent gave it a negative rating of any kind. Thirty-six percent gave it either a +4 or a +5. Things are surely different now. A number of survey organizations regularly ask their respondents whether they approve or disapprove of the way Congress is doing its job. The proportions bounce around, depending on the overall national mood and the latest headlines on congressional doings. But with a few brief exceptions, one of which was at the onset of the Gulf War, the proportions saying they approve Congress's performance has remained in the range of one-fourth to one-third of the public. In 64 iterations of this question for the period from 1989 through January 1994, only 27 percent of respondents, on average, put themselves in the "approve" column.

Today Americans' complaints about governmental performance are generally sweeping. The expectations of government from this highly ambivalent and conflicted public seems reasonably well heeded by the current system. Looking at the almost $1.5 trillion federal budget enacted for FY '94, it's hard to make the case that governmental action has been throttled. At the same time, a public that is dubious about government's performance and about the wisdom of expanding state action further may be well served by a system that puts substantial checks and limits on the development of new programs.

The founders of the American system sought to establish and sustain a type of government at once energetic and limited. This admixture of seeming opposites is in a sense jarring, but it has received the continuing support of much of the populace. The levels of government today are far higher than they were in the past, but the same admixture pertains. The American system continues to produce government that is extraordinarily energetic and highly constrained.

Knowing What's Best

If Americans are ambivalent about government's proper role and reluctant to issue the call, "Charge!" and if they show no signs of wanting to strengthen political parties, why should we urge upon them steps toward a stronger and "more responsible" party system? The only defensible answer would be: because, though much of the public doesn't know it, the absence of a stronger party system is a major reason why so many people are so dissatisfied with governmental performance. Is that answer valid?

One reason to doubt its validity is the fact that dissatisfaction with government's performance is evident in nearly all of the world's industrial democracies, not just the United States. Indeed, the United States does not rank at all high comparatively on many of these measures. If many countries with strong party systems manifest as much or more dissatisfaction with governmental institutions and performance as the

United States does, the idea that strengthening our party system is likely to contribute to increased satisfaction and confidence is dubious. Admittedly, it does not necessarily reject such strengthening, since many other factors can shape confidence levels.

Today, majorities of record or near-record proportions are expressing dissatisfaction with or pessimism about their country's political and economic performance and their own personal prospects. In France, for example, a country with strong and disciplined political parties, economic pessimism is rampant, and the entire political class has come under intense criticism. The ruling Socialists were dealt a massive defeat in the 1993 elections for the National Assembly. With only a couple of exceptions, politicians of all the parties got low marks. In Great Britain, Prime Minister John Major has some of the lowest approval ratings of any British prime minister. Labour fares better, but its showing in the recent local elections where the Liberal Democrats bested it reveals a real lack of enthusiasm for the country's other major party.

The argument on behalf of stronger parties needs to be examined in three distinct arenas—party organization, party in government, and party in the electorate. The case for stronger parties in the first two seems very weak. What's more, the argument runs in precisely the opposite direction from that which the public says it wants. The public's criticism, as seen clearly in survey data, is that politics is too much captured by political insiders—for example, by the elected Democratic and Republican politicians in the national legislature—and in general that "the system" is too insulated from meaningful day-to-day popular control. The call is somehow to check and limit the political class.

The last thing this public wants is stronger party organization and stronger party apparatus in government. Its present discontents push it in a direction similar to that pursued by the Progressive Movement early in this century. The Progressives believed that the principal institutions of American representative democracy—political parties, legislatures, city councils, and the like—had been captured by "the interests," were riddled with corruption, and often had been wrested from popular control. Muckraking journalists, among them Ida M. Tarbell and Lincoln Steffens, graphically portrayed the venality and unresponsiveness that they saw as all too common in the nation's political life.

Many in the Progressive Movement concluded that the only way to cure these ills was to give individual citizens new authority to override and control representative institutions. They backed and saw enacted a host of "direct democracy" reforms: the direct primary to take nominations away from party "bosses"; initiatives and referenda, to allow the people to make laws directly; the recall, to permit voters to "kick the bums out" when they were performing badly, even before their regular terms were up. The success that the reformers had makes clear that they tapped a deep lode of resentment.

Today public frustrations resemble those of the Progressive Era and probably surpass anything between that era and our own. As in the Progressive Era, dissatisfaction gets expressed in increased backing for direct democracy. The American political culture is strongly individualistic, and we are always sympathetic to the idea of direct citizenry intervention above and beyond elections. But when things are seen going poorly in terms of the institutions' performance, direct democracy's appeal gets a special boost.

Many of the innovations of the Progressive Era, such as referenda and primaries, are in wide use today. And the public would now extend them further. But today's direct democracy agenda finds other expressions. Backing for term limits is one. Support for the Perot movement is another.

Appropriate Individualism

Political science has long favored a strengthening of parties, as opposed to more direct democracy, to deal with governmental unresponsiveness and increase popular control. The public plainly doesn't agree. Some might dismiss its evident disagreement with anything that smacks of augmenting the party apparatus and control as simply the unthinking response of a highly individualist culture. The culture *is* highly individualist. And that's not going to change, so practical politics suggests that improvements be made within its dictates. But beyond this, if Americans are at times excessively obedient to individualist assertions, it's not at all clear that they are wrong on the proper role of party organization and party machinery in government. Party leaders *are* political insiders. As modern government has mushroomed, the political class *has* become more insulated. Finding ways to check it further might permit ordinary voters to intervene more effectively and extensively in setting public policy.

The United States may not be beset by the old-fashioned venality and corruption that the Progressives faced, but the primary representative institutions often seem worlds apart from the general public, responding to insider agendas. Politics as usual inside the Beltway is highly insulated and in a sense isolated. The interests that dominate "Beltway politics" differ from those that the Progressives battled, but they may be no less insensitive to popular calls for change. The old Progressive answer of extending direct citizen authority and intervention deserves careful reconsideration as a partial answer to present-day insufficiencies and shortcomings in representative democracy.

Appropriate Party Bolstering

The one area where a strong case can be made for modest steps to strengthen the party presence involves the electorate. One of the most unusual features of the contemporary party system is the frequency with which split results are attained—for example, the Republicans winning the presidency pretty regularly, but not controlling both houses of Congress since 1954. This condition seems to have two quite different sources—one involving something that much of the public intends, but the other quite unintentional and indeed fundamentally unwanted.

The intended dimension, what I call cognitive Madisonianism, starts from the fact that Americans have historically been less troubled than their counterparts in other democracies about divided control. It accords with the general thrust and biases of separation of powers. Into this, however, it seems that something new has been added. The high measure of ambivalence that so many citizens have about government's role, and from this the doubts they entertain about both political parties, seems to be well served by electoral outcomes that frequently give each of the major parties a piece of the action.

Today's public wants somewhat contradictory things of the modern state. And it sees the Democrats and Republicans as differing significantly on the issue of government's role. Cognitive Madisonianism insists that the two parties' competing views on government's proper role be pitted one against another, as when a Republican executive pushes one way and a Democratic legislature the other. The empirical work needed to explore cognitive Madisonianism satisfactorily has not been done—despite extensive surveys on related topics. We do know that high degrees of ambivalence concerning government's role have been present over the last 25 years, but survey data show nothing comparable for earlier periods, and large segments of the public express broad approval of divided government.

Those who see evidence of cognitive Madisonianism in two-tier voting must acknowledge nonetheless that more is at work. Even in the face of pronounced voter dissatisfaction with Congress, for example, historically unprecedented majorities of incumbents of both parties have been winning reelection, and House of Representative incumbents typically win by big margins. Underlying this development are several notable features of contemporary electioneering: (1) incumbents generally enjoy huge advantages in campaign contributions, and (2) they also enjoy a big advantage in government-provided resources—notably in the very large staffs given members through the "reforms" of the late 1960s and early 1970s. House members' staff was tripled, and many members have put a large bloc of their new assistants to work back in their districts— little electoral machines available to them year-round at public expense. Finally, whereas in races for governor and U.S. senator, as well as for president, many voters know something substantial about the candidates' policy stands and records, they usually don't have much information of this kind on House members. They are likely, though, to have some vaguely favorable image of him or her, while having no impression at all of the challenger.

Getting voters to pay a bit more attention to party labels is the one thing that could upset this present dynamic. A voter might not know anything about a member of Congress's voting record, but still vote against him or her in favor of a challenger who is less known because the voter wanted to change party control, to give the "outs" a chance. There is abundant evidence that this is exactly what has happened historically. But over the last quarter-century, as incumbents have gained election resources far greater than ever before, the proportion of voters bound by significant "party awareness" has declined precipitously. "Vote for the person, not the party," is in many ways laudable. It conforms entirely to the American individualist tradition of democratic governance. Nonetheless, it sometimes works poorly, especially when large numbers of voters know little of consequence about the person. What's more, the person in Congress usually votes with his party these days. The pronounced decline of "party thinking" leaves many voters ill-equipped to express effectively the dissatisfaction they clearly feel. Voters don't like important aspects of legislative performance, for example, but voting "for the person" denies them a means of doing much to address their dissatisfaction.

As for a revival of what we have called party thinking, those who believe it is needed ultimately have to make the case. The Republicans, notably, appear to have suffered electorally from the absence of greater party thinking in a broad array of less visible legislative races. If they haven't suffered thus—that is, if much of the electorate on cognitive Madisonian or other grounds wants an essentially permanent Democratic majority in the House of Representatives—the Republicans will undoubtedly be unable to make this case successfully, regardless of the adroitness of their efforts.

A Substantial Party Presence

More than three decades ago, political scientist and historian Clinton Rossiter wrote eloquently on the virtues of a "mixed" party system, one that gives a large role to the institutional parties and at the same time to individual voters. The current assumption in political science, though, is that the mixed system is no more because the party presence has declined so markedly. This is an excessive response to current trends and an unbalanced reading of them. Some developments have reduced the party presence. The media, for example, play a much larger role in political communication generally and in the process of candidate choice than ever before—mostly at the parties' expense.

But at the same time, in other areas we have actually moved toward stronger and in a way more disciplined political parties. The vehicle of the new "discipline" isn't institutional sanctions—party leaders being able to "punish" recalcitrant members—but rather growing ideological homogeneity within each of the two major parties. Thirty years ago when Rossiter wrote *Parties and Politics in America*, the Democratic congressional party was highly irresponsible and undisciplined. It carried within it competing wings or factions, each resting on a firm local base, which could agree upon little about how the country should be governed except that they wanted the Democratic party to organize the Congress. *Congressional Quarterly* introduced in 1957 the concept "conservative coalition" votes in Congress—defining them as ones in which a majority of southern Democrats vote with a majority of Republicans against a majority of northern Democrats. "Conservative coalition voting scores" for individual members were a key *CQ* tally. The Democratic party was, then, highly irresponsible, in the sense that its southern wing often worked for aims contrary to what the national party proclaimed. As for the Republicans, while they lacked a split as wide and deep as that between the Democrats' northern and southern wings, liberal, moderate, and conservative blocs detracted from the programmatic coherence of congressional Republicanism as well.

In recent years, however, there has been a powerful movement toward greater "discipline," through the vehicle of internal philosophical agreement. Congressional Democrats today are much more coherently a liberal party, and congressional Republicans much more a conservative one than ever before. We can see this from the splendid roll-call analysis done regularly by political scientist William Schneider and his colleagues at *National Journal*. In their January 1991 report, for example, Richard E. Cohen and William Schneider noted that "bipartisanship was a rare commodity on key congressional votes in 1990. And divisions within each party narrowed, according to *National Journal*'s annual congressional vote ratings. . . . Southern Democrats and eastern Republicans, the traditional centers of ideological moderation in both the House and Senate, moved further apart in 1990. Their shifts (the southern Democrats to the Left and the eastern Republicans to the Right) were another sign of the increased partisanship [i.e., united parties arrayed against each other] in both chambers." The 1994 report by Cohen and Schneider reiterated similar findings and gave powerful evidence on the newfound responsibility of both congressional parties.

A Final Word

Today's "mixed" system is different from the one Rossiter described. But the present party system contains its own distinctive strengths as well as new elements of weakness. The parties are much more programmatically coherent and internally disciplined by ideological agreement today than in Rossiter's time. They present far clearer choices for all who care to pay attention. Advocates of stronger and more responsible parties have for the most part failed to call attention to the marked party strengthening evident in the data on the new internal coherence of the congressional Republican and Democratic parties.

The United States needs a mixed system, and it has one. Parties have been weakened in some regards but strengthened in others. They remain a substantial presence in American political life. They remain about as much of a presence as the public wants or will abide. And it is far from clear that groups such as the Committee on Party Renewal, which seek a general strengthening of parties in the electorate, as organizations, and in government, address the principal source of voter complaint—partisan unresponsiveness and a politics too dominated by institutions inside the Beltway.

DISCUSSION QUESTIONS

1. Ladd suggests that stronger parties are related to bigger government. Does the rejuvenated Republican party in Congress contradict this assertion? That is, can strong parties be used to cut the size of government? Explain.

2. Is responsible party government a realistic possibility in today's political climate? Does divided government in which one party controls the presidency and the other party controls Congress, pose an insurmountable obstacle? Why or why not?

3. What are the advantages and disadvantages of responsible party government?

CHAPTER 11

Groups and Interests

56
"Political Association in the United States"
from *Democracy in America*

ALEXIS DE TOCQUEVILLE

The right of political association has long been a cornerstone of American democracy. Alexis de Tocqueville, a French citizen who studied early nineteenth-century American society, argued that the right to associate provides an important check on a majority's power to suppress a political minority. Tocqueville pointed out that allowing citizens to associate in a variety of groups with a variety of crosscutting interests provides a political outlet for all types of political interests, and enables compromises to be reached as each interest group attempts to build support among shifting coalitions. "There is a place for individual independence," Tocqueville argued, in the American system of government. "[A]s in society, all the members are advancing at the same time toward the same goal, but they are not obliged to follow exactly the same path."

Better use has been made of association and this powerful instrument of action has been applied to more varied aims in America than anywhere else in the world.

* * *

The inhabitant of the United States learns from birth that he must rely on himself to combat the ills and trials of life; he is restless and defiant in his outlook toward the authority of society and appeals to its power only when he cannot do without it. The beginnings of this attitude first appear at school, where the children, even in their games, submit to rules settled by themselves and punish offenses which they have defined themselves. The same attitude turns up again in all the affairs of social life. If some obstacle blocks the public road halting the circulation of traffic, the neighbors at once form a deliberative body; this improvised assembly produces an executive authority which remedies the trouble before anyone has thought of the possibility of some previously constituted authority beyond that of those concerned. Where enjoyment is concerned, people associate to make festivities grander and more orderly. Finally, associations are formed to combat exclusively moral troubles: intemperance is fought in common. Public security, trade and industry, and morals and religion all provide the aims for associations in the United States. There is no end which the human will despairs of attaining by the free action of the collective power of individuals.

* * *

The right of association being recognized, citizens can use it in different ways. An association simply consists in the public and formal support of specific doctrines by a certain number of individuals who have undertaken to cooperate in a stated way in order to make these doctrines prevail. Thus the right of association can almost be identified with freedom to write, but already associations are more powerful than the press. When some view is represented by an association, it must take clearer and more precise shape. It counts its supporters and involves them in its cause; these supporters get to know one another, and numbers increase zeal. An association unites the energies of divergent minds and vigorously directs them toward a clearly indicated goal.

Freedom of assembly marks the second stage in the use made of the right of association. When a political association is allowed to form centers of action at certain important places in the country, its activity becomes greater and its influence more widespread. There men meet, active measures are planned, and opinions are expressed with that strength and warmth which the written word can never attain.

But the final stage is the use of association in the sphere of politics. The supporters of an agreed view may meet in electoral colleges and appoint mandatories to represent them in a central assembly. That is, properly speaking, the application of the representative system to one party.

* * *

In our own day freedom of association has become a necessary guarantee against the tyranny of the majority. In the United States, once a party has become predominant, all public power passes into its hands; its close supporters occupy all offices and have control of all organized forces. The most distinguished men of the opposite party, unable to cross the barrier keeping them from power, must be able to establish themselves outside it; the minority must use the whole of its moral authority to oppose the physical power oppressing it. Thus the one danger has to be balanced against a more formidable one.

The omnipotence of the majority seems to me such a danger to the American republics that the dangerous expedient used to curb it is actually something good.

Here I would repeat something which I have put in other words when speaking of municipal freedom: no countries need associations more— to prevent either despotism of parties or the arbitrary rule of a prince —than those with a democratic social state. In aristocratic nations secondary bodies form natural associations which hold abuses of power in check. In countries where such associations do not exist, if private people did not artificially and temporarily create something like them, I see no other dike to hold back tyranny of whatever sort, and a great nation might with impunity be oppressed by some tiny faction or by a single man.

*   *   *

In America the citizens who form the minority associate in the first place to show their numbers and to lessen the moral authority of the majority, and secondly, by stimulating competition, to discover the arguments most likely to make an impression on the majority, for they always hope to draw the majority over to their side and then to exercise power in its name.

Political associations in the United States are therefore peaceful in their objects and legal in the means used; and when they say that they only wish to prevail legally, in general they are telling the truth.

*   *   *

The Americans . . . have provided a form of government within their associations, but it is, if I may put it so, a civil government. There is a place for individual independence there; as in society, all the members are advancing at the same time toward the same goal, but they are not obliged to follow exactly the same path. There has been no sacrifice of will or of reason, but rather will and reason are applied to bring success to a common enterprise.

DISCUSSION QUESTIONS

1. Tocqueville argues that "freedom of association has become a necessary guarantee against the tyranny of the majority." While freedom of association is clearly a central part of any free society, what changes in our political system would suggest a rethinking of this benign view?

2. Can you think of any instances where the influence of groups should be limited (for example, political extremists such as the various militia groups, or large political action committees in political campaigns)? Explain.

57

"The Logic of Collective Action" from
The Rise and Decline of Nations

Mancur Olson

Americans organize at a tremendous rate to pursue common interests in the political arena. Yet not all groups are created equal, and some types of political organizations are much more common than others. In particular, it is far easier to organize groups around narrow economic interests than it is to organize around broad "public goods" interests. Why do some groups organize while others do not?

The nature of collective goods, according to the economist Mancur Olson, explains this phenomenon. When a collective good is provided to a group, no member of the group can be denied the benefits of the good. For example, if Congress passes a law that subsidizes a new telecommunications technology, any company that produces that technology will benefit from the subsidy. The catch is, any company will benefit even if they did not participate in the collective effort to win the subsidy. Olson argues that "the larger the number of individuals or firms that would benefit from a collective good, the smaller the share of the gains . . . that will accrue to the individual or firm." Hence, the less likely any one member of the group will contribute to the collective effort to secure the collective benefit. For smaller groups, the collective good is larger and more meaningful, and the more likely any one member of the group will be willing to make an individual sacrifice to provide a benefit shared by the entire group.

The logic helps to explain the greater difficulty "public interest groups" have in organizing and staying organized to provide such collective goods as clean air, consumer product safety, and banking regulations aimed at promoting inner city investments by banks. These goods benefit very large numbers of people, but the benefit to any one person, Olson would argue, is not sufficient for them to sacrifice time or money for the effort to succeed. This is especially true if the individual believes that he are she will benefit from the collective good, even if they do not contribute. Olson identifies "selective incentives" as one way in which these larger groups are able to overcome the incentive to "free ride" and instead contribute to the collective effort.

The Logic

The argument of this book begins with a paradox in the behavior of groups. It has often been taken for granted that if everyone in a group of individuals or firms had some interest in common, then there would be a tendency for the group to seek to further this interest. Thus many students of politics in the United States for a long time supposed that citizens with a common political interest would organize and lobby to serve that interest. Each individual in the population would be in one or more groups and the vector of pressures of these competing groups explained the outcomes of the political process. Similarly, it was often supposed that if workers, farmers, or consumers faced monopolies harmful to their interests, they would eventually attain countervailing power through organizations such as labor unions or farm organizations that obtained market power and protective government action. On a larger scale, huge social classes are often expected to act in the interest of their members; the unalloyed form of this belief is, of course, the Marxian contention that in capitalist societies the bourgeois class runs the government to serve its own interests, and that once the exploitation of the proletariat goes far enough and "false consciousness" has disappeared, the working class will in its own interest revolt and establish a dictatorship of the proletariat. In general, if the individuals in some category or class had a sufficient degree of self-interest and if they all agreed on some common interest, then the group would to some extent also act in a self-interested or group-interested manner.

If we ponder the logic of the familiar assumption described in the preceding paragraph, we can see that it is fundamentally and indisputably faulty. Consider those consumers who agree that they pay higher prices for a product because of some objectionable monopoly or tariff, or those workers who agree that their skill deserves a higher wage. Let us now ask what would be the expedient course of action for an individual consumer who would like to see a boycott to combat a monopoly or a lobby to repeal the tariff, or for an individual worker who would like a strike threat or a minimum wage law that could bring higher wages. If the consumer or worker contributes a few days and a few dollars to organize a boycott or a union or to lobby for favorable legislation, he or she will have sacrificed time and money. What will this sacrifice obtain? The individual will at best succeed in advancing the cause to a small (often imperceptible) degree. In any case he will get only a minute share of the gain from his action. The very fact that the objective or interest is common to or shared by the group entails that the gain from any sacrifice an individual makes to serve this common purpose is shared with everyone in the group. The successful boycott or strike or lobbying action will bring the better price or wage for everyone in the relevant category, so the individual in any large group with a common interest will reap only a minute share of the gains from whatever sacrifices the individual makes to achieve this common interest. Since any gain goes to everyone in the group, those who contribute nothing to the effort will get just as much as those who made a contribution. It pays to "let George do it," but George has little or no incentive to do anything in the group interest either, so (in the absence of factors that are completely left out of the conceptions mentioned in the first paragraph) there will be little, if any, group action. The paradox, then, is that (in the absence of special arrangements or circumstances to which we shall turn later) large groups, at least if they are composed of rational individuals, will *not* act in their group interest.

This paradox is elaborated and set out in a way that lets the reader check every step of the logic in a book I wrote entitled *The Logic of Collective Action.*

* * *

Organizations that provide collective goods to their client groups through political or market action . . . are . . . not supported because of the collective goods they provide, but rather because they have been fortunate enough to find what I have called *selective incentives*. A selective incentive is one that applies selectively to the individuals depending on whether they do or do not contribute to the provision of the collective good.

A selective incentive can be either negative or positive; it can, for example, be a loss or punishment imposed only on those who do *not* help provide the collective good. Tax payments are, of course, obtained with the help of negative selective incentives, since those who are found not to have paid their taxes must then suffer both taxes and penalties. The best-known type of organized interest group in modern democratic societies, the labor union, is also usually supported, in part, through negative selective incentives. Most of the dues in strong unions are obtained through union shop, closed shop, or agency shop arrangements which make dues paying more or less compulsory and automatic. There are often also informal arrangements with the same effect; David McDonald, former president of the United Steel Workers of America, describes one of these arrangements used in the early history of that union. It was, he writes, a technique

> which we called . . . visual education, which was a high-sounding label for a practice much more accurately described as dues picketing. It worked very simply. A group of dues-paying members, selected by the district director (usually more for their size than their tact) would stand at the plant gate with pick handles or baseball bats in hand and confront each worker as he arrived for his shift.[1]

As McDonald's "dues picketing" analogy suggests, picketing during strikes is another negative selective incentive that unions sometimes need; although picketing in industries with established and stable unions is usually peaceful, this is because the union's capacity to close down an enterprise against which it has called a strike is clear to all; the early phase of unionization often involves a great deal of violence on the part of both unions and anti-union employers and scabs.

* * *

Positive selective incentives, although easily overlooked, are also commonplace, as diverse examples in *The Logic* demonstrate. American farm organizations offer prototypical examples. Many of the members of the stronger American farm organizations are members because their dues payments are automatically deducted from the "patronage dividends" of farm cooperatives or are included in the insurance premiums paid to mutual insurance companies associated with the farm organizations. Any number of organizations with urban clients also provide similar positive selective incentives in the form of insurance policies, publications, group air fares, and other private goods made available only to members. The grievance procedures of labor unions usually also offer selective incentives, since the grievances of active members often get most of the attention. The symbiosis between the political power of a lobbying organization and the business institutions associated with it often yields tax or other advantages for the business institution, and the publicity and other information flowing out of the political arm of a movement often generates patterns of preference or trust that make the business activities of the movement more remunerative. The surpluses obtained in such ways in turn provide positive selective incentives that recruit participants for the lobbying efforts.

Small groups, or occasionally large "federal" groups that are made up of many small groups of socially interactive members, have an additional source of both negative and positive selective incentives. Clearly most people value the companionship and respect of those with whom they interact. In modern societies solitary confinement is, apart from the rare death penalty, the harshest legal punishment. The censure or even ostracism of those who fail to bear a share of the burdens of collective action can sometimes be an important selective incentive. An extreme example of this occurs when British unionists refuse to speak to uncooperative colleagues, that is, "send them to Coventry." Similarly, those in a socially interactive group seeking a collective good can give special respect or honor to those who distinguish themselves by their sacrifices in the interest of the group and thereby offer them a positive selective incentive. Since most people apparently prefer relatively like-minded or agreeable and respectable company, and often prefer to associate with those whom they especially admire, they may find it costless to shun those who shirk the collective action and to favor those who over-subscribe.

Social selective incentives can be powerful and inexpensive, but they are available only in certain situations. As I have already indicated, they have little applicability to large groups, except in those cases in which the large groups can be federations of small groups that are capable of social interaction. It also is not possible to organize most large groups in need of a collective good into small, socially interactive subgroups, since most individuals do not have the time needed to maintain a huge number of friends and acquaintances.

The availability of social selective incentives is also limited by the social heterogeneity of some of the groups or categories that would benefit from a collective good. Everyday observation reveals that most socially interactive groups are fairly homogeneous and that many people resist extensive social interaction with those they deem to have lower status or greatly different tastes. Even Bohemian or other nonconformist groups often are made up of individuals who are similar to one another, however much they differ from the rest of society. Since some of the categories of individuals who would benefit from a collective good are socially heterogeneous, the social interaction needed for selective incentives sometimes cannot be arranged even when the number of individuals involved is small.

*   *   *

In short, the political entrepreneurs who attempt to organize collective action will accordingly be more likely to succeed if they strive to organize relatively homogeneous groups. The political managers whose task it is to maintain organized or collusive action similarly will be motivated to use indoctrination and selective recruitment to increase the homogeneity of their client groups. This is true in part because social selective incentives are more likely to be available to the more nearly homogeneous groups, and in part because homogeneity will help achieve consensus.

Information and calculation about a collective good is often itself a collective good. Consider a typical member of a large organization who is deciding how much time to devote to studying the policies or leadership of the organization. The more time the member devotes to this matter, the greater the likelihood that his or her voting and advocacy will favor effective policies and leadership for the organization. This typical member will, however, get only a small share of the gain from the more effective policies and leadership: in the aggregate, the other members will get almost all the gains, so that the individual member does not have an incentive to devote nearly as much time to fact-finding and thinking about the organization as would be in the group interest. Each of the members of the group would be better off if they all could be coerced into spending more time finding out how to vote to make the organization best further their interests. This is dramatically evident in the case of the typical voter in a national election in a large country. The gain to such a voter from studying issues and candidates until it is clear what vote is truly in his or her interest is given by the difference in the value to the individual of the "right" election outcome as compared with the "wrong" outcome, *multiplied by the probability a change in the individual's vote will alter the outcome of the election.* Since the probability that a typical voter will change the outcome of the election is vanishingly small, the typical citizen is usually "rationally ignorant" about public affairs. Often, information about public affairs is so interesting or entertaining that it pays to acquire it for these reasons alone—this appears to be the single most important source of exceptions to the generalization that *typical* citizens are rationally ignorant about public affairs.

Individuals in a few special vocations can receive considerable rewards in private goods if they acquire exceptional knowledge of public goods. Politicians, lobbyists, journalists, and social scientists, for example, may earn more money, power, or prestige from knowledge of this or that public business. Occasionally, exceptional knowledge of public policy can generate exceptional profits in stock exchanges or other markets. Withal, the typical citizen will find that his or her income and life chances will not be improved by zealous study of public affairs, or even of any single collective good.

The limited knowledge of public affairs is in turn necessary to explain the effectiveness of lobbying. If all citizens had obtained and digested all pertinent information, they could not then be swayed by advertising or other persuasion. With perfectly informed citizens, elected officials would not be subject to the blandishments of lobbyists, since the constituents would then know if their interests were betrayed and defeat the unfaithful representative at the next election. Just as lobbies provide collective goods to special-interest groups, so their effectiveness is explained by the imperfect knowledge of citizens, and this in turn is due mainly to the fact that information and calculation about collective goods is also a collective good.

* * *

The fact that the typical individual does not have an incentive to spend much time studying many of his choices concerning collective goods also helps to explain some otherwise inexplicable individual contributions toward the provision of collective goods. The logic of collective action that has been described in this chapter is not immediately apparent to those who have never studied it; if it were, there would be nothing paradoxical in the argument with which this chapter opened, and students to whom the argument is explained would not react with initial skepticism. No doubt the practical implications of this logic for the individual's own choices were often discerned before the logic was ever set out in print, but this does not mean that they were always understood even at the intuitive and practical level. In particular, when the costs of individual contributions to collective action are very small, the individual has little incentive to investigate whether or not to make a contribution or even to exercise intuition. If the individual knows the costs of a contribution to collective action in the interest of a group of which he is a part are trivially small, he may rationally not take the trouble to consider whether the gains are smaller still. This is particularly the case since the size of these gains and the policies that would maximize them are matters about which it is usually not rational for him to investigate.

This consideration of the costs and benefits of calculation about public goods leads to the testable prediction that voluntary contributions toward the provision of collective goods for large groups without selective incentives will often occur when the costs of the individual contributions are negligible, but that they will *not* often occur when the costs of the individual contributions are considerable. In other words, when the costs of individual action to help to obtain a desired collective good are small enough, the result is indeterminate and sometimes goes one way and sometimes the other, but when the costs get larger this indeterminacy disappears. We should accordingly find that more than a few people are willing to take the moment of time needed to sign petitions for causes they support, or to express their opinions in the course of discussion, or to vote for the candidate or party they prefer. Similarly, if the argument here is correct, we should not find many instances where individuals voluntarily contribute substantial sums of resources year after year for the purpose of obtaining some collective good for some large group of which they are a part. Before parting with a large amount of money or time, and particularly before doing so repeatedly, the rational individual will reflect on what this considerable sacrifice will accomplish. If the individual is a typical individual in a large group that would benefit from a collective good, his contribution will not make a perceptible difference in the amount that is provided. The theory here predicts that such contributions become less likely the larger the contribution at issue.

Even when contributions are costly enough to elicit rational calculation, there is still one set of circumstances in which collective action can occur without selective incentives. This set of circumstances becomes evident the moment we think of situations in which there are only a few individuals or firms that would benefit from collective action. Suppose there are two firms of equal size in an industry and no other firms can enter the industry. It still will be the case that a higher price for the industry's product will benefit both firms and that legislation favorable to the industry will help both firms. The higher price and the favorable legislation are then collective goods to this "oligopolistic" industry, even though there are only two in the group that benefit from the collective goods. Obviously, each of the oligopolists is in a situation in which if it restricts output to raise the industry price, or lobbies for favorable legislation for the industry, it will tend to get half of the benefit. And the cost-benefit ratio of action in the common interest easily could be so favorable that, even though a firm bears the whole cost of its action and gets only half the benefit of this action, it could still profit from acting in the common interest. Thus if the group that would benefit from collective action is sufficiently small and the cost-benefit ratio of collective action for the group sufficiently favorable, there may well be calculated action in the collective interest even without selective incentives.

* * *

Untypical as my example of equal-sized firms may be, it makes the general point intuitively obvious: other things being equal, *the larger the number of individuals or firms that would benefit from a collective good, the smaller the share of the gains from action in the group interest that will accrue to the individual or firm that undertakes the action. Thus, in the absence of selective incentives, the incentive for group action diminishes as group size increases, so that large groups are less able to act in their common interest than small ones.* If an additional individual or firm that would value the collective good enters the scene, then the share of the gains from group-oriented action that anyone already in the group might take must diminish. This holds true whatever the relative sizes or valuations of the collective good in the group.

* * *

The significance of the logic that has just been set out can best be seen by comparing groups that would have the same net gain from collective action, if they could engage in it, but that vary in size. Suppose there are a million individuals who would gain a thousand dollars each, or a billion in the aggregate, if they were to organize effectively and engage in collective action that had a total cost of a hundred million. If the logic set out above is right, they could not organize or engage in effective collective action without selective incentives. Now suppose that, although the total gain of a billion dollars from collective action and the aggregate cost of a hundred million remain the same, the group is composed instead of five big corporations or five organized municipalities, each of which would gain two hundred million. Collective action is not an absolute certainty even in this case, since each of the five could conceivably expect others to put up the hundred million and hope to gain the collective good worth two hundred million at no cost at all. Yet collective action, perhaps after some delays due to bargaining, seems very likely indeed. In this case any one of the five would gain a hundred million from providing the collective good even if it had to pay the whole cost itself; and the costs of bargaining among five would not be great, so they would sooner or later probably work out an agreement providing for the collective action. The numbers in this example are arbitrary, but roughly similar situations occur often in reality, and the contrast between "small" and "large" groups could be illustrated with an infinite number of diverse examples.

The significance of this argument shows up in a second way if one compares the operations of lobbies or cartels within jurisdictions of vastly different scale, such as a modest municipality on the one hand and a big country on the other. Within the town, the mayor or city council may be influenced by, say, a score of petitioners or a lobbying budget of a thousand dollars. A particular line of business may be in the hands of only a few firms, and if the town is distant enough from other markets only these few would need to agree to create a cartel. In a big country, the resources needed to influence the national government are likely to be much more substantial, and unless the firms are (as they sometimes are) gigantic, many of them would have to cooperate to create an effective cartel. Now suppose that the million individuals in our large group in the previous paragraph were spread out over a hundred thousand towns or jurisdictions, so that each jurisdiction had ten of them, along with the same proportion of citizens in other categories as before. Suppose also that the cost-benefit ratios remained the same, so that there was still a billion dollars to gain across all jurisdictions or ten thousand in each, and that it would still cost a hundred million dollars across all jurisdictions or a thousand in each. It no longer seems out of the question that in many jurisdictions the groups of ten, or subsets of them, would put up the thousand-dollar total needed to get the thousand for each individual. Thus we see that, if all else were equal, small jurisdictions would have more collective action per capita than large ones.

Differences in intensities of preference generate a third type of illustration of the logic at issue. A small number of zealots anxious for a particular collective good are more likely to act collectively to obtain that good than a larger number with the same aggregate willingness to pay. Suppose there are twenty-five individuals, each of whom finds a given collective good worth a thousand dollars in one case, whereas in another there are five thousand, each of whom finds the collective good worth five dollars. Obviously, the argument indicates that there would be a greater likelihood of collective action in the former case than in the latter, even though the aggregate demand for the collective good is the same in both. The great historical significance of small groups of fanatics no doubt owes something to this consideration.

The argument in this chapter predicts that those groups that have access to selective incentives will be more likely to act collectively to obtain collective goods than those that do not, and that smaller groups will have a greater likelihood of engaging in collective action than larger ones. The empirical portions of *The Logic* show that this prediction has been correct for the United States.

* * *

DISCUSSION QUESTIONS

1. Does our individual calculation of the benefits and costs associated with participating in a collective endeavor explain why some groups organize and others do not? Can you think of other considerations that would play a role? Explain.

2. Think of your own decisions to join or not join a group. Have you ever been a "free rider"? If so, what would it have taken to get you to join?

3. Are you more likely to "free ride" if the group is large (a national environmental group) or small (a fraternity or sorority)?

4. What does Olson's argument say about Tocqueville's view about the role of groups in overcoming the potential tyranny of majority?

NOTES

1. David J. McDonald, *Union Man* (New York: Dutton, 1969), p. 121.

58

"Connections Still Count"

W. John Moore

Just as some groups are more likely to organize and stay organized to pursue their agenda in the political process, some groups will have more access to the political process to express their views. It has become standard practice in political campaigns to attack the influence of "special interests" and the insider access of their lobbyists. Interest groups across the political and policy spectrum hire lobbyists to present their concerns to elected officials, but some lobbyists have more access than others. W. John Moore argues that despite the rhetoric of candidates concerned about special interest group influence and their highly paid lobbyists, what still matters most are the connections individual lobbyists have with members of Congress and with the White House. The influence of lobbyists' various clients—from industry-wide organizations to individual corporations to groups with social and ideological agendas—depends on the access of their lobbyists. Such an intimate approach to political influence might be very effective and efficient for the groups hiring the lobbyists, but it clearly raises questions about the individual voter's access to, and influence on, the governing process.

Clara Nomee, chairwoman of the Crow Tribal Council, came to Washington last fall seeking approval for treaty changes that would bring millions of dollars to her Montana tribe. She visited Capitol Hill, talked to Interior Department officials and met with top White House officials.

But the highlight of Nomee's trip was a visit to the Oval Office. President Clinton wasn't there, but she wrapped her arms around his chair and prayed aloud in Crow, beseeching the Great Spirit, Akabaadatea, to watch over the President and the American people.

Nomee's precious minutes in the inner sanctum were arranged by Betsey Wright, executive vice president of the Wexler Group, a Washington public affairs firm that represents the Crow council.

Wright is new to the lobbying business. But she was Clinton's chief of staff during most of his 12 years in the Arkansas governor's office and was a key aide and troubleshooter during his 1992 presidential campaign. As a result, she knows many members of the White House staff. Her telephone calls are returned. And she gets Wexler's clients into the White House.

For all the talk that lobbying has evolved into a science like astrophysics or a skill like throwing a split-fingered fastball, the successful Washington influence merchant still needs what one top lobbyist calls "stroke." Connections still count.

Wright is among a handful of rookie Washington lobbyists who have parlayed brains, experience, savvy and—yes, access—into thriving careers.

"It's always been easy to throw a rock through any window in downtown Washington and hit someone with a great story to tell," veteran lobbyist Charlie McBride said. "But unless you have access to somebody willing to hear your story, it doesn't do you much good."

Friends of Bill have descended on Washington, much as Californians did during the Reagan years and Georgians did during the Carter era. The Rose Law Firm in Little Rock, Ark., former home of Hillary Rodham Clinton and several top Administration officials, has opened a Washington office. The Washington lobbying firm Global USA just hired a former roommate of the President's, Paul Berry, who now represents several health care companies.

Or consider former Rep. Beryl F. Anthony Jr., D-Ark., who joined the Washington office of the Chicago-based law firm of Winston & Strawn after being defeated for reelection in 1992.

Anthony, a former Ways and Means Committee member and onetime chairman of the Democratic Congressional Campaign Committee, has been spotted with Clinton at Georgetown University basketball games. On election night in 1992, he watched the returns with Bill and Hillary in the Arkansas governor's mansion. The President picked Anthony's wife, Sheila Foster Anthony, to be the Justice Department's top lobbyist.

Congressional ethics rules prohibited Anthony from lobbying on Capitol Hill for a year after leaving office. But corporate clients still flocked to him. For example, four drug companies reportedly paid him $400,000 to lobby the White House to keep tax breaks for companies doing business in Puerto Rico.

In an interview, Anthony said that he has talked with a number of White House officials, including chief of staff Thomas F. (Mack) McLarty III, "although not as often as you would suspect." His style, he said, is to contact high-level officials when an issue is close to being resolved. "Then you make your argument, and they can accept it or reject it," he added.

Lobbyists familiar with Anthony's effort to preserve the Puerto Rico tax break said he used that strategy to perfection for his pharmaceutical company clients. "Beryl really knows how to play the game," a drug company lobbyist said.

Anthony said that he did not talk to McLarty specifically about the Puerto Rico tax issue. Nevertheless, McLarty helped press a compromise on Sen. David Pryor, D-Ark., a key Finance Committee member and a chief foe of the tax break, whom Anthony could not have contacted directly.

And Anthony's Clinton connections are clearly on the minds of his clients. A spokesman for the American Hospital Association said last year that the group hired Anthony because of his knowledge of the Clinton Administration.

And what prospective client wouldn't be impressed by this scenario: At a recent ceremony marking the signing of the Brady gun control bill, Clinton heralded Anthony as a hero for supporting legislation that might have cost him his congressional seat.

"When the President of the United States gets up and pays tribute to you at a bill signing, you don't have to worry about getting your phone calls returned," lobbyist McBride marveled.

"Access and influence flourish in Washington. If you served in the government or the campaign and you know a lot of people, you are going to make a lot of money," said Charles Lewis, executive director of the Center for Public Integrity, a Washington-based group that monitors government ethics. "Things have not changed one whit."

Or, as a Washington lobbyist put it recently as he finished a lunch of *agnolotti* at Tiberio's: "Clout happens."

Snaring Clients

Some lobbyists say that their business has changed markedly in recent years. The days of booze, money and women are mostly gone. Access is only part of the game: subtlety and decorum are treasured; blatant abuse of connections seldom works. The style "is no longer Dodge City. It is more Madison Avenue," said Michael Colopy, a Washington lobbyist with the Minneapolis-based law firm of O'Connor & Hannan.

Still, the rewards for new lobbyists with good Capitol Hill or executive branch contacts continue to grow. At Winston & Strawn, Anthony has teamed up with Dennis E. Eckart of Ohio, a House Democrat who left office a year ago and was the target of unusually heavy wooing by law and lobbying firms. In less than a year, the dynamic duo has brought Winston & Strawn almost 25 new clients, almost all of them blue-chip corporations and major trade associations embroiled in megabattles over such issues as health care reform and the superfund program.

Another star is Robert J. Leonard, the former chief counsel and staff director of the House Ways and Means Committee. Leonard formed a law firm with two seasoned lobbyists, William C. Oldaker and Thomas M. Ryan, early last year. The firm has already landed a raft of clients, including the Alliance for Managed Competition, a coalition of the nation's five largest health insurance companies. The group's success or failure in lobbying on health care reform will be determined in large measure by Leonard's old committee.

* * *

In a report released in September, Public Citizen Inc.'s Congress Watch, a Washington-based watchdog group, found that 180 former executive and legislative branch officials had become lobbyists or Washington lawyers since Election Day 1992. The report contained "profiles in chutzpah" of Anthony, Eckart and others who had neatly sidestepped ethics laws to become top lobbyists.

But many lobbyists say that Public Citizen is hopelessly naive. They argue that talent, not connections, produces clients. Many former Members and aides flop as lobbyists. The successful newcomers "understand the system and they like politics, so it is no surprise that they are doing well," said Joel Jankowsky, a Washington lobbyist with the law firm of Akin, Gump, Strauss, Hauer & Feld.

The best lobbyists package their skills with their connections. Tax lobbyist John P. Winburn, a partner in the Washington law firm of Winburn & Jenkins, likens Washington lobbying to representing a drunk driver in a southern town. You hire a lawyer with a winning record, Winburn said. But you also look for somebody who's on the town council or— better yet—a deacon at the local church.

Winburn should know: His law partner is former Rep. Ed Jenkins, D-Ga., an influential Ways and Means member who retired at the end of 1992 and has already assembled a stable of clients, mostly companies based in Atlanta.

Another Ways and Means veteran who is assembling an impressive client list is former Rep. Thomas J. Downey, D-N.Y., who now has his own Washington consulting business and represents several health care clients and Joseph E. Seagram & Sons Inc.

Democrats aren't the only rookies who've done well: Former Rep. Norman F. Lent, R-N.Y., the ranking minority member of the Energy and Commerce Committee until his retirement a year ago, has set up a lobby shop with a former aide, Michael Scrivner, that has snared some big clients. And Nicholas Calio, who was President Bush's congressional liaison, has gone into business with Lawrence F. O'Brien III, a tax lobbyist with strong Democratic credentials.

Arkansas lawyers with friends in the Clinton White House have seen their business improve, too. S. Hubert Mayes of the Little Rock law firm of Mitchell, Williams, Selig, Gates & Woodyard was recruited by the Alliance of American Insurers to work on health care reform. One of Mayes's partners, Thomas (Ark) Monroe, a former Arkansas insurance commissioner who oversees the firm's Washington practice from Little Rock, was enlisted by Metropolitan Life Insurance Co. to work on health care.

The Wright Stuff

But when it comes to Clinton connections, almost no one can beat Wright, who has legions of friends throughout the Administration and is invited to the White House for private showings of first-run movies with the First Family. "It's nice to be friends with the President," Wright admitted in an interview.

Wright isn't the first Wexler Group partner to have enjoyed easy access to the White House. During the Reagan Administration, it was Nancy C. Reynolds, a confidant of Nancy Reagan's and former aide to then-California Gov. Ronald Reagan. During the Bush years, it was Craig L. Fuller, who had been Bush's chief of staff when he was Vice President. (Reynolds and Fuller subsequently left the firm.) "Administration-proof" is how chairman Anne Wexler once described her firm.

Wright has arranged White House appointments for a number of Wexler clients, including the American Forest and Paper Association. Last summer, the trade group was fighting parts of a proposed executive order that would have required the federal government to use recycled paper produced without chlorine. Paper company executives said that imposition of the no-chlorine requirement would cost the industry $13 billion by 1998.

"I helped them because they were having difficulty in getting an appointment and I tried to get through" the red tape, Wright said of her work for the group. Officials of the group and executives of major paper companies met with the White House's director of environmental policy, Kathleen A. McGinty. Although industry lost most of its other battles over the recycling order, the chlorine-free provision was dropped.

"I found amusing her characterization of her role as one allowing all sides an opportunity to weigh in," Richard Dennison, a senior scientist at the Environmental Defense Fund, said of Wright. "That's an argument not usually raised by industry interests."

For another Wexler client, the American Dietetics Association, Wright obtained a meeting between association officials and Carol H. Rasco, assistant to the President for domestic policy. Wright was Rasco's boss when both worked for then-Gov. Clinton. Wright also has chatted with Hillary Clinton about the need to include nutrition in the health care package. "Nutrition is an issue that the Clintons and I share a great personal interest in," she said.

Wright has also scheduled meetings at the White House and with Cabinet officials for the Los Angeles-based Century Council, a group sponsored by alcoholic beverage manufacturers that fights underage drinking and alcohol abuse.

"I don't know," Wright answered when asked how many times she has called the White House on behalf of clients. Many of her White House calls are not for paying clients, she added, but for groups that she believes deserve a top-level airing of their views. When calling for clients, she added, "I have as hard a time getting my calls returned as anyone else."

But when the Minneapolis *Star Tribune* asked in an interview in October whether she gets special attention from the White House, Wright responded: "Gosh . . . I hope so. . . . I hope working for Bill Clinton helped."

Wright confirms the accuracy of the quote. "I don't want to say Bill Clinton treats me like a stranger," she said.

Critics contend that Wright's connection to Clinton is the main reason that Wexler brought her on board. "She knows Bill Clinton as well as probably only five people in the world," Lewis of the Center for Public Integrity said. "You can't tell me she has an intricate, detailed knowledge of federal affairs."

But Wright's defenders say that she has an unparalleled understanding of what makes the Clinton White House tick. In an Administration where titles can be misleading, Wright knows how to connect the dots between the officials who actually shape policy. "She's a Clintonologist," an admiring lobbyist said.

Dale W. Snape, the Wexler Group's vice president and general manager, said that Wright was not brought on board as a "rainmaker" or to provide access to Clinton. She was hired because "she understands the decision-making apparatus in the White House. She knows how the boxes interact and how the people interact," he said. The firm has not hyped the addition of Wright in its marketing efforts, he added.

Perception and Reality

Some lobbyists warn that clients who spend big to buy access may not get their money's worth. "There is so much ignorance about how this town works," a veteran lobbyist said. "The consumer of legal and lobbying services still thinks that if you hire someone for access that you have hired a successful advocate." That explains why so many companies are hiring "the new kids on the block," the lobbyist said.

Sour grapes? Perhaps. But as former House Democratic whip Tony Coelho put it: "You don't have to have real clout to be successful. But you have to have perceived clout."

Even lobbyists who aren't trying to sell their connections are thriving. Take Peter S. Knight, a lawyer in the Washington firm of Wunder, Diefenderfer, Cannon & Thelen. A former Cornell University football player who was Albert Gore Jr.'s first Washington hire when he was elected to the House, Knight has seen his stock soar virtually overnight. He was chairman of Gore's vice presidential campaign in 1992 and deputy director for personnel on the presidential transition team. Gore's role as the Administration's point man on telecommunications boosts Knight's value even more, at a time when telecommunications has moved to the federal policy forefront.

Does Knight's connection to Gore matter? "Clients perceive it as effective, and Peter may well get some benefit from it," said Richard E. Wiley, the dean of the telecommunications bar and a partner at the law firm of Wiley, Rein & Fielding. Wiley and other lobbyists point out that Knight was considered a skilled advocate before Gore became Vice President. Still, when Bell Atlantic Corp., now [1993] locked in the hottest takeover battle in years, went looking for a Washington lawyer recently, it hired Knight.

Knight says he doesn't know whether his relationship with Gore matters much to prospective clients. "I think people rely on your judgment because you know the issues and you work hard on them and you are a straight shooter. And I like to think that I am in that category," he said.

In fact, Knight has shocked some fellow lobbyists by declining to take some clients for fear of appearing to cash in on his connections. "If people think they can hire me to gain access to a certain person, then that is not the kind of work I will undertake," he said.

But Gore's election as Vice President, a job he could have for seven more years, and the possibility that he could someday be President, augur well for Knight. "Peter is someone who has 15 years worth of perceived and real power," said Coelho, who's now a New York City investment banker.

Would Bell Atlantic have hired Knight without his connections? "Absolutely not," Coelho said. "That does not mean Peter Knight is not smart and it does not mean that he does not have ability; he does. But that is the way Washington works."

Still, lobbyists note that getting in the door is only part of their job. Once inside, they still must promote their clients' interests. "It's so much a substantive game now that there is no forgiveness for not having the brights to deliver the message," warned Lindsay D. Hooper, head of the Washington lobbying group of Hooper Hooper Owen & Gould.

Consider the credentials of Leonard, the former Ways and Means aide who is considered by many lobbyists to be the most talented staff member to leave Capitol Hill in years. "He has seen every tax bill and knows every legal theory. Any firm in the city would love to have him," said William Mike House, a lobbyist with the Washington law firm of Hogan & Hartson.

Leonard is considered such a sure bet that even if his former boss, Ways and Means chairman Dan Rostenkowski, D-Ill., were to leave Congress [as he did in 1995], it would have little impact on his lobbying future. "Rob knows the leadership as well as the Ways and Means Committee members," fellow tax lobbyist Winburn said. "He's a guy who is a treasure house of knowledge."

In fact, Leonard's prospects were so good when he left Capitol Hill that instead of joining an established firm he created a new one with Oldaker and Ryan. Such small firms could be the wave of the future, lobbyists said, because overhead is low and there are no associates to share the booty. So far, Oldaker, Ryan & Leonard is a huge success.

House ethics rules barred Leonard from lobbying his old committee for a year after he left it at the end of 1992. So what was he doing during that year? Leonard declined repeated requests for an interview. But the rules are loose enough in their definition of lobbying that Leonard could have advised clients who had business before the committee.

The ethics rules also permit ex-Members and aides to lobby the Administration and to devise legislative strategy and tactics. Former Rep. Eckart, for example, is in the middle of a titanic lobbying battle over changes in the superfund toxic-waste cleanup legislation that he helped draft as a young Member in 1986. Eckart and Anthony now represent the American Insurance Association's (AIA's) Superfund Improvement Project.

"I hear his name mentioned very frequently as a key player in all the discussions around town on an issue that is extremely important," said Rena I. Steinzor, a lawyer with the Washington firm of Spiegel & McDiarmid who represents cities in the superfund debate. "AIA hired him because he is a well-respected player around town."

Winston & Strawn beat out a handful of other law firms for the lucrative AIA contract because of Anthony and Eckart. "The expertise Beryl and Dennis brought to us on superfund was simply unmatched" by other firms, Mike McGavick, director of the AIA's Superfund Improvement Project said. The duo was hired, he emphasized, "for their counsel, not their contacts."

Eckart has caught some flak from environmental and public-interest groups that contend he is working to undercut a law that he helped draft. But in an interview, Eckart said that he recognized two years ago that the superfund was providing millions of dollars in lawyers' fees while doing little to clean up waste sites. The insurance industry wants changes that would reduce their liability for cleanup costs.

Eckart emphasized that he is a counselor, not a lobbyist, for the AIA.

"I think I am making a natural segue from public citizen to private citizen who still cares about the public business," added Eckart, who also teaches at Kent State University in Ohio and is a television commentator in Cleveland and in Washington. "I don't think I should be disenfranchised."

Winston & Strawn's hiring of Eckart was widely considered one of the recruiting coups of the year, even at a reported salary of $500,000 a year. Eckart, 43, was considered a rising star in Congress and is one of the youngest former Members to go through the revolving door. "His potential has not even begun to be tapped," Coelho said. "There are not many people like him at his age, with his ability and these connections. That is what makes him such a superstar."

Going the Distance

Despite his attacks on Washington lobbyists during the 1992 campaign, Clinton has helped create boom times for them. In Clinton, they got an energetic President whose activist agenda on the budget, health care and the North American Free Trade Agreement translates into happy days on K Street. According to the Senate's Office of Records and Registration, lobbyists gained 2,974 new clients in 1993. There are 7,867 individuals and firms registered to lobby, up from 7,633 in 1992.

"It's the irony of ironies," said the Center for Public Integrity's Lewis. After capitalizing on public frustration and bitterness toward lobbyists, he said, Clinton has produced "a greater bonanza for them than any other President has provided in a couple of decades."

Of course, any change in Administration produces some new business for lobbyists. And after 12 years of Republican occupancy in the White House, Clinton's arrival created plenty of opportunities for lobbyists with Democratic connections.

The President issued an order barring his top aides from lobbying the White House for five years after they leave their jobs. But such restrictions have a limited impact. Two top aides, deputy chief of staff Roy M. Neel and legislative affairs director Howard G. Paster, left after less than 11 months to take jobs with groups that lobby. Neel will make $500,000 a year as chief of the U.S. Telephone Association; Paster reportedly will make $1 million annually as the top executive of Hill and Knowlton Inc.

Moreover, Clinton's attacks on lobbyists may have lost a bit of their sting amid recent press reports that several years ago his wife may have lobbied an Arkansas bank regulator appointed by Gov. Clinton on behalf of a savings and loan executive who was a Clinton campaign contributor.

The ultimate test for the new crop of lobbyists probably will not come until several years down the road. That's when a whole new set of rookies with even better connections will arrive on K Street.

"Access is a short-lived phenomenon," a Washington lawyer warned. Firms such as Oldaker, Ryan & Leonard, with no associates to do the grunt work, could make an early killing but then suffer as time goes by, the lawyer added.

Burnout is another factor, especially among ex-Members, who may simply decide they don't want to lobby. A new Administration could also produce a flood of refugees—including planeloads of people "flying coach" back to Little Rock, a lobbyist joked.

But the rules of the lobbying game remain the same. "The only thing that changes is whom to need access to and to whom you go to provide that access," lobbyist McBride said. As the issues change, he added, the players change. "If I wanted to go see [top White House aide] Bruce Lindsey, I wouldn't hire Clark Clifford to do that."

Knowledge is valuable. Credibility is vital. But, a public relations expert said, "who will return your phone calls is a very important measure of your success in this town."

DISCUSSION QUESTIONS

1. Many commentators have focused on the success of "grass-roots" lobbying, which relies on mass responses from constituents, rather than the "insider lobbying" described by Moore. Which approach to lobbying seems to be more effective as a means of influencing political outcomes? Why?

2. Which approach is more consistent with Olson's argument? Explain.

3. What are the implications for the representative process of insider lobbying? Should the average citizen be concerned about the influence of lobbyists? Why?

THE DEBATE: PACS AND POLITICS: WAS MADISON RIGHT?

The Framers were suspicious of factions—this is one reason why most of them disliked the idea of political parties, which were seen as simply large factions. To combat the "mischief of faction," Madison argues in *The Federalist*, No. 10, one must eliminate the sources of factions (which was impossible, in his view), eliminate their effects by constraining liberty (possible, but unacceptable), or mitigate their effects by creating a republic where such groups could proliferate. Expanding the size of the country and instituting a system of separation of powers and indirect representation minimizes the threat that any single faction would become so large and powerful as to pose a threat. Factions were eminent where liberty thrived, but the "mischief" of factions could be checked by the multiplicity of factions in a diverse country and a system of representation based on varied constituencies. The competition of diverse minority interests could generate compromise and balanced public policy. In other words, the more factions the better. *The Federalist*, No. 10 is considered a brilliant exposition of what is known as the "pluralist theory": the idea that the competition among groups in society for political power produces the best approximation of overall public good.

Was Madison right? In the excerpt from *The Governmental Process* (1951), David Truman answers with an emphatic yes. Truman argues that despite the popular criticism of "special" interests, such groups have been a common feature of American government since the time of the founders—indeed, the formation of special interests was the topic of *The Federalist*, No. 10. What critics of group influence fail to recognize, however, is the fact that people have "multiple or overlapping membership" in groups so that "no tolerably normal person is totally absorbed in any group in which he participates." There is the possibility of balance, in other words, to the views any one member brings to any organization and ultimately to the political process. Further, the potential for group formation is always present, and "[s]ometimes it may be this possibility of organization that alone gives the potential group a minimum of influence in the political process." Just because someone is not a member of an organized group, in other words, does not mean he or she has no influence in the political process. The result, as Madison argued, is a balanced approach to the diverse interests that must compromise to form public policy.

Jonathan Rauch disagrees; he sees the proliferation of interest groups as having a profoundly negative impact on national politics. Unlike Madison and Truman, who argued that competition among numerous groups produces balance and compromise, Rauch sees what he calls "hyperpluralism:" an explosion of groups making claims on government power and resources. The problem is that it is easier to stop government action than it is to see it through. As a result, interest groups formed around particular government programs (social security, farm subsidies, tax breaks) can easily stop any attempt to reorient public priorities. When elected officials attempt, for example, to reduce budget deficits or to shift expenditures, they are overwhelmed by the pressures of a wide range of groups. As a result, government programs are never terminated or restructured; tough budget cuts or tax changes are rarely made; and a very rich, democratic nation and its government become immobilized.

59
The Federalist, No. 10

JAMES MADISON

To the People of the State of New York:

Among the numerous advantages promised by a well-constructed Union, none deserves to be more accurately developed than its tendency to break and control the violence of faction. The friend of popular governments never finds himself so much alarmed for their character and fate, as when he contemplates their propensity to this dangerous vice. He will not fail, therefore, to set a due value on any plan which, without violating the principles to which he is attached, provides a proper cure for it. The instability, injustice, and confusion introduced into the public councils, have, in truth, been the mortal diseases under which popular governments have everywhere perished; as they continue to be the favorite and fruitful topics from which the adversaries to liberty derive their most specious declamations. The valuable improvements made by the American constitutions on the popular models, both ancient and modern, cannot certainly be too much admired; but it would be an unwarrantable partiality, to contend that they have as effectually obviated the danger on this side, as was wished and expected. Complaints are everywhere heard from our most considerate and virtuous citizens, equally the friends of public and private faith, and of public and personal liberty, that our governments are too unstable; that the public good is disregarded in the conflicts of rival parties; and that measures are too often decided, not according to the rules of justice and the rights of the minor party, but by the superior force of an interested and overbearing majority. However anxiously we may wish that these complaints had no foundation, the evidence of known facts will not permit us to deny that

Handwritten annotations:

- can be good if they don't control gov. + oppress the people

- factions - negative but necessary (lightly)
- restrict either causes or effects
- move to balance
- have a lot of factions + balanced thought

- 2 ways to eliminate by causes
  1 - eliminate liberty
  2 - make everyone have the same opinion
  (can't eliminate causes, only effects)

- if a faction is a minority, no problem, majority is a problem. Gov must prevent this
- bigger population = more politicians = better gov. union is bigger

they are in some degree true. It will be found, indeed, on a candid review of our situation, that some of the distresses under which we labor have been erroneously charged on the operation of our governments; but it will be found, at the same time, that other causes will not alone account for many of our heaviest misfortunes; and, particularly, for that prevailing and increasing distrust of public engagements, and alarm for private rights, which are echoed from one end of the continent to the other. These must be chiefly, if not wholly, effects of the unsteadiness and injustice with which a factious spirit has tainted our public administrations.

By a faction, I understand a number of citizens, whether amounting to a majority or minority of the whole, who are united and actuated by some common impulse of passion, or of interest, adverse to the rights of other citizens, or to the permanent and aggregate interests of the community.

There are two methods of curing the mischiefs of faction: the one, by removing its causes; the other, by controlling its effects. *2 solutions:*

There are again two methods of removing the causes of faction: the *removing causes* one, by destroying the liberty which is essential to its existence; the other, *controlling* by giving to every citizen the same opinions, the same passions, and the *effects* same interests.

It could never be more truly said than of the first remedy, that it is *cause:* worse than the disease. Liberty is to faction what air is to fire, an aliment -*destroying* without which it instantly expires. But it could not be less folly to abolish *liberty* liberty, which is essential to political life, because it nourishes faction, -*everyone* than it would be to wish the annihilation of air, which is essential to *some* animal life, because it imparts to fire its destructive agency. *interests*

The second expedient is as impracticable as the first would be unwise. As long as the reason of man continues fallible, and he is at liberty to exercise it, different opinions will be formed. As long as the connection subsits between his reason and his self-love, his opinions and his passions will have a reciprocal influence on each other; and the former will be objects to which the latter will attach themselves. The diversity in the faculties of men, from which the rights of property originate, is not less an insuperable obstacle to a uniformity of interests. The protection of these faculties is the first object of government. From the protection of different and unequal faculties of acquiring property, the possession of different degrees and kinds of property immediately results; and from the influence of these on the sentiments and views of the respective proprietors, ensues a division of the society into different interests and parties.

The latent causes of faction are thus sown in the nature of man; and we see them everywhere brought into different degrees of activity, according to the different circumstances of civil society. A zeal for different opinions concerning religion, concerning government, and many other

than states therefore union is better & stronger

points, as well of speculation as of practice; an attachment to different leaders ambitiously contending for pre-eminence and power; or to persons of other descriptions whose fortunes have been interesting to the human passions, have, in turn, divided mankind into parties, inflamed them with mutual animosity, and rendered them much more disposed to vex and oppress each other than to co-operate for their common good. So strong is this propensity of mankind to fall into mutual animosities, that where no substantial occasion presents itself, the most frivolous and fanciful distinctions have been sufficient to kindle their unfriendly passions and excite their most violent conflicts. But the most common and durable source of factions has been the various and unequal distribution of property. Those who hold and those who are without property have ever formed distinct interests in society. Those who are creditors, and those who are debtors, fall under a like discrimination. A landed interest, a manufacturing interest, a mercantile interest, a moneyed interest, with many lesser interests, grow up of necessity in civilized nations, and divide them into different classes, actuated by different sentiments and views. The regulation of these various and interfering interests forms the principal task of modern legislation, and involves the spirit of party and faction in the necessary and ordinary operations of the government.

No man is allowed to be a judge in his own cause, because his interest would certainly bias his judgment, and, not improbably, corrupt his integrity. With equal, nay with greater reason, a body of men are unfit to be both judges and parties at the same time; yet what are many of the most important acts of legislation, but so many judicial determinations, not indeed concerning the rights of single persons, but concerning the rights of large bodies of citizens? and what are the different classes of legislators but advocates and parties to the causes which they determine? Is a law proposed concerning private debts? It is a question to which the creditors are parties on one side and the debtors on the other. Justice ought to hold the balance between them. Yet the parties are, and must be, themselves the judges; and the most numerous party, or, in other words, the most powerful faction must be expected to prevail. Shall domestic manufactures be encouraged, and in what degree, by restrictions on foreign manufactures? are questions which would be differently decided by the landed and the manufacturing classes, and probably by neither with a sole regard to justice and the public good. The apportionment of taxes on the various descriptions of property is an act which seems to require the most exact impartiality; yet there is, perhaps, no legislative act in which greater opportunity and temptation are given to a predominant party to trample on the rules of justice. Every shilling with which they overburden the inferior number is a shilling saved to their own pockets.

It is in vain to say that enlightened statesmen will be able to adjust these clashing interests and render them all subservient to the public good. Enlightened statesmen will not always be at the helm. Nor, in many cases, can such an adjustment be made at all without taking into view indirect and remote considerations, which will rarely prevail over the immediate interest which one party may find in disregarding the rights of another or the good of the whole.

The inference to which we are brought is, that the *causes* of faction cannot be removed, and that relief is only to be sought in the means of controlling its *effects*.

If a faction consists of less than a majority, relief is supplied by the republican principle, which enables the majority to defeat its sinister views by regular vote. It may clog the administration, it may convulse the society; but it will be unable to execute and mask its violence under the forms of the Constitution. When a majority is included in a faction, the form of popular government, on the other hand, enables it to sacrifice to its ruling passion or interest both the public good and the rights of other citizens. To secure the public good and private rights against the danger of such a faction, and at the same time to preserve the spirit and the form of popular government, is then the great object to which our inquiries are directed. Let me add that it is the great desideratum [desire] by which this form of government can be rescued from the opprobrium under which it has so long labored, and be recommended to the esteem and adoption of mankind.

By what means is this object attainable? Evidently by one of two only. Either the existence of the same passion or interest in a majority at the same time must be prevented, or the majority, having such coexistent passion or interest, must be rendered by their number and local situation unable to concert and carry into effect schemes of oppression. If the impulse and the opportunity be suffered to coincide, we well know that neither moral nor religious motives can be relied on as an adequate control. They are not found to be such on the injustice and violence of individuals, and lose their efficacy in proportion to the number combined together, that is, in proportion as their efficacy becomes needful.

From this view of the subject it may be concluded that a pure democracy, by which I mean a society consisting of a small number of citizens, who assemble and administer the government in person, can admit of no cure for the mischiefs of faction. A common passion or interest will, in almost every case, be felt by a majority of the whole; a communication and concert result from the form of government itself; and there is nothing to check the inducements to sacrifice the weaker party or an obnoxious individual. Hence it is that such democracies have ever been spectacles of turbulence and contention; have ever been found incompatible with personal security or the rights of property; and have in general been as short in their lives as they have been violent in their deaths. Theoretic politicians, who have patronized this species of government, have erroneously supposed that by reducing mankind to a perfect equality in their political rights, they would, at the same time, be perfectly equalized and assimilated in their possessions, their opinions, and their passions.

A republic, by which I mean a government in which the scheme of representation takes place, opens a different prospect, and promises the cure for which we are seeking. Let us examine the points in which it varies from pure democracy, and we shall comprehend both the nature of the cure and the efficacy which it must derive from the Union.

The two great points of difference between a democracy and a republic are: first, the delegation of the government in the latter to a small number of citizens elected by the rest; secondly, the greater number of citizens and greater sphere of country over which the latter may be extended.

The effect of the first difference is, on the one hand, to refine and enlarge the public views, by passing them through the medium of a chosen body of citizens, whose wisdom may best discern the true interest of their country, and whose patriotism and love of justice will be least likely to sacrifice it to temporary or partial considerations. Under such a regulation, it may well happen that the public voice, pronounced by the representatives of the people, will be more consonant to the public good than if pronounced by the people themselves, convened for the purpose. On the other hand, the effect may be inverted. Men of factious tempers, of local prejudices, or of sinister designs, may by intrigue, by corruption, or by other means, first obtain the suffrages, and then betray the interests of the people. The question resulting is, whether small or extensive republics are more favorable to the election of proper guardians of the public weal; and it is clearly decided in favor of the latter by two obvious considerations.

In the first place, it is to be remarked that, however small the republic may be, the representatives must be raised to a certain number in order to guard against the cabals of a few; and that, however large it may be, they must be limited to a certain number in order to guard against the confusion of a multitude. Hence, the number of representatives in the two cases not being in proportion to that of the two constituents, and being proportionally greater in the small republic, it follows that, if the proportion of fit characters be not less in the large than in the small republic, the former will present a greater option and consequently a greater probability of a fit choice.

In the next place, as each representative will be chosen by a greater number of citizens in the large than in the small republic, it will be more difficult for unworthy candidates to practise with success the vicious arts by which elections are too often carried; and the suffrages of the people being more free, will be more likely to centre in men who possess the most attractive merit and the most diffusive and established characters.

It must be confessed that in this, as in most other cases, there is a mean, on both sides of which inconveniences will be found to lie. By enlarging too much the number of electors, you render the representative too little acquainted with all their local circumstances and lesser interests: as by reducing it too much, you render him unduly attached to these, and too little fit to comprehend and pursue great and national objects. The federal Constitution forms a happy combination in this respect; the great and aggregate interests being referred to the national, the local and particular to the State legislatures.

The other point of difference is, the greater number of citizens and extent of territory which may be brought within the compass of republican than of democratic government; and it is this circumstance principally which renders factious combinations less to be dreaded in the former than in the latter. The smaller the society, the fewer probably will be the distinct parties and interests composing it; the fewer the distinct parties and interests, the more frequently will a majority be found of the same party; and the smaller the number of individuals composing a majority, and the smaller the compass within which they are placed, the more easily will they concert and execute their plans of oppression. Extend the sphere, and you take in a greater variety of parties and interests; you make it less probable that a majority of the whole will have a common motive to invade the rights of other citizens; or if such a common motive exists, it will be more difficult for all who feel it to discover their own strength and to act in unison with each other. Besides other impediments, it may be remarked that, where there is a consciousness of unjust or dishonorable purposes, communication is always checked by distrust in proportion to the number whose concurrence is necessary.

Hence, it clearly appears that the same advantage which a republic has over a democracy in controlling the effects of faction is enjoyed by a large over a small republic,—is enjoyed by the Union over the States composing it. Does the advantage consist in the substitution of representatives whose enlightened views and virtuous sentiments render them superior to local prejudices and to schemes of injustice? It will not be denied that the representation of the Union will be most likely to possess these requisite endowments. Does it consist in the greater security afforded by a greater variety of parties, against the event of any one party being able to outnumber and oppress the rest? In an equal degree does the increased variety of parties comprised within the Union, increase this security. Does it, in fine, consist in the greater obstacles opposed to the concert and accomplishment of the secret wishes of an unjust and interested majority? Here, again, the extent of the Union gives it the most palpable advantage.

The influence of factious leaders may kindle a flame within their particular States, but will be unable to spread a general conflagration through the other States. A religious sect may degenerate into a political faction in a part of the Confederacy; but the variety of sects dispersed over the entire face of it must secure the national councils against any danger from that source. A rage for paper money, for an abolition of debts, for an equal division of property, or for any other improper or wicked project, will be less apt to pervade the whole body of the Union than a particular member of it; in the same proportion as such a malady is more likely to taint a particular county or district, than an entire State.

In the extent and proper structure of the Union, therefore, we behold a republican remedy for the diseases most incident to republican government. And according to the degree of pleasure and pride we feel in being republicans, ought to be our zeal in cherishing the spirit and supporting the character of Federalists. Publius

60
"The Alleged Mischiefs of Faction" from
The Governmental Process

David B. Truman

Most accounts of American legislative sessions—national, state, or local—are full of references to the maneuverings and iniquities of various organized groups. Newspaper stories report that a legislative proposal is being promoted by groups of business men or school teachers or farmers or consumers or labor unions or other aggregations of citizens. Cartoonists picture the legislature as completely under the control of sinister, portly, cigar-smoking individuals labeled "special interests," while a diminutive John Q. Public is pushed aside to sulk in futile anger and pathetic frustration. A member of the legislature rises in righteous anger on the floor of the house or in a press conference to declare that the bill under discussion is being forced through by the "interests," by the most unscrupulous high-pressure "lobby" he has seen in all his years of public life. An investigating committee denounces the activities of a group as deceptive, immoral, and destructive of our constitutional methods and ideals. A chief executive attacks a "lobby" or "pressure group" as the agency responsible for obstructing or emasculating a piece of legislation that he has recommended "in the public interest."

* * *

Such events are familiar even to the casual student of day-to-day politics, if only because they make diverting reading and appear to give the citizen the "low-down" on his government. He tends, along with many of his more sophisticated fellow citizens, to take these things more or less for granted, possibly because they merely confirm his conviction that "as everybody knows, politics is a dirty business." Yet at the same time he is likely to regard the activities of organized groups in political life as somehow outside the proper and normal processes of government, as the lapses of his weak contemporaries whose moral fiber is insufficient to prevent their defaulting on the great traditions of the Founding Fathers. These events appear to be a modern pathology.

Group Pressures and the Founding Fathers

Group pressures, whatever we may wish to call them, are not new in America. One of the earliest pieces of testimony to this effect is essay number 10 of *The Federalist*, which contains James Madison's classic statement of the impact of divergent groups upon government and the reasons for their development. He was arguing the virtues of the proposed Union as a means to "break and control the violence of faction," having in mind, no doubt, the groups involved in such actions of the debtor or propertyless segment of the population as Shays's Rebellion. He defined faction in broader terms, however, as "a number of citizens, whether amounting to a majority or minority of the whole, who are united and actuated by some common impulse of passion, or of interest. . . ."

* * *

[Madison's] analysis is not just the brilliant generalization of an armchair philosopher or pamphleteer; it represents as well the distillation from Madison's years of acquaintance with contemporary politics as a member of the Virginia Assembly and of [the Continental] Congress. Using the words "party" and "faction" almost interchangeably, since the political party as we know it had not yet developed, he saw the struggles of such groups as the essence of the political process. One need not concur in all his judgments to agree that the process he described had strong similarities to that of our own day.

The entire effort of which *The Federalist* was a part was one of the most skillful and important examples of pressure group activity in American history. The State ratifying conventions were handled by the Federalists with a skill that might well be the envy of a modern lobbyist. It is easy to overlook the fact that "unless the Federalists had been shrewd in manipulation as they were sound in theory, their arguments could not have prevailed."

* * *

Alexis de Tocqueville, perhaps the keenest foreign student ever to write on American institutions, noted as one of the most striking characteristics of the nation the penchant for promoting a bewildering array of projects through organized societies, among them those using political means. "In no country in the world," he observed, "has the principle of association been more successfully used or applied to a greater multitude of objects than in America."[1] De Tocqueville was impressed by the organization of such groups and by their tendency to operate sometimes upon and sometimes parallel to the formal institutions of government. Speaking of the similarity between the representatives of such groups and the members of legislatures, he stated: "It is true that they [delegates of these societies] have not the right, like the others, of making the laws; but they have the power of attacking those which are in force and of drawing up beforehand those which ought to be enacted."[2]

Since the modern political party was, in the Jackson period, just taking the form that we would recognize today, De Tocqueville does not always distinguish sharply between it and other types of political interest groups. In his discussion of "political associations," however, he gives an account of the antitariff convention held in Philadelphia in October of 1831, the form of which might well have come from the proceedings of a group meeting in an American city today:

> Its debates were public, and they at once assumed a legislative character; the extent of the powers of Congress, the theories of free trade, and the different provisions of the tariff were discussed. At the end of ten days the Convention broke up, having drawn up an address to the American people in which it declared: (1) that Congress had not the right of making a tariff, and that the existing tariff was unconstitutional; (2) that the prohibition of free trade was prejudicial to the interests of any nation, and to those of the American people especially.[3]

Additional evidence might be cited from many quarters to illustrate the long history of group politics in this country. Organized pressures supporting or attacking the charter of the Bank of the United States in Jackson's administration, the peculations surrounding Pendleton's "Palace of Fortune" in the pre–Civil War period, the operations of the railroads and other interests in both national and state legislatures in the latter half of the last century, the political activities of farm groups such as the Grange in the same period—these and others indicate that at no time have the activities of organized political interests not been a part of American politics. Whether they indicate pathology or not, they are certainly not new.

* * *

The political interest group is neither a fleeting, transitory newcomer to the political arena nor a localized phenomenon peculiar to one member of the family of nations. The persistence and the dispersion of such organizations indicate rather that we are dealing with a characteristic aspect of our society. That such groups are receiving an increasing measure of popular and technical attention suggests the hypothesis that they are appreciably more significant in the complex and interdependent society of our own day than they were in the simpler, less highly developed community for which our constitutional arrangements were originally designed.

Many people are quite willing to acknowledge the accuracy of these propositions about political groups, but they are worried nevertheless. They are still concerned over the meaning of what they see and read of the activities of such organizations. They observe, for example, that certain farm groups apparently can induce the Government to spend hundreds of millions of dollars to maintain the price of food and to take "surplus" agricultural produce off the market while many urban residents are encountering painful difficulty in stretching their food budgets to provide adequately for their families. They observe that various labor organizations seem to be able to prevent the introduction of cheaper methods into building codes, although the cost of new housing is already beyond the reach of many. Real estate and contractors' trade associations apparently have the power to obstruct various governmental projects for slum clearance and low-cost housing. Veterans' organizations seem able to secure and protect increases in pensions and other benefits almost at will. A church apparently can prevent the appropriation of Federal funds to public schools unless such funds are also given to the schools it operates in competition with the public systems. The Government has declared that stable and friendly European governments cannot be maintained unless Americans buy more goods and services abroad. Yet American shipowners and seamen's unions can secure a statutory requirement that a large proportion of the goods purchased by European countries under the Marshall Plan* must be carried in American ships. Other industries and trade associations can prevent the revision of tariff rates and customs regulations that restrict imports from abroad.

In all these situations the fairly observant citizen sees various groups slugging it out with one another in pursuit of advantages from the Government. Or he sees some of them co-operating with one another to their mutual benefit. He reads of "swarms" of lobbyists "putting pressure on" congressmen and administrators. He has the impression that any group can get what it wants in Washington by deluging officials with mail and telegrams. He may then begin to wonder whether a governmental system like this can survive, whether it can carry its responsibilities in the world and meet the challenges presented by a ruthless dictatorship. He wants to see these external threats effectively met. The sentimental nonsense of the commercial advertisements aside, he values free speech, free elections, representative government, and all that these imply. He fears and resents practices and privileges that seem to place these values in jeopardy.

* [The U.S. European Recovery Plan after World War II]

A common reaction to revelations concerning the more lurid activities of political groups is one of righteous indignation. Such indignation is entirely natural. It is likely, however, to be more comforting than constructive. What we seek are correctives, protections, or controls that will strengthen the practices essential in what we call democracy and that will weaken or eliminate those that really threaten that system. Uncritical anger may do little to achieve that objective, largely because it is likely to be based upon a picture of the governmental process that is a composite of myth and fiction as well as of fact. We shall not begin to achieve control until we have arrived at a conception of politics that adequately accounts for the operations of political groups. We need to know what regular patterns are shown by group politics before we can predict its consequences and prescribe for its lapses. We need to re-examine our notions of how representative government operates in the United States before we can be confident of our statements about the effects of group activities upon it. Just as we should not know how to protect a farm house from lightning unless we knew something of the behavior of electricity, so we cannot hope to protect a governmental system from the results of group organization unless we have an adequate understanding of the political process of which these groups are a part.

* * *

There are two elements in this conception of the political process in the United States that are of crucial significance and that require special emphasis. These are, first, the notion of multiple or overlapping membership and, second, the function of unorganized interests, or potential interest groups.

The idea of overlapping membership stems from the conception of a group as a standardized pattern of interactions rather than as a collection of human units. Although the former may appear to be a rather misty abstraction, it is actually far closer to complex reality than the latter notion. The view of a group as an aggregation of individuals abstracts from the observable fact that in any society, and especially a complex one, no single group affiliation accounts for all of the attitudes or interests of any individual except a fanatic or a compulsive neurotic. No tolerably normal person is totally absorbed in any group in which he participates. The diversity of an individual's activities and his attendant interests involve him in a variety of actual and potential groups. Moreover, the fact that the genetic experiences of no two individuals are identical and the consequent fact that the spectra of their attitudes are in varying degrees dissimilar means that the members of a single group will perceive the group's claims in terms of a diversity of frames of reference. Such heterogeneity may be of little significance until such time as these multiple memberships conflict. Then the cohesion and influence of the affected group depend upon the incorporation or accommodation of the conflicting loyalties of any significant segment of the group, an accommodation that may result in altering the original claims. Thus the leaders of a Parent-Teacher Association must take some account of the fact that their proposals must be acceptable to members who also belong to the local taxpayers' league, to the local chamber of commerce, and to the Catholic Church.

* * *

We cannot account for an established American political system without the second crucial element in our conception of the political process, the concept of the unorganized interest, or potential interest group. Despite the tremendous number of interest groups existing in the United States, not all interests are organized. If we recall the definition of an interest as a shared attitude, it becomes obvious that continuing interaction resulting in claims upon other groups does not take place on the basis of all such attitudes. One of the commonest interest group forms, the association, emerges out of severe or prolonged disturbances in the expected relationships of individuals in similar institutionalized groups. An association continues to function as long as it succeeds in ordering these disturbed relationships, as a labor union orders the relationships between management and workers. Not all such expected relationships are simultaneously or in a given short period sufficiently disturbed to produce organization. Therefore only a portion of the interests or attitudes involved in such expectations are represented by organized groups. Similarly, many organized groups—families, businesses, or churches, for example—do not operate continuously as interest groups or as political interest groups.

Any mutual interest, however, any shared attitude, is a potential group. A disturbance in established relationships and expectations anywhere in the society may produce new patterns of interaction aimed at restricting or eliminating the disturbance. Sometimes it may be this possibility of organization that alone gives the potential group a minimum of influence in the political process. Thus . . . the Delta planters in Mississippi "must speak for their Negroes in such programs as health and education,"[4] although the latter are virtually unorganized and are denied the means of active political participation.*

* * *

Obstacles to the development of organized groups from potential ones may be presented by inertia or by the activities of opposed groups, but the possibility that severe disturbances will be created if these submerged, potential interests should organize necessitates some recognition

* [Until the 1960s, most southern blacks were denied the right to vote.]

of the existence of these interests and gives them at least a minimum of influence.

More important for present purposes than the potential groups representing separate minority elements are those interests or expectations that are so widely held in the society and are so reflected in the behavior of almost all citizens that they are, so to speak, taken for granted. Such "majority" interests are significant not only because they may become the basis for organized interest groups but also because the "membership" of such potential groups overlaps extensively the memberships of the various organized interest groups. The resolution of conflicts between the claims of such unorganized interests and those of organized interest groups must grant recognition to the former not only because affected individuals may feel strongly attached to them but even more certainly because these interests are widely shared and are a part of many established patterns of behavior the disturbance of which would be difficult and painful. They are likely to be highly valued.

* * *

It is thus multiple memberships in potential groups based on widely held and accepted interests that serve as a balance wheel in a going political system like that of the United States. To some people this observation may appear to be a truism and to others a somewhat mystical notion. It is neither. In the first place, neglect of this function of multiple memberships in most discussions of organized interest groups indicates that the observation is not altogether commonplace. Secondly, the statement has no mystical quality; the effective operation of these widely held interests is to be inferred directly from verbal and other behavior in the political sphere. Without the notion of multiple memberships in potential groups it is literally impossible to account for the existence of a viable polity such as that in the United States or to develop a coherent conception of the political process. The strength of these widely held but largely unorganized interests explains the vigor with which propagandists for organized groups attempt to change other attitudes by invoking such interests. Their importance is further evidenced in the recognized function of the means of mass communication, notably the press, in reinforcing widely accepted norms of "public morality."

* * *

Thus it is only as the effects of overlapping memberships and the functions of unorganized interests and potential groups are included in the equation that it is accurate to speak of governmental activity as the product or resultant of interest group activity. As [political scientist Arthur F.] Bentley has put it:

There are limits to the technique of the struggle, this involving also limits to the group demands, all of which is solely a matter of empirical observation. ... Or, in other words, when the struggle proceeds too harshly at any point there will become insistent in the society a group more powerful than either of those involved which tends to suppress the extreme and annoying methods of the groups in the primary struggle. It is within the embrace of these great lines of activity that the smaller struggles proceed, and the very word struggle has meaning only with reference to its limitations.[5]

To assert that the organization and activity of powerful interest groups constitutes a threat to representative government without measuring their relation to and effects upon the widespread potential groups is to generalize from insufficient data and upon an incomplete conception of the political process. Such an analysis would be as faulty as one that, ignoring differences in national systems, predicted identical responses to a given technological change in the United States, Japan, and the Soviet Union.

Notes

1. Alexis de Tocqueville, *Democracy in America*, ed. by Phillips Bradley (New York: Knopf, 1945), Volume I, p. 191.
2. Tocqueville, p. 193.
3. Tocqueville, p. 194.
4. V. O. Key, *Southern Politics in State and Nation* (New York: Knopf, 1949), p. 235.
5. Arthur F. Bentley, *The Process of Government* (Chicago: University of Chicago Press, 1908), p. 372.

61
"The Hyperpluralism Trap"

Jonathan Rauch

Anyone who believes Washington needs to get closer to the people ought to spend a little time with Senator Richard Lugar, the Indiana Republican. "Take a look at the people coming into my office on a normal Tuesday and Wednesday," Lugar said in a speech not long ago. "Almost every organization in our society has a national conference. The typical way of handling this is to come in on a Monday, rev up the troops, give them the bill number and send them up to the Hill. If they can't get in on Tuesday, strike again on Wednesday. I regularly have on Tuesday as many as fifteen constituent groups from Indiana, all of whom have been revved up by some skillful person to cite bills that they don't understand, have never heard of prior to that time, but with a score sheet to report back to headquarters whether I am for or against. It is so routine, it is so fierce, that at some point you [can't be] immune to it."

This is the reality of modern government. The rhetoric of modern politics, alas, is a little different. Take today's standard-issue political stem-winder, which goes something like this: "I think perhaps the most important thing that we understand here in the heartland . . . is the need to reform the political system, to reduce the influence of special interests and give more influence back to the kind of people that are in this crowd tonight by the tens of thousands." That stream of boilerplate is from Bill Clinton (from his election-night speech), but it could have come from almost any politician. It's pitched in a dominant key of political rhetoric today: *standard populism*—that is, someone has taken over the government and "we" must take it back, restore government to the people, etc. But who, exactly, are those thousands of citizens who troop weekly through Senator Lugar's suite, clutching briefing packets and waving scorecards? Standard populism says they are the "special interests," those boils on the skin of democracy, forever interposing themselves between the American people and the people's servants in Washington.

Well, fifty years ago that analysis may have been useful, but not anymore. In America today, the special interests and "the people" have become objectively indistinguishable. Groups are us. As a result, the populist impulse to blame special interests, big corporations and political careerists for our problems—once a tonic—has become Americans' leading political narcotic. Worse, it actually abets the lobbying it so righteously denounces.

Begin with one of the best known yet most underappreciated facts of our time: over the past three or four decades we have busily organized ourselves into interest groups—lobbies, loosely speaking—at an astonishing rate. Interest groups were still fairly sparse in America until about the time of World War II. Then they started proliferating, and in the 1960s the pace of organizing picked up dramatically.

Consider, for instance, the numbers of groups listed in Gale Research's *Encyclopedia of Associations*. The listings have grown from fewer than 5,000 in 1956 to well over 20,000 today. They represent, of course, only a small fraction of America's universe of interest groups. Environmental organizations alone number an estimated 7,000, once you count local clean-up groups and the like; the Washington *Blade*'s resource directory lists more than 400 gay groups, up from 300 at the end of 1990. Between 1961 and 1982 the number of corporate offices in Washington increased tenfold. Even more dramatic was the explosion in the number of public-interest organizations and grass-roots groups. These barely existed at all before the 1960s; today they number in the tens of thousands and collect more than $4 billion per year from 40 million individuals, according to political scientist Ronald Shaiko of American University.

Well, so what? Groups do many good things—provide companionship for the like-minded, collect and disseminate information, sponsor contests, keep the catering industry solvent. Indeed, conventional political theory for much of the postwar period was dominated by a strain known as pluralism, which holds that more groups equals more representation equals better democracy. Yet pluralism missed something. It assumed that the group-forming process was self-balancing and stable, as opposed to self-feeding and unstable. Which is to say, it failed to grasp the danger of what American University political scientist James Thurber aptly calls hyperpluralism.

In economics, inflation is a gradual increase in the price level. Up to a point, if the inflation rate is stable, people can plan around it. But if the rate starts to speed up, people start expecting more inflation. They hoard goods and dump cash, driving the inflation still faster. Eventually, an invisible threshold is crossed: the inflation now feeds on its own growth and undermines the stability of the whole economic system.

What the pluralists missed is that something analogous can happen with interest groups. People see that it pays to organize into groups and angle for benefits, so they do it. But as more groups make more demands, and as even more hungry groups form to compete with all the other groups, the process begins to feed on itself and pick up momentum. At some point there might be so many groups that they choke the political system, sow contention and conflict, even erode society's governability. That's hyperpluralism. And if it is less destabilizing than hyperinflation, it may be more insidious.

The pattern is most visible in smaller social units, such as local school districts, where groups colonize the curriculum—sex education for liberals, values instruction for conservatives, recycling lessons for environmentalists, voluntary silent prayer for Christians. But even among the general population the same forces are at work. Fifty years ago the phrase "the elderly" denoted a demographic category; today, thanks largely to federal pension programs and the American Association of Retired Persons (AARP), it denotes a giant and voracious lobby. In the 1930s the government set up farm-subsidy programs, one per commodity; inevitably, lobbies sprang up to defend each program, so that today American agriculture is fundamentally a collection of interest groups. With the help of group organizers and race-based benefits, loose ethnic distinctions coalesce into hard ethnic lobbies. And so on.

Even more depressing, any attempt to fight back against the proliferating mass of subdivision is foiled by the rhetoric of standard populism and its useful stooge: the special interest. The concept of a "special interest" is at the very core of standard populism—the "them" without which there can be no "us." So widely accepted is this notion, and so useful is it in casual political speech, that most of us talk routinely about special interests without a second thought. We all feel we know a special interest when we see one, if only because it is a group of which we are not a member. Yet buried in the special interest idea is an assumption that is no longer true.

The concept of the special interest is not based on nothing. It is, rather, out of date, an increasingly empty relic of the time of machine politics and political bosses, when special interests were, quite literally, special. Simply because of who they were, they enjoyed access that was available to no one else. But the process of everyone's organizing into more and more groups can go only so far before the very idea of a special interest loses any clear meaning. At some point one must throw up one's hands and concede that the hoary dichotomy between special interests and "us" has become merely rhetoric.

According to a 1990 survey conducted for the American Society of Association Executives, seven out of ten Americans belong to at least one association, and one in four Americans belongs to four or more. Practically everyone who reads these words is a member of an interest group, probably several. Moreover, formal membership tallies omit many people whom we ordinarily think of as being represented by lobbies. For example, the powerful veterans' lobbies enroll only perhaps one-seventh of American veterans, yet the groups lobby on behalf of veterans as a class, and all 27 million veterans share in the benefits. Thus the old era of lobbying by special interests—by a well-connected, plutocratic few—is as dead now as slavery and Prohibition. We Americans have achieved the full democratization of lobbying: influence-peddling for the masses.

The appeal of standard populism today comes precisely from the phony reassurance afforded by its real message: "Other people's groups are the special interests. Less for them—more for you!" Spread that sweet manure around and the natural outgrowth is today's tendency, so evident in the Clinton style, to pander to interest groups frantically while denouncing them furiously. It is the public's style, too: sending ever more checks to the AARP and the National Rifle Association and the National Federation of Independent Business and the National Wildlife Federation and a million others, while railing against special interests. Join and join, blame and blame.

So hyperpluralism makes a hash of the usual sort of standard populist prescription, which calls for "the people" to be given more access to the system, at the expense of powerful Beltway figures who are alleged to have grown arrogant or corrupt or out of touch. Activists and reformers who think the answer to democracy's problems is more access for more of the people need to wake up. Uncontrolled access only breeds more lobbies. It is axiomatic that "the people" (whatever that now means) do not organize to seek government benefits; lobbies do. Every new door to the federal treasury is an opportunity for new groups to queue up for more goodies.

Populists resolutely refuse to confront this truth. Last year, for example, Republicans and the editors of *The Wall Street Journal* campaigned fiercely—and successfully—for new congressional rules making it easier for legislators and groups to demand that bottled-up bills be discharged from committee. The idea was to bring Congress closer to "the people" by weakening the supposedly high-handed barons who rule the Hill. But burying the Free Christmas Tree for Every American Act (or whatever) in committee—while letting members of Congress say they *would* have voted for it—was one of the few remaining ways to hold the door against hungry lobbies clamoring for gifts.

A second brand of populism, *left-populism*, is even more clueless than the standard brand, if that's possible. Many liberals believe the problem is that the wrong groups—the rich, the elites, the giant corporations, etc.—have managed to out-organize the good guys and take control of the system. One version of this model was elaborated by William Greider in his book *Who Will Tell the People*. The New Deal legacy, he writes, "rests upon an idea of interest group bargaining that has gradually been transformed into the random deal-making and permissiveness of the present. The alterations in the system are decisive and . . . the ultimate effects are anti-democratic. People with limited resources, with no real representation in the higher levels of politics, are bound to lose in this environment." So elaborate is the Washington machine of lobbyists, consultants, P.R. experts, political action committees and for-hire think tanks, says Greider, that "powerful economic interests," notably corporations and private wealth, inevitably dominate.

What's appealing about this view is the truism from which it springs: the wealthy enjoy a natural advantage in lobbying, as in almost everything else. Thus many lobbies—even liberal lobbies—are dominated by the comfortable and the wealthy. Consider the case of environmental groups. Anyone who doubts they are major players in Washington today need only look at the massive 1990 Clean Air Act, a piece of legislation that business gladly would have done without. Yet these groups are hardly battalions of the disfranchised. "Readers of *Sierra*, the magazine of the Sierra Club, have household incomes twice that of the average American," notes Senior Economist Terry L. Anderson of the Political Economy Research Center. And *The Economist* notes that "in 1993 the Nature Conservancy, with $915 million in assets, drew 73 percent of its income from rich individuals." When such groups push for emissions controls or pesticide rules, they may be reflecting the priorities of people who buy BMWs and brie more than the priorities of people who buy used Chevies and hamburger. So left-populism's claim to speak for "the people" is often suspect, to say the least.

The larger problem with left-populism, however, is its refusal to see that it is feeding the very problem it decries. Left-populism was supposed to fix the wealth-buys-power problem by organizing the politically disadvantaged into groups: unions, consumer groups, rainbow coalitions and so on. But the strategy has failed. As the left (the unions, the environmentalists) has organized ever more groups, the right (the bosses, the polluters) has followed suit. The group-forming has simply spiralled. This makes a joke of the left-populist prescription, which is to form more "citizens' groups" on the Naderite model, supposedly reinvigorating representative democracy and giving voice to the weak and the silenced. Greider proposes giving people subsidies to spend on political activism: "Giving individual citizens the capacity to deploy political money would inevitably shift power from existing structures and disperse it among the ordinary millions who now feel excluded."

Inevitably, it would do no such thing. Subsidies for activism would perforce go straight into the waiting coffers of (what else?) interest groups, new and old. That just makes matters worse, for if one side organizes more groups, the other side simply redoubles its own mobilization ad infinitum. That escalating cycle is the story of the last three decades. The only winner is the lobbying class. Curiously, then, left-populism has come to serve the very lobbying elites—the Washington lawyers and lobby shops and P.R. pros and interest group execs—whom leftists ought, by rights, to loathe.

The realization that the lobbying class is, to a large extent, both entrepreneurial and in business for itself has fed the third brand of populism, *right-populism*. In the right-populist model, self-serving political careerists have hijacked government and learned to manipulate it for profit. In refreshing contrast to the other two brands of populism, however, this one is in touch with reality. Washington *is* in business for itself, though not only for itself. Legislators and lobbies have an interest in using the tax code to please their constituents, but they also have an interest in churning the tax code to generate campaign contributions and lobbying fees. Luckily for them, those two imperatives generally coincide: the more everyone hunts for tax breaks, the more lobbying jobs there are. Right-populism has tumbled to the fact that so-called public interest and citizens' groups are no more immune to this self-serving logic of lobbying—create conflict, reap rewards—than is any other sort of professional lobby.

Yet right-populism fails to see to the bottom of the problem. It looks into the abyss but flinches. This is not to say that term limits and other procedural fine-tunes may not help; such reforms are no doubt worth trying. But even if noodling with procedures succeeded in diluting the culture of political careerism, it would help (or hurt) mainly at the margins. No, tinkering with the process isn't the answer. What we must do is go straight at the beast itself. We must attack and weaken the lobbies—that is, the *people*'s lobbies.

It sounds so simple: weaken the lobbies! Shove them aside, reclaim the government! "It's just that simple," twinkles Ross Perot. But it's not that simple. Lobbies in Washington have clout because the people who scream when "special interests" are attacked are Medicare recipients defending benefits, farmers defending price supports, small businesses defending subsidized loans, racial groups defending set-asides and so on. Inherently, challenging these groups is no one's idea of fun, which is why politicians so rarely propose to do it. The solution is to strip away lobbies' protections and let competition hammer them. In practice, that means:

Balance the federal budget. It is a hackneyed prescription, but it is the very first thing we should do to curtail the lobbies' ability to rob the future. Deficits empower lobbies by allowing them to raid the nation's scarce reserves of investment capital. Deprived of that ability, they will be forced to compete more fiercely for money, and they'll be unable to steal from the future.

Cut the lobbies' lifelines. Eliminate subsidies and programs, including tax loopholes, by the hundreds. Killing a program here or there is a loser's game; it creates a political uproar without actually making a noticeable difference. The model, rather, should be the 1986 tax reform measure, which proved that a wholesale housecleaning really is possible. Back then, tax loopholes were cleared away by the truckload. The trick was—and is—to do the job with a big package of reforms that politicians can tout back home as real change. That means ditching whole Cabinet departments and abolishing virtually all industry-specific subsidies. Then go after subsidies for the non-needy—wholesale, not retail.

Promote domestic perestroika. Lobbies live to lock benefits in and competition out, so government restraints on competition should be removed—not indiscriminately, but determinedly. President Carter's deregulation of transportation industries and interest rates, though imperfectly executed, were good examples. Air travel, trucking and rail shipping are cheaper *and* safer. The affected industries have been more turbulent, but that's exactly the point. Domestic competition shakes up interest groups that settle cozily into Washington.

Encourage foreign competition. This is most important of all. The forces that breed interest groups never abate, and so fighting them requires a constant counterforce. Foreign competition is such a counterforce. Protection invariably benefits the industries and groups with the sharpest lobbyists and the fattest political action committees; stripping away protection forces them to focus more on modernizing and less on lobbying.

No good deed, they say, goes unpunished. We sought to solve pressing social problems, so we gave government vast power to reassign resources. We also sought to look out for ourselves and bring voices to all of our many natures and needs, so we built countless new groups to seek government's resources. What we did not create was a way to control the chain reaction we set off. Swarming interest groups excited government to perpetual activism, and government activism drew new groups to Washington by the thousands. Before we knew it, society itself was turning into a collection of ravenous lobbies.

Why was this not always a problem? Because there used to be control rods containing the chain reaction. Smoke-filled rooms, they were called. On Capitol Hill or in Tammany Hall, you needed to see one of about six people to have any hope of getting what you wanted, and those six people dispensed (and conserved) favors with parsimonious finesse. Seen from today's vantage, smoke-filled rooms and political machines did a creditable job of keeping a lid on the interest group frenzy—they just didn't do it particularly fairly. That's why we opened up access to anyone who wants to organize and lobby, and opened up power to subcommittee chairs and caucus heads and even junior legislators. In doing so, we abolished the venal gatekeepers. But that was only the good news. The bad news was that we also abolished the gate.

No, we shouldn't go back to smoke-filled rooms. But the way forward is harder than it ever was before. The maladies that now afflict government are ones in which the public is wholly, enthusiastically implicated. Still, there are sprigs and shoots of encouragement all around. There was the surprisingly strong presidential bid of former Senator Paul Tsongas, which built something of a constituency for straight talk. There's the rise of a school of Democrats in Congress—among them Senator Bob Kerrey and retiring Representative Tim Penny—who are willing to drag the White House toward sterner fiscal measures. There was the Clinton-led triumph of NAFTA last year. Those developments show promise of a political movement that is counterpopulist yet also popular. Maybe—is it too much to hope?—they point beyond the desert of populism.

DISCUSSION QUESTIONS

1. Why was Madison concerned about factions? What solutions to the "mischiefs of faction" did he suggest?

2. What would David Truman say to Common Cause and the other reformers who want to eliminate PAC contributions in federal campaigns?

3. Can you think of examples of the crosscutting memberships in groups that Truman describes? Does this help prevent majority tyranny? Why or why not?

4. Even if you are not a member of an organized interest group, can you think of any such groups who speak for you? If so, are any of them examples of crosscutting memberships?

5. What does the Clinton presidency tell us about the power of interest groups? Can you think of examples where they have altered the policy outcome? Explain.

PART IV

Public Policy

CHAPTER 12

Politics and Policy

62
"The Science of 'Muddling Through' "

CHARLES E. LINDBLOM

Today's national government plays a role in virtually every aspect of our lives. It provides health insurance for the elderly and the poor, welfare assistance, veterans' benefits, student loans, and a tax break for homeowners paying a mortgage. It regulates the activities of the stock markets, industrial pollution, worker safety and worker rights, the quality of our food, and air traffic. These programs and regulatory policies are all designed and implemented by the government to achieve particular goals—such as an expanding economy, healthy citizens, college education, and home ownership. It is important that we know just how the government goes about formulating and implementing public policy, and the consequences of those efforts. Who plays a role in the making of public policy besides elected officials, and what motivates their decision making? Who are the beneficiaries of various public policies, and is the "public interest" being served?

In the article below, the economist and political scientist Charles Lindblom argued that the efforts of scholars to study and improve on the policy process were flawed because they were based on the assumption that public policy could be made in a "rational" manner. The problem, according to Lindblom, is that decision making for public policy normally proceeds incrementally: policymakers are incapable of defining and developing alternatives that encompass all possible means of achieving explicitly defined goals. Rather, decision makers start with what already exists, goals defined in part by what is known to work and by the most vocal and powerful interests. Changes are then made at the margin to achieve these various ends. Further, the way we evaluate any given policy is heavily dependent on our values and beliefs about what government ought to do and how it ought to be achieved. There is rarely, according to Lindblom, a clear objective standard of a "good" policy that all policymakers and analysts can agree on. Lindblom's article, originally printed in 1959, was groundbreaking

*in that it challenged conventional wisdom among analysts that rational com-
prehensive analysis was possible for purposes of formulating public policy.*

Suppose an administrator is given responsibility for formulating policy
with respect to inflation. He might start by trying to list all related
values in order of importance, e.g., full employment, reasonable business
profit, protection of small savings, prevention of a stock market crash.
Then all possible policy outcomes could be rated as more or less efficient
in attaining a maximum of these values. This would of course require a
prodigious inquiry into values held by members of society and an
equally prodigious set of calculations on how much each value is equal
to how much of each other value. He could then proceed to outline all
possible policy alternatives. In a third step, he could undertake systematic comparison of his multitude of alternatives to determine which attains the greatest amount of values.

In comparing policies, he would take advantage of any theory available that generalized about classes of policies. In considering inflation,
for example, he would compare all policies in the light of the theory of
prices. Since no alternatives are beyond his investigation, he would consider strict central control and the abolition of all prices and markets on
the one hand and elimination of all public controls with reliance completely on the free market on the other, both in the light of whatever
theoretical generalizations he could find on such hypothetical economies.

Finally, he would try to make the choice that would in fact maximize
his values.

An alternative line of attack would be to set as his principal objective,
either explicitly or without conscious thought, the relatively simple goal
of keeping prices level. This objective might be compromised or complicated by only a few other goals, such as full employment. He would
in fact disregard most other social values as beyond his present interest,
and he would for the moment not even attempt to rank the few values
that he regarded as immediately relevant. Were he pressed, he would
quickly admit that he was ignoring many related values and many possible important consequences of his policies.

As a second step, he would outline those relatively few policy alternatives that occurred to him. He would then compare them. In comparing his limited number of alternatives, most of them familiar from past
controversies, he would not ordinarily find a body of theory precise
enough to carry him through a comparison of their respective consequences. Instead he would rely heavily on the record of past experience
with small policy steps to predict the consequences of similar steps extended into the future.

Moreover, he would find that the policy alternatives combined objectives or values in different ways. For example, one policy might offer
price level stability at the cost of some risk of unemployment; another
might offer less price stability but also less risk of unemployment. Hence,

the next step in his approach—the final selection—would combine into one the choice among values and the choice among instruments for reaching values. It would not, as in the first method of policy-making, approximate a more mechanical process of choosing the means that best satisfied goals that were previously clarified and ranked. Because practitioners of the second approach expect to achieve their goals only partially, they would expect to repeat endlessly the sequence just described, as conditions and aspirations changed and as accuracy of prediction improved.

By Root or by Branch

For complex problems, the first of these two approaches is of course impossible. Although such an approach can be described, it cannot be practiced except for relatively simple problems and even then only in a somewhat modified form. It assumes intellectual capacities and sources of information that men simply do not possess, and it is even more absurd as an approach to policy when the time and money that can be allocated to a policy problem is limited, as is always the case. Of particular importance to public administrators is the fact that public agencies are in effect usually instructed not to practice the first method. That is to say, their prescribed functions and constraints—the politically or legally possible—restrict their attention to relatively few values and relatively few alternative policies among the countless alternatives that might be imagined. It is the second method that is practiced.

Curiously, however, the literatures of decision-making, policy formulation, planning, and public administration formalize the first approach rather than the second, leaving public administrators who handle complex decisions in the position of practicing what few preach. For emphasis I run some risk of overstatement. True enough, the literature is well aware of limits on man's capacities and of the inevitability that policies will be approached in some such style as the second. But attempts to formalize rational policy formulation—to lay out explicitly the necessary steps in the process—usually describe the first approach and not the second.

The common tendency to describe policy formulation even for complex problems as though it followed the first approach has been strengthened by the attention given to, and success enjoyed by, operations research,* statistical decision theory,† and systems analysis.‡ The hall-

---

* *Operations research:* type of analysis, based on mathematical models, used to determine the most efficient use of resources for a set of goals.

† *Statistical decision theory:* theory that allows one to make choices between alternatives by objectifying problems and analyzing them quantitatively. Also called Bayesian decision theory after Thomas Bayes (1702–1761), who developed the mathematical foundation of inference, the method of using information on a sample to infer characteristics about a population.

‡ *Systems analysis:* analysis of systemic data by means of advanced quantitative techniques to aid in selecting the most appropriate course of action among a series of alternatives.

marks of these procedures, typical of the first approach, are clarity of objective, explicitness of evaluation, a high degree of comprehensiveness of overview, and, wherever possible, quantification of values for mathematical analysis. But these advanced procedures remain largely the appropriate techniques of relatively small-scale problem-solving where the total number of variables to be considered is small and value problems restricted. Charles Hitch, head of the Economics Division of RAND Corporation, one of the leading centers for application of these techniques, has written:

> I would make the empirical generalization from my experience at RAND and elsewhere that operations research is the art of sub-optimizing, i.e., of solving some lower-level problems, and that difficulties increase and our special competence diminishes by an order of magnitude with every level of decision making we attempt to ascend. The sort of simple explicit model which operations researchers are so proficient in using can certainly reflect most of the significant factors influencing traffic control on the George Washington Bridge, but the proportion of the relevant reality which we can represent by any such model or models in studying, say, a major foreign-policy decision, appears to be almost trivial.[1]

Accordingly, I propose in this paper to clarify and formalize the second method, much neglected in the literature. This might be described as the method of *successive limited comparisons*. I will contrast it with the first approach, which might be called the rational-comprehensive method. More impressionistically and briefly—and therefore generally used in this article—they could be characterized as the branch method and root method, the former continually building out from the current situation, step-by-step and by small degrees; the latter starting from fundamentals anew each time, building on the past only as experience is embodied in a theory, and always prepared to start completely from the ground up.

Let us put the characteristics of the two methods side by side in simplest terms.

Rational-Comprehensive (Root)

1a. Clarification of values or objectives distinct from and usually prerequisite to empirical analysis of alternative policies.

2a. Policy-formulation is therefore approached through means-end analysis: First the ends are isolated, then the means to achieve them are sought.

3a. The test of a "good" policy is that it can be shown to be the most appropriate means to desired ends.

4a. Analysis is comprehensive; every important relevant factor is taken into account.

5a. Theory is often heavily relied upon.

Assuming that the root method is familiar and understandable, we proceed directly to clarification of its alternative by contrast. In explaining the second, we shall be describing how most administrators do in fact approach complex questions, for the root method, the "best" way as a blueprint or model, is in fact not workable for complex policy questions, and administrators are forced to use the method of successive limited comparisons.

Intertwining Evaluation and Empirical Analysis (1B)

The quickest way to understand how values are handled in the method of successive limited comparisons is to see how the root method often breaks down in *its* handling of values or objectives. The idea that values should be clarified, and in advance of the examination of alternative policies, is appealing. But what happens when we attempt it for complex social problems? The first difficulty is that on many critical values or objectives, citizens disagree, congressmen disagree, and public administrators disagree. Even where a fairly specific objective is prescribed for the administrator, there remains considerable room for disagreement on sub-objectives. Consider, for example, the conflict with respect to locating public housing, described in Meyerson and Banfield's study of the Chicago Housing Authority—disagreement which occurred despite the clear objective of providing a certain number of public housing units in the city. Similarly conflicting are objectives in highway location, traffic control, minimum wage administration, development of tourist facilities in national parks, or insect control.

Successive Limited Comparisons (Branch)

1b. Selection of value goals and empirical analysis of the needed action are not distinct from one another but are closely intertwined.
2b. Since means and ends are not distinct, means-end analysis is often inappropriate or limited.
3b. The test of a "good" policy is typically that various analysts find themselves directly agreeing on a policy (without their agreeing that it is the most appropriate means to an agreed objective).
4b. Analysis is drastically limited: i) Important possible outcomes are neglected. ii) Important alternative potential policies are neglected. iii) Important affected values are neglected.
5b. A succession of comparisons greatly reduces or eliminates reliance on theory.

Administrators cannot escape these conflicts by ascertaining the majority's preference, for preferences have not been registered on most issues; indeed, there often *are* no preferences in the absence of public discussion sufficient to bring an issue to the attention of the electorate.

Furthermore, there is a question of whether intensity of feeling should be considered as well as the number of persons preferring each alternative. By the impossibility of doing otherwise, administrators often are reduced to deciding policy without clarifying objectives first.

Even when an administrator resolves to follow his own values as a criterion for decisions, he often will not know how to rank them when they conflict with one another, as they usually do. Suppose, for example, that an administrator must relocate tenants living in tenements scheduled for destruction. One objective is to empty the buildings fairly promptly, another is to find suitable accommodation for persons displaced, another is to avoid friction with residents in other areas in which a large influx would be unwelcome, another is to deal with all concerned through persuasion if possible, and so on.

How does one state even to himself the relative importance of these partially conflicting values? A simple ranking of them is not enough; one needs ideally to know how much of one value is worth sacrificing for some of another value. The answer is that typically the administrator chooses—and must choose—directly among policies in which these values are combined in different ways. He cannot first clarify his values and then choose among policies.

A more subtle third point underlies both the first two. Social objectives do not always have the same relative values. One objective may be highly prized in one circumstance, another in another circumstance. If, for example, an administrator values highly both the dispatch with which his agency can carry through its projects *and* good public relations, it matters little which of the two possibly conflicting values he favors in some abstract or general sense. Policy questions arise in forms which put to administrators such a question as: Given the degree to which we are or are not already achieving the values of dispatch and the values of good public relations, is it worth sacrificing a little speed for a happier clientele, or is it better to risk offending the clientele so that we can get on with our work? The answer to such a question varies with circumstances.

The value problem is, as the example shows, always a problem of adjustments at a margin. But there is no practicable way to state marginal objectives or values except in terms of particular policies. That one value is preferred to another in one decision situation does not mean that it will be preferred in another decision situation in which it can be had only at great sacrifice of another value. Attempts to rank or order values in general and abstract terms so that they do not shift from decision to decision end up by ignoring the relevant marginal preferences. The significance of this third point thus goes very far. Even if all administrators had at hand an agreed set of values, objectives, and constraints, and an agreed ranking of these values, objectives, and constraints, their marginal values in actual choice situations would be impossible to formulate.

Unable consequently to formulate the relevant values first and then choose among policies to achieve them, administrators must choose directly among alternative policies that offer different marginal combinations of values. Somewhat paradoxically, the only practicable way to disclose one's relevant marginal values even to oneself is to describe the policy one chooses to achieve them. Except roughly and vaguely, I know of no way to describe—or even to understand—what my relative evaluations are for, say, freedom and security, speed and accuracy in governmental decisions, or low taxes and better schools than to describe my preferences among specific policy choices that might be made between the alternatives in each of the pairs.

In summary, two aspects of the process by which values are actually handled can be distinguished. The first is clear: evaluation and empirical analysis are intertwined; that is, one chooses among values and among policies at one and the same time. Put a little more elaborately, one simultaneously chooses a policy to attain certain objectives and chooses the objectives themselves. The second aspect is related but distinct: the administrator focuses his attention on marginal or incremental values. Whether he is aware of it or not, he does not find general formulations of objectives very helpful and in fact makes specific marginal or incremental comparisons. Two policies, X and Y, confront him. Both promise the same degree of attainment of objectives a, b, c, d, and e. But X promises him somewhat more of f than does Y, while Y promises him somewhat more of g than does X. In choosing between them, he is in fact offered the alternative of a marginal or incremental amount of f at the expense of a marginal or incremental amount of g. The only values that are relevant to his choice are these increments by which the two policies differ; and, when he finally chooses between the two marginal values, he does so by making a choice between policies.

As to whether the attempt to clarify objectives in advance of policy selection is more or less rational than the close intertwining of marginal evaluation and empirical analysis, the principal difference established is that for complex problems the first is impossible and irrelevant, and the second is both possible and relevant. The second is possible because the administrator need not try to analyze any values except the values by which alternative policies differ and need not be concerned with them except as they differ marginally. His need for information on values or objectives is drastically reduced as compared with the root method; and his capacity for grasping, comprehending, and relating values to one another is not strained beyond the breaking point.

* * *

Successive Comparison as A System

Successive limited comparisons is, then, indeed a method or system; it is not a failure of method for which administrators ought to apologize.

None the less, its imperfections, which have not been explored in this paper, are many. For example, the method is without a built-in safeguard for all relevant values, and it also may lead the decision-maker to overlook excellent policies for no other reason than that they are not suggested by the chain of successive policy steps leading up to the present. Hence, it ought to be said that under this method, as well as under some of the most sophisticated variants of the root method—operations research, for example—policies will continue to be as foolish as they are wise.

Why then bother to describe the method in all the above detail? Because it is in fact a common method of policy formulation, and is, for complex problems, the principal reliance of administrators as well as of other policy analysts. And because it will be superior to any other decision-making method available for complex problems in many circumstances, certainly superior to a futile attempt at superhuman comprehensiveness. The reaction of the public administrator to the exposition of method doubtless will be less a discovery of a new method than a better acquaintance with an old. But by becoming more conscious of their practice of this method, administrators might practice it with more skill and know when to extend or constrict its use. (That they sometimes practice it effectively and sometimes not may explain the extremes of opinion on "muddling through," which is both praised as a highly sophisticated form of problem-solving and denounced as no method at all. For I suspect that in so far as there is a system in what is known as "muddling through," this method is it).

One of the noteworthy incidental consequences of clarification of the method is the light it throws on the suspicion an administrator sometimes entertains that a consultant or adviser is not speaking relevantly and responsibly when in fact by all ordinary objective evidence he is. The trouble lies in the fact that most of us approach policy problems within a framework given by our view of a chain of successive policy choices made up to the present. One's thinking about appropriate policies with respect, say, to urban traffic control is greatly influenced by one's knowledge of the incremental steps taken up the present. An administrator enjoys an intimate knowledge of his past sequences that "outsiders" do not share, and his thinking and that of the "outsider" will consequently be different in ways that may puzzle both. Both may appear to be talking intelligently, yet each may find the other unsatisfactory. The relevance of the policy chain of succession is even more clear when an American tries to discuss, say, antitrust policy with a Swiss, for the chains of policy in the two countries are strikingly different and the two individuals consequently have organized their knowledge in quite different ways.

If this phenomenon is a barrier to communication, an understanding of it promises an enrichment of intellectual interaction in policy formulation. Once the source of difference is understood, it will sometimes be stimulating for an administrator to seek out a policy analyst whose recent experience is with a policy chain different from his own.

This raises again a question only briefly discussed above on the merits of like-mindedness among government administrators. While much of organization theory argues the virtues of common values and agreed organizational objectives, for complex problems in which the root method is inapplicable, agencies will want among their own personnel two types of diversification: administrators whose thinking is organized by reference to policy chains other than those familiar to most members of the organization and, even more commonly, administrators whose professional or personal values or interests create diversity of view (perhaps coming from different specialties, social classes, geographical areas) so that, even within a single agency, decision-making can be fragmented and parts of the agency can serve as watchdogs for other parts.

DISCUSSION QUESTIONS

1. When you decide which pair of pants or type of shirt you will buy, do you use a the "root" or "branch" method of decision making? How about when you decided which college you would go to or which career you might choose? Explain.

2. Do you see any problems with incremental decision making? What types of decisions does it tend to favor? Is this a good or a bad thing? Explain.

3. Is the comprehensive method of decision making possible, or is it too taxing for the human brain, as Lindblom suggests? Explain.

NOTES

1. "Operations Research and National Planning—A Dissent," *Operations Research* 5 (October 1957), p. 718.

63
"American Business, Public Policy, Case Studies, and Political Theory"

Theodore J. Lowi

Before Lowi's article appeared in 1964, many social scientists analyzed public policy through case studies that focused on one particular policy and its implementation. Lowi argued that what the social sciences lacked was a means to cumulate, compare, and contrast the diverse findings of these studies. We needed, in other words, a typology of policymaking. In the article below, Lowi argues that different types of public policies produce different patterns of participation. Public policies can be classified as distributive, regulatory, or redistributive, each with its own distinctive "arena of power." For example, public policies that provide benefits to a single congressional district, group, or company can be classified as distributive. In the distributive arena of power, policy beneficiaries are active in seeking to expand or extend their benefits, but there is no real opposition. Rather, legislators build coalitions premised on "mutual noninterference"—interests and their representatives seek particular benefits such as a research and development contract, a new highway, or a farm subsidy, but they do not oppose the similar requests of others.

The regulatory and redistributive policy arenas also display distinctive dynamics and roles that participants in the process play. Lowi's work was important not only for providing a classification scheme by which social scientists could think more systematically about different public policies, but for proposing that we study "politics" as a consequence of different types of public policy. Traditionally, social scientists have studied the politics to see what kind of policies are produced.

. . . What is needed is a basis for cumulating, comparing, and contrasting diverse findings. Such a framework or interpretative scheme would bring the diverse cases and findings into a more consistent relation to each other and would begin to suggest generalizations sufficiently close to the data to be relevant and sufficiently abstract to be subject to more broadly theoretical treatment.

* * *

The scheme is based upon the following argument: (1) The types of relationships to be found among people are determined by their expectations—by what they hope to achieve or get from relating to others. (2) In politics, expectations are determined by governmental outputs or policies. (3) Therefore, a political relationship is determined by the type of policy at stake, so that for every type of policy there is likely to be a distinctive type of political relationship. If power is defined as a share in the making of policy, or authoritative allocations, then the political relationship in question is a power relationship or, over time, a power structure.

* * *

There are three major categories of public policies in the scheme: distribution, regulation, and redistribution. These types are historically as well as functionally distinct, distribution being almost the exclusive type of national domestic policy from 1789 until virtually 1890. Agitation for regulatory and redistributive policies began at about the same time, but regulation had become an established fact before any headway at all was made in redistribution.

These categories are not mere contrivances for purposes of simplification. They are meant to correspond to real phenomena—so much so that the major hypotheses of the scheme follow directly from the categories and their definitions. Thus, *these areas of policy or government activity constitute real arenas of power.* Each arena tends to develop its own characteristic political structure, political process, elites, and group relations. What remains is to identify these arenas, to formulate hypotheses about the attributes of each, and to test the scheme by how many empirical relationships it can anticipate and explain.

Areas of Policy Defined

(1) In the long run, all governmental policies may be considered redistributive, because in the long run some people pay in taxes more than they receive in services. Or, all may be thought regulatory because, in the long run, a governmental decision on the use of resources can only displace a private decision about the same resource or at least reduce private alternatives about the resource. But politics works in the short run, and in the short run certain kinds of government decisions can be made without regard to limited resources. Policies of this kind are called "distributive," a term first coined for nineteenth-century land policies, but easily extended to include most contemporary public land and resource policies; rivers and harbors ("pork barrel") programs; defense procurement and R & D; labor, business, and agricultural "clientele" services; and the traditional tariff. Distributive policies are characterized by the ease with which they can be disaggregated and dispensed unit by small unit, each unit more or less in isolation from other units and from any general rule. "Patronage" in the fullest meaning of the word can be taken as a synonym for "distributive." These are policies that are

virtually not policies at all but are highly individualized decisions that only by accumulation can be called a policy. They are policies in which the indulged and the deprived, the loser and the recipient, need never come into direct confrontation. Indeed, in many instances of distributive policy, the deprived cannot as a class be identified, because the most influential among them can be accommodated by further disaggregation of the stakes.

(2) Regulatory policies are also specific and individual in their impact, but they are not capable of the almost infinite amount of disaggregation typical of distributive policies. Although the laws are stated in general terms ("Arrange the transportation system artistically." "Thou shalt not show favoritism in pricing."), the impact of regulatory decisions is clearly one of directly raising costs and/or reducing or expanding the alternatives of private individuals ("Get off the grass!" "Produce kosher if you advertise kosher!"). Regulatory policies are distinguishable from distributive in that in the short run the regulatory decision involves a direct choice as to who will be indulged and who deprived. Not all applicants for a single television channel or an overseas air route can be propitiated. Enforcement of an unfair labor practice on the part of management weakens management in its dealings with labor. So, while implementation is firm-by-firm and case-by-case, policies cannot be disaggregated to the level of the individual or the single firm (as in distribution), because individual decisions must be made by application of a general rule and therefore become interrelated within the broader standards of law. Decisions cumulate among all individuals affected by the law in roughly the same way. Since the most stable lines of perceived common impact are the basic sectors of the economy, regulatory decisions are cumulative largely along sectoral lines; regulatory policies are usually disaggregable only down to the sector level.

(3) Redistributive policies are like regulatory policies in the sense that relations among broad categories of private individuals are involved and, hence, individual decisions must be interrelated. But on all other counts there are great differences in the nature of impact. The categories of impact are much broader, approaching social classes. They are, crudely speaking, haves and have-nots, bigness and smallness, bourgeoisie and proletariat. The aim involved is not use of property but property itself, not equal treatment but equal possession, not behavior but being. The fact that our income tax is in reality only mildly redistributive does not alter the fact of the aims and the stakes involved in income tax policies. The same goes for our various "welfare state" programs, which are redistributive only for those who entered retirement or unemployment rolls without having contributed at all. The nature of a redistributive issue is not determined by the outcome of a battle over how redistributive a policy is going to be. Expectations about what it *can* be, what it threatens to be, are determinative.

Arenas of Power

Once one posits the general tendency of these areas of policy or governmental activity to develop characteristic political structures, a number of hypotheses become compelling. And when the various hypotheses are accumulated, the general contours of each of the three arenas begin quickly to resemble, respectively, the three "general" theories of political process identified earlier. The arena that develops around distributive policies is best characterized in the terms of [E. E.] Schattschneider's findings. The regulatory arena corresponds to the pluralist school, and the school's general notions are found to be limited pretty much to this one arena. The redistributive arena most closely approximates, with some adaptation, an elitist view of the political process.

(1) The distributive arena can be identified in considerable detail from Schattschneider's case-study alone. What he and his pluralist successors did not see was that the traditional structure of tariff politics is also in largest part the structure of politics of all those diverse policies identified earlier as distributive. The arena is "pluralistic" only in the sense that a large number of small, intensely organized interests are operating. In fact, there is even greater multiplicity of participants here than the pressure-group model can account for, because essentially it is a politics of every man for himself. The single person and the single firm are the major activists.

* * *

When a billion-dollar issue can be disaggregated into many millions of nickel-dime items and each item can be dealt with without regard to the others, multiplication of interests and of access is inevitable, and so is reduction of conflict. All of this has the greatest of bearing on the relations among participants and, therefore, the "power structure." Indeed, coalitions must be built to pass legislation and "make policy," but what of the nature and basis of the coalitions? In the distributive arena, political relationships approximate what Schattschneider called "mutual non-interference"—"a mutuality under which it is proper for each to seek duties [indulgences] for himself but improper and unfair to oppose duties [indulgences] sought by others."[1] In the area of rivers and harbors, references are made to "pork barrel" and "log-rolling," but these colloquialisms have not been taken sufficiently seriously. A log-rolling coalition is not one forged of conflict, compromise, and tangential interest but, on the contrary, one composed of members who have absolutely nothing in common; and this is possible because the "pork barrel" is a container for unrelated items. This is the typical form of relationship in the distributive arena.

The structure of these log-rolling relationships leads typically, though not always, to Congress; and the structure is relatively stable because all who have access of any sort usually support whoever are the leaders. And there tend to be "elites" of a peculiar sort in the Congressional committees whose jurisdictions include the subject-matter in question. Until recently, for instance, on tariff matters the House Ways and Means Committee was virtually the government. Much the same can be said for Public Works on rivers and harbors.[22] It is a broker leadership, but "policy" is best understood as cooptation rather than conflict and compromise.

* * *

(2) The regulatory arena could hardly be better identified than in the thousands of pages written for the whole polity by the pluralists. But, unfortunately, some translation is necessary to accommodate pluralism to its more limited universe. The regulatory arena appears to be composed of a multiplicity of groups organized around tangential relations or David Truman's "shared attitudes." (see p. 454) Within this narrower context of regulatory decisions, one can even go so far as to accept the most extreme pluralist statement that policy tends to be a residue of the interplay of group conflict. This statement can be severely criticized only by use of examples drawn from non-regulatory decisions.

As I argued before, there is no way for regulatory policies to be disaggregated into very large numbers of unrelated items. Because individual regulatory decisions involve direct confrontations of indulged and deprived, the typical political coalition is born of conflict and compromise among tangential interests that usually involve a total sector of the economy. Thus, while the typical basis for coalition in distributive politics is uncommon interests (log-rolling), an entirely different basis is typical in regulatory politics. The pluralist went wrong only in assuming the regulatory type of coalition is *the* coalition.

* * *

What this suggests is that the typical power structure in regulatory politics is far less stable than that in the distributive arena. Since coalitions form around shared interests, the coalitions will shift as the interests change or as conflicts of interest emerge. With such group-based and shifting patterns of conflict built into every regulatory issue, it is in most cases impossible for a Congressional committee, an administrative agency, a peak association governing board, or a social elite to contain all the participants long enough to establish a stable power elite. Policy outcomes seem inevitably to be the residue remaining after all the reductions of demands by all participants have been made in order to extend support to majority size. But a majority-sized coalition of shared interests on one issue could not possibly be entirely appropriate for some other issue. In regulatory decision-making, relationships among group leadership elements and between them on any one or more points of governmental access are too unstable to form a single policy-making elite. As a consequence, decision-making tends to pass from administrative agencies and Congressional committees to Congress, the place where uncertainties in the policy process have always been settled. Congress as an institution is the last resort for breakdowns in bargaining over policy, just as in the case of parties the primary is a last resort for breakdowns in bargaining over nominations. No one leadership group can contain the conflict by an almost infinite subdivision and distribution of the stakes. In the regulatory political process, Congress and the "balance of power" seem to play the classic role attributed to them by the pluralists.

* * *

(3) Issues that involve redistribution cut closer than any others along class lines and activate interests in what are roughly class terms. If there is ever any cohesion within the peak associations, it occurs on redistributive issues, and their rhetoric suggests that they occupy themselves most of the time with these. In a ten-year period just before and after, but not including, the war years [World War II], the Manufacturers' Association of Connecticut, for example, expressed itself overwhelmingly more often on redistributive than on any other types of issues.

* * *

Where the peak associations, led by elements of Mr. Mills's power elite*, have reality, their resources and access are bound to affect power relations. Owing to their stability and the impasse (or equilibrium) in relations among broad classes of the entire society, the political structure of the redistributive arena seems to be highly stabilized, virtually institutionalized. Its stability, unlike that of the distributive arena, derives from shared interests. But in contrast to the regulatory arena, these shared interests are sufficiently stable and clear and consistent to provide the foundation for ideologies.

* * *

. . . Finally, just as the nature of redistributive policies influences politics towards the centralization and stabilization of conflict, so does it further influence the removal of decision-making from Congress. A decentralized and bargaining Congress can cumulate but it cannot balance, and redistributive policies require complex balancing on a very large scale. What [William] Riker has said of budget-making applies here: ". . . legislative governments cannot endure a budget. Its finances must be totted up by party leaders in the legislature itself. In a complex fiscal system, however, haphazard legislative judgments cannot bring revenue

---

* [According to C. Wright Mills, a small network of individuals, which he called the power elite, controls the economy, the political system, and the military.]

into even rough alignment with supply. So budgeting is introduced—which transfers financial control to the budget maker. . . ."[2] Congress can provide exceptions to principles and it can implement those principles with elaborate standards of implementation as a condition for the concessions that money-providers will make. But the makers of principles of redistribution seem to be the holders of the "command posts."

None of this suggests a power elite such as Mills would have had us believe existed, but it does suggest a type of stable and continual conflict that can only be understood in class terms. The foundation upon which the social-stratification and power-elite school rested, especially when dealing with national power, was so conceptually weak and empirically unsupported that its critics were led to err in the opposite direction by denying the direct relevance of social and institutional positions and the probability of stable decision-making elites. But the relevance of that approach becomes stronger as the scope of its application is reduced and as the standards for identifying the scope are clarified. But this is equally true of the pluralist school and of those approaches based on a "politics of this-or-that policy."

* * *

Discussion Questions

1. Provide examples of each type of policy that Lowi discusses (distributive, regulatory, and redistributive). Explain your choices.

2. If you were a member of Congress, which type of policy would you try to emphasize if your main interest was in getting reelected? Why?

3. Are there any types of policies that do not seem to fit Lowi's framework? Do some policies fit in more than one category? If so, provide examples.

Notes

1. E. E. Schattschneider, *Politics, Pressure and the Tariff* (New York: 1935), pp. 135–6.
2. William Riker, *Democracy in the United States* (New York: 1953), p. 216.

64
"Why Our Democracy Doesn't Work"

WILLIAM A. NISKANEN

William Niskanen looks at the politics that create our public policies. His argument is a familiar one among critics of the public policy process, but Niskanen states it in particularly bold terms: "An oligarchy [of special interests] is using democratic processes to exploit the majority, and is governing in the name of the people but for those who have a special influence on the government." The problem, Niskanen argues, is inherent in our political system.

Public opinion polls and voting behavior indicate that most Americans are in favor of lower public spending, but Americans are even more vocal in securing public spending for programs from which they benefit. Interest groups organized around the continuation of a particular public policy place powerful demands upon elected officials to continue programs, often without representation of the broader public, who is footing the bill. And members of Congress, despite voters' demands for lower government spending in general, are rewarded with reelection when they provide special benefits to their districts or to supportive interest groups. There is also no incentive for the political parties to endorse lower spending, across the board. Democrats, Niskanen argues, are predisposed to bigger government, and it is what Democratic constituents expect. Republicans, on the other hand, fear being branded as "unrealistic, reactionary, irresponsible, uncaring, etc.," if they advocate huge spending cuts. The result is continued spending without any restraint.

Interestingly, Niskanen wrote this article before the 1994 midterm elections, which produced a Republican House and Senate for the first time in more than forty years. The Republicans did indeed pursue the kinds of spending cuts advocated by Niskanen, but the effort has cooled dramatically in the wake of tremendous political pressure brought to bear by the beneficiaries and advocates of many federal programs.

American government does not serve us very well. Moreover, because our periodic elections are only a weak error-correcting process, this has been the case for a long time.

This is an awkward conclusion for a political economist who is not inclined to a radical perspective. Our conventional model of democratic government assumes that, given competitive parties and majority rule, the government will act as an agent of the median voter. The government described by this model has several characteristic problems, especially when there are no effective constitutional limits on its powers, but it is supposed to serve the interests of a majority of the voters quite well.

I have now come to a belief that our conventional model of democratic government is a romantic rationalization of our high school civics lessons. What has led me to this conclusion? The scope and scale of American government are now substantially larger than is consistent with the interests of the majority of voters. Let me briefly summarize the evidence:

- The popular vote for the presidential and gubernatorial candidates of the incumbent party has generally *declined* in response to an increase in real per capita government spending since the prior election. The candidate of the incumbent party is often elected (or reelected), despite an increase in government spending, because voters prefer continuity and because they credit the incumbent party for an improvement in general economic conditions.
- People also vote by moving. State population data reflect a general pattern of net migration from states with high per capita government spending to states with lower spending. Similarly, population changes among our major cities are a negative function of the level of per capita government spending.

These types of evidence are strongly inconsistent with the view that the growth of government reflects a broad popular demand for more government services.

Other types of evidence reinforce this perspective.

- Federal spending is more closely related to the capacity to tax and borrow than to objective measures of the demand for federal services. Estimates of the demand for government services based on regression analysis of cross-state data, for example, explain only about one-half of the increase in real per capita government spending over time. Looking at the country as a whole, the government spending share of GNP has increased at a remarkably steady annual rate (the variation that has occurred has been due largely to changes in the unemployment rate and the number of armed forces overseas).
- When the federal government gives a grant to a state or local government, the recipient government increases its expenditures by an amount equal to most or all of the grant. When the same grant is given directly to the population (say, for instance, the federal government decides to supplement the income of the residents of a particular locality), the recipient government still ends up spending more money —since the amount collected in taxes goes up—but the increase in spending is much less than if the grant were given directly to the government. (The response of national governments to foreign aid is quite similar.) The magnitude of this "flypaper effect" is an indirect indica-

tion of the ability of government officials to implement their own spending preferences.
- Legislatures routinely approve measures that would not be approved by a popular referendum. For example, several weeks after Congress approved the Clean Air Act Amendments of 1990, voters rejected all but a few of about 200 environmental measures on state and local ballots. Last year, Congress approved a substantial increase in federal taxes, even though voters rejected nine of the ten major tax measures on state ballots in 1992. Congress also approved an increase in domestic spending, even though a recent public opinion poll indicates that more than 60 percent of those polled would prefer fewer government services and lower taxes to more services and higher taxes. In Europe, there is a similar pattern—as evidenced by the reluctance of most governments to subject the Maastricht treaty [1991 treaty approving European union] to a popular referendum.
- Every president elected since 1968 has "run against Washington," but the federal share of GNP has continued to increase.
- And many national and regional governments have continued the pursuit of destructive economic policies, without substantial reversal except in the case of financial collapse.

The dilemma posed by the evidence from both political behavior and polls of opinion is that while most people oppose a higher level of total government spending, they are even more vocal in support of spending for programs from which they especially benefit! The calculus of concentrated benefits and diffused costs creates a strong incentive to organize political activity in support of specific programs, even if the sum of the diffused costs is much greater than the benefits. As a consequence, almost all the witnesses at legislative hearings favor higher spending for the specific program being reviewed. The federal budget now finances everything from babysitting to midnight basketball.

I read this broad body of evidence to suggest that the processes of representative democracy lead to a level of government spending, taxes, and regulation that is higher than that preferred by a majority of voters. An oligarchy is using democratic processes to exploit the majority, and is governing in the name of the people but for those who have a special influence on the government.

This perspective contrasts sharply with the more characteristic conservative concern that a populist majority will exploit the property-owning minority. Much redistribution, it turns out, is not from the rich to the poor but from the general population to those to whom the agenda-setters are most responsive. Our government is now a democratic leviathan in which voter approval is treated as a constraint rather than as an objective, a difference that is important primarily because our major parties are not very competitive. For the most part, in other words,

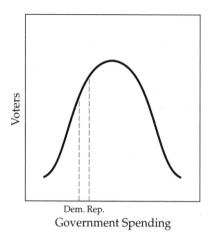

Dem. Rep.
Government Spending

politicians serve the interests of voters only to the extent necessary for election. And the weak competition between the parties allows politicians substantial discretion to pursue other interests.

What We Want vs. What We Get

The figure [above] summarizes my unconventional perspective on contemporary American politics. The vertical axis measures the number (or percentage) of voters who favor a specific level of government spending. The horizontal axis measures the level of government spending. The distribution of preferences at a specific time, in turn, is a function of the distribution of expected tax shares and the level and distribution of current spending. My judgment, in addition, is that the characteristic position of Republican candidates is somewhat closer to the preferred level of spending but that the characteristic position of both major party candidates is to the "left" of the preferred level. This perspective is consistent with the evidence summarized above, but it raises some very awkward questions:

  1) Why do the Republicans lose so many elections? The simple but incomplete answer is that the Republicans, as in 1992, are often "the stupid party." A more informative answer is that the popular vote is a function of conditions other than the level of government spending and that the Republicans have often not been effective in promoting or identifying with these other conditions. In the elections for governor and president, the other major condition is the change in real per capita income since the prior election, and the effect of this condition on the popular vote is substantially larger than the effect of government spending. As a consequence, a substantial increase in government spending is consistent with the election of a candidate of the incumbent party if general economic conditions are satisfactory.

Similarly, in the elections for state legislatures and Congress, the other major condition is the effectiveness of the incumbent as an intermediary with the bureaucracy and in securing preferences for the interests in his or her district. Again, a substantial increase in spending is consistent with the election of a candidate of the incumbent party if the incumbent has been effective in these roles. The 1992 election revealed both a broad discontent with the general performance of Congress and an endorsement of the performance of most individual members. Although congressional term limits were approved in every state in which the issue was on the ballot, almost every member of Congress running in the general election was reelected.

In summary, the popular vote is a vote for (or against) a *package* of conditions specific to each candidate and party. Voters do not appear to have endorsed a higher level of spending, but politicians usually can be elected if their performance or position on other important conditions is satisfactory.

2) Why don't the Republicans move to the right? The simple answer is that Republicans can win elections without endorsing lower spending as long as the Democrats are a high spending party. The more complex answer is that almost all of the agenda setters in American politics—the interest groups, the bureaucracy, the intellectual community, and the media—have a stake in big government, and any move to the right on spending issues is broadly criticized as unrealistic, reactionary, irresponsible, uncaring, etc. The political calculus of concentrated benefits and diffused costs assures that the advocates of big government will continue to dominate the "culture of spending."

3) Why don't the Democrats endorse lower spending? The simple answer is that the Democrats can win elections as long as the Republicans make serious mistakes on issues other than spending. The more complex answer is that the Democrats are dependent on party activists who have an ideological or pecuniary stake in big government. Similarly, the role of party activists has led the Republican Party to endorse a position on some social issues that is substantially different from the vote-maximizing position. The role of both party activists and money in elections limits the opportunity for a party to chose a vote-maximizing position on those issues of most concern to these groups. There have been very few major shifts in party positions in American history, but it would be useful to study the conditions that led to these shifts. The Democrats, for example, were generally the small government party through the nineteenth century and were the low tariff party until the 1980s. And in this century, the Republicans were the small defense party until the 1980s.

4) Why doesn't a third party arise on the right? In fact, the largest third party votes in the period since World War II were for candidates on the right, George Wallace in 1968 and Ross Perot in 1992. The Amer-

ican electoral system, however, is strongly biased against third parties. A third party can be successful only when one or both of the major parties splits on a major issue, such as slavery. As a rule, the two major parties can move substantially from the vote-maximizing position without significant risk from a third party. Ross Perot, for example, won 19 percent of the popular vote without winning one electoral vote. The large third party vote on the right, however, supports my view that both major parties are to the left of the policies preferred by the majority.

The Political Cartel

Our conventional model of democratic government assumes competitive, non-ideological parties that will endorse any policy position that promises to increase their prospect for election. My increasingly grumpy perspective is that our major parties operate as an implicit cartel between ideological Democrats and accommodationist Republicans, in which the Democrats accept the basic structure of the economy and the Republicans accept the major activities of the modern state. The intellectual community and the media reinforce this cartel by dismissing any candidate who challenges this understanding. Ronald Reagan was the only presidential candidate to successfully challenge this cartel, winning the contempt of the self-appointed censors and broad popular approval by the voters.

This alternative perspective is not an adequate guide to the future, however, because it is consistent with two quite different outlooks. In my grumpy outlook, the cartel survives. Democrats continue to promote ever higher spending, taxes, and regulation to meet newly discovered public needs and human rights. And the Republicans acquiesce to avoid the charge of being greedy or uncaring. Every president is regarded as a failure, Congress continues to be an object of contempt, a populist and nativist third party rumbles on the right, voters are increasingly alienated, and the economy stagnates—but the cartel survives.

My optimistic outlook is based on the recognition that a government that does not serve the interests of the general population is often much more fragile than is superficially apparent—the most dramatic examples of this, of course, are the recent collapses of most of the world's communist regimes. The accumulating evidence suggests the potential for a major transformation of American politics, a majority coalition for limited, constitutional, *smaller* government.

Nor is this only a recent possibility. The Republicans have long had the potential to exploit it but, as often as not, they have been part of the problem. Federal domestic spending and regulation, for example, increased rapidly under both Richard Nixon and George Bush. Moreover, the Republicans' capacity to lead a broad coalition for smaller government has often been undermined by various errors:

- carelessness about economic growth in 1960 and 1992
- the major political scandal of Watergate
- actions and statements that reinforce the perception that the Republican Party is a class party with a rigid position on social issues (1992) or a dangerous position on military issues (1964).

The immediate challenge for the Republican Party, of course, is to enlist the support of most of the Perot voters without endorsing Perot's more bizarre positions. A coalition of libertarians, conservatives, and populists will not agree on some issues, nor will any other coalition broad enough to elect a president. For the moment, however, only this type of coalition has the potential to constrain our democratic leviathan.

Discussion Questions

1. Have attempts at cutting the budget since Niskanen wrote his article (in 1994) supported or undermined his conclusions? Explain.

2. Is cutting spending as impossible as he claims? Why or why not?

3. Who else is to blame in this process other than interest groups? Explain.

THE DEBATE: DOES THE DEFICIT MATTER?

Perhaps the most important public policy document of any government is the annual budget, and no public policy debate has a longer history of controversy than the practice of deficit spending by the national government. When the government spends more than it gathers in taxes and borrows to cover the deficit each year, is it an immoral and irresponsible act that will burden future generations? Or is deficit spending and borrowing a practical investment in the future for building a national infrastructure and educating our children?

Senator Larry Craig (R.-Idaho) and the economist James Buchanan argue in favor of a constitutional amendment requiring a balanced budget (or preventing the government from deficit spending) on two slightly different grounds. Craig points to the immoral burden of deficit spending (and the year-to-year accumulation of the national debt) for future generations, the billions of dollars each year that go toward paying interest on the debt rather than investment through the private sector, and the large segments of the national debt owned by foreign investors. Buchanan bases his argument in public choice theory. The theory, simply put, argues that politicians, like all people, will take actions that reflect their self-interest. Members of Congress want to secure lots of votes, so they make budget decisions that will be popular with the maximum number of voters. Keynesian theory, which argued that deficit spending could be used to fine-tune the economy, was embraced by economists and politicians alike in the 1940s, but its flaw was a failure to recognize that taxation and spending issues are decided by elected officials seeking reelection, rather than the fine tuning of the macro economy. For both Craig and Buchanan, only a balanced budget amendment would provide the necessary discipline to bring the growing federal debt under control.

Robert Eisner stands in opposition to the amendment. He argues that in fact a significant portion of the national government's debt is owned by Americans. This, according to Eisner, is a very good thing. Citing Abraham Lincoln, Eisner argues that "The great advantage of citizens being creditors as well as debtors, with relation to the public debt, is obvious. Men can readily perceive that they cannot be much oppressed by a debt which they owe themselves." While proponents of a balanced budget amendment often point out that every American family, business, and state and local government must balance its budget each year, Eisner points out that in fact most American families, businesses, and subnational governments in fact have two budgets—one for current expenditures, and one for longer-term capital investments such as a home mortgage or college educations, new equipment or facilities, or the building of structures such as roads and septic systems. The inability of the national government to invest in the future would be worse for America, Eisner argues, than the annual accumulation of deficits—which have in fact decreased over the past five years.

65
"Should the Senate Pass a Balanced Budget Constitutional Amendment?"

LARRY E. CRAIG AND JAMES M. BUCHANAN

Statement of Larry E. Craig

From testimony before the Senate Judiciary Committee during January 5, 1995 hearings on a balanced budget constitutional amendment.

I am testifying today on behalf of S.J. Res. 1, the bipartisan, bicameral, consensus balanced budget amendment to the Constitution, introduced here in the Senate yesterday by Majority Leader [Robert] Dole [KS-R].

We have steadily forged the language of this measure over the years, carefully crafting an amendment which, having been created over a period of time, would be able to withstand the test of time as part of the supreme law of our land.

All the elements are in place now. This is something the public has supported overwhelmingly and consistently for some years. The challenge to us is to place into our Constitution, our most revered public document, a provision which even some of our Founders recognized immediately as a serious omission: a balanced budget amendment.

Consideration of a balanced budget amendment is a fitting way to begin a new era for our Federal Government. By its very definition, a proposed amendment to our Constitution requires a supermajority [two-thirds vote] of both Houses of Congress. And then the measure will travel in all directions from the U.S. Capitol to the capitals of every State in the Union.

Passing a balanced budget amendment on to the State legislatures sends clear messages to the people across the land.

We hear voters' demands that the government control the way it spends the taxpayers' dollars. In the United States of America, it is the people who control their government, and not the other way around.

An extended debate on the proper role and scope of government is long overdue in this Nation. There is no better way to ensure that debate takes in every coffee shop and shopping mall across the country than to send a balanced budget amendment to all 50 States.

What the voters did in November of last year is part of this Nation's plan for ongoing revolution. They said they were fed up with the way the majority parties had represented them in Washington and they acted on that.

The battle cry for those voters should be familiar to us. It was the same one which rang out across the 13 colonies more than 200 years ago: taxation without representation. Just as King George and Parliament taxed their American subjects without giving them a say, the government is today taxing future generations to pay for government programs which we cannot afford today.

Looking forward to the 21st century, Americans have said loudly and clearly that they want a better world, a stronger American economy, more opportunity for their children, not stagnation or decline.

I am confident this new Congress will respect the right to representation which belongs to the American people.

Our founders and other leaders have clearly outlined that sound fiscal management of the Federal Government went hand in hand with the right to representation. In this century, Woodrow Wilson, the President and eminent scholar, said it well: "Money being spent without new taxation and appropriation without accompanying taxation is as bad as taxation without representation."

The moral imperative that government spend no more than it had was clear to Thomas Jefferson: "The question whether one generation has the right to bind another by the deficit it imposes is a question of such consequence as to place it among the fundamental principles of government. We should consider ourselves unauthorized to saddle posterity with our debts, and morally bound to pay them ourselves."

Jefferson, Wilson, and others recognized long ago what we commonly accept in our homes and businesses today. You cannot spend what you do not have for very long. It is just a matter of time before those bills come due.

Those bills are coming due now for the Federal Government. We are beginning to see standards of living drop because money which would go back into the economy pays interest on the Federal debt. We need to enact a balanced budget amendment now before it is too late to reverse this trend.

No one states our case better than Jefferson: "I wish it were possible to obtain a single amendment to our Constitution. I would be willing to depend on that alone for the reduction of the administration of our government to the genuine principles of its Constitution; I mean an additional article taking from the Federal Government the power of borrowing."

A number of critics of this effort argue that Federal deficits and re-sulting debt are short-term distortions in our governing system. They seem to think that if we just wait this out, somehow the problem will solve itself.

That position often accompanies an underlying attitude that the U.S. Government is so deeply in debt we should not even try to pay it off.

Others have honorably faced up to the nature of this problem and have tried to solve it, but with simple statutes. Despite heroic efforts, every one of these attempts has failed.

Our recent history is littered with the tattered remnants of acts which were intended to stop the financial bleeding from the Federal Treasury.

President Clinton exhorted us about deficit reduction, but the Federal debt still will grow by more than $2 trillion during his term of office. Sadly, his Administration has declared that no more deficit reduction really was necessary until after 1996.

In 1990, then President Bush made a deal with Congress which prom-ised reduced deficits. It too fell short.

We all remember Gramm-Rudman-Hollings II, and before that the original Gramm-Rudman-Hollings law. But because they did not carry the ultimate authority of the Constitution they were swept aside uncer-emoniously. Both worked—but that was the problem. What Congress enacts by statute can just as easily be amended, postponed, suspended, or repealed.

These efforts demonstrate that we face a fundamental omission in our governing document. If it was a problem that a simple statute could resolve, any of these statutes would have worked.

The balanced budget amendment is not the first important omission we've acted to resolve. It took nearly a century after ratification of the Constitution to add the Thirteenth and Fourteenth Amendments, abol-ishing slavery and granting citizenship to all native or naturalized Americans.

The balanced budget amendment has been an issue for two centuries. As the role of government has been evolving and redefined over the last 60 years, this amendment has moved from being appropriate to being absolutely essential. Let us be grateful we have the opportunity to ad-dress this flaw through the very process that the original framers of the Constitution provided.

The warnings about Federal Government debt are everywhere.

After hitting a 30-year low, interest rates have begun marching back upward and easily could continue in that direction. Whether or not the cost of borrowing money climbs, as the national debt grows, we face an exploding burden in interest payments on that debt.

Nearly 20 percent of our interest payments are transfers of wealth from the U.S. to overseas owners of the debt.

The nonpartisan General Accounting Office (GAO) reported in 1992 that unless prompt action was taken to reduce annual deficits, Americans faced potential losses in standard of living. In contrast, GAO reported balancing the Federal budget by 2001 would lead to a 35 percent increase in standard of living.

Losses in standard of living represent the cruelest possible tax. Those who have the least are hurt the most, and they never stop paying.

The Federal Reserve Bank of New York reported that the deficits of the 1980s depressed our standard of living by 5 percent.

Even President Clinton acknowledges the damage we're doing to our children and grandchildren. His *Analytical Perspectives* on the FY [fiscal year] 1995 budget projects future generations will lose as much as 82 percent of their lifetime incomes to taxes, while paying off tax and spend policies.

Even if the budget could be balanced next year, that would still leave our children, grandchildren, and great grandchildren with a debt of $5 trillion or more hanging over their heads. Under current trends, the debt will be about $9 billion a decade from now.

Even if we don't add any more to the debt, the annual gross interest on that debt is already more than $300 billion a year, and climbing. That makes these interest payments the second largest Federal spending item following Social Security. It's also equal to about half of all personal income taxes paid to the Federal Government.

Placed in context, the U.S. faces a looming crisis in our ability to defend ourselves against overseas threats we haven't even identified. Can we afford to equip and train our military men and women, give them a fighting chance, if we're paying so much in interest?

Speaking of Social Security, can any one of us guarantee that the Nation will have the resources to keep that system sound, if interest on the government's debt is nipping at the heels of Social Security because of ever-growing borrowing needs?

To those who continue to argue that these deficits are just a temporary problem which will correct itself over time, I say face reality. Most of the figures on interest which we have right now are based on the optimistic view that the phenomenally low interest rates of a year ago would prevail. However, just since we had this debate in early 1994, interest rates have climbed several percentage points and show few signs of slowing down. The situation is best symbolized by the timer on a bomb, steadily ticking downward toward an explosion. This balanced budget amendment is the only chance we have to halt that timer.

Deficits are not a short-term occurrence as many would have you believe. Our Nation has a little over 200 years of history since ratification of this Constitution. In 57 of the last 65 years, the government has spent more than it took in. That's over a fourth of our existence. Through Republican and Democratic administrations we've been unable to balance the books. This clearly indicates an area of constitutional omission which must be addressed through an amendment.

I am cosponsor of this version of the amendment because I know what it says, and what it does not say. All the ambiguities have been hammered out.

The balanced budget eliminates questionable definitions of what the government spends and what it takes in by stipulating the measure will be total outlays against total receipts in each fiscal year.

Presidents are required to submit budget proposals each year which meet the same standard.

The balanced budget amendment does not threaten to bind Congress and the President in time of war.

There is no stronger enforcement mechanism in a constitutional democracy than an amendment like this one. The balanced budget amendment is a direct charge to constitutional officers who are required to swear an oath they will uphold the Constitution.

Enabling legislation has been under consideration in Congress for as long as the proposed amendment itself has been debated. The Chief Executive, like Members of Congress, swears to "preserve, protect, and defend the Constitution." In addition, the same checks and balances which protect Americans from other abuses of government will protect them from overspending.

The legal decisions and precedent for judicial review of matters under a balanced budget amendment show arguments about judicial entanglement to be unfounded. This proposal neither precludes very limited and appropriate judicial review, nor encourages irresponsible litigation.

Above all else, a balanced budget amendment will remove the finger pointing and other political games played with the government over budgeting. The Constitution becomes the arbiter of whether government is spending more than it takes in.

And finally, where many laws intending to do what the balanced budget amendment will do have come and gone, this proposal will bring a permanence to budgetary discipline which statutory relief has consistently failed to do.

It seems like a simple idea really; to require that the government live within its means, just as individual Americans and businesses do. It's a painfully simple principle which, until now, the representatives of the people have not had the courage to embrace.

I call on all Members of this body, and of the House, to rise against the threat of fiscal collapse as Americans have always risen in unity against threats to our economic and physical security overseas. In America, that which is good and just and proper wins in the end.

Statement of James M. Buchanan

From testimony before the Senate Judiciary Committee during January 5, 1995 hearings on a balanced budget constitutional amendment.

As Thomas Jefferson recognized only a decade after its adoption, the U.S. Constitution is seriously flawed in its failure to restrict government borrowing. This procedural flaw should be corrected.

Why do we need a balanced budget amendment now, when there was no such provision for two centuries? I suggest that the effective fiscal constitution did include a balanced budget rule until the middle of this century. The rule was, however, embedded in the moral attitudes of both the public and the politicians. Prior to World War II, it was thought to be grossly immoral for politicians to create deficits except in periods of war or extreme national crisis.

The moral rule against fiscal irresponsibility was effectively repealed by the Keynesian revolution in economics. By the 1940s, economists were converted to the Keynesian notion that deficits should be used to fine tune the economy in order to guarantee full employment. By the 1960s, politicians had come to incorporate the Keynesian doctrines in their excuses for increased spending.

The Keynesian doctrines were flawed in their failure to recognize that tax and expenditure decisions are made politically, through the actions of elected representatives of citizens, who are themselves responsible to constituencies. The natural proclivity of politicians who seek to satisfy constituency demands is to expand rates of spending and to reduce taxes. Hence, given any plausible excuse, they will act out this proclivity, with the predicted result. Deficits came to be a permanent feature of our economic-fiscal environment. The initial Keynesian logic was simply left behind in the cacophony of special interest claims for differential spending favors.

The tendency of democratic processes to create deficits is the simplest of all predictions that emerge from elementary public choice theory.

Unfortunately, we cannot reinstate moral rules. We must, therefore, substitute formal constitutional constraints that are aimed at the same purpose.

I emphasize that the problem is procedural, not political. The regime of deficit financing cannot be eliminated by electing different politicians and different majorities in Congress. Any actions taken toward fiscal responsibility in current budgeting may simply provide space for the benefits to be dissipated by later Congresses.

Opponents of the balanced budget amendment allege that particular economic policies should not be written into the Constitution. But the amendment does not imply any economic policy. The procedural requirement is only that the budget be balanced. The amendment does not restrict the power or ability of Congress to spend and to tax. The amendment amounts to nothing more than honesty in budgeting.

In one sense, of course, we always pay for what we spend through government, as anywhere else. But those who pay for the government spending that is financed by borrowing are taxpayers in future years, those who must pay the taxes to meet the ever-mounting interest obligations that are already far too large an item in the Federal budget. The immorality of the intergenerational transfer that deficit financing represents cries out for correction.

The balanced budget rule should stand alone on its own merits. To include a tax or spending limit proposed constitutional amendment would, I think, make the proposal vulnerable to the charge that a particular economic attitude is to be constitutionalized.

Opponents also claim that a constitutional balanced budget rule would be unenforceable. We can acknowledge that any rule, any law, whether constitutional or other, sets up incentives for evasion. But recognition of this fact does not, in any way, imply that constraints do not constrain. The constitutional rule would constrain spending growth, of that we can be certain.

Let me refer to some general effects of a balanced budget rule. In 1962, I wrote a paper entitled "Easy Budgets and Tight Money" in which I argued that the proclivity of modern democracies to run deficits makes it necessary for central banks to keep interest rates high to avoid inflation. A balanced budget regime would surely allow for lower rates of interest in future years, which would channel scarce savings into productive private investment rather than into the financing of current government consumption.

When all is said and done, there is no rational argument against the balanced budget amendment. Simple observation of the fiscal record over recent years tells us that the procedures through which fiscal choices are made are not working. The problem is not one that involves political leaders or parties. The problem is one where those whom we elect are required to function under the wrong set of rules, the wrong procedures. It is high time to get our fiscal house in order.

We can only imagine the increase in investor and business confidence, domestic and foreign, that enactment of a balanced budget amendment would produce. More importantly, we might begin to regain confidence in ourselves, as a free people under responsible constitutional government.

66
"The Balanced Budget Crusade"

ROBERT EISNER

A "balanced budget," no matter that few know what it means, particularly by archaic federal accounting rules, seems to be an American icon. Republicans and President Clinton now both proclaim it as a
goal, differing only on timing and the means of achieving it.

The politics of all this seem overwhelming. Republicans think they
have an issue to gain the support of most of the 20 million 1992 Perot
voters who seem obsessed over the deficit and the debt it creates. Democrats, apparently scared witless that the Republicans are right on the
politics, are reduced largely to saying, "Me too, but not your way!"

It has not always been so. In his 1864 annual message to Congress,
Abraham Lincoln said:

> The public debt on the first day of July last, as appears by the books of the
> treasury, amounted to $1,740,690,489.49. Probably, should the war continue
> for another year, that amount may be increased by not far from five hundred
> million dollars. Held as it is for the most part, by our own people, it has
> become a substantial branch of national, though private, property. For obvious
> reasons, the more nearly this property can be distributed among all the people
> the better. . . . The great advantage of citizens being creditors as well as
> debtors, with relation to the public debt, is obvious. Men can readily perceive
> that they cannot be much oppressed by a debt which they owe themselves.

In 1962, President John F. Kennedy declared, "Obviously deficits are
sometimes dangerous—and so are surpluses. . . . What we need is not
labels and cliches but more basic discussion of the sophisticated and
technical questions involved in keeping a great economic machine moving ahead." And, in 1981, Congressman Jack Kemp stated, "The Republican party no longer worships at the altar of a balanced budget."

Everybody tells the pollster that a balanced budget is good, until it is
learned how it might be balanced and whom it will hurt. That many
would be hurt is clear. Senate Republicans, in the fall of 1995, put forth
proposals that take large bites out of prospective outlays for Medicare,
Medicaid, education, research, and countless other programs. House Republicans were generally ready to go their Senate colleagues one better
by adding more massive tax cuts, thus necessitating still more draconian
cuts in spending.

But it is not just the "special interests" of those directly affected that
may be hurt by budget cuts. Slashing productive public investment—in

human capital and in physical infrastructure—can have damaging effects on the private economy and our present and future welfare. And, if the loss of purchasing power, whether due to the government giving the public less as it reduces outlays or taking from it more as it raises taxes, depresses the economy or brings us into a recession, the damage will be enormous.

False Alarm

By conventional measures, the deficit has, in fact, dramatically decreased, from $290 billion or 4.9 percent of Gross Domestic Product (GDP) in 1992 to $203 billion or 3.1 percent of GDP in 1994 and to $164 billion or 2.3 percent of GDP in 1995. The debt, which increases each year by the amount of the deficit, is no longer growing faster than the nation's income.

If we look at budgets of other leading nations, we find that almost all of them have larger deficits—in proportion to the size of their economies—than we do. Indeed, the Maastricht agreement for the European Economic Union sets a limit on deficits of no more than 3 percent of GDP, a figure that we will be well below this year and, even by conservative (or alarmist?) Congressional Budget Office projections, below this entire century.

If we account for capital outlays the way the federal budget does, we would find that most cities and states frequently, if not chronically, run deficits. And composite balance sheets of American households and businesses would show that both add hugely to their debt every year, which means, by federal accounting rules, that they are running massive deficits, generally greater than that of the federal government. Why then should the federal government balance its budget, particularly if to do so will entail massive sacrifice by such "special interests" as the elderly, the ill, the young, the poor, businessmen, farmers, veterans—indeed, the great bulk of the population?

Most of the simplistic arguments for a balanced budget are without merit. First, we will not go "bankrupt." The deficit contributes not to a national debt owed to other countries but to a federal government debt overwhelmingly owed to its own people in our own currency. A sovereign government can always get or create the money necessary to roll over such a debt or to pay it off.

Second, the deficit and debt are not adding to the burdens of our children. As President Lincoln knew—and it was hardly original with him—for every debtor there is a creditor, and our children will eventually be just as much creditors as debtors. Every savings bond and Treasury bill, note, and bond constituting the debt, except for the minor portion owned by foreigners, will be an asset of our posterity. If we are putting an extra burden on our children, it is not in those pieces of paper, which will in fact be their inheritance of wealth.

Third, our deficits are not causing others to lose confidence in us and, hence, driving down the value of the dollar. We remain the greatest and strongest economy in the world. If a balanced budget "strengthens" the dollar, it will only do so because it slows the economy so that we import less and, hence, supply fewer dollars to the rest of the world.

Fourth, our deficits are not driving up inflation or interest rates. The historical relation between deficits and interest rates is murky indeed. Federal Reserve policy, the state of the economy, and expected inflation are what really matter.

How a Balanced Budget Hurts

What then do analytical economists see as the role of the deficit and its possible effect on the current economy and our future? Conservative economist Robert Barro of Harvard University and his many follow-ers argue for "Ricardian Equivalence,"* which holds that, as a first ap-proximation, it does not matter whether government expenditures are financed by current taxes or by current borrowing—a deficit. The reasoning is that, if taxes are cut, thus creating a deficit, taxpayers' be-havior will not be affected. They will say to themselves that the resulting debt will have to be serviced and/or paid off in the future. Hence, their lower taxes now will be matched by higher taxes later. They will not therefore spend the money they are no longer paying in taxes. They will either set it aside to pay their higher taxes in the future themselves or they will leave the money to their children to pay the taxes.

Most professional economists, however, believe that Ricardian Equiv-alence is of limited applicability and reject the argument that deficits do not matter. Contradicting Barro's views, most of us apparently feel richer when, other things being equal, we own our share of $3.5 trillion dollars of Treasury obligations than when we don't. And we feel still richer if deficits increase our real holdings of those assets. Hence, we generally spend more on consumption.

If we are already buying everything our economy is capable of producing—we are operating at full employment and full capacity—production of more goods to satisfy our consumption demand can only come at the expense of production of investment goods. We may then put a burden on our children by leaving them less productive because we leave them fewer capital goods. But suppose, as in most of our his-tory except during wartime, we are not producing at full capacity. Then, more spending induced by deficits can, and is likely to, increase consumption and, concomitantly, to increase business investment and

---

* [Named after the seventeenth-century economist David Ricardo]

production, thus providing for the increased consumption. Far from burdening our children, we are actually aiding them even as we help ourselves.

Further, increased holdings of government debt will induce us to spend more of our incomes only if our holdings have risen in real terms adjusted for inflation and, more fundamentally, have *risen relative to our incomes*. Since the debt held by the public averaged about $3,500 billion in fiscal year 1995, inflation, at the roughly 3 percent of the past year, would mean that holders of that debt suffered a loss in its purchasing power or real value equal to (approximately) 3 percent of $3,500 billion, or some $100 billion. Thus the real increase in the debt, and therefore the real deficit, is only the nominal deficit of $164 billion minus $100 billion, or $64 billion. And, with national income growing at 6 percent per year, the debt would have to grow at more than 6 percent of that $3.5 trillion—a nominal deficit of more than $210 billion or some $50 billion *more* than last year's $164 billion—to cause us to spend a larger proportion of our incomes.

A "balanced budget" would hardly be balanced in a growing economy. It would imply a debt-to-income ratio declining by about 6 percent per year, thus reducing our spending and bringing the risk of recession.

If our concern is that we provide properly for the future, it is absurd to try to balance a budget that makes no distinction between government expenditures for current consumption and government expenditures of an investment nature—for physical infrastructure, basic research and the development of new technology, the education of our children, and the health of our people. We might well wish to balance a current operating budget and restrict our borrowing to net investment, borrowing and investing enough, as a rule of thumb, to have a total deficit that keeps the ratio of debt to national income or GDP constant. But balancing the budget at the expense of our public investment in the future is one way that we really borrow from our children—and never pay them back.

Will a balanced budget drive down interest rates, perhaps abetted by the Federal Reserve, so that we have more private investment? That is a dicey proposition. Lower interest rates tend to encourage investment, particularly in housing, although they also lower the interest income of millions of households. But the loss of $200 billion of purchasing power *each year* is likely to slow the economy so much that private investment, despite the best efforts of the Fed, will be less, not more.

Some Deficit Hawks

What are the arguments in favor of balancing the budget, even as it is currently measured? Perhaps the most important one does not really relate to budget balancing at all but to reducing the role of government. Nobel Laureates Milton Friedman of the Hoover Institution and James

Buchanan of George Mason University see the discipline of a balanced budget as preventing excessive government spending. Friedman and Buchanan, and many others, believe that in a representative form of government such as ours there are major incentives for our legislators to enact programs that may not even be in the long-term interests of the groups that promote them, much less society as a whole. The public is, however, notoriously reluctant to support higher taxes. If the programs had to be paid for by tax increases, the legislators would not dare to enact them. Economists arguing for a balanced budget on the grounds that it is necessary to reduce the role of government are not therefore arguing for a balanced budget per se. They generally disapprove of raising taxes to balance budgets more than they do of deficits.

"Supply-side economists" would reduce taxes, particularly marginal tax rates, regardless of their effect on the deficit (although some have claimed that the lower rates will increase taxable income so much that tax revenues would rise and, hence, reduce the deficit). The application of their views, along with the military buildup and the recession of 1982–1983, contributed to the large, much decried Reagan deficits. It may well be argued that those deficits, by pumping purchasing power into the economy, were a major factor in the recovery from that recession.

Many economists, including such prominent figures as Charles Schultze of the Brookings Institution, chairman of the Council of Economic Advisers under President Carter, Nobel Laureate Franco Modigliani of MIT, and Benjamin Friedman, chairman of Harvard's Economics Department, argue that deficits crowd out private investment. They claim that deficits reduce the nation's productivity and place a burden on future generations. When it is pointed out that, despite (or because of?) our recent deficits, gross private domestic investment has soared to record heights, both in absolute real terms and as a percentage of GDP, the reply is that this investment has been financed by foreigners. And this, we are told, has its cost: The interest and dividends on this investment will be paid to foreigners over the years ahead.

Budget deficits, by my estimates, do indeed contribute to trade or current account deficits with other nations. Essentially, they do so by raising our GDP and national income, thereby increasing our imports. If balancing the domestic budget were to eliminate those international deficits, they would do so by slowing our own economy. We would buy fewer Toyotas (the variety made in Japan, not Kentucky) but fewer Chryslers and Fords as well. And, further, it must be pointed out, even current account deficits averaging $100 billion a year for the next five years would add only $500 billion to net foreign claims on the United States. At a 4 percent real rate of return, that would cost us $20 billion per year, less than 0.3 percent of our GDP, hardly a burden worth risking a recession over. In the long run, we should expect a lower exchange rate to balance our current accounts, at least to a point where foreign claims become a constant proportion of our GDP.

On the larger question of deficits crowding out the total of all investment, domestic and foreign, the critical issue is how much slack there is in the economy. What Schultze, Modigliani, and Benjamin Friedman apparently have in mind is an economy that, over the long run, is essentially at full employment or, at least, at a level of employment—some call it the "natural rate"—that deficits and aggregate demand cannot generally affect. Increased government demand or consumption demand has no free resources to draw upon. The consequence will be increased inflation. It is not clear why this alone would reduce private investment. But, if the response of the Federal Reserve to the inflation is to increase nominal *and* real interest rates, the result may be expected to be a reduction in real investment and an increased burden on the future.

If, however, the economy is at less than full employment, the increased effective demand resulting from a structural deficit will increase total output, carrying increased investment to meet the increased demand for consumer goods. My own research has indicated that this is exactly what is happening. Correctly measured, real structural deficits have been followed by lower unemployment, greater output, and more consumption *and* private investment. They have also been accompanied by more *public* investment. Far from contributing to an increased burden on our future, they have provided for greater well-being for our children and our grandchildren.

Dissident Voices

Many economists agree that deficit reduction is desirable in the appropriate circumstances. But they view the current crusade for a balanced budget under current federal accounting rules that do not separate out capital expenditures—let alone a constitutional amendment that would put the economy into a fiscal straight jacket—as misguided and ill-informed. The list of dissidents includes Nobel Laureates (and past presidents of the American Economic Association) Kenneth Arrow of Stanford University, Gérard Debreu of the University of California, Berkeley, Lawrence Klein of the University of Pennsylvania, Franco Modigliani and Robert M. Solow of MIT, and James Tobin of Yale University. Also included are Moses Abramovitz of Stanford, William Baumol of New York University, Charles P. Kindleberger of MIT, John Kenneth Galbraith of Harvard University, William Vickrey of Columbia University, all past presidents of the American Economic Association, and Hyman Minsky of the Levy Economic Institute, Robert Heilbroner of the New School for Social Research, Peter Bernstein, formerly with Shearson-Lehman, Paul Davidson of the University of Tennessee, and many others. Many have spoken out, but their voices have not broken through.

Some economists think that, while changing the level and composition of government expenditures may matter, a balanced budget will do no good or harm to the economy as a whole. Others think it can do serious harm. Whichever group is right, the sacrifice to attain that "balance" will be as useful as the ancient sacrifices to propitiate pagan gods—or those Western religious crusades of yesteryear.

DISCUSSION QUESTIONS

1. How big a problem is the budget deficit? How does it affect you as a taxpayer and citizen? Why should we try to get rid of it?

2. How can the budget deficit problem be solved? Are major changes in the structure of political institutions, such as a balanced budget amendment to the Constitution, needed to solve the problem?

3. Which of the possible solutions to the deficit problem are most likely to be enacted? Explain.

4. Do you agree with the distinction Eisner makes between different kinds of deficit spending? Why or why not?

CHAPTER 13

Government and the Economy

67
"Call for Federal Responsibility"

FRANKLIN D. ROOSEVELT

The national government has always played a role in the economy. Since the late 1700s the government has provided property for private development, enforced contracts and prohibited the theft of private property, provided subsidies to encourage the growth of particular industries, and regulated trade. The question that commands the attention of political leaders and citizens alike today is what the limits of government involvement in the economy ought to be.

This debate reached a peak during the Great Depression, as the nation struggled to define government's role in reviving the economy, and played a critical role in the 1932 presidential election between the Democratic candidate, Franklin D. Roosevelt, and the Republican president, Herbert Hoover. In the campaign speech reprinted here, FDR argued that the federal government should play a role in unemployment insurance, housing for the poor, and public works programs to compensate for the hardship of the Great Depression. Hoover, on the other hand, was very much opposed to altering the relationship between government and the private sector which was "builded [sic] up by 150 years of toil of our fathers." It was the extension of freedom and the exercise of individual initiative, Hoover claimed, which made the American economic system strong and which would gradually bring about economic recovery. Roosevelt prevailed, and the resulting New Deal changed the face of government.

The first principle I would lay down is that the primary duty rests on the community, through local government and private agencies, to take care of the relief of unemployment. But we then come to a situation where there are so many people out of work that local funds are insufficient.

It seems clear to me that the organized society known as the State comes into the picture at this point. In other words, the obligation of government is extended to the next higher unit.

I practise what I preach. In 1930 the state of New York greatly increased its employment service and kept in close touch with the ability of localities to take care of their own unemployed. But by the summer of 1931 it became apparent to me that actual state funds and a state-supervised system were imperative.

I called a special session of the legislature, and they appropriated a fund of $20 million for unemployment relief, this fund to be reimbursed to the state through the doubling of our income taxes. Thus the state of New York became the first among all the states to accept the definite obligation of supplementing local funds where these local funds were insufficient.

The administration of this great work has become a model for the rest of the country. Without setting up any complex machinery or any large overhead, the state of New York is working successfully through local agencies, and, in spite of the fact that over a million people are out of work and in need of aid in this one state alone, we have so far met at least the bare necessities of the case.

This past spring the legislature appropriated another $5 million, and on November 8 the voters will pass on a $30 million bond issue to tide us over this winter and at least up to next summer.

* * *

I am very certain that the obligation extends beyond the states and to the federal government itself, if and when it becomes apparent that states and communities are unable to take care of the necessary relief work.

It may interest you to have me read a short quotation from my message to the legislature in 1931:

> What is the State? It is the duly constituted representative of an organized society of human beings, created by them for their mutual protection and well-being. One of the duties of the State is that of caring for those of its citizens who find themselves the victims of such adverse circumstances as make them unable to obtain even the necessities of mere existence without the aid of others.
>
> In broad terms, I assert that modern society, acting through its government, owes the definite obligation to prevent the starvation or the dire want of any of its fellowmen and women who try to maintain themselves but cannot. To these unfortunate citizens aid must be extended by the government, not as a matter of charity but as a matter of social duty.

That principle which I laid down in 1931, I reaffirm. I not only reaffirm it, I go a step further and say that where the State itself is unable successfully to fulfill this obligation which lies upon it, it then becomes the positive duty of the federal government to step in to help.

In the words of our Democratic national platform, the federal government has a "continuous responsibility for human welfare, especially for the protection of children." That duty and responsibility the federal government should carry out promptly, fearlessly, and generously.

It took the present Republican administration in Washington almost three years to recognize this principle. I have recounted to you in other speeches, and it is a matter of general information, that for at least two years after the crash, the only efforts made by the national administration to cope with the distress of unemployment were to deny its existence.

When, finally, this year, after attempts at concealment and minimizing had failed, it was at last forced to recognize the fact of suffering among millions of unemployed, appropriations of federal funds for assistance to states were finally made.

I think it is fair to point out that a complete program of unemployment relief was on my recommendation actually under way in the state of New York over a year ago; and that in Washington relief funds in any large volume were not provided until this summer, and at that they were pushed through at the demand of Congress rather than through the leadership of the President of the United States.

At the same time, I have constantly reiterated my conviction that the expenditures of cities, states, and the federal government must be reduced in the interest of the nation as a whole. I believe that there are many ways in which such reduction of expenditures can take place, but I am utterly unwilling that economy should be practised at the expense of starving people.

We must economize in other ways, but it shall never be said that the American people have refused to provide the necessities of life for those who, through no fault of their own, are unable to feed, clothe, and house themselves. The first obligation of government is the protection of the welfare and well-being, indeed the very existence, of its citizens.

* * *

The next question asks my attitude toward appropriations for public works as an aid to unemployment. I am perfectly clear as to the principles involved in this case also.

From the long-range point of view it would be advisable for governments of all kinds to set up in times of prosperity what might be called a nest egg to be used for public works in times of depression. That is a policy which we should initiate when we get back to good times.

But there is the immediate possibility of helping the emergency through appropriations for public works. One question, however, must be answered first because of the simple fact that these public works cost money.

We all know that government treasuries, whether local or state or federal, are hard put to it to keep their budgets balanced; and, in the case of the federal Treasury, thoroughly unsound financial policies have made its situation not exactly desperate but at least threatening to future stability if the policies of the present administration are continued.

All public works, including federal, must be considered from the point of view of the ability of the government Treasury to pay for them. There are two ways of paying for public works. One is by the sale of bonds. In principle, such bonds should be issued only to pay for self-sustaining projects or for structures which will without question have a useful life over a long period of years. The other method of payment is from current revenues, which in these days means in most cases added taxes. We all know that there is a very definite limit to the increase of taxes above the present level.

From this point, therefore, I can go on and say that, if funds can be properly provided by the federal government for increased appropriations for public works, we must examine the character of these public works. I have already spoken of that type which is self-sustaining. These should be greatly encouraged. The other type is that of public works which are honestly essential to the community. Each case must rest on its own merits.

It is impossible, for example, to say that all parks or all playgrounds are essential. One may be and another may not be. If a school, for instance, has no playground, it is obvious that the furnishing of a playground is a necessity to the community. But if the school already has a playground and some people seek merely to enlarge it, there may be a very definite question as to how necessary that enlargement is.

Let me cite another example. I am much interested in providing better housing accommodations for the poor in our great cities. If a slum area can be torn down and new modern buildings put up, I should call that almost a human necessity; but, on the other hand, the mere erection of new buildings in some other part of the city while allowing the slums to remain raises at once a question of necessity. I am confident that the federal government working in cooperation with states and cities can do much to carry on increased public works and along lines which are sound from the economic and financial point of view.

Now I come to another question. I am asked whether I favor a system of unemployment insurance reserves made compulsory by the states, supplemented by a system of federally coordinated state employment offices to facilitate the reemployment of jobless workers.

The first part of the question is directly answered by the Democratic platform which advocates unemployment insurance under state laws.

This is no new policy for me. I have advocated unemployment insurance in my own state for some time, and, indeed, last year six Eastern governors were my guests at a conference which resulted in the drawing up of what might be called an idea plan of unemployment insurance.

This type of insurance is not a cure-all but it provides at least a cushion to mitigate unemployment in times of depression. It is sound if, after starting it, we stick to the principle of sound insurance financing. It is only where governments, as in some European countries, have failed to live up to these sound principles that unemployment insurance has been an economic failure.

As to the coordinated employment offices, I can only tell you that I was for the bills sponsored by Senator Wagner of my own state and passed by the Congress. They created a nationally coordinated system of employment offices operated by the individual states with the advisory cooperation of joint boards of employers and employees.

To my very great regret this measure was vetoed by the President of the United States. I am certain that the federal government can, by furnishing leadership, stimulate the various states to set up and coordinate practical, useful systems.

68
"Against the Proposed New Deal"

HERBERT HOOVER

This campaign is more than a contest between two men. It is more than a contest between two parties. It is a contest between two philosophies of government.

We are told by the opposition that we must have a change, that we must have a new deal. It is not the change that comes from normal development of national life to which I object but the proposal to alter the whole foundations of our national life which have been builded through generations of testing and struggle, and of the principles upon which we have builded the nation. The expressions our opponents use must refer to important changes in our economic and social system and our system of government, otherwise they are nothing but vacuous words. And I realize that in this time of distress many of our people are asking whether our social and economic system is incapable of that great primary function of providing security and comfort of life to all of the firesides of our 25 million homes in America, whether our social system provides for the fundamental development and progress of our people, whether our form of government is capable of originating and sustaining that security and progress.

This question is the basis upon which our opponents are appealing to the people in their fears and distress. They are proposing changes and so-called new deals which would destroy the very foundations of our American system.

Our people should consider the primary facts before they come to the judgment—not merely through political agitation, the glitter of promise, and the discouragement of temporary hardships—whether they will support changes which radically affect the whole system which has been builded up by 150 years of the toil of our fathers. They should not approach the question in the despair with which our opponents would clothe it.

Our economic system has received abnormal shocks during the past three years, which temporarily dislocated its normal functioning. These shocks have in a large sense come from without our borders, but I say to you that our system of government has enabled us to take such strong action as to prevent the disaster which would otherwise have come to our nation. It has enabled us further to develop measures and programs which are now demonstrating their ability to bring about restoration and progress.

We must go deeper than platitudes and emotional appeals of the public platform in the campaign if we will penetrate to the full significance of the changes which our opponents are attempting to float upon the wave of distress and discontent from the difficulties we are passing through. We can find what our opponents would do after searching the record of their appeals to discontent, group and sectional interest. We must search for them in the legislative acts which they sponsored and passed in the Democratic-controlled House of Representatives in the last session of Congress. We must look into measures for which they voted and which were defeated. We must inquire whether or not the presidential and vice-presidential candidates have disavowed these acts. If they have not, we must conclude that they form a portion and are a substantial indication of the profound changes proposed.

And we must look still further than this as to what revolutionary changes have been proposed by the candidates themselves.

We must look into the type of leaders who are campaigning for the Democratic ticket, whose philosophies have been well known all their lives, whose demands for a change in the American system are frank and forceful. I can respect the sincerity of these men in their desire to change our form of government and our social and economic system, though I shall do my best tonight to prove they are wrong. I refer particularly to Senator Norris, Senator La Follette, Senator Cutting, Senator Huey Long, Senator Wheeler, William R. Hearst and other exponents of a social philosophy different from the traditional American one. Unless these men feel assurance of support to their ideas, they certainly would not be supporting these candidates and the Democratic Party. The seal of these men indicates that they have sure confidence that they will have voice in the administration of our government.

I may say at once that the changes proposed from all these Democratic principals and allies are of the most profound and penetrating character.

If they are brought about, this will not be the America which we have known in the past.

Let us pause for a moment and examine the American system of government, of social and economic life, which it is now proposed that we should alter. Our system is the product of our race and of our experience in building a nation to heights unparalleled in the whole history of the world. It is a system peculiar to the American people. It differs essentially from all others in the world. It is an American system.

It is founded on the conception that only through ordered liberty, through freedom to the individual, and equal opportunity to the individual will his initiative and enterprise be summoned to spur the march of progress.

It is by the maintenance of equality of opportunity and therefore of a society absolutely fluid in freedom of the movement of its human particles that our individualism departs from the individualism of Europe. We resent class distinction because there can be no rise for the individual through the frozen strata of classes, and no stratification of classes can take place in a mass livened by the free rise of its particles. Thus in our ideals the able and ambitious are able to rise constantly from the bottom to leadership in the community.

This freedom of the individual creates of itself the necessity and the cheerful willingness of men to act cooperatively in a thousand ways and for every purpose as occasion arises; and it permits such voluntary co-operations to be dissolved as soon as they have served their purpose, to be replaced by new voluntary associations for new purposes.

There has thus grown within us, to gigantic importance, a new conception. That is, this voluntary cooperation within the community. Cooperation to perfect the social organization; cooperation for the care of those in distress; cooperation for the advancement of knowledge, of scientific research, of education; for cooperative action in the advancement of many phases of economic life. This is self-government by the people outside of government; it is the most powerful development of individual freedom and equal opportunity that has taken place in the century and a half since our fundamental institutions were founded.

It is in the further development of this cooperation and a sense of its responsibility that we should find solution for many of our complex problems, and not by the extension of government into our economic and social life. The greatest function of government is to build up that cooperation, and its most resolute action should be to deny the extension of bureaucracy. We have developed great agencies of cooperation by the assistance of the government which promote and protect the interests of individuals and the smaller units of business. The Federal Reserve System, in its strengthening and support of the smaller banks; the Farm Board, in its strengthening and support of the farm cooperatives; the Home Loan Banks, in the mobilizing of building and loan associations and savings banks; the Federal Land Banks, in giving independence and strength to land mortgage associations; the great mobilization of relief to distress, the mobilization of business and industry in measures of recovery, and a score of other activities are not socialism—they are the essence of protection to the development of free men.

The primary conception of this whole American system is not the regimentation of men but the cooperation of free men. It is founded upon the conception of responsibility of the individual to the community, of the responsibility of local government to the state, of the state to the national government.

It is founded on a peculiar conception of self-government designed to maintain this equal opportunity to the individual, and through decentralization it brings about and maintains these responsibilities. The centralization of government will undermine responsibilities and will destroy the system.

Our government differs from all previous conceptions, not only in this decentralization but also in the separation of functions between the legislative, executive, and judicial arms of government, in which the independence of the judicial arm is the keystone of the whole structure.

It is founded on a conception that in times of emergency, when forces are running beyond control of individuals or other cooperative action, beyond the control of local communities and of states, then the great reserve powers of the federal government shall be brought into action to protect the community. But when these forces have ceased, there must be a return of state, local, and individual responsibility.

The implacable march of scientific discovery with its train of new inventions presents every year new problems to government and new problems to the social order. Questions often arise whether, in the face of the growth of these new and gigantic tools, democracy can remain master in its own house, can preserve the fundamentals of our American system. I contend that it can; and I contend that this American system of ours has demonstrated its validity and superiority over any other system yet invented by human mind.

It has demonstrated it in the face of the greatest test of our history— that is the emergency which we have faced in the past three years.

When the political and economic weakness of many nations of Europe, the result of the World War and its aftermath, finally culminated in collapse of their institutions, the delicate adjustment of our economic and social life received a shock unparalleled in our history. No one knows that better than you of New York. No one knows its causes better than you. That the crisis was so great that many of the leading banks sought directly or indirectly to convert their assets into gold or its equivalent with the result that they practically ceased to function as credit institutions; that many of our citizens sought flight for their capital to other countries; that many of them attempted to hoard gold in large amounts. These were but indications of the flight of confidence and of the belief that our government could not overcome these forces.

Yet these forces were overcome—perhaps by narrow margins—and this action demonstrates what the courage of a nation can accomplish under the resolute leadership in the Republican Party. And I say the Republican Party, because our opponents before and during the crisis, proposed no constructive program; though some of their members patriotically supported ours. Later on the Democratic House of Representatives did develop the real thought and ideas of the Democratic Party, but it was so destructive that it had to be defeated, for it would have destroyed, not healed.

In spite of all these obstructions, we did succeed. Our form of government did prove itself equal to the task. We saved this nation from a quarter of a century of chaos and degeneration, and we preserved the savings, the insurance policies, gave a fighting chance to men to hold their homes. We saved the integrity of our government and the honesty of the American dollar. And we installed measures which today are bringing back recovery. Employment, agriculture, business—all of these show the steady, if slow, healing of our enormous wound.

I therefore contend that the problem of today is to continue these measures and policies to restore this American system to its normal functioning, to repair the wounds it has received, to correct the weaknesses and evils which would defeat that system. To enter upon a series of deep changes, to embark upon this inchoate new deal which has been propounded in this campaign, would be to undermine and destroy our American system.

DISCUSSION QUESTIONS

1. Do you agree with the Republican party in Congress today that the government plays too much of role in economic affairs? If there ought to be less government activity, what should the government stop doing?

2. Are there any activities the government does that you consider essential? Why?

69
"It's *Not* the Economy, Stupid"

CHARLES R. MORRIS

Few things are more crucial to a president's popularity and success than the state of the economy. Presidents who preside over a growing economy are typically assured of reelection. A recession usually means a president will have the opportunity to write his memoirs after an early and involuntary retirement mandated by the voters. Yet two aspects of the relationship between presidential standing and the economy are curious. First, voter perceptions of how the economy is doing can be more important than objective indicators of the economy. Between March 1991 and September 1992, President George Bush suffered the steepest and fastest drop in popularity ever recorded, and he lost the 1992 election in large part because the public perceived him as indifferent to the economic woes of the time. By historical standards, though, the recession of 1990–1992 was mild, and it ended well before election day.

The second curiosity, as Charles R. Morris argues in this essay, is that presidents actually have very little control over macroeconomic conditions such as inflation, unemployment, and interest rates. The image of the president actively "managing" economic affairs, enacting policy to foster growth or counteract recessions, is, in Morris's words, "a sham." The institution with the greatest short term influence over the economy is the Federal Reserve Board, and it is structured to be independent of presidential influence. Morris argues that the complexities of the U.S. economy are beyond the capacity of economists truly to understand, and even farther beyond the ability of presidents to control.

As all the world knows, "the economy" was the overriding issue in the 1992 presidential election. President George Bush "mishandled" the economy. He lost. Bill Clinton promised to handle it more skillfully. He won. I will argue that he won on a false issue, and that the main criterion on which our presidential elections have come to be decided— managing the economy—is a sham.

The assumption that the President manages the economy is the core of prevailing political wisdom, dinned into the public mind by a generation of pundits, a convention of discourse endlessly repeated but rarely examined. The fact is, presidential elections have become referenda on the business cycle, whose fortuitous turnings are personified in the President—thus the "Bush recession" yields to the "Clinton recovery." This is not economics, it is anthropology—an exercise in collective magic. Presidents are properly accountable for their executive and leg-islative performance, and there is no question that federal actions can affect the economy, sometimes profoundly. Eliminating the budget def-icit in four years, for example, might create a nasty recession or a run-away boom—economists, as always, disagree. But the effects would almost certainly be substantial, however unpredictable. Modern political campaigns, however, are fought on the premise that Presidents can *man-age* the economy, that they can take detailed actions that have a precise result—such as raising productivity, reducing unemployment, or in-creasing investment. In that sense, how much control do Presidents re-ally have over the economy? The answer is very, very little.

Mind over Matter

The "economy" itself is really just a metaphor for the enormously com-plex stew of daily personal and commercial transactions among some 250 million Americans. The deceptively precise numbers that purport to measure "savings" or "growth" or "income" are crude approximations compounded from a slag heap of samples, surveys, estimates, interpo-lations, seasonal adjustments, and plain guesses. It takes months, even years, for economists to sort through the numbers and figure out what really happened—if they ever do. There is still no consensus on what caused the Great Depression. The most recent returns on the U.S. econ-omy show signs of respectable growth. But economists are arguing fiercely over whether it is too little or too much, the morning lark of a solid long-term recovery or just a dead-cat bounce. And, of course, they disagree even more fiercely on the policy prescriptions that flow from their prejudices: "Do something or things will get worse!" Or, "*If* you do something, things will get worse!"

Clinton's ill-fated economic-stimulus program exemplifies the confu-sion. Certainly it was small: at $16 billion, hardly more than the rounding error in the national accounts. And no one could argue with a straight face that a porridge of new playgrounds, vaccination programs, and Headstart dollars would visibly improve the economy. But while the Nobel laureate economists James Tobin and Robert Solow warned that the stimulus was too small, Wall Street worried that the President would spook the bond market. If bondholders decided that the economy was growing too fast, or the government was borrowing too much, and in-flation was heading up, interest rates would rise and undercut the re-covery—the last thing Clinton wanted.

At one point Secretary of Labor Robert Reich, a key designer of the Clinton economic strategy, argued that the "psychological impact" of the stimulus program was what really counted. The emphasis on changing people's *minds* about the economy sounded a little like official expla-nations of American policy in Vietnam—bombing just enough to discourage the enemy. The resemblance, in fact, is no accident, for both the image of the President as button-pusher in the economic engine room and the heavily psychologized tactics in Vietnam are squarely in a peculiarly American tradition of thinking about society and the economy.

Pulling Levers

Pan the camera back almost a hundred years: there stands an aging Henry Adams, the historian and descendant of Presidents, agape before a giant electrical dynamo at the Great Paris Exposition of 1900, ready to fall on his knees, "bewildered and helpless, as in the fourth century, a priest of Isis before the Cross of Christ." Transported by this Damascene vision, Adams set out to construct a "dynamic theory of history," seeking the fundamental laws, like those of electricity or magnetism or the kinetic theory of gases, that govern the affairs of men.

Adams's search for a scientific history was tempered by self-mocking irony. But to minds less steeped in the past, America's leap into the Machine Age and the mighty transformations of American social and industrial relations opened entirely new intellectual vistas. The new "scientific" outlook was thoroughly positivist (nothing existed, or at least was worth talking about, if it could not be measured); it was atomistic (all things were condensed from identical particles); and it was statistical (the intricate but predictable dance of countless freely colliding molecules of gas was choreographed by a few simple, immutable laws). In a series of easy stages the same logic was applied to virtually the entire field of human endeavor.

To begin with, the mapping from a mechanistic physics to the burgeoning science of economics seemed entirely natural, precise, and complete: correct prices, for instance, arose from the statistical interaction of countless atomized market participants obeying the simple canons of rational self-interest. Around the turn of the century American universities developed a defense of American liberal capitalism as the regime most consistent with a scientific outlook, and the economist's style of thinking rapidly colonized the rest of the social sciences. Franklin Giddings, at Columbia; Edward A. Ross, at the University of Wisconsin; and Charles Horton Cooley, at the University of Michigan, pushed the still-nascent study of sociology toward statistics and measurement. (Ross and Cooley started their careers as economists.) The program of the American Sociological Society, organized in 1905, was entirely "scientific," seeking the basic forces, or "sympathy," that bound society together, trying to discover a praxis of "social control" for a liberal society, teasing out the rules of the "social equilibrating-apparatus." By the 1920s all of political science was being recast into a study of the market behavior of utility-maximizing individuals. The same behaviorist faith inspired John Dewey's confidence that schools could be organized like "great factories," to turn out self-reliant citizens who would people Dewey's vision of a liberal democracy.

After a period of eclipse during the Depression, the scientific pretensions of American economics and its sister social studies were powerfully reinforced by the sweeping triumph of Keynesianism. Ignoring Keynes's own warnings about the waywardness of real markets, American academics forged a rigidly mechanistic vision of the economic apparatus: pull this lever and investment rises, turn this flywheel and consumption goes up—all the pieces clicking smoothly into place like stainless-steel tumblers. Faith in a *deus in machina** prompted John Kennedy's wildly unprescient declaration in 1962 that there were no ideological issues left to solve; the country faced only "technical problems . . . administrative problems."

The economist's vision of the rational actor was formalized in John von Neumann and Oskar Morgenstern's *Theory of Games and Economic Behavior* (1944). Game theory supplied a metaphysics for the arms race, and led Robert McNamara in his will-o'-the-wisp pursuit of a precise equilibrium of "mutual assured destruction" with the Soviets, as if nuclear arms were a problem of tariffs and quotas, like trade. Since rational actors in rational games reach mutually beneficial accommodations through signaling, it was forever a puzzlement to the civilian theorists in the Pentagon that Ho Chi Minh obdurately persisted in misinterpreting their carefully calibrated bombing campaigns.

Even American ethics has become hardly more than a branch of economics. Dewey always struggled, if not very successfully, against the economist's equation of values with mere *wants*, although it seemed an obvious implication of his pragmatist teachings. There is no such struggle in John Rawls's *A Theory of Justice*, the most discussed ethical work of the past generation. Rawls proceeds by constructing a system of goods-maximizing choices by highly rational atomized individuals who lack any history or social ties. The same economistic bias also explains much of the American obsession with personal rights and legalistic procedure: if all wants are theoretically equal, there is nothing left for moralists to do but tinker with process. Economists, after all, care only that the corn auction works; whatever price emerges will *ipso facto* [by the fact itself] be the right one.

The interventionist bias of the early Keynesians has created a leftish aura around the more "scientific" social theories. But the same empiricist, atomistic view of society, the insistence on equating choices with values, is a major theme of American conservatism, from Milton Friedman's willingness to legalize drugs to the current "school choice" movement. Thomas Sowell and Robert Nozick take issue with Rawls using exactly the same microeconomic tools that Rawls uses—they just wind

* [Literally god in a machine, a sudden solution.]

up with diametrically different results. The philosophic differences between the left and the right in America, that is, most often reduce to a barren instrumentalism: Should government pull the levers, or do the levers move themselves?

The reach and power of the economic paradigm in America is impressive enough; but what makes it all the more remarkable is that there is almost no compelling reason to believe that it works any better in economics than it did in guerrilla warfare, let alone in sociology, politics, or morals.

Economics in the Real World

Financial-market professionals often take for granted the practical uselessness of economists. Recently, for example, Robert Beckwitt, a bond manager at Fidelity Investments, the big mutual-funds company, tracked the success of Wall Street's economists in forecasting interest rates. Bond values depend critically on interest rates, and bond traders basically make bets on whether interest rates will rise or fall when they buy and sell bonds. One of a Wall Street economist's most important tasks, therefore, is to forecast rate trends, and many hours of analytic energy and vast amounts of computer power are lavished on the problem. According to Beckwitt's data, however, the best bond-investment strategy over the past decade would have been to do exactly the opposite of what the consensus recommended: when the economists said "Sell," the wise investor bought—and achieved, in fact, quite outstanding returns. Charles Wolf, at the Rand Corporation, once compiled a box score for the major economic forecasters; the fit between most forecasts and actual outcomes was approximately random. A running joke at *The Wall Street Journal* is a regular feature that pits top stock pickers against a portfolio compiled by throwing darts at a wall: year after year the dart board is neck and neck with the analysts.

Forecasting in economics is not the same as plotting the path of a planet. Fundamental axioms in economics have a disturbing tendency to flip upside down with little warning, as if gravity suddenly made objects float. For many years it was received wisdom in economics textbooks that if the Federal Reserve increased the money supply (by loosening the credit reins), interest rates would fall. In theory, money is a commodity like any other, and if there is more of it, its price, or the rate of interest, should fall. For years, in the main, the theory held true. Then, at some elusive moment in the 1970s, investors decided that loose credit caused inflation, which was also arguably true. The Ford and Carter Administrations had greatly expanded credit to help cushion the 1970s oil-price shocks, and inflation was rising rapidly. If lenders expect inflation, they will insist on higher interest rates to protect the value of their money. Almost overnight the financial headlines executed an about-face: if the

Federal Reserve loosened credit, it was thenceforth taken for granted that interest rates would rise, not fall. The earth, having been round, was now flat, and the economic astrolabes were adjusted accordingly.

Alan Greenspan, the chairman of the Federal Reserve, was recently lectured by a Senate committee for not pushing interest rates down faster to spur an economic expansion. (Lower interest rates presumably induce greater borrowing and therefore greater economic activity.) In fact Greenspan had been pushing interest rates down very aggressively for more than a year. But the Federal Reserve controls only short-term rates, primarily through its overnight lending to member banks. So while short-term rates fell very rapidly during 1992, longer-term rates—the ones investors mainly care about—hardly budged. Investors didn't know which law applied. Would Greenspan's aggressive loosening make money plentiful and lower rates? Or would it trigger inflation and raise rates? The result was a kind of paralysis: short-term rates went down and long-term rates stayed up. The beneficiaries were the banks, who could suddenly borrow very cheaply from the government and lend the money right back at much higher interest, by buying longer-term government bonds. The whole point of the exercise, of course, had been to increase bank lending to business; but since banks could make so much money playing the Treasury market, lending to business actually dropped.

There is no escaping the pervasive influence of the federal behemoth. About one out of every four dollars spent in the land is spent by, or put in the pocket of the spender by, the federal government. If the government lurches left or yaws right, a big chunk of the economy lurches or yaws with it. But it is hardly a surgical policy instrument; there are few obvious levers to pull. At bottom the government engages in four kinds of economic activity. Half a trillion dollars or so is passed out to citizens each year, either directly, as in Social Security payments, or in the form of medical services. Some $300 billion finances the global sprawl of the U.S. military. Another $300 billion pays for the three-million-strong army of federal civil servants and a ragout of federal programs, from Headstart ($2.7 billion) to dusty relics like the Rural Electrification Administration ($1.2 billion). Finally, the government borrows some $300 billion each year from banks, insurance companies, and pension funds and then cycles most of it back as interest on the debt—a majestically rotating wheel of money.

Any economic actor as big as the federal government can, like John Steinbeck's Lennie,* clearly do some Very Important Bad Things, whether it intends to or not. In 1982, for example, Congress and the Reagan Administration chickened out on a $10 billion savings-and-loan crisis. Instead of paying the tab and closing down the industry, they

---

* [A mentally challenged character from Steinbeck's novel *Of Mice and Men*.]

covered it up with phony accounting and looser rules, and turned it into a $150 billion problem just a few years later—managing along the way to create a vast supply of unusable commercial real estate, and to roil all the world's financial markets by unleashing a great flood of federal borrowing for the sake of unlucky depositors. By the same token, a complicated but very different series of policy decisions in Japan during the 1980s has created an almost identical American-scale S&L-style crisis there. Once in a while, on the other hand, an opportunity arises to do a Very Important Good Thing. Actually fixing the U.S. health-care system, so that costs were brought under control, the uninsured received minimal benefits, and workers could change jobs without fear of losing coverage (if all that is indeed possible), would be just such an Important Good Thing.

But for the most part the federal apparatus trundles irresistibly ahead, a vast, splayfooted creature moving pretty much under its own power. A web of laws, regulations, long-term procurement contracts, treaties, jealously guarded congressional prerogatives, and deference to hallowed practice collectively overbear the occasional deflecting obstacle. Gentle nudges, pluckings at the coat sleeves, are of no avail against such tremendous inertial force; a minor initiative like the Clinton stimulus program is simply lost underfoot. Only very occasionally an utterly determined and utterly resourceful President, as Richard Nixon was, can bend the machinery to his will. Fearing for his re-election in 1972, with the economy slowing and inflation rising, Nixon and his Treasury Secretary, John Connally, engaged in a bravura performance of economic browbeating. They slapped on wage and price controls, broke the link between the dollar and gold, gunned up the money supply, and managed to wring out a year of strong growth with low inflation just before the election—at the price of triggering a huge recession during Nixon's short-lived second term. The economy, that is, *can* be managed over the short term, but only by relentless and violent clubbing, not by pushing buttons, and not by Presidents who are queasy about their methods or care about the consequences.

Truly important economic decisions, as often as not, zip by unnoticed by the public, probably by the President, because their consequences can take such a long time to become clear. For example, housing prices rose strongly through most of the 1980s, partly in response to severe supply problems in the early part of the decade. The housing shortage is usually attributed to the Baby Boomers' entering adulthood. The population entering retirement, however, was almost as big, and their housing behavior was something new in history. In 1973 Nixon and the Democratic Congress had sharply increased Social Security payments and indexed them to rise faster than inflation. For the first time, a retiring population had the wherewithal to keep their homes, and by and large they did so, instead of moving in with their children as previous generations had done. A substantial share of the nation's housing stock was thus withdrawn from the normal inventory-refreshment cycle, precipitating a boom in housing construction a decade later.

The new independence of the elderly, in fact, has had a long list of profound consequences: the growth of retirement villages, the boom in states like Florida and Arizona, new nursing-care patterns for the failing aged (the proverbial youngest daughter now typically lives in another city), and much more. Many of these changes, of course, represent progress. The point is merely that putting a greater share of national income in the hands of oldsters has had powerful effects far beyond the simple shifting of relative poverty indices among age cohorts.

Such examples are numerous. The country's economic structure has been profoundly affected by three decades of federal, state, and insurance-company policies aimed at expanding third-party coverage of health services. Last year the number of U.S. hospital workers increased by about as many people as are employed by all American computer makers. The Pentagon's aggressive search for miniaturized weapons technologies in the 1950s and early 1960s funded a host of unconventional electronics geniuses, helped create California's Silicon Valley and, by extension, the American venture-capital industry, and is still the source of much of the U.S. edge in advanced computer technologies. Economic models, by and large, just skate by issues like these. They're messy and unpredictable, and they involve tremendous effects from seemingly small actions—wars won or lost because of a missing horseshoe. And they are, depressingly enough for the traditional "scientific" economists, the way the real world works.

Complexity

The beauty of machines lies in regularity and order—the predictable harmonies of the Newtonian solar system, the eternal canons of a clockmaker God. Specify the initial conditions of any system—say, a table of billiard balls. Introduce a force—the moving cue ball—into the system and calculate the angles and forces of the subsequent collisions, and you will have specified the future position of the balls. That is the fundamental premise of the modern study of economics. But billiard balls don't work like that.

The celestial machine of Newtonian physics is a simple system, a small number of bodies revolving around a single massive body. But systems with many interacting elements, "complex" systems, do not behave like simple systems. You may specify the initial position of the billiard balls to any arbitrary level of precision—the sphericity of the balls, the smoothness of the surface, the trueness of the bumpers. But there will be some level of imprecision remaining, some element of the unknown, some fleeting shadow of randomness. If you strike successive "identical" tables of balls identically, their final positions will vary widely after only a very small number of collisions. Very tiny degrees of randomness, fed through a very small number of collisions, will lead to radically varying outcomes. If God removed an electron from the end of the universe, it would change the collision pattern of the air molecules in my room. A few days later there might be a storm in a neighboring state.

The real world is messily complex. Water flows in turbulent patterns; tiny variations in the flow quickly build up to big structures—eddies, riptides, vortices—that merge, expand, disappear. Molecules in a cell accrete tiny electrical variations and patterns of connections with other molecules. Suddenly a threshold is crossed and huge events are triggered—the cell divides, or pours forth viruses, or becomes cancerous, or dies. Mutations build up invisibly in the fossil record, and suddenly there is an enormous fluorescence of new species and life forms; the face of the earth changes. Real financial transactions are rarely structured like the rational two-person game so beloved of economic theorists: add just one more player and create a modest range of choices, and the computer simulations spin out a rich new world of shifting combinations and co-alitions. Chess is a game between only two players, with only moderately complex rules, but it quickly spirals into an infinity of outcomes. Scientists are just now developing the super-computers and the mathematical tools needed for problems like these. Even planetary orbits, it turns out, are much less stable and predictable than was once assumed.

Is the economy a complex system? Put even more radically, is the economy "computable"? That is, is it hopeless even to *try* to model it? The center of thinking about such issues is a small think tank in the foothills of the Rockies—the Santa Fe Institute, devoted to exploring the new understanding of complexity. Since the mid-1980s it has facilitated a remarkable dialogue between scholars such as the Nobel Prize–winning scientists Murray Gell-Man and Philip Anderson and the economist Kenneth Arrow, a Nobel laureate and perhaps the country's finest mathematical economist. W. Brian Arthur, a professor of economics at Stanford, and John Holland, of the University of Michigan, who was trained as a computer scientist, both Santa Fe fellows, are intensely involved in re-evaluating conventional economics in the light of complexity theory.

Both Holland and Arthur are interested in the local microformations in the economy, the vortices in the turbulent stream. Arthur points to the "QWERTY" typewriter keyboard, originally designed to slow typists down so that mechanical keys wouldn't jam. There are many more-efficient configurations, but QWERTY is now the unassailable standard, just as the Netherlands, a northern country with a short growing season, is the world's tulip center. Any economic system, that is, may have a very large number of possible equilibrium points, which flies in the face of traditional theory. Worse, raw chance may play a major role in the final equilibrium. "Economic data," Arthur says, "give an illusion of a stable, long-term trend line, but underneath that apparent stability is a constant turnover of structures. Some regions become rich, some stay poor, and often there's no obvious reason why. We need to understand those processes, how they work in the real world, from the ground up." (The idea of looking at smaller structures has immediate relevance. Recent national economic reports have been significantly influenced by recessionary conditions in a few states, such as New York and California. Politically distributed national stimulus programs are, at the very least, an inefficient response.)

Holland points out that the economy is an adaptive system, which increases its unpredictability. Unlike the molecules in a gas, economic agents learn from experience. There is indeed a kind of Heisenberg principle of economic management. If the federal government starts focusing on, say, the money supply as a tool for controlling the economy, the relationship between the money supply and the rest of the economy will surely change, vitiating the original policy assumptions. Biological systems, Holland suggests, are better than Newtonian mechanics as analogues for an economy. "The amount of biomass and its complexity seem to have been increasing at a steady, slow rate, for an extremely long period of time, although there is enormous variation in the successful life forms in any particular period. Economies may work that way. But there may also be some stable solutions; fish, porpoises, and ichthyosaurs at different times developed the same solution—hydrodynamic bodies." Arthur cautions, however, that there are nine or ten solutions to the problem of evolving an eye—pinholes, lens arrays, and the like—and that decidedly *un*hydrodynamic mollusks and crabs have been very successful colonizers of the seas.

The notion that economies are complex systems—more biological than Newtonian—has powerful intuitive appeal. But it will be a long time before complexity theory will be of much help to policy makers. One frustrating problem is a lack of data. Physicists are used to working with thousands, even tens of thousands, of observations. Industrialized countries have been collecting reasonably consistent economic statistics for only about fifty years; their quality is often poor, and their content changes subtly over the years. Financial-market data are somewhat better, and there is some tantalizing but inconclusive evidence that market behavior may mirror that of complex natural systems. Drop grains of sand, one after another, on the same spot; they will form a pile with a regular shape. Every so often a single grain will start an avalanche; most of the avalanches will be small, but once in a while, and quite unpredictably, one will be catastrophically large, wiping out whole sections of the pile. The market movements of most interest to Wall Street may be just avalanches in a sand pile. For the moment, however, the value of complexity theory in economics and finance is primarily as a cautionary metaphor, a pinprick to the pretensions of pundits, a warning that, at least occasionally, well-intended policies could, as the physicist David Ruelle put it, lead to "wild . . . fluctuations" with "possibly quite disastrous effects."

Economic Discourses

There is no escaping economic policy. The federal government is too large a presence in the American living room to be ignored, too insistent a claimant when the pie is divided. A President who feigned not having an economic policy would be engaging in as empty, and as damaging, a pretense as the most enthusiastic economic micromanager. The element of unpredictability in economic systems counsels caution, not nihilism, humility rather than despair.

The problem is one of domains of discourse. At least since John Kennedy's 1960 campaign to get "America moving again," Presidents have been obliged to adopt the pose of day-to-day managers. Day-to-day responsibilities imply day-to-day results; the press demands them, and the voters are trained to expect them. But let's face it, all the factory whistle-stops in a campaign notwithstanding, Presidents can't do much to create new jobs for machinists in Topeka. Rather than admit that, Presidents and press exchange cant, and voters sink into cynicism.

Discourse needs to shift toward "stewardship" and away from "management." We are a grown-up nation, with an educated, sophisticated press corps. It should be possible, although it will certainly not be easy, to set reasonable goals for political stewardship of the economy, and develop some reasonable scorecard on the important issues. Guidelines for sound stewardship might include, for instance, a list like the following.

Skepticism about one's own cleverness is usually a good policy starting point. In America, at least, markets mostly work, after their fashion. That is, although they almost never produce optimum results, and often take an uncomfortably long time to work, market outcomes are usually more nuanced, more subtly adapted to underlying complexities, than a priori designs. When Presidents Carter and Reagan decontrolled oil prices at the outset of the 1980s, supply, demand, and prices all came into a fair degree of balance with surprising speed after almost a decade of administrative floundering. Therefore a good initial bias is perpetually raised eyebrows toward complicated nonmarket solutions.

Pandering produces bad policy. There is an emerging consensus, even among quite conservative economists, that only the federal government can solve the health-care conundrum; indeed, it may be the Administration's single most important economic issue, affecting business and consumers alike. Solving the problem will be enormously difficult, requiring some measure of pain all around. The temptation to opt for politically expedient solutions with severely damaging long-term consequences may be overwhelming. The democratic principle presumes that the public will listen to arguments, consistently and persistently delivered, in favor of doing the right thing. Perhaps it is just a long time since an Administration has tried.

All important policies are long-term. The quandary facing elected officials is that anything important takes more than four years. Even successful health-care reform would not pay visible dividends sooner than the end of the decade. The benefits from careful deficit reduction will never be quantified. Even an Administration resolved to do the right thing over the long term, as the Clinton Administration seems to be, will be cruelly torn between its own decent instincts and the clamor of political advisers for short-term results.

And finally, *Presidents should trust their instincts over models.* Arguments against deficit spending are almost always cast in instrumentalist terms—its effects on interest rates, inflation, and investment. The truth is that none of these effects can be consistently demonstrated. Deficits, for example, have been rising steadily for ten years, and interest rates and inflation have been falling just as steadily: ten-year and thirty-year bonds have recently been at two-decade lows. A recent Goldman Sachs study found no relation between deficits and interest rates in most industrial countries, and only a weak, and fading, relation in England and America. There is no question that large deficits have economic consequences; it's just hard to prove what they are. It's an example of the complexity problem. The background noise—the effects of recessions, technology cycles, global capital flows, savings rates, monetary policy, commodity shortages, political disruptions—overwhelms our ability to trace the consequences of change in a single variable.

The clashes of economists on the meaning of deficits, unfortunately, obscure the truly important, if "unscientific," reason why they should be eliminated. Deficits are moral hazards. They are fundamentally anti-democratic; they allow government to increase spending without the implicit referendum of a tax increase. It has long been a settled principle of Western civil government that state borrowing leads to profligacy and irresponsibility. If revenues cannot constrain spending, government itself will be unrestrained. We need to eliminate deficit spending not because someone's computer says it will create more investment in 1996, or whenever, but to restore the integrity of our political system.

To President Clinton's great credit, his first economic speeches, stripped of the patina of economistic jargon, really do seem to have been appeals to citizens to do the right thing—to endure some pain in order to bring the appetites of government back into line with its resources, to forgo some personal benefits for a greater good. And judging from the first polls, people have reacted very positively, just as one might hope. But by so badly appealing to principle, Clinton has assumed a heavy burden of faith-keeping. If taxes go up and the deficit does *not* go down, it will be a breach of trust not likely to be forgiven or forgotten, and the backwash of voter cynicism could poison the political system for years. Unfortunately, as the specifics of the Clinton program become clearer, the danger of precisely such a result seems very real.

The public and its elected politicians need to reinforce each others' best instincts, not their worst ones. Presidents will perform up to the standard the public sets for them. Dropping our insistence that our Presidents spout cant and pretend to be daily miracle workers, shifting the focus to the long term, and helping to search out the right principles of action are the least we owe our Presidents, and ourselves.

Discussion Questions

1. If the economy isn't under presidential direction, does Congress exert any influence? If so, how?

2. If the president is unable to direct the economy, should we conclude that government economic policy is irrelevant to the operation of the U.S. economy?

70

"If the GDP Is Up, Why Is America Down?"

Clifford Cobb, Ted Halstead, and Jonathan Rowe

The gross domestic product, the standard measure of overall economic activity, is familiar to any American who watches the news or reads a paper. Yet as Cobb, Halstead and Rowe point out in the following article, the GDP tells us nothing about wealth or value; it is simply, in their words, a measure of "money changing hands." More GDP is not necessarily better, and the emphasis policy makers place on it can lead to poor economic policy.

The problem, according to the three, is that the GDP is a statistic ground in an economic theory that is no longer tenable for today's generation—an economic theory that views any kind of economic growth as a positive outcome, no matter what the social or environmental costs might be. What we need, these authors argue, are "better ways to measure our achievements as a nation."

Throughout the tumult of the elections last year [1994] political commentators were perplexed by a stubborn fact. The economy was performing splendidly, at least according to the standard measurements. Productivity and employment were up; inflation was under control. The World Economic Forum, in Switzerland, declared that the United States had regained its position as the most competitive economy on earth, after years of Japanese dominance.

The Clinton Administration waited expectantly, but the applause never came. Voters didn't *feel* better, even though economists said they should. The economy as economists define it was booming, but the individuals who compose it—or a great many of them, at least—were not. President Bill Clinton actually sent his economic advisers on the road to persuade Americans that their experience was wrong and the indicators were right.

This strange gap between what economists choose to measure and what Americans experience became the official conundrum of the campaign season. "PARADOX OF '94: GLOOMY VOTERS IN GOOD TIMES," *The New York Times* proclaimed on its front page. "BOOM FOR WHOM?" read the cover of *Time* magazine. Yet reporters never quite got to the basic question—namely, whether the official indicators are simply wrong, and are leading the nation in the wrong direction.

The problem goes much deeper than the "two-tiered" economy—prosperity at the top, decline in the middle and at the bottom—that received so much attention. It concerns the very definition of prosperity itself. In the apt language of the nineteenth-century writer John Ruskin, an economy produces "illth" as well as wealth; yet the conventional measures of well-being lump the two together. Could it be that even the upper tier was—and still is—rising on the deck of a ship that is sinking slowly into a sea of illth, and that the nation's indicators of economic progress provide barely a clue to that fact?

Ample attention was paid to the symptoms: People were working longer hours for less pay. The middle class was slipping while the rich were forging ahead. Commutes were more harried. Crime, congestion, and media violence were increasing. More families were falling apart. A *Business Week*/Harris poll in March imparted the not surprising news that more than 70 percent of the public was gloomy about the future.

Sounding much like the guidance department of a progressive New York grammar school, the Clinton Administration said that Americans were simply suffering the anxieties of adjustment to a wondrous new economy. Speaking in similar terms, Alan Greenspan, the chairman of the Federal Reserve Board, told a business gathering in San Francisco this past February that "there seemingly inexplicably remains an extraordinarily deep-rooted foreboding about the [economic] outlook" among the populace.

Those silly people. But could it be that the nation's economic experts live in a statistical Potemkin village* that hides the economy Americans are actually experiencing? Isn't it time to ask some basic questions about the gauges that inform expert opinion, and the premises on which those gauges are based?

Economic indicators are the main feedback loop to national policy. They define the economic problems that the political arena seeks to address. If the nation's indicators of economic progress are obsolete, then they consign us to continually resorting to policies that cannot succeed because they aren't addressing the right problems.

Today the two political parties differ somewhat in regard to means, but neither disputes that the ultimate goal of national policy is to make the big gauge—the gross domestic product—climb steadily upward. Neither questions that a rising GDP will wash away the nation's ills: if Americans feel unsettled despite a rising GDP, then clearly even more growth is needed.

This was clear in the months after the election, as the media continued to report economy up, people down stories that never quite managed to get to the crucial question: What is "up," anyway? In July, *Business Week* ran a cover story called "The Wage Squeeze" that got much closer than most. The article showed remarkable skepticism regarding the conven-

---

* [From late-eighteenth-century Russian history. Potemkin created the look of prosperity in a village that Catherine the Great was visiting, hiding the actual deplorable conditions.]

tional wisdom. But the magazine's editorial writers retreated quickly. Why aren't workers doing better even as corporate profits and "the economy" are up? "America just may not be growing fast enough," they said.

Furthermore, the GDP and its various proxies—rates of growth, expansion, recovery—have become the very language of the nation's economic reportage and debate. We literally cannot think about economics without them. Yet these terms have increasingly become a barricade of abstraction that separates us from economic reality. They tell us next to nothing about what is actually going on.

The GDP is simply a gross measure of market activity, of money changing hands. It makes no distinction whatsoever between the desirable and the undesirable, or costs and gain. On top of that, it looks only at the portion of reality that economists choose to acknowledge—the part involved in monetary transactions. The crucial economic functions performed in the household and volunteer sectors go entirely unreckoned. As a result the GDP not only masks the breakdown of the social structure and the natural habitat upon which the economy—and life itself—ultimately depend; worse, it actually portrays such breakdown as economic gain.

Yet our politicians, media, and economic commentators dutifully continue to trumpet the GDP figures as information of great portent. There have been questions regarding the accuracy of the numbers that compose the GDP, and some occasional tinkering at the edges. But there has been barely a stirring of curiosity regarding the premise that underlies its gross statistical summation. Whether from sincere conviction or from entrenched professional and financial interests, politicians, economists, and the rest have not been eager to see it changed.

There is an urgent need for new indicators of progress, geared to the economy that actually exists. We are members of Redefining Progress, a new organization whose purpose is to stimulate broad public debate over the nature of economic progress and the best means of attaining it. Accordingly, we have developed a new indicator ourselves, to show both that it can be done and what such an indicator would look like. This new scorecard invites a thorough rethinking of economic policy and its underlying premises. It suggests strongly that it is not the voters who are out of touch with reality.

* * *

The GDP Today: How Down Becomes Up

If the chief of your local police department were to announce today that "activity" on the city streets had increased by 15 percent, people would not be impressed, reporters least of all. They would demand specifics.

Exactly *what* increased? Tree planting or burglaries? Volunteerism or muggings? Car wrecks or neighborly acts of kindness?

The mere quantity of activity, taken alone, says virtually nothing about whether life on the streets is getting better or worse. The economy is the same way. "Less" or "more" means very little unless you know *of what*. Yet somehow the GDP manages to induce a kind of collective stupor in which such basic questions rarely get asked.

By itself the GDP tells very little. Simply a measure of total output (the dollar value of finished goods and services), it assumes that everything produced is by definition "goods." It does not distinguish between costs and benefits, between productive and destructive activities, or between sustainable and unsustainable ones. The nation's central measure of well-being works like a calculating machine that adds but cannot subtract. It treats everything that happens in the market as a gain for humanity, while ignoring everything that happens outside the realm of monetized exchange, regardless of the importance to well-being.

By the curious standard of the GDP, the nation's economic hero is a terminal cancer patient who is going through a costly divorce. The happiest event is an earthquake or a hurricane. The most desirable habitat is a multibillion-dollar Superfund site. All these add to the GDP, because they cause money to change hands. It is as if a business kept a balance sheet by merely adding up all "transactions," without distinguishing between income and expenses, or between assets and liabilities.

The perversity of the GDP affects virtually all parts of society. In 1993 William J. Bennett, who had been the Secretary of Education in the Reagan Administration, produced a study of social decline. He called it "The Index of Leading Cultural Indicators," a deliberate counterpoint to the Commerce Department's similarly named regular economic report. His objective was to detail the social erosion that has continued even as the nation's economic indicators have gone up.

The strange fact that jumps out from Bennett's grim inventory of crime, divorce, mass-media addiction, and the rest is that much of it actually adds to the GDP. Growth can be social decline by another name. Divorce, for example, adds a small fortune in lawyers' bills, the need for second households, transportation and counseling for kids, and so on. Divorce lawyers alone take in probably several billion dollars a year, and possibly a good deal more. Divorce also provides a major boost for the real-estate industry. "Unfortunately, divorce is a big part of our business. It means one [home] to sell and sometimes two to buy," a realtor in suburban Chicago told the *Chicago Tribune*. Similarly, crime has given rise to a burgeoning crime-prevention and security industry with revenues of more than $65 billion a year. The car-locking device called The Club adds some $100 million a year to the GDP all by itself, without counting knock-offs. Even a gruesome event like the Oklahoma City bombing becomes an economic uptick by the strange reckonings of the

GDP. "Analysts expect the share prices [of firms making anti-crime equipment] to gain during the next several months," *The Wall Street Journal* reported a short time after the bombing, "as safety concerns translate into more contracts."

Bennett cited the chilling statistics that teenagers spend on average some three hours a day watching television, and about five minutes a day alone with their fathers. Yet when kids are talking with their parents, they aren't adding to the GDP. In contrast, MTV helps turn them into ardent, GDP-enhancing consumers. Even those unwed teenage mothers are bringing new little consumers into the world (where they will quickly join the "kiddie market" and after that the "teen market," which together influence more than $200 billion in GDP). So while social conservatives like Bennett are rightly deploring the nation's social decline, their free-marketeer counterparts are looking at the same phenomena through the lens of the GDP and breaking out the champagne.

Something similar happens with the natural habitat. The more the nation depletes its natural resources, the more the GDP increases. This violates basic accounting principles, in that it portrays the depletion of capital as current income. No businessperson would make such a fundamental error. When a small oil company drains an oil well in Texas, it gets a generous depletion allowance on its taxes, in recognition of the loss. Yet that very same drainage shows up as a gain to the nation in the GDP. When the United States fishes its cod populations down to remnants, this appears on the national books as an economic boom—until the fisheries collapse. As the former World Bank economist Herman Daly puts it, the current national-accounting system treats the earth as a business in liquidation.

Add pollution to the balance sheet and we appear to be doing even better. In fact, pollution shows up twice as a gain: once when the chemical factory, say, produces it as a by-product, and again when the nation spends billions of dollars to clean up the toxic Superfund site that results. Furthermore, the extra costs that come as a consequence of that environmental depletion and degradation—such as medical bills arising from dirty air—also show up as growth in the GDP.

This kind of accounting feeds the notion that conserving resources and protecting the natural habitat must come at the expense of the economy, because the result can be a lower GDP. That is a lot like saying that a reserve for capital depreciation must come at the expense of the business. On the contrary, a capital reserve is essential to ensure the future of the business. To ignore that is to confuse mere borrowing from the future with actual profit. Resource conservation works the same way, but the perverse accounting of the GDP hides this basic fact.

No less important is the way the GDP ignores the contribution of the social realm—that is, the economic role of households and communities. This is where much of the nation's most important work gets done, from caring for children and older people to volunteer work in its many forms. It is the nation's social glue. Yet because no money changes hands in this realm, it is invisible to conventional economics. The GDP doesn't count it at all—which means that the more our families and communities decline and a monetized service sector takes their place, the more the GDP goes up and the economic pundits cheer.

Parenting becomes child care, visits on the porch become psychiatry and VCRs, the watchful eyes of neighbors become alarm systems and police officers, the kitchen table becomes McDonald's—up and down the line, the things people used to do for and with one another turn into things they have to buy. Day care adds more than $4 billion to the GDP; VCRs and kindred entertainment gear add almost $60 billion. Politicians generally see this decay through a well-worn ideological lens: conservatives root for the market, liberals for the government. But in fact these two "sectors" are, in this respect at least, merely different sides of the same coin: both government and the private market grow by cannibalizing the family and community realms that ultimately nurture and sustain us.

These are just the more obvious problems. There are others, no less severe. The GDP totally ignores the distribution of income, for example, so that enormous gains at the top—as were made during the 1980s—appear as new bounty for all. It makes no distinction between the person in the secure high-tech job and the "downsized" white-collar worker who has to work two jobs at lower pay. The GDP treats leisure time and time with family the way it treats air and water: as having no value at all. When the need for a second job cuts the time available for family or community, the GDP records this loss as an economic gain.

Then there's the question of addictive consumption. Free-market fundamentalists are inclined to attack critics of the GDP as "elitists." People buy things because they want them, they say, and who knows better than the people themselves what adds to well-being? It makes a good one-liner. But is the truth really so simple? Some 40 percent of the nation's drinking exceeds the level of "moderation," defined as two drinks a day. Credit-card abuse has become so pervasive that local chapters of Debtors Anonymous hold forty-five meetings a week in the San Francisco Bay area alone. Close to 50 percent of Americans consider themselves overweight. When one considers the $32 billion diet industry, the GDP becomes truly bizarre. It counts the food that people wish they didn't eat, and then the billions they spend to lose the added pounds that result. The coronary-bypass patient becomes almost a metaphor for the nation's measure of progress: shovel in the fat, pay the consequences, add the two together, and the economy grows some more.

So, too, the O.J. Simpson trial. When *The Wall Street Journal* added up the Simpson legal team ($20,000 a day), network-news expenses, O.J. statuettes, and the rest, it got a total of about $200 million in new GDP, for which politicians will be taking credit in 1996. "GDP OF O.J. TRIAL OUTRUNS THE TOTAL OF, SAY, GRENADA," the *Journal*'s headline writer proclaimed. One begins to understand why politicians prefer to talk about growth rather than what it actually consists of, and why Prozac alone adds more than $1.2 billion to the GDP, as people try to feel a little better amid all this progress.

*   *   *

. . . [N]o field has grown more tightly shut than economics, whose basic orthodoxies have persisted for at least a hundred years. Unless history stops cold, these, too, will eventually yield, and the time is now propitious. The generation that developed the GDP, and for which the GDP distilled an entire world view, is now mainly retired. The students and disciples of that generation are well into their middle years, rumbling along on mental capital from long ago. For the generation that is replacing them, the defining traumas were not the Depression and the Second World War but rather the material glut and environmental and social disintegration of which many in the old guard served as unwitting boosters and engineers.

To be sure, the old order does not lack acolytes. But for a growing number of economists, the conceptual tools and measurements of the neoclassical model—Keynesian twists included—are no longer adequate. These economists are demanding that their profession start to take account of the larger economy in which the market is grounded—the natural and social spheres, which they have in the past dismissed as the netherworlds of externality. In a survey in the 1980s of economists at fifty major universities two thirds acknowledged a sense of "lost moorings" in the profession.

In recent decades this kind of critique has been associated mainly with the ecological camp. Herman Daly, Hazel Henderson, Kenneth Boulding, and other writers have pointed out that in a world of finite physical resources the possibility of endless material expansion is not something we should count on. What is new today is that a similar argument is coming from certain quarters on the right: specifically that the pursuit of GDP has been undermining traditional values and social cohesion, much as it has been destroying the natural habitat.

Americans are conditioned to see ecology and social conservatism as occupying opposite ends of the political spectrum. But that is largely an optical illusion, reinforced by an antiquated national accounting system. The fact is that adherents at both ends deplore the way the pursuit of GDP can undermine the realm of their concern. Much as this pursuit turns ancient forests into lumber and beaches into sewers, so it turns families into nodes of consumption and the living room into a marketing free-fire zone. Both camps speak from the standpoint of *values* against the moral relativism and opportunism of the market. "If you read the

New Testament or the Pope's encyclical, it's no cheers for socialism and one and a half or two for capitalism," William Bennett, who was Reagan's Secretary of Education, observes. "Socialism treats people as a cog in the machine of the state; capitalism tends to treat people as commodities."

This strain of conservatism, partly rooted in traditional Christian teachings, was largely dormant during the Cold War, when the greater enemy communism predominated. But with the fall of the Soviet bloc it has reawakened, and the result has been a widening gap on the right between social conservatives and libertarian free-marketeers. This gap was easily overlooked in the Republican triumph last November, but it may well become as important as the one between the Republicans and the Democrats they replaced.

It can be seen, for example, in the diverging views of that archetypal Republican era, the Reagan eighties. Martin Anderson, who was Reagan's domestic-policy adviser, gave the rapturous libertarian view in his book *Revolution* (1988). "It was the greatest economic expansion in history," Anderson wrote. "Wealth poured from the factories of the United States, and Americans got richer and richer."

But does richer mean better—even assuming that all Americans shared in this bounty, which they didn't? For libertarians, as for many Keynesian liberals, the question isn't relevant. For social conservatives, however, it is *the* question. Bennett does not disparage the economic achievements of the Reagan years. Nor does he dispute that more family income can mean better schooling, medical care, and the like. But recently he has been calling attention to the social decay that has continued despite (and often in the name of) economic growth. "Would you rather have kids raised by rich people with lousy values, or by good people who just don't have much money?" he asks. "A lot of us would say we want the values right."

What the right calls "family values" is one arena in which the latent conflict between market and nonmarket values is coming out into the open. In a long article in *The Washington Post* last November, Edward Luttwak, of the Center for Strategic and International Studies, a conservative think tank in Washington, D.C., pointed out that much family disruption today arises from the "creative destruction" of the market that free-market economists adore. The failure to acknowledge this, Luttwak wrote, is "the blatant contradiction at the very core of what has become mainstream Republican ideology."

In an interview Luttwak argued that people need stability more than they need much of the new stuff that makes the GDP go up. Yet economists talk about stability "in entirely negative terms," he said. Conservation becomes a dirty word. One would think that conservatives would be the first to point this out; stability, after all, is what families and communities are for. But the political right is muzzled on these issues,

Luttwak said, by the economic interests of its major funders. "Any conservative who wishes to conserve will not be funded."

This split has a distinct similarity to the tension that arose in the Democratic Party in the seventies between environmentalists and the growth-boosting Keynesian mainstream. It could betoken the beginning of a new politics in which the popular currents represented by social conservatives and environmentalists increasingly find common cause. Some writers have made the connection already. For example, Fred Charles Iklé, who was an undersecretary of defense in the Reagan Administration, wrote an article for the *National Review* in which he criticized the "growth utopians" of the right. "Citizens who fear for our vanishing patrimony in nature," Iklé wrote, "drink from a wellspring of emotions that nourishes the most enduring conservative convictions." (He also tweaked the magazine's right-wing readers by pointing out that economic growth almost invariably leads to bigger government.)

Just a few years ago a confluence of the environmental and social-conservative impulses would have seemed unlikely. But the political seas are changing rapidly. The coalition that came together to oppose NAFTA and GATT—environmentalists and anti-corporate populists like Ralph Nader on the one hand, and social conservatives like Pat Buchanan on the other—seemed an oddity to most pundits. But something similar happened when the Walt Disney Company proposed a new theme park near the Civil War battlefield in Manassas, Virginia. Buchanan and numerous other tradition-minded conservatives joined environmentalists in blasting the proposal. In his syndicated newspaper column Buchanan demanded, "Conservatives who worship at the altar of an endlessly rising GNP should tell us: What is it they any longer wish to conserve?"

The two camps have converged in opposing the so-called "takings" bills, which would require the taxpayers to compensate property owners for restrictions on the use of their property. The Reverend Donald E. Wildemon, the president of the American Family Association, in Tupelo, Mississippi, has called such a proposal in his state the "porn owners' relief measure," because it could restrict the ability of local governments to control such things as topless bars. Environmentalists of course worry about the implications for the protection of wetlands, open space, and the like. The two camps agree that "growth" is not an end in itself but must serve larger values that are not economic in the usual sense.

We may be witnessing the opening battles in a new kind of politics that will raise basic questions about growth—questions that defy the conventional left-right divide. Where the old politics was largely concerned with the role of government—with the relation between public and private sectors—the emerging one will be more concerned with such issues as central versus local, market culture versus family and community culture, material accretion versus quality and values. The new politics will not be anti-growth, because to be categorically against growth is as nonsensical as to be categorically for it. Rather, it will begin with Luttwak's sane observation that when your goal is simply to increase GDP, then "what you increase isn't necessarily good." It will insist that growth—and economics generally—must be a means to an end, and not an end in itself.

This is not to suggest that such a new alliance is around the corner. But although the differences between the social-conservative and environmentalist camps are still large, they are probably etched more sharply among leaders in Washington than in the nation as a whole. These groups are converging on one crucial issue—namely, the ends of economic life. In their different ways they are expressing the feeling, widespread among the public, that the pronouncements from economic experts are fundamentally out of sync with the experience of their own lives; that economics must be about more than just the production and consumption of stuff; and that we need larger goals and better ways to measure our achievements as a nation.

Of course, this instinct could play out in many ways. But at least one thing is clear: boosting the GDP is no longer a sufficient aim for a great nation, nor one that America can continue to endure.

Discussion Questions

1. Suppose you are an employee of the Commerce Department charged with finding new ways to measure the value of the U.S. economy. What kinds of things would you consider? How would you take into account (meaning how would you measure, in economic terms) the health of the family, communities and the natural habitat?

The Debate: The Role of Government in the Economy

In the following debate between E. J. Dionne and John Hood over the government's regulatory role, Hood maintains that "free enterprise" does not need government protection to survive, drawing on the lessons of regulating urban transportation systems to make his point. Where the government places limits on the number of taxicabs allowed to service the city, for example, a gray market evolves—one that eludes government regulation—in order to fill the consumer demand for cheaper and more service. In his view, free enterprise is akin to a greased pig: Government tries to corner it, tame it, and influence its behavior, but it slips away and takes its own direction.

To Dionne, Hood's argument is simplistic, and it ignores the nurturing role government can play in a free-enterprise system. Dionne claims that the government's efforts to protect freedom have allowed "innovators to experiment, the scientists to discover, societies to create forms of organization appropriate to their needs." While many Americans voted for the Republican party in 1994 in order to "get government off our back," Dionne argues that Americans will want it to hop on again as the consequences of its withdrawal become clear.

71
"Gray Markets and Greased Pigs"

John Hood

Hailing a taxi in Boston can be tricky. It helps to be pushy, even rude. Tight city regulation of taxicabs has kept their number at 1,525 since 1934. Because government has prevented supply from rising to meet growing demand, there's an artificial taxi shortage.

But the story doesn't end there. Business travelers and tourists can still find transportation in Boston. Hotels, such as the Bostonian Hotel downtown, have begun operating their own limousines to take guests to airports, eateries, or other destinations around town. "I could not in good conscience sit there in the hotel watching guests stand on the street for 30 minutes to get to an airport that is five minutes away," Tim Kirwan, manager of the Bostonian, told *The Washington Post.*

Markets are resilient. Try as they might, government and the special interests they protect (in this case, the cab companies) can't completely suppress the forces of competition. By limiting one particular choice, they only direct enterprising people toward others. The result is either a black market, in which completely illegal transactions occur, or what might be called a "gray" market, in which firms substitute legal options for banned ones—either with the tacit acceptance of authorities or without their knowledge—thus defeating the intent of regulation.

Gray markets exist in many areas, such as zoning regulation (where business- or residential-only labels are routinely circumvented), but are perhaps most visible in the transportation field. In New York, for example, about 15,000 "gypsy cabs" operate in poor, minority communities, mainly in Queens, Brooklyn, and the Bronx. Strict regulation for half a century has limited the number of cabs in New York to 11,787. Consequently, over 600 "black car" livery companies have sprung up to bridge the gap between demand and legal supply.

Such companies are supposed to cater only to phoned-in customers, but many drivers take off their livery license plates (designed to help taxi commission inspectors spot them) and cruise the streets as "gypsies." These cabs do business not only because of the general taxi scarcity throughout the city, but also because some yellow cabs won't venture into unsafe areas to pick up minority customers.

Phone-in livery services are becoming a competitive force in many cities that regulate the number of taxicabs, such as Chicago and Atlanta. While not really illegal, they do circumvent the intent of regulations by giving taxis a run for their money.

Another form of competition—jitneys—has sprung up in Pittsburgh and Los Angeles. A jitney is a station wagon or small van that makes better use of miles traveled by carrying more than one passenger at a time. They were prevalent across the country in the early 1900s, but threatened transit and cab companies succeeded in outlawing them in most cities.

Their illegal status doesn't hinder them much. In Pittsburgh, for instance, jitneys dominate the transport market: if the jitneys cut prices, the legal taxis do, too. And like New York's gypsy cabs, jitneys provide service to neighborhoods shunned by the regular taxi fleets.

Of course, though governments may not be able to eliminate certain products or services from a market, they can make them more expensive. A "gypsy" ride in New York can sometimes cost two or three times what the same trip would cost in a yellow cab. Cab owners in Atlanta were even able to get a price floor codified in law: $50 a trip for limousines and $40 a trip for corporate cars, about three times what each would cost in a free market. (Jitneys, though, can sometimes offer lower prices than taxis, because they can carry more than one passenger at a time.)

Like alcohol and drug prices during times of prohibition, prices for illegal services rise because of increased risks to providers and lack of consumer information. Established interests count on the higher prices to reduce their competition, if they can't get outright bans enacted and enforced. Even so, services that circumvent regulations—like New

York's gypsy cabs—flourish. Consumers are willing to pay more to get the services regulated monopolies won't provide.

The artificially higher prices, though, do mean a loss of efficiency in the market. Consumers still buy more in goods and services from regulated industries, like the taxi companies, than they would if competition were freer.

Black and gray markets may seem a bit unseemly and corrupting, but they actually make up a large and crucial segment of our mixed economy. In some Third World countries they produce most of the goods and services, including food and other essentials. In such countries, government power is employed not only excessively but arbitrarily to favor political cronies. Enemies are taxed into bankruptcy, while valuable assets and capital are seized for "the good of the state." This creates so much uncertainty that businesses either leave (if possible) or go underground.

It may appear that the state, able to drive a business underground with its power to tax and regulate, exerts great control over the country's economic life. But that misses the point—that there is always an underground, even in totalitarian societies like the [former] Soviet Union, to which embattled businesses may flee.

A Losing Battle

Government is fighting a losing battle when it grapples with the discipline of the market. There's no real mystery about why this is so. Free enterprise is not some fragile, delicate experiment in constant need of protection. It does not have to be imposed or fostered. It is, in short, the natural order of things.

Coercive government, on the other hand, needs constant attention and tinkering. Consider how difficult it is for government to maximize its revenues. As supply-siders have shown, hiking tax rates won't always increase revenues because, among other factors, higher-income taxpayers lose their incentive to work and invest. Any increase in tax rates, in fact, sets off a market reaction that can actually reduce tax revenues. Witness, for example, the current controversy over capital gains taxes. The same principle applies to regulation. There is no shortage of ways to compete with a regulated monopoly, but there's a limited number of ways government can restrict competition. Insulate an industry from competition, and the resulting price increases and drops in service encourage consumers to substitute other products or services. And rest assured—firms will pop up to provide them. Frustrated regulators must feel like they're chasing a greased pig.

Government action can't eliminate market forces; it can only distort them. Sure, government's attempt to tax or regulate producers out of existence has disastrous side effects. But they are, indeed, only side ef-

fects. The goal—to drive "illegal" competition out of the marketplace—
is rarely achieved. Government just can't catch the pig.

72
"The Era of 'Big' Government: Why You'd Miss It If It Went"

E. J. Dionne, Jr.

The new radicalism in American politics, exemplified by the Republican *Contract with America*, means that the debate in 1996 and beyond is not simply a contest between political parties. It's a confrontation between fundamentally different approaches to economic turbulence, moral uncertainty, and international disorder. American politics has been unsettled in recent years because most Americans sense that the country has not adapted well to these changes, and because they are ambivalent about them. They see enormous potential in technological change and the global economic revolution, but also know that both carry high costs, challenge old values, and threaten the living standards of many. Like most people facing comparable choices in other times, Americans would like to reap their gains from the new era and minimize the costs it will impose. The central political question is whether such a tradeoff can be managed, and how.

It is Newt Gingrich's genius to be the first major Republican politician to pose many of these questions explicitly. His strategy would make technological change itself the priority and push government aside. "We do have an economic game plan," said the House Republicans in their post-contract manifesto, *Restoring the Dream*, "and its central theme is to get bureaucratic government off of America's back and out of the way." What has been called Third Wave conservatism posits that virtually all the constructive changes in the next era will take place in the private marketplace.

This new conservatism harks back not to Ronald Reagan but to the Gilded Age of the 1890s. "Today," wrote Paul Starr in *The American Prospect*, "the forces of the nineteenth century are laying siege to the accomplishments of the twentieth century in the name of the twenty-first." The new conservatives would resolve the country's political crisis by shrinking government. They would resolve the economic crisis by accelerating the economic transition. Denying any link between economic developments and the country's moral state, they would leave the solution of the moral crisis to traditional institutions, limiting the government's charitable endeavors in the hope that this would revive religiously based programs for social and personal uplift. All this would resolve the international crisis by transforming the United States, in Newt Gingrich's memorable phrase, into "the decisive economic power on the planet, which is the most competitive nation, which is capable of leading the human race, and which has reestablished here at home a culture that works."

The new conservatism will fail not because it isn't bold—it is *very* bold to try to restore nineteenth-century doctrines—but because it seeks to define away almost all the problems that Americans want politicians to grapple with. The new conservatism is premised on the idea that there is no tradeoff in the new era, that if only economic change goes forward unfettered, everyone will be better off. But most Americans don't believe that. Nor do most Americans define the moral crisis simply in terms of the misbehavior of others and presume that more and better preaching will solve the problem. They experience the moral crisis in their own lives, in worries about whether their own work will be rewarded and how they will raise their children. There is overwhelming distrust of government, but this does not translate into the overweening confidence in the corporate sector that so characterizes the new conservatism. The popular anger at government reflects not simply an impatience with bureaucrats but also a disappointment at government's failure to help citizens who are working their way through a difficult economic period. Americans want some protection from *both* the government and the market to preserve space in which families, voluntary associations, churches, and the other institutions of civil society can thrive.

If the old liberals seemed too eager to have the government usurp the authority of those institutions, the new conservatives appear blissfully unaware of how the economic marketplace can encroach on their prerogatives.

The central evasion in the program of the new conservatism is its effort to deny that even the most conservative government will constantly be making rules—through tax laws, regulations, or trade agreements—and that these rules have consequences. The new conservatism speaks the language of a joyful anarchism. In fact, it is like most conventional political movements, simply reshaping government to serve particular purposes and interests. If in the name of "deregulation" the government weakens environmental protections, the new rules it creates will powerfully affect how individuals and companies treat the environment. Repealing worker safety rules changes the incentives for employers who face enormous pressures from the marketplace to cut corners—even when they would prefer not to. If income from investments is treated more favorably for tax purposes than income from employment, the government is making a powerful statement about the relative importance of investment and labor. Trade agreements affect the lives and job prospects of millions. Even agreements promoting free trade are thousands of pages long, containing scores of new rules that reshape the economy.

Thus the new conservatism's emphasis on a battle between "big government" and "small government" is a misleading and false choice because it disguises what is at state: not merely the size of government but the *direction* of government policy—the incentives government will be offering and the values that will dominate policy making. The central issue in American politics in 1996 and beyond is thus not *whether* new rules will be written but what those rules will be and the extent to which they will make it easier or harder for average Americans—and especially those in the Anxious Middle—to prosper in a new era.

There is a final difficulty with the new conservatism that goes largely undiscussed: Its program has been tried before and found wanting. That is the importance of realizing that the new *laissez faire* is simply Gilded Age conservatism dressed up in the finery of a high-tech age. Both doctrines cast all worker protections as "socialism" and any effort by government to write rational rules for a new style of competition as an attack on property rights.

Throughout this century American voters knew better. They understood that a free-market economy could not function properly in the absence of rules, workers' rights, government spending on public goods, and continuing public investments to enhance the skills and opportunities of the workforce. This understanding was not confined to liberals or Democrats. It was accepted also by most Republicans. It was Dwight Eisenhower, after all, who sponsored the Interstate Highway System, one of the great public works in American history, and sponsored the first student loan program to help poor and middle-class Americans go to college. Much of the American business community came to welcome government's role in preventing chaos in the marketplace and redressing social wrongs. This understanding of politics, drawn from America's Progressive tradition, defined the center of gravity in *both* parties.

The logic of the new high-technology era demands not the dismantling of this tradition that is now under way in Congress, but its revival and renewal. Not since the industrial transition at the turn of the century and the mass dislocation of the Great Depression have Americans felt a greater desire for creative approaches to governing.

Contemporary liberals have failed to meet this demand, and Americans have paid a high price for their loss of imagination. It is visible in the political fatalism of millions of working Americans who once looked to Washington in their efforts to achieve self-sufficiency. In casting ballots for Roosevelt and Truman, Kennedy and Johnson, these Americans sensed they were part of historic, and effective, political movement. Now, politics lies discredited and with it the hope that democratic government can respond effectively to change. The responsibility for this failure is widely shared. It encompasses "New Democrats" who said they would revitalize government, traditional liberals who claimed to speak for "average Americans," moderate Republicans who now face a choice of being isolated in their party or capitulating to its new disposition, and a Left that lost its way in the controversies surrounding multiculturalism and deconstruction and gave up on democratic politics.

But the game is not played out. Indeed, it is just beginning. The demand for a new Progressive departure will not go away, and all these groups have an opportunity to define the project.

By casting "government" and "the market" as the main mechanisms of social organization, the conventional political debate thus leaves out the most important institutions in people's lives—family, church, neighborhood, workplace organizations, and a variety of other voluntary institutions ranging from sports clubs and youth groups to privately organized child-care centers and the loose fellowships created at taverns like Cheers of television fame. All are places where, as the theme song of "Cheers" tells us, everybody knows your name. The great flaw in the binary choice between government and the market is described brilliantly by the sociologist Alan Wolfe in his book *Whose Keeper?*: "The opposition between individual freedom and state authority that guides so much of contemporary political theory . . . is a false opposition. [C]ivil society, not the individual, is the better alternative to government in modern society." Wolfe notes that while "believers in *laissez faire* complain that the state has grown at the expense of individuals, and advocates of a stronger state sometimes bemoan individualism, the truth is that the decline of obligations once associated with civil society strengthens both individualism and governmental authority."

Conservatives, both old and new, have done a good job of reminding us of the Progressives' sometimes excessive eagerness for replacing the mechanisms of private charity and communal responsibility—family, church, and mutual assistance societies—with the often clumsier mechanisms of government. What conservatives, especially the new conservatives, refuse to recognize is the extent to which these organizations are effective precisely because they do not operate according to the logic of free markets, but according to an older moral logic that predated capitalism. Following Wolfe, one can begin to see how the moral crisis Americans are experiencing grows not simply from the "countercultural" or "permissive" ideas that developed in the 1960s. Its roots lie deeper, in a society built on purely individualistic and market values that steadily cut away the bonds of solidarity, morality, and trust.

If profit is all that matters, filmmakers or music producers will not think twice about filling the marketplace with products that foster amoral or dysfunctional values among the young. If all personal ties between employer and employee are deemed to be "irrational" or "sentimental" when compared to the competitive needs of the marketplace, employers need not think at all about how work schedules might affect the ability of employees to rear their children or how cutbacks in medical coverage might affect their employees' lives. And if government gives no protection for those many employers who *do* care about such things, it risks forcing them out of business as they are undercut by competitors for whom cost and price are the only factors in business decisions. As David Broder has pointed out, one of the terrible ironies of the health-care battle is that the *minority* of employers who do not offer health insurance took control of the political debate from the vast *majority* of businesses that do. A debate that might have been over how business and individuals might fairly share the obligation of providing help for the sick became instead a fight over government "compulsion," as if government itself had created the need for health insurance.

The central irony of our time that so many of the new conservatives wish to avoid is this: *A capitalist society depends on noncapitalist values in order to hold together and prosper.* Adam Smith certainly recognized this. It is what Daniel Bell has referred to as "the cultural contradictions of capitalism." More recently, Francis Fukuyama has written of "the social virtues" behind "the creation of prosperity."

If the problem is cast this way, the purpose of Progressivism is not to use government to wreck the free market, but precisely the opposite: to create the social conditions in which the market can work well in its proper sphere. The Progressives' goal is not to strengthen government for government's sake, but to use government where possible to strengthen the institutions of civil society.

Progressives—liberals—thus need to embrace a politics of liberty and community. They cannot leave the definition of liberty to their conservative adversaries. They need to contest the negative definition of liberty as incomplete. Yes, individuals need to be protected against omnipotent, abusive government. But they also have a right to look to government to help in defending their autonomy and expanding the possibilities of self-reliance. Government should not weaken the bonds of civil society. But government can step in to strengthen civil society and protect it against the disruptions created by the normal workings of the economic market. Surely anyone who claims to believe in "family values" should want to relieve families of some of the pressures placed upon them by work and economic distress.

A New Progressivism that would operate in accord with these principles would take seriously Republican strategist Bill Kristol's talk about "the politics of liberty and the sociology of virtue." But it would contest the effectiveness of the new conservative program supported by Kristol and his allies, arguing that liberty and virtue require not only freedom from government coercion, but also the active support of a government that understands both its obligations and its limits. It is not enough to preach virtue to a family that finds its living standard falling despite its own best efforts to work, save, invest, and care for its children. Such a family surely deserves some support for its own efforts to expand its opportunities—and, at the least, some insurance against the worst economic catastrophes that might befall it.

Alternatives to the new conservatism will thus arise simply because the voters will demand them. One can see in the responses to Pat Buchanan's nationalism and to Ross Perot's anti-Washington pronouncements the rumblings of an Anxious Middle prepared to be radicalized by economic frustrations, moral unease, and impatience with government's failures. Thus the basic inspiration behind the broad Progressive project remains relevant—a belief in the use of government to expand individual choice and protect communities, an effort to improve living standards across the society, and an understanding that a democratic society works best with a broad and thriving middle class. Progressives do not seek absolute equality or anything like it; but they also know that rising inequality can be dangerous for democracy.

The tragedy of President Bill Clinton's term, especially his first two years, is that he raised many of the right issues without producing either the results he promised or a set of political alliances that could carry on a long-term project of social reconstruction. He did not encourage New and Old Democrats to work together; if anything, rifts in his party seemed to widen. He did not draw in moderate Republicans, many of whom still have impulses shaped by their party's progressive tradition. He did not convince the Left that he shared its goals of social justice and social equality. And he did not succeed in nurturing a progressive wing within the business community that accepted the need for government action to solve problems that the free market neither would nor could solve on its own. Clinton's most obvious failure was personal; that none of the wings of the potential Progressive alliance fully trusted him. It was a personal failure that had repercussions across almost every area of policy.

Yet precisely because Clinton was on the right track in the questions he asked and in some of the solutions he offered, many of the issues of the Clinton term will need revisiting—perhaps even by Clinton himself.

In an otherwise brilliant dissection of the great economic and political transformations of our era, ("The Age of Social Transformation," *Atlantic*, November 1994) the social thinker Peter Drucker asserts flatly that "if this century proves one thing, it is the futility of politics." He argues that the large changes of the twentieth century had nothing to do with the "headline-making political events" and everything to do with social and economic changes that operated "like ocean currents deep below the hurricane-tormented surface of the sea." These, he says, have had "the lasting, indeed the permanent, effect."

Drucker goes on to describe with great clarity the agricultural revolution, the declining role of agricultural employment, the rise of industrialism, and the emergence of the blue-collar worker, "the first lower class in history that could be organized and could stay organized." He speaks of urbanization and the fact that cities in this age, unlike cities in earlier ages, actually *improve* public health. This was, he writes, primarily because the factory produced higher living standards, but also because of "new public health measures: purification of water, collection and treatment of wastes, quarantine against epidemics, inoculation against disease." The new era, with the rise of the "knowledge worker," Drucker concludes, will demand "social and political innovations"—particularly in education, because the new period will put a premium on "the quality of knowledge and the productivity of knowledge."

What is so striking about Drucker's view is that his detailed and insightful analysis of developments in commerce, science, and society flies in the face of his insistence on "the futility of politics." *That is because he takes democratic politics for granted.* The truth is that almost none of the advances Drucker describes could have happened absent the victories of democracy and free government. The freedom accorded by democracy allowed the innovators to experiment, the scientists to discover, societies to create forms of organization appropriate to their needs. Social protections, through government and private organizations, allowed prosperity to be shared under conditions of social peace. Industrialization did not have that same bracing effect in other places where it went forward rapidly, notably the Soviet Union, largely because the political conditions were different.

Moreover, Drucker's entirely accurate assertion about the effective organization of blue-collar workers is a statement about politics itself. The twentieth century turned out for the better in significant part because ordinary people were able to use politics in free societies to do extraordinary things—first to organize themselves and then to demand and win improvements in their living standards, create opportunities for their children, and insist on a basic social equality that is the essence of democracy as a way of life. This century, far from proving the futility of politics, is a history of the triumph of *democratic politics*. At the end of the century, the central problem confronting the democracies is not excessive government or a lack of economic and technical inventiveness, but a decay in the sort of social and political inventiveness and organization that gave power to ordinary citizens, shaped the economy into an engine of mass prosperity, and strengthened democracy.

The overriding need in the United States and throughout the democratic world is for a new engagement with democratic reform, the political engine that made the industrial era as successful as it was. The technologies of the information age will not on their own construct a successful society, any more than industrialism left to itself would have made the world better. The industrial age needed to be rescued from those who thought that technology on its own could save the human race. Now the information age must also be saved from the cyberutopians. Even the most extraordinary breakthroughs in technology and the most ingenious applications of the Internet will not save us from social breakdown, crime, or injustice. Only politics, which is the art of how we organize ourselves, can even begin to take on such tasks.

Politics and government cannot raise children, write love songs, create computer languages, invent the technology after the microchip, or discover a cure for cancer. But politics and government do shape the conditions under which such acts of creativity are made easier or harder, more likely or less likely. Politics has everything to do with building a more just, more civil, more open society. Those who rallied to Progressivism, the cause of those who believe that democratic government has the capacity to improve society, always understood this. Their time has come again.

Discussion Questions

1. Can you think of other instances where governmental regulations have been undermined by "gray markets"? Explain.

2. When is regulation of the market necessary? Explain.

CHAPTER 14

Government and Society

73
"A Program for Social Security"

FRANKLIN D. ROOSEVELT

Just as the New Deal was a historic transition in the relationship between government and the economy, much of what we consider the modern welfare state got its start during the 1930s when President Franklin D. Roosevelt responded to the economic hardship of the Great Depression with a variety of social insurance and economic security programs. In 1934, Roosevelt sent Congress legislation that established Social Security and Aid to Families with Dependent Children and unemployment insurance, and strengthened public health programs. In the message to Congress, Roosevelt set out some principles which, he argued, should guide government action: the programs should start small, so as "to avoid any danger of permanently discrediting the sound and necessary policy of federal legislation for economic security by attempting to apply it on too ambitious a scale before actual experience has provided guidance for the permanently safe direction of such efforts"; the insurance programs should be self-sustaining ones that would not require "the proceeds of general taxation"; the programs should be managed by the states (except for Social Security); and the federal government should maintain control over program funds.

Despite the small scale of the proposal, it was controversial, and opponents of Social Security immediately challenged the program as unconstitutional (the Supreme Court upheld the legislation in 1937). And even though Roosevelt proposed only modest spending—$100 million, or about $1.5 billion in today's dollars—funding levels grew over time, especially for Social Security, as organized constituencies fought to preserve and bolster the programs. In 1995, the federal government spent more than $300 billion on Social Security alone.

In addressing you on June 8, 1934, I summarized the main objectives of our American program. Among these was, and is, the security of the men, women, and children of the nation against certain hazards and vicissitudes of life. This purpose is an essential part of our task. In my annual message to you I promised to submit a definite program of action. This I do in the form of a report to me by a Committee on Economic Security, appointed by me for the purpose of surveying the field and of recommending the basis of legislation.

I am gratified with the work of this committee and of those who have helped it: The Technical Board of Economic Security, drawn from various departments of the government; the Advisory Council on Economic Security, consisting of informed and public-spirited private citizens; and a number of other advisory groups, including a Committee on Actuarial Consultants, a Medical Advisory Board, a Dental Advisory Committee, a Hospital Advisory Committee, a Public Health Advisory Committee, a Child Welfare Committee, and an Advisory Committee on Employment Relief. All of those who participated in this notable task of planning this major legislative proposal are ready and willing at any time to consult with and assist in any way the appropriate congressional committees and members with respect to detailed aspects.

It is my best judgment that this legislation should be brought forward with a minimum of delay. Federal action is necessary to and conditioned upon the actions of states. Forty-four legislatures are meeting or will meet soon. In order that the necessary state action may be taken promptly, it is important that the federal government proceed speedily.

The detailed report of the committee sets forth a series of proposals that will appeal to the sound sense of the American people. It has not attempted the impossible nor has it failed to exercise sound caution and consideration of all of the factors concerned: the national credit, the rights and responsibilities of states, the capacity of industry to assume financial responsibilities, and the fundamental necessity of proceeding in a manner that will merit the enthusiastic support of citizens of all sorts.

It is overwhelmingly important to avoid any danger of permanently discrediting the sound and necessary policy of federal legislation for economic security by attempting to apply it on too ambitious a scale before actual experience has provided guidance for the permanently safe direction of such efforts. The place of such a fundamental in our future civilization is too precious to be jeopardized now by extravagant action. It is a sound idea—a sound ideal. Most of the other advanced countries of the world have already adopted it, and their experience affords the knowledge that social insurance can be made a sound and workable project.

Three principles should be observed in legislation on this subject. In the first place, the system adopted, except for the money necessary to initiate it, should be self-sustaining in the sense that funds for the payment of insurance benefits should not come from the proceeds of general taxation. Second, excepting in old-age insurance, actual management should be left to the states, subject to standards established by the federal government. Third, sound financial management of the funds and the reserves and protection of the credit structure of the nation should be assured by retaining federal control over all funds through trustees in the Treasury of the United States.

At this time, I recommend the following types of legislation looking to economic security:

First, unemployment compensation.

Second, old-age benefits, including compulsory and voluntary annuities.

Third, federal aid to dependent children through grants to states for the support of existing mother's pension systems and for services for the protection and care of homeless, neglected, dependent, and crippled children.

Fourth, additional federal aid to state and local public-health agencies and the strengthening of the federal Public Health Service. I am not at this time recommending the adoption of so-called health insurance, although groups representing the medical profession are cooperating with the federal government in the further study of the subject, and definite progress is being made.

With respect to unemployment compensation, I have concluded that the most practical proposal is the levy of a uniform federal payroll tax, 90 percent of which should be allowed as an offset to employers contributing under a compulsory state unemployment compensation act. The purpose of this is to afford a requirement of a reasonably uniform character for all states cooperating with the federal government and to promote and encourage the passage of unemployment compensation laws in the states. The 10 percent not thus offset should be used to cover the costs of federal and state administration of this broad system. Thus, states will largely administer unemployment compensation, assisted and guided by the federal government.

An unemployment compensation system should be constructed in such a way as to afford every practicable aid and incentive toward the larger purpose of employment stabilization. This can be helped by the intelligent planning of both public and private employment. It also can be helped by correlating the system with public employment so that a person who has exhausted his benefits may be eligible for some form of public work as is recommended in this report. Moreover, in order to encourage the stabilization of private employment, federal legislation should not foreclose the states from establishing means for inducing industries to afford an even greater stabilization of employment.

In the important field of security for our old people, it seems necessary to adopt three principles—first, noncontributory old-age pensions for those who are now too old to build up their own insurance; it is, of course, clear that for perhaps thirty years to come funds will have to be provided by the states and the federal government to meet these pensions. Second, compulsory contributory annuities, which in time will establish a self-supporting system for those now young and for future generations. Third, voluntary contributory annuities by which individual initiative can increase the annual amounts received in old age. It is proposed that the federal government assume one-half of the cost of the old-age pension plan, which ought ultimately to be supplanted by self-supporting annuity plans.

The amount necessary at this time for the initiation of unemployment compensation, old-age security, children's aid, and the promotion of public health, as outlined in the report of the Committee on Economic Security, is approximately $100 million.

The establishment of sound means toward a greater future economic security of the American people is dictated by a prudent consideration of the hazards involved in our national life. No one can guarantee this country against the dangers of future depressions, but we can reduce these dangers. We can eliminate many of the factors that cause economic depressions and we can provide the means of mitigating their results. This plan for economic security is at once a measure of prevention and a method of alleviation.

We pay now for the dreadful consequence of economic insecurity— and dearly. This plan presents a more equitable and infinitely less expensive means of meeting these costs. We cannot afford to neglect the plain duty before us. I strongly recommend action to attain the objectives sought in this report.

DISCUSSION QUESTIONS

1. Does the current welfare state support or undermine the principles outlined by FDR in this article? Explain.

2. How is today's debate over welfare reform (discussed later in this chapter) reflected in this discussion by FDR? Explain.

74
"The Next New Deal"

Neil Howe and Philip Longman

Who benefits from the welfare state? The question is central to discussions of public policy, as well as to the current debate over the deficit and who should bear the burden of cutbacks in government programs. Neil Howe and Philip Longman argue that, contrary to widespread public perception, government benefits are tilted heavily in favor of the middle class and the wealthy, not the poor (Warren Rudman and Paul Tsongas, founders of the Concord Coalition, press this point as well). Social security, government pensions, Medicare, and various tax deductions and credits provide benefits without regard to need. According to the authors, these programs distort social policy by diverting funding to the already well-off. In 1994, for example, $8 billion in Social Security payments went to households with incomes over $100,000. The solution offered by Howe and Longman is gradually to phase out benefit payments and tax deductions as income rises—a controversial proposal, given the political clout of groups such as the American Association of Retired Persons (AARP), which will surely try to protect their favorite programs.

With the coming of the next New Deal, Americans will look back and marvel at what became of our old welfare state—that tangle of inequity and dysfunction once known as federal entitlements. Why did the public tolerate a system that wound up distributing most of its benefits to the well-off? And how did the economy survive its costs?

History books will no doubt concentrate on a few choice examples of the conditions that finally forced a wholesale reform. Readers may learn, for instance, that by 1991 the federal government's largest housing subsidy program was providing an average of $3,000 a year to each of the six million wealthiest households in America, while offering nothing to the 36 million Americans in poverty.

To qualify for this particular benefit, called the home-mortgage deduction, you had to borrow using your first or second home as collateral. And the more you borrowed, even if it was to finance a chalet in Aspen—or just a ski trip to Aspen—the more subsidy you would receive from other taxpayers. By 1991 the cost of the home-mortgage deduction had risen to $37 billion, of which 81 percent went directly to households with incomes over $50,000. Meanwhile, economists bemoaned the anemic U.S. personal savings rate, which in the late 1980s fell to its lowest level since the 1930s.

The U.S. health-care system a quarter century after the announcement of the Great Society will also provide future historians with rich examples of the conditions that led to the next New Deal. How to explain that the U.S. economy staggered under the highest per capita health-care costs on earth, and still 23 million Americans under the age of thirty-five were uninsured for any medical care at all?

Stranger yet was what happened to these uninsured Americans, and to everyone else, if they happened to live to be sixty-five. After that birthday a citizen, regardless of income, became entitled to take part in a program called Medicare, which would pay for everything from CAT scans to pacemakers, from chiropractic to orthopedic recliners. In 1991 Medicare spent nearly $19 billion subsidizing the health care of households earning $50,000 or more. That year government experts projected that the mounting cost of Medicare would cause the program to collapse within fifteen years, and that if current trends continued, total health-care spending would rise to an economy-shattering 44 percent of the gross national product by 2030. No one listened.

Gold-plated pensions for federal employees will also no doubt be held up by future historians as emblematic of the decadence of late-twentieth-century political culture. By what accident of history were military and civil-service retirees with incomes over $100,000 collecting $9.2 billion from the U.S. Treasury in 1991? For half this sum the official poverty rate for all American elderly could have been reduced to zero. At the very least, Congress could have done something about the $1.4 trillion in unfunded federal pension liabilities on the books. But the House of Representatives was busy with other business at the time—such as voting itself a controversial pay hike that would later be remembered for its explosive impact on pension costs. Retiring in 1991, a typical congressman looked forward to $1,098,735 in lifetime benefits; by 1993 the figure had risen to $1,523,263.

Finally, there was the program originally designed to offer all Americans what President Franklin Roosevelt's brain trusters called "a floor of protection" against destitution in old age. But over the course of more than half a century Social Security had evolved into something radically different. By 1991 the system was distributing more than $55 billion a year, or more than a fifth of its benefits, to households with incomes above $50,000 a year. For that much money the government could have provided every American with cradle-to-grave insurance against poverty—including the one American child in twenty who lived in a household reporting a cash income during 1991 of less than $5,000.

For many years the worsening inefficiency and inequity of the U.S. social-welfare system seemed to make little impression on American political opinion. Political leaders as diverse as Newt Gingrich, George

Bush, Bill Clinton, and Daniel Patrick Moynihan expressed alarm at the moral hazard of providing welfare benefits to poor unwed mothers. But few political leaders worried about the moral hazard—and incomparably larger cost—of subsidizing home-equity loans for rising young stockbrokers, granting free medical care, PX cards, and half pay for life to ex-colonels at age forty-two, passing out farm payments to affluent agribusiness owners, or writing checks to globe-trotting senior citizens which got forwarded to Bermuda. It was convenient to assume that free lunches corrupted only the underclass.

As the 1990–1992 recession lingered, forcing local governments to cut teachers' pay, ignore the raving homeless, and fence off sagging bridges, state governors turned to Washington, where politicians shrugged their shoulders and pointed to a budget bursting with entitlement programs running on autopilot. Meanwhile, ordinary Americans wondered what was happening to their nation's public sector. It could afford neither to build for the future nor to care for the needy—despite unprecedented borrowing, a near-record level of taxation, and sinking defense outlays that by the fall of 1992 had reached their lowest share of GNP since Harry Truman ran for President. With the vaunted post–Cold War "peace dividend" evaporating, the United States found itself unable to invest adequately in either its infrastructure or its children. Eventually people began to talk of another Great Depression, before the coming of the next New Deal.

A Welfare State for the Affluent

Rudolf Goldscheid, the socialist economist, once observed, "The budget is the skeleton of the state stripped of all misleading ideologies." By now federal entitlement spending has become so pervasive in American life —not just among the poor but most notably among the middle class and the affluent—that one cannot make sense of our politics or the condition of our economy without considering how this spending rearranges the nation's resources and defines our choices as a society.

Ever since the early 1980s, when the United States lost control of its fiscal policy, the term "entitlements"—referring to all federal benefit payments to individuals—has been part of the American political lexicon. Today the twelve-digit numbers that first worried budget experts back in the late 1970s look positively quaint—although events have proved that the growth of entitlements is indeed the leading cause of the nation's long-term structural deficits. This year the cost of federal benefits is larger than was the entire federal budget when Ronald Reagan arrived in Washington with a mandate to slash the welfare state.

All told, entitlements have become a trillion-dollar river. The main current includes more than $700 billion in direct outlays, received by at least one member of roughly half the nation's households. These expenditures account for more than 45 percent of all federal spending, and are more than twice as large as the amount consumed by defense. Another flow of nearly $200 billion is distributed in the form of tax subsidies to individuals, such as the home-mortgage deduction and the exclusion for employer-paid health care. These explicit breaks in the tax code are the moral and fiscal equivalent of the government's simply mailing a check. To pay for them, other people's taxes have to be raised, other benefits have to be cut, or the deficit has to be increased.

The accumulating burden is not about to ease. Our economy shows no sign of "outgrowing" the cost of entitlements, as many partisans of Reaganomics, along with many liberals, once hoped. Though the relative cost typically rises and falls with the business cycle, it has always emerged from each new recession larger than it emerged from the last. In fiscal year 1992 federal benefit outlays alone will exceed 12 percent of GNP, the second highest level ever. Including tax benefits, the total cost of federal entitlements amounts to well over 15 percent of GNP, and Congress now projects that it will climb steadily through the late 1990s. For the first time, the economy should not expect any post-recession relief.

Who benefits from this spending? Until recently no one really knew. Budget experts, to be sure, have always pointed to a few eyebrow-raising numbers. Consider the fact that of all federal benefit outlays, only a quarter flows through programs that require any evidence of financial need —and that even this "means-tested" quarter includes such middle-class staples as student loans and VA hospital care. Consider also that only one of every eight federal benefit dollars actually reaches Americans in poverty. But reliable income figures for all recipient households have simply not been available. Cash-income surveys conducted by the Census Bureau are plagued by high rates of underreporting (especially by the wealthy). Tax-return data from the Internal Revenue Service are more accurate, but do not cover the entire population (especially the poor).

Several years ago, however, growing curiosity on Capitol Hill persuaded the nonpartisan Congressional Budget Office to try to unravel the mystery. By merging the Census and IRS data sources, CBO economists ultimately arrived at reliable and comprehensive estimates of benefits by household income. The estimates were circulated behind closed doors during the 1990 budget summit and have since been updated— though they have never yet been published. The benefit-income statistics we cite throughout this article are based on these CBO estimates, which cover about 80 percent of all federal benefit outlays.

These numbers destroy any ideological myths Americans may cling to about who gets what from government. They offer an accurate glimpse of that "skeleton of the state"—which has too long been locked in the political closet.

The CBO research demonstrates, in fact, that the most affluent Americans actually collect slightly more from the welfare state than do the poorest Americans. It shows that last year U.S. households with incomes over $100,000 received, on average, $5,690 worth of federal cash and in-kind benefits, while the corresponding figure for U.S. households with incomes under $10,000 was $5,560. Quite simply, if the federal government wanted to flatten the nation's income distribution, it would do better to mail all its checks to random addresses. The problem is not that poverty programs don't target the poor. More than 85 percent of the benefits from AFDC [Aid to Families with Dependent Children], SSI [Supplemental Security Insurance], and food stamps do indeed go to households with incomes under $20,000. But their impact is neutralized by all the other programs, which tilt the other way and are, of course, much greater in size.

The trend over time is also unsettling. Liberals sometimes attribute the growing disparity of income in America to Reagan-era cuts in targeted poverty programs. Among the very poorest households that is indeed one cause. From 1980 to 1991, in constant dollars, the average federal benefit received by households with incomes under $10,000 declined by seven percent. Yet liberals typically overlook the gentrification of America's untargeted nonpoverty programs, which has been pushing even more powerfully to widen the gap between rich and poor. During those same eleven years, among households with incomes over $200,000 the real value of average benefits received (mostly Social Security, Medicare, and federal pensions) fully doubled.

But thus far we have been considering only direct outlays. When we include the value of entitlements conveyed through the tax code, the bias in favor of the well-off becomes even more pronounced.

Tax Expenditures and Other Subsidies

Such tax subsidies date back to 1918, when patriotic fervor for U.S. troops in Europe was running high. Political leaders in Washington felt they should do something dramatic to reward the doughboys. Facing a tight budget, Congress hesitated to raise veterans' benefits directly. But then someone on Capitol Hill took a look at the five-year-old federal income-tax system and came up with a nifty idea: Why not "raise" veterans' benefits simply by exempting such benefits from the tax?

Over the years many more "tax expenditures" have followed, nearly all of them—like the first—created entirely off budget, without estimating eventual cost and far from the scrutiny that normally accompanies direct appropriations. Several, including the exemptions for Social Security benefits and for employer-paid health care, were created not by Congress but by offhand IRS rulings in the 1930s and 1940s. At the time, no one paid them much notice, because tax rates were low, Social Security benefits were modest, and company health plans were rare. But in fiscal year 1992 these two rulings alone are costing the federal government nearly $90 billion, which is more than the Pentagon's total budget for weapons procurement.

Though tax expenditures as a political art were invented during the First World War, the term itself dates back only to the mid-1960s, when it was coined by Stanley S. Surrey, a Harvard Law don who served as assistant secretary of the Treasury for tax policy in the Kennedy and Johnson Administrations. In the course of his battles with Congress over tax policy, Surrey was struck by the fact that Congress was increasingly using selective tax reductions for specific groups of people, rather than direct appropriations, as a means of distributing public resources.

Surrey's favorite example was the deduction for medical expenses. He explained that this tax provision had precisely the same impact, both on the budget and on the public, as a multibillion-dollar benefit program that heavily favored the very rich (because they pay taxes at the highest rates) and that entirely excluded the very poor (because they don't pay taxes at all). There was indeed only one big difference: the same Congress that created the tax provision would never dare to create the benefit program.

Although the tax-expenditure concept has been widely accepted by economists over the past thirty years, it strikes many Americans the wrong way. A common complaint is that the concept somehow assumes that government "owns" all your income before doing you the favor of letting you keep part of it. This is not the case. The concept simply assumes that each person owes the government according to a general rate schedule superimposed on every person's ability to pay. Whatever violates such equal treatment is deemed the equivalent of a benefit outlay —the same, that is, as a check in the mail.

From the dogmatic insistence that there is no such thing as a tax expenditure, any number of absurdities must follow: for instance, that a public policy exempting all circus clowns from paying income taxes would not be a public benefit to circus clowns—who would simply be keeping more of "their own" money. Who cares if keeping more of "their" money means taking more of someone else's? Or if it means bankrupting everyone's kids? The ultimate thrust of this line of reasoning is to deny that a society can consent to and act upon any equitable principle of public sacrifice. Accordingly, all taxation is inherently unjust, and though cheating on your taxes may be legally wrong, it cannot be morally wrong.

It is no surprise that many well-off Americans, uneasy about their nation's loss of fiscal discipline, find consolation in this pugnacious illogic. What is surprising is to hear conservatives leading the chorus. Back in the early 1970s, strange to say, many of these same intellectuals pushed Nixon's ill-fated "negative income tax," the very premise of which is that less tax is the precise equivalent of more income. But during the 1980s they have become the preachers of a selective civic virtue—austerity for targeted benefits to the poor and indulgence toward shot-gun tax favors to the affluent.

Today, even though the government publishes estimates of the cost of different tax expenditures, this form of spending still attracts comparatively little attention. But by now the numbers involved, and their social and economic effects, are too large to ignore. Honest people can and do differ over what constitutes a genuine tax expenditure, as opposed to "equitable" treatment—say, for investment income or charitable donations. According to some, ability to pay should be measured by what a person earns; according to others, by what a person consumes. But even if we confine our list of tax expenditures to those that contradict any principle of ability to pay—that is, to those that nearly all economists can agree on—the total fiscal cost comes to at least $170 billion. Those tax expenditures arbitrarily reward millions of lucky people for such endeavors as financing a built-in sauna, hiring an au pair, or getting the boss to pay for the therapist.

This spending is regressive in the strictest sense of the word. Even when poorer households qualify for these benefits (and often they do not), what they receive is smaller, relative to their income, than what goes to the affluent. According to the congressional Joint Committee on Taxation, for example, last year the average value of the mortgage-interest deduction for taxpayers with incomes over $100,000 was $3,469. In contrast, the same deduction was worth an average of only $516 for taxpayers in the $20,000 to $30,000 bracket who qualified to take the benefit—and of course many, including renters and those who opted for the standard deduction, did not.

When we add together all the tax expenditures and all the direct outlays for which we have 1991 income data—and this is about 80 percent of each type of entitlement—an unambiguous picture emerges. On average, households with incomes under $10,000 collected a total of $5,690 in benefits. On average, households with incomes over $100,000 collected $9,280. In terms of total fiscal cost, moreover, the aggregate amounts received by the non-needy in 1991 were staggering. One half (at least $400 billion) of all entitlements went to households with incomes over $30,000. One quarter (at least $200 billion) went to households with incomes over $50,000. These are the facts—regardless of what our political folktales might say.

How did our entitlement system wind up delivering most of its benefits to people who are clearly not in need? Obviously, the overall spending pattern does not conform to any master plan. Congress never passed a "Comprehensive Welfare for the Well-Off Act." Rather, the system we see today is the inadvertent legacy of thousands of why-not-please-everybody votes on Capitol Hill—together with economic and demographic trends that no one anticipated.

Nor does any conspiracy lie behind the way Americans have chosen over the past decade to finance the growth of entitlements. They have done so through deficit spending—the result of a persistent ideological deadlock between cutting spending and raising taxes. Each side, unfortunately, has reason to regret the outcome. On the one hand, those who prevented significant reform in the welfare state have worsened any prevailing trend toward inequity by income and class. On the other hand, those who urged that it is better to finance the welfare state through debt than through taxes have burdened Americans with a new layer of inequity by age and generation.

These are the conditions leading to the coming of the next New Deal—a new deal that is needed to restore both fairness and efficiency to our trillion-dollar entitlement budget. The U.S. social-welfare system has by now come to resemble a ramshackle mansion on a hill, with squeaky back stairways and barren hallways leading to musty, sealed-off chambers.

Open this door and behold the federal railroad retirement system—a Christmas gift from Congress to the railroad industry in 1935, still chugging after all these years, at an annual cost of $7.8 billion. That crowing in the pantry is the sound of $50,000, on average, in direct federal payments being snatched up by each of the 30,000 biggest-grossing farmers in America. Not one of them looks like Pa Joad. And down this hall you'll find the bonanza-baby nursery, filled with Americans born from 1910 through 1916, whose Social Security benefit levels are higher than those of anyone born before or after. Can anyone remember why? What about that thumping noise? Maybe it's the so-called one-percent "kicker" from the 1970s, which still inflates civil-service pensions.

This is a structure, leaky and drafty and wildly expensive to heat, that was tolerably suited to its previous owners but now requires radical remodeling. What would FDR, architect of the original New Deal, have said if he had learned that by 1991 a fifth of American children would be living in poverty—still ill housed and ill nourished—while a fifth of the dollars spent by major federal benefit programs went to households earning $50,000 or more?

Fortunately, the system can be made to work again. But before the next New Deal can happen, Americans will have to start viewing entitlements as a whole, and debating comprehensive reforms.

Welfare for the Well-Off

Even if our current entitlement system were sustainable well into the twenty-first century—and it is not—most Americans would still have good reason to demand a new deal. Consider how little we as a nation are getting back for the money we are spending: no national health-insurance plan, no maternity benefits or family allowances such as are available in Germany and France, no guarantee against falling into poverty or even becoming homeless—in old age or at any other time of life.

In 1990, for example, the federal government handed out an average of $11,400 worth of benefits to every American aged sixty-five or over —more than ten times what it gave to each child—yet 3.7 million senior citizens still languished below the poverty line. Many of the latter receive a "means-tested" benefit—Supplemental Security Income. But for an elderly person living alone in 1990 the federal SSI program offered a maximum cash benefit of 74 percent of the poverty level, or $4,632 annually. That same year, while 18 million Americans earning less than $15,000 at full-time, year-round jobs "contributed" their FICA dollars, a CEO and spouse could retire and expect to receive more than $24,000 annually in tax-sheltered Social Security and Medicare benefits, in addition to their corporate pension and "medigap" plan, and sundry forms of private investment income.

Why doesn't the welfare state do a better job of actually insuring against poverty? The bottom-line reason is that we divert too many resources to the affluent.

The most stunning illustrations of welfare for the well-off come in the form of entitlements conveyed through the tax code. Consider, for example, the exclusion from taxation of most Social Security income along with the insurance value of Medicare benefits, which together cost the Treasury about $34 billion last year. The households that receive the largest favor are those with the most income. In fact, both these tax expenditures may be regarded as especially insidious forms of back-door spending, since they simply add to the already top-heavy distribution of Social Security and Medicare benefits. For the 37 percent of senior citizens who regularly vacation abroad, these tax subsidies are enough to pay for a few extra days of shopping in tropical ports of call. But they do little for another 40 percent of senior citizens who owe no tax on their Form 1040 because they aren't as well off. This is why every other major industrial nation regards all or nearly all of its social-insurance benefits as taxable income.

The same point applies to the child-care credit, which cost the government more than $3 billion last year. Households with incomes below $10,000 received virtually no benefit from this tax subsidy. Those with incomes above $50,000, however, received $1.2 billion to help pay for nannies and other child-care expenses.

For the really big bucks, take a look at the exclusion for employer-paid health care. Under this provision, those Americans fortunate enough to receive health-care insurance from their employers are allowed to exclude the value of their insurance from both income and payroll taxation. Last year this single tax expenditure cost the U.S. Treasury $60 billion in forgone revenue.

Who benefited? Obviously, no one among the 35 million people not covered by any form of health insurance or among the 32 million people who pay for their plans out of their own pockets. These 67 million Americans are twice as likely to live in poverty as are all other Americans. But that is only part of the inequity. Among households that were covered by employer-paid health-care plans, the average benefit for those in the highest income brackets was many times larger than the average for those in the lowest income brackets. Moreover, most economists agree that such large subsidies encourage their beneficiaries to overconsume health-care services, and thus put even more inflationary pressure on a system already in crisis. Who will argue with an employer who offers a "Gold Plan" package that provides generous coverage for every medical contingency, from orthodontia to nose jobs to psychoanalysis, as long as it's tax-free?

It is much the same story with most other entitlements conveyed through the tax code. Not only are they inequitable in their distribution of benefits but also they contribute to gross distortions in how the U.S. economy allocates resources. In addition to overconsuming health care, for example, affluent Americans tend to overconsume powder rooms and swimming pools and vacation homes at the expense of more-productive investments—thanks to the mortgage deduction and other tax subsidies for owner-occupied real estate. One result of all these tax favors: the hospitals and homes of Grosse Point and other affluent suburbs of Detroit are far more luxurious than any to be found in, say, the suburbs of Yokohama or Stuttgart. But only in Detroit do the suburbs surround a burned-out, deindustrializing core. Not coincidentally, every major industrial society except the United States pays for little (or none) of its health care with tax-sheltered insurance, and tightly restricts (or prohibits) any deductions for interest on home mortgages.

To the rule that says most tax subsidies go to the wealthy, there is one exception: the Earned Income Tax Credit. First enacted in 1975, the EITC is the closest America has ever come to a negative income tax. But its effect on the overall picture is negligible. Even after including the EITC with all the other tax expenditures mentioned above, the bottom line is still that the rich receive by far the largest benefits.

Households with incomes below $10,000, for example, receive an average of $131 a year from all these tax-subsidy programs combined. Middle-class households do better: those with incomes in the $30,000 to $50,000 range receive tax benefits averaging $1,483. But it is the truly affluent who receive the greatest subsidy: the average benefit for households with incomes over $100,000 is $3,595 a year, or nearly thirty times what goes to households most in need.

The Weight of Reality Upon Ideology

Why have Americans put up for so long with such flagrant malfunctioning of their social-welfare system? Part of the explanation must lie in today's political culture, which by the standards of FDR's crusading generation has remained exceptionally cautious in its thinking about the major institutions of the welfare state, and preoccupied with mere process issues. Meanwhile, as the decades have passed, the earth has been slowly shifting beneath the major monuments of the first New Deal. The old assumptions will not hold.

When Social Security first started paying out benefits, for example, the elderly were by far the most destitute age group in American society. As recently as 1969, 25 percent of American elderly were officially designated "poor"—as were only 14 percent of children under age eighteen. Today the relative positions of the very old and the very young are just about reversed: in 1990, 12 percent of the elderly and 21 percent of children were poor. Other indicators, such as noncash income, financial assets, and homeownership rates, also show that the typical elderly household is now considerably better off than the typical young family. At the same time, as we have seen, millions of the elderly continue to live in poverty. And yet Social Security continues to distribute none of its benefits on the basis of need.

We live in a world radically different from that of FDR's generation. How touching it is for the historian to read that New Deal planners once projected that Social Security's survivors' and unemployment benefits would steadily reduce means-tested family assistance. The assumption, of course, was that widows were the only single mothers struggling to raise children. That 13 million children would be living with single non-widowed mothers in 1990 was simply unthinkable. And how maddening it is for today's married woman to learn that she won't receive Social Security benefits based on her earnings unless she makes at least half her husband's salary throughout her working life. It should come as no surprise that a social-welfare system designed to serve the America of Benny Goodman and Norman Rockwell now stands in need of serious structural repair.

We also live in a world radically different from that of the Johnson and Nixon presidencies, when the steepest increases in entitlement spending took place. In that era renowned economists wrote books about the "challenge of abundance" and testified before Congress about how Americans would soon enjoy a twenty-two-hour workweek. In 1972, on the eve of Social Security's largest single benefit hike, the system's actuaries projected that henceforth real U.S. wages would forever rise at the rate of 56 percent every two decades—an assumption that made almost anything affordable. Looking back, that sort of economic euphoria seems as dated as *2001: A Space Odyssey*. What has in fact happened over the twenty years since 1972 is that real wages, as defined by the actuaries, have grown by hardly more than four percent. Polls indicate that most Americans are no longer confident that today's children will do as well economically as their parents—and indeed they will not, unless the country frees up the resources it needs to undertake wide-scale investments in improving productivity.

Sixty years after the New Deal there is virtually no connection between the pattern of entitlement spending and any coherent public purpose. So why is reform so often regarded as impossible?

Part of the reason is ideological. Throughout the Reagan years the allure of supply-side economics persuaded many conservatives that reforming entitlements was no longer necessary; with tax cuts and deregulation, the nation could simply "outgrow" them. The party that once fought losing battles against the New Deal could thereby dish the Whigs and painlessly rid itself of its plutocratic reputation. Liberals, meanwhile, have been slow to grasp how an ideal that was once taken as the nation's highest expression of community has evolved into a system that serves the interests of economic royalists at the expense of the common man.

Today reality is gradually wearing away these ideological misconceptions. Still, the reform of any single entitlement program is blocked by highly organized special-interest groups, from the gray-power and pension lobbies to the agribusiness, construction, and health-care industries. Even affluent beneficiaries who may be uncomfortable accepting government money don't like feeling singled out for sacrifice. The Palm Beach retiree, for example, won't go along with higher taxes on his Social Security benefits just so that the yuppie down the street can get another tax break.

What is needed is a comprehensive approach to entitlement reform—one that cuts not only direct spending but also tax expenditures for the well-off. In this way entitlement reform could avoid becoming a contest between generations. By putting every form of government spending on the table, America could also end that long-running, sterile debate between those who want to cut spending and those who want to cut taxes. Genuine reform could at last be what it should be: a more equitable and productive redirection of the nation's limited resources.

The Peace Dividend Is Not Enough

But couldn't we get by, many readers will ask, with just staying the course? Won't the end of the Cold War free up enough resources so that we won't need to take on entitlement reform?

The short answer is no. A world at peace won't be enough to right the nation's fiscal imbalance.

As we mentioned earlier, benefit outlays accounted for 45 percent of all federal spending in calendar year 1991. Yet this conventional measure of the cost of entitlements, large as it is, underestimates their practical importance. First, it includes only the benefits themselves, not the cost of administering them. Add on a minimal five percent overhead, and the total rises to 48 percent of the budget. Second, a fair measure would compare entitlements only with other types of spending that are adjustable, not with spending that is entirely beyond anyone's control. So let's subtract net interest payments on the national debt ($199.4 billion) and last year's [1991's] payments on the S&L bailout ($101.8 billion). Both are obligations that must be met in order to avoid a devastating financial panic. Now the total rises to 60 percent of the budget. Finally, let's figure in the $170 billion in benefit-like tax expenditures. This pushes the total up to just over 65 percent of the budget.

The bottom line might be summarized this way: Entitlements, defined as the full cost of both direct and tax-code benefits, amount to two thirds of the federal spending over which government has some control.

A large part of the remaining third is defense spending. The cuts now scheduled will help, but alone they are clearly insufficient. Consider that even eliminating the entire Marine Corps would not defray the annual cost of military pensions. In fact, even if the Department of Defense were abolished and all the armed forces disbanded, the U.S. Treasury would still not be able to pay this year's bills without borrowing. As for the small corner of the budget still dedicated to "discretionary" civilian projects—everything from running parks, regulating polluters, and sheltering runaway children to building highways, testing superconductors, and arresting drug traffickers—as a share of GNP that corner has been smaller since the late 1980s than at any other time since the late 1950s. It is unlikely that Americans could achieve major savings in this catchall budget area without curtailing some of the vital core services they expect from government. Most policy discussions instead favor more of this type of spending, which no doubt would already be larger today were it not perpetually crowded out by the metastasizing of universal benefits.

Another question, still sometimes heard in post-Reagan America, is "Why reform entitlements or even worry about the deficit when we can always just raise taxes?" But the answer is clear enough: The revenue option won't work because it won't happen. One can find many polls showing that most Americans favor the concept of a means test for benefits. But one cannot find any poll showing that more than a small minority of Americans favor a large, general-purpose tax hike.

This anti-tax sentiment is linked to widespread cynicism about government, especially the federal government, which should make many liberals think twice before dismissing entitlement reform. Quite simply, those who want more taxes and bigger budgets must first demonstrate that government can apply commonsense priorities to the money it is already spending. Anyone waiting for public attitudes to change spontaneously should take a closer look at America's rising generation of voters under thirty—not just at their Republican sympathies, which incline them against taxes anyway, but at their intense distrust of unkeepable promises, breakable chain letters, and crocodile tears. What the typical new voter most distrusts, in short, is just the sort of rhetoric that still enshrouds our welfare state.

Unfavorable Demographics

Each decade since the first New Deal, from the 1930s through the 1980s, entitlement spending has grown faster than the economy. Under our current system it is certain to do so in future decades as well, especially once the oldest members of the enormous postwar Baby Boom generation begin reaching retirement age, just sixteen years from now. Today more than 60 percent of all federal benefit spending flows to the 12 percent of Americans who are age sixty-five or older. As long as the welfare state allocates most benefits on the basis of seniority alone, the cost will grow geometrically as the size of the elderly population increases. In combination with the aging of the population, improvements in medical technology will likely cause per capita health-care costs to continue growing several times as fast as per-worker GNP.

Demographic data easily numb the mind, but one can gain an intuitive sense of what all this means for government spending by considering just how favorable demographic trends have been for the United States in recent years. During the 1980s the 76 million members of the Baby Boom generation moved into their prime productive years—old enough to have mastered job skills but too young to retire. The result was an automatic surge in federal revenue—especially since the women of this generation have been far more likely than their mothers to work for wages, and therefore to contribute taxes.

Meanwhile, demographics have also been favorable to the spending side of the budget. The growth rate of the retirement-age population has actually been slowing down since the mid-1980s, owing to the declining birth rates of the late 1920s. Yet the United States is still running enormous budget deficits. What will happen when these favorable demographic trends turn into unfavorable trends, beginning around 2010?

Since 1960, federal benefit outlays alone have grown from roughly five percent to 12 percent of GNP. No one knows, of course, what the future may bring. But if one adopts the economic, demographic, and medical assumptions used by the Social Security Administration and the Health Care Financing Administration, the total cost will rise much further over the next fifty years, perhaps to 21 percent of GNP (best case) or to 30 percent of GNP (most plausible case). And this assumes not a single new program or eligibility provision. Outlays of this magnitude would threaten to crowd out not only all forms of public and private investment but also any hope that government might respond to new social needs. Ultimately, even huge tax hikes would merely cover the growing cost of programs whose original intentions had long been forgotten.

Well before we reach such nightmare fiscal scenarios, moreover, the income inequity of the U.S. welfare state will become painfully obvious. Look ahead to the year 2000, when today's unusually affluent Americans in their fifties begin to retire. This is a cohort of lifelong upward mobility whose average household wealth in retirement (according to the economists Frank Levy and Richard Michel) is likely to exceed that of all living Americans born either before or after them. Then consider the position of today's young adults—handicapped by unstable family backgrounds, an inferior education, and stagnating entry-level wages. By the year 2000, while raising families amid growing talk of yet another hike in the payroll tax, they will cast searching eyes at the abundance of their elders. In her recent book *Social Insecurity* the former Social Security commissioner Dorcas Hardy does not hesitate to link the issues of age, income, and race. "As we move into the next century," she asks, "will the minorities of this country—immigrants and otherwise—come to see the Social Security system as a mechanism by which the government robs their children of a better future, in order to support a group of elderly white people in a retirement that is both too luxurious and too long?"

Take it from someone who once ran the system: the entitlement crisis is not about to go away if we just ignore it.

A Comprehensive Reform

Overhauling the U.S. welfare state so that it serves our national goals will entail enormous changes, most likely including a wholesale restructuring of the U.S. health-care system. But in the meantime we Americans can make federal entitlements much more equitable, and free up the resources we need to cut our fiscal deficits and boost our national savings, by acting on a simple if far-reaching principle. The principle is that one's benefits should be proportional to one's need—whether the subsidy comes in the form of health insurance or a farm subsidy or a mortgage-interest deduction or a Social Security check.

How might such a principle be applied to the existing welfare state, and how much money would it save? Any reform package should satisfy the three most common objections to a cost-control effort. First, it should not reduce the income of any household that is anywhere near the poverty line. More precisely, the half of all U.S. households that report incomes over $30,000 should be asked to bear nearly all the extra burden.

Second, any reform package should adjust benefits according to a graduated scale, so that middle- and upper-income households do not become net losers just because they happen to rise a few dollars above a certain threshold. Nor should earning a high income become a disqualification for receiving any subsidy. To preserve the universal character of our major entitlement programs, members of every household, regardless of income, should still stand to gain some benefits, albeit in proportion to their needs.

Third, any comprehensive reform must take into account the quasi-contractual nature of at least some entitlement programs. This last proviso is the toughest to accommodate, but not as tough as is sometimes thought.

Strongly rooted in American political folklore, for example, is the idea that Social Security recipients are only "getting their money back," that Social Security is an "inviolable contract," and so forth. But such claims have no financial or even legal basis, however much certain politicians and interest groups may claim otherwise. True enough, the original Social Security Act of 1935 included a "money back" guarantee (with some interest) on all employee contributions, and called for benefit levels to be calculated on the basis of the lifetime covered wages earned by each individual. But the guarantee was eliminated by Congress in 1939, and the link between benefit levels and years of participation, after being weakened in 1939, was entirely discarded in 1950.

Ever since, the U.S. Supreme Court has repeatedly ruled that no covered worker retains any right, contractual or otherwise, over taxes paid into the system. In fact, the Social Security Administration keeps no direct records of how much each person contributes. It just keeps records of each person's wage history, to which a politically determined benefit formula is applied when that person retires. Today's retirees, as it happens, receive benefits worth two to ten times what they would have earned had they invested all their lifetime Social Security taxes (both their own and their employer's) in Treasury bonds. Meanwhile, largely because of the very steep increases in Social Security taxes in recent years, most economists agree that under current law Social Security will not offer large categories of younger participants anything approaching a fair market return on what they paid into the system.

So there is no reason that Social Security benefits for the well-off cannot be reduced if a majority of Americans decide that their collective resources should be used for different purposes. The same is true for civil-service and military pensions, although here the case is much stronger that an implied contract exists between well-off pensioners and the government.

Before the 1970s federal employees worked for lower wages than their counterparts in the private sector. One reason they did so was the expectation of receiving government pensions far more generous than any offered by private-sector employers. Even today, no private pension offers benefits at such an early age, at such a high percentage of pay, with such lenient provisions for disability, or with such generous indexing. Moreover, because these government pension programs were never funded on an actuarially sound basis, current taxpayers are now unjustly stuck with a huge tab for yesterday's unwise policy. Still, these benefits are part of the compensation that was promised at the time—a distinction that makes a moral if not a legal difference and ought to limit benefit reductions even to the most affluent federal pensioner.

Applying our simple principle would not require a big new bureaucracy. All means-testing could be achieved exclusively through tax returns, much as we now handle the limited taxation of Social Security for households with adjusted gross incomes over $25,000. Each filer would be required to enter all benefits received, which could be checked against federal records. Above certain limits the total would trigger a "benefit-withholding" liability, which the filer would send back to the IRS along with any outstanding income-tax liability. As a practical matter, federal benefits could be withheld just as wages are withheld, based on a tax filer's previous experience.

How would benefit-withholding rates be set? Here are a few illustrative options, with estimates of how much money they would have saved in calendar year 1991 alone.

- For all cash and in-kind entitlement programs except federal-employee pension plans: Withhold 7.5 percent of any benefits that cause total household income to exceed $30,000, and withhold an additional five percent at the margin for each additional $10,000 in household income. The maximum reduction of benefits would be 85 percent, applicable to households with incomes of $190,000 or more. Total savings: $33.5 billion.
- For civil-service and military pensions: Same as above, but with a much lower maximum withholding rate, in deference to the quasi-contractual nature of these benefits. The maximum reduction of benefits would be 25 percent, for households earning $70,000 a year or more. Total savings: $7.6 billion.
- For all major entitlement benefits conveyed through the tax code except benefit exclusions: Limit the amount of such tax expenditures received by upper-income households to the average expenditure per household within the $30,000 to $50,000 bracket. In 1991, for example, this would have limited the total allowable mortgage-interest deduction to roughly $2,500. Total savings: $34.7 billion.
- For benefit tax exclusions: Get rid of all income thresholds and make Social Security just as taxable as any other cash income—except for 15 percent of pre-reform benefits. This untouched residual will offer, to even the wealthiest of today's retirees, at least a five percent tax-free return on all contributions they have personally paid into the system. Also, for households with incomes from $30,000 to $50,000, phase out half of the tax exclusion on the insurance value of Medicare (net of Medicare Part B premiums). Total savings: $16.9 billion.

Altogether, these provisions, if they had been in place in 1991, would have freed up $93 billion in the federal budget. To be sure, no one would advocate instituting all of them in one year, especially in a bad recession year. But imagine that they were phased in over four years—starting, say, in 1993. Assuming that income brackets were adjusted for inflation, and using official budget and revenue projections, total annual savings would rise to $149 billion by 1996. That would be enough to ensure that the next recovery is a genuine investment-led expansion, not another borrow-and-consume bacchanalia.

The budget savings could be considerably higher. The figures noted here reflect only about 80 percent of all federal entitlements and tax expenditures, those for which income distributions are known. The extra 20 percent included, total budget savings in 1996 could rise to more than $186 billion. Furthermore, trimming subsidies to the affluent reduces their incentive to take advantage of available benefits. Thus, to the extent that it would prompt middle- and upper-income Americans to forgo benefits altogether—for example, by retiring later, or by opting for less tax-sheltered health insurance and housing—the measure would clearly save taxpayers more than the amount a static calculation would indicate.

Because all the savings would be collected through the tax code, a single piece of legislation, falling under the jurisdiction of the tax committee in each house, would be sufficient to implement the reform. Imagine doing the same job by amending every benefits statute: the process would snake through dozens of committees, grind on for years if not decades, and ultimately be undone by interest groups.

This approach also has the virtue of treating all Americans fairly, according to their individual circumstances, unlike most other reform proposals—for example, limiting all cost-of-living adjustments (COLAs). Even a COLA freeze that discriminated against large monthly benefits would lead to obvious inequities. For a widow receiving no income other than one large Social Security check, a COLA may be essential to keep food on the table. For a triple-dipping federal pensioner receiving the minimum Social Security benefit, that same COLA may be just enough to cover the annual rise in greens fees at the club. An income-based approach takes account of the difference. Unlike most government agencies, moreover, the Internal Revenue Service is well trained in tracking dollars no matter how far they travel. Even the farm subsidy that filters down through five partnerships before appearing as personal income will have to show up, earmarked, on someone's Form 1040.

Politically, this approach balances the sacrifices asked of elderly and working-age Americans, without raising tax rates and without burdening the poor or even most of the middle class. Moreover, the plan would reduce specific programs in rough proportion to their overall size in the budget. Roughly half the savings would come from Social Security and Medicare and the related taxation of benefits. An additional 40 percent would come from other programs and tax expenditures, especially employer-paid health care and mortgage interest. Another eight to nine percent would come from federal pensions.

Would such a reform in and of itself constitute another New Deal? Hardly. The measures it would comprise are, however, the essential preconditions for the next New Deal. Without them the United States will simply see more and more of its options as a nation crowded out by the compounding costs of our subsidies to the well-off.

As always, every area of federal spending should be scrutinized. Missionless bombers must be cut. Pork-barrel waterways must be eliminated. Welfare programs targeting the poor must undergo further changes, to require the able-bodied to work and to reduce the cycle of dependency. But none of these areas is where the big money is, and it is not by reforming them that the United States will free up the resources it needs to build a more just and productive society in the next century.

Whenever one's vision of that new society—whether it includes a national health service or means-tested health vouchers, a negative income tax or a 15 percent flat tax, green cars running on hydrogen or mag-lev trains humming from city to city—to get something new, one must give up something old. A society that cannot find the resources to pay for sixty-cent tuberculosis vaccinations for ten-year-olds must ask itself why it is offering subsidized health care and housing to millionaires. Call it a rendezvous with destiny.

DISCUSSION QUESTIONS

1. Do you think any of the suggestions by Howe and Longman will be taken up by politicians in the next few years? Explain.

2. Should there be means testing of entitlement programs such as Medicare and Social Security? Why or why not?

75

"Remaking U.S. Social Policies
for the 21st Century" from
Social Policy in the United States

THEDA SKOCPOL

In a chapter from her book, Social Policy in the United States, *Theda Skocpol criticizes the Concord Coalition's position advocating a dramatic restructuring of the social welfare system that is heavily biased toward middle class and wealthy individuals in retirement (see Howe and Longman, above). Restructuring Social Security might ease "the $4 trillion noose of national debt we have put around the necks of our progeny," but Skocpol argues the proposal is politically and economically unsound. Politically, most Americans claim a stake in social security from years of contributions and would oppose changes that reduced their own future benefits. Skocpol maintains that the Coalition recommendations would force "more and more elderly people into full- or part-time employment," while federal and state programs are forcing welfare recipients to take low-wage jobs, and more women who are wives and mothers need jobs. This greater competition in the labor market might have the negative effect of reducing wages and benefits.*

As the turn of a new century approaches, Americans are looking critically at the scope and purposes of their nation's social policies. Signs of fundamental reconsideration cut across partisan and ideological lines, and go beyond particular policy areas. Experts, journalists, advocacy groups, and politicians now repeatedly ask whether "too much" is being done for elderly citizens, while the needs of younger people are insufficiently addressed by existing public programs.

Of course, social policies in the United States have been controversial for quite some time. From the 1960s to the 1980s, matters of poverty, race, and class were at the forefront of discussion. Americans argued about the War on Poverty and the Great Society, and then about the allegedly excessive tax burdens that government was placing upon the hardworking middle class to pay for "welfare handouts" to the undeserving poor. Issues such as these, replete with racial tensions, fueled the rise of conservatism after 1964; and they continue to simmer today. Yet since the middle of the 1980s, the terms of public debate have shifted perceptibly toward matters of generational equity, highlighting the divergent fates of young and old in relation to existing public policies. Many conservatives and liberals agree that fundamental reconstructions may be necessary to achieve generational equity as the nation prepares for the dawn of the next century.

*   *   *

The Concord Coalition is nominally bipartisan, co-chaired by two retired U.S. Senators, Republican Warren Rudman and Democrat Paul Tsongas. Peter G. Peterson elaborated the ideas of the Concord Coalition in his 1993 book *Facing Up: How to Restore the Economy from Crushing Debt and Restore the American Dream.* The book's Foreword is written by Rudman and Tsongas, and its dust jacket declares that its royalties will be donated to the Concord Coalition. As Peterson explains, the Concord Coalition aims to mobilize middle-class public opinion to urge politicians in Washington, D.C., into "doing the right thing" for America's children and our national future by fundamentally revamping existing social policies.

Entitlements for the elderly—especially Social Security, Medicare, and federal pensions—account for much of current federal spending. Peterson holds them responsible for the large federal deficit, and he projects taxes and entitlement spending for decades into the future in dramatic charts that suggest that the nation is certain to "go bankrupt." In sharp contrast to the good fortune enjoyed by people who came of age after the Great Depression and World War II, young adults today are losing out on the American Dream of rising incomes, home ownership, and upward social mobility. Their children—"our grandchildren"—will do even worse, Peterson asserts, suffering under massive tax burdens to pay for entitlements going to overindulged middle-class people, especially the elderly.

The answer to the nation's debt "crisis," according to Peterson and the Concord Coalition, is to drastically cut public spending on "middle-class entitlements." Various specific reforms are proposed, including turning Social Security and Medicare into means-tested programs only for the needy. Resources should be shifted into what Peterson calls "real investments"—that is, privately managed funds. *Facing Up*, in short, invokes the well-being of future generations and offers a grand moral argument on behalf of a call to cut back the public sector in favor of private capital. "More than two centuries ago," Peterson perorates,

> Thomas Jefferson wrote a letter to James Madison in which he warned of the utter inappropriateness in a democracy of a value system that allows the debts of one generation to burden the next. . . . Jefferson would be shocked, saddened, and ashamed to see the $4 trillion noose of national debt we have put around the necks of our progeny—not to mention the trillions more in unfunded federal benefit liabilities we are passing on to future workers. . . . To place the weight of these trillions upon unborn children is to rob them of

what Jefferson and the founding fathers promised us: life, liberty, and the pursuit of happiness.[1]

*   *   *

Peterson's *Facing Up* starts with his disarming acknowledgment that he has been a lifelong Republican, but within a few pages he launches into a scathing critique of Ronald Reagan and his policies of the 1980s. Along with other fiscal conservatives and moderate Republicans, Peterson fears the huge federal budget deficits that President Reagan's initiatives helped to create. In this view, Reagan is to be faulted for cutting federal taxes without accomplishing commensurate cuts in the largest domestic social spending programs—especially such "middle-class entitlements" as Social Security, Medicare, veterans' pensions, and mortgage subsidies. For Peterson, the 1972 amendments to Social Security were equally abhorrent. He argues that they put the entire American middle class "on the dole." The elderly in Peterson's portrayal are selfishly robbing their children and grandchildren, and the American Association of Retired Persons is presented as the biggest and most sinister "special interest group" in U.S. politics.[2]

Peterson and the Concord Coalition are taking a new approach to achieving a long-standing objective of U.S. conservatives—making sure that federal social spending is kept to a minimum and is means-tested, targeted only on the most needy. Conservatives understand well that marginal social programs for the poor also are not very politically popular; it is easier to keep them from expanding in a democratic polity. Back in the formative years of the Social Security system, Peterson's conservative forerunners waged a losing struggle to abolish universal social insurance in favor of marginal public spending on the very poor elderly alone. During the presidency of Ronald Reagan, conservatives again became hopeful that "middle-class entitlements" would be restructured. But after briefly raising the possibility of such reforms, President Reagan and his Budget Director, David Stockman, quickly retreated from middle-class programs, and concentrated most of their rhetorical and budgetary fire on means-tested social spending for the poor. Now Peterson and his fiscal conservative allies are taking a quite different approach to what they see as the problem of overly generous federal spending. Instead of appealing to middle-class hostility against blacks and welfare clients, Peterson and the Concord Coalition are appealing to middle-class anxieties and idealism about the national future, and to the interests of working-aged adults as taxpayers.

Leaders of the Concord Coalition are trying to reduce middle-class public support for the Social Security system by arguing that it is really just a set of heavy taxes on working-aged adults to support many non-needy elderly people. Besides, it is suggested, the system is bound to go bankrupt before today's middle-class workers can collect anything, so why should they support it? Concord Coalition critics also argue that if Social Security is cut back into a less expensive means-tested program, money will be saved for programs helping the "truly needy," for federal deficit reduction, and for enhanced private investments that will cause the economy to grow faster. Peterson all but promises that, if only Social Security and other social programs inclusive of the middle class are removed, most middle-class people will be net beneficiaries because renewed national economic growth will create new opportunities for job mobility and private income growth. Like the "supply-side" economists who surrounded President Reagan, the Concord Coalition projects a wonderful future if only the domestic functions of the federal government can be further chopped back in the United States.

Political Possibilities for the Future

What is likely to happen to U.S. social policies as America enters the twenty-first century? Will the arguments of the Concord Coalition prevail? . . . Are other strategies possible? Of course the future is now in the making, through public debates and political conflicts whose outcomes are indeterminate. But we can briefly explore some of the alternative possibilities.

* * *

The Concord Coalition's criticisms of universal entitlements are gaining currency just as many adult middle-income and lower-middle-income workers do, in fact, feel hard-pressed by the large payroll taxes that are collected for Social Security. The attempt to extend a top-down antitax alliance from attacks on welfare to fundamental restructuring of social insurance for the elderly has its best hope of success if mid-career workers can be persuaded that they have little stake, or else only a negative stake, in the Social Security system—in short, if they see themselves as Peter Peterson portrays them, primarily as burdened taxpayers rather than as beneficiaries.

Still, there are likely to be severe limits to the popularity and legislative viability of the Concord Coalition's message. The huge and resourceful American Association of Retired Persons is not the only probable opponent. Most Americans feel that they have built up a stake in the retirement insurance system, and will profoundly resent politicians who go back on what is popularly understood as a sacred social contract. In addition, mid-career, middle-income working Americans often have elderly parents, in whose economic security, indeed comfort and independence, they have a considerable stake. At one point in *Facing Up*, Peterson argues that the United States needs a new entitlement system that "will encourage us to save more for the future, care more for our children and parents. . . ."[3] How many middle-class women, already overwhelmed with the burdens of combining wage-work and child-rearing, will be enticed by the notion that they should also take added responsibility for their aging parents?

Interestingly, Peterson's book presents a profoundly patriarchal image of how the economy and families work. He lauds his Greek-immigrant father for running a 24-hour-a-day, 365-day-a-year restaurant, while hardly ever appearing at home. Peterson's mother is hardly mentioned, except as someone who lived out her elderly years on income from rental properties bought by the father's savings. Whatever one may think of this portrayal of Peterson's parental family, its gender and economic realities are far indeed from those of the middle-income Americans of today that the Concord Coalition is attempting to mobilize.

As the 1994 Bipartisan Commission gives greater political visibility to the ideas of the Concord Coalition, they are likely to be scrutinized by skeptical experts as well as politically opposed groups. The economic disadvantages of Peter Peterson's ideas will be probed. Would sudden cuts in federal spending really propel national economic growth? What would be the effects on labor markets and wage rates? For example, Peterson recommends delays and cuts in elderly pension benefits that he agrees would have the effect of forcing more and more elderly people into full- or part-time employment. Yet this would happen even as more and more American wives and mothers need jobs, and even as the federal and state governments are pushing welfare clients into low-wage labor markets. Meanwhile, the U.S. private economy is generating fewer jobs with incomes adequate to sustain either one-parent or two-parent families. Ironically, steep cutbacks in retirement benefits could actually backfire on younger working parents and their children—by creating more competition for jobs and further lowering private wages and fringe benefits that are already under downward pressure.

*   *   *

Certainly, Bill Clinton's presidency has had a very difficult time politically. Some of the reasons have nothing to do with social policy. The President's call for universalism in health care reform, and his touting of work rather than open-ended welfare payments, have been very popular. Yet President Clinton's difficulties in getting even popular social policy ideas through Congress underline that progressives are bound to have a hard time working within the institutions and circumstances of U.S. politics at the close of the twentieth century. As a moderate Democrat committed to revitalizing government's capacity to deal with national economic and social problems, Bill Clinton was elected with only a plurality of the popular and electoral vote. He heads (if that is the right word) a Democratic Party that has little unity and hardly any capacity for grass-roots political mobilization. His presidency has had to contend with the rock-hard realities of a huge, inherited federal budget deficit in an era when most elected politicians are unwilling to discuss taxes and the public distrusts government and politicians.

In this situation, President Clinton has understandably had a very difficult time in revamping U.S. social policies to offer more support for working families—especially for those "in the middle" between rich and poor. He has, nevertheless, done a good job of highlighting the importance of moving in this direction. Whether or not Clinton loses ground in Congress after 1994, and whether or not he is reelected in 1996, he has already pointed the way toward a promising agenda for U.S. progressive politics and social policy at the dawn of the new century.

In the name of the broadly shared values of work and parental responsibility, all Americans can be asked to contribute as workers, caregivers, and taxpayers. In return, the nation can afford to offer a modicum of economic security and social support to all families, not just in retirement, but throughout their active years of employment and the rearing of "our children." . . .

DISCUSSION QUESTIONS

1. Do you agree with Howe and Longman's assessment of the entitlement problem, or Skocpol's? Explain.

2. If you agree with Skocpol, what do you think should be done to solve the long-term problems with entitlement problems?

NOTES

1. Peter G. Peterson, *Facing Up: How to Rescue the Economy from Crushing Debt and Restore the American Dream* (New York: Simon and Schuster, 1993), 43–4.
2. Peterson, *Facing Up*, p. 82.
3. Peterson, *Facing Up*, p. 114.

THE DEBATE: WELFARE REFORM

Welfare reform—specifically, reform of the federal programs that provide aid to families with dependent children, food stamps, health care, child care, and job-training skills for welfare recipients—was a key item in the Contract with America. President Clinton also promised welfare reform in his 1992 presidential campaign. The current system, as both Republicans and Democrats recognize, is broken, with many recipients never leaving welfare to become self-sufficient, more than 80 percent of children from low-income families being born to fatherless homes, and steadily increasing costs. When President Roosevelt proposed a social welfare system, he warned, as Senator John Shelby of Alabama points out below, against creating a system that fostered dependency as opposed to providing individuals and families with a bridge toward independence. But a system of dependency, critics argue, is precisely what the government has created.

In March of 1995, the Republicans introduced a welfare reform bill in the House of Representatives based on three principles: "personal responsibility, work, and returning power over welfare to the States and communities where the needy can be helped in the most efficient way." Recipients could be cut off from benefits after five years, and all recipients would be expected to find work. Responding to the frustrations of mayors and governors caught in the massive restrictions that accompany federal welfare dollars, the bill also proposed bundling welfare money into block grants and giving subnational governments greater flexibility in developing welfare systems of their own. Critics of the legislation, including Representative William J. Coyne (D.-Pa.), argue that if mothers are forced to go to work, children will be left home alone; if food and medical benefits are cut, children will go hungry and without medical attention; and if benefits are cut after five years, the abortion rate will increase. The onus, in other words, would fall directly on children—a burden made all the more troublesome, Coyne argues, by the tax breaks being advocated by Republicans for the nation's wealthiest families.

A less partisan yet critical look at the welfare reform effort is offered by Jeffry Katz, who points out the difficulty of training welfare recipients for jobs that are scarce and that pay enough to end the cycle of dependency. For the states, which will be responsible for implementing the jobs programs, the challenge is acute. As Katz points out in the article, many states would prefer a reduction in the cash benefits they receive from the federal government as opposed to the obligation of implementing jobs programs that are bureaucratically costly, complex, and seldom successful. Further, certain welfare recipients will not be employable, or live in economically depressed areas that do not have elastic job markets. Katz reports on the liberal critics who argue the result will simply be more homeless families and, especially, more homeless children.

76
"Putting Recipients to Work Will Be the Toughest Job"

JEFFREY L. KATZ

The Republican welfare bills making their way through Congress [in 1995] have three main goals: limit federal spending, hand welfare programs to the states and put welfare recipients to work.

The first two goals can be accomplished by legislative fiat. But putting people to work is more complicated.

Congress can write laws requiring work. It can limit the amount of time that welfare recipients can receive benefits. It can even order states to place a certain percentage of their welfare caseload in jobs. Republicans have put those provisions, and much more, in the welfare overhaul measures (HR 4) approved by the Senate Finance Committee (S Rept 104-96) and passed by the House. . . .

But none of those requirements offer any assurances that more welfare recipients will actually work. And getting them to work is arguably the only way to truly transform the welfare state and meet the public's hopes for reform.

Republicans hope to change the welfare equation by giving states unprecedented control over the programs and relying on them to link welfare recipients to work.

The states have undeniably become the focus of welfare-to-work efforts in the past decade. State experiments have included subsidizing jobs, conditioning benefits on willingness to perform community service, and forcing recipients to sign contracts requiring them to take more responsibility for their lives.

But since 1988, when putting people to work became a main goal of the welfare program, the states have had only modest success. Only about 9 percent of the roughly 5 million adults now receiving Aid to Families with Dependent Children (AFDC), the nation's main cash welfare program, are working.

Improving on that record depends not only on motivating recipients, many welfare experts say, but also on committing sufficient resources to local welfare offices. It is there that, with the proper expertise and wherewithal, welfare recipients can be matched with the jobs, child care and career counseling that can get them into the work force and keep them there.

Most GOP lawmakers believe that getting the federal government out of the way will allow welfare programs to be customized to fit local needs. They also count on motivating welfare recipients by requiring them to work within two years of receiving benefits and denying any welfare checks after five years. In addition, they would set specific work goals for states.

"What we're looking for is an attitudinal change across the entire country," said Rep. E. Clay Shaw Jr., R-Fla., chairman of the House Ways and Means Human Resources Subcommittee and a leading proponent of the House welfare bill. The idea, he said, is to make welfare "not a way of life, but simply a short-term bridge over tough times."

But moving people from welfare to work depends on some elements that cannot be legislated. Time limits and work requirements may be enough to spur some welfare recipients to work, but their jobs might be temporary and the pay insufficient to move them out of poverty or off welfare. For others—especially those who lack skills, job experience and education—the task is more challenging.

Moreover, finding jobs would not be easy even under the best circumstances. "It's not like America needs 5 million single mothers looking for work at the low end of the labor market," said Judith M. Gueron, president of the Manpower Demonstration Research Corp., which evaluates social programs for the disadvantaged.

State efforts to help welfare recipients get jobs and keep them has initially required more money for such things as child care and administrative oversight. Reorienting welfare offices from places that mainly verify eligibility into placement centers for the hard-core unemployed will not be easy.

Even as GOP lawmakers relish the notion of cutting the federal welfare bureaucracy to reduce costs, their hopes of moving welfare recipients into the work force depend partly on spending those funds to reorient local offices.

Lawrence M. Mead, a visiting professor at the Woodrow Wilson School at Princeton University, summed up successful welfare-to-work programs in Wisconsin, pointing out that "reforming welfare may save money on balance, but it requires more bureaucracy rather than less."

And these qualified welfare managers are hard to come by, added Robert Rector, a senior policy analyst at the Heritage Foundation and an influential conservative on this issue among GOP lawmakers.

"A lot of the success of these programs has to come from high-level or midlevel bureaucrats who are committed to making the programs work," Rector said. "We may have a shortage of those."

Troubled Program

The federal government's current thinking on welfare-to-work programs is embodied in the Family Support Act of 1988 (PL 100-485). It requires states to run a Job Opportunities and Basic Skills (JOBS) program, providing welfare recipients with work, remedial education and training.

The law is credited with advancing the idea that in exchange for receiving benefits, welfare recipients must take steps to improve their lives. In practice, though, JOBS has had limited success—partly because of the economy and partly because of flaws in the program.

Never envisioned as a quick fix, the legislation was hampered by the 1990 recession: First, the weak economy contributed to an explosion of welfare rolls. Then the drain on state revenues limited states' ability to pay for education, training and job placement. The welfare rolls also swelled from the continued rise of out-of-wedlock births which, particularly among teenagers, is often associated with long-term stays on welfare.

Some analysts have also faulted the JOBS programs themselves. A General Accounting Office (GAO) report released in May said most JOBS programs failed to move welfare recipients to work. Local administrators cited insufficient staff and resources, as well as recipients' discouragement about taking low-paying jobs. They also said they wanted more flexibility to subsidize jobs and give recipients more on-the-job experience.

The report also concluded that many JOBS programs "emphasize preparing participants for employment without also making strong efforts to help them get jobs."

Some states have conducted welfare experiments by obtaining waivers from federal laws, an approach that started under President Ronald Reagan and then accelerated. These waivers have, for example, given certain states more leeway to impose time limits on benefits and to transform AFDC or food stamp benefits into wage subsidies.

"Despite very cumbersome federal laws and waiver processes, the states have been leaders in the last decade in changing public welfare from a 50-year-old program in income maintenance toward one that has a new goal of self-sufficiency and reducing dependence," said A. Sidney Johnson III, executive director of the American Public Welfare Association, which represents state social service departments and local welfare agencies.

The nation's most widely heralded JOBS program is in Riverside County, Calif. Single-parent participants in the program there earned an average of $3,562 a year, or 40 percent more per person than those not in the program, according to a 1994 study by Manpower. Because of these earnings, the state reduced annual AFDC payments to participants by an average of $584, paying them 17 percent less than those not in JOBS.

Among the keys to Riverside's success, Gueron said, were getting welfare recipients into jobs quickly, relying heavily on job searches, strictly enforcing participation rules and maintaining close links to area businesses.

A subsequent study released July 7 [1995] by Manpower found that participants in JOBS programs in Riverside, Atlanta and Grand Rapids, Mich., which strongly emphasized immediate employment, needed 22 percent less in AFDC benefits and 14 percent less in food stamps than those not in JOBS programs. Participants also were 24 percent more likely to be employed and had 26 percent higher earnings than others.

Even so, Gueron has cautioned lawmakers that large numbers of welfare recipients across the country are unlikely to move quickly into the work force. Many welfare recipients will be unable to earn enough to get off welfare, she said, and those who do work can easily lose their jobs. Others, perhaps one-quarter of welfare recipients, lack the skills, experience or stability to maintain unsubsidized jobs.

Can States Get the Job Done?

Under the GOP welfare bills, states would be given broad flexibility to use federal money to help find jobs for welfare recipients. But how they would use these funds is unclear.

Federal welfare money now essentially goes to states in two pots. One provides welfare checks, mainly through AFDC. The federal share of AFDC benefits and administrative costs was $14.1 billion in fiscal 1994; states paid $11.9 billion.

Another fund provides matching funds to states to run job training and placement programs through JOBS. That amounted to $786 million in federal funds and $514 million in state money in fiscal 1994.

The House and Senate GOP welfare bills would consolidate these funds, so that states would receive one block grant from which to provide checks and pay for work programs. The House version of HR 4 would consolidate AFDC and three related programs into a block grant worth $15.4 billion annually for five years. The Senate version would consolidate AFDC and six related programs into a $16.8 billion block grant.

But under those circumstances, states might give work programs short shrift. It would be cheaper, at least in the short run, to hand checks to welfare recipients than to provide what they might need to help them get jobs: placement assistance, child care, wage subsidies, and remedial education or training. The Finance Committee bill, but not the House bill, would require states to provide child care to welfare recipients who have children younger than 6 and who need it to work.

Money is a critical element in helping welfare recipients find work, said Mark S. Greenberg, a senior staff attorney at the Center for Law and Social Policy, a liberal public research group. States already can require nearly 80 percent of welfare recipients to take part in a JOBS program, Greenberg said, but only about 13 percent participate.

"The principal barrier to expanding JOBS participation has not been federal rules," he said. "It has been the cost of increasing the number of participants."

How then can states be expected to react to a welfare system with restraints on federal funding and time limits on benefits? Or as Gueron put it, "Under fiscal pressure and with a short time horizon, will states make the upfront investments that we know can produce the longer term savings?"

No, according to the nonpartisan Congressional Budget Office (CBO). It concluded that 44 states would be unable to place half their welfare caseload into work or training programs by fiscal 2001, as required by the Senate Finance Committee bill.

John W. Tapogna, a CBO analyst, told the Finance Committee on May 26 that most states would simply accept a reduction of up to 5 percent of their welfare block grant rather than meet the work requirement.

Other observers say there are limits to the effectiveness of even well-funded work programs, and they say only a tough approach will get people off welfare.

Rector of the Heritage Foundation played down the importance of job preparation programs such as JOBS, saying that states respond best to requirements that they find work for a certain percentage of welfare recipients. Beyond that, he said, the only sure way to reduce welfare is to minimize the number of out-of-wedlock births that lead families into poverty.

Gary Burtless, a senior fellow at the Brookings Institution, noted the limited success of the approaches used in Riverside. Even if they were duplicated across the country, he said, "I would not anticipate lots and lots of people moving off the rolls." That, Burtless said, would be accomplished by time limits on benefits.

How Best to Find Jobs

Republicans are counting on the time limits and work requirements to motivate welfare recipients, creating a stronger expectation that they find jobs. That leaves open the question of the proper route for welfare recipients—gaining experience by accepting the first job offer or gaining skills through training and education.

To some extent, welfare recipients can be motivated by higher expectations. Johnson said that in Oregon, for example, case workers are instructed to ask from the outset, "How can I help you get a job?" rather than trying primarily to verify eligibility for benefits. "It sounds like not a big difference," Johnson said. "But it sets up quite different expectations."

Elsewhere, welfare recipients are being challenged to take practical steps to improve themselves even if they might be unable to hold a full-time job.

In inner-city Chicago, a welfare-to-work program known as Project Match assumes that all welfare recipients can help themselves. Working mainly with residents of the Cabrini Green public housing development, Project Match helps recipients with even the barest job skills become more self-sufficient. It encourages them to become better parents and to do volunteer work if they are unprepared for full-time jobs, and it gives wide discretion to caseworkers.

"We feel people should be doing something," said Toby Herr, director of Project Match. "What they should do should be flexible." Caseworkers assist welfare recipients even after they obtain jobs, because many recipients quit their jobs or are fired after the first setback at home or at work.

Project Match stresses practical experience as a stepping stone toward working, rather than emphasizing education. "If they saw there was a link between education and income," Herr said, "they would have stayed in school in the first place."

That sentiment seems to fit with the growing sense that education and training are less important than gaining on-the-job experience as quickly as possible. "If people have failed conspicuously to prosper in school between the ages of 6 and 18," Burtless said, "the notion that when they're 25 they're suddenly going to be receptive and able to absorb a good education is far-fetched."

But Greenberg said that point can be overstated. He maintained that education and training can improve the earnings of welfare recipients, particularly for those who already have some work experience.

He cited evidence from the Manpower study of California's JOBS program. Riverside County, which emphasized work, increased the employment rate of welfare recipients—but not necessarily their pay. By contrast, a JOBS program in Alameda County that relied more on vocational training and post-secondary education had more success than Riverside in increasing earnings.

"It is important to continue to focus on approaches that can raise the earnings and reduce the poverty of families," Greenberg said. "The idea of 'work first' may be entirely appropriate for a parent with little or no work history. But many of the parents who enter the welfare system have substantial prior work experience but in low-wage jobs with little mobility."

Are Recipients Employable?

Ultimately, the question becomes: How many welfare recipients are likely to become permanently employed? Can the labor market even absorb a large number of them?

"Yes," said Mead, the Princeton welfare analyst, "provided it's not done overnight." He said the labor market could stretch to accommodate new employees, though many jobs would be low paying. But he acknowledged that analysts "really don't know how many of the mothers are employable because we haven't tried to make them work until recently, and only in certain localities."

Mead said he is unsure whether welfare recipients are likely to earn enough to get off welfare, something that is nominally easier to do in states with low welfare benefits such as Mississippi (where a mother and two children can get up to $120 monthly) than in states with high benefits such as California (where they can get up to $607).

Shaw expressed confidence that jobs were available to most of those who want one. "I'm always hearing from people who can't fill $5- and $6-an-hour jobs," he said. "The reason is people who know how to really game the system can get a lot more from welfare."

Burtless has said that most labor economists believe that employers could find work for 2 million to 3 million AFDC recipients, especially if they were willing to accept low-wage jobs with few fringe benefits.

Overall, Burtless said that about a quarter or more of the welfare mothers who would be pushed into the work force when their benefits ran out would succeed in maintaining a job, earning at least as much as they now receive on welfare.

But about half the mothers pushed off welfare would be worse off than they are now, earning less than they now get on welfare.

And another one-quarter of recipients are "going to be in such severe difficulty that they will have to give up their children or, in trying to keep their families together, they will spend time as homeless people."

It is the thought of this last group—of welfare mothers and their children sent into the streets to fend for themselves—that energizes liberal critics of the GOP approach. They say that states would find it cheaper to withhold job assistance and simply drop welfare recipients from the rolls when they hit the time limit rather than help them get jobs.

Rector maintains that public pressure will keep that from happening to any large degree. "The ability of states to kick highly dependent people off the rolls is highly limited," he said, because widespread media coverage of hapless welfare recipients would stop officials from neglecting them.

But clearly not all welfare recipients will find jobs, something that Shaw acknowledged would be particularly true in poverty-stricken areas.

"In some areas this is going to be a problem," Shaw said. "We're going to have to monitor the situation very closely, particularly where you've got large pockets of unemployment and poverty in the inner cities."

And in words rarely used this year by key Republicans as they talk about welfare, Shaw said that dealing with the situation in these neighborhoods would be "a federal responsibility."

77
Debate on the Senate Floor
on Welfare Reform

SENATORS JOHN SHELBY (R.-ALA.) AND
ORRIN HATCH (R.-UTAH)

MR. SHELBY. Mr. President, I rise in strong support of the conference report on H.R. 4. This bill is the most significant piece of welfare reform legislation to come before Congress in more than three decades. The current welfare system is destroying the hopes and opportunities of thousands of Americans by trapping them in cycles of dependency. President Roosevelt, the hero of liberal welfare advocates, warned us what would happen if we structured our welfare system in a way that fostered reliance on the Government. Listen to what he said in his 1935 annual message to Congress:

> The lessons of history, confirmed by the evidence immediately before me, show conclusively that continued dependence upon relief induces a spiritual and moral disintegration fundamentally destructive to the national fiber. To dole out relief in this way is to administer a narcotic, a subtle destroyer of the human spirit.

Mr. President, that is exactly what the architects of the modern welfare state have done. They have created a welfare system that encourages people to view welfare as a way of life. The typical welfare family has already spent 6½ years on welfare, and will end up spending a total of 13 years on the rolls. Thirteen years, Mr. President. After 13 years on welfare, the average family has received at least $150,000 of taxpayers' money. No wonder President Roosevelt said this type of welfare was a narcotic that destroyed the human spirit.

The reason welfare has become so addictive is because it completely destroys any incentive to work or become self-sufficient. The current system essentially says to its potential victims, if you do not want to work, have a child you are not able to support. If you do this, the Government will send you a check every month, pay your food bills, give you some free child care, pay all of your health care bills, your heating bills, your college bills, give you some WIC money, pay for your children's breakfast and lunch at school, and possibly provide you with your own apartment.

In other words, Mr. President, the message is the Government will take care of you. You do not need to take care of yourself. You simply need to sit at home and do nothing. That is a very cruel form of assistance. It destroys the natural inclination in every human being to reach their full potential. No private charity operates in that manner. No private charity simply mails people checks for having children they are not able to support.

The bill before us today will begin to repair the broken welfare State; it will restore healthy incentives in our welfare system. It does not abandon poor Americans or their children. Rather, it requires adult welfare recipients to work in exchange for their benefits. If passed, these work requirements will be the first serious work requirements ever passed by Congress. This is not only healthy for the recipients, but it is good for their children to be raised in an environment where they see their parents getting up and going to work every day. Work will become the norm among those receiving welfare, not the exception.

While I am very optimistic about the results of the strong work requirements in this bill, I want to express my concerns with the lack of provisions to address the most serious problem facing our country today: the breakdown of the traditional family. Eighty percent of children in many low-income communities are born in fatherless homes and welfare is the dominant feature of these homes.

For many poor people, the current welfare system makes bearing children out of wedlock a very practical alternative to the traditional method of raising a family—getting a job, a work skill, and finding a spouse committed to raising a family before having a child. If a young woman has a child before she has a work skill and a spouse, it will be almost impossible for her to ever escape the welfare trap. Mr. President, I regret that this legislation does not replace cash payments to teenagers with services to care for the child. But, I am glad we were able to at least give States the option to do that. It is my sincere hope that many States will pursue that option and will enact other policies to address the crisis of illegitimacy. I am glad that we were able to include the national prohibition against increasing cash payments to welfare recipients who have additional children while on welfare. Mr. President, if we do not contain the epidemic of illegitimacy, it will destroy the fabric of our society. America simply cannot survive without a strong family unit.

This legislation represents real reform. It is a carefully constructed balance between those who would advocate a complete end to public assistance and those who would seek to expand the current welfare

State. It is the boldest reform we could have taken in the current political environment, and I hope for the sake of our Nation's future, that all of my colleagues will support this bill and the President will sign it into law.

MR. HATCH. Mr. President, we stand here today to debate and vote on a very important piece of legislation, one that could change the lives of America's needy families.

Not since the Economic Opportunity Act was signed into law by President Lyndon Johnson on August 20, 1964, have we had such broad-sweeping and radical change in our welfare system.

Mr. President, we all know that the current war on poverty has not been successful. Since the war began, the number of children on the welfare rolls has grown from 3.3 million to 9.6 million in 1993. This was not the result of negligence, or a lack of trying. The combined Federal, State, and local spending on welfare in constant dollars increased from $38.4 billion in 1965 to $324.3 billion in 1993.

The current system is not working. What was designed with good intent, has become a trap pulling the needy families of America into a cycle of dependency that eats at their self-esteem and their ability to become self-sufficient.

The legislation before us today would change all that. This legislation moves the Federal Government out of the paper-pushing bureaucracy and moves it into a facilitator for families moving into self-sufficiency.

This legislation will help empower our families, not pull them into perpetual dependency. Gone will be the days of welfare checks for nothing. Beneficiaries will now have to engage in work activities in order to receive assistance.

This legislation retains the role of the Federal Government in overseeing the allocation of Federal money, but also gives the authority for designing the systems to the States. The States are in the best position to know the needs and environment of their unique constituencies. This legislation will allow them to design programs that coordinate resources and support families rather than just lead them through the blind maze of bureaucracy.

Mr. President, we all agree that the current system must be changed. This legislation turns the welfare programs of this country into a cohesive system flexible enough to meet the varying demands of individual States and areas while protecting our families and our children. I urge my colleagues and the President to take the chance we have today to make good on President Clinton's campaign promise to "change welfare as we know it." Let us pass this legislation and enable it to become public law.

78
"Should the House Pass H.R. 4, the Personal Responsibility Act?"

Representatives Bill Archer (R.-Tex.), Michael Collins (R.-Ga.), and William J. Coyne (D.-Pa.)

Mr. Archer. The Republican welfare revolution is at hand. Today begins the demise of the failed welfare state that has entrapped the Nation's needy for too long. Today we begin to replace that disaster in social engineering with a reform plan that brings hope to the poor of this Nation and relief to the Nation's taxpayers. Working Americans who carry the load will get relief.

Government has spent $5.3 trillion on welfare since the war on poverty began—the most expensive war in the history of this country—and the Census Bureau tells us we have lost the war. The bill we bring to the floor today constitutes the broadest overhaul of welfare ever proposed.

The status quo welfare state is unacceptable.

Today we have the chance to move beyond the rhetoric of previous years of endless campaign promises to end welfare as we know it. Today there must be no doubt. The rhetoric is stopping, the solution is beginning.

Our bill is constructed on three principles which strike at the very foundations of the Nation's failed welfare state. The three principles are: personal responsibility, work, and returning power over welfare to our States and communities where the needy can be helped in the most efficient way.

The first and most fundamental principle, captured by the title of our bill, is personal responsibility, the character trait that built this country.

The current welfare system destroys families and undermines the work ethic. It traps people in a hopeless cycle of dependency. Our bill replaces this destructive welfare system with a new system based on work and strong families.

Virtually every section of the bill requires more personal responsibility. Recipients are required to work for their benefits. Drug addicts and alcoholics are no longer rewarded with cash payments that are often spent on their habit. Aliens who were allowed into the country because they promised to be self-supporting are held to their promises; fathers who do not live with their children are expected to pay child support or suffer severe consequences; and welfare can no longer be a way of life. After five years, no more cash benefits will be provided.

This bill will reverse the decades-long Federal policy of rewarding unacceptable and self-destructive behavior. We will no longer reward for doing the wrong thing.

The second underlying principle of our bill flows naturally from the first. Able-bodied adults on welfare must work for their benefits. Here it appears that the Democrats have surrendered completely to Republican philosophy. On work we are all Republicans now, but it was not always so.

During the welfare debate of 1987 and 1988, Democrats perpetuated a system in which able-bodied adults could stay on welfare year after year without doing anything. Now the Clinton Administration and Democrats in the House are finally claiming they want mandatory work too, but the substitutes they will offer later do not require serious work.

If the Democrats were serious about welfare reform, they would have taken action last year when they had the chance. House Republicans signed a *Contract With America* that promised we would provide a vote on the House floor on true welfare reform, and we are now fulfilling that promise within less than 80 days. The third principle which forms the foundation of our bill is our commitment to shrink the Federal Government by returning power and flexibility to the States and communities where the needy can be helped the most. My own mayor in Houston, Texas, a Democrat, talked to me several weeks ago and said you can cut the amount of Federal money coming to Houston by 25 percent, but give me the flexibility without the Federal regulations and I will do more with 25 percent less.

Some say, however, that only those in their ivory towers in Washington care enough to help the needy and aid the poor; the only caring people in all of government throughout the United States are here in Washington. That is what they say. They say you cannot trust the States. These people seem to think that the governors are still standing in the schoolhouse doors not letting people in. But rather, it is the Democrats in Washington who are standing in the doors of our Nation's ghettos and not letting people out.

The current regulatory morass is shown on the chart standing next to me. It shows that the welfare system Republicans inherited consists of at least 336 programs in eight domains of welfare policy. The Federal Government expects to spending $125 billion on these programs this year. Here it is, proof of the ridiculous tangle of overlapping bureaucratic programs that have been thrust upon the Nation since the beginning of the war on poverty, and the worst part is that the American taxpayers, working Americans, are paying the bill.

But these 336 programs are only the tip of the iceberg. Imagine how many regulations had to be written to implement these 336 programs. Just let me show you. These are the regulations from just two of the 336 programs. They are standing right next to me here on the desk. They weigh 62.4 pounds.

I can think of no more fitting symbol of the failed welfare state than these pounds of Federal regulations. It is time to remove the Federal middleman from the welfare system. We can cut these unnecessary regulations, eliminate Federal bureaucrats, and give our States and communities the freedom they need to help their fellow citizens. Our bill will end 40 of the biggest and fastest growing programs and replace them with five block grants. By ending counterproductive, overlapping, and redundant programs, we will win half the battle. We are proud, though, that we have hit upon a much better approach to helping the poor than this top-heavy Federal system.

The laboratories of democracy are in the States, not Washington, D.C. Block grants will bring the decisions closer to the people affected by them. They will give governors more responsibility and resources to design and run their own programs.

And once we have given the States this flexibility and eliminated the need for them to beg Washington for permission to operate outside the stack of rules in that pile on the desk, the reforms they have implemented thus far will be dramatically expanded and spread to every State.

Welfare today has left a sad mark on the American success story. It has created a world in which children have no dreams for tomorrow and grownups have abandoned their hopes for today.

The time has come to replace this failed system with a new system that uplifts our Nation's poor, a new system that turns the social safety net from a trap into a trampoline, a new system that rewards work and personal responsibility in families, a new system that lifts a load off working, taxpaying Americans. It represents a historic shift, long overdue.

* * *

MR. COLLINS. The President, during his campaign, ran on the platform of changing welfare. In fact, he said, "We're going to end welfare as we know it today."

To end it does not mean you reform it. It means you change it. Because to reform it only changes the shape of it and leaves the same substance. Is change necessary? It is long overdue. The answer is yes.

Why? It is because 26 percent of the families in this country are in some way, shape, or fashion drawing some type of government benefit that comes under the entitlement of welfare. What is the real problem with welfare? It is called cash—the old saying, cash is the root of all evil. Cash has been the real problem, and is the real problem, in welfare.

What is the history of cash in welfare? It goes back to the mid-1930s. In fact, it was called Aid to Dependent Children, later called AFDC. It was actually created in 1935 as a cash grant to enable States to aid needy children, children who did not have fathers at home.

Was the AFDC program intended to be an indefinite program? No, it was not to last forever. The priority of it was to help children whose fathers were either deceased or disabled or unable to work. The program was supposed to sunset after the Social Security laws were changed.

When AFDC was created, no one ever imagined that a father's desertion and out-of-wedlock births would replace the father's death or disability as the most prevalent reason for triggering the need for assistance. No one ever dreamed that fathers would abandon children as they have.

In order to facilitate the sunset of the AFDC program, in 1939, the Federal Government expanded Social Security benefits by adding survivors benefits. This was to help wives and children of workers who died at any early age.

In 1956, the Federal Government added disability to Social Security to try to cover those children whose fathers were unable to work because of some severe disability. But rather than sunset AFDC, the program continued to grow and has ballooned in recent years, because the very nature of the program has encouraged illegitimacy and irresponsible behavior.

Let me give Members a few statistics. In 1940, for 41 percent of children on AFDC, their father had died. The fathers had abandoned 20 percent of the children. The fathers were disabled to work for 27 percent.

In 1992, 1.6 percent of the children's fathers have died; for 86 percent of children on AFDC, their fathers have abandoned them; and for only 4.1 percent, their fathers are disabled to work.

The AFDC system has created a real problem. It has encouraged irresponsible behavior by embracing a philosophy that says the government will take care of a child if a father won't. H.R. 4 stops this problem. It stops cash benefits in certain years, requires personal responsibility, and gives the States the flexibility, the very same thing that was supposed to happen in 1935, to handle the situation.

* * *

MR. COYNE.   I rise in strong opposition to the welfare reform package brought to the floor today by the Republican Majority. This mean-spirited attack on children and poor families in America fails every test of true welfare reform.

The Republican bill is tough on children and weak on work. This plan will punish children who happen to be born into poverty. At the same time, this plan cuts child care funding and other programs that are essential if an adult on welfare is to get a job and leave the welfare rolls.

Instead of fixing welfare and moving Americans from welfare to work, the Republican bill is simply an exercise in cutting programs that serve children, the disabled, and families living in poverty.

What can possibly be the motive for launching such a cruel attack on the children of America? The answer is the Republican Majority will cut programs for the poor to provide tax cuts for the wealthy. Cuts in child care, school lunches, and programs for the poor will be used to finance tax breaks like the capital gains tax cut. We are literally short-changing America's children to give tax breaks to individuals with incomes over $100,000 a year.

The Republican bill will punish over 15 million innocent American children. It would punish children who are born out of wedlock to a mother under the age of 18. It punishes any child who happens to be born to a family already on welfare. This bill does not guarantee that a child will have safe child care when their parents work. It cuts SSI [Supplemental Security Insurance] benefits to over 680,000 disabled children. Under this bill, State accountability for the death of a child is limited simply to reporting the child's death. Finally, this bill adds to the injuries of abused and neglected children by cutting $2 billion from Federal programs to care for these children.

The Republican bill will increase the risk of a child in poverty suffering from abuse and neglect. And yes, the result will be that some mothers who want to give birth to a child will be pushed to consider ending their pregnancy.

The Republican bill is a cruel attack on America's children, but it also fails to provide the essential tools needed by parents who want to move from welfare to work. A mother who takes a minimum wage job can only do so if she has access to safe child care. Unfortunately, this bill will cut Federal funds for child care by 25 percent in the year 2000. This means that over 400,000 fewer children will receive Federal child care assistance. Pennsylvania alone will lose $25.7 million in Federal child care assistance funding by the year 2000. That means that over 15,000 children in Pennsylvania will be denied Federal assistance for safe child care.

* * *

The legislation will result in America's poor children being left home alone. Mothers who are required by the State to work will no longer be guaranteed child care. States that seek to provide child care assistance will have to make up for Federal child care cuts by raiding other State programs or increasing State taxes.

Again, the Republican bill is tough on children and weak on work. It allows States to push a person off the welfare rolls and then count that person toward meeting the Republicans' so-called work requirement. There is no requirement for education, training, and support services for individuals who need help moving from welfare to a job. In fact, nearly $10 billion for job training programs have been cut from the first Republican welfare plan. Apparently, these funds were needed more to pay for tax cuts for upper income Americans.

* * *

DISCUSSION QUESTIONS

1. There clearly are no easy answers to the problem of welfare reform. We will always need a social welfare system, but how do we construct one that generates hope and opportunity rather than dependency? Is the Republican approach an appropriate means to reform the system? What would you suggest for reform?

2. Is welfare a right to which people in poverty are entitled? Or is it something that can be legitimately taken away?

3. What are the implications of transferring more power on welfare policy to the states? Is this a good or a bad idea? Can you think of lessons that have been learned from other policy areas that would help answer this question?

CHAPTER 15

Foreign Policy and World Politics

79
"The Sources of Soviet Conduct"

"X" [GEORGE KENNAN]

This article, which George Kennan wrote while serving as a State Department planner, set out the policy of containment that was to guide U.S. Cold War policy toward the Soviet Union. Kennan felt that contemporary thinking about the Soviet Union was caught between two unrealistic poles: hard core anti-Communists who feared creeping Socialism within the United States, and accommodationists such as Henry Wallace who felt that the United States could induce the Soviets to pursue a more cooperative stance. Neither side accurately read Soviet intentions, Kennan felt. He argued that the Soviet leaders were authoritarian as well as pragmatic, and they were more concerned with power and control than any ideological purity. Therefore, the Soviets would respond to consistent U.S. counterpressure: "firm and vigilant containment," he concluded, would keep the Soviets from expanding their influence too far beyond their borders. To Kennan's dismay, his article was widely interpreted as confirming a Soviet drive for global domination, which was not his intent.

The political personality of Soviet power as we know it today [in 1947] is the product of ideology and circumstances: ideology inherited by the present Soviet leaders from the movement in which they had their political origin, and circumstances of the power which they now have exercised for nearly three decades in Russia. There can be few tasks of psychological analysis more difficult than to try to trace the interaction of these two forces and the relative role of each in the determination of official Soviet conduct. Yet the attempt must be made if that conduct is to be understood and effectively countered.

* * *

Now the outstanding circumstance concerning the Soviet régime is that down to the present day this process of political consolidation has never been completed and the men in the Kremlin have continued to be predominantly absorbed with the struggle to secure and make absolute the power which they seized in November 1917. They have endeavored to secure it primarily against forces at home, within Soviet society itself. But they have also endeavored to secure it against the outside world. For ideology, as we have seen, taught them that the outside world was hostile and that it was their duty eventually to overthrow the political forces beyond their borders. The powerful hands of Russian history and tradition reached up to sustain them in this feeling. Finally, their own aggressive intransigence with respect to the outside world began to find its own reaction.

*   *   *

Now it lies in the nature of the mental world of the Soviet leaders, as well as in the character of their ideology, that no opposition to them can be officially recognized as having any merit or justification whatsoever. Such opposition can flow, in theory, only from the hostile and incorrigible forces of dying capitalism. As long as remnants of capitalism were officially recognized as existing in Russia, it was possible to place on them, as an internal element, part of the blame for the maintenance of a dictatorial form of society. But as these remnants were liquidated, little by little, this justification fell away; and when it was indicated officially that they had been finally destroyed, it disappeared altogether. And this fact created one of the most basic of the compulsions which came to act upon the Soviet régime: since capitalism no longer existed in Russia and since it could not be admitted that there could be serious or widespread opposition to the Kremlin springing spontaneously from the liberated masses under its authority, it became necessary to justify the retention of the dictatorship by stressing the menace of capitalism abroad.

*   *   *

[T]he innate antagonism between capitalism and Socialism . . . has become imbedded in foundations of Soviet power. It has profound implications for Russia's conduct as a member of international society. It means that there can never be on Moscow's side any sincere assumption of a community of aims between the Soviet Union and powers which are regarded as capitalist. It must invariably be assumed in Moscow that the aims of the capitalist world are antagonistic to the Soviet régime, and therefore to the interests of the peoples it controls. If the Soviet Government occasionally sets its signature to documents which would indicate the contrary, this is to be regarded as a tactical manœuvre permissible in dealing with the enemy (who is without honor) and should be taken in the spirit of *caveat emptor* ["let the buyer beware"]. Basically, the antagonism remains. It is postulated. And from it flow many of the phenomena which we find disturbing in the Kremlin's conduct of foreign policy: the secretiveness, the lack of frankness, the duplicity, the wary suspiciousness, and the basic unfriendliness of purpose. These phenomena are there to stay, for the foreseeable future. There can be variations of degree and of emphasis. When there is something the Russians want from us, one or the other of these features of their policy may be thrust temporarily into the background; and when that happens there will always be Americans who will leap forward with gleeful announcements that "the Russians have changed," and some who will even try to take credit for having brought about such "changes." But we should not be misled by tactical manœuvres. These characteristics of Soviet policy, like the postulate from which they flow, are basic to the internal nature of Soviet power, and will be with us, whether in the foreground or the background, until the internal nature of Soviet power is changed.

This means that we are going to continue for a long time to find the Russians difficult to deal with. It does not mean that they should be considered as embarked upon a do-or-die program to overthrow our society by a given date. The theory of the inevitability of the eventual fall of capitalism has the fortunate connotation that there is no hurry about it.

*   *   *

This brings us to the second of the concepts important to contemporary Soviet outlook. That is the infallibility of the Kremlin. The Soviet concept of power, which permits no focal points of organization outside the Party itself, requires that the Party leadership remain in theory the sole repository of truth. For if truth were to be found elsewhere, there would be justification for its expression in organized activity. But it is precisely that which the Kremlin cannot and will not permit.

The leadership of the Communist Party is therefore always right, and has been always right ever since in 1929 Stalin formalized his personal power by announcing that decisions of the Politburo were being taken unanimously.

On the principle of infallibility there rests the iron discipline of the Communist Party. In fact, the two concepts are mutually self-supporting. Perfect discipline requires recognition of infallibility. Infallibility requires the observance of discipline. And the two together go far to determine the behaviorism of the entire Soviet apparatus of power. But their effect cannot be understood unless a third factor be taken into account: namely, the fact that the leadership is at liberty to put forward for tactical purposes any particular thesis which it finds useful to the cause at any particular moment and to require the faithful and unquestioning acceptance of that thesis by the members of the movement as a whole. This means that truth is not a constant but is actually created, for all intents and purposes, by the Soviet leaders themselves. It may vary from week to week, from month to month. It is nothing absolute and immutable—nothing which flows from objective reality. It is only the most recent manifestation of the wisdom of those in whom the ultimate wisdom is supposed to reside, because they represent the logic of history.

The accumulative effect of these factors is to give to the whole subordinate apparatus of Soviet power an unshakeable stubbornness and steadfastness in its orientation. This orientation can be changed at will by the Kremlin but by no other power. Once a given party line has been laid down on a given issue of current policy, the whole Soviet governmental machine, including the mechanism of diplomacy, moves inexorably along the prescribed path, like a persistent toy automobile wound up and headed in a given direction, stopping only when it meets with some unanswerable force. The individuals who are the components of this machine are unamenable to argument or reason which comes to them from outside sources. Their whole training has taught them to mistrust and discount the glib persuasiveness of the outside world. Like the white dog before the phonograph, they hear only the "master's voice." And if they are to be called off from the purposes last dictated to them, it is the master who must call them off. Thus the foreign representative cannot hope that his words will make any impression on them. The most that he can hope is that they will be transmitted to those at the top, who are capable of changing the party line. But even those are not likely to be swayed by any normal logic in the words of the bourgeois representative. Since there can be no appeal to common purposes, there can be no appeal to common mental approaches. For this reason, facts speak louder than words to the ears of the Kremlin; and words carry the greatest weight when they have the ring of reflecting, or being backed up by, facts of unchallengeable validity.

But we have seen that the Kremlin is under no ideological compulsion to accomplish its purposes in a hurry. Like the Church, it is dealing in ideological concepts which are of long-term validity, and it can afford to be patient. It has no right to risk the existing achievements of the revolution for the sake of vain baubles of the future. The very teachings of Lenin himself require great caution and flexibility in the pursuit of Communist purposes. Again, these precepts are fortified by the lessons of Russian history: of centuries of obscure battles between nomadic forces over the stretches of a vast unfortified plain. Here caution, circumspection, flexibility and deception are the valuable qualities; and their value finds natural appreciation in the Russian or the oriental mind. Thus the Kremlin has no compunction about retreating in the face of superior force. And being under the compulsion of no timetable, it does not get panicky under the necessity for such retreat. Its political action is a fluid stream which moves constantly, wherever it is permitted to move, toward a given goal. Its main concern is to make sure that it has filled every nook and cranny available to it in the basin of world power. But if it finds unassailable barriers in its path, it accepts these philosophically and accommodates itself to them. The main thing is that there should always be pressure, unceasing constant pressure, toward the desired goal. There is no trace of any feeling in Soviet psychology that that goal must be reached at any given time.

These considerations make Soviet diplomacy at once easier and more difficult to deal with than the diplomacy of individual aggressive leaders like Napoleon and Hitler. On the one hand it is more sensitive to contrary force, more ready to yield on individual sectors of the diplomatic front when that force is felt to be too strong, and thus more rational in the logic and rhetoric of power. On the other hand it cannot be easily defeated or discouraged by a single victory on the part of its opponents. And the patient persistence by which it is animated means that it can be effectively countered not by sporadic acts which represent the momentary whims of democratic opinion but only by intelligent long-range policies on the part of Russia's adversaries—policies no less steady in their purpose, and no less variegated and resourceful in their application, than those of the Soviet Union itself.

In these circumstances it is clear that the main element of any United States policy toward the Soviet Union must be that of a long-term, patient but firm and vigilant containment of Russian expansive tendencies. It is important to note, however, that such a policy has nothing to do with outward histrionics: with threats or blustering or superfluous gestures of outward "toughness." While the Kremlin is basically flexible in its reaction to political realities, it is by no means unamenable to considerations of prestige. Like almost any other government, it can be placed by tactless and threatening gestures in a position where it cannot afford to yield even though this might be dictated by its sense of realism. The Russian leaders are keen judges of human psychology, and as such they are highly conscious that loss of temper and of self-control is never a source of strength in political affairs. They are quick to exploit such evidences of weakness. For these reasons, it is a *sine qua non* [essential condition] of successful dealing with Russia that the foreign government in question should remain at all times cool and collected and that its demands on Russian policy should be put forward in such a manner as to leave the way open for a compliance not too detrimental to Russian prestige.

In the light of the above, it will be clearly seen that the Soviet pressure against the free institutions of the western world is something that can be contained by the adroit and vigilant application of counter-force at a series of constantly shifting geographical and political points, corresponding to the shifts and manœuvres of Soviet policy, but which cannot be charmed or talked out of existence. The Russians look forward to a duel of infinite duration, and they see that already they have scored great successes.

* * *

It is clear that the United States cannot expect in the foreseeable future to enjoy political intimacy with the Soviet régime. It must continue to regard the Soviet Union as a rival, not a partner, in the political arena. It must continue to expect that Soviet policies will reflect no abstract love of peace and stability, no real faith in the possibility of a permanent happy coexistence of the Socialist and capitalist worlds, but rather a cautious, persistent pressure toward the disruption and weakening of all rival influence and rival power.

Balanced against this are the facts that Russia, as opposed to the western world in general, is still by far the weaker party, that Soviet policy is highly flexible, and that Soviet society may well contain deficiencies which will eventually weaken its own total potential. This would of itself warrant the United States entering with reasonable confidence upon a policy of firm containment, designed to confront the Russians with unalterable counter-force at every point where they show signs of encroaching upon the interests of a peaceful and stable world.

But in actuality the possibilities for American policy are by no means limited to holding the line and hoping for the best. It is entirely possible for the United States to influence by its actions the internal developments, both within Russia and throughout the international Communist movement, by which Russian policy is largely determined. This is not only a question of the modest measure of informational activity which this government can conduct in the Soviet Union and elsewhere, although that, too, is important. It is rather a question of the degree to which the United States can create among the peoples of the world generally the impression of a country which knows what it wants, which is coping successfully with the problems of its internal life and with the responsibilities of a World Power, and which has a spiritual vitality capable of holding its own among the major ideological currents of the time. To the extent that such an impression can be created and maintained, the aims of Russian Communism must appear sterile and quixotic, the hopes and enthusiasm of Moscow's supporters must wane, and added strain must be imposed on the Kremlin's foreign policies. For the palsied decrepitude of the capitalist world is the keystone of Communist philosophy. Even the failure of the United States to experience the early economic depression which the ravens of the Red Square [site of the Kremlin] have been predicting with such complacent confidence since hostilities ceased would have deep and important repercussions throughout the Communist world.

By the same token, exhibitions of indecision, disunity and internal disintegration within this country have an exhilarating effect on the whole Communist movement. At each evidence of these tendencies, a thrill of hope and excitement goes through the Communist world; a new jauntiness can be noted in the Moscow tread; new groups of foreign supporters climb on to what they can only view as the band wagon of international politics; and Russian pressure increases all along the line in international affairs.

It would be an exaggeration to say that American behavior unassisted and alone could exercise a power of life and death over the Communist movement and bring about the early fall of Soviet power in Russia. But the United States has it in its power to increase enormously the strains under which Soviet policy must operate, to force upon the Kremlin a far greater degree of moderation and circumspection than it has had to observe in recent years, and in this way to promote tendencies which must eventually find their outlet in either the break-up or the gradual mellowing of Soviet power. For no mystical, Messianic movement—and particularly not that of the Kremlin—can face frustration indefinitely without eventually adjusting itself in one way or another to the logic of that state of affairs.

Thus the decision will really fall in large measure in this country itself. The issue of Soviet-American relations is in essence a test of the over-all worth of the United States as a nation among nations. To avoid destruction the United States need only measure up to its own best traditions and prove itself worthy of preservation as a great nation.

Surely, there was never a fairer test of national quality than this. In the light of these circumstances, the thoughtful observer of Russian-American relations will find no cause for complaint in the Kremlin's challenge to American society. He will rather experience a certain gratitude to a Providence which, by providing the American people with this implacable challenge, has made their entire security as a nation dependent on their pulling themselves together and accepting the responsibilities of moral and political leadership that history plainly intended them to bear.

DISCUSSION QUESTIONS

1. How accurate were Kennan's predictions regarding the eventual fate of the Soviet Union?

2. Do you think the containment policy Kennan favored played a role in the Soviet Union's collapse? Explain.

80
"An Outward-Looking Economic Nationalism"

ROBERT B. REICH

In the post–Cold War world, economic affairs have asumed greater importance relative to military issues as a component of national strength. And, as international borders become more permeable, what happens to the international economy has more impact on domestic economic events. Reich traces the impact these phenomena have on what the national government can do to protect domestic interests, using trade policy as his focus. He notes that the debate over trade policy is dominated by two opposing camps. "Neo-mercantilists" want the government actively to protect domestic industries from foreign competition through import restrictions; this group argues that free trade will destroy American jobs as lower costs abroad make it impossible for U.S. companies to compete. "Laissez-faire cosmopolitans" on the other hand, want the government to stay out of the fray and support free trade and the globalization of economic affairs.

In Reich's view, neither group has the right answer to the question of how to protect U.S. interests. He advocates a combination of the two policies, arguing that the government should not abandon the economy to market forces, while at the same time recognizing that some forms of intervention are worse than others. Instead of trade barriers and protection of specific industries, Reich advocates a policy of "economic nationalism" along with steps to insure that domestic economic strength does not come at the expense of other countries. Economic strength is best assured through investment in infrastructure, education, and research and development.

The debate grows louder and more strident with each passing trade statistic: On the one side, neo-mercantilists, comprising a growing coalition of American firms and trade unions, urge that government advance American enterprise—even at the expense of others around the globe. In this view, unless we become more assertive, foreigners will continue to increase market shares at America's expense in industry after industry—exploiting our openness, gaining competitive advantage over us, ultimately robbing us of control over our destinies. On the other side, laissez-faire cosmopolitans, comprising most Wall Street bankers, professional economists, and officials at the highest reaches of the Bush Administration, argue that government should stay out. In their view, profit-seeking individuals and enterprises are far better able to decide what gets produced where. Governments only mess things up. Free movement of all factors of production across national boundaries will ultimately improve everyone's lot—ours *and* theirs.

Which side has the better case? Neither. What's being lost from the debate is a third position superior to both: outward-looking economic nationalism, in which each nation takes responsibility for improving the wealth-creating capacities of its citizens, but works with other nations to ensure that these improvements not come at others' expense. The third position is not laissez-faire, because governments actively encourage new technologies and industries, smooth the transition from older industries, educate their work forces, invest in infrastructure, and create international rules of fair play for accomplishing all these things. But neither is it neo-mercantilist, because the overarching goal is to enhance global welfare rather than to advance one nation's well-being by reducing another's.

First, a typical debate. No doubt you have heard parts of it before, but in order to define the third position it is necessary to set out what the other two are arguing about.

The unsophisticated laissez-faire cosmopolitan's opening gambit: Don't you realize that every nation will be better off if each specializes in what it does best, and then can trade with others? The English economist David Ricardo discovered the law of comparative advantage almost two centuries ago when he showed that England and Portugal would each benefit from sticking to natural endowments, textiles and wine respectively. History has shown that attempts to meddle with this logic only deprive citizens in both nations of potential improvements in their welfare.

The unsophisticated neo-mercantilist's reply: The law of comparative advantage is nice in theory, but it doesn't describe the modern world. Nations are wealthy to the extent that they have advanced industries and well-paying jobs. Other nations subsidize their industries. We can't just afford to let industries like steel and autos go down the drain, even if some other countries price their cars and their steel more cheaply than ours.

The slightly more sophisticated laissez-faire cosmopolitan's rejoinder: Stop and think. Steel-making jobs may pay well, but if foreigners can make steel more efficiently than American steel makers, it's crazy for the rest of us to pay extra by blocking foreign steel imports. By doing that we're merely transferring our hard-earned cash to American steel makers. Why are they so special that they deserve to be subsidized by the rest of us? What about all the American producers of cars, appliances, and machine tools that would become more profitable and competitive if they could buy cheaper foreign steel? These industries provide good jobs, too. And by the way, don't forget about Third-World nations that might otherwise become the lowest-cost steel producers of all if we don't protect our markets. With earnings from steel they could buy our cars, appliances, and machine tools—and any other products we make more efficiently than steel. Incidentally, some of these Third World nations borrow money from us and would find repayment considerably easier if we allowed them to sell us their steel.

The slightly more sophisticated neo-mercantilist's answer: You don't get it. Let's say we agree that free trade really is the best of all worlds. But it isn't the world we live in. Most other countries don't believe in free trade, or practice it. We have to play hardball in order to get a level playing field. If they don't open their markets to us, we shouldn't give them a free ride in the American market. I'd like to be a free trader, too. But in the real world, sometimes you have to use mercantilist means to obtain cosmopolitan ends. In the modern world, nations acquire comparative advantage when their engineers, entrepreneurs, and workers learn by doing. What kind of "factor endowments" does Japan have other than an industrial policy? Private industry doesn't invest enough in learning-by-doing. The gap between private and social needs has to be filled in by the state.

And here's where they're beating us. Through tariffs and non-tariff barriers (like industrial standards, health and safety regulations, and complex distribution systems) and outright subsidies, they're nurturing on-the-job skills that will allow them to dominate the *next* generations of industry and technology. So not only are we failing to get as much of this knowledge and experience as we would if government were filling in the gap between private and social returns—we're not even gaining the private returns! American companies see no point to investing in such industries and technologies as long as foreign markets are closed and foreign exports are subsidized. There's no other choice: We either beat them at this game or get beaten by them. We should close our markets until we get reciprocity, subsidize our firms, and stop foreigners from grabbing our technologies and buying our companies.

The sophisticated laissez-faire cosmopolitan's response: Who are you kidding? I understand politics as well as you do. Once these protectionist measures are in place, they're almost never rescinded. Protected industries become dependent on them, and gain the political clout to keep them. Meanwhile, our so-called retaliation prompts the other nation to counterretaliate, and before you know it protectionist barriers are higher than ever. "Cosmopolitan ends" my foot.

The sophisticated neo-mercantilist's coup de grace [decisive stroke]: Other countries manage to use mercantilist strategies effectively, without making their industries sheltered and lazy. Maybe they have a comparative advantage in mercantilism. Japan kept out American steel in the fifties, but they used that period of protection to create the world's most dynamic steel industry. You and David Ricardo are ignoring one key fact. In the modern world, comparative advantage can be created. Just consider Japan's surge into auto, micro-electronics, and other forms of advanced manufacturing. Look at South Korea, Taiwan, Hong Kong and Singapore. You think the invisible hand did this?

The exasperated laissez-faire cosmopolitan's conversation stopper: What century are you living in anyway? You talk as if nations still counted. But today, national markets are collapsing into one giant world market. Since money crosses borders at the speed of an electronic impulse, the cost of capital is rapidly converging. Technologies move from computers in one nation to satellites and then down to computers in another, so everyone gains access to new technological insights at about the same time. And global companies are doing everything everywhere.

If the Japanese people want to work their fannies off making complex gadgets that never fall apart and selling them to us at bargain-basement prices, taking our IOUs in return, let them go ahead and we'll enjoy the benefits. You see, my friend, national economies no longer exist. There's no such thing as national economic interest.

The Zero-Sum Fallacy

Both of these standard positions, even in their most sophisticated versions, are wrongheaded. To begin, the neo-mercantilist's zero-sum premise—either they win or we win—is simply incorrect. As one nation's workers become more insightful about new technologies they are able to add more wealth to the world. To this limited extent the cosmopolitan is right: Everyone on the planet benefits from smaller and more powerful semiconductor chips regardless of who makes them, and the knowledge of how to make them inevitably migrates to other workers in other nations.

Of course, the nation whose workers first gain the insights may benefit disproportionately. That advantage may cause other nations' citizens to experience a relative decline in wealth, notwithstanding their absolute gain. Sociologists have long known of "relative deprivation" whereby people evaluate their well-being relative to the wealth of others. There is also the political reality that power flows to those nations that gain large economic leads over others. For both these reasons, nations may be willing to forego absolute gains in welfare to prevent their rivals from enjoying even larger gains. While understandable, such zero-sum impulses are hardly to be commended as a principle of international economic behavior. Since economic advances rarely benefit all nations in equal proportion, such an approach, if widely adapted, would legitimize the blocking of most efforts to enhance global wealth.

In any event, economic interdependence now runs so deep that any zero-sum strategy is likely to boomerang, as the members of OPEC discovered in the 1970s when their sky-high oil prices plunged the world into recession and reduced the demand for oil. Today no nation's central bank can control its money supply or the value of its currency without the help of other nations' central banks, nor can a nation unilaterally raise its interest rates or run large budget surpluses or deficits without others' cooperation or acquiescence. These days, every advanced nation depends on others as a market for, and source of, its goods. The Japanese need a strong and prosperous America as a market for their goods and a place to invest their money. Any step they took that precipitated a steep economic decline in America would have disastrous results for them.

The "America first" premises of neo-mercantilism, moreover, are uncomfortably close to the "America first" premises of Cold War militarism, and, if implemented, would be likely to have similar consequences. History offers ample evidence of the danger: zero-sum nationalism in whatever form tends to corrode public values to the point where citizens support policies that marginally improve their welfare while harming everyone else on the planet, and thus invite other nations to do the same. Whether the issue is global warming, immigration and refugees, the drug trade, Third World debt, population control, energy use, management of the macroeconomy, the spread of nuclear weapons, or any number of other things linked to species survival, global cooperation is essential. But zero-sum habits and attitudes render it all the more difficult to achieve.

But what if foreigners dominate a major technology, as the Japanese are on the way to doing in advanced semiconductors, high-definition television, and a dozen other gadgets? What if they freeze us out? Their mastery of particular technologies won't freeze us out of technological progress. Technologies aren't like commodities for which world demand is finite, nor do they come in fixed quantities that either they get or we get. Technologies are domains of knowledge. They are like the outer branches of a giant bush on which countless other branches are growing all the time. While it's true that the American work force needs direct experience in designing and fabricating technologies on outer branches if it will share in their future growth, they need not be exactly the same branches as occupied by the Japanese or any other nation's work force. We already occupy branches they don't—complex software, airframes, cinematography, and biotechnology, to name only a few.

It should also be noted that *they* are *here*, training American workers to be more productive in the branches that foreigners already occupy. Ten percent of American manufacturing workers are employed by foreign-owned firms. Those firms are now creating more jobs in the United States than are American manufacturers and at higher average wages (in 1986, $32,887, as compared to an American average of $28,954). Foreign firms come here not just because American assets are now so cheap, but because the foreign firms can be more productive in the United States than can their American-owned rivals. (The wave of foreign investment in the United States began in the mid-1970s rather than from the start of the current-account deficit in 1982, and the two leading foreign investors have been the British and the Dutch rather than the trade-surplus rich Japanese and West Germans.) After Bridgestone Tire took over Firestone, productivity soared. The same thing happened at the General Motors–Toyota joint venture in Fremont, California, where Toyota transformed what had been a troubled GM plant into a model facility through retooling and retraining.

Given the choice of either foreign managers and the financial capital that comes with them, or American managers and capital that accompanies them, American workers in many industries do better making foreign-engineered and managed products. Japanese and Western European managers, for example, take lower salaries and benefits for themselves relative to their workers, encourage substantially more worker participation, and provide workers with greater job security, than do their American counterparts. Wall Street demands faster paybacks—and thus tolerates less experimentation, long-term research, worker training, and product development—than do many foreign sources of capital.

The specter of foreign management and ownership nevertheless frightens many Americans, who believe that foreign executives will be less sensitive to national needs than are American executives. Even if foreign firms are now retooling their American plants and training their American workers to be more productive, some fear that they might nonetheless bias their strategies to reduce American competitiveness. They might even withdraw their investments from the United States and leave us stranded.

This line of reasoning assumes that American executives and American-owned firms will, by contrast, put national interests ahead of the interests of their shareholders. Yet, apart from wartime or other periods of national emergency, this is hardly the case. In fact, American-owned and managed firms are setting up shop abroad at as fast a pace as foreign firms are coming here. American companies increased their foreign capital spending by 24 percent in 1988, 13 percent in 1989—far above their domestic levels of capital investments (11 and 8 percent, respectively). Much of this foreign investment abroad went for high value added production. In fact, American firms increased their overseas research and development spending by 33 percent between 1986 and 1988, compared with a 6 percent increase in R&D spending in the United States. They are going wherever they must to maximize profits.

American executives who sacrificed profits for the sake of national goals would make themselves vulnerable to a takeover or liable for breach of fiduciary duty to their shareholders. Were American managers knowingly to sacrifice profits for the sake of presumed national goals, they would be acting without authority, on the basis of their own views of what such goals might be, and without accountability to shareholders or to the public. Obviously, American corporations have an incentive to display good "corporate citizenship" by making charitable contributions and investing in their communities, as long as such acts improve their corporations' image and thus contribute to higher profits in the future. But foreign-owned and managed firms can be expected to engage in similar eleemosynary activities for the same reason. Indeed, they are apt to be even more charitable than are American-owned and managed firms, given their conspicuous need to build public trust. Meanwhile, American firms feel a similar compulsion to act as good citizens in their host countries. Robert W. Galvin, chairman of Motorola, noted recently that, should it become necessary for Motorola to close some of its factories, it would not close its Southeast Asian plants before it closed its American ones. "We need our Far Eastern customers," said Galvin, "and we cannot alienate the Malaysians. We must treat our employees all over the world equally."

Our national economic goal should be to increase the value of what American citizens add to the world economy—and thus to improve the American standard of living. To the extent that foreign-owned firms help us to accomplish this, they should be welcomed. By the same token, American-owned firms—rapidly becoming global entities—should have no special claim on the nation's resources.

The Laissez-Faire Fallacy

The laissez-faire cosmopolitans are only half right, however. While they correctly disavow zero-sum objectives, they fail to comprehend the importance of public-sector involvement in the nation's economic development. To equate such involvement with zero-sum outcomes is simply wrong.

The American work force needs much more help than what can be supplied by foreign firms with superior technology, capital, or management skill. Because of the "public goods" nature of research and development, education, training and retraining, job search and relocation assistance (as well as infrastructure such as roads, ports, bridges, sewage treatment), public investment is critical. Indeed, the justification for public-sector expenditure is even more potent than the standard "public goods" observation that because the benefits of such investments can't be apportioned according to who pays for them, we can't rely on the market to do it. In an increasingly integrated world economy, the fruits of such investments aren't limited to American corporations, which, as I have stressed, are going global at a rapid pace. Nor for that matter are they limited to Americans. Again: new technologies inevitably leak out beyond national borders; educated and trained workers create new wealth that's shared with the rest of the world; modern transportation and communication systems increase the speed and efficiency with which goods and services can be shipped into and out of the nation from other nations. Everyone benefits from such investments, at least to a small degree—even foreigners.

Thus a strong argument, in theory, for public sector investment. But the argument also presents a practical political dilemma. For if the benefits of such wealth creating investments are enjoyed in the first instance by an entire nation's work force, and then to an increasing extent by many foreigners, why should an individual taxpayer willingly pay for them? Why not seek to reduce taxes, then withdraw into a small enclave bounded by family and friends, paying only what's necessary to ensure that everyone within that enclave is well educated and has access to the infrastructure he or she needs?

Loyalty to place—to one's city or region or nation—once provided an answer to this question. Individual citizens supported taxes to pay for education, roads, and other civic improvements, even when the individual taxpayer was likely to enjoy but a fraction of what was paid out. He or she did so out of a sense of obligation to improve the well-being of everyone else within the same political and geographic unit. To be sure, such civic boosterism, pride, and patriotism were founded upon an enlightened self-interest. As Tocqueville noted, American patriotism was "confounded with the personal interest of the citizen. A man comprehends the influence which the prosperity of his country has upon his own welfare; he is aware that the laws authorize him to contribute his assistance to that prosperity, and he labors to promote it as a portion of his right." As our fellow citizens grew wealthier and more productive we benefitted by their ability to give us more in exchange for what we offered them. We also benefitted from the social tranquility induced in a population adequately clothed, housed, and fed.

Now that local, state, and even national economies are becoming regions of a global economy, however, their borders no longer clearly define areas of special economic interdependence. To take an extreme example, the American executive of a global corporation, linked to his worldwide operations by computer, modem, and fax, is far more dependent on the firm's design engineers in Kuala Lumpur, fabricators in Taiwan, bankers in Bonn, and sales and marketing specialists in Paris, London, Frankfurt, and Tokyo than on his neighbors next door or on the workers in the factory on the other side of town. And the security guards that patrol his condominium (itself located within an enclave far removed from crime-ridden areas of the region) can assure him a reasonable degree of tranquility, even if people on the other side of town are starving. While this example is hardly typical, it does portray a growing segment of the population for whom there is no longer much enlightened self-interest in patriotism.

It is in this setting that rootless cosmopolitanism is especially mischievous. We have little left but the sentiment of loyalty to inspire sacrifice for the greater good. A sense of national purpose—of historic, cultural, and principled connection to a common political endeavor—must transcend cosmopolitan economic ties if it is to elicit investment in the nation's future. Paradoxically, such nationalist sentiments result in greater global wealth than do cosmopolitan sentiments founded upon loyalty to no nation. Like the villagers whose diligence in tending to their own gardens results in a bounteous harvest for all, citizens that feel a special obligation to cultivate the talents and abilities of their compatriots end up contributing to the well-being of compatriots and non-compatriots alike.

Towards Outward-Looking Nationalism

Note, however, the difference between this kind of nationalist sentiment and the zero-sum nationalism that animates neo-mercantilism. Here, one nation's well-being is not contingent upon another's loss. To the contrary, national well-being depends upon its and every other nation's investments in the productive capacities of people. To extend the metaphor, while each garden-tender may feel competitive with every other, each also understands that the success of the total harvest requires cooperation. While each has primary responsibility to tend his own garden, each has a secondary responsibility to ensure that all gardens flourish.

Thus, outward-looking economic nationalism would eschew obstacles to the movement of goods, money, and technology across borders. Even were such obstacles enforceable (which is less and less the case), they would reduce the capacity of each nation's work force to enjoy the fruits of investments made in them, and in others. But not all government intervention would be eschewed. To the contrary, this approach would encourage public spending within each nation in any manner than enhanced the capacity of each work force to add more value to the world economy—including pre-school care, education, training and retraining, infrastructure, and research and development.

Outward-looking economic nationalism also would tolerate—even invite—national subsidies to firms that undertook within their borders high value-added production (complex design engineering, production engineering, fabrication, systems integration, and so forth) so that the nation's work force could gain sophisticated on-the-job skills. But to ensure against zero-sum games in which nations bid against one another to attract the same set of global firms and related technologies, nations would negotiate over appropriate levels and targets of such subsidies.

The result would be a kind of "GATT for direct investment"—setting out the rules by which nations could bid for high value-added investments by global corporations. Barred would be threats to close the domestic market unless certain investments were undertaken within it, for such threats would likely degenerate into zero-sum contests. Instead, the rules would seek to define fair tactics, depending upon the characteristics of the national economy and the type of investment being sought. For example, the amount of permissible subsidy might be directly proportional to the size of the nation's work force but inversely proportional to its average skills. Thus nations with large and relatively unskilled work forces would be allowed greater leeway in bidding for global investment than nations with smaller and more highly-skilled workers.

Other subsidies would be pooled and parceled out to where they could do the most good, as the European Community has begun to do regionally. For example, nations would jointly fund basic research and development whose fruits were likely to travel almost immediately across international borders—projects such as the high-energy particle accelerator, the human genome, and the exploration of space. How such funds were apportioned, and toward what ends, would of course be a subject of negotiation.

Another example: Outward-looking economic nationalism would encourage subsidies designed to ease the transition of a work force out of older industries and technologies in which there was worldwide overcapacity. Such subsidies might take the form of severance payments, relocation assistance, extra training grants, extra unemployment insurance, regional economic aid, and funds for retooling or upgrading machinery toward higher value-added production. Since every nation benefits when overcapacity anywhere else is reduced, such subsidies might come from a common fund established by all nations. Payments could be apportioned according to how much of that particular industry's capacity lay within each nation's borders at the start.

Finally, outward-looking economic nationalism would seek to develop the capacities of the work force of the Third World—not as a means of forestalling world communism or stabilizing Third World regimes so that global companies can safely extract raw materials and sell products within them—but as a means of enhancing global wealth. To this end, the shift of high-volume, commodity industries to Third World nations would be welcomed, and markets in advanced economies would be open to them. The Third World's debt burden would be reduced, and new lending made available.

A Global Mixed Economy

In the aftermath of the devastation of World War Two, the United States took the lead in creating a new international economic system to guide the growth of the world economy—a system of fixed exchange rates to minimize currency fluctuations, an International Monetary Fund to ensure liquidity, a World Bank to aggregate and direct development finance, and a GATT to ensure an open trading system. In effect, these innovations were designed to reduce the likelihood of zero-sum contests and to enhance world trade and finance directed at growth for all. By almost any standard the system was a spectacular success. The years 1945 to 1970 witnessed the most dramatic and widely shared economic growth in the history of mankind. World GNP grew from $300 billion to over $2,000 billion. Even allowing for inflation, real income tripled; world trade quadrupled.

These innovations were not the products of laissez-faire thinking. They represented bold interventions into the market. Nor were they the products of zero-sum nationalistic impulse. They worked because it was in the interest of every participating nation to make them work. Thus a marriage of positive-sum cosmopolitanism with enlightened nationalism.

My purpose in these pages has been to suggest a further step along this same path. The world economy has evolved during the past forty-five years. In particular, the transition from basic industries to advanced technologies now requires huge capital investments, yet also demands cumulative knowledge and skills that easily leak out beyond the private sector firm making such investments. In addition, national corporations are rapidly becoming global entities, lacking any special connection or responsibility to particular nations. Thus most governments are assisting their economies, not by protecting "national" firms but by improving the quality of their work forces, luring direct investment by global corporations, easing the transition out of mature industries, nurturing new technologies. If such interventions are to enhance world wealth rather than merely rearrange it, new international rules to guide such interventions must be devised, and soon. Thus the case for outward-directed economic nationalism as an alternative both to zero-sum neo-mercantilism and to laissez-faire cosmopolitanism.

But unlike the economically and politically preeminent United States at the close of World War Two, which could justify to its citizens and foreigners alike the short-term sacrifices and dislocations that new international institutions would entail, there is no longer a single world leader capable of striking the deal. Nor is there a natural private constituency for this third approach, either here or abroad.

The pressures of sudden economic change have made neo-mercantilism attractive both to organized labor, threatened by cheaper foreign labor, and to domestic businesses, threatened by the superior scale and market power of global corporations. Their champions in the United States are politicians who view the new-found economic prowess of Japan, the "four tigers" of East Asia, and the potential prowess of a united Europe, as threats to America's security and autonomy. Their remedy: protection of the domestic market (often masquerading as "voluntary restraint agreements," anti-dumping levies, countervailing duties, agreements by other nations to import certain quantities of American goods, "Buy American" provisions within federal procurement regulations, and assorted obstacles to foreign direct investment).

Meanwhile the possibilities for large windfall gains have rendered laissez-faire cosmopolitanism especially attractive to global businesses headquartered in the United States, Wall Street bankers, and economists who inhabit the upper reaches of Republican administrations. Their champions are politicians who insist that the global market is best run by the "invisible hand."

In other words, organized economic interests threatened by global competition feel that they have much to lose and little to gain from an outward-looking approach that seeks to enhance world wealth. Organized economic interests already benefitting from the blurring of national borders, on the other hand, sense that they have much to lose and little to gain from government intervention intended to spread such benefits.

The trick—both within the United States and within other advanced economies—will be to persuade each group that outward-directed economic nationalism is the best deal they can hope to extract from the other. A new generation of leaders here and abroad will have to point out to the neo-mercantilists that they will be more imperiled by laissez-faire cosmopolitanism, and to the cosmopolitans that they will be more disrupted by neo-mercantilism, than either will be by the outward-directed alternative.

Ideally, a compromise will work to the world's advantage. All of us stand to benefit more from nationalists with cosmopolitan vision than from either cosmopolitans or nationalists lacking global perspective. But in political economics, that we all stand to gain has rarely been reason enough. Perhaps in this new era of global possibility, we will find the imagination and the will to appreciate our common interests.

DISCUSSION QUESTIONS

1. Reich's policies would produce mostly long-term benefits; it takes some time for education and training to show any results on a national scale. What are the implications of this for the practicality of his suggestions, or the likelihood that they will be adopted?

2. Who are the direct beneficiaries of Reich's policies? Think through the same questions for trade barriers (import quotas, tariffs, and so on).

THE DEBATE: AMERICAN FOREIGN POLICY: ISOLATIONISM OR INVOLVEMENT?

The end of the Cold War has altered perceptions of what the United States' goals are with respect to the rest of the world. As long as there was a Soviet Union, our interests seemed clear: containment of Soviet expansion and support of anti-Communism around the world (as Kennan advocated in his article). Minor security conflicts that were otherwise irrelevant became important when viewed through the lens of U.S.–Soviet rivalry. The collapse of the Soviet Union has changed the debate: It is no longer clear, for example, that international power depends directly on military strength, because economic forces play a larger role in determining national well-being. The military's role has changed as well. During the Cold War, the military was oriented toward deterring and, if necessary, defeating Soviet military activity. Now the emphasis has shifted toward smaller-scale conflicts and nontraditional military operations such as peace keeping, humanitarian assistance, and promoting democratization.

Yet there are still no clear strategic principles that guide U.S. policy, and those who support a continued U.S. presence in international affairs must contend with a strong isolationist sentiment among the public. When problems and crises arise in the new environment, as they have in Bosnia, Somalia, Rwanda, and Haiti, how should the U.S. respond? How do we determine what our interests are in these conflicts? Should we use military force only when our national security interests are directly threatened, or should we commit troops to combat civil violence and genocide even when our interests may be only peripherally involved? Most important, what price are we willing to pay in money and lives? The following two readings take contrasting positions. Barry M. Blechman is sympathetic toward U.S. intervention, but he argues that the strong pressure to intervene in the face of a crisis is not matched with a willingness to do what is necessary to succeed. He maintains that we need to take a broader view of what our interests are when civil strife erupts around the world, and that we should recognize that nonintervention has costs of its own. Charles Krauthammer's article highlights the difficulties in moving from the abstract to the particular. In arguing that the role of a superpower is to intervene only when "global stability [is] threatened," he concludes that U.S. military presence in the former Yugoslavia—and, indeed, using troops for peace-keeping missions in general—is a fundamental misuse of U.S. power.

81
"The Intervention Dilemma"

Barry M. Blechman

With the end of the Cold War and, with it, the risk that interventions abroad could result in confrontation, crisis, and even war between the nuclear-armed superpowers, Americans have begun to rethink the norms governing U.S. involvements in the affairs of other states. Contradictory impulses have dominated this debate. The typical American urge to export democratic and humanitarian values has encouraged activist policies and resulting involvements in many countries. But the traditional American antipathy toward "overseas entanglements" and, particularly, a distaste for military interventions, have diminished support for many individual expeditions that implied a serious risk of U.S. casualties or even significant expenditures.

The resulting policy dilemma caused difficulties for President George Bush and has bedeviled President Bill Clinton. Both administrations sought to escape from the dilemma by turning to the United Nations (UN), both to legitimate interventions and to spread the burden to a wider group of countries. As a result, the world organization's traditional peacekeeping functions have been transformed into more muscular "peace operations." But UN peace operations have had only mixed results, and the few clear failures have led to legislative initiatives that would severely curtail U.S. participation in UN peace operations and possibly cripple the organization's ability to sustain more than a traditional peacekeeping role.

Lost in the furor have been the facts that the UN has had more successes than failures in its expanded security role, and that the UN's apparent failures have not been completely its fault, to say nothing of the possibility that steps could be taken to greatly strengthen the UN's potential to contribute to international security through peace operations.

Contradictory Impulses

The belief that governments have a right, even obligation, to intervene in the affairs of other states seems to have gained great currency in recent years. Of course, modern communications have made people everywhere more aware of situations that seem to cry out for intervention, and more familiar with the personal tragedies that accompany these horrible calamities. Technology, too, has provided more ready means of intervention—whether for diplomats to mediate, for observers to monitor elections, for paramilitary forces to enforce economic sanctions, or for armed forces to carry out military operations—removing in many cases the excuse of infeasibility. The governments of the great powers, and particularly the U.S. government, have the means to intervene today, whether they choose to do so or not.

Yet, far more than the physical means of awareness and intervention has changed. The norms governing intervention themselves have evolved. The sanctity once accorded to state boundaries has eroded considerably. The interdependence and penetrability of states need no elaboration. Serious crises anywhere in the world cause financial markets and currency rates to reverberate, affecting investors' confidence and the business climate overall. Companies large and small depend on foreign investors, components, markets, and technologies. Individuals are both affected more directly by turmoil in distant lands and more familiar with foreign countries. Ordinary citizens interact more frequently with people living abroad. People exercise rights to visit and conduct business in foreign countries routinely, almost without thinking about the legal boundaries that have been crossed.

Most important, however, profound changes have occurred in popular expectations. After decades of little more than formal intonation, the belief that governments can be expected to adhere to certain universal standards of behavior, even within their own borders, seems to have taken hold. This is certainly not to say that all people in all parts of the world already hold this belief. The view has penetrated populations to different degrees—most profoundly in Europe and North America, to a lesser degree in other parts of the world—but the trend is very clear, particularly among the economic and social elites that dominate politics in most countries.

What is the basis for the new view? Apparently, increasing numbers of people are willing to act on what must be an implicit belief that sovereignty does not reside with an abstraction called the state, and certainly not with self-appointed military or civilian dictatorships, but with the people of a country themselves. Even more, the view seems to hold, the power of all governments, even those popularly elected, is limited: individuals have inalienable rights that must be observed and protected by all governments. As a result, according to this increasingly powerful view, all governments can be held to certain standards of behavior involving basic human rights and democratic processes. In addition, when a country falls into such disarray that no governing body can end a humanitarian tragedy, the world community itself is accountable. When such events occur, the view continues, all people in other countries, and their governments, have not only the right, but the obligation, to intervene on behalf of both oppressed peoples and innocent bystanders.

Historically, when murderous civil wars or large-scale abuses of human rights occurred in a country, powerful governments with direct interests in that state sometimes intervened. Today, as a result of the greater currency of the views described above, great powers often feel compelled to intervene in domestic conflicts even when their direct stakes are limited. Sometimes, the officials of a great power hold to the views just described—and see intervention as a humanitarian responsibility. But at other times, if governments hesitate, and if the events in question are of sufficient magnitude, various constituencies exert political pressures for action—action to end the slaughter, to feed the refugees, to restore democracy, to at least save the lives of the children. Often, these days, private citizens and organizations become involved in these situations before governments even contemplate acting. Religious charities, humanitarian organizations, and activist political rights groups are involved on the ground in virtually all troubled nations. Their reports and activities reinforce, and sometimes help to create, popular pressures in foreign capitals for some kind of official action.

Thus, in the contemporary world, major powers react when troubles occur in even the most remote parts of the globe. Diplomats are dispatched, good offices tendered, observers emplaced, and political and economic campaigns of isolation launched. Sometimes, if exercised with persistence and skill, these peaceful means of conflict resolution work. More often, they do not: dictators stubbornly cling to power, powerful elites continue to oppress the masses, ethnic factions continue to revenge historic slaughters with the even greater slaughters made possible by modern weaponry.

Why do peaceful means fail? Many factors, no doubt, are responsible, but one stands out. In the contemporary age, intervening governments can only rarely use peaceful instruments of conflict resolution knowing that they could credibly threaten military intervention should peaceful means fail. This is the intervention dilemma. Even as the proclivity of major powers to intervene in domestic conflicts in foreign nations has grown, the natural reluctance of populations to pay the price of such interventions, if challenged, has also gathered steam. This reluctance takes two forms: pressures in many democratic states against the use of public funds for foreign operations; and, more pointed, popular opposition in democratic states to the use of military power in most circumstances.

Thus, increasingly, even while powerful political constituencies demand action by democratic governments to resolve domestic conflicts in foreign nations, even more powerful constituencies resist the use of the one form of intervention that often is the only realistic means of accomplishing the first constituency's demands—the threat or actual use of force. In an international system with no central authority, the absence of credible military threats curtails the effectiveness of all forms of coercive diplomacy and limits the effectiveness of even peaceful means of conflict resolution.

Formally, of course, countless treaties and agreements concluded over decades have proscribed the use of military force except in self-defense. Such morally based constraints no doubt continue to motivate many in their opposition to the use of force. Even more powerful, however, are more tangible constraints. Increasingly, the citizens of democratic nations appear unwilling to underwrite military interventions with either blood or treasure. When one looks at the history of the twentieth century, it is clear that the moral basis for restraint in the use of force has carried only limited weight. It has been the coupling of these ethical concerns with the current unwillingness to sacrifice either money or lives for government objectives that seems to have turned the tide against military interventions.

In the 1950s, for example, the populations of most European powers expressed clearly their unwillingness to support military operations in most parts of the world, the one possible exception being a direct attack on themselves. Even the French proved unwilling in 1958 to continue paying the very high price of France's colonialist military intervention in Algeria.*

The watershed for the United States came 10 years later in Southeast Asia. The popularity of U.S. military operations in Grenada, Panama, and Kuwait may seem to contradict this assertion, but a look at the complete record of U.S. military operations since the withdrawal from Vietnam makes it clear that popular support for military interventions seems to hinge on their brevity, bloodlessness, and immediate—and evident—success. The abrupt U.S. withdrawals from Beirut in 1983–84 and Somalia in 1993–94, following isolated, if dramatic, incidents in which U.S. forces suffered casualties, demonstrate clearly the U.S. public's opposition to interventions that appear to be either difficult or costly.

Nor is the phenomenon restricted to popular attitudes. Episodes like Beirut and Somalia seem to have impressed both the executive and legislative branches of the U.S. government, and both major political parties, profoundly. How else to explain the sudden termination of Operation Desert Storm short of its logical strategic objective of deposing the source of the problem, Saddam Hussein? And how else to explain the current bipartisan hesitancy to undertake even the most minor military tasks, such as restoring the democratically elected government in Haiti?

The unpopularity of military operations helps to explain why the United States and European governments came to believe in the early 1990s that interventions should be carried out through the UN. Trapped in the dilemma—popular pressures to intervene more frequently in the

---

* [Algeria revolted against the French in 1958.]

affairs of other states, but even more powerful forces poised to oppose the threat or use of military force—the U.S. and European nations turned decidedly away from unilateral actions and toward multinational activities sanctioned, and often managed, by the UN.

The greater cooperativeness of the Soviet Union that began in the late 1980s made the turn to the UN feasible, of course, but it did not necessitate this major shift in policy. Indeed, as the Soviet military threat receded and the United States emerged increasingly as the world's sole military superpower, one might have thought that the United States would have demonstrated a greater propensity to act unilaterally, or at least in coalition with its traditional allies. All else being equal, it is certainly less complicated to act in one of these modes than under the UN's aegis [sponsorship]. Just the opposite has occurred, however, with both the Bush and Clinton administrations turning to the UN in virtually every relevant situation.

Governments turned to the UN for several reasons. First, the democracies have shared the goal of creating effective collective means of resolving conflicts since World War II. When the Soviet Union began in the mid-1980s to use its veto power far less frequently, achieving this goal appeared to be possible for the first time.

Second, on more practical grounds, acting through the UN is a means of sharing the burdens of maintaining international stability—both the tangible burden in money and lives, and the political burden of imposing one's will on others. The United States may pay close to one-third the cost of UN peacekeeping operations, but that is still better than the three-thirds costs of unilateral actions. Action through the UN, moreover, both legitimates and sanctions military interventions in the eyes of domestic and foreign audiences. As was demonstrated in the Kuwait case, for example, recourse to the UN's formal procedures for the exercise of collective self-defense was essential both to retain popular support in the United States and to hold together the coalition of nations that actually fought the war.

There is, however, a third reason for the turn to the UN, which, even if not perceived by decision makers, has also motivated more frequent recourse to the world body. When government officials find themselves confronting the intervention dilemma—pressures to act, but a distinctly remote possibility of acting successfully due to the difficulty of credibly threatening the use of force—they have an additional incentive to turn to the UN.

Dealing with civil conflicts through the UN enables government decision makers to shift the locus of responsibility. Introducing the issue in the Security Council, cajoling action by the world body, is itself a means of satisfying those constituencies demanding intervention. Turning to the UN, in effect, says, "We are acting, we are drawing attention to the issue, we are writing resolutions, stepping up pressures, persuading others to join us, etc." At the same time, if UN diplomacy and political pressures prove inadequate and the situation remains unacceptable, it appears not to be the government's failure, but the failure of the world body. Government officials in many countries have been more than willing to practice such scapegoating, as if the UN were able to act more effectively or ambitiously than its key members permit.

Naturally, this attempt to sidestep the intervention dilemma by acting through the UN failed in many cases. The paper demonstration of action provided by activity in the UN Security Council proved of only limited value in stanching political pressures for effective interventions in conflicts in foreign nations. At the same time, the cloak of respectability conferred by the UN proved of only limited utility in confronting the popular reluctance to undertake military tasks of any substantial difficulty or cost.

In most civil conflict situations, if political constraints make recourse to military force infeasible, the intervenor's leverage is limited. If a civil war is not ripe for resolution, if contending factions are not yet convinced that the price of continued warfare exceeds any potential gain, mediators cannot succeed regardless of their skills. In such cases, only a willingness to separate the combatants forcefully and impose a settlement has even a chance of ending the war, and then only so long as the intervenor is willing to continue sitting on the belligerents.

Similarly, as has been seen repeatedly in recent years, neither political nor economic pressures are typically powerful enough to dislodge dictators who see everything to lose, and little to gain, by stepping down peacefully. If the use of military power is not a credible instrument of last resort, then the intervenor's objective is often impossible from the outset. In many situations, without a credible threat of effective military action, UN diplomats and mediators are no more effective than national representatives in similarly constrained circumstances.

The UN has been a useful vehicle for taking limited military actions to help mitigate the more visible aspects of conflict situations—ensuring the delivery of humanitarian assistance, implementing cease-fires, and so forth—but the use of real force to impose solutions has almost always been ruled out. The prospect of significant financial costs and, particularly, loss of life, has proven just as powerful a deterrent to forceful interventions in foreign nations under the UN flag as under national insignia. As a result, in most UN peace operations, the rules of engagement have carefully specified constraints that both ensured that UN forces remained out of harm's way and made it impossible for them to enforce solutions. In the one case in which such constraints were eased [Somalia], and casualties occurred, the haste with which even the world's greatest military power withdrew doomed the mission to failure and proved to many the weaknesses of the UN.

Emerging from the Dilemma

Currently, both the administration and most members of Congress who have addressed the issue are seeking to restrain the number and scope of military interventions by the UN. The greater emphasis now being placed on "realism" in deciding when and how to intervene, as spelled out in the administration's 1994 peacekeeping policy, is essentially an attempt to break out of the intervention dilemma by mustering pragmatism as the first line of defense against the political impulse to intervene. Rwanda was the first clear demonstration of the new policy. Following the brutal intensification of the civil war in that troubled country in April 1994, the United States worked to maintain realistic boundaries on the strengthening of the UN mission there.

A greater emphasis on realism in approving UN interventions is clearly appropriate at present, given the huge expansion in the organization's agenda over the past few years and its clear inability to carry out many of the tasks that have already been assigned to it. But the United States should not define a realistic intervention policy too narrowly, for failures to intervene are not without their own costs. By committing itself to making the changes that would make the UN an effective instrument for containing world conflict, the United States would make possible, eventually, a more ambitious definition of what is realistic.

The United States and most other great powers may not have significant, tangible interests in Rwanda, but they do have economic and political stakes in other places that have been, or might in the future be, rent by civil conflicts. The realism that long delayed military intervention in Haiti cost the United States dearly, for example, in terms of losses for Americans who do business in Haiti, in terms of the cost of dealing with Haitian refugees on the seas and in the United States, and, more important, in terms of the impact that U.S. timidity had on perceptions around the world of the nation's fitness to lead the world community.

In other cases, too, realism defined too narrowly could have profound long-term effects. The jury is still out on the effects of the U.S. and European failure to intervene decisively in the civil wars in the former Yugoslavia. The U.S. decision was right not to put troops on the ground there without a peace agreement, excepting the deterrent force in Macedonia, but the consequences of this realism are not yet clear. The potential for new conflicts in the Balkans, and for the broadening of old ones, remains high. Such contingencies could engulf the entire region in war and trigger even broader and longer-term conflicts among the great powers.

And, finally, there is a moral cost of nonintervention that should not be ignored. The impulse for intervention is not some fad, nor a plot foisted on innocent populations by a liberal clique, as some have maintained. It reflects the deeply held humanitarian values of democratic populations in the contemporary age. Five hundred thousand people may have died prematurely in Rwanda in 1994, many of them children. How do Americans feel about that tragedy? Could it have been prevented or, at least, restrained in its consequences? How would Americans feel if it were the case that an investment of a few hundred million dollars could have prevented one-half the Rwandan deaths? Every person evaluates such trade-offs, or potential trade-offs, differently. They not only have to judge the cost to Rwandans against the cost to themselves, but must also reach a judgment about the likely effectiveness of the intervention. There is no single right or wrong answer.

Civil conflicts and humanitarian tragedies affect every American by indicating a failure in fundamental human values. They also affect Americans more tangibly, by diminishing business activity, by disrupting financial markets, by stimulating population movements that impose economic burdens and political disruptions on neighboring countries, by posing risks of broader conflicts that would upset world peace and prosperity in momentous terms. If the United States could prevent such conflicts for free, and for certain, citizens would clearly want the government to act. Judging when it is realistic to act is a more tricky endeavor, which requires hardheaded assessments of options *and* interests.

The recent failures of the UN in a number of interventions—more properly, the failures of the members of the UN in a number of interventions—should cause Americans to be modest in their estimates of what is realistic. This is understandable. But the United States can, and should, push the boundaries of realism, by working to make the UN a more effective instrument for interventions in conflicts. If the United States had greater confidence in the UN's abilities, it would be more ambitious in what it considered realistic. Any number of reports have spelled out the reforms that are required.

- Most important, the UN needs to be taken seriously as an institution and reorganized and professionalized accordingly. Necessary reforms go well beyond the symbolically important step of establishing an independent inspector general, the keystone of current U.S. demands for UN reform. To become an effective organization, the UN requires, at a minimum, a streamlined bureaucracy beginning at the most senior levels, the appointment of a deputy secretary general to manage the organization and coordinate its component agencies, the assignment of clear responsibilities to senior officials, and the imposition of a professional personnel system grounded firmly on merit.
- The financial aspects of peacekeeping and other UN military activities need to be handled in a more routine manner. The budgets for peace operations should be placed in a single account and integrated into the regular UN budget. Their costs should be apportioned to member

states on the basis of the same formula used for other organizational expenses.

• The UN also needs to be given the means of conducting military operations effectively. This includes the financial resources necessary to build an infrastructure capable of providing effective command, training, and logistical capabilities, and sufficient resources to carry out the mandates of individual missions effectively. Member states need to earmark military units for potential use in UN operations and to give them the specialized training and equipment they need to be effective. Consideration also should be given to permitting the Security Council, through an organization governed by the Military Staff Committee, to recruit a small quick reaction force composed of individual volunteers. Such a force would make it possible to establish the vanguard of a new peace force promptly after a Security Council decision to intervene.

UN reform has long been discussed, but little has been accomplished. The time is ripe for a far-reaching initiative. All that is required is a coherent U.S. position with the support of both the president and Congress, determined and persistent U.S. leadership, and a little common sense.

Finally, the executive branch would be in a better position to judge when interventions are realistic—and when they are not—if it worked more closely with Congress on these issues, long before it reached the point of decision. Legislators necessarily know more than the executive about the beliefs of their constituents—about the balance in any one situation between the interventionary impulse and the bias against the use of military force. This is not to say that executive branch decisions should always be determined by opinion polls. Consultations with Congress can help to reveal not only what the public believes, but also what actions and policies might encourage positive changes in public opinion.

Closer coordination between the branches on these issues also has the potential to build political support either for interventions or for decisions not to intervene, whichever is relevant. Congress clearly believes that its financial powers are short-circuited when the administration supports the initiation of UN missions without real consultations and then hands the bill to the legislature. The leadership group and ranking members of key committees clearly should be consulted prior to U.S. approval of any UN mission. A more serious problem concerns those UN missions that will include U.S. combat forces. In these cases, any administration is well advised, in its own interest and in the interest of sustaining its policy, to seek formal congressional approval of the commitment of U.S. forces.

Although the consultative process between the branches on UN peacekeeping and potential military interventions improved during 1994, the accession of a Republican majority in Congress has led to legislative initiatives that would make it virtually impossible for the United States to make use of UN peace operations to advance its own interest in a more stable and humane world. Such legislation has already been passed by the House and will be taken up by the Senate later this year [1995]. It would be tragic if the House bill, particularly its provisions that would sharply cut back U.S. contributions to UN peace operations, were permitted to stand.

As the branch of government most directly attuned to currents in public opinion, and necessarily most responsive to them, Congress can play a special role in helping the executive branch to break out of the intervention dilemma. A more forthcoming position by the executive branch on the establishment of formal consultative procedures might help to avoid the passage of crippling legislation, enabling the United States to move beyond the current debate and on to more constructive actions to strengthen the UN's ability to carry out peace operations.

82
"Why America Must Not Go into Bosnia"

Charles Krauthammer

Now that we are marching into Bosnia [1995], we will hear endless debate about the rights and wrongs and origins of the war. Everyone has a theory of what went wrong and why. The most plausible, in my view, is that the seminal mistake was the West's recognition of Croatia and Slovenia and then Bosnia—in effect, the de-recognition of the Yugoslav federation—without having first demanded, as a condition for recognition, ironclad provisions for respecting the rights of minorities and prior agreement with the other member republics of Yugoslavia on final frontiers.

It is, nonetheless, far too late for history. The issue looming before the nation today has the potential to create an entirely new history whose origins will not at all be obscure—the history of the peace "implementation force" (IFOR) that the administration wishes to dispatch to Bosnia to enforce the peace accords initialed last week in Dayton.

My view is quite straightforward: The deployment of 20,000 or so American ground troops to police a cease-fire in Bosnia would be a serious mistake for the United States.

This is a no-win situation for the U.S. Such a deployment can end in one of two ways. First, a humiliating retreat, as in Somalia, but with the stakes higher and the commitment larger, after some incident involving a major loss of American life and cries from the Congress and from the American people for withdrawal. Or, more likely, we will persevere, indeed escalate our involvement, send more troops to protect existing troops and be caught in a long-term, static, and defensive deployment with painful losses, ambiguous rules of engagement, escalating friction among NATO allies—most of whom do not want to remain there but would do so under American leadership—and no way out.

These practical, tactical reasons are obvious and have been well rehearsed in the current debate on a Bosnian peace force: no definable objective, no identifiable enemy, no exit strategy. But there is a larger strategic reason to be wary of a Bosnian involvement. And that is: To use heavily armed, combat-ready American ground troops as peacekeepers is to fundamentally misunderstand America's role as the world's sole remaining superpower, and to fundamentally miscast the finest, most powerful military in the world.

A sole superpower is the ultimate balancer of power in the world, or, to put it another way, the balancer of last resort. Its geopolitical role is to intervene militarily when a regional balance has been catastrophically overthrown and global stability threatened. Iraq's conquest of Kuwait and its looming threat to the rest of the Arabian peninsula was just such an event. It could be reversed only by American will and American action. And it was so reversed.

That is the role of a superpower. It is decidedly *not* the role of a superpower to place itself between the combatants in a civil war of marginal importance to the world balance of power—indeed of marginal importance to the regional balance of power—among unreconciled parties who have already shown a propensity for killing and kidnapping peacekeepers, and who will have a much greater incentive to do exactly that when the peacekeepers are wearing the uniform of the most powerful and, one might add, the most mediagenic country in the world.

When America sends peacekeepers, it is not sending peacekeepers. It is sending targets. There is a reason why, for the last 50 years, Americans have generally not been used in peacekeeping operations. Peacekeeping is the job of small countries with no particular interest in the outcome of a conflict; who are of no particular geopolitical importance to the combatants; whose very marginality is an affirmation of credible neutrality.

It is far, far harder for a superpower to remain neutral, and even harder still to be perceived as neutral, in most conflicts. And in the Bosnian war, in particular, the United States has been decidedly not neutral. We have made our sympathies with the Bosnian Muslim side abundantly clear in our declarations, in our use of air power, and indeed in our promises to arm the Bosnian government even as we act as peace-keepers—an absurd contradiction of the very idea of peacekeeping.

Imagine a president who came before Congress and said that the Israeli-Palestinian peace process required the presence of 20,000 American troops on the ground in the West Bank to separate the combatants and help them make peace. He would be summarily shown the door. And yet he is asking the Congress to approve a similar deployment in not a two-sided but a three-sided civil war that has been conducted with a much higher level of ferocity than any Israeli-Palestinian encounter of the last 25 years.

Well, you might say, don't we have American peacekeepers in the Sinai? Yes, but they are observers. They do not use heavy tanks. Their basic weapons are binoculars and cell phones. If all that was required of the U.S. in Bosnia was a token observer force as in Sinai, to lend the prestige and the moral support of the U.S. to some settlement agreed to by the warring parties, I could see no objection to that. It would be lightly armed, easily deployed, and easily withdrawn. Its function would not be to fight or to prevent others from fighting, but simply to give the imprimatur of the United States to a self-enforcing agreement among the parties themselves.

And that is the key point. If the combatants in Bosnia are serious about ending the fighting and accepting roughly the distribution of territory and roughly the balance of power now on the ground, then they should do it and enforce it themselves, perhaps with the help of a few blue helmets from truly neutral countries. If they are not, then there is no peace to keep. And between such antagonists is no place to interpose American troops.

What about the final argument, the case based on purely American national interests? Most advocates of Bosnia intervention have given up arguing that the United States has any significant inherent interest in Bosnia. They base their national interest argument, instead, on the collateral damage non-deployment would do to less disputable American interests: NATO cohesion, European stability, and American credibility. Take them in turn:

NATO. There is no doubt and no denying that non-deployment would be a blow to NATO. Indeed, the single most powerful argument *in favor* of deployment invokes NATO: To renege on this promise of American relief for our NATO allies already trapped in Bosnia would be the worst blow Clinton has yet dealt to NATO cohesion. Whatever the strategic folly of having our troops in Bosnia, the argument goes, our allies expect us now to take the lead on the ground—a reasonable and powerful expectation that is based on a presidential promise.

Yes, reneging on such a promise would be a blow. Nonetheless, following through and actually sending the troops would be worse. No good outcome of such a deployment is foreseeable. Either it results, as I indicated above, in humiliating retreat—in which case our allies are left high and dry and betrayed. Or it lingers painfully: We persist in a thankless, unwinnable, and costly operation, a source of constant recrimination and resentment among the allies that erodes and finally exhausts the alliance's 50-year store of solidarity. There is no good way out. Better, therefore, to inflict one blow to NATO now than an inevitable series of blows in agonizing succession later.

Yet one does not abandon a promise blithely. We should—and can—demonstrate concern for our allies and assuage whatever feelings of disappointment or betrayal might follow our decision not to deploy a peacekeeping force. How? By offering the immediate deployment of American ground troops in sizable number with the sole objective of evacuating any ally who wishes to withdraw now that we would not be going in.

This, at least, would be a mission with a beginning and an end, with a clear operational objective and a clear political objective as well. It would demonstrate to our allies—particularly our Gulf War allies, the British and the French—that our decision not to send 20,000 ground troops on peacekeeping duty is animated neither by timidity nor by any unconcern about them. Indeed, we would risk our own soldiers to extricate them. But not to join them in a quagmire.

EUROPE. The second national-interest argument is that we must intervene in Bosnia because of the continuing, indeed, intensifying threat the war poses to European stability. This one, a staple of the congressional testimony offered by administration officials pushing the peacekeeping force, is nonsense. The threat of the Bosnian war spreading to the rest of Europe has been raised monthly for the last four years. It proves more hollow by the day. With the Croatian reconquest of the Krajina in August [1995] and the recent Serb-Croat accord on Eastern Slavonia, the war is in fact *contracting*. There are warnings all the time about the war spreading to Macedonia or Kosovo or Albania or even Greece and Turkey. Where is the evidence for the spread of this war?

Yes, there was 1914. But this is not 1914: There is no Austria-Hungarian empire on the verge of collapse. There is no Ottoman empire waiting to be carved up. There is no drive for territorial expansion among the European powers. Imperialism is now 50 years dead. The idea of great European powers occupying other countries for the glory of God and country exists only in parody and old movies. There is no European interest in the Balkans other than staying out of the morass. The idea of the Great Powers going to war over the control of this cursed, tragic piece of land is simply absurd.

Which leaves us with the last question:

AMERICAN CREDIBILITY. Yes, whenever the United States makes a commitment and then reneges on it, its credibility is damaged. That is a cost of refusing to deploy, and it must not be denied. But the responsibility for that cost lies squarely with the administration that made that foolish promise without proper reflection, not with a Congress trying to avert the consequences of that ill-considered promise.

Moreover, one has to weigh what would happen to American credibility were we to deploy and then withdraw under pressure after a demonstration of impotence as in Mogadishu or Beirut. Ask yourself: Is American credibility greater after our entry and then withdrawal from Somalia than it would have been had we never gone into Somalia in the first place?

Credibility is not just the weakest reason for intervention. It is the most dangerous. It is weak because it is circular: We are going in because we have said we are going in. It is dangerous because it can only be vindicated by success, and thus is a spur to continuous escalation in pursuit of success.

By severing American involvement from any concrete national interest, the credibility argument creates a new interest of ever expanding demands. Yet Bosnia is a situation where even the most ardent advocates of intervention are so skeptical of success that they promise to leave in one year. That is a tacit way of saying "no escalation." But then what kind of credibility are we demonstrating when the greatest power on the globe injects itself massively into a small war pledging in advance to slink away on a railroad timetable regardless of the outcome?

What should the Congress do? It should reject the idea of sending a large, heavily armed American combat presence to be an active peacekeeping or implementation force in Bosnia. Yes, this will occasion great diplomatic difficulty. It may cause the current agreement, based on an expectation of American involvement, to unravel. That would be an unfortunate result, but it would have to be laid at the feet of the Bosnian parties themselves. They cannot expect the United States to impose a peace that they are unwilling to make on their own.

What will happen if Dayton unravels because we are unwilling to enforce it? What will happen is that, if the parties are interested in peace, they will have to reconvene in Dayton or elsewhere. We will have to go back to them and redo any agreement until it becomes one that can stand on its own, with perhaps a token NATO observer force or even some UN blue helmets to act as the local constabulary and police a separation zone.

We make the parties this offer: Make a real peace as in Sinai and we will support you. But nothing less. It is your choice. It is your country. But these are our soldiers.

Discussion Questions

1. In your view, what constitutes the greatest threats to U.S. national security? What is the single most important threat?

2. Do you support U.S. military involvement (putting American lives at risk) in humanitarian missions? To quell civil unrest and ethnic warfare? To protect traditional allies against attack? If you do, would you be willing to fight? If you do not, what might be the consequences of refusing to become involved?

Appendix of Supreme Court Cases

Marbury v. Madison (1803)

The power of judicial review—the authority of the federal courts to determine the constitutionality of state and federal legislative acts—was established early in the nation's history in the case of Marbury v. Madison *(1803). While the doctrine of judicial review is now firmly entrenched in the American judicial process, the outcome of* Marbury *was by no means a sure thing. The doctrine had been outlined in* The Federalist *No. 78, and had been relied upon implicitly in earlier, lower federal court cases, but there were certainly sentiments among some of the Founders to suggest that only Congress ought to be able to judge the constitutionality of its acts.*

[The facts leading up to the decision in Marbury v. Madison *tell an intensely political story. Efforts to reform the federal judiciary had been ongoing with the Federalist administration of President Adams. Following the defeat of the Federalist party in 1800, and the election of Thomas Jefferson as president, the Federalist Congress passed an act reforming the judiciary. The act gave outgoing President Adams authority to appoint several Federalist justices of the peace before Jefferson's term as president began. This would have enabled the Federalist party to retain a large measure of power.*

Marbury was appointed to be a justice of the peace by President Adams, but his commission, signed by the president and sealed by the secretary of state, without which he could not assume office, was not delivered to him before President Jefferson took office March 4, 1803. Jefferson refused to order James Madison, his secretary of state, to deliver the commission. Marbury, in turn, filed an action in the U.S. Supreme Court seeking an order—called a writ of mandamus—directing the secretary of state to compel the delivery of the commission.

The Constitution grants the Supreme Court original jurisdiction in only a limited number of cases—those involving ambassadors, public ministers, and those in which a state is a party; in the remaining cases, the Court has authority only as an appellate court. When it acts according to its original jurisdiction, the Court exercises initial authority over a controversy, just like a trial court, as distinguished from the more limited authority it exercises when a case is presented as an appeal from a lower court's decision.

In 1789, Congress passed legislation setting up the federal courts, called the Judiciary Act of 1789. That legislation gave the Supreme Court the original authority to "issue writs of mandamus in cases warranted by the principles and usage of law. . . ." Thus, the ultimate question in Marbury v. Madison *was whether Congress could, by statute, enlarge the original jurisdiction of the Court.*

The Court first considered whether Marbury's appointment was complete—and therefore irrevocable—before Jefferson took office. Under the law, the appointment was deemed complete when the president signed the commission and the secretary of state sealed it; the appointment was a completed fact at that time, and was not dependent upon delivery. Therefore, the Court found that Marbury was entitled to his commission. The Court then decided that by withholding the commission, Secretary of State Madison was violating Marbury's legal rights. The remaining question was whether the Supreme Court could issue an order compelling the delivery of the commission.]

CHIEF JUSTICE MARSHALL delivered the opinion of the Court.

. . . It is, then, the opinion of the Court,

1st. That by signing the commission of Mr. Marbury, the President of the United States appointed him a justice of peace for the county of Washington, in the District of Columbia; and that the seal of the United States, affixed thereto by the Secretary of State, is conclusive testimony of the verity of the signature, and of the completion of the appointment, and that the appointment conferred on him a legal right to the office for the space of five years.

2d. That, having this legal title to the office, he has a consequent right to the commission; a refusal to deliver which is a plain violation of that right, for which the laws of his country afford him a remedy.

It remains to be inquired whether,

3d. He is entitled to the remedy for which he applies. This depends on,

1st. The nature of the writ applied for; and,

2d. The power of this court.

* * *

This . . . is a plain case for a mandamus, either to deliver the commission, or a copy of it from the record; and it only remains to be inquired,

Whether it can issue from this court.

The act to establish the judicial courts of the United States authorizes the Supreme Court "to issue writs of mandamus in cases warranted by the principles and usages of law, to any courts appointed, or persons holding office, under the authority of the United States."

The Secretary of State, being a person holding an office under the authority of the United States, is precisely within the letter of the description, and if this court is not authorized to issue a writ of mandamus to such an officer, it must be because the law is unconstitutional, and therefore absolutely incapable of conferring the authority, and assigning the duties which its words purport to confer and assign.

The constitution vests the whole judicial power of the United States in one Supreme Court, and such inferior courts as congress shall, from time to time, ordain and establish. This power is expressly extended to all cases arising under the laws of the United States; and, consequently, in some form, may be exercised over the present case; because the right claimed is given by a law of the United States.

In the distribution of this power it is declared that "the Supreme Court shall have original jurisdiction in all cases affecting ambassadors, other public ministers and consuls, and those in which a state shall be a party. In all other cases, the Supreme Court shall have appellate jurisdiction."

* * *

To enable this court, then, to issue a mandamus, it must be shown to be an exercise of appellate jurisdiction, or to be necessary to enable them to exercise appellate jurisdiction.

* * *

It is the essential criterion of appellate jurisdiction, that it revises and corrects the proceedings in a cause already instituted, and does not create that cause. . . . [Y]et to issue such a writ to an officer for the delivery of a paper, is in effect the same as to sustain an original action for that paper, and, therefore, seems not to belong to appellate, but to original jurisdiction.

The authority, therefore, given to the Supreme Court, by the act establishing the judicial courts of the United States, to issue writs of mandamus to public officers, appears not to be warranted by the constitution; and it becomes necessary to inquire whether a jurisdiction so conferred can be exercised.

The question, whether an act, repugnant to the constitution, can become the law of the land, is a question deeply interesting to the United States; but, happily, not of an intricacy proportioned to its interest. It seems only necessary to recognize certain principles, supposed to have been long and well established, to decide it.

That the people have an original right to establish, for their future government, such principles, as, in their opinion, shall most conduce to their own happiness is the basis on which the whole American fabric has been erected. The exercise of this original right is a very great exertion; nor can it, nor ought it, to be frequently repeated. The principles, therefore, so established, are deemed fundamental. And as the authority from which they proceed is supreme, and can seldom act, they are designed to be permanent.

This original and supreme will organizes the government, and assigns to different departments their respective powers. It may either stop here, or establish certain limits not to be transcended by those departments.

The government of the United States is of the latter description. The powers of the legislature are defined and limited; and that those limits may not be mistaken, or forgotten, the constitution is written. To what purpose are powers limited, and to what purpose is that limitation committed to writing, if these limits may, at any time, be passed by those intended to be restrained? The distinction between a government with limited and unlimited powers is abolished, if those limits do not confine the persons on whom they are imposed, and if acts prohibited and acts allowed, are of equal obligation. It is a proposition too plain to be contested, that the constitution controls any legislative act repugnant to it; or, that the legislature may alter the constitution by an ordinary act.

Between these alternatives there is no middle ground. The constitution is either a superior paramount law, unchangeable by ordinary means, or it is on a level with ordinary legislative acts, and, like other acts, is alterable when the legislature shall please to alter it.

If the former part of the alternative be true, then a legislative act contrary to the constitution is not law: if the latter part be true, then written constitutions are absurd attempts, on the part of the people, to limit a power in its own nature illimitable.

Certainly all those who have framed written constitutions contemplate them as forming the fundamental and paramount law of the nation, and, consequently, the theory of every such government must be, that an act of the legislature, repugnant to the constitution, is void.

This theory is essentially attached to a written constitution, and, is consequently, to be considered, by this court, as one of the fundamental principles of our society. It is not therefore to be lost sight of in the further consideration of this subject.

If an act of the legislature, repugnant to the constitution, is void, does it, notwithstanding its invalidity, bind the courts, and oblige them to give it effect? Or, in other words, though it be not law, does it constitute a rule as operative as if it was a law? This would be to overthrow in fact what was established in theory; and would seem, at first view, an absurdity too gross to be insisted on.

*　*　*

It is emphatically the province and duty of the judicial department to say what the law is. Those who apply the rule to particular cases, must of necessity expound and interpret that rule. If two laws conflict with each other, the courts must decide on the operation of each.

So if a law be in opposition to the constitution; if both the law and the constitution apply to a particular case, so that the court must either decide that case conformably to the law, disregarding the constitution; or conformably to the constitution, disregarding the law; the court must determine which of these conflicting rules governs the case. This is of the very essence of judicial duty.

If, then, the courts are to regard the constitution, and the constitution is superior to any ordinary act of the legislature, the constitution, and not such ordinary act, must govern the case to which they both apply.

Those, then, who controvert the principle that the constitution is to be considered, in court, as a paramount law, are reduced to the necessity of maintaining that courts must close their eyes on the constitution, and see only the law.

This doctrine would subvert the very foundation of all written constitutions. It would declare that an act which, according to the principles and theory of our government, is entirely void, is yet, in practice, completely obligatory. It would declare that if the legislature shall do what is expressly forbidden, such act, notwithstanding the express prohibition, is in reality effectual. It would be giving to the legislature a practical and real omnipotence, with the same breath which professes to restrict their powers within narrow limits. It is prescribing limits, and declaring that those limits may be passed at pleasure.

That it thus reduces to nothing what we have deemed the greatest improvement on political institutions, a written constitution, would of itself be sufficient, in America, where written constitutions have been viewed with so much reverence, for rejecting the construction. But the peculiar expressions of the constitution of the United States furnish additional arguments in favour of its rejection.

The judicial power of the United States is extended to all cases arising under the constitution.

Could it be the intention of those who gave this power, to say that in using it the constitution should not be looked into? That a case arising under the constitution should be decided without examining the instrument under which it arises?

This is too extravagant to be maintained.

In some cases, then, the constitution must be looked into by the judges.

. . . [I]t is apparent, that the framers of the constitution contemplated that instrument as a rule for the government of courts, as well as of the legislature.

Why otherwise does it direct the judges to take an oath to support it? This oath certainly applies in an especial manner, to their conduct in their official character. How immoral to impose it on them, if they were to be used as the instruments, and the knowing instruments, for violating what they swear to support!

The oath of office, too, imposed by the legislature, is completely demonstrative of the legislative opinion on this subject.

* * *

Why does a judge swear to discharge his duties agreeably to the constitution of the United States, if that constitution forms no rule for his government? If it is closed upon him, and cannot be inspected by him?

If such be the real state of things, this is worse than solemn mockery. To prescribe, or to take this oath, becomes equally a crime.

It is also not entirely unworthy of observation, that in declaring what shall be the supreme law of the land, the constitution itself is first mentioned; and not the laws of the United States generally, but those only which shall be made in pursuance of the constitution, have that rank.

Thus, the particular phraseology of the constitution of the United States confirms and strengthens the principle, supposed to be essential to all written constitutions, that a law repugnant to the constitution is void; and that courts, as well as other departments, are bound by that instrument.

McCulloch v. Maryland (1819)

Early in the nation's history, the United States Supreme Court interpreted the powers of the national government expansively. The first Supreme Court case to directly address the scope of federal authority under the Constitution was McCulloch v. Maryland *(1819). The facts were straightforward: Congress created the Bank of the United States—to the dismay of many states who viewed the creation of a national bank as a threat to the operation of banks within their own state borders. As a result, when a branch of the Bank of the United States was opened in Maryland, that state attempted to limit the bank's ability to do business under a law that imposed taxes on all banks not chartered by the state.*

In an opinion authored by Chief Justice Marshall, the Court considered two questions: whether Congress had the authority to create a national bank; and whether Maryland could in turn tax it. Marshall's answer to these two questions defends an expansive theory of implied powers for the national government and propounds the principle of national supremacy with an eloquence rarely found in judicial decisions.

CHIEF JUSTICE JOHN MARSHALL delivered the opinion of the Court.

The first question made in the cause is, has Congress power to incorporate a bank? The power now contested was exercised by the first Congress elected under the present constitution. The bill for incorporating the Bank of the United States did not steal upon an unsuspecting legislature, and pass unobserved. Its principle was completely understood, and was opposed with equal zeal and ability. . . . In discussing this question, the counsel for the state of Maryland have deemed it of some importance, in the construction of the constitution, to consider that instrument not as emanating from the people, but as the act of sovereign and independent states. The powers of the general government, it has been said, are delegated by the states, who alone are truly sovereign; and must be exercised in subordination to the states, who alone possess supreme dominion. . . . No political dreamer was ever wild enough to think of breaking down the lines which separate the states, and of compounding the American people into one common mass. Of consequence, when they act, they act in their states. But the measures they adopt do not, on that account, cease to be the measures of the people themselves, or become the measures of the state governments.

From these conventions the constitution derives its whole authority. The government proceeds directly from the people; is "ordained and established" in the name of the people; and is declared to be ordained, "in order to form a more perfect union, establish justice, insure domestic tranquility, and secure the blessings of liberty to themselves and to their posterity." The assent of the states, in their sovereign capacity, is implied in calling a convention, and thus submitting that instrument to the people. But the people were at perfect liberty to accept or reject it; and their act was final. It required not the affirmance, and could not be negatived, by the state governments. The constitution, when thus adopted, was of complete obligation, and bound the state sovereignties.

The government of the Union, then (whatever may be the influence of this fact on the case), is, emphatically, and truly, a government of the people. In form and in substance it emanates from them. Its powers are granted by them, and are to be exercised directly on them, and for their benefit.

This government is acknowledged by all to be one of enumerated powers. The principle, that it can exercise only the powers granted to it, is now universally admitted. But the question respecting the extent of the powers actually granted, is perpetually arising, and will probably continue to arise, as long as our system shall exist. The government of the United States though limited in its powers, is supreme; and its laws, when made in pursuance of the constitution, form the supreme law of the land, "anything in the constitution or laws of any state to the contrary notwithstanding."

* * *

A constitution, to contain an accurate detail of all the subdivisions of which its great powers will admit, and of all the means by which they may be carried into execution, would partake of the prolixity of a legal code, and could scarcely be embraced by the human mind. It would probably never be understood by the public. Its nature, therefore, requires, that only its great outlines should be marked, its important objects designated, and the minor ingredients which compose those objects be deduced from the nature of the objects themselves. . . . in considering this question, then, we must never forget, that it is a constitution we are expounding.

Although, among the enumerated powers of government, we do not find the word "bank" or "incorporation," we find the great powers to lay and collect taxes; to borrow money; to regulate commerce; to declare and conduct a war; and to raise and support armies and navies. The sword and the purse, all the external relations, and no inconsiderable portion of the industry of the nation, are entrusted to its government. . . . [I]t may with great reason be contended, that a government, entrusted with such ample powers, on the due execution of which the happiness and prosperity of the nation so vitally depends, must also be entrusted with ample means for their execution. The power being given, it is the interest of the nation to facilitate its execution. It can never be their interest, and cannot be presumed to have been their intention, to clog and embarrass its execution by withholding the most appropriate means. . . . It is, then, the subject of fair inquiry, how far such means may be employed.

The government which has a right to do an act, and has imposed on it the duty of performing that act, must, according to the dictates of reason, be allowed to select the means.

* * *

But the constitution of the United States has not left the right of Congress to employ the necessary means, for the execution of the powers conferred on the government, to general reasoning. To its enumeration of powers is added that of making "all laws which shall be necessary and proper, for carrying into execution the foregoing powers, and all other powers vested by this constitution, in the government of the United States, or in any department [or officer] thereof."

The counsel for the state of Maryland have urged various arguments, to prove that this clause . . . is really restrictive of the general right, which might otherwise be implied, of selecting means for executing the enumerated powers.

. . . [Maryland argues that] Congress is not empowered by it to make all laws, which may have relation to the powers conferred on the government, but such only as may be "necessary and proper" for carrying them into execution. The word "necessary" is considered as controlling the whole sentence, and as limiting the right to pass laws for the execution of the granted powers, to such as are indispensable, and without which the power would be nugatory. That it excludes the choice of means, and leaves to Congress, in each case, that only which is most direct and simple.

Is it true, that this is the sense in which the word "necessary" is always used? . . . We think it does not. If reference be had to its use, in the common affairs of the world, or in approved authors, we find that it frequently imports no more than that one thing is convenient, or useful, or essential to another. To employ the means necessary to an end, is generally understood as employing any means calculated to produce the end, and not as being confined to those single means, without which the end would be entirely unattainable.

Let this be done in the case under consideration. The subject is the execution of those great powers on which the welfare of a nation essentially depends. It must have been the intention of those who gave these powers, to insure, as far as human prudence could insure, their beneficial execution. This could not be done by confiding the choice of means to such narrow limits as not to leave it in the power of Congress to adopt any which might be appropriate, and which were conducive to the end. This provision is made in a constitution intended to endure for ages to come, and consequently, to be adapted to the various crises of human affairs. To have prescribed the means by which government should, in all future time, execute its powers, would have been to change, entirely, the character of the instrument, and give it the properties of a legal code. It would have been an unwise attempt to provide, by immutable rules, for exigencies which, if foreseen at all, must have been seen dimly, and which can be best provided for as they occur. To have declared that the best means shall not be used, but those alone without which the power given would be nugatory, would have been to deprive the legislature of the capacity to avail itself of experience, to exercise its reason, and to accommodate its legislation to circumstances. If we apply this principle of construction to any of the powers of the government, we shall find it so pernicious in its operation that we shall be compelled to discard it.

* * *

We admit, as all must admit, that the powers of the government are limited, and that its limits are not to be transcended. But we think the sound construction of the constitution must allow to the national legislature that discretion, with respect to the means by which the powers it confers are to be carried into execution, which will enable that body to perform the high duties assigned to it, in the manner most beneficial to the people. Let the end be legitimate, let it be within the scope of the constitution, and all means which are appropriate, which are plainly adapted to that end, which are not prohibited, but consist with the letter and spirit of the constitution, are constitutional.

* * *

It being the opinion of the court that the act incorporating the bank is constitutional, and that the power of establishing a branch in the state of Maryland might be properly exercised by the bank itself, we proceed to inquire: Whether the state of Maryland may, without violating the constitution, tax that branch?

That the power of taxation is one of vital importance; that it is retained by the states; that it is not abridged by the grant of a similar power to the government of the Union; that it is to be concurrently exercised by the two governments; are truths which have never been denied. But, such is the paramount character of the constitution that its capacity to withdraw any subject from the action of even this power, is admitted. . . . [T]he paramount character [of the Constitution] would seem to restrain, as it certainly may restrain, a state from such other exercise of this power as is in its nature incompatible with, and repugnant to, the constitutional laws of the Union. A law, absolutely repugnant to another, as entirely repeals that other as if express terms of repeal were used.

* * *

This great principle is, that the constitution and the laws made in pursuance thereof are supreme; that they control the constitution and laws of the respective states, and cannot be controlled by them. From this, which may be almost termed an axiom, other propositions are adduced as corollaries, on the truth or error of which, and on their application to this case, the cause has been supposed to depend. These are, 1st. That a power to create implies a power to preserve. 2d. That a power to destroy, if wielded by a different hand, is hostile to, and incompatible with, these powers to create and to preserve. 3d. That where this repugnance exists, that authority which is supreme must control, not yield to that over which it is supreme.

. . . [T]axation is said to be an absolute power, which acknowledges no other limits than those expressly prescribed in the constitution, and like sovereign powers of every other description, is trusted to the discretion of those who use it. But the very terms of this argument admit that the sovereignty of the state, in the article of taxation itself, is subordinate to, and may be controlled by the constitution of the United States. How far it has been controlled by that instrument must be a question of construction. In making this construction, no principle not declared can be admissible, which would defeat the legitimate operations of a supreme government.

* * *

All subjects over which the sovereign power of a state extends, are objects of taxation; but those over which it does not extend, are, upon the soundest principles, exempt from taxation. . . . The sovereignty of a state extends to everything which exists by its own authority, or is introduced by its permission; but does it extend to those means which are employed by Congress to carry into execution—powers conferred on that body by the people of the United States? We think it demonstrable that it does not. Those powers are not given by the people of a single state. They are given by the people of the United States, to a government whose laws, made in pursuance of the constitution, are declared to be supreme. Consequently, the people of a single state cannot confer a sovereignty which will extend over them.

If we apply the principle for which the state of Maryland contends, to the constitution generally, we shall find it capable of changing totally the character of that instrument. We shall find it capable of arresting all the measures of the government, and of prostrating it at the foot of the states. The American people have declared their constitution, and the laws made in pursuance thereof, to be supreme; but this principle would transfer the supremacy, in fact, to the states. If the controlling power of the states be established; if their supremacy as to taxation be acknowledged; what is to restrain their exercising this control in any shape they may please to give it? Their sovereignty is not confined to taxation. That is not the only mode in which it might be displayed. The question is, in truth, a question of supremacy; and if the right of the states to tax the means employed by the general government be conceded, the declaration that the constitution, and the laws made in pursuance thereof, shall be the supreme law of the land, is empty and unmeaning declamation.

* * *

We are unanimously of opinion, that the law passed by the legislature of Maryland, imposing a tax on the Bank of the United States, is unconstitutional and void. This opinion does not deprive the states of any resources which they originally possessed. It does not extend to a tax paid by the real property of the bank, in common with other real property within the state, nor to a tax imposed on the interest which the citizens of Maryland may hold in this institution, in common with other property of the same description throughout the state. But this is a tax on the operations of the bank, and is, consequently, a tax on the operation of an instrument employed by the government of the Union to carry its powers into execution. Such a tax must be unconstitutional.

Reversed.

Barron v. Baltimore (1833)

The declaration made in Barron v. Baltimore *(1833) that citizenship had a dual aspect—state and national—set the terms of the Supreme Court's interpretation of the Bill of Rights for nearly 150 years. The reasoning of the case proved persuasive even after the adoption of the Fourteenth Amendment, as the federal courts refused to extend the protections of the federal Constitution to citizens aggrieved by the actions of state or local governments.*

[*Barron brought suit in a federal court claiming that the city of Baltimore had appropriated his property for a public purpose without paying him just compensation. He asserted that the Fifth Amendment to the Constitution operated as a constraint upon both state and federal governments.*]

CHIEF JUSTICE JOHN MARSHALL delivered the opinion of the Court.

. . . The question presented is, we think, of great importance, but not of much difficulty. The constitution was ordained and established by the people of the United States for themselves, for their own government, and not for the government of the individual states. Each state established a constitution for itself, and in that constitution, provided such limitations and restrictions on the powers of its particular government, as its judgment dictated. The people of the United States framed such a government for the United States as they supposed best adapted to their situation and best calculated to promote their interests. The powers they conferred on this government were to be exercised by itself; and the limitations on power, if expressed in general terms, are naturally, and, we think, necessarily, applicable to the government created by the instrument. They are limitations of power granted in the instrument itself; not of distinct governments, framed by different persons and for different purposes.

If these propositions be correct, the fifth amendment must be understood as restraining the power of the general government, not as applicable to the states. In their several constitutions, they have imposed such restrictions on their respective governments, as their own wisdom suggested; such as they deemed most proper for themselves. It is a subject on which they judge exclusively, and with which others interfere no further than they are supposed to have a common interest.

* * *

Had the people of the several states, or any of them, required changes in their constitutions; had they required additional safe-guards to liberty from the apprehended encroachments of their particular governments; the remedy was in their own hands, and could have been applied by themselves. A convention could have been assembled by the discontented state, and the required improvements could have been made by itself.

. . . Had Congress engaged in the extraordinary occupation of improving the constitutions of the several states, by affording the people additional protection from the exercise of power by their own governments, in matters which concerned themselves alone, they would have declared this purpose in plain and intelligible language.

But it is universally understood, it is a part of the history of the day, that the great revolution which established the constitution of the United States, was not effected without immense opposition. Serious fears were extensively entertained, that those powers which the patriot statesmen, who then watched over the interests of our country, deemed essential to union, and to the attainment of those unvaluable objects for which union was sought, might be exercised in a manner dangerous to liberty. In almost every convention by which the constitution was adopted, amendments to guard against the abuse of power were recommended. These amendments demanded security against the apprehended encroachments of the general government—not against those of the local governments. In compliance with a sentiment thus generally expressed, to quiet fears thus extensively entertained, amendments were proposed by the required majority in congress, and adopted by the states. These amendments contain no expression indicating an intention to apply them to the state governments. This court cannot so apply them.

We are of opinion, that the provision in the fifth amendment to the constitution, declaring that private property shall not be taken for public use, without just compensation, is intended solely as a limitation on the exercise of power by the government of the United States, and is not applicable to the legislation of the states. We are, therefore, of opinion, that there is no repugnancy between the several acts of the general assembly of Maryland, given in evidence by the defendants at the trial of this cause, in the court of that state, and the constitution of the United States. This court, therefore, has no jurisdiction of the cause, and it is dismissed.

This cause came on to be heard, on the transcript of the record from the court of appeals for the western shore of the state of Maryland, and was argued by counsel: On consideration whereof, it is the opinion of this court, that there is no repugnancy between the several acts of the general assembly of Maryland, given in evidence by the defendants at the trial of this cause in the court of that state, and the constitution of the United States; whereupon, it is ordered and adjudged by this court, that this writ of error be and the same is hereby dismissed, for the want of jurisdiction.

Viability =
23 to 24
wks.

Roe v. Wade (1973) – *woman's right until the 3rd trimester*

One of the most significant changes in constitutional interpretation in the last or
twenty-five years has been the Court's willingness to look beyond the explicit after
language of the Bill of Rights to find unenumerated rights, such as the right to (s?)

privacy. In discovering such rights, the Court has engaged in what is known as substantive due process analysis—defining and articulating fundamental rights—distinct from its efforts to define the scope of procedural due process, when it decides what procedures the state and federal governments must follow to be fair in their treatment of citizens. The Court's move into the substantive due process area has generated much of the political discussion over the proper role of the Court in constitutional interpretation.

The case that has been the focal point for this debate is Roe v. Wade, *the 1973 case which held that a woman's right to privacy protected her decision to have an abortion. The right to privacy in matters relating to contraception and childbearing had been recognized in the 1965 decision of* Griswold v. Connecticut, *and was extended in subsequent decisions culminating in* Roe. *The theoretical issue of concern here relates back to the incorporation issue: Should the Supreme Court be able to prohibit the states not only from violating the express guarantees contained in the Bill of Rights, but its implied guarantees as well?*

[Texas law prohibited abortions except for "the purpose of saving the life of the mother." Plaintiff challenged the constitutionality of the statute, claiming that it infringed upon her substantive due process right to privacy.]

JUSTICE BLACKMUN delivered the opinion of the Court.

. . . [We] forthwith acknowledge our awareness of the sensitive and emotional nature of the abortion controversy, of the vigorous opposing views, and the deep and seemingly absolute convictions that the subject inspires. One's philosophy, one's experiences, one's exposure to the raw edges of human existence, one's religious training, one's attitudes toward life and family and their values, and the moral standards one establishes and seeks to observe, are all likely to affect one's thinking [about] abortion. In addition, population growth, pollution, poverty, and racial overtones tend to complicate and not to simplify the problem. Our task, of course, is to resolve the issue by constitutional measurement, free of emotion and of predilection. We seek earnestly to do this, and, because we do, we have inquired into, and in this opinion place some emphasis upon, medical and medical-legal history and what that history reveals about man's attitudes toward the abortion procedure over the centuries.

* * *

[The Court here reviewed ancient and contemporary attitudes toward abortion, observing that restrictive laws date primarily from the late nineteenth century. The Court also reviewed the possible state interests in restricting abortions,

including discouraging illicit sexual conduct, limiting access to a hazardous medical procedure, and the states' general interests in protecting fetal life. The Court addressed only the third interest as a current legitimate interest of the state.]

. . . The Constitution does not explicitly mention any right of privacy. In a line of decisions, however, . . . the Court has recognized that a right of personal privacy, or a guarantee of certain areas or zones of privacy, does exist under the Constitution. . . . This right of privacy, whether it be founded in the Fourteenth Amendment's concept of personal liberty and restrictions upon state action, as we feel it is, or, as the District Court determined, in the Ninth Amendment's reservation of rights to the people, is broad enough to encompass a woman's decision whether or not to terminate her pregnancy. The detriment that the State would impose upon the pregnant woman by denying this choice altogether is apparent. Specific and direct harm medically diagnosable even in early pregnancy may be involved. Maternity, or additional offspring, may force upon the woman a distressful life and future. Psychological harm may be imminent. Mental and physical health may be taxed by child care. There is also the distress, for all concerned, associated with the unwanted child, and there is the problem of bringing a child into a family already unable, psychologically and otherwise, to care for it. In other cases, as in this one, the additional difficulties and continuing stigma of unwed motherhood may be involved. All these are factors the woman and her responsible physician necessarily will consider in consultation.

On the basis of elements such as these, appellants and some amici [friends of the Court] argue that the woman's right is absolute and that she is entitled to terminate her pregnancy at whatever time, in whatever way, and for whatever reason she alone chooses. With this we do not agree. Appellants' arguments that Texas either has no valid interest at all in regulating the abortion decision, or no interest strong enough to support any limitation upon the woman's sole determination, is unpersuasive. The Court's decisions recognizing a right of privacy also acknowledge that some state regulation in areas protected by that right is appropriate. As noted above, a State may properly assert important interests in safeguarding health, in maintaining medical standards, and in protecting potential life. At some point in pregnancy, these respective interests become sufficiently compelling to sustain regulation of the factors that govern the abortion decision. The privacy right involved, therefor, cannot be said to be absolute. In fact, it is not clear to us that the claim asserted by some amici that one has an unlimited right to do with one's body as one pleases bears a close relationship to the right of privacy previously articulated in the Court's decisions.

* * *

We therefore conclude that the right of personal privacy includes the abortion decision, but that this right is not unqualified and must be considered against state interests in regulation.

Where certain "fundamental rights" are involved, the Court has held that regulation limiting these rights may be justified only by a "compelling state interest," and that legislative enactments must be narrowly drawn to express only the legitimate state interests at stake.

. . . The District Court held that the appellee failed to meet his burden of demonstrating that the Texas statute's infringement upon Roe's rights was necessary to support a compelling state interest. . . . Appellee argues that the State's determination to recognize and protect prenatal life from and after conception constitutes a compelling state interest. As noted above, we do not agree fully with either formulation.

The appellee and certain amici argue that the fetus is a "person" within the language and meaning of the Fourteenth Amendment. In support of this they outline at length and in detail the well-known facts of fetal development. If this suggestion of personhood is established, the appellant's case, of course, collapses, for the fetus' right to life is then guaranteed specifically by the Amendment. The appellant conceded as much on reargument. On the other hand, the appellee conceded on reargument that no case could be cited that holds that a fetus is a person within the meaning of the Fourteenth Amendment.

The Constitution does not define "person" in so many words. Section 1 of the Fourteenth Amendment contains three references to "person." The first, in defining "citizens," speaks of "persons born or naturalized in the United States." The word also appears both in the Due Process Clause and in the Equal Protection Clause. "Person" is used in other places in the Constitution. . . . But in nearly all these instances, the use of the word is such that it has application only postnatally. None indicates, with any assurance, that it has any possible pre-natal application.

All this, together with our observation, that throughout the major portion of the 19th century prevailing legal abortion practices were far freer than they are today, persuades us that the word "person," as used in the Fourteenth Amendment, does not include the unborn.

. . . The pregnant woman cannot be isolated in her privacy. She carries an embryo and, later, a fetus, if one accepts the medical definitions of the developing young in the human uterus. . . . The situation therefore is inherently different from marital intimacy, or bedroom possession of obscene material, or marriage, or procreation, or education, with which [earlier cases defining the right to privacy] were concerned. As we have intimated above, it is reasonable and appropriate for a State to decide that at some point in time another interest, that of health of the mother or that of potential human life, becomes significantly involved. The woman's privacy is no longer sole and any right of privacy she possesses must be measured accordingly.

Texas urges that, apart from the Fourteenth Amendment, life begins at conception and is present throughout pregnancy, and that, therefore, the State has a compelling interest in protecting that life from and after conception. We need not resolve the difficult question of when life begins. When those trained in the respective disciplines of medicine, philosophy, and theology are unable to arrive at any consensus, the judiciary, at this point in the development of man's knowledge, is not in a position to speculate as to the answer.

. . . In view of all this, we do not agree that, by adopting one theory of life, Texas may override the rights of the pregnant woman that are at stake. We repeat, however, that the State does have an important and legitimate interest in preserving and protecting the health of the pregnant woman, whether she be a resident of the State or a nonresident who seeks medical consultation and treatment there, and that it has still *another* important and legitimate interest in protecting the potentiality of human life. These interests are separate and distinct. Each grows in substantiality as the woman approaches term and, at a point during pregnancy, each becomes "compelling."

With respect to the State's important and legitimate interest in the health of the mother, the "compelling" point, in the light of present medical knowledge, is at approximately the end of the first trimester. This is so because of the now established medical fact . . . that until the end of the first trimester mortality in abortion is less than mortality in normal childbirth. It follows that, from and after this point, a State may regulate the abortion procedure to the extent that the regulation reasonably relates to the preservation and protection of maternal health. Examples of permissible state regulation in this area are requirements as to the qualifications of the person who is to perform the abortion; as to the licensure of that person; as to the facility in which the procedure is to be performed, that is, whether it must be a hospital or may be a clinic or some other place of less-than-hospital status; as to the licensing of the facility; and the like.

This means, on the other hand, that, for the period of pregnancy prior to this "compelling" point, the attending physician, in consultation with his patient, is free to determine, without regulation by the State, that in his medical judgment the patient's pregnancy should be terminated. If that decision is reached, the judgment may be effectuated by an abortion free of interference by the State.

With respect to the State's important and legitimate interest in potential life, the "compelling" point is at viability. This is so because the fetus then presumably has the capability of meaningful life outside the mother's womb. State regulation protective of fetal life after viability thus has both logical and biological justifications. If the State is interested in pro-

- Compelling pt. is end of 1st trimester
- prior to this the woman can choose
- Compelling pt. is @ viability

tecting fetal life after viability, it may go so far as to prescribe abortion during that period except when it is necessary to preserve the life or health of the mother.

Measured against these standards, the Texas Penal Code, in restricting legal abortions to those "procured or attempted by medical advice for the purpose of saving the life of the mother," sweeps too broadly. The statute makes no distinction between abortions performed early in pregnancy and those performed later, and it limits to a single reason, "saving" the mother's life, the legal justification for the procedure. The statute, therefore, cannot survive the constitutional attack made upon it here.

* * *

Reversed.

Brown v. Board of Education (1954)

over-turned
Plessy v. Ferguson

Brown v. Board of Education *(1954) was a momentous opinion, invalidating the system of segregation that had been established under* Plessy v. Ferguson *(1896). However, the constitutional pronouncement only marked the beginning of the struggle for racial equality, as federal courts got more and more deeply involved in trying to prod recalcitrant state and local governments into taking steps to end racial inequalities. The* Brown *decision follows.*

denied to public schools: separate but unequal

[*The* Brown *case involved appeals from several states. In each case, the plaintiffs had been denied access to public schools designated only for white children under a variety of state laws. They challenged the* Plessy v. Ferguson (1896) *"separate but equal" doctrine, contending that segregated schools were by their nature unequal.*

Chief Justice Warren first discussed the history of the Fourteenth Amendment's equal protection clause, finding it too inconclusive to be of assistance in determining how the Fourteenth Amendment should be applied to the question of public education.]

CHIEF JUSTICE WARREN writing for the majority.

. . . The doctrine of "separate but equal" did not make its appearance in this Court until 1896, in the case of Plessy v. Ferguson, involving not education but transportation. American courts have since labored with the doctrine for over a half a century. In this Court, there have been six cases involving the "separate but equal" doctrine in the field of public education.

* * *

In the instant cases, [the question of the application of the separate but equal doctrine to public education] is directly presented. Here, . . . there are findings below that the Negro and white schools involved have been equalized, or are being equalized, with respect to buildings, curricula, qualifications and salaries of teachers, and other "tangible" factors. Our decision, therefore, cannot turn on merely a comparison of these tanglible factors in the Negro and white schools involved in each of the cases. We must look instead to the effect of segregation itself on public education.

In approaching this problem, we cannot turn the clock back to 1868 when the [Fourteenth] Amendment was adopted, or even to 1896 when Plessy v. Ferguson was written. We must consider public education in the light of its full development and its present place in American life throughout the Nation. Only in this way can it be determined if segregation in public schools deprives these plaintiffs of the equal protection of the laws.

Today, education is perhaps the most important function of state and local governments. Compulsory school attendance laws and the great expenditures for education both demonstrate our recognition of the importance of education to our democratic society. It is required in the performance of our most basic responsibilities, even service in the armed forces. It is the very foundation of good citizenship. Today it is a principal instrument in awakening the child to cultural values, in preparing him for later professional training, and in helping him to adjust normally to his environment. In these days, it is doubtful that any child may reasonably be expected to succeed in life if he is denied the opportunity of an education. Such an opportunity, where the state has undertaken to provide it, is a right which must be made available to all on equal terms.

We come then to the question presented: Does segregation of children in public schools solely on the basis of race, even though the physical facilities and other "tangible" factors may be equal, deprive the children of the minority group of equal educational opportunities? We believe that it does.

In Sweatt v. Painter, in finding that a segregated law school for Negroes could not provide them equal educational opportunities, this Court relied in large part on "those qualities which are incapable of objective measurement but which make for greatness in a law school." In McLaurin v. Oklahoma State Regents, the Court, in requiring that a Negro admitted to a white graduate school be treated like all other students, again resorted to intangible considerations: ". . . his ability to study, to engage in discussions and exchange views with other students, and, in general, to learn his profession." Such considerations apply with added force to children in grade and high schools. To separate them from others of similar age and qualifications solely because of their race generates a feeling of inferiority as to their status in the community that may affect their hearts and minds in a way unlikely ever to be undone. The effect of this separation on their educational opportunities was well stated by a finding in the Kansas case by a court which nevertheless felt compelled to rule against the Negro plaintiffs:

"Segregation of white and colored children in public schools has a detrimental effect upon the colored children. The impact is greater when it has the sanction of the law; for the policy of separating the races is usually interpreted as denoting the inferiority of the Negro group. A sense of inferiority affects the motivation of a child to learn. Segregation with the sanction of law, therefore, has a tendency to [retard] the educational and mental development of Negro children and to deprive them of some of the benefits they would receive in a racial[ly] integrated school system." Whatever may have been the extent of psychological knowledge at the time of Plessy v. Ferguson, this finding is amply supported by modern authority. Any language in Plessy v. Ferguson contrary to this finding is rejected.

We conclude that in the field of public education the doctrine of "separate but equal" has no place. Separate educational facilities are inherently unequal. Therefore, we hold that the plaintiffs and others similarly situated for whom the actions have been brought are, by reason of the segregation complained of, deprived of the equal protection of the laws guaranteed by the Fourteenth Amendment. This disposition makes unnecessary any discussion whether such segregation also violates the Due Process Clause of the Fourteenth Amendment.

Because these are class actions, because of the wide applicability of this decision, and because of the great variety of local conditions, the formulation of decrees in these cases presents problems of considerable complexity. On reargument, the consideration of appropriate relief was necessarily subordinated to the primary question—the constitutionality of segregation in public education. We have now announced that such segregation is a denial of the equal protection of the laws.

United States v. Nixon (1974)

The Supreme Court has had few occasions to rule on the constitutional limits of executive authority. The Court is understandably reluctant to articulate the boundaries of presidential and legislative power, given the Court's own somewhat ambiguous institutional authority. In the case that follows, however, the Court looked at one of the ways in which the Constitution circumscribes the exercise of presidential prerogative.

United States v. Nixon (1974) involves claims to executive authority. President Richard Nixon was implicated in a conspiracy to cover up a burglary of the Democratic Party Headquarters at the Watergate Hotel in Washington, D.C., during the 1972 re-election campaign. The Special Prosecutor assigned to investigate the break-in and file appropriate criminal charges asked the trial court to order the President to disclose a number of documents and tapes related to the cover-up in order to determine the scope of the President's involvement. The President produced edited versions of some of the materials, but refused to comply with most of the trial court's order, asserting that he was entitled to withhold the information under a claim of "executive privilege."

CHIEF JUSTICE BURGER delivered the opinion of the Court.

In the District Court, the President's counsel argued that the court lacked jurisdiction to issue the subpoena because the matter was an intra-branch dispute between a subordinate and superior officer of the Executive Branch and hence not subject to judicial resolution. That argument has been renewed in this Court with emphasis on the contention that the dispute does not present a "case" or "controversy" which can be adjudicated in the federal courts. The President's counsel argues that the federal courts should not intrude into areas committed to the other branches of Government. He views the present dispute as essentially a "jurisdictional" dispute within the Executive Branch which he analogizes to a dispute between two congressional committees. Since the Executive Branch has exclusive authority and absolute discretion to decide whether to prosecute a case, it is contended that a President's decision is final in determining what evidence is to be used in a given criminal case.

. . . Although his counsel concedes the President has delegated certain specific powers to the Special Prosecutor, he has not "waived nor delegated to the Special Prosecutor the President's duty to claim privilege as to all materials which fall within the President's inherent authority to refuse to disclose to any executive officer." The Special Prosecutor's demand for the items therefore presents, in the view of the President's counsel, a political question since it involves a "textually demonstrable" grant of power under Art. II. . . .

The demands of and the resistance to the subpoena present an obvious controversy in the ordinary sense, but that alone is not sufficient to meet constitutional standards. In the constitutional sense, controversy means more than disagreement and conflict; rather it means the kind of controversy courts traditionally resolve. Here at issue is the production or non-production of specified evidence deemed by the Special Prosecutor to be relevant and admissible in a pending criminal case. It is sought by one official of the Government within the scope of his express authority; it is resisted by the Chief Executive on the ground of his duty to preserve the confidentiality of the communications of the President. Whatever the correct answer on the merits, these issues are "of a type which are traditionally justiciable."

* * *

. . . We turn to the claim that the subpoena should be quashed because it demands "confidential conversations between a President and his close advisors that it would be inconsistent with the public interest to produce." The first contention is a broad claim that the separation of powers doctrine precludes judicial review of a President's claim of privilege. The second contention is that if he does not prevail on the claim of absolute privilege, the court should hold as a matter of constitutional law that the privilege prevails over the subpoena. . . .

* * *

[The Court discussed its authority to interpret the Constitution, concluding that it had full power to interpret a claim of executive privilege.]

In support of his claim of absolute privilege, the President's counsel urges two grounds one of which is common to all governments and one of which is peculiar to our system of separation of powers. The first ground is the valid need for protection of communications between high government officials and those who advise and assist them in the performance of their manifold duties; the importance of this confidentiality is too plain to require further discussion. Human experience teaches that those who expect public dissemination of their remarks may well temper candor with a concern for appearances and for their own interests to the detriment of the decisionmaking process. Whatever the nature of the privilege of confidentiality of presidential communications in the exercise of Art. II powers the privilege can be said to derive from the supremacy of each branch within its own assigned area of constitutional duties. Certain powers and privileges flow from the nature of enumerated powers; the protection of the confidentiality of presidential communications has similar constitutional underpinnings.

The second ground asserted by the President's counsel in support of the claim of absolute privilege rests on the doctrine of separation of powers. Here it is argued that the independence of the Executive Branch within its own sphere, insulates a president from a judicial subpoena in an ongoing criminal prosecution, and thereby protects confidential presidential communications.

However, neither the doctrine of separation of powers, nor the need for confidentiality of high level communications, without more, can sustain an absolute, unqualified presidential privilege of immunity from judicial process under all circumstances. The President's need for complete candor and objectivity from advisers calls for great deference from the courts. However, when the privilege depends solely on the broad, undifferentiated claim of public interest in the confidentiality of such conversations, a confrontation with other values arises. Absent a claim of need to protect military, diplomatic or sensitive national security secrets, we find it difficult to accept the argument that even the very important interest in confidentiality of presidential communications is significantly diminished by production of such material for *in camera* inspection with all the protection that a district court will be obliged to provide.

The impediment that an absolute, unqualified privilege would place in the way of the primary constitutional duty of the judicial branch to do justice in criminal prosecutions would plainly conflict with the function of the courts under Art. III. In designing the structure of our Government and dividing and allocating the sovereign power among three coequal branches, the Framers of the Constitution sought to provide a comprehensive system, but the separate powers were not intended to operate with absolute independence. To read the Art. II powers of the President as providing an absolute privilege as against a subpoena essential to enforcement of criminal statutes on no more than a generalized claim of the public interest in confidentiality of nonmilitary and nondiplomatic discussions would upset the constitutional balance of "a workable government" and gravely impair the role of the court under Art. III.

Since we conclude that the legitimate needs of the judicial process may outweigh presidential privilege, it is necessary to resolve those competing interests in a manner that preserves the essential functions of each branch. The rights and indeed the duty to resolve that question does not free the judiciary from according high respect to the representations made on behalf of the President. The expectation of a President to the confidentiality of his conversations and correspondence, like the claim of confidentiality of judicial deliberations, for example, has all the values to which we accord deference for the privacy of all citizens and added to those values the necessity for protection of the public interest in his responsibilities against the inroads of such a privilege on the fair administration of criminal justice. The interest in preserving confidentiality is weighty indeed and entitled to great respect. However we cannot conclude that advisers will be moved to temper the candor of their remarks by the infrequent occasions of disclosure because of the possibility that such conversations will be called for in the context of a criminal prosecution.

On the other hand, the allowance of the privilege to withhold evidence that is demonstrably relevant in a criminal trial would cut deeply into the guarantee of due process of law and gravely impair the basic function of the courts. A President's acknowleged need for confidentiality in the communications of his office is general in nature, whereas the constitutional need for production of relevant evidence in a criminal proceeding is specific and central to the fair adjudication of a particular ciriminal case in the administration of justice. Without access to specific facts a criminal prosecution may be totally frustrated. The President's broad interest in confidentiality of communications will not be vitiated by disclosure of a limited number of conversations preliminarily shown to have some bearing on the pending criminal cases.

We conclude that when the ground for asserting privilege as to subpoenaed materials sought for use in a criminal trial is based only on the generalized interest in confidentiality, it cannot prevail over the fundamental demand of due process of law in the fair administration of criminal justice. The generalized assertion of privilege must yield to the demonstrated, specific need for evidence in a pending criminal trial.

* * *

In this case the President challenges a subpoena served on him as a third party requiring the production of materials for use in a criminal prosecution on the claim that he has a privilege against disclosure of confidential communications. He does not place his claim of privilege on the ground they are military or diplomatic secrets. As to these areas of Art. II duties the courts have traditionally shown the utmost deference to presidential responsibilities. No case of the Court, however, has extended this high degree of deference to a President's generalized interest in confidentiality. Nowhere in the Constitution, as we have noted earlier, is there any explicit reference to a privilege of confidentiality; yet to the extent this interest relates to the effective discharge of a President's powers, it is constitutionally based.

* * *

[*The Court distinguished this case from cases involving claims against the president while acting in an official capacity.*]

Mr. Chief Justice Marshall sitting as a trial judge in the *Burr* case was extraordinarily careful to point out that: "[I]n no case of this kind would a Court be required to proceed against the President as against an ordinary individual." Marshall's statement cannot be read to mean in any sense that a President is above the law, but relates to the singularly unique role under Art. II of a President's communications and activities, related to the performance of duties under that Article. Moreover, a President's communications and activities encompass a vastly wider range of sensitive material than would be true of any "ordinary individual." It is therefore necessary in the public interest to afford presidential confidentiality the greatest protection consistent with the fair administration of justice. The need for confidentiality even as to idle conversations with associates in which casual reference might be made concerning political leaders within the country or foreign statesmen is too obvious to call for further treatment. We have no doubt that the District Judge will at all times accord the presidential records that high degree of deference suggested in *United States v. Burr*, and will discharge his responsibility to see to it that until released to the Special Prosecutor no *in camera* [private] material is revealed to anyone. This burden applies with even greater force to excised material; once the decision is made to excise, the material is restored to its privileged status and should be returned under seal to its lawful custodian.

Affirmed.

Planned Parenthood of Southeastern Pennsylvania v. Casey (1992)

In Roe v. Wade *(1973), the Court held that the right to privacy encompassed a woman's right to choose to have an abortion. In the twenty years since* Roe *was decided, a number of states have passed statutes attempting to limit that right and the Court indicated that it would uphold regulations on abortions so long as they did not place an "undue burden" upon a woman's right to choose an abortion. This was a less restrictive test for evaluating the constitutionality of the regulations than might have been applied, and which allowed for a broad interpretation by the states. Therefore, when a Pennsylvania law imposing significant restrictions on abortion "on demand" was passed in the early 1990s, Planned Parenthood of SEPA sued the state's Governor, Tom Casey, for violating a woman's right to an abortion.*

The Court in Planned Parenthood v. Casey *reaffirmed* Roe *by a bare majority. A prominent factor in the majority's opinion was the extent to which the Court should be willing to upset a prior holding. The majority opinion discussed in detail the conditions under which a departure from a settled interpretation ought to be considered, and expressed concern about perceptions of institutional legitimacy that might result if it acted too precipitously to overturn a prior decision. The dissent argued just as strongly that the Court was not compelled to save* Roe, *since the initial decision was ill considered.*

JUSTICE O'CONNOR, JUSTICE KENNEDY, AND JUSTICE SOUTER announce the judgment of the Court.

I

After considering the fundamental constitutional questions resolved by *Roe* [*v. Wade, . . .*], principles of institutional integrity, and the rule of *stare decisis,* [precedent] we are led to conclude this: the essential holding of *Roe v. Wade* should be retained and once again reaffirmed.

It must be stated at the outset and with clarity that *Roe's* essential holding, the holding we reaffirm, has three parts. First is a recognition of the right of the woman to choose to have an abortion before viability

[handwritten margin notes: ① woman's right to abortion b/f viability ② after viability the state can restrict ③ state must protect woman & fetus]

and to obtain it without undue interference from the State. Before viability, the State's interests are not strong enough to support a prohibition of abortion or the imposition of a substantial obstacle to the woman's effective right to elect the procedure. Second is a confirmation of the State's power to restrict abortions after fetal viability, if the law contains exceptions for pregnancies which endanger a woman's life or health. And third is the principle that the State has legitimate interests from the outset of the pregnancy in protecting the health of the woman and the life of the fetus that may become a child. These principles do not contradict one another; and we adhere to each.

* * *

II

Our law affords constitutional protection to personal decisions relating to marriage, procreation, contraception, family relationships, child rearing, and education. Our cases recognize "the right of the individual, married or single, to be free from unwarranted governmental intrusion into matters so fundamentally affecting a person as the decision whether to bear or beget a child." *Eisenstadt v. Baird*, . . . Our precedents "have respected the private realm of family life which the state cannot enter." *Prince v. Massachusetts*, . . . These matters, involving the most intimate and personal choices a person may make in a lifetime, choices central to personal dignity and autonomy, are central to the liberty protected by the Fourteenth Amendment. At the heart of liberty is the right to define one's own concept of existence, of meaning, of the universe, and of the mystery of human life.

* * *

While we appreciate the weight of the arguments made on behalf of the State in the case before us, arguments which in their ultimate formulation conclude that *Roe* should be overruled, the reservations any of us may have in reaffirming the central holding of *Roe* are outweighed by the explication of individual liberty we have given combined with the force of *stare decisis*. We turn now to that doctrine.

III

A [W]hen this Court reexamines a prior holding, its judgment is customarily informed by a series of prudential and pragmatic considerations designed to test the consistency of overruling a prior decision with the ideal of the rule of law, and to gauge the respective costs of reaffirming and overruling a prior case. Thus, for example, we may ask whether the rule has proved to be intolerable simply in defying practical workability; whether the rule is subject to a kind of reliance that would lend a special hardship to the consequences of overruling and add inequity to the cost of repudiation; whether related principles of law have so far developed as to have left the old rule no more than remnant of abandoned doctrine; or whether facts have so changed or come to be seen so differently, as to have robbed the old rule of significant application or justification[.]

Although *Roe* has engendered opposition, it has in no sense proven "unworkable," representing as it does a simple limitation beyond which a state law is unenforceable[.]

We have seen how time has overtaken some of *Roe's* factual assumptions: advances in maternal health care allow for abortions safe to the mother later in pregnancy than was true in 1973, and advances in neonatal care have advanced viability to a point somewhat earlier. But these facts go only to the scheme of time limits on the realization of competing interests, and the divergences from the factual premises of 1973 have no bearing on the validity of *Roe's* central holding, that viability marks the earliest point at which the State's interest in fetal life is constitutionally adequate to justify a legislative ban on nontherapeutic abortions. The soundness or unsoundness of that constitutional judgment in no sense turns on whether viability occurs at approximately 28 weeks, as was usual at the time of *Roe*, at 23 to 24 weeks, as it sometimes does today, or at some moment even slightly earlier in pregnancy, as it may if fetal respiratory capacity can somehow be enhanced in the future. Whenever it may occur, the attainment of viability may continue to serve as the critical fact, just as it has done since *Roe* was decided; which is to say that no change in *Roe's* factual underpinning has left its central holding obsolete, and none supports an argument for overruling it.

B In a less significant case, *stare decisis* analysis could, and would, stop at the point we have reached. But the sustained and widespread debate *Roe* has provoked calls for some comparison between that case and others of comparable dimension that have responded to national controversies and taken on the impress of the controversies addressed.

*   *   *

[*The Court reviewed two earlier lines of cases involving major reversals of doctrine, holding that there had been no similar changes in the factual assumptions underpinning the decision here.*]

. . . In constitutional adjudication as elsewhere in life, changed circumstances may impose new obligations, and the thoughtful part of the Nation could accept each decision to overrule a prior case as a response to the Court's constitutional duty.

Because the case before us presents no such occasion it could be seen as no such response. Because neither the factual underpinnings of *Roe's* central holding nor our understanding of it has changed (and because no other indication of weakened precedent has been shown) the Court could not pretend to be reexamining the prior law with any justification beyond a present doctrinal disposition to come out differently from the Court of 1973[.]

. . . In the present case, . . . as our analysis to this point makes clear, [a] terrible price would be paid for overruling. Our analysis would not be complete, however, without explaining why overruling *Roe*'s central holding would not only reach an unjustifiable result under principles of *stare decisis*, but would seriously weaken the Court's capacity to exercise the judicial power and to function as the Supreme Court of a Nation dedicated to the rule of law[.]

The underlying substance of [the Court's] legitimacy is . . . expressed in the Court's opinions, and our contemporary understanding is such that a decision without principled justification would be no judicial act at all. But even when justification is furnished by apposite legal principle, something more is required. Because not every conscientious claim of principled justification will be accepted as such, the justification claimed must be beyond dispute. The Court must take care to speak and act in ways that allow people to accept its decisions on the terms the Court claims for them, as grounded truly in principle, not as compromises with social and political pressures having, as such, no bearing on the principled choices that the Court is obliged to make. Thus, the Court's legitimacy depends on making legally principled decisions under circumstances in which their principled character is sufficiently plausible to be accepted by the Nation.

* * *

The Court's duty in the present case is clear. In 1973, it confronted the already-divisive issue of governmental power to limit personal choice to undergo abortion, for which it provided a new resolution based on the due process guaranteed by the Fourteenth Amendment. Whether or not a new social consensus is developing on that issue, its divisiveness is no less today than in 1973, and pressure to overrule the decision, like pressure to retain it, has grown only more intense. A decision to overrule *Roe*'s essential holding under the existing circumstances would address error, if error there was, at the cost of both profound and unnecessary damage to the Court's legitimacy, and to the Nation's commitment to the rule of law. It is therefore imperative to adhere to the essence of *Roe*'s original decision, and we do so today.

IV

From what we have said so far it follows that it is a constitutional liberty of the woman to have some freedom to terminate her pregnancy. We conclude that the basic decision in *Roe* was based on a constitutional analysis which we cannot now repudiate. The woman's liberty is not so unlimited, however, that from the outset the State cannot show its concern for the life of the unborn, and at a later point in fetal development the State's interest in life has sufficient force so that the right of the woman to terminate the pregnancy can be restricted.

That brings us, of course, to the point where much criticism has been directed at *Roe*, a criticism that always inheres when the Court draws a specific rule from what in the Constitution is but a general standard. . . . And it falls to us to give some real substance to the woman's liberty to determine whether to carry her pregnancy to full term.

We conclude the line should be drawn at viability, so that before that time the woman has a right to choose to terminate her pregnancy. We adhere to this principle for two reasons. First, as we have said, is the doctrine of *stare decisis*. Any judicial act of line-drawing may seem somewhat arbitrary, but *Roe* was a reasoned statement, elaborated with great care. We have twice reaffirmed it in the face of great opposition. Although we must overrule those parts of *Thornburgh* and *Akron I* which, in our view, are inconsistent with *Roe's* statement that the State has a legitimate interest in promoting the life or potential life of the unborn, the central premise of those cases represents an unbroken commitment by this Court to the essential holding of *Roe*. It is that premise which we reaffirm today.

The second reason is that the concept of viability, as we noted in *Roe*, is the time at which there is a realistic possibility of maintaining and nourishing a life outside the womb, so that the independent existence of the second life can in reason and all fairness be the object of state protection that now overrides the rights of the woman. Consistent with other constitutional norms, legislatures may draw lines which appear arbitrary without the necessity of offering a justification. But courts may not. We must justify the lines we draw. And there is no line other than viability which is more workable.

*   *   *

The woman's right to terminate her pregnancy before viability is the most central principle of *Roe v. Wade*. It is a rule of law and a component of liberty we cannot renounce.

*   *   *

Though the woman has a right to choose to terminate or continue her pregnancy before viability, it does not at all follow that the State is prohibited from taking steps to ensure that this choice is thoughtful and informed. Even in the earliest stages of pregnancy, the State may enact rules and regulations designed to encourage her to know that there are philosophic and social arguments of great weight that can be brought to bear in favor of continuing the pregnancy to full term and that there are procedures and institutions to allow adoption of unwanted children as well as a certain degree of state assistance if the mother chooses to raise the child herself. "The Constitution does not forbid a State or city, pursuant to democratic processes, from expressing a preference for normal childbirth." *Webster v. Reproductive Health Services* [(1989)]. It follows that States are free to enact laws to provide a reasonable framework for a woman to make a decision that has such profound and lasting meaning. This, too, we find consistent with *Roe*'s central premises, and indeed the inevitable consequence of our holding that the State has an interest in protecting the life of the unborn.

We reject the trimester framework, which we do not consider to be part of the essential holding of *Roe*. . . . The trimester framework suffers from these basic flaws: in its formulation it misconceives the nature of the pregnant woman's interest; and in practice it undervalues the State's interest in potential life, as recognized in *Roe*.

* * *

Because we set forth a standard of general application to which we intend to adhere, it is important to clarify what is meant by an undue burden.

A finding of an undue burden is a shorthand for the conclusion that a state regulation has the purpose or effect of placing a substantial obstacle in the path of a woman seeking an abortion of a nonviable fetus. . . . [W]e answer the question, left open in previous opinions discussing the undue burden formulation, whether a law designed to further the State's interest in fetal life which imposes an undue burden on the woman's decision before fetal viability could be constitutional. The answer is no.

Some guiding principles should emerge. What is at stake is the woman's right to make the ultimate decision, not a right to be insulated from all others in doing so. Regulations which do no more than create a structural mechanism by which the State, or the parent or guardian of a minor, may express profound respect for the life of the unborn are permitted, if they are not a substantial obstacle to the woman's exercise of the right to choose. Unless it has that effect on her right of choice, a state measure designed to persuade her to choose childbirth over abortion will be upheld if reasonably related to that goal. Regulations designed to foster the health of a woman seeking an abortion are valid if they do not constitute an undue burden.

Even when jurists reason from shared premises, some disagreement is inevitable. . . . We do not expect it to be otherwise with respect to the undue burden standard. We give this summary:

(a) To protect the central right recognized by *Roe v. Wade* while at the same time accommodating the State's profound interest in potential life, we will employ the undue burden analysis as explained in this opinion. An undue burden exists, and therefore a provision of law is invalid, if its purpose or effect is to place a substantial obstacle in the path of a woman seeking an abortion before the fetus attains viability.

(b) We reject the rigid trimester framework of *Roe v. Wade*. To promote the State's profound interest in potential life, throughout pregnancy the State may take measures to ensure that the woman's choice is informed, and measures designed to advance this interest will not be invalidated as long as their purpose is to persuade the woman to choose childbirth over abortion. These measures must not be an undue burden on the right.

(c) As with any medical procedure, the State may enact regulations to further the health or safety of a woman seeking an abortion. Unnecessary health regulations that have the purpose or effect of presenting a substantial obstacle to a woman seeking an abortion impose an undue burden on the right.

(d) Our adoption of the undue burden analysis does not disturb the central holding of *Roe v. Wade*, and we reaffirm that holding. Regardless of whether exceptions are made for particular circumstances, a State may not prohibit any woman from making the ultimate decision to terminate her pregnancy before viability.

(e) We also reaffirm *Roe*'s holding that "subsequent to viability, the State in promoting its interest in the potentiality of human life may, if it chooses, regulate, and even proscribe, abortion except where it is necessary, in appropriate medical judgment, for the preservation of the life or health of the mother."

United States v. Lopez (1995)

How far does Congress's authority extend with respect to the states? Since the 1930s, when a liberalization of Supreme Court doctrine cleared the way for an expansion of federal authority, Congress has relied on a loose interpretation of the Commerce Clause to justify extensive involvement in state and local affairs. (Congress can also shape what states do, for example, by placing conditions upon the receipt of federal funds). In 1990, Congress enacted the Gun-Free School Zones Act, making possession of a firearm in designated school zones a federal crime. When Alfonso Lopez, Jr., was convicted of violating the act, his lawyer challenged the constitutionality of the law, arguing that it was "invalid as beyond the power of Congress under the Commerce Clause." In a striking reversal of interpretation, the Supreme Court agreed and declared the law invalid, holding that banning guns in schools was too far removed from any effect on interstate commerce to warrant federal intervention. Critics of the decision argued that the Court's reasoning might invalidate a large body of federal crime and drug legislation that relies on the connection between regulated activity and interstate commerce. Supporters maintained that the decision marked a new era of judicial respect for federalism and state autonomy.

CHIEF JUSTICE REHNQUIST delivered the opinion of the Court.

In the Gun-Free School Zones Act of 1990, Congress made it a federal offense "for any individual knowingly to possess a firearm at a place that the individual knows, or has reasonable cause to believe, is a school zone." The Act neither regulates a commercial activity nor contains a requirement that the possession be connected in any way to interstate commerce. We hold that the Act exceeds the authority of "Congress to regulate Commerce . . . among the several States. . . ." (U.S. Constitution Art. I, 8, cl. 3).

On March 10, 1992, respondent, who was then a 12th-grade student, arrived at Edison High School in San Antonio, Texas, carrying a concealed .38 caliber handgun and five bullets. Acting upon an anonymous tip, school authorities confronted respondent, who admitted that he was carrying the weapon. He was arrested and charged under Texas law with firearm possession on school premises. The next day, the state charges were dismissed after federal agents charged respondent by complaint with violating the Gun-Free School Zones Act of 1990.

A federal grand jury indicted respondent on one count of knowing possession of a firearm at a school zone, in violation of 922(q) [the relevant section of the Act of 1990]. Respondent moved to dismiss his federal indictment on the ground that 922(q) "is unconstitutional as it is beyond the power of Congress to legislate control over our public schools." The District Court denied the motion, concluding that 922(q) "is a constitutional exercise of Congress' well-defined power to regulate activities in and affecting commerce, and the 'business' of elementary, middle and high schools . . . affects interstate commerce." Respondent waived his right to a jury trial. The District Court conducted a bench trial, found him guilty of violating 922(q), and sentenced him to six months' imprisonment and two years' supervised release.

On appeal, respondent challenged his conviction based on his claim that 922(q) exceeded Congress' power to legislate under the Commerce Clause. The Court of Appeals for the Fifth Circuit agreed and reversed respondent's conviction. It held that, in light of what it characterized as insufficient congressional findings and legislative history, "in the full reach of its terms, is invalid as beyond the power of Congress under the Commerce Clause." Because of the importance of the issue, we granted *certiorari* and we now affirm.

We start with first principles. The Constitution creates a Federal Government of enumerated powers. As James Madison wrote, "[t]he powers delegated by the proposed Constitution to the federal government are few and defined. Those which are to remain in the State governments are numerous and indefinite." (*The Federalist*, No. 45). This constitutionally mandated division of authority was adopted by the Framers to ensure protection of our fundamental liberties. Just as the separation and independence of the coordinate branches of the Federal Government serves to prevent the accumulation of excessive power in any one branch, a healthy balance of power between the States and the Federal Government will reduce the risk of tyranny and abuse from either front.

[For the next several pages Rehnquist reviews the evolution of interpretations of the Commerce Clause, starting with *Gibbons v. Ogden* (1824). This case established the relatively narrow interpretation of the Commerce Clause in which the Court prevented *states* from interfering with interstate commerce. Very rarely did cases concern Congress's power. The 1887 Interstate Commerce Act and the 1890 Sherman Antitrust Act expanded Congress's power to regulate intrastate commerce "where the interstate and intrastate aspects of commerce were so mingled together that full regulation of interstate commerce required incidental regulation of intrastate commerce," arguing that the Commerce Clause authorized such regulation. Several New Deal era cases, *NLRB v. Jones & Laughlin Steel Corp.* (1937), *United States v. Darby* (1941), and *Wickard v. rn* (1942) broadened the interpretation of the Commerce Clause].

Jones & Laughlin Steel, Darby, and Wickard ushered in an era of Commerce Clause jurisprudence that greatly expanded the previously defined authority of Congress under that Clause. In part, this was a recognition of the great changes that had occurred in the way business was carried on in this country. Enterprises that had once been local or at most regional in nature had become national in scope. But the doctrinal change also reflected a view that earlier Commerce Clause cases artificially had constrained the authority of Congress to regulate interstate commerce.

But even these modern-era precedents which have expanded congressional power under the Commerce Clause confirm that this power is subject to outer limits. In Jones & Laughlin Steel, the Court warned that the scope of the interstate commerce power "must be considered in the light of our dual system of government and may not be extended so as to embrace effects upon interstate commerce so indirect and remote that to embrace them, in view of our complex society, would effectually obliterate the distinction between what is national and what is local and create a completely centralized government." Since that time, the Court has heeded that warning and undertaken to decide whether a rational basis existed for concluding that a regulated activity sufficiently affected interstate commerce.

* * *

Consistent with this structure, we have identified three broad categories of activity that Congress may regulate under its commerce power. First, Congress may regulate the use of the channels of interstate commerce. Second, Congress is empowered to regulate and protect the instrumentalities of interstate commerce, or persons or things in interstate commerce, even though the threat may come only from intrastate activities. Finally, Congress' commerce authority includes the power to regulate those activities having a substantial relation to interstate commerce, those activities that substantially affect interstate commerce.

Within this final category, admittedly, our case law has not been clear whether an activity must *affect* or *substantially affect* interstate commerce in order to be within Congress' power to regulate it under the Commerce Clause. We conclude, consistent with the great weight of our case law, that the proper test requires an analysis of whether the regulated activity *substantially affects* interstate commerce.

We now turn to consider the power of Congress, in the light of this framework, to enact 922(q) [The Gun-Free School Zones Act]. The first two categories of authority may be quickly disposed of: 922(q) is not a regulation of the use of the channels of interstate commerce, nor is it an attempt to prohibit the interstate transportation of a commodity through the channels of commerce; nor can 922(q) be justified as a regulation by which Congress has sought to protect an instrumentality of interstate commerce or a thing in interstate commerce. Thus, if 922(q) is to be sustained, it must be under the third category as a regulation of an activity that substantially affects interstate commerce.

First, we have upheld a wide variety of congressional Acts regulating intrastate economic activity where we have concluded that the activity substantially affected interstate commerce. Examples include the regulation of intrastate coal mining; intrastate extortionate credit transactions, restaurants utilizing substantial interstate supplies, inns and hotels catering to interstate guests, and production and consumption of homegrown wheat. These examples are by no means exhaustive, but the pattern is clear. Where economic activity substantially affects interstate commerce, legislation regulating that activity will be sustained.

Even Wickard, which is perhaps the most far reaching example of Commerce Clause authority over intrastate activity, involved economic activity in a way that the possession of a gun in a school zone does not. Roscoe Filburn operated a small farm in Ohio, on which, in the year involved, he raised 23 acres of wheat. It was his practice to sow winter wheat in the fall, and after harvesting it in July to sell a portion of the crop, to feed part of it to poultry and livestock on the farm, to use some in making flour for home consumption, and to keep the remainder for seeding future crops. The Secretary of Agriculture assessed a penalty against him under the Agricultural Adjustment Act of 1938 because he harvested about 12 acres more wheat than his allotment under the Act permitted. The Act was designed to regulate the volume of wheat moving in interstate and foreign commerce in order to avoid surpluses and shortages, and concomitant fluctuation in wheat prices, which had previously obtained. The Court said, in an opinion sustaining the application of the Act to Filburn's activity, "One of the primary purposes of the Act in question was to increase the market price of wheat and to that end to limit the volume thereof that could affect the market. It can hardly be denied that a factor of such volume and variability as home-consumed wheat would have a substantial influence on price and market conditions. This may arise because being in marketable condition such wheat overhangs the market and, if induced by rising prices, tends to flow into the market and check price increases. But if we assume that it is never marketed, it supplies a need of the man who grew it which would otherwise be reflected by purchases in the open market. Home-grown wheat in this sense competes with wheat in commerce" (317 U.S., at 128).

Section 922(q) is a criminal statute that by its terms has nothing to do with *commerce* or any sort of economic enterprise, however broadly one might define those terms. Section 922(q) is not an essential part of a larger regulation of economic activity, in which the regulatory scheme could be undercut unless the intra-state activity were regulated. It cannot, therefore, be sustained under our cases upholding regulations of activities that arise out of or are connected with a commercial transaction, which viewed in the aggregate, substantially affects interstate commerce.

Second, 922(q) contains no jurisdictional element which would ensure, through case-by-case inquiry, that the firearm possession in question affects interstate commerce. . . . 922(q) has no express jurisdictional element which might limit its reach to a discrete set of firearm possessions that additionally have an explicit connection with or effect on interstate commerce.

* * *

The Government's essential contention, in fine, is that we may determine here that 922(q) is valid because possession of a firearm in a local school zone does indeed substantially affect interstate commerce. The Government argues that possession of a firearm in a school zone may result in violent crime and that violent crime can be expected to affect the functioning of the national economy in two ways. First, the costs of violent crime are substantial, and, through the mechanism of insurance, those costs are spread throughout the population. Second, violent crime reduces the willingness of individuals to travel to areas within the country that are perceived to be unsafe. The Government also argues that the presence of guns in schools poses a substantial threat to the educational process by threatening the learning environment. A handicapped educational process, in turn, will result in a less productive citizenry. That, in turn, would have an adverse effect on the Nation's economic well-being. As a result, the Government argues that Congress could rationally have concluded that 922(q) substantially affects interstate commerce.

We pause to consider the implications of the Government's arguments. The Government admits, under its "costs of crime" reasoning, that Congress could regulate not only all violent crime, but all activities that might lead to violent crime, regardless of how tenuously they relate to interstate commerce. Similarly, under the Government's "national productivity" reasoning, Congress could regulate any activity that it found was related to the economic productivity of individual citizens: family law (including marriage, divorce, and child custody), for example. Under the theories that the Government presents in support of 922(q), it is difficult to perceive any limitation on federal power, even in areas such as criminal law enforcement or education where States historically have been sovereign. Thus, if we were to accept the Government's arguments, we are hard-pressed to posit any activity by an individual that Congress is without power to regulate.

Although Justice Breyer argues that acceptance of the Government's rationales would not authorize a general federal police power, he is unable to identify any activity that the States may regulate but Congress may not. Justice Breyer posits that there might be some limitations on Congress' commerce power such as family law or certain aspects of education. These suggested limitations, when viewed in light of the dissent's expansive analysis, are devoid of substance.

Justice Breyer focuses, for the most part, on the threat that firearm possession in and near schools poses to the educational process and the potential economic consequences flowing from that threat. Specifically, the dissent reasons that (1) gun-related violence is a serious problem; (2) that problem, in turn, has an adverse effect on classroom learning; and (3) that adverse effect on classroom learning, in turn, represents a substantial threat to trade and commerce. This analysis would be equally applicable, if not more so, to subjects such as family law and direct regulation of education.

For instance, if Congress can, pursuant to its Commerce Clause power, regulate activities that adversely affect the learning environment, then, a fortiori, it also can regulate the educational process directly. Congress could determine that a school's curriculum has a "significant" effect on the extent of classroom learning. As a result, Congress could mandate a federal curriculum for local elementary and secondary schools because what is taught in local schools has a significant "effect on classroom learning," and that, in turn, has a substantial effect on interstate commerce.

Justice Breyer rejects our reading of precedent and argues that "Congress . . . could rationally conclude that schools fall on the commercial side of the line." Again, Justice Breyer's rationale lacks any real limits because, depending on the level of generality, any activity can be looked upon as commercial. Under the dissent's rationale, Congress could just as easily look at child rearing as "fall[ing] on the commercial side of the line" because it provides a "valuable service" namely, to equip [children] with the skills they need to survive in life and, more specifically, in the workplace. We do not doubt that Congress has authority under the Commerce Clause to regulate numerous commercial activities that substantially affect interstate commerce and also affect the educational process. That authority, though broad, does not include the authority to regulate each and every aspect of local schools.

Admittedly, a determination whether an intrastate activity is commercial or noncommercial may in some cases result in legal uncertainty. But, so long as Congress' authority is limited to those powers enumerated in the Constitution, and so long as those enumerated powers are interpreted as having judicially enforceable outer limits, congressional legislation under the Commerce Clause always will engender "legal uncertainty." As Chief Justice Marshall stated in *McCulloch v. Maryland*, (1819), "The [federal] government is acknowledged by all to be one of enumerated powers. The principle, that it can exercise only the powers granted to it . . . is now universally admitted. But the question respecting the extent of the powers actually granted, is perpetually arising, and will probably continue to arise, as long as our system shall exist." The Constitution mandates this uncertainty by withholding from Congress a plenary police power that would authorize enactment of every type of legislation. Congress has operated within this framework of legal uncertainty ever since this Court determined that it was the judiciary's duty "to say what the law is." Any possible benefit from eliminating this "legal uncertainty" would be at the expense of the Constitution's system of enumerated powers.

* * *

These are not precise formulations, and in the nature of things they cannot be. But we think they point the way to a correct decision of this case. The possession of a gun in a local school zone is in no sense an economic activity that might, through repetition elsewhere, substantially affect any sort of interstate commerce. Respondent was a local student at a local school; there is no indication that he had recently moved in interstate commerce, and there is no requirement that his possession of the firearm have any concrete tie to interstate commerce.

To uphold the Government's contentions here, we would have to pile inference upon inference in a manner that would bid fair to convert congressional authority under the Commerce Clause to a general police power of the sort retained by the States. Admittedly, some of our prior cases have taken long steps down that road, giving great deference to congressional action. The broad language in these opinions has suggested the possibility of additional expansion, but we decline here to proceed any further. To do so would require us to conclude that the

Constitution's enumeration of powers does not presuppose something not enumerated, and that there never will be a distinction between what is truly national and what is truly local. This we are unwilling to do.

For the foregoing reasons the judgment of the Court of Appeals is Affirmed.

Acknowledgments

From *The Origins of the American Constitution* by Michael Kammen, editor. Copyright © 1986 by Michael Kammen. Used by permission of Viking Penguin, a division of Penguin Books USA Inc.

The Federalist, No. 15, by Alexander Hamilton from the NAL-Dutton collection edited by Clinton Rossiter (1961).

From *The Paranoid Style in American Politics and Other Essays* by Richard Hofstadter. Copyright 1952, © 1964, 1965 by Richard Hofstadter. Reprinted by permission of Alfred A. Knopf, Inc.

Reprinted with the permission of Simon & Schuster from *An Economic Interpretation of the Constitution of the United States* by Charles Beard. Copyright 1935 by Macmillan Publishing Company; Copyright renewed © 1963 by William Beard and Miriam Vagts Beard.

Brown, Robert E.; *Charles Beard and the Constitution: A Critical Analysis of "An Economic Interpretation of the Constitution."* Copyright renewed © 1956 by Princeton University Press. Reprinted with permission of Princeton University Press.

The Federalist, Nos. 51 and 46, by James Madison from the NAL-Dutton collection edited by Clinton Rossiter (1961).

"The Price of Early Federalism," from *The Price of Federalism* by Paul Peterson (1995). Reprinted by permission of the Brookings Institution.

"Guns, the Commerce Clause, and the Courts" by Robert Katzmann from the *Brookings Review*, Summer 1995. Reprinted by permission.

Rules Committee Report on the Unfunded Mandate Reform Act of 1995.

"Unfunded Mandates" by James R. St. George from the *Brookings Review*, Spring 1995. Reprinted by permission.

"It Ain't Broke" by Charles A. Jones from *Back to Gridlock: Government in the Clinton Years*, edited by James Sundquist (1995). Reprinted by permission of the Brookings Institution.

"A Rationale" by Donald L. Robinson from *Back to Gridlock: Government in the Clinton Years*, edited by James Sundquist (1995). Reprinted by permission of the Brookings Institution.

"Letter from Birmingham Jail, 1963" by Martin Luther King, Jr. Reprinted by arrangement with The Heirs to the Estate of Martin Luther King, Jr., c/o Writers House, Inc., as agent for the proprietor. Copyright 1963 by Martin Luther King, Jr., copyright renewed 1991 by Coretta Scott King.

"In Defense of Prejudice" by Jonathan Rauch. Copyright © 1995 by *Harper's Magazine*. All rights reserved. Reproduced from the May issue by special permission.

"The War on Drugs Is Lost" by William F. Buckley and "The War on Drugs Is Lost" by Steven B. Duke from *National Review*, February 12, 1996. Copyright © 1996 by National Review, Inc., 150 East 35th Street, New York, NY 10016. Reprinted by permission.

"Legalization Madness" by James A. Inciardi and Christine A. Saum. Reprinted with permission of the author and *The Public Interest*, Spring 1996, pp. 72–82, © 1996 by National Affairs, Inc.

From *Congress: The Electoral Connection* by David R. Mayhew. Copyright © 1974 by Yale University Press. Reprinted by permission.

"Too Representative Government" by Steven Stark from the *Atlantic Monthly*, May 1995. Reprinted by permission.

"By the Numbers" by Viveca Novak from *National Journal*, February 12, 1994. Copyright 1994 by National Journal, Inc. All rights reserved. Reprinted by permission.

"Slaying the Dinosaur: The Case for Reforming the Senate Filibuster" by Thomas E. Mann and Sarah A. Binder from the *Brookings Review*, Summer 1995. Reprinted by permission.

"Defending the Dinosaur: The Case for Not Fixing the Filibuster" by Bill Frenzel from the *Brookings Review*, Summer 1995. Reprinted by permission.

From Richard Neustadt, *Presidential Power*. Copyright © 1960. All rights reserved. Reprinted/adapted by permission of Allyn & Bacon.

"The Search for the Perfect President" from *The Economist*, November 18, 1995. Copyright © 1995 The Economist Newspaper Group, Inc. Reprinted with permission.

"Presidents and Economics: One-Star Generalizations" by Herbert Stein from the *American Enterprise*, January/February 1996. Reprinted by The American Enterprise, a national magazine of politics, business, and culture, based in Washington, D.C.

"Perspectives on the Presidency" from *The Presidency in a Separate System* by Charles O. Jones (1994). Reprinted by permission of the Brookings Institution.

"The Out-of-Control Presidency" by Michael Lind from the *New Republic*, August 14, 1995. Reprinted by permission of the *New Republic*, © 1995, The New Republic, Inc.

"The Study of Administration" by Woodrow Wilson. Reprinted with permission from *Political Science Quarterly*, vol. 2, no. 2 (June, 1887): 197–222.

From *Bureaucracy: What Government Agencies Do and Why They Do It* by James Q. Wilson. Copyright © 1989 by Basic Books, Inc. Reprinted by permission of Basic Books, a division of HarperCollins Publishers, Inc.

"National Performance Review: An Analysis" by Donald Kettl from *LaFollette Policy Report*, Fall 1994 (vol. 6, no. 2). Reprinted with permission.

From "Report Regarding the Internal Investigation of Shootings at Ruby Ridge, Idaho, during the Arrest of Randy Weaver" by the Department of Justice.

From "The National Performance Review" by Albert Gore.

The Federalist, No. 78, by Alexander Hamilton from the NAL-Dutton collection edited by Clinton Rossiter (1961).

From *Storm Center: The Supreme Court in American Politics*, Third Edition, by David M. O'Brien. Copyright © 1993, 1990, 1986 by David M. O'Brien. Reprinted with permission of W. W. Norton & Company, Inc.

"The Color-Blind Court" by Jeffrey Rosen from the *New Republic*, July 31, 1995. Reprinted by permission of the *New Republic*, © 1995, The New Republic, Inc.

Reprinted with the permission of The Free Press, a division of Simon & Schuster from *The Tempting of America: The Political Seduction of the Law* by Robert H. Bork. Copyright © 1990 by Robert H. Bork.

"Who's Right about the Constitution? Meese v. Brennan" by Stuart Taylor, Jr. from the *New Republic*, January 6 & 13, 1986. Reprinted by permission of the *New Republic*, © 1986, the New Republic, Inc.

"Polling the Public" from *Public Opinion in a Democracy* by George Gallup. Published under the University Extension Fund, Herbert L. Baker Foundation, Princeton University, 1939.

"Why Americans Hate Politics and Politicians" by Michael Nelson from *Virginia Quarterly Review*, Autumn 1994. Reprinted by permission.

"The Presidency and the Press" by Charles Jones from the *Harvard International Journal of Press/Politics*, 1: 2 (Fall, 1996), pp. 116–20. Copyright © 1996 by the President and Fellows of Harvard College and the Massachusetts Institute of Technology. Reprinted with permission.

"Why Americans Hate the Media" from *Breaking the News* by James Fallows. Copyright © 1996 by James Fallows (originally appeared in the *Atlantic Monthly*). Reprinted by permission of Pantheon Books, a division of Random House, Inc.

"Civic Journalism: Involving the Public" by Margaret T. Gordon from the *Seattle Times*, April 7, 1996. Reprinted by permission of the author.

"When News Media Go to Grass Roots, Candidates Often Don't Follow" by Howard Kurtz from the *Washington Post*, June 4, 1996. © 1996 The Washington Post. Reprinted with permission.

Reprinted by permission of the publisher from *The Responsible Electorate* by V. O. Key, Cambridge, Mass.: Harvard University Press. Copyright © 1966 by the President and Fellows of Harvard College.

" 'Give 'em Hell' These Days Is a Figure of Speech" by Eileen Shields West from *Smithsonian*, October 1988. Reprinted by permission of the author.

"What I Learned about How We Pick a President" by Lamar Alexander from the *Weekly Standard*, March 15, 1996. Reprinted by permission.

"Take the Wealth Primarily to Court" by John Bonifax from *Social Policy*, Fall 1995. Published by Social Policy Corporation, New York, New York 10036. Copyright 1995 by Social Policy Corporation. Reprinted by permission.

"The Decline of Collective Responsibility in American Politics" by Morris P. Fiorina reprinted by permission of *Daedalus*, Journal of the American Academy of Arts and Sciences, from the issue entitled, "The End of the Consensus?" Summer 1980, vol. 109, no. 3.

"The People vs. The Parties" by Kevin Phillips. Reprinted with permission from the *American Prospect* Fall 1994. © New Prospect, Inc.

Forum: "A Revolution, or Business as Usual?" Copyright © 1995 by *Harper's Magazine*. All rights reserved. Reproduced from the March issue by special permission.

"Third Party Candidates Face a High Hurdle in the Electoral College" by Walter Berns and "Third Party Candidates Won't Necessarily Bring Reform" by Gordon S. Black from the *American Enterprise*, January/February 1996. Reprinted by The American Enterprise, a national magazine of politics, business, and culture, based in Washington, D.C.

"A Report of the Committee on Political Parties: Toward a More Responsible Two-Party System" from *American Political Science Review*, September 1950.

"Of Political Parties Great and Strong: A Dissent" by Everett Carll Ladd from the *American Enterprise*, July/August 1994. Reprinted by The American Enterprise, a national magazine of politics, business, and culture, based in Washington, D.C.

"Political Association in the United States" from *Democracy in America* by Alexis de Tocqueville. Edited by J. P. Mayer and Max Lerner. Translated by George Lawrence. English translation copyright © 1965 by Harper & Row, Publishers, Inc. Copyright renewed. Reprinted by permission of HarperCollins Publishers, Inc.

"The Logic of Collective Action" from *The Rise and Decline of Nations* by Mancur Olson, Copyright © 1982 by Yale University Press. Reprinted by permission.

"Connections Still Count" by W. John Moore from *National Journal*, January 8, 1994. Copyright 1994 by National Journal, Inc. All rights reserved. Reprinted by permission.

The Federalist, No. 10, by James Madison from the NAL-Dutton collection edited by Clinton Rossiter (1961).

"The Alleged Mischiefs of Faction" from *The Governmental Process* by David Truman. Published by Alfred A. Knopf © 1963. Reprinted by permission of the author.

"The Hyperpluralism Trap" by Jonathan Rauch from the *New Republic*, June 6, 1994. Reprinted by permission of the *New Republic*, © 1994, The New Republic, Inc.

"The Science of 'Muddling Through,' " by Charles E. Lindblom from *Public Administration Review*, Spring 1959. Reprinted with permission from *Public Administration Review* © by the American Society for Public Administration (ASPA), 1120 G Street NW, Suite 700, Washington, D.C. 20005. All rights reserved.

"American Business and Public Policy, Case-Studies, and Political Theory" by Theodore J. Lowi from *World Politics*, Vol. 16 (1964). Reprinted by permission of the Johns Hopkins University Press.

"Why Our Democracy Doesn't Work" by William A. Niskanen. Reprinted with permission of the author and the *Public Interest*, Summer 1994, pp. 88–95 © 1994 by National Affairs, Inc.

"Should the Senate Pass A Balanced Budget Constitutional Amendment?" by Larry E. Craig and James M. Buchanan from *Congressional Digest*, February 1995, pp. 42–52. Reprinted by permission.

"The Balanced Budget Crusade" by Robert Eisner. Reprinted with permission of the author and the *Public Interest*, Writer 1996, pp. 85–92 © 1996 by National Affairs, Inc.

"It's Not the Economy, Stupid" by Charles R. Morris. Reprinted by the permission of Russell & Volkening as agents for the author. This piece was originally published in the *Atlantic Monthly*. Copyright © 1993 by Charles R. Morris.

"If the GDP Is Up, Why Is America Down?" by Clifford Cobb, Ted Halstead, and Jonathan Rowe. Copyright 1995, by Clifford Cobb, Ted Halstead, and Jonathan Rowe of Redefining Progress, as first published in the *Atlantic Monthly*. Reprinted by permission.

"Gray Markets and Greased Pigs" by John Hood from the *Freeman: Ideas on Liberty*, vol. 39, no. 8 (August 1989). Reprinted by permission.

"The Era of 'Big' Government: Why You'd Miss It If It Went" by E. J. Dionne from *Commonwealth*, February 23, 1996. Copyright © 1996 by the Commonwealth Foundation. Reprinted by permission.

"The Next New Deal" by Neil Howe and Philip Longman from the *Atlantic Mothly*, April 1992. Reprinted by permission of the authors.

"Remaking U.S. Social Policies for the 21th Century," from *Social Policy in the United States* by Theda Skocpol. Copyright © 1995 by Princeton University Press. Reprinted by permission of Princeton University Press.

"Putting Recipients to Work Will Be the Toughest Job" by Jeffrey L. Katz from *Congressional Quarterly Weekly Report*, vol. 53, no. 27. Reprinted by permission.

Debate on the Senate Floor on Welfare Reform with Senators John Shelby (R.-Ala.) and Orrin Hatch (R.-Utah), *Congressional Record*, December 2, 1995, S19159–S19160. Reprinted by permission.

"Should the House Pass H.R. 4, the Personal Responsibility Act?" by Representatives Bill Archer (R.-Tex.), Michael Collins (R.-Ga.), and William J. Coyne, *Congressional Record*, March 21, 1995. Reprinted by permission.

"The Sources of Soviet Conduct" by "X" [George Kennan] from *Foreign Affairs* (Spring 1947).

"An Outward-Looking Economic Nationalism" by Robert Reich. Reprinted with permission from the *American Prospect* Spring 1990. © New Prospect, Inc.

"The Intervention Dilemma" by Barry M. Blechman from the *Washington Quarterly*, 18: 3 (Summer, 1995), pp. 63–73. © 1995 by the Center for Strategic and International Studies (CSIS) and the Massachusetts Institute of Technology. Reprinted by permission.

"Why America Must Not Go into Bosnia" by Charles Krauthammer from the *Weekly Standard*, December 5, 1995. Reprinted by permission of the author.